Frommer's®

Walt Disney World® & Orlando 2012

by Laura Miller

WILEY

John Wiley & Sons, Inc.

ABOUT THE AUTHOR

Laura Miller is a freelance writer based out of Orchard Park, New York. She's spent countless hours scouring Central Florida's various theme parks, hotels, resorts, and restaurants over the years (too many to count)—both with and without her five children. A family-travel expert who religiously travels to the Land the Mouse Built several times a year, she also operates **mouseearsandmore.com**, a website dedicated to Central Florida and the art of family travel.

Published by:

JOHN WILEY & SONS, INC.

111 River St.
Hoboken, NJ 07030-5774

ISBN 978-1-118-02750-9 (paper); ISBN 978-1-118-16803-5 (ebk); ISBN 978-1-118-16804-2 (ebk); ISBN 978-1-118-16805-9 (ebk)

Editor: Leslie Shen, with Naomi P. Kraus
Production Editor: Katie Robinson
Cartographer: Roberta Stockwell
Photo Editor: Richard Fox
Production by Wiley Indianapolis Composition Services
Front cover photo: Big Thunder Mountain Railroad at Magic Kingdom; ©Gary Bogdon Photography.
Back cover photo: The Wizarding World of Harry Potter, Islands of Adventure. © 2010 Universal Orlando Resort. All rights reserved. HARRY POTTER, characters, names and related indicia are trademarks of and © Warner Bros. Entertainment Inc. Harry Potter Publishing Rights © JKR. (s10)

For information on our other products and services or to obtain technical support, please contact our Customer Care Department within the U.S. at 877/762-2974, outside the U.S. at 317/572-3993 or fax 317/572-4002.

Wiley also publishes its books in a variety of electronic formats. Some content that appears in print may not be available in electronic formats.

Manufactured in the United States of America

5 4 3 2 1

CONTENTS

LIST OF MAPS

ACKNOWLEDGMENTS

I'd like to thank Amy Voss at the Orlando/Orange County Convention & Visitors Bureau; Dave Herbst and Michelle Baumann at Walt Disney World; Tom Schroder and Brittany Tollerton at Universal Orlando; and Dagmar Cardwell at SeaWorld, not to mention all the marketing and PR reps at the countless hotels and resorts, for all of their research assistance as well as their continued support during the many trips I made to the Orlando area while writing this book.

Thanks to my family, especially my five kids—Ryan, Austin, Nicolas, Hailey, and Davis—and my sister Cindy. They all in some way, shape, or form played a part in this endeavor, whether it was spending endless hours touring the parks, hunting through the many hotels, helping to review the various restaurants, or simply making sure I was free to travel whenever necessary. Thank you to my agent, Julie Hill—your continued support and encouragement are invaluable.

And a special thanks to Naomi Kraus and Leslie Shen, my editors, not only for the enormous amount of time and effort they put into helping me with this endeavor, but for their valuable input, helpful advice, guidance, and patience they offered along the way—all of which I so greatly appreciate.

—Laura Miller

HOW TO CONTACT US

In researching this book, we discovered many wonderful places—hotels, restaurants, shops, and more. We're sure you'll find others. Please tell us about them, so we can share the information with your fellow travelers in upcoming editions. If you were disappointed with a recommendation, we'd love to know that, too. Please write to:

Frommer's Walt Disney World® & Orlando 2012
John Wiley & Sons, Inc. • 111 River St. • Hoboken, NJ 07030-5774
frommersfeedback@wiley.com

ADVISORY & DISCLAIMER

Travel information can change quickly and unexpectedly, and we strongly advise you to confirm important details locally before traveling, including information on visas, health and safety, traffic and transport, accommodations, shopping, and eating out. We also encourage you to stay alert while traveling and to remain aware of your surroundings. Avoid civil disturbances, and keep a close eye on cameras, purses, wallets, and other valuables.

While we have endeavored to ensure that the information contained within this guide is accurate and up-to-date at the time of publication, we make no representations or warranties with respect to the accuracy or completeness of the contents of this work and specifically disclaim all warranties, including without limitation warranties of fitness for a particular purpose. We accept no responsibility or liability for any inaccuracy or errors or omissions, or for any inconvenience, loss, damage, costs, or expenses of any nature whatsoever incurred or suffered by anyone as a result of any advice or information contained in this guide.

The inclusion of a company, organization, or website in this guide as a service provider and/or potential source of further information does not mean that we endorse them or the information they provide. Be aware that information provided through some websites may be unreliable and can change without notice. Neither the publisher nor author shall be liable for any damages arising herefrom.

FROMMER'S STAR RATINGS, ICONS & ABBREVIATIONS

Every hotel, restaurant, and attraction listing in this guide has been ranked for quality, value, service, amenities, and special features using a **star-rating system.** In country, state, and regional guides, we also rate towns and regions to help you narrow down your choices and budget your time accordingly. Hotels and restaurants are rated on a scale of zero (recommended) to three stars (exceptional). Attractions, shopping, nightlife, towns, and regions are rated according to the following scale: zero stars (recommended), one star (highly recommended), two stars (very highly recommended), and three stars (must-see).

In addition to the star-rating system, we also use **seven feature icons** that point you to the great deals, in-the-know advice, and unique experiences that separate travelers from tourists. Throughout the book, look for:

special finds—those places only insiders know about

fun facts—details that make travelers more informed and their trips more fun

kids—best bets for kids and advice for the whole family

special moments—those experiences that memories are made of

overrated—places or experiences not worth your time or money

insider tips—great ways to save time and money

great values—where to get the best deals

The following abbreviations are used for credit cards:

AE   American Express   DISC   Discover   V   Visa

DC   Diners Club   MC   MasterCard

TRAVEL RESOURCES AT FROMMERS.COM

Frommer's travel resources don't end with this guide. Frommer's website, **www.frommers. com**, has travel information on more than 4,000 destinations. We update features regularly, giving you access to the most current trip-planning information and the best airfare, lodging, and car-rental bargains. You can also listen to podcasts, connect with other Frommers.com members through our active-reader forums, share your travel photos, read blogs from guidebook editors and fellow travelers, and much more.

THE BEST OF WALT DISNEY WORLD & ORLANDO

In the beginning, Orlando may have been a sleepy little Southern town filled with farmland as far as the eye could see, orange groves galore, and only two attractions to its name (a water-ski show and some great big gators). Then came the Mouse. More specifically, a mouse named Mickey and his creator, a man of fantastic imagination and vision named Walt Disney. Life in Orlando would never be the same. Since the opening of Walt Disney World back in 1971, Orlando has grown to become one of the world's top vacation destinations. Almost 45 million people from all parts of the world make their way to this city each year to sample its unending array of exciting, unique, and diverse activities. Those of us who continue to return year after year can count on each visit to provide a host of new experiences and memories.

When Disney World first opened its gates to the public, I doubt if anyone but Walt Disney, the original Imagineer, could have predicted what lay ahead. Disney, searching for an East Coast location for his second theme park, decided Orlando was just the place he was looking for. In 1964, in a covert operation that would have made James Bond proud, Walt Disney began quietly purchasing large quantities of land in and around the Orlando area, and within months he had acquired property nearly twice the size of Manhattan. In 1965, Walt announced to the public his plans to bring to Orlando the world's most spectacular theme park. Fashioned after Disneyland in California, construction soon began on Disney's Magic Kingdom. Unfortunately, Walt Disney was never able to see his dream come to life, as he passed away in 1966, just 5 years shy of the opening of what, to this day, is still the world's most spectacular theme park—Walt Disney World.

Disney's legacy, while commercialized over the years, has practically become a rite of passage, not to mention a national shrine to which visitors flock by the millions. And if you have kids, a visit here is almost a requirement. The opening of Walt Disney World's Magic Kingdom started a tourist boom in Central Florida the likes of which has never been seen elsewhere. Today, the Kingdom That Walt Built entices visitors with four

By the Numbers

While attendance levels continue to remain relatively steady at Disney, and attendance at Universal Orlando has increased exponentially (thanks to the addition of the Wizarding World of Harry Potter), SeaWorld hasn't been so lucky. Across the board, Orlando's theme parks (including Disney, and even Universal to some extent) continue to feel the effects of the economic downturn. Though predictions state that attendance levels will continue to rise over the next few years, they will likely do so at a much slower pace (with Universal's wildly high attendance figures likely to drop as the newness of the Wizarding World begins to wear off). The parks, however, continue to entice visitors to return and to stay longer by offering special deals, discounts, and the addition of wild and wonderfully new attractions. Here are the 2010 attendance estimates (and their national rankings) for all of the major Orlando parks according to TEA, Inc., and Economic Research Associates:

- No. 1: Magic Kingdom, 17 million (–1.5%)
- No. 3: Epcot, 11 million (–1.5%)
- No. 4: Disney's Animal Kingdom, 9.7 million (+1%)
- No. 5: Disney's Hollywood Studios, 9.6 million (–.1%)
- No. 7: Islands of Adventure, 5.9 million (+30.2%)
- No. 8: Universal Studios Florida, 5.9 million (+6.1%)
- No. 9: SeaWorld, 5.1 million (–12%) (Disneyland and Disney's California Adventure rank 2nd and 6th, respectively.)

theme parks; a dozen smaller attractions; a shopping, dining, and entertainment district; tens of thousands of hotel rooms; a vacation club (otherwise known as timeshares); scores of restaurants; and even three cruise ships (soon to be four). Universal Orlando adds to the dizzying array with two theme parks, three luxury resorts, and an entertainment complex that's home to several unique restaurants, clubs, shops, and entertainment venues. SeaWorld tosses in three theme parks and a small entertainment, dining, and shopping district of its own. And those are just the major players. All in all, there are just shy of 100 attractions, both large and small, that will keep you coming back for more. There are also plenty of restaurants, ranging from fine dining to on-the-fly fast food; many of the more casual restaurants are as themed as the parks themselves. And the city doesn't lack for hotels and resorts either, with roughly 119,000 rooms, villas, and suites to go around by the end of 2012. If you can believe it, the landscape is still changing, evolving, growing, and expanding to ensure your experiences will do the same each and every time you stay and play in Orlando.

Beyond the fast-paced excitement, glitz, and glitter of Orlando's theme parks, you'll find Central Florida's more natural side, with hidden treasures just waiting to be discovered. More than 300 lakes, springs, and rivers are here to be explored and enjoyed. There are numerous parks and gardens, many with trails for walking and hiking, and the area's wildlife sanctuaries and zoos showcase Florida's animal inhabitants. The number of recreational opportunities—picnics in parks, boating along waterways, fishing, biking, and hiking, to name a few—is almost limitless. And Orlando's rich history and culture come to life through its many museums, galleries, and theaters.

Where to go, what to do, when to do it . . . with so many decisions to make, you may very well find your head spinning. Because of the vast quantity of offerings, a vacation to Orlando necessitates a reasonable amount of planning, not to mention budgeting. The sheer number of attractions and available activities requires that you narrow down your choices to fit both your schedule and your budget. Entrance fees can be daunting (a 1-day ticket to one of the major parks averages around $85 for adults and $79 for kids 3–9), and when you add in the costs of dining, accommodations, and souvenirs, sticker shock at the high price tag is not out of the question. A typical family of four could easily end up spending several hundred dollars a day! Some parks have begun offering deals to bring down the average daily price of your ticket if you buy multiday passes, but don't give them too much credit—the parks are wagering they'll generate additional revenue with all of the money you'll spend on extra hotel nights and meals. But even if you do have deep pockets, Orlando offers so much to experience that to take it all in properly would require far more time than the average vacation would allow. I doubt if even two or three vacations could do the trick.

That's exactly why this book was written: to make available to you the most up-to-date and detailed information on what Orlando has to offer. A mix of options that takes into account every budget and taste is included in each chapter so you can make the most informed decisions possible. With this book, you'll have the tools to plan ahead and ensure that your family has the best vacation possible. I have traveled to Central Florida more times than I can count in the past 25 years. Single, married, with kids, and without, I've stood in all the lines, ridden the rides, and dined in the restaurants—even during the height of summer and spring break. In other words, I've done all of the hard work so you don't have to, and I give realistic and practical travel tips throughout this book in order to help you enjoy a more magical vacation. At the same time, I also give you options to help make your vacation more affordable and to keep expenses to a minimum while still having the maximum amount of fun.

THE best ORLANDO EXPERIENCES

- **Explore Disney's Animal Kingdom.** Explore Disney's most spectacular and wildest Imagineering to date. Trek through the jungles of Africa along the Pangani Forest Exploration Trail or set out on safari across the savanna with Kilimanjaro Safaris. Journey through the exotic lands of Asia and embark on an expedition to the peaks of Expedition Everest; then explore the mysteries of Anandapur while wandering the Maharajah Jungle Trek. Be sure not to miss Finding Nemo—The Musical or the Festival of the Lion King, absolutely the best shows in all of WDW. See p. 226.

- **Go Globe-Trotting at Epcot.** You can travel around the world in only an afternoon at the World Showcase pavilions, rocket through space on a thrilling mission to Mars at Mission: Space, travel back in time to the age of the dinosaurs at the Universe of Energy, and dive deep below the sea to explore the ocean's inhabitants at the Seas with Nemo & Friends. And there's no better way to cap your day off than watching Epcot's IllumiNations, a spectacular show of fireworks, laser lights, and fountains. See p. 197.

1 | Orlando Theme Parks

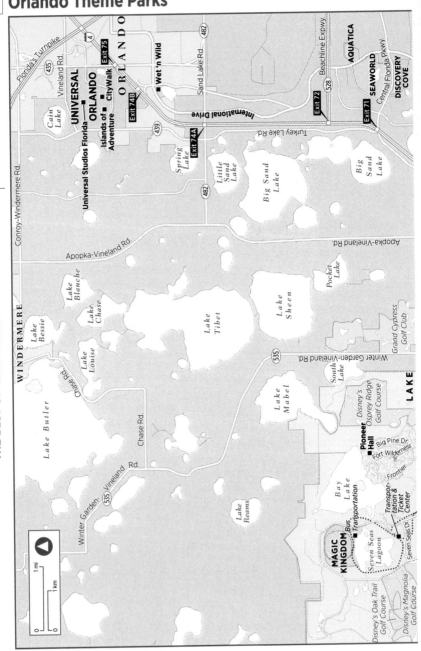

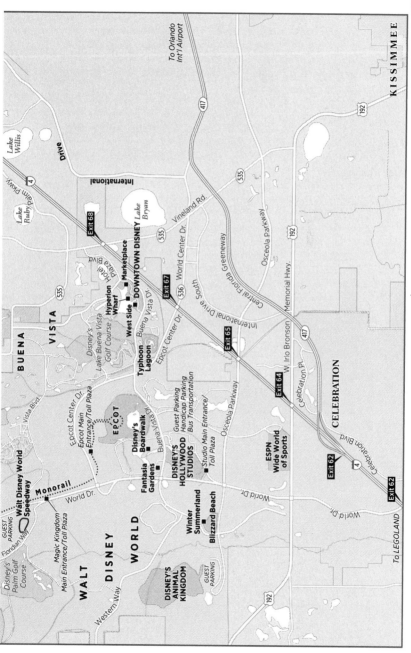

o **Take Center Stage at Disney's Hollywood Studios.** Though it is more grown-up than the Magic Kingdom, it has plenty of great shows to entertain the kids and attractions to thrill movie buffs. Don't miss Toy Story Mania, the American Idol Experience, Star Tours (overhauled in 2011), Twilight Zone Tower of Terror, Rock 'n' Roller Coaster, and Fantasmic!—an innovative, after-dark mix of live action, waterworks, fireworks, and laser lights that rivals IllumiNations. See p. 214.

o **Escape to the Magic Kingdom.** It may seem an obvious choice, but Disney's oldest is still the most magical of Orlando's theme parks. Speed through the universe on Space Mountain, watch Donald's antics at Mickey's PhilharMagic, laugh out loud at the Monsters, Inc. Laugh Floor, or wave hello to the ghouls of the Haunted Mansion. Cap your day with the impressive Wishes fireworks display. There's plenty here to entertain all ages. *Note:* At press time, the Magic Kingdom was in the midst of an extensive 3-year expansion slated for completion in late 2012. See p. 174.

o **Experience Universal Orlando.** Universal Studios Florida and its sister, Islands of Adventure, are both chock-full of thrilling rides and spectacular shows that combine cutting-edge technology, high-tech special effects, and incredible imagination and creativity. The attention to detail throughout the parks is amazing—check out the street sets at USF and the wildly unique landscapes of IOA (including the Wizarding World of Harry Potter) and you'll see what I mean. For thrill seekers, not-to-be-missed attractions include Hollywood Rip Ride Rockit, Revenge of the Mummy, Men in Black Alien Attack, the Dragon Challenge, the Forbidden Journey, the Incredible Hulk Coaster, the Amazing Adventures of Spider-Man, and Dudley Do-Right's Ripsaw Falls. See chapter 6.

o **Dive into the Eco-Edutainment of SeaWorld, Discovery Cove, and Aquatica.** Your kids may never realize just how much they're learning as they explore their way through these theme parks' eco-exhibits and experiences. With the addition of Manta, Journey to Atlantis, and Kraken, **SeaWorld** (p. 277) added a bit of zip and zing to the lineup, ensuring that those in need of an adrenaline rush aren't left out in the cold (or over at the other parks). But it's still the hands-on encounters, such as touching silky rays as they glide by you in droves, and up-close views of animals ranging from polar bears and penguins to killer whales, that draw the crowds. **Discovery Cove** (p. 288) is more of an island retreat than a theme park, where the big draw is the chance to take a dip with the dolphins. Rest and relax on the beach, swim along with the fishes, or explore the Grand Reef (the park's latest addition, slated to make its debut just as this book goes to print). **Aquatica** (p. 290) combines high-speed thrills (with raft rides and racing tunnels), up-close animal encounters (with Commerson's dolphins, colorful fish, brilliant macaws, and more), and a whimsical South Pacific atmosphere to create an eco-themed water park unlike any other.

o **Go Wild at Gatorland.** Located between Orlando and Kissimmee, this throwback park is a great way to spend a half-day (an especially good choice for that extra time on your day of arrival) and costs less than a third of the price of some of the major theme parks. In addition to the animal exhibits, Gator Jumparoo, a signature show since the park opened in 1949, and Gator Wrestlin' are worth a look. Thrill seekers with a bit of extra cash can even zip along high above the crocs and gators (and lush grounds) below—the park's zipline adventure made its debut in summer 2011. Other options include a train ride, water playground, and aviary. If you have some extra spending money for a once-in-a-lifetime experience, consider becoming a Trainer for a Day. See p. 292.

○ **Pamper Yourself with a Spa Treatment.** Rest, relax, and rejuvenate—you may very well need to if you intend on surviving all of the fast-paced activities you've planned. After a few days at the parks, it should almost be a requirement. **Disney's Grand Floridian Resort & Spa** (℗ **407/934-7639** or 407/824-3000), the **Mandara Spa** at Universal's Portofino Bay Hotel (℗ **888/322-5541** or 407/503-1000) and at the WDW Dolphin (℗ **407/934-4000**), the **Spa by Guerlain** at the Waldorf Astoria (℗ **407/597-5360** or 407/352-4000), the **Neu Lotus Spa** at the Renaissance Orlando at SeaWorld (℗ **407/351-5555**), and the **Spa at the Peabody** (℗ **407/345-4431** or 407/586-0000) all offer an array of fabulous treatments, some with salon services to boot.

THE best THRILL RIDES

Orlando lays claim to some of the biggest and baddest thrill rides and roller coasters anywhere—certainly one of the largest collections of them in any one locale. So if your idea of fun is to twist and turn at speeds only a jet should reach, dive uncontrollably from dizzying heights to below ground level and back, or see just how far up into your throat your stomach can go—this is the place for you. Here are the city's top stomach churners and G-force generators.

○ **Harry Potter and the Forbidden Journey** (Islands of Adventure): The queue, as much a part of the experience as the ride itself, is signature Universal—and, like the ride, simply brilliant. The thrills, however, come once you board: The robotic arm swings and swirls, whooshes and whirls past the gigantic spherical screen, is immersed in spectacular special effects, and brings riders face to face with some of the Wizarding World's scariest characters. It's by far the best ride in Orlando. See p. 274.

○ **Manta** (SeaWorld): Gliding, swooping, and diving (this one's a very smooth ride) at speeds of up to 56 mph, you'll fly face-down and headfirst (yikes!) along some 3,359 feet of twisted steel track. You'll spin through four inversions (including inline spins, flat spins, and a pretzel loop) and drop a heart-pounding 113 feet to within feet of the water below before it's over (which is in just under 3 min.)—in the end throwing out a spray of water some 14 feet high and some 60 feet long. See p. 285.

○ **Hollywood Rip Ride Rockit** (Universal Studios): You're the star as this high-speed, musically themed multisensory thriller has riders rocking out (while being recorded by a sophisticated on- and off-board video system) at speeds of up to 65 mph, twisting and turning, dipping and diving along the intertwining track set some 17 stories above the walkways of Universal Studios and the CityWalk lagoon. And did I mention the record-breaking noninverted loop? It's the world's largest. So crank up the tunes (you get to pick 'em ahead of time) and enjoy the ride; after it's over, you can pick up a copy (for a fee) of your ride—think music video with a high-tech twist. See p. 256.

○ **Incredible Hulk Coaster** (Islands of Adventure): It's the smoothest ride in town, but you'll still blast from 0 to 40 mph in 2 seconds flat (on your way up to 60 mph), spin upside-down more than 100 feet above the ground, dive straight back down only to spin your way through seven rollovers, and then drop deep below ground on this big, green, mean machine. (You might glow as green as the coaster when you're done.) See p. 268.

o **Rock 'n' Roller Coaster** (Disney's Hollywood Studios): You'll launch from 0 to 60 mph in 2.8 seconds, heading straight into the first of several inversions as 120 speakers in your "stretch limo" blast Aerosmith at (yeeeow!) 32,000 watts right into your ears. To add to the thrill of this indoor coaster, the entire experience takes place in the dark. See p. 222.

o **Dragon Challenge** (Islands of Adventure): Regardless of which dragon you choose—the Chinese Fireball or the Hungarian Horntail—your legs will dangle below as you sharply twist and turn through five inversions at speeds of 55 to 60 mph. The two intertwined coasters come within inches of each other (12 to be exact), only just missing a collision, not two but three times. See p. 273.

o **Summit Plummet** (Disney's Blizzard Beach): This one starts slow, with a lift ride (even in Florida's 100°F/38°C dog days) to the 120-foot summit. But it finishes with the (self-proclaimed) world's fastest body slide—a test of your courage and swimsuit—as it goes virtually straight down and has you moving sans vehicle at 60 mph by the end. See p. 239.

o **Twilight Zone Tower of Terror** (Disney's Hollywood Studios): The name says it all. The ride transports guests into the Twilight Zone as a haunted hotel's service elevator slowly rises—only to plummet 13 stories, terrifying those inside. But the freefall fun doesn't end there. The tower's computer program randomly alternates drop sequences to make sure you never experience the same ride twice. When you get off and your legs finally stop shaking, *some* of you will want to ride again. See p. 224.

o **The Amazing Adventures of Spider-Man** (Islands of Adventure): Combining the best of all worlds—3-D movie effects, a moving simulator car, and live action—this is the second-best ride in Orlando (coming in right behind the Forbidden Journey). Your vehicle spins, twists, pitches, and dives through elaborate sets as Spider-Man tries to save the world (and you) from total annihilation. The chase ends in a dramatic, simulated 400-foot drop that feels an awful lot like the real thing. It doesn't offer the same type of thrills as a coaster, but it's sure to get your Spidey senses tingling. See p. 267.

o **Kraken** (SeaWorld): Named for a mythological creature, this stomach-churning ride is a beast! This floorless, open-sided coaster reaches speeds of up to 65 mph as it combines steep climbs, deep drops, and seven tremendous loops reaching high above water before plunging below the ground, to make it one of the most aggressive and intense coasters anywhere. See p. 284.

THE best WATER RIDES

o **Splash Mountain** (Magic Kingdom): You'll follow the adventure of Brer Rabbit and his friends, based on the 1946 movie *The Song of the South,* before taking a 52-foot vertical plunge straight down to the water below. See p. 184.

o **Dudley Do-Right's Ripsaw Falls** (Islands of Adventure): Dudley Do-Right and Snidely Whiplash are once again at odds, and you're caught right in the middle. This flume sends you plummeting not once but twice, and that second drop sends you 15 feet below the surface of the water before you make your escape. See p. 269.

o **Jurassic Park River Adventure** (Islands of Adventure): A seemingly calm tour through the age of the dinosaurs suddenly takes a turn for the worse. Before you know it, your only escape route involves a dramatic 85-foot drop almost straight down—it's touted as the "longest, steepest, fastest water descent ever built." See p. 270.

THE BEST OF WALT DISNEY WORLD & ORLANDO

The Best Water Rides

Considering that Orlando welcomes nearly 45 million visitors each year, it should come as no surprise that hundreds of websites are devoted to vacationing here. These include information on just about everything, from the history of Walt Disney World to getting around town.

There are several sites written by Disney fans, employees, and self-proclaimed experts. A favorite is all about **Hidden Mickeys** (www.hiddenmickeys.org), a park tradition (see "Find the Hidden Mickeys," p. 220). These subtle Disney images can be found scattered throughout the realm, though they sometimes are in the eye, or imagination, of the beholder. **Deb's Unofficial Walt Disney World Information Guide** (www.allearsnet.com) is the best around, loaded with great tips and information on everything Disney, from the parks and resorts to the restaurants, nightlife, and much more. It now includes information on Universal Orlando as well.

Definitely take a look at Disney's official site, **www.disneyworld.com**, if you're planning a pilgrimage to the House of Mouse. The website recently got a top-to-bottom overhaul, making it easier to navigate and much more informative. It's loaded with photos and 360-degree views of Disney's resorts, rooms, parks, and more. **Magical Gatherings,** available on the Disney site, is a free downloadable online tool allowing you to plan your group's Disney vacation, via computer, with other family members (or friends), no matter where they live. You can plan itineraries, take group polls, list everyone's favorites, and even chat to come up with the perfect

plan. **My Disney Vacation,** also available on the Disney site, allows you to plan your entire Disney vacation from start to finish—you can even create your very own customized theme-park maps to mirror the itinerary you've planned out online.

If you're looking to save a few dollars, try **Mousesavers** (www.mousesavers.com), which features insider Disney tips and exclusive discounted deals for area hotels, resorts, and packages.

If a trip to one of Universal Orlando's theme parks or CityWalk is on your dance card, then stop at **www.universalorlando.com**. You can order tickets (including exclusive Internet-only deals), make resort reservations, and find out about special events, among other things. Fish fans can get in the know about SeaWorld at **www.seaworld.com** and Discovery Cove at **www.discoverycove.com**.

Though a relative newcomer, **www.mouseearsandmore.com** is filled with travel tips, in-depth reviews, and information on Disney, Universal Orlando, and SeaWorld. Also included are reviews of the area's kid-friendliest restaurants and resorts, a boon for parents.

For general information about the city, accommodations, dining, nightlife, or special events, head to the Orlando/Orange County Convention & Visitors Bureau site at **www.visitorlando.com**. The *Orlando Weekly* (**www.orlandoweekly.com**) offers reviews and recommendations for arts, movies, music, restaurants, and more. The *Orlando Sentinel* (**www.orlandosentinel.com**) features Go2Orlando, a section loaded with information on the area's dining, attractions, shopping, and more.

○ **Popeye & Bluto's Bilge-Rat Barges** (Islands of Adventure): Up to 12 riders splash and churn through a wacky series of twists and turns and dips and drops (some pretty intense) in order to help Popeye save his sweetie, Olive Oyl, from the dastardly clutches of Bluto. No one will walk away from this one without getting completely soaked—it's the wettest and wildest raft ride in town. See p. 270.

o **Journey to Atlantis** (SeaWorld): This flume ride sends you careening around the sharpest of curves as the forces of good and evil battle to claim Atlantis for their own. Before you know it, you're being thrown into total darkness, emerging only to find yourself plummeting down several steep, watery drops. See p. 283.

THE best ROMANTIC HIDEAWAYS

o **Courtyard at Lake Lucerne** (Downtown; ✆ 800/444-5289 or 407/648-5188): This charming B&B is an eclectic mix of some of Orlando's oldest homes—each impeccably restored and meticulously furnished. Ask for the honeymoon suite for a truly romantic getaway; just off the main room is a quaint little glass-enclosed porch—the perfect spot to watch the sunset or sip a glass of wine. See p. 95.

o **Disney's Wilderness Lodge** (Lake Buena Vista; ✆ 407/934-7639 or 407/938-4300): This grand resort is reminiscent of the lodge at Yellowstone National Park. The spewing geyser out back, the mammoth stone hearth in the lobby, the Artist's Point 360-degree view of Bay Lake, and the towering forest sheltering the resort from the rest of the world are just a few reasons to stay here. Some guest rooms have patios or balconies overlooking the lake, woodlands, or meadow. See p. 58.

o **Disney's Animal Kingdom Lodge** (Lake Buena Vista; ✆ 407/934-7639 or 407/938-3000): This uniquely themed resort, home to Jambo House (the original lodge) and the Kidani Village (Disney's newest vacation club villas), is set against a Disneyesque version of the African savanna. The grand lobby—with its thatched roof, ornate shield chandeliers, and large stone fireplace—is just a sampling of the spectacular architecture and decor that runs throughout this remotely located resort. Have a romantic meal at one of the resort's great restaurants; then catch the sunset over the savanna. See p. 57.

o **Portofino Bay Hotel** (Universal Orlando; ✆ 888/322-5541 or 407/503-1000): This enchanting resort re-creates the romantic atmosphere and architecture of its namesake town in Italy. Lounge in the ultracomfy rooms, the state-of-the-art spa, or one of the three heated pools. And it's only a stroll away from both of Universal Orlando's theme parks. See p. 86.

o **Villas of Grand Cypress** (Orlando; ✆ 800/835-7377 or 407/239-4700): This luxury villa-style resort offers lush grounds dotted with bougainvillea and hibiscus, lakes fat with largemouth bass and bream, and grounds speckled with trumpeter swans, wood ducks, and the occasional fox or bobcat. It shares a golf academy, racquet club, and equestrian center with the Hyatt Regency Grand Cypress. Best of all, the woodsy grounds make you feel as if you're far, far from Disney, which is right next door. See p. 70.

THE best LUXURY RESORTS

o **Disney's Grand Floridian Resort & Spa** (Orlando; ✆ 407/934-7639 or 407/824-3000): This magnificent Victorian inn—Disney's best hotel—has an opulent five-story lobby complete with a Chinese Chippendale aviary. An orchestra plays big-band music every evening near Victoria & Albert's, the resort's five-star restaurant. See p. 52.

- **Gaylord Palms** (Lake Buena Vista; ☎ 877/677-9352 or 407/586-2000): This destination resort features impeccable service, themed guest rooms (the Emerald Bay rooms are the best) with luxe amenities, a lush 4½-acre glass-topped atrium, and (best of all) a branch of the renowned Relâche Spa. See p. 70.

- **Hyatt Regency Grand Cypress Resort** (Orlando; ☎ 800/233-1234 or 407/239-1234): This standout has some impressive treats, including a half-acre pool with a dozen waterfalls and 3 spas, 12 tennis courts, 4 Jack Nicklaus–designed golf courses, and a 45-acre nature walk. All that adds up to luxury, pure and simple. See p. 69.

- **The Peabody Orlando** (Orlando; ☎ 800/732-2639 or 407/352-4000): Adding to the main hotel's classically elegant ambience is the new $450-million Peabody Tower, featuring chic rooms with posh touches (miniature LCD TVs embedded in the bathroom mirrors, among them), a full-service spa, and a sophisticated piano lounge. Add to that the Peabody's signature pampering, and the end result is an impressive and luxe lineup. See p. 84.

- **Reunion Resort Orlando** (Reunion; ☎ 888/418-9611 or 407/662-1000): Lavish villas, stunning private homes, and the posh Wyndham Grand Resort are just the tip of the iceberg at this luxury pick. The personalized service will simply spoil you, while the extensive recreational facilities—top-notch golf courses, a full-service spa, water park, and kids' club—will make you think twice about ever wanting to leave. See p. 78.

- **Ritz-Carlton Orlando** (Grande Lakes; ☎ 800/576-5760 or 407/206-2400): Perks at this posh getaway, set in the Grande Lakes Resort, include luxurious rooms with first-class amenities, a 40,000-square-foot spa, a championship golf course, excellent child-care facilities, and a lazy river pool. See p. 87.

- **Waldorf Astoria Orlando** (Lake Buena Vista; ☎ 800/925-3673 or 407/597-5500): The elegance of New York's original Waldorf Astoria is not lost at this, the second of only four Waldorf Astoria resorts in the world. Boasting an impressive address (surrounded on three sides by Disney World and nestled against the Bonnet Creek Nature Preserve), this grand hotel brings with it luxurious rooms, unmatched service, a formal cabana-lined pool, a Guerlain Spa, a championship golf course, a variety of dining options, and even private transportation to Disney. See p. 55.

THE best MODERATELY PRICED ACCOMMODATIONS

- **Disney's Port Orleans Resort** (Lake Buena Vista; ☎ 407/934-7639 or 407/934-5000): Here's a good value by Disney standards. It has dual Southern charm in its French Quarter and Riverside areas, and the pool has a water slide curving from the mouth of a colorful dragon. See p. 60.

- **Hilton in the Walt Disney World Resort** (Lake Buena Vista; ☎ 407/827-4000): It's the only official resort on Hotel Plaza Boulevard to offer Disney's Extra Magic Hour option. Other pluses include a huge variety of services, two pools, and spacious junior suites. And it has a great location next to Downtown Disney. See p. 67.

- **Staybridge Suites Lake Buena Vista** (Lake Buena Vista; ☎ 800/866-4549 or 407/238-0777): Close to the action of Downtown Disney and the theme parks, this resort's one- and two-bedroom suites have full kitchens and are larger and more comfortable than most of the competition. And breakfast is on the resort—a complimentary buffet of hot and cold items is set out daily so you don't have to deal with the hassle of dining elsewhere. See p. 76.

o **Lake Buena Vista Resort Village & Spa** (Lake Buena Vista; ℂ **866/401-2699** or 407/597-0214): Off the beaten path yet close to Disney, this upscale resort's oversized two-, three-, and four-bedroom suites have full kitchens, washers and dryers, and plasma TVs. A 7,500-square-foot pirate-themed pool will keep the kids entertained, while the full-service spa ensures the adults will remain relaxed. See p. 73.

THE best THEME RESTAURANTS

Orlando has elevated themed dining to an art form. The food at these restaurants may not be the best in town (though it won't be terrible either), but you can't beat the atmosphere.

o **World Showcase Restaurants** (Epcot; ℂ **407/939-3463**): Epcot's World Showcase is home to Orlando's best collection of theme restaurants in one setting. Dine in Italy, chow down in China, or watch a belly dancer do her thing as you eat couscous in Morocco. You'll have a blast no matter which spot you choose. See p. 207.

o **Sci-Fi Dine-In Theater Restaurant** (Disney's Hollywood Studios; ℂ **407/939-3463**): Your table is set inside a 1950s-era convertible, your carhop (umm . . . waitress) serves you popcorn as an appetizer, and you can zone out on sci-fi flicks on a giant movie screen while you eat. It's an out-of-this-world experience. See p. 122.

o **50's Prime Time Café** (Disney's Hollywood Studios; ℂ **407/939-3463**): Ozzie and Harriet would feel right at home inside this replica of Mom's kitchen (ca. 1950), where classic TV shows play on black-and-white screens. Servers may threaten to withhold dessert (choices include s'mores!) if you don't finish your meatloaf, so clean that plate. See p. 121.

o **T-Rex Cafe** (Downtown Disney Marketplace; ℂ **407/828-8739**): Set some million or so years in the past, this paleontologist's playground is waiting to be explored—especially if you're dining with the kids. Bubbling geysers, a fossil dig site, life-sized animatronic dinosaurs, an hourly meteorite shower, eerily glowing rooms, and themes of fire and ice—it's all here. It's definitely one of the most creative dining spots at Disney. See p. 133.

THE best PLACES FOR ADULTS

Let's face it: Orlando and the theme-park zones usually crawl with kids. That's fine if you have your own in tow, but if you're looking for some quality adult time (or at least a place not necessarily swarming with children), you do have some options. Some people are incredulous when informed that Orlando is the honeymoon capital of the U.S., but it happens to be true; so be assured that there are activities, hotels, and so on that are geared to adults here (though, admittedly, avoiding kids altogether is tough). Aside from the romantic hideaways discussed above, here are some good bets for adults.

- **Visit Epcot.** Of all the major theme parks in Orlando, this one, thanks to its scientific and cultural themes, is the most adult-oriented of the bunch. Shop, stroll, and dine your way through the nations of the World Showcase; take a behind-the-scenes tour of the park's horticulture or architecture; or explore the technological- and scientific-themed attractions of Future World. See p. 197.

- **Swim with Dolphins at Discovery Cove.** It's popular with families, but thanks to the park's limit on guest entry (a mere 1,000 people per day), adults won't get overwhelmed by kids at SeaWorld's sister park. There are plenty of places to catch rays in relative serenity, and the dolphin swim's a thrill at any age. See p. 288.

- **Dine in an Upscale Restaurant.** Though it's not a firm rule (especially inside the theme parks), generally speaking, the more you pay for dinner, the more likely it is that you won't encounter children at your meal. So if you're looking for a romantic dinner, save up and splurge (and I mean splurge). Great options for a special dinner include **Victoria & Albert's** (p. 127), **Emeril's** (p. 138), **Tchoup Chop** (p. 138), **California Grill** (p. 125), **Ocean Prime** (p. 141), and **Flying Fish Café** (p. 126). For a great brunch, head to **La Coquina** (p. 136). For other options, check out chapter 4, "Where to Eat."

- **Explore Winter Park.** This upscale town north of Orlando oozes old money and Southern charm. And the pace here is decidedly slower than the mad rush of the theme parks (adults usually love it; kids get bored). Stroll Park Avenue's shops and restaurants, or take a boat tour along the lake. See p. 312.

- **Party the Night Away at Universal CityWalk or the Disney Resorts.** With the closing of Pleasure Island's clubs for "re-imagining," Universal's nighttime entertainment district is now the place to hang for the 21-and-older set. Top clubs include **the groove, Rising Star, Pat O'Brien's,** and the **Red Coconut Club.** See the "At CityWalk" section in chapter 8, "Walt Disney World & Orlando After Dark." Over at the resorts, in this case Disney's Coronado Springs, **Rix** (p. 327) is the hottest place to party the night away for a 30-something crowd and visiting celebs and VIPs.

- **Head for the Circus.** Cirque du Soleil, that is. Forget about finding any animals, though. Cirque's stylish La Nouba combines theatrics, acrobatics, and the incredible style for which the Montreal-based troupe is known. It's an incredible (albeit pricey) way to spend an evening in Orlando. See p. 324.

- **Rev Your Engines at the Richard Petty Driving Experience and the Indy Racing Experience.** If you've ever watched the Daytona 500 or the Indy 500 race and imagined yourself at the wheel, this attraction is for you. Ride shotgun in a real NASCAR race car, or drive yourself (after a crash classroom course—no pun intended). It's an adrenaline-pumper you won't find in a theme park, and nobody under 18 is allowed (height and weight restrictions apply). See p. 242.

WALT DISNEY WORLD & ORLANDO IN DEPTH

2

I t's hard to believe that Walt Disney World first opened its gates some 40 years ago. After the Magic Kingdom's unveiling back in 1971, an incredible upsurge in development immediately followed, bringing not only additional theme parks, but also a slew of smaller attractions, world-class hotels, top-notch restaurants, and premier shopping venues that all combine to ensure Orlando is indisputably one of the world's preeminent vacation destinations.

Things to Do   **Disney** boasts four major theme parks, two water parks, and a shopping/dining/entertainment district. But the Mouse's House is not the only game in town. Take in the action-packed thrills of **Universal Studios Florida** and **Islands of Adventure** (the latter home to the wildly popular **Wizarding World of Harry Potter**), as well as the excitement of Universal's nightclub/restaurant district, **CityWalk.** If you prefer a bit less hustle and bustle, the eco-adventure parks at **SeaWorld, Discovery Cove,** and **Aquatica** feature a more laid-back experience. **Gatorland,** a throwback attraction, lets you take in the beauty of the natural surroundings at a leisurely pace. And the new **LEGOLAND Florida** immerses visitors in everything LEGO. Orlando also offers recreational activities galore, among them golf (with some of the country's top courses right nearby), indoor surfing, and zipline adventures.

Shopping   High-end malls such as the **Mall at Millenia** feature a dizzying array of designer boutiques, while architecturally inviting open-air outlet malls (most notably the **Premium Outlets** at Vineland and at International Dr.) and an eclectic array of theme-park shops will all give your wallet a workout.

Restaurants & Dining   Celebrity chefs and themed restaurants ensure that dining out is an experience in itself. Sit back and sip a signature martini, soak up sounds of Sinatra, and sink your teeth into a melt-in-your-mouth filet at **Ocean Prime** (located along the famed **Restaurant Row** on Sand Lake Rd.), or experience the exotic Asian-inspired surroundings of **Emeril's Tchoup Chop,** at Universal's Royal Pacific.

Nightlife & Entertainment Hang out at the clubs at Universal's **CityWalk** (including **Latin Quarter, Red Coconut Club,** and **Jimmy Buffett's Margaritaville**), the lounges at Disney (such as **Rix** and the **Outer Rim**), or even as far out as downtown Orlando, where bars and dance clubs can be found along Wall Street and Church Street Station. Comedy clubs (**Fat Fish Blue, Sak Comedy Club,** and even the theatrical antics at **Sleuths Mystery Dinner Show**) will keep you laughing well into the night.

ORLANDO 101: WHAT HAPPENED WHEN THE MOUSE MOVED IN

You can't truly understand Orlando without finding out how it came to be a tourism behemoth in the first place. Orlando may have begun life as a sleepy little Southern town, but it sure didn't stay that way for long. Over the years, the city has dramatically transformed itself into an international vacation destination and the theme-park capital of the world. Orlando welcomes nearly 50 million visitors annually from all over the globe. What began with plantations, cattle ranches, and orange groves now boasts the world's greatest collection of thrill rides, fine dining, luxury accommodations, and superior shopping—not to mention an array of cultural and natural attractions. This, however, did not all happen overnight. Over the years, Orlando has felt its fair share of growing pains, even during its earliest days.

SETTLERS VS. SEMINOLES: THE ROAD TO STATEHOOD Florida history dates to 1513—more than a century before the Pilgrims landed at Plymouth Rock—when Ponce de León, a sometimes misguided explorer, spied the shoreline and lush greenery of Florida's Atlantic coast while looking for "the fountain of youth." He named it *La Florida*—"the place of flowers." After years of alternating Spanish, French, and British rule, the territory was ceded (by Spain) to the United States in 1821. Lost in the international shuffle were the Seminole Indians. After migrating from Georgia and the Carolinas in the late 18th century to some of Florida's richest farmlands, they were viewed by the *new* Americans as an obstacle to white settlement. A series of compromise treaties and violent clashes between settlers and the Seminoles continued through 1832, when a young warrior named Osceola strode up to the bargaining table, slammed his knife into the papers on it, and, pointing to the quivering blade, proclaimed, "The only treaty I will ever make is this!"

With that dramatic statement, the hostilities worsened. The Seminoles' guerrilla-style warfare thwarted the U.S. Army's attempt to remove them for almost 8 years, during which time many of the resisters drifted south into the interior of Central Florida. In what today is the Orlando area, the white settlers built Fort Gatlin in 1838 to offer protection to pioneer homesteaders. The Seminoles kept up a fierce rebellion until 1842, when, undefeated, they accepted a treaty whereby their remaining numbers (about 300) were given land and promised peace. The same year, the Armed Occupation Act offered 160 acres to any pioneer willing to settle in the area for a minimum of 5 years. The land was fertile: Wild turkeys and deer abounded in the woods, grazing land for cattle was equally plentiful, and dozens of lakes provided fish for settlers and water for livestock. In 1843, what had been Mosquito County was more invitingly renamed Orange County. And with the Seminoles more or less out of

15

the picture (though sporadic uprisings still occurred), the Territorial General Legislature petitioned Congress for statehood. On March 3, 1845, President John Tyler signed a bill making Florida the 27th state.

Settlements and statehood notwithstanding, at the middle of the 19th century, the Orlando area (then named Jernigan for one of its first settlers) consisted largely of pristine lakes and pine-forested wilderness. There were no roads, and you could ride all day (if you could find a trail) without meeting a soul. The Jernigans successfully raised cattle, and their homestead was given a post office in 1850. It became a way stop for travelers and the seat of future development. In 1856, the boundaries of Orange County were revised, and, thanks to the manipulations of resident James Gamble Speer, a member of the Indian Removal Commission, Fort Gatlin (Jernigan) became its official seat.

How the fledgling town came to be named Orlando is a matter of some speculation. Some say Speer renamed the town after a dearly loved friend, whereas other sources say it was named after a Shakespearean character in *As You Like It*. But the most accepted version is that the town was named for plantation owner Orlando Reeves (or Rees), whose homestead had been burned out in a skirmish. For years, it was thought a marker discovered near the shores of Lake Eola, in what is now downtown, marked his grave. But Reeves died later, in South Carolina. It's assumed the name carved in the tree was a marker for others who were on the Indians' trail. Whatever the origin, Orlando was officially recognized by the U.S. postmaster in 1857.

THE 1860S: CIVIL WAR/CATTLE WARS Throughout the early 1860s, cotton plantations and cattle ranches became the hallmarks of Central Florida. A cotton empire ringed Orlando. Log cabins went up along the lakes, and the pioneers eked out a somewhat lonely existence, separated from each other by miles of farmland. But there were troubles brewing in the 31-state nation that soon devastated Orlando's planters. By 1859, it was obvious that only a war would resolve the slavery issue. In 1861, Florida became the third state to secede from the Union, and the modest progress it had achieved came to a standstill. The Stars and Bars flew from every flagpole, and local men enlisted in the Confederate army, leaving the fledgling town

DATELINE

1843 Mosquito County in Central Florida is renamed Orange County.

1856 Orlando becomes the seat of Orange County.

1875 Orlando is incorporated as a municipality.

1880 The South Florida Railroad paves the way for the expansion of Orlando's agricultural markets. Swamp cabbage hits an all-time high on the commodities market.

1884 Fire destroys much of Orlando's fledgling business district.

1894-95 Freezing temperatures destroy the citrus crops, wreaking havoc on the groves and causing many growers to lose everything.

1910-25 A land boom hits Florida. Fortunes are made overnight.

1926 The land boom goes bust. Fortunes are lost overnight.

1929 An invasion of Mediterranean fruit flies devastates Orlando's citrus industry. But, who cares? Here comes the stock market crash.

1939-45 World War II revives Orlando's ailing economy.

of Orlando in poverty. A federal blockade made it difficult to obtain necessities, and many slaves fled. In 1866, the Confederate troops of Florida surrendered, the remaining slaves were freed, and a ragtag group of defeated soldiers returned to Orlando. They found a dying cotton industry, unable to function without slave labor. In 1868, Florida was readmitted to the Union.

Its untended cotton fields having gone to seed, Orlando concentrated on cattle ranching, a business heavily taxed by the government, and one that ushered in an era of lawlessness and violence. A famous battle involving two families, the Barbers and the Mizells, left at least nine men dead in 2 months in a Florida version of the Hatfields and McCoys.

A Fountain of Fruit

Legend has it that Florida's citrus industry has its roots in seeds spit onto the ground by Ponce de León and his followers as they traversed the state searching for the fountain of youth. The seeds supposedly germinated in the rich Florida soil.

Like frontier cattle towns out West, post–Civil War Orlando was short on civilized behavior. Gunfights, brawls, and murders were commonplace. But as the 1860s came to an end, large-herd owners from other parts of the state moved into the area and began organizing the industry in a less chaotic fashion. Branding and penning greatly reduced rustling, though they didn't totally eliminate the problem. Even a century later—as recently as 1973—soaring beef prices caused a rash of cattle thievery. Some traditions die hard. Even today, there are a number of rustling complaints each year.

AN ORANGE TREE GROWS IN ORLANDO   In the 1870s, articles in national magazines began luring large numbers of Americans to Central Florida with promises of fertile land and a warm climate. In Orlando, public roads, schools, and churches sprang up to serve the newcomers, many of whom replanted defunct cotton fields with citrus groves. Orlando was incorporated under state law in 1875, and boundaries and a city government were established.

1964   Walt Disney begins surreptitiously buying Central Florida farmland, purchasing more than 28,000 acres for nearly $5.5 million.

1965   Disney announces his plan to build the world's most spectacular theme park in Orlando.

1966   Walt Disney dies of lung cancer.

1971   The Magic Kingdom opens its gates for the first time.

1972   A new 1-day attendance mark is set December 27, when 72,328 people visit the Magic Kingdom. It will be broken almost every year thereafter.

1973   SeaWorld opens with a splash in Orlando.

1982   Epcot opens with vast hoopla.

1989   WDW launches Disney–MGM Studios (offering a behind-the-scenes look at Tinseltown), Typhoon Lagoon (a 56-acre water theme park), and Pleasure Island (a nightclub district for adults).

1990   Universal Studios Florida opens, bringing the movies to life for all who enter its gates.

1993   SeaWorld expands, and Universal Studios unleashes the fearsome Jaws.

continues

New settlers poured in from all over the country, businesses flourished, and by the end of the year the town had its first newspaper, the *Orange County Reporter*. The first locomotive of the South Florida Railroad chugged into town in 1880, sparking a building and land boom—the first of many. Orlando got sidewalks and its first bank in 1883, the same year the town voted itself dry in hopes of averting the fistfights and brawls that ensued when cowboys crowded into local saloons every Saturday night for some rowdy R&R. For many years, the city continued to vote itself alternately wet and dry, but it made little difference. Legal or not, liquor was always readily available.

FIRE & ICE   In January 1884, a grocery fire that started at 4am wiped out blocks of businesses, including the *Orange County Reporter*. But 19th-century Orlando was a bit like a Frank Capra movie. The town rallied, providing a new location for the paper and presenting its publisher, Mahlon Gore, with $1,200 in cash to help defray losses and $300 in new subscriptions. The paper not only survived, it flourished. And the city, realizing the need, created its first fire brigade. By August 1884, a census revealed a population of 1,666. That same year, 600,000 boxes of oranges were shipped from Florida to points north—most of those boxes originating in Orlando. By 1885, Orlando was a viable town, boasting as many as 50 businesses. This isn't to say it was New York. Razorback hogs roamed the streets and alligator wrestling was major entertainment.

Disaster struck a week after Christmas in 1894, when the temperature plummeted to an unseasonable 24°F (–4°C). Water pipes burst and orange blossoms froze, blackened, and died. The freeze continued for 3 days, wrecking the citrus crop for the year.

Many grove owners went bust, and those who remained were hit with a second devastating freeze the following year. Tens of thousands of trees died in the killing frost. Small growers were wiped out, but large conglomerates that could afford to buy up the small growers' properties at bargain prices and wait for new groves to mature assured the survival of the industry.

SPECULATION FEVER: GOOD DEALS, BAD DEALS . . .   As Orlando entered the 20th century, citrus and agriculture surpassed cattle ranching as the mainstays of the local economy. Stray cows no longer had to be shooed from the

1998 Disney starts its own cruise line and opens most of Animal Kingdom. Universal opens CityWalk, a vast new entertainment complex. Disney's West Side, Pleasure Island, and Disney Village Marketplace become known as Downtown Disney.

1999 Islands of Adventure, Universal Orlando's second theme park, featuring stomach-churning thrill rides, opens. The final section of Animal Kingdom, Asia, opens. The Disney Cruise Line launches Good Ship No. 2, the *Wonder*.

2000 SeaWorld opens its second park, Discovery Cove, offering a chance to swim with the fishes, er, dolphins. SeaWorld also delivers its first roller coaster, Kraken.

2001 Church Street Station closes its doors for good. The tourist industry takes a blow due to the September 11, 2001, terrorist attacks.

2003 The Waterfront entertainment district makes a splashy debut at SeaWorld.

2004 Cypress Gardens reopens as Cypress Gardens Adventure Park,

railway tracks. Streets were being paved and electricity and telephone service installed. The population at the turn of the 20th century was 2,481. In 1902, the city passed its first automobile laws, which included an in-town speed limit of 5 mph. In 1904, the city flooded. And in 1905, it suffered a drought that ended—miraculously or coincidentally—on a day when all faiths united at the local First Baptist Church to pray for rain. By 1910, prosperity returned, and Orlando, with a population of nearly 4,000, was in a small way becoming a tourism and convention center. World War I brought further industrial growth and a real-estate boom, not just to Orlando, but to all of Florida. Millions of immigrants, speculators, and builders descended on the state in search of a quick buck. As land speculation reached a fever pitch and property was bought and resold almost overnight, many citrus groves gave way to urbanization. Preeminent Orlando builder and promoter Carl Dann described the action: "It finally became nothing more than a gambling machine, each man buying on a shoestring, betting dollars a bigger fool would come along and buy his option."

Quite suddenly, the bubble burst. A July 1926 issue of the *Nation* provided the obituary for the Florida land boom: "The world's greatest poker game, played with lots instead of chips, is over. And the players are now . . . paying up." Construction slowed to a trickle, and many newcomers who came to Florida to jump on the bandwagon fled to their homes in the North. Though Orlando wasn't quite as hard hit as Miami—scene of the greediest land grabs—some belt-tightening was in order. Nevertheless, the city managed to build a municipal airport in 1928. Then came a Mediterranean fruit-fly infestation that crippled the citrus industry. Hundreds of thousands of acres of land in quarantined areas had to be cleared of fruit, and vast quantities of boxed fruit were destroyed. The 1929 stock market crash that precipitated the Great Depression added an exclamation point to Florida's ruined economy.

Liquor Ain't Quicker

The wet/dry battle in Orlando continued until 1998, when the city removed "blue laws" that restricted the sale of liquor on Sunday within the city limits.

featuring new thrill rides, water shows, concerts, and its famous botanical gardens.

2006 Expedition Everest becomes the first true thrill ride to debut at Animal Kingdom. SeaWorld debuts a new Shamu whale show.

2007 Disney–MGM Studios becomes Disney's Hollywood Studios.

2008 SeaWorld opens Aquatica. Disney shuts down the clubs at Pleasure Island.

2009 SeaWorld opens Manta—its third real thrill ride. Universal Studios rocks out with a new coaster, Hollywood Rip Ride Rockit. The American Idol Experience debuts at Disney's Hollywood Studios.

2010 Aquatica opens Omaka Rocka—a half-pipe-inspired water slide. The Wizarding World of Harry Potter is revealed at Islands of Adventure. The *Disney Wonder* sets sail for Alaska as the *Disney Dream* makes its maiden voyage.

continues

...& NEW DEALS   President Franklin D. Roosevelt's New Deal helped the state climb back on its feet. The Works Progress Administration (WPA) put 40,000 unemployed Floridians back to work—work that included hundreds of public projects in Orlando. Of these, the most important was the expansion and resurfacing of the city's airport. By 1936, the tourist trade had revived somewhat, construction was up once again, and the state began attracting a broader range of visitors. But the event that finally lifted Florida—and the nation—out of the Depression was World War II.

Orlando had weathered the Great Depression. Now it prepared for war with the construction of army bases, housing for servicemen, and training facilities. Enlisted men poured into the city. The airport was again enlarged and equipped with barracks, a military hospital, administration buildings, and mess halls. By 1944, Orlando had a second airport and was known as "Florida's Air Capital," home to major aircraft and aviation-parts manufacturers. Thousands of servicemen did part of their hitch in Orlando, and, when the war ended, many returned to settle here.

POSTWAR PROSPERITY   By 1950, Orlando, with a population of 51,826, was the financial and transportation hub of Central Florida. The city shared the bullish economy of the 1950s with the rest of the nation. In the face of the Cold War, the Orlando air base remained and grew, funneling millions of dollars into the local economy. Florida's population increased by a whopping 79% during the decade— making it America's 10th-most-populated state—and tourists came in droves, nearly 4.5 million in 1950.

One reason for the influx was the advent of the air-conditioner, which made life in Florida infinitely more pleasant. Also fueling Orlando's economy was a brand-new industry arriving in nearby Cape Canaveral in 1955—the government-run space program. Cape Canaveral became NASA's headquarters, including the Apollo rocket program that eventually blasted Neil Armstrong toward his "giant leap for mankind." During the same decade, the Glenn L. Martin Company (later Martin Marietta), builder of the Matador Missile, purchased 10 square miles for a plant 4 miles south of Orlando. Its advent sparked further industrial growth, and property values soared. More than 60 new industries moved to the area in 1959. But even the most

2011   The Grand Reef opens at Discovery Cove, bringing with this expansion the SeaVenture underwater walking tour. Star Tours reopens at Disney's Hollywood Studios, taking guests on an updated 3-D adventure across the galaxy. Halfway around the world, Aulani, Disney's newest Vacation Club Resort & Spa, opens in Hawaii. The Disney Cruise Line adds three new ports (New York, Seattle, and Galveston), 2-night cruises, and a slew of new itineraries. Disney breaks ground on the Shanghai Disney Resort.

optimistic Orlando boosters couldn't foresee the glorious future that was the city's ultimate destiny.

THE DISNEY DECADES In 1964, Walt Disney began secretly buying millions of dollars worth of Central Florida farmland. As vast areas of land were purchased in lots of 5,000 acres here, 20,000 there—at remarkably high prices—rumors flew as to who needed so much land and had the money to acquire it. Some thought it was Howard Hughes; others, the space program. Speculation was rife almost to the very day, November 15, 1965 ("D" Day for Orlando), when Uncle Walt arrived in town and announced his plans to build the world's most spectacular theme park ("bigger and better than Disneyland"). In a 2-year construction effort, Disney employed 9,000 people. Land speculation reached unprecedented heights, as hotel chains and restaurateurs grabbed up property near the proposed park. Mere swampland sold for millions. The total cost of the project by its October 1971 opening was $400 million. Mickey Mouse escorted the first visitor into the Magic Kingdom, and numerous celebrities, from Bob Hope to Julie Andrews, took part in the opening ceremonies. In Walt Disney World's first 2 years, the attraction drew 20 million visitors and employed 13,000 people. The sleepy citrus-growing town of Orlando had become the "Action Center of Florida," and the fastest-growing city in the state.

In the Words of Walt Disney

Why be a governor or a senator when you can be king of Disneyland? You can dream, create, design, and build the most wonderful place in the world . . . but it requires people to make the dream a reality.

Additional attractions multiplied faster than fruit flies, and hundreds of firms relocated their businesses to the area. SeaWorld, a major theme park, came to town in 1973. All the while, Walt Disney World continued to grow and expand, adding Epcot in 1982 and Disney–MGM Studios (now Disney's Hollywood Studios) in 1989, along with water parks; more than a dozen "official" resorts; a shopping, dining, and entertainment district; campgrounds; a vast array of recreational facilities; and several other adjuncts that are thoroughly described in this book. In 1998, Disney opened yet another theme park, this one dedicated to zoological entertainment and aptly called Animal Kingdom.

Universal Orlando, whose Universal Studios Florida park opened in 1990, continues to expand and keep the stakes high. In late 1998, it unveiled a new entertainment district, CityWalk, and in 1999, it opened Islands of Adventure, a second theme park including attractions dedicated to Dr. Seuss, Marvel Comics, and Jurassic Park. Also in 1999, it opened the Portofino Bay Hotel, a 750-room Loews property. In 2001, the curtain went up on the Hard Rock Hotel, and in summer 2002, the Royal Pacific resort opened as Universal announced plans to add two more hotels to the property in the next decade (plans that have thus far gone nowhere).

SeaWorld, too, got in on the action when it opened its $100-million sister park, Discovery Cove, in 2000. Now visitors have the chance to swim with dolphins even in landlocked Orlando.

While the tourist economy suffered for almost 2 years after the September 11, 2001, terrorist attacks and took a battering after a trio of hurricanes touched down in Central Florida in the summer of 2004, the industry has regained much of its strength as the years have passed. Indeed, one unfortunate casualty of the economic slowdown, Cypress Gardens, closed its doors in 2003 (and again, albeit only briefly, in 2008), reopened under new management with a new lineup of attractions, only to close its doors for good in 2009. Taking its place is the world's largest LEGOLAND (which at press time was preparing to open).

Disney, Universal, and SeaWorld, as usual, are in a building mode, albeit not quite as enthusiastically as they were during the late 1990s. All the parks have added new attractions, ranging from Soarin' at Epcot to Universal's Fear Factor Live to Sea-World's new entertainment and dining district, the Waterfront. In 2005, in honor of California sibling Disneyland's 50th anniversary, Disney World unveiled new shows, services, rides, and attractions. The year 2006 brought with it the addition of Expedition Everest, Animal Kingdom's first real thrill ride. And in 2007, the Cinderella Castle Suite (where lucky visitors can actually stay overnight inside the Magic Kingdom) was unveiled as part of Disney's Year of a Million Dreams celebration. New shows, attractions, and an after-hours Pirate and Princess Party debuted at the parks. Universal Orlando created a permanent home for the Blue Man Group at Universal Studios Florida. In 2008, Disney's Year of a Million Dreams continued, Disney–MGM Studios became Disney's Hollywood Studios, and even more new shows and attractions (including Toy Story Mania and a Disneyesque version of *American Idol*) debuted. Disney also closed its clubs on Pleasure Island in order to "re-imagine" the district. Aquatica (SeaWorld's eco-themed water park) became the first new park to open in over 8 years.

The year 2009 brought with it an economic upheaval that took a huge toll on tourism in Orlando, leaving the hotels, restaurants, and parks scrambling for business. Despite the slowdown, two new mega-coasters still managed to emerge: Manta, an undersea-themed thriller, debuted at SeaWorld, while up the road at Universal Studios, Hollywood Rip Ride Rockit, a combination rock concert, music video, and coaster ride, opened. Disney kicked off a new year-long celebration aptly named What Will You Celebrate, with free admission (to a single Disney park) as the bonus for guests visiting on their actual birthday. Downtown Disney began adding new shops, restaurants, and smaller attractions, slowly filling the "re-imagined" space where Pleasure Island's clubs once stood. New resorts continued to spring up in and around Orlando (including Disney's Treehouse Villas, Disney's Bay Lake Tower, and the nearby Waldorf Astoria, among others), but a slowdown in construction is expected in upcoming years.

Amid the continuing economic slump, Universal Orlando completed a massive expansion in 2010 as the Wizarding World of Harry Potter made its debut at Islands of Adventure. Disney inspired visitors to give back to the community with the Give a Day Get a Disney Day program, rewarding volunteers with a free day at a Disney theme park for their efforts. Disney's Wide World of Sports became the ESPN Wide World of Sports; the Electrical Parade returned, lighting up Main Street (in the Magic Kingdom) for the first time in almost 10 years; and dining options at Epcot expanded to include a Neapolitan Pizzeria (at the Italy Pavilion) and a Mexican Cantina (at the Mexico Pavilion). New resorts continue to open (the Holiday Inn in the Walt Disney World Resort, Marriott's Lakeshore Reserve at Grande Lakes, the Coco Key Hotel, Element Orlando Convention Center, and the Peabody Tower among them); however, as projected, construction has now slowed to a snail's pace, with not a single resort opening in 2011. Only two resorts, Disney's Art of Animation Resort and the Drury Inn & Suites (on Sand Lake Road), are slated to open this year. The Four

Seasons at the Walt Disney World Resort, originally set to open in 2012, remains on the books, but with an opening date "TBD."

With 2011 came signs of a slight upswing in the economy, tourism exhibiting the most visible signs of life. Hotels began filling rooms at a rate not seen in several years (with significant increases over the last year alone). Airport traffic and attraction attendance was on the rise, with tourists (and the theme parks) beginning to once again spend money. Disney began construction at levels almost unheard of in recent years. A major expansion began at the Magic Kingdom—with the size of Fantasyland to be doubled by the end of this year—and detailed plans were revealed for a re-imagined Pleasure Island, the abandoned clubs (standing empty since 2008) demolished to make way for what will soon become Hyperion Wharf. Also revealed were details regarding Disney's secretive billion-dollar investment in next-gen technology and experiences—though sketchy (and slated to roll out over the next several years), plans include bypassing hotel check-in, reserving ride times right from your computer, and a slew of personalized interactive experiences yet to be revealed. In addition, Disney kicked off Let the Memories Begin, the resorts' latest year-long celebration that has park-goers taking center stage, their images projected on Cinderella Castle each night for all to see. Also in 2011, Discovery Cove opened the Grand Reef, expanding its lineup of underwater attractions—including a walking tour that takes guests (donning diving helmets) along a series of underwater pathways. Even Gatorland got in on the expansion action, debuting a wild zipline experience that takes adventurous guests zipping across the park's preservelike grounds, high above the crocs and gators that lurk in the marshes below.

Regardless, the pace of progress in this ever-changing city continues to move forward—albeit more slowly than in the past—and it's a sure bet that these newcomers will be joined by even newer rides, resorts, and shopping and dining experiences in the coming years.

RECOMMENDED READING

The best Walt Disney World and Orlando guidebook on the planet (yes, this one) covers almost everything most travelers need and want to know. But there are a few areas where I bow to the expertise of less-than-mainstream or special-interest books. Interests and intent vary—some may want to discover the secret behind Disney's business strategy, others may find the region's historical timeline more to their liking, and still others may simply want to prepare their toddler for an upcoming trip. So here are a few additional books that may be available in your local library or bookstore.

○ *Florida's Ghostly Legends and Haunted Folklore* (2005, Pineapple Press) contains strange tales of the supernatural, revealing Florida's slightly spookier side. Move over, Haunted Mansion; this is the real deal. Ghost stories, legends, and accounts of strange occurrences may make you think twice about turning out the lights.

○ *National Audubon Society Field Guide to Florida* (1998, Knopf) is a handy back-pocket guide that delivers a wonderful education on the state's flora and fauna, parks and preserves, land, weather, natural phenomena, and much more. Plus, it's dripping with pictures to help newcomers and natives alike tell a yellow-bellied slider from a cooter.

o *A Photo Journey to Central Florida* (1992, AAA Publications), though some-what hard to find, features some rather nice photos of the area's architecture, historical sites, and scenic spots, along with pictures of the parks and attractions. It offers a brief glimpse into Florida and its natural beauty alongside the more commercial aspects of Orlando.

o *Vegetarian Walt Disney World and Greater Orlando, 2nd Edition* (2003, Vegetarian World Guides), is the most comprehensive and enterprising guide around for vegetarians, vegans, or mainstream diners looking for a break from carnivorous menus. Susan Shumaker and Than Saffel review 275 restaurants and hotels, more than half of which are on Disney soil. They also give tips about what to eat going to and from Orlando, as well as the dos and don'ts of ethnic dining in Central Florida. There's also a section on kids' dining.

o *Cooking with Mickey* (2000, Walt Disney Company) is a collection of the Mouse's most requested recipes. Do note that another way to take home some of the flavor of WDW is to simply ask for the recipe of a dish that you enjoyed. In some (but not all) cases, Disney will be happy to e-mail the instructions and a list of ingredients to you at home.

o *Delicious Disney Just for Kids* (2011, Disney Editions) is filled cover to cover with contributions from Disney chefs (from Disney World, Disneyland, and the Disney Cruise Line). The kid-friendly cookbook has recipes that kids will enjoy making as much as they will eating—including macaroni and cheese (from Jiko) and BLT tomato soup (from the Sci-Fi Dine-In Theater).

o *Mickey's Gourmet Cookbook* (1994, Disney Editions) is full of some of the most popular recipes from the House of Mouse—a few culinary secrets that Disney is willing to share. You can keep your vacation going even after you get home—provided you can cook.

o *Hidden Mickeys, 3rd Edition: A Field Guide to Walt Disney World's Best Kept Secrets* (2007, Intrepid Traveler) is filled with trivia and, of course, those Hidden Mickeys—including tips on where and how to look for them.

o *Kingdom Keepers* (2005–11, Disney Hyperion) is a seven-book series that takes young readers on a fantastic adventure, pitting the main characters against a familiar assortment of Disney villains as they try to take over the park. The books highlight actual attractions and locations throughout the Walt Disney World resort.

o *Popping Up Around Walt Disney World* (2004, Disney Editions) is fun for kids (and even adults). This colorful and detailed pop-up book offers a tour through the world of Disney. It takes readers through the parks, details some of the attractions, and tosses in a bit of trivia, too.

o *Weird Florida: Your Travel Guide to Florida's Local Legends and Best Kept Secrets* (2009, Sterling) is a mix of historical accounts, wacky rumors, myths, and urban legends—a showcase of Florida's more unusual side.

o *Be Our Guest* (2004, Disney Editions) is a how-to guide to the hospitality industry that business gurus will appreciate.

o *Designing Disney* (2009, Disney Editions) highlights the tremendous contributions made by John Hench, one of Disney's original and most influential Imagineers whose legendary concepts were key in designing Disney's theme parks.

o *Since the World Began: Walt Disney World: The First 25 Years* (1996, Disney Editions) is a must for Disney fanatics. The title was originally intended to celebrate Disney World's 25th anniversary, and readers will find page after page filled with drawings and photos, along with a detailed history of the park's creation.

○ **Spinning Disney's World** (2007, Intrepid Traveler) looks back at the career of a Disney original: Charles Ridgeway, one of Disney's first and foremost PR personalities. He fondly recollects his years at Disney, from his days working directly with Walt to the present.

○ **Walt Disney: The Triumph of the American Imagination** (2007, Vintage) recounts in great detail the life of Walt Disney himself, from his early childhood to his years at Disney Studios and beyond.

○ **Walt Disney Imagineering: A Behind the Dreams Look at Making More Magic Real** (2010, Disney Editions), a sequel to *Walt Disney Imagineering: A Behind the Dreams Look at Making the Magic Real,* introduces readers to Disney's creative dream team as the Imagineers themselves reveal who they are, what they do, and how they do it. Highlights include sketches and concept art of Disney's newest attractions, as well as a hint at future projects.

WHEN TO GO

Orlando is the theme-park capital of the world, and you could almost argue that there really is no off season here, though the busiest seasons are whenever kids are out of school. Late May to just past Labor Day, long holiday weekends, winter holidays (mid-Dec to early Jan), and most especially spring break (late Mar to Apr) are very busy. Do, however, keep in mind that kids in other hemispheres follow a completely different schedule altogether. Obviously, an Orlando vacation—and especially a Disney vacation—is most enjoyed when the crowds are at the thinnest and the weather is the most temperate. Hotel rooms (likely the largest chunk of your vacation bill) are also priced lower (albeit only slightly) during the off season, though don't expect that period to follow the traditional winter/summer patterns of most areas.

Peak-season rates can go into effect during large conventions and special events, either of which may occur at any time of the year. Even something as remote as Bike Week in Daytona Beach (about an hour's drive away) can raise prices. These kinds of events will especially impact the moderately priced hotels and resorts located off Walt Disney World.

Best times: Try the week after Labor Day until the week before Thanksgiving, when the kids have just returned to school; the week after Thanksgiving until mid-December; and the 6 weeks before and after school spring vacations (which generally occur around Easter).

Worst times: The absolute worst time of year to visit is during spring break—usually the 2 weeks prior to and after Easter. The crowds are unbelievable, the lines are unbearable (my kids have waited upwards of 2 hr. to hop on some of the most popular attractions), waiting times at local restaurants can lead to starvation, and traffic—particularly on International Drive—will give you a headache. The December holidays and summer, when out-of-state visitors take advantage of school breaks and many locals bring their families to the parks (the latter also flock to the parks during Florida resident discount months, which usually fall in May and Nov), can also prove a challenge. Packed parking lots are the norm during the week before and after Christmas, and the summer brings with it oppressive heat and humidity.

Seriously consider pulling your kids out of school for a few days around an off-season weekend to avoid the long lines. (You may be able to keep them in their schools' good graces by asking teachers to let them write a report on an educational element of the vacation. Epcot, SeaWorld, and the Orlando Museum of Science offer the most in the way of educational exhibits.) Even during these periods, though, the number of international visitors guarantees you won't be alone.

One other time-related hazard: For several weeks in May and September, you will find yourself in the midst of the dreaded "love bug" season in Central Florida. These small flylike insects emerge twice a year, get into practically everything, and like nothing more than to commit suicide on your car windshield, leaving a messy splatter. They don't bite, but they are a serious nuisance. If you can avoid them, I highly recommend it.

Weather

It's not uncommon for the skies to open up on Orlando, even when the day begins with the sun ablaze. Florida is well known for its afternoon downpours, so don't be too concerned—storms don't usually last too long. Most people simply run for temporary cover, and then resume their activities when the rain slows to a drizzle or stops altogether. It is wise, however, to bring along some type of rain gear, as storms can spring up rather quickly. A small fold-up umbrella can protect you until you can get to shelter. If you forget your gear, rain ponchos can be purchased throughout the parks for about $6 for a child-size poncho, or $8 for an adult size. The child-size poncho also happens to cover the average stroller quite well, protecting camera equipment and souvenirs—not to mention the child sitting inside it.

Don't let a rainy afternoon spoil your fun. Crowds are dramatically thinner on these days, and there are plenty of indoor attractions to enjoy, particularly at Epcot, Disney's Hollywood Studios, and Universal Studios Florida, where many of the attractions are actually indoors. The flip side, of course, is that many of the outdoor rides and attractions at Disney, Universal, and SeaWorld are temporarily closed during downpours and lightning storms.

Note: If you're taking advantage of a land/cruise package (see "Disney Cruise Packages," later in this chapter), make sure you take into account hurricane season, which generally runs from around June 1 to November 30 (when the majority of Central Florida's afternoon downpours tend to occur). Inland, the worst is usually only sheets of rain and enough wind to wipe the smile right off your face. That said, the summer of 2004 (when three hurricanes passed through the area) was a noticeable reminder that the worst can happen, and 2005 brought with it what seemed like an endless number of storms, extending the rainy season well beyond the normal timeline. And while 2006 was relatively quiet weather-wise, tornados touched down and devastated areas just north of Orlando in 2007. Although the past few years have been relatively quiet, forecasters predict an increased number of storms in 2012—but how many will actually reach land (or affect areas as far inland as Orlando) is unknown. The moral of this story: Be prepared, because almost anything can happen. If you are on the coastal areas or at sea, you will likely be at the point where the storms hit their hardest, making them extremely dangerous. Tornadoes and lightning—two particularly active summer curses—should also not be taken lightly.

Central Florida Average Temperatures

	JAN	FEB	MAR	APR	MAY	JUNE	JULY	AUG	SEPT	OCT	NOV	DEC
High (°F)	71	73	78	83	88	91	92	92	90	85	79	73
High (°C)	22	23	26	28	31	33	33	33	32	29	26	23
Low (°F)	49	50	55	60	66	72	73	73	73	66	58	51
Low (°C)	9	10	13	16	19	22	23	23	23	19	14	11

Holidays

Banks, government offices, post offices, and many stores, restaurants, and museums are closed on the following legal national holidays: January 1 (New Year's Day), the third Monday in January (Martin Luther King, Jr., Day), the third Monday in February (Presidents' Day), the last Monday in May (Memorial Day), July 4 (Independence Day), the first Monday in September (Labor Day), the second Monday in October (Columbus Day), November 11 (Veterans' Day/Armistice Day), the fourth Thursday in November (Thanksgiving Day), and December 25 (Christmas). The Tuesday after the first Monday in November is Election Day, a federal government holiday in presidential-election years (held every 4 years, and next in 2012).

Orlando Area Calendar of Events

For an exhaustive list of events beyond those listed here, check **http://events.frommers. com**, where you'll find a searchable, up-to-the-minute roster of what's happening in not only Orlando, but in cities all over the world.

JANUARY

Capital One Florida Citrus Bowl. New Year's Day kicks off with this football game in downtown Orlando. It pits the second-ranked teams from the Southeastern and Big Ten conferences against each other. Tickets range from $50 to $90. Club seats ($225) and club suites are available as well. Call ✆ **800/297-2695** or 407/423-2476 for information, or **Ticketmaster** at ✆ **800/745-3000** for tickets (on the Internet, visit www.fcsports.com). Pep rallies and a free downtown parade are held a few days before the game, featuring marching bands and floats.

Walt Disney World Marathon. About 90% of the 16,000 runners finish this 26.2-mile "sprint" through the resort area and parks. It's open to anyone 18 and older, including runners with disabilities, as long as they are able to maintain the 16-minute-mile pacing requirements. If you are unable to do so, you'll be picked up and transported to the finish line. The registration fee ($140-$160, depending on when you register) includes race entry, a T-shirt, and a program—those who finish receive a medal, other souvenir extras, and complimentary admission to a Disney park on the Monday after the race. The final registration deadline is usually in early November (but is often at capacity several months earlier), and preregistration is required. There's also a half-marathon ($140-$160), Goofy's Race-and-a-Half Challenge (includes registration for both marathons; $310-$350), a two-person team marathon relay ($280-$320), a Family Fun Run 5K for both kids and adults ($50; $55 with a child in a stroller), and Mickey's Marathon Kid Fest, which includes the Mickey Mile ($25 per child) and a handful of shorter races for the 13-and-under set—including a diaper dash ($10 per child). Call ✆ **407/ 939-7810,** or go to **www.disneysports. com**. Early January.

Zora Neale Hurston Festival. This 4-day celebration in Eatonville, the first incorporated African-American town in America, highlights the life and works of the author and is usually held the last weekend in January. Eatonville is 25 miles north of the theme parks. Admission is free, though tickets ($5-$100) are required for select lectures, seminars, concerts, and events. Call ☎ **407/647-3959,** or check out **www.zorafestival.com**.

FEBRUARY

Atlanta Braves. The Braves have been holding spring training at ESPN Wide World of Sports Complex since 1998. There are 18 home games during the 1-month season. The team arrives in mid-February; games begin in early March. Tickets are $10 to $42. You can get more information at ☎ **407/939-GAME** (4236) or www.espn wwos.com/atlantabraves. To purchase tickets, call Ticketmaster at ☎ **800/745-3000.** You can also get online information at **www.atlantabraves.com** or **www.majorleaguebaseball.com**.

Houston Astros. The Astros train at Osceola County Stadium, 1000 Bill Beck Blvd., Kissimmee. Tickets are $10 to $27. Get them through Ticketmaster at ☎ **800/745-3000.** Games begin in late February and run through March. For information, check the Astros' website at **www.astros.com**.

Mardi Gras at Universal Orlando. Floats, stilt walkers, live entertainment, and beads thrown to the crowd add to the fun of this event. A party to rival the original held in New Orleans, it's definitely geared toward an adult crowd, with plenty of drinking and carousing. Special discounted tickets are available allowing entrance to the park only after 5pm ($54.99); otherwise, it's included in regular park admission ($85 adults). The celebration runs 1 night a week—usually Saturday—from mid-February to mid-April. For information, call ☎ **888/389-4783** or 407/363-8000, or go online to **www.universalorlando.com**.

Silver Spurs Rodeo. It features real yippee-I-O cowboys in calf roping, bull riding, barrel racing, and more. This rodeo is the largest in the eastern United States. It's held at the Silver Spurs Arena, 1875 E. Irlo Bronson Memorial Hwy. (U.S. 192), Kissimmee. It runs for 3 days in February and again for 3 days in June. Tickets cost $15 (kids 10 and under are free with a paying

adult). Call ☎ **407/677-6336,** or visit **www.silverspursrodeo.com** for details.

MARCH

Arnold Palmer Invitational. Hosted by Arnold Palmer and featuring top-ranked players including Ernie Els and Orlando-based golfer Tiger Woods, this PGA Tour event is held at the Bay Hill Club, 9000 Bay Hill Blvd. Daily admission is $35 to $45 and up for adults, $15 for ages 11 to 17. Call ☎ **866/764-4843** or 407/876-7774, or check out **www.arnoldpalmerinvitational.com**.

Sidewalk Arts Festival. Held in Winter Park's Central Park, this 3-day exhibition draws artists from all over North America on the third weekend in March. The festival is consistently named one of the best in the nation by *Sunshine Artist* magazine. Admission is free, though you may have to pay for parking. Call ☎ **407/672-6390,** or go to **www.wpsaf.org** for details.

APRIL

Florida Film Festival. The Enzian Theater has been showcasing American independent and foreign films for more than a decade. This annual event was named one of the top 10 such events in the world by *The Ultimate Film Festival Survival Guide, 2nd Edition* (Lone Eagle). Single tickets run $10. Call ☎ **407/644-6579,** or check out **www.floridafilmfestival.com**.

Epcot International Flower & Garden Festival. This 6-week-long event showcases gardens, topiary characters, floral displays, speakers, seminars, and nightly entertainment. The festival is free with regular park admission ($85 adults, $79 kids 3–9). For more information, call ☎ **407/934-7639** or visit **www.disneyworld.com**. The festival kicks off in late April and goes through early June.

Viva La Musica. This celebration of Latin culture and music is held annually at Sea-World. Festivities include concerts, crafts, and food displays throughout the park. There is no extra charge to join in the fun, which happens on select Saturdays in April and May. For more information and exact dates, head online to **www.seaworld.com**.

Orlando International Fringe Festival. More than 100 diverse acts from around the world participate in this eclectic event, held for 10 days in May at various venues in downtown Orlando. Entertainers present drama, comedy, political satire, and experimental theater. Everything performed on outdoor stages, from sword swallowing to *Hamlet,* is available free to Fringe attendees after they purchase a festival button for about $6. Ticket prices for indoor events vary, but most are less than $10. Call ✆ **407/648-0077,** or visit **www.orlando fringe.org** for details.

Star Wars Weekends. Every year, Disney features a fan-fest full of activities for *Star Wars* fanatics. Characters are on hand for up-close meet-and-greets, as well as a handful of *Star Wars* actors. Games, parades, and special entertainment top off the festivities. The celebrations run for 5 consecutive weekends beginning in May and are included in park admission ($85 adults, $79 kids).

JUNE

Gay Days. The first weekend in June attracts tens of thousands of gays and lesbians to Central Florida for what amounts, with add-ons, to a week of festivities. It grew out of "Gay Day," held unofficially at Disney World since the early 1990s and drawing some 100,000 people to the area. Special events at Disney, Universal, and SeaWorld cater to gays and lesbians. Look for online information on discounts, packages, hosts, and more at **www.gaydays.com.** Also see "Fast Facts: Orlando: LGBT Travelers," on p. 380.

Silver Spurs Rodeo. See the description under "February," above.

JULY

Independence Day. Disney adds a bit of sparkle to the fireworks displays at all the Disney parks, which stay open later than normal. Call ✆ **407/934-7639,** or surf over to **www.disneyworld.com** for details. **SeaWorld** (✆ **407/351-3600;** www.sea world.com) features a dazzling laser/fireworks spectacular. There's also a free fireworks display in downtown Orlando at Lake Eola Park. For information, call ✆ **407/246-2827.** Other fireworks events are listed in the local newspaper, the *Orlando Sentinel.*

SEPTEMBER

Night of Joy. The first weekend (Thurs–Sun) in September, the Magic Kingdom hosts a festival of contemporary Christian music featuring top artists. This is a very popular event, so obtain tickets early. Performers also make an appearance at Long's Christian Bookstore in College Park, about 20 minutes north of Disney. Admission (if you buy in advance) to the concert is $51.95 for 1 night (7:30pm–12:30am), or $92.95 for 2 nights; single-night admission at the gate is $59.95. Use of Magic Kingdom attractions is included. For concert details, call ✆ **407/934-7639;** for information about the free appearance at Long's, call ✆ **407/422-6934.**

Universal has gone head-to-head with Disney on this one, scheduling its **Rock the Universe** concert the same weekend (✆ **866/788-4636**). Big-name Christian bands and speakers headline the event. Tickets (which include admission to the parks after 4pm) cost $59.99 for 1 night, or $85.99 for both nights of the event. Packages including both nights of celebration and 3 days of admission to the parks are available as well ($105.99).

OCTOBER

Orlando Magic. The NBA team plays half of its 82-game regular season between October and April at the Amway Arena, 600 W. Amelia St. Ticket prices range from $18 to $150 (higher for premium seats). A few tickets, usually single seats, are often available the day before games involving lesser known NBA challengers. Call ✆ **407/916-2400** for details, or 866/448-7849 or 407/839-3900 for tickets. On the Internet, go to **www.nba.com/magic.**

Halloween Horror Nights. Universal Orlando's Islands of Adventure (✆ **888/389-4783** or 407/363-8000; www.universal orlando.com) transforms its grounds on select nights during October and into

November into haunted attractions. Live entertainment and special shows, hundreds of ghouls and goblins roaming the streets, and specially designed haunted houses make for a truly terrifying experience. The park essentially closes at dusk, reopening in a new macabre form from 7pm to midnight or later. Full admission ($85 adults) is charged for this event, which is definitely geared to grown-ups (as the liquor flows freely and the frightfulness is *truly* that). Note that guests are not permitted to wear costumes (so that Universal employees can spot their peers).

Mickey's Not-So-Scary Halloween Party. The Magic Kingdom (℗ **407/934-7639;** www.disneyworld.com) invites you to join Mickey and his pals for a far-from-frightening time. In this one, you can come in costume and trick-or-treat throughout the Magic Kingdom from 7pm to midnight on any of 10 or so nights. The alcohol-free party includes parades, live music, and storytelling. The climax is a bewitching fireworks spectacular. Unlike the celebration at Universal Studios, this one is completely family-friendly. A separate admission fee is charged ($59.95–$67.95 adults, $53.95–$62.95 kids 3–9, depending on the night), and you should get tickets well in advance (saving you $6 per ticket).

Children's Miracle Network Golf Classic. Top PGA tour players compete at WDW golf courses during the month of October. Many tour professionals, including Stephen Ames, Brian Davis, and Tiger Woods (who calls Orlando home) participate, ensuring that there's usually plenty of first-rate talent on display. Daily ticket prices range from $15 to $35. Tickets for the 4-day event run about $50. For information, contact Walt Disney World Golf Sales, P.O. Box 10000, Lake Buena Vista, FL 32830 (℗ **407/824-2250;** www.disneyworld.com). You also can get tickets through the Children's Miracle Network at **www.childrensmiraclenetworkclassic.com**.

Epcot International Food & Wine Festival. Here's your chance to sip and savor the food and beverages of more than 20 cultures. More than 100 wineries from across the United States participate. Events include wine tastings for adults, seminars, food, dinners, concerts, and celebrity-chef cooking demonstrations. Tickets for the seminars, lunches, and wine tastings run approximately $35 to $130, including gratuity; signature dinners and vertical wine tastings range from $100 to $375 (sometimes more). The event also features 25 food-and-wine marketplaces where appetizer-size portions of dishes ranging from pizza to escargot (and everything in between) sell for less than $8 each. Entrance to the festival is included in park admission. Call ℗ **407/934-7639,** or check out **www.disneyworld.com** for details. Early October to mid-November.

NOVEMBER

Walt Disney World Festival of the Masters. One of the largest art shows in the South takes place at Downtown Disney Marketplace for 3 days during the second weekend in November. The exhibition features more than 150 top artists, photographers, and craftspeople, all winners of juried shows throughout the country. You can listen to the music of the jazz festival or enjoy one of the many family activities, all for free. Call ℗ **407/934-7639,** or visit **www.disneyworld.com**.

The Osborne Family Spectacle of Lights. This classic holiday attraction returned by popular demand after being closed down for renovations in 2004 and 2005. Lighting up the nights at Disney's Hollywood Studios are millions of sparkling bulbs acquired from a family whose Christmas-light collection got a bit too bright for their neighbors. Sadly, Jennings Osborne, the man originally responsible for creating this spectacular display, passed away in 2011—but his twinkling and dancing lights remain a shining reminder of the holiday spirit he shared with the world. The holiday display runs from November to early January.

DECEMBER

Christmas at Walt Disney World. During the holiday festivities, Main Street in the Magic Kingdom is lavishly decked out with twinkling lights and Christmas holly, all while carolers are greeting visitors throughout the park. Epcot, Disney's Hollywood Studios, and Animal Kingdom also offer special embellishments and entertainment throughout the holiday season, and the Disney resorts are decked out with towering Christmas trees, wreaths, boughs, and bows.

Some holiday highlights include **Mickey's Very Merry Christmas Party,** an after-dark (7pm–midnight) ticketed event ($62.95 adults, $57.95 kids 3–9). This takes place on select nights at the Magic Kingdom and offers a festive parade, fireworks, special shows, and admission to a handful of rides. Also included are cookies, cocoa, and a souvenir photo.

Holidays Around the World and the **Candlelight Procession** at Epcot feature hundreds of carolers, storytellers from a host of international countries, celebrity narrators telling the Christmas story, a 450-voice choir, and a 50-piece orchestra in a very moving display. Fireworks are included. Regular admission ($85 adults, $79 kids 3–9) is required. Call ✆ **407/934-7639** for details on all of the above, or go to **www.disneyworld.com**. The holiday fun lasts from mid-December to early January.

Macy's Holiday Parade. That's not a typo! Universal and Macy's (the latter a tenant at the Mall at Millenia, p. 314) offer a smaller version of **Macy's Thanksgiving Day Parade** at Universal Studios Florida. It runs from mid-December to early January, featuring several of the floats and gigantic balloons from the original New York City parade (✆ **407/363-8000;** www.universalorlando.com). Park admission ($85 adults, $79 kids 3–9) is required. Over at Islands of Adventure, even the Grinch celebrates the holidays at Seuss Landing, which is decked out like Whoville for the holidays, including wintry decorations and Whos running all about to create a festive mood.

Walt Disney World New Year's Eve Celebration. For 1 night a year, the Magic Kingdom stays open until the wee hours for a massive fireworks explosion. In the past, other New Year's festivities in WDW have included a special Hoop-Dee-Doo Musical Revue at Fort Wilderness, as well as guest performances by well-known musical groups at Disney's Hollywood Studios and Epcot. Call ✆ **407/934-7639,** or visit **www.disneyworld.com** for details. December 31.

RESPONSIBLE TRAVEL

While sustainable travel may not be the first thing you think of when heading to the theme-park capital of the world, Orlando takes the environment quite seriously—understandable for an area that's impacted so heavily by the millions of tourists who visit from around the world (a number that far exceeds the number of actual area residents). As the city's largest employers, Disney, Universal, and SeaWorld (among others) actively encourage eco-friendly practices—on their own part as well as on the part of the millions of guests who pass through their gates, eat at their restaurants, and stay at their hotels.

Disney, in addition to ensuring that its hotels are "green" certified properties (see "Green Hotels," below), has announced that over the next several years the company will continue to decrease greenhouse emissions (though the goal is to eliminate them altogether down the road) and will

Disney in December

No snow? No problem. Although there may be a lack of the white stuff in Orlando during the month of December (or any other month, for that matter), WDW more than makes up for it by decking the halls as only Disney can do: 11 miles of garlands, 3,000 wreaths, and 1,500 Christmas trees in all decorate Walt Disney World during the holiday season.

decrease its electrical use by 10%. Other lofty goals include the reduction of solid waste (cut by 50% by the year 2013).

Universal is doing its part as well. All three of its on-site hotels have been "green" certified. Universal has also begun using alternative fuels in its service vehicles in an effort to reduce toxic emissions; the cooking oil used in its restaurants is recycled, as are the paper and cardboard products used throughout the resort.

At SeaWorld (and its sister parks), hydrogen fuels power shuttles, dinnerware and utensils are made from sugarcane and vegetable starch, and seafood (even for its animal inhabitants) is purchased from sustainable fisheries. SeaWorld has partnered with the Rainforest Alliance to ensure that foods purchased are farmed and harvested in ways that protects area wildlife, habitats, and people. Roughly 50% of park waste (animal, food, and construction) is recycled. Visitors (and residents) are encouraged to recycle while exploring the theme parks thanks to the addition of special bins for the disposal of cans and bottles, with others for actual trash.

Using public transportation (most notably Disney's vast array of buses, monorails, and water taxis; Universal's water taxis and buses; International Dr.'s I-Ride Trolley system, and so forth) contributes to getting more cars off the street, making for cleaner air. In Orlando, it's even possible to hire a pedicab; the **Redi Pedi Pedicab** (© **407/403-5511**) and **5 Star Pedicab** (© **407/566-7527**) are the two largest companies serving the Orlando area.

In addition, several hotels, among them the entire collection of official Walt Disney World resorts and all of the Universal Orlando resorts, have signed on to the Florida Green Lodge program, which requires hotels to become more energy efficient in all areas of operation, from conserving water to reducing unsorted waste (see "Green Hotels," below). Hotels that meet the standard are awarded one-, two-, or three-palm certification.

General Ecotourism Resources

Sustainable tourism is defined as conscientious travel—in other words, being careful with the environments you explore and respecting the communities you visit. Two overlapping components of sustainable travel are **ecotourism** and **ethical tourism.** The **International Ecotourism Society (TIES)** defines ecotourism as responsible travel to natural areas that conserves the environment and improves the well-being of local people. TIES suggests that ecotourists follow these principles:

- Minimize environmental impact.
- Build environmental and cultural awareness and respect.
- Provide positive experiences for both visitors and hosts.
- Provide direct financial benefits for conservation and for local people.
- Raise sensitivity to host countries' political, environmental, and social climates.
- Support international human rights and labor agreements.

You can find some eco-friendly travel tips and statistics, as well as touring companies and associations—listed by destination under "Your Travel Choice"—at the **TIES** website, **www.ecotourism.org**. Also check out **Ecotravel.com,** which lets you search for sustainable touring companies in several categories (water based, land based, spiritually oriented, and so on).

Responsible Travel (www.responsibletravel.com) is a great source of sustainable travel ideas; the site is run by a spokesperson for ethical tourism in the travel industry.

"green" HOTELS

Quite a number of Orlando hotels have received "green" certification by the Florida Department of Environmental Protection and are designated as Green Lodge hotels. In order to be considered for the certification, hotels must adhere to a set list of requirements, including conservation of water through the use of low-flow plumbing fixtures, a linen reuse program, and the use of energy-efficient and programmable thermostats. Waste-reduction criteria must also be met. In addition, all Green Lodges must use green cleaning supplies and high-efficiency air filters.

Green Lodge resorts can (and do) range from mom-and-pop motels to five-star luxury resorts in Orlando. For more on the program and a complete list of the hotels in and around Orlando that are green (there are several, including all official WDW resorts and all official Universal resorts), go to **www.dep. state.fl.us/greenlodging**.

Sustainable Travel International (www.sustainabletravelinternational.org) promotes ethical tourism practices and manages a directory of sustainable properties and tour operators around the world.

Carbonfund (www.carbonfund.org), **TerraPass** (www.terrapass.org), and **Carbon Neutral** (www.carbonneutral.org) provide information on carbon offsetting, or offsetting the greenhouse gases emitted during flights.

While much of the focus of ecotourism is about reducing impacts on the natural environment, ethical tourism concentrates on ways to preserve and enhance local economies and communities, regardless of location. You can embrace ethical tourism by staying at a locally owned hotel or shopping at a store that employs local workers and sells locally produced goods.

Animal-Rights Issues

While most know **SeaWorld** only as an adventure park, it is in fact a huge supporter of both the environment and its inhabitants. A good deal of the work it does behind the scenes revolves around the rescue and rehabilitation of the ocean's wildlife. At the same time, its attractions are meant to help educate the public about the inhabitants of the world's vast oceans and the importance of keeping their environments (and ours) safe for them (and us) to live in. In addition, the **SeaWorld Wildlife Fund** focuses its resources on species research, habitat protection, animal rescue and rehabilitation, and conservation education. Since its launch, it has granted $5 million to more than 350 projects in 60 countries, including global organizations such as World Wildlife Fund, the Nature Conservancy, and Conservation International, along with smaller grassroots organizations. For those concerned about the dolphin-swim programs, additional information about the ethics of swimming with dolphins and other outdoor activities can be found by visiting the websites of the **Whale and Dolphin Conservation Society** (www.wdcs.org) and **Tread Lightly** (www.treadlightly.org).

Over at Walt Disney World, **Disney's Worldwide Conservation Fund** (established back in 1995 as a global awards program for the study and protection of the world's wildlife and ecosystems), in association with Disney's Animal Kingdom, now contributes financially by supporting some 750 projects with more than $12 million in grants to organizations and individuals working in 110 countries for the protection and study of wildlife and ecosystems—many of which are biological hot spots rich in plant and animal life at risk of imminent destruction. Locally, Disney's Animal Program has played a significant and integral part in the propagation of several species and the rescue of injured wildlife. Not only does the Animal Kingdom oversee the health and well-being of all animals at Walt Disney World, but it is also responsible for thousands of animals, including 33 endangered and threatened species throughout the area. Veterinary services, science, and animal-care teams work together to ensure that each animal receives the best possible care. Disney's Animal Kingdom and the Seas at Epcot are both accredited by the Association of Zoos and Aquariums.

ORIENTATION
Visitor Information

Once you've arrived, you can stop in at the **Orlando/Orange County Convention & Visitors Bureau (Orlando CVB),** 8723 International Dr., Ste. 101, Orlando; however, it's best to call ahead (📞 **800/972-3304** or 407/363-5872; www.visit orlando.com) for information on the area's offerings. Staffers at the CVB can help answer your questions, as well as send out maps, brochures, and coupons good for discounts or freebies. The CVB sells discount tickets to several attractions. Savings on multiday passes to Universal run about $10, while SeaWorld savings run about $2 on a 1-day ticket (and at times includes a second day free), and up to $15 on multipark tickets; only Disney's 4-day or longer passes are discounted, with savings from $5 to $15 depending on the ticket (some include free upgrades, increasing the savings even more). The CVB's multilingual staff can also make dinner reservations and hotel referrals for you. The CVB is open daily from 8:30am to 6:30pm, except Christmas. From I-4, take exit 74A east 2 blocks, turn south on International Drive, and continue 1 mile. The center is on the left, at the corner of I-Drive and Austrian Row.

The **Kissimmee Convention & Visitors Bureau** is located at 1925 E. Irlo Bronson Memorial Hwy./U.S. 192, Kissimmee (📞 **407/742-8200;** www.visit kissimmee.com). It also offers maps, brochures, and discount coupons. From I-4, take exit 64A/U.S. 192 east about 12 miles to Bill Beck Boulevard, and then go left into the CVB's parking lot. It's open Monday through Friday from 8am to 5pm. Again, you can call and have these items sent to you ahead of time so you can do some planning at home.

Five tourism centers around Florida have statewide information. They're located 4 miles north of Jennings on I-75 south; 3 miles north of Campbellton on Highway 231; 7 miles north of Yulee on I-95; 16 miles west of Pensacola on I-10 east; and at the capitol in Tallahassee.

Finally, nearly all hotel lobbies and many restaurants, highway rest stops, and attractions have racks brimming with brochures for area activities (except for Disney brochures—they're only available at Disney-owned and -operated hotels, "official" Disney hotels along Hotel Plaza Blvd., and designated "Good Neighbor" hotels). Many are filled with dining discounts and cost-cutting coupons, so cover your bases and pick up a few of everything.

INFORMATION (& MORE) AT THE AIRPORT

Passengers arriving at or departing from Orlando International Airport can stroll over to one of two Disney shops. The **Magic of Disney** (📞 **407/825-2360**) is in the

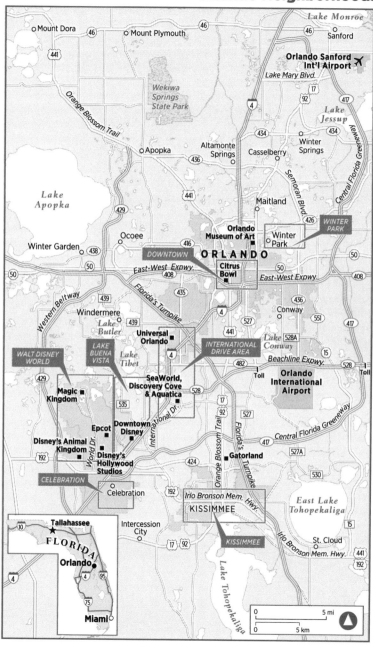

main terminal, third level, right behind the Northwest Airlines ticket desk. **Disney Earport** (☎ **407/825-2339**) is in the main terminal, across from the Hyatt Regency. They sell WDW multiday tickets, arrange dinner-show and hotel reservations at Disney resorts, and provide brochures and assistance. They're open daily, usually from 7am to 9 or 10pm, but know that the airport stores are filled with a rather run-of-the-mill selection of Disney merchandise; unless you're on your way home and forgot to buy that must-have Mickey for Auntie Gertrude, you'll find a far better selection elsewhere.

The **Universal Studios Stores** (☎ **407/825-2473**), usually open daily from 7am to 9pm, sell park tickets at two locations: Airside A, main terminal, and Airside B, Delta side, before security—both on the third level. **SeaWorld** stores, at airsides A and B, are open daily from 6am to 9pm (☎ **407/825-2614**). For space buffs coming through town, **Kennedy Space Center** (☎ **407/445-1788**) has two locations at the airport, in both the East and West halls. Even the **Ron Jon Surf Shop** (☎ **407/825-2217**) has an airport outpost (daily 7am–9pm).

Orlando Neighborhoods in Brief

Walt Disney World Though Walt Disney World and Orlando are often considered synonymous, WDW isn't situated in Orlando (surprise!). It's actually located southwest of the city in Lake Buena Vista and is a municipal entity in its own right. WDW encompasses more than 47 square miles and claims four major theme parks, two smaller water parks, several smaller attractions, numerous themed resorts, a plethora of restaurants and shops, and an entertainment district.

Downtown Disney Though not actually a neighborhood, Downtown Disney is certainly large enough to be distinguished as such. It encompasses Disney's entertainment districts—Downtown Disney West Side and the recently re-imagined Pleasure Island (soon to become Hyperion Wharf)—as well as its shopping and dining complex, the Downtown Disney Marketplace. The area is filled with entertainment venues, restaurants, shops, and smaller attractions. You can experience the circus, ride in a gigantic tethered balloon, shop till you drop, and tempt your taste buds—all in the space of a single evening.

Lake Buena Vista Lake Buena Vista actually encompasses all of WDW, but also includes much of the area bordering the resort. Here you can find the "official" (but not Disney-owned) hotels situated along Hotel Plaza Boulevard. The area along 535

(known locally as Apopka–Vineland) is home to its own share of resorts and restaurants. Though the region is bustling, many of its resorts, restaurants, and shops are set along alcoves and tree-lined side streets, far from the main thoroughfare, to maintain a quieter, more charming atmosphere.

Celebration As you drive through this quaint little town—full of beautiful homes trimmed in gingerbread, some of them with white-picket fences, shade trees, and some of the loveliest landscaping around—you may find yourself musing about this 4,900-acre community's seeming perfection. The fact that Disney had a hand in its creation should then come as no great surprise—experts that they are at creating the perfect version of almost anything. The Market Street area's charming collection of shops, restaurants, and even its own small hotel is reminiscent of a bygone era—and an upscale version at that.

Kissimmee Brought back to life by a multimillion-dollar "Rebeautivacation" project several years back, U.S. 192, Kissimmee's main tourist strip, sports extrawide sidewalks, colorful (and plentiful) streetlamps, landscaping, and location markers. Though many areas are weathering a bit poorly, there are plans in the works to revitalize and re-create the area's identity, as I-Drive has done; these could eventually include a

Package Deals

Just about everybody seems to be in the business of package deals these days. Although Disney itself offers a handful of package options, the discounts aren't usually that considerable. However, do ask reservations clerks about the latest and greatest promotion, or what may be running at the time you intend to visit. Promotions tend to run for a limited time, so be sure to get all the details—when it runs, what it includes, what it doesn't, and so on. You should also search the Disney website (www.disneyworld.com) for special deals and promotions.

For up-to-date coverage of promotional offerings and discount codes good at Disney World, check out **www. mousesavers.com.** The site also offers its own slate of Disney specials.

shuttle similar to the I-Ride Trolley, though substantially smaller. The roadway itself has been improved to handle traffic more easily and safely (in part due to the recent construction of new exits and access roads leading directly to Disney). Kissimmee is lined practically end to end with a variety of budget and moderate resorts and hotels, most of which cater to families (though a few more upscale options have sprung up along its outer edges as well as to the south); a plentitude of casual restaurants; and a handful of minor attractions.

International Drive Area (Hwy. 536) Known as **I-Drive,** this busy tourist zone is home to more than 100 resorts and hotels (a number that continues to grow almost exponentially), countless restaurants, attractions both big and small, shopping, entertainment, and even its own transportation system—the I-Ride Trolley. There literally is something here for everybody. The areas north of Sand Lake Road are by far the most congested, filled to capacity with T-shirt shops, tourist traps, resorts, restaurants, and attractions. If you head south, toward the intersection at S.R. 528 (also known as the Beachline Expwy.), it's still chock-full of restaurants and hotels, but the landscaping is far more appealing, and tree-lined walkways offer a more pleasant place to walk. The driving, however, is still slow going at best.

Downtown Orlando Orlando is a lot smaller than most major U.S. cities but has a charm all its own. The downtown area is about 20 miles northeast of Walt Disney World, which ensures it's far less congested with tourists than the theme-park zones. Here you'll find chic restaurants, trendy clubs, upscale hotels, and a cultural center that's filled with theaters, museums, the very visitor-friendly Orlando Science Center, and more. Shopping is plentiful, as downtown streets are dotted with boutiques and antiques shops (especially along "Antique Row" on Orange Ave. near Lake Ivanhoe).

Winter Park Those who make the effort to get up to Winter Park, located just north of downtown (Orlando, that is), will enjoy its upscale ambience and quaint Southern charm. The town's biggest draw is Park Avenue, with its collection of chic shops and restaurants set along tree-lined cobblestone streets. Many of Florida's moneyed snowbirds used to hang out in Winter Park for the winter, and this part of the suburbs is a great adult getaway and a good place to relax and escape the WDW, Universal, and I-Drive crowds. It's not, however, a good place to take the kids.

VACATION & CRUISE PACKAGES

The number and diversity of package tours to Orlando is staggering. If Disney is on your agenda, head to **www.disneyworld.com** (where you'll find loads of information

A MICKEY MOUSE AFFAIR: getting married AT WALT DISNEY WORLD

Want to fly up the aisle on Aladdin's magic carpet? Arrive in a glass coach pulled by six white horses? Or take the plunge, literally and figuratively, on the Twilight Zone Tower of Terror?

If you've always dreamed of a fairy-tale wedding, Disney is happy to oblige for a price (though often a large one). Recognizing WDW's popularity as a honeymoon destination—each year, more honeymooners head here than to any other spot in America—Disney, in 1995, cut out the middleman and officially went into the wedding business. And, oh, what big business it is!

Disney's first step was building the multimillion-dollar nondenominational chapel in the middle of the Seven Seas Lagoon. The next step was letting the world know the Disney wedding chapel was open for business. The first nuptials were televised live on the Lifetime television network. (Construction was still in progress at the chapel, so the bride and groom wore white hard hats.) Since it opened, more than 35,000 couples (approximately 1,500 couples each year), hailing from every state and a number of foreign countries, have mixed matrimony with Disney magic at the chapel, which resembles a Victorian summerhouse. You'll have to cough up at least $1,991 just to have the ceremony here (not including the minimum expenditure of $10,000–$20,000 required for a custom wedding—or the minimum 4-night stay that's also required).

An intimate "Escape" wedding for two starts at about $4,750 (not including the 4-night minimum stay at one of Disney's resorts) and includes a daylight ceremony at one of several Disney resort locations, a wedding cake, a bouquet for the bride, a marriage certificate signed by Mickey himself, and a host of other trimmings (at Disney's Wedding Pavilion, prices start at $5,750). "Custom Wishes" weddings start at $10,000. The average Disney wedding costs $28,000 and has 100 guests (Prince Charming not included). A la carte add-ons range from $800 for a 30-minute visit from your favorite Disney character to $2,700 to arrive in Cinderella's glass coach. It would cost at least $25,000 to have your ceremony at the Magic Kingdom (minimum food, beverage, and hotel expenditures are required and are at an additional cost). The introduction of the Disney Couture wedding collection (by David Tutera), a unique honeymoon registry, and a line of princess-inspired designer wedding gowns (available only in select Florida locations at press time) bring additional elements of elegance that only Disney could create to the wedding mix. If you can imagine it, Disney can likely do it—as long as your wallet matches your imagination.

For details, call ✆ **321/939-4 610** (✆ **800/370-6009** for honeymoons only), or go to **www.disney weddings.com**.

and can book a package as well). Disney's array of choices can include airfare, accommodations on or off Disney property, theme-park passes, a rental car, meals, a Disney cruise, and/or a stay at Disney's beach resorts in Vero Beach or Hilton Head, South Carolina. Some packages are tied to a season, while others are for special-interest vacationers, including golfers, honeymooners, or spa aficionados. For more information, or to book a Disney vacation package, call ✆ **407/939-6244.**

Although not on the same scale as Disney's options, Universal Orlando packages have improved greatly with the addition of the Islands of Adventure theme park, the

CityWalk food-and-club district, and Universal's Loews-run hotels (along with several off-site hotel partners added in recent years). The options include lodging, VIP access to Universal's theme parks, and discounts to other non-Disney attractions. Some include round-trip airfare. Contact **Universal Vacations** at ℂ **877/801-9720,** or go to **www.universalorlando.com**.

SeaWorld also offers packages that include rooms from a choice of a handful of SeaWorld-area hotels, car rental, and tickets to SeaWorld. Call ℂ **800/557-4268,** or go to **www.seaworldvacations.com**.

For linksters, **Golf Getaways** (ℂ **800/800-4028;** www.golfgetaways.com) and **Golfpac Vacations** (ℂ **800/327-0878;** www.golfpacinc.com) offer play-and-stay packages.

For more information on package tours and for tips on booking your trip, see **www.frommers.com/planning**.

Disney Cruise Packages

There's hardly a Florida tourist market that WDW hasn't successfully tapped. Ocean-going vacations are no exception. **Disney Cruise Line** (ℂ **800/951-3532;** www.disneycruise.com) launched the *Magic, Wonder,* and *Dream* in 1998, 1999, and 2011, respectively, and will debut the *Fantasy* in 2012. It didn't take long before the line made it all the way to the top of the family cruising market.

The *Magic* is Art Deco in style, with Mickey in the three-level lobby and a *Beauty and the Beast* mural in its top restaurant, Lumiere's. The *Wonder's* decor is Art Nouveau. Ariel commands its lobby, and its featured eatery, Triton's, sports a mural from *The Little Mermaid.*

Subtle differences aside, these are nearly identical twins. Both are 83,000 tons with 12 decks, 875 cabins, and room for 2,400 guests. There are some adults-only areas, including **Palo,** an intimate and romantic Italian restaurant; however, both ships have extensive kids' and teens' programs that take up almost an entire deck. They're broken into four age groups: the **Flounder's Reef Nursery** for ages 3 months to 3 years; **Disney's Oceaneer Club** and **Disney's Oceaneer Lab** for ages 3 to 12 (on the *Wonder*) and 3 to 10 (on the *Magic*). **Ocean Quest** (on the *Magic*) is the newest addition; filled with activities for almost every age, it features video games, plasma TVs, and a simulator that allows kids to steer the ship in and out of ports of call. Additional children's activities are now offered by interest rather than by age—allowing your kids to choose exactly which activities they wish to participate in.

Restaurants, shows, and other onboard activities are extremely family-oriented. One of the line's unique features is a dine-around option that lets you move among main restaurants (each ship has four) from night to night while keeping the same servers.

Debuting in January 2011, the *Dream* is reminiscent of the grand ocean liners that sailed in the 1920s and '30s, oozing elegance and stylish sophistication, accented by whimsical Disneyesque touches. Practically dwarfing the *Magic* and *Wonder,* the *Dream* stands two decks taller and features 1,250 staterooms (and a capacity for up to 4,000 guests). Innovations on board include a first-of-its-kind water coaster (located on the upper deck), along with imaginative tech-y touches such as virtual portholes, an interactive play-floor, living characters, and enchanted art (think real-time animation). Like its older siblings, the *Dream* offers numerous dining options and an extensive array of onboard activities (including supervised childcare); the difference here, however, is that activities are arranged by interest rather than by age.

2

WALT DISNEY WORLD & ORLANDO IN DEPTH

Vacation & Cruise Packages

Avoid the Ups & Downs

Nothing spoils a cruise like a storm—or worse. In the first case, consider avoiding hurricane season altogether (June–Nov, though the peak is July to mid-Oct). These unpredictable storms can both spoil your fun and upset the strongest of stomachs. The stormy seasons aside, pack a few motion-sickness pills or patches just in case.

Speaking of spoiling a cruise, several cruise ships, including the *Disney* *Magic,* have had outbreaks of a virus that caused stomach flu-like symptoms in the past. This is no ill reflection on any one line: Cruise ships are closed environments, and sometimes a passenger brings the illness on board. For an Internet rating by the **Centers for Disease Control,** go to www.cdc.gov/nceh/vsp/default.htm. Note, however, that the site is often weeks out of date.

The *Dream* sails out of Port Canaveral (at least for the next few years), with cruises to The Bahamas and the Caribbean.

In 2012, the *Fantasy* will set sail, bringing with it even more innovative touches and experiences than the *Dream*—an AquaDuck water coaster, magic portholes, and enchanted artwork (all on the *Dream* as well) will be complemented by unique dinner shows and dining experiences, an adult entertainment district with chic clubs and lounges, and even a Bibbidi Bobbidi Boutique (among plenty of other kid-friendly entertainment options and activities).

Sailing out of Port Canaveral, which is about an hour east of Orlando by car, 3-night voyages visit Nassau, Bahamas, and Castaway Cay, Disney's own private island; 5-night cruises add Key West. There are also 7-night eastern Caribbean (St. Thomas, Tortola, and Castaway Cay) and 7-night western Caribbean (Key West, Grand Cayman, Cozumel, and Castaway Cay) itineraries. If you buy a land-sea package, transportation to and from Orlando is included; 7-night land-sea packages include 3 or 4 days afloat, with the rest of the week at a WDW resort. Prices depend on your choice of stateroom and resort. Packages are available that add round-trip air and unlimited admission to the WDW parks and other Disney attractions. You can get discounted fares if you book well in advance and go during nonpeak periods; specials or "Magic Rates" run periodically as well. Call for details and rates, or check with a travel agent.

From other ports, Alaskan cruises (5-, 6-, and 7-day), cruises to the Mexican Riviera (7-, 8-, and 10-day), and transatlantic Mediterranean cruises (8-, 10-, 11-, and 14-day) are offered as well. Mediterranean cruises (aboard the *Magic*) feature stops in such ports of call as Ajaccio, Corsica; Barcelona, Spain; Naples, Italy; Madeira, Portugal; and Gibraltar, U.K., among several others. Northern European cruises (8- to 14-night cruises aboard the *Magic*) feature stops in such ports as Cherbourg, France; Oslo, Norway; Helsinki, Finland; and St. Petersburg, Russia, among others. For more information on these and other sailings, call © **888/325-2500.**

Beginning in 2012, the Disney Cruise Line will set sail from three new ports (in addition to its existing ports): New York, Seattle, and Galveston, Texas.

The Disney *Magic*, once repositioned from Port Canaveral to New York, will sail 20 cruises from New York—including 8-night cruises to The Bahamas and 5-night cruises along the New England coast to Canada. It will also include 2-night cruises for those wanting to cruise for only a short time (with rates starting at $370 per person). Cruises to The Bahamas will, as always, include a day at Disney's private island, Castaway Cay; Nassau, Bahamas; and a stop at Port Canaveral (all guests receiving a 1-day Park Hopper ticket and round-trip transportation between the ship and their Disney resort). Rates for the new 8-night Bahamian cruise (departing from New York) start at $1,240 per person. Five-night cruises up the New England coast will stop at Halifax, Nova Scotia, and Saint John, New Brunswick. Rates start at $715 per person. Seven-night cruises from the Port of Galveston to the western Caribbean will also be offered. Ports of call include Grand Cayman and Mexico's Costa Maya and Cozumel. Rates start at $840 per person.

The Disney *Wonder* will sail a total of 14 7-night cruises from the Port of Seattle to Tracy Arm, Skagway, Juneau, and Ketchikan, Alaska, as well as Victoria, British Columbia. Rates start at $917 per person. The *Wonder* will continue sailing Mexican Riviera cruises from the Port of Los Angeles, as well as 7-night Pacific Coast cruises that stop in San Francisco, San Diego, and Ensenada, Mexico. Rates start at $707 per person on either route. In addition, the *Wonder* will set sail on a 15-night voyage to Hawaii (departing from Los Angeles) that stops in Hilo, on the Big Island; Kahului, Maui; Honolulu, Oahu; Nawiliwili, Kauai; and Ensenada, Mexico. Rates start at $1,800 per person.

The Disney *Dream* will sail 3-, 4- and 5-night cruises from Port Canaveral to The Bahamas and Disney's private island, Castaway Cay. Five-night itineraries include two stops at Castaway Cay. Rates start at $471 per person.

The Disney *Fantasy* will make her maiden voyage in March 2012, sailing out of Port Canaveral on 7-night Caribbean itineraries (alternating eastern and western routes). Rates start at $959 per person.

For more information, call Disney Cruise Line or check out its very informative website, which also allows you to plan and reserve shore excursions before you go. Another excellent source of detailed information on both cruising and the Disney line is *Frommer's Cruises & Ports of Call.*

WHERE TO STAY

There seemed to be no end to Orlando's hotel boom just a few years back. Almost 4,000 new rooms were added every year through the year 2000—but the economic upheaval in the years that followed took its toll, and construction began to slow dramatically. It wasn't until 2007, when tourism once again began to thrive, that the city's vast and varied inventory of accommodations experienced an increase not seen in nearly a decade, with roughly 5,000 rooms added in 2008 alone. The year 2009 brought with it an additional 2,558 rooms; however, just over 1,000 rooms were added in 2010, new construction all but coming to a halt—a reflection of the most recent economic downturn. In 2011, not a single room was added, though extensive renovations, refits, and refurbishments continued to ensure that visitors could lay their head in comfortable and constantly updated surroundings. The area's budget hotels, theme-park resorts, and high-end luxury resorts all kicked it up a notch or two in an effort to vie for business (trendy decor, high-tech gadgets, soothing spas, and extensive pool and play areas were among the most common additions). New construction once again picked up in 2012—an additional 2,884 rooms are projected to open by the end of the year (some with pirate, princess, character, or even lifestyle themes). All in all, Orlando will boast roughly 119,000 rooms varying in both size and style, and ranging from basic lodging (including only the essentials) to luxurious accommodations (bursting with lavish amenities and over-the-top extravagances), including scores of places located in or near the major-league tourist draws: Walt Disney World, Universal Orlando, SeaWorld, and the rest of International Drive. Disney alone claims 36 resorts (including the resort scheduled to open later this year), timeshares, and "official" hotels.

THE best HOTEL BETS

For more of my favorite Central Florida hotels and motels, see chapter 1, "The Best of Walt Disney World & Orlando."

- **Best for Families:** Every Disney resort caters to families, with special menus for kids, video-game arcades, free transportation to the parks, extensive recreational facilities, and, in some cases, character meals. Some, however, stand out in particular. **Disney's Beach Club Resort** (p. 50) boasts a laid-back seaside charm, a multitude of kid-friendly dining options, and one of the coolest pools on Disney property, making it a favorite with families—and did I mention that Epcot is literally just steps away? To enjoy wilderness of a different kind, try **Disney's Animal King-dom Lodge** (p. 57), where the animals of the African savanna seemingly come right up to your doorstep. If you prefer the rustic and woodsy feel of the Pacific Northwest's national parks, head to **Disney's Wilderness Lodge** (p. 58).

Outside the House of Mouse, the **Nickelodeon Family Suites** (p. 74) features two- and three-bedroom Kid Suites, multilevel water slides, extensive play areas, and an all-Nickelodeon decor. **Floridays Resort Orlando** (p. 74) features two- and three-bedroom suites with all the comforts of home, an inviting pool and play area, and grocery delivery. After top-to-bottom renovations and a change in ownership, the **DoubleTree by Hilton Orlando at SeaWorld** (p. 91) offers redesigned rooms with kitchenettes, spacious suites, beautifully landscaped grounds, a multitude of pools, play areas, and on-site dining options for the entire family, all within a minute or two of SeaWorld and I-Drive's various offerings.

- **Best Inexpensive Hotels:** That's easy: If you're going to stay on WDW property, you can't beat the prices at **Disney's All-Star Movies Resort, Disney's All-Star Music Resort, Disney's All-Star Sports Resort,** and **Disney's Pop Century Resort** (listings begin on p. 61). Outside of Disney, the **Comfort Suites Main-gate Resort** (p. 82) offers spacious rooms and plenty of amenities at reasonable rates. It's one of the nicest inexpensive properties in the Kissimmee area and is only 1½ miles west of Disney.

- **Best Budget Motels:** The **Fairfield Inn & Suites Orlando at SeaWorld** (p. 93) offers a complimentary breakfast, a Shamu pool and splash zone, clean and comfortable rooms, a location close to I-Drive's attractions and restaurants, and rates that won't bust your budget. The new **SpringHill Suites Orlando at SeaWorld** (p. 93) sports oversized suites (with space for up to six), a chic and stylish decor, and a location that's practically on SeaWorld's doorstep. If you want to stay closer to Mickey, the **Holiday Inn Main Gate East** (p. 80) offers tons of recreational activities for kids and adults, good rooms, and a free shuttle service to the theme parks—all at bargain rates.

- **Best for Business Travelers:** The **Gaylord Palms** (p. 70), **Marriott Orlando World Center** (p. 72), and **Peabody Orlando** (p. 84) offer full concierge service, excellent restaurants, spacious lounges, and an extensive array of business services, while the **Hyatt Place Universal** (p. 92) is a good option for the more budget-conscious business set.

- **Best Location: Disney's Grand Floridian Resort & Spa** (p. 52), **Disney's Polynesian Resort** (p. 54), **Disney's Contemporary Resort** (p. 51), and **Disney's Bay Lake Tower** (p. 52) are on the WDW monorail route, providing easy access to the parks. The **Portofino Bay Hotel** (p. 86), **Hard Rock Hotel** (p. 88), and **Royal Pacific Resort** (p. 89) are within walking distance of both Universal Orlando parks, and there's also boat service to the dock at CityWalk.

- **Best Service:** The elegant **Peabody Orlando** (p. 84) offers attentive pampering from one of the best staffs in the area. At the **Reunion Resort Orlando** (p. 78), a personal concierge ensures guests are treated to top-notch service. At the **Waldorf Astoria Orlando** (p. 55), attentive service is legendary, with a concierge staff trained to follow the standards of Les Clefs d'Or, an elite group of the world's top concierges.

- **Best Pools:** All of the Walt Disney World resorts have wonderfully whimsical, themed swimming pools, and usually of Olympic size. Arguably, the best is shared by **Disney's Beach Club Resort** (p. 50) and **Disney's Yacht Club Resort**

WHAT YOU'LL really PAY

The prices quoted here are for hotels' rack rate, the maximum that it charges; it is, however, seriously unlikely that you'll end up paying that rate in Orlando unless you arrive around Christmas or Easter. You can typically find discounts of up to 20% when booking through websites such as Hotels.com or Expedia; see "Practical Information," at the end of this chapter, for more tips. During slow times, it's not impossible to obtain a room at an expensive property for the same rate as a more moderate one. Rack rates at the Orlando Marriott World Center start at $349, but in December 2011, just a cursory search of the usual discount sites revealed that the going rate was actually closer to $160.

If you're the gambling type, you can bid for a room on Priceline. In July, a room at the deluxe Hyatt Regency Grand Cypress (rack rates start at $179) was snagged on Priceline for $80. Sometimes all you have to do is contact the hotel directly and negotiate. For example, in October, the Comfort Inn Lake Buena Vista was advertising a weekday rate of $59 on its own website, but a spot check of the major discounters (Priceline, Hotels.com, Expedia, Travelocity) yielded a price of $45. When I told the hotel what I'd been quoted online, I was offered the same rate on the spot.

The hotels listed in this chapter are divided by location and price category. As you might expect, many of the inexpensive properties are the farthest from the action and/or have the most spartan, unimaginative accommodations.

Keep in mind, however, that this isn't one of the world's best bargain destinations. Unlike other Florida tourist areas, there are few under-$60 motels that meet the standards demanded for listing in this book. That's why I've raised the price bar. The listings in the **inexpensive** category charge an average of less than $100 per night for a double room. Those offering rooms for $100 to $200 make up the **moderate** category, rooms for $200 to $300 are listed as **expensive,** and anything more than $300 is listed as **very expensive.** Any included extras (such as breakfast) are listed for each property. *Note:* Quoted discount rates almost never include breakfast, hotel tax, or any applicable resort fees.

Orlando's peak and low seasons are often complicated, as the peak times are sporadically disbursed throughout the calendar. Even remote events such as the International Sweet Potato Growers convention in Orlando can raise off-season prices. These events especially impact moderately priced properties outside WDW.

Keep in mind that rates are per night double unless otherwise noted, and they don't include hotel taxes of up to 14.5%. Also, most Orlando hotels and motels let **kids younger than 12 (and usually younger than 17) stay free** with a parent or guardian, if you don't exceed maximum room occupancy. But to be safe, ask for details when booking your room.

(p. 55). Stormalong Bay, a 3-acre free-form pool and water park, stretches between them, including a shipwreck for exploring and sand-bottom pools for a toe-tickling experience. Outside the Disney complex, the best resort pool in Orlando can be found at the **Hyatt Regency Grand Cypress Resort** (p. 69). It's a half-acre, lagoonlike, water-world pool that flows through rock grottoes, is spanned by a rope bridge, and has 12 waterfalls and two steep water slides. The 24,000-square-foot lazy river pool shared by the **Ritz-Carlton** and **JW Marriott Orlando** at Grande Lakes (p. 87), however, definitely provides some stiff competition. Not to be ignored is the rock-'n'-roll pool at Universal's **Hard Rock Hotel** (p. 88), with its underwater sound system and fantastic landscaping, or the super kid-friendly water park–style pools at the **Nickelodeon Family Suites** (p. 74).

IN & AROUND WALT DISNEY WORLD

The resorts in this section are either Disney-owned or "official" Disney hotels that offer many of the same perks. All are on the Disney Transportation System, which means those of you who don't want to venture too far (and are okay with the occasional scheduling inconvenience) will be able to do without a car. If you do decide to bring or rent a car, you'll get free self-parking at your hotel and at the Disney parks.

If you decide that Disney is your destination, come up with a short list of preferred places to stay, and then call CRO (✆ **407/934-7639**) for up-to-the-minute rates. Web surfers can get information at **www.disneyworld.com**.

Those who come by auto will find large signs along all of the major roads on Disney property pointing the way to the various resorts. You'll find these hotels listed on the "Walt Disney World & Lake Buena Vista Hotels" map in this section.

Individual resorts don't have their own **golf courses,** but WDW has 99 holes situated along the northern end of the property (see "Hitting the Links," in chapter 6). The same goes for **kennels;** resort guests can board their pets during the day or overnight at Disney's Best Friends Pet Care center. The luxury pet facility (opened in the summer of 2010) caters to the pampered-pet set and is centrally located on the Bonnet Creek Parkway (and replaces the numerous facilities once located near the theme-park entrances). The new kennel offers a wide range of services and amenities, the most basic of which include day care, grooming, and overnight boarding.

Prices in the following listings reflect the range available at each resort when this guide was published. Rates vary depending on season and room location, but the numbers should help you determine which places fit your budget.

Note: Most hotels and resorts, Disney or otherwise, have a limited number of cribs (or portable cribs) available at no extra charge. Rollaway beds or cots are usually available for around $10 to $25 per night. Refrigerators (mini ones, anyway) are sometimes available, though some hotels may charge up to $15 per night for the privilege. All Orlando hotels also offer nonsmoking rooms (while offering at least some rooms for smokers), and **all of Disney's hotels went smoke-free** in 2007, with **all three of Universal Orlando's resorts following suit** on May 11, 2011 (they do, however, offer a small number of designated outdoor smoking areas).

Best for: Visitors who intend on spending all (or at least most) of their time at Walt Disney World.

Drawbacks: Prices are often much higher for the most desirable accommodations (those closest to the theme parks); and Disney transportation, albeit free, can be difficult to manage with kids, strollers and all the associated gear—not to mention painstakingly slow, depending on the location of your resort.

Walt Disney World & Lake Buena Vista Hotels

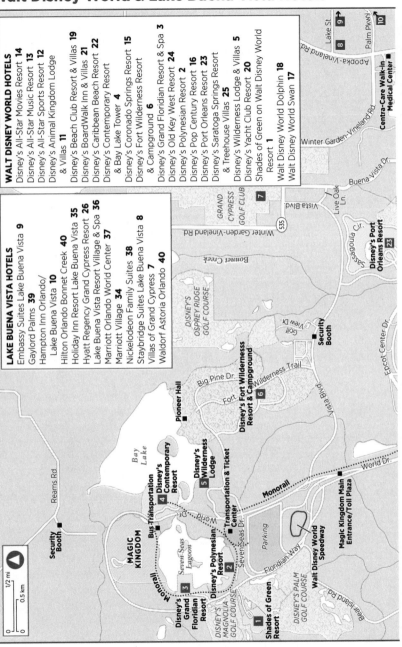

WALT DISNEY WORLD HOTELS

Disney's All-Star Movies Resort **14**
Disney's All-Star Music Resort **13**
Disney's All-Star Sports Resort **12**
Disney's Animal Kingdom Lodge & Villas **11**
Disney's Beach Club Resort & Villas **19**
Disney's BoardWalk Inn & Villas **21**
Disney's Caribbean Beach Resort **22**
Disney's Contemporary Resort & Bay Lake Tower **4**
Disney's Coronado Springs Resort **15**
Disney's Fort Wilderness Resort & Campground **6**
Disney's Grand Floridian Resort & Spa **3**
Disney's Old Key West Resort **24**
Disney's Polynesian Resort **2**
Disney's Pop Century Resort **16**
Disney's Port Orleans Resort **23**
Disney's Saratoga Springs Resort & Treehouse Villas **25**
Disney's Wilderness Lodge & Villas **5**
Disney's Yacht Club Resort **20**
Shades of Green on Walt Disney World Resort **1**
Walt Disney World Dolphin **18**
Walt Disney World Swan **17**

LAKE BUENA VISTA HOTELS

Embassy Suites Lake Buena Vista **9**
Gaylord Palms **39**
Hampton Inn Orlando/ Lake Buena Vista **10**
Hilton Orlando Bonnet Creek **40**
Holiday Inn Resort Lake Buena Vista **35**
Hyatt Regency Grand Cypress Resort **26**
Lake Buena Vista Resort Village & Spa **36**
Marriott Orlando World Center **37**
Marriott Village **34**
Nickelodeon Family Suites **38**
Staybridge Suites Lake Buena Vista **8**
Villas of Grand Cypress **7**
Waldorf Astoria Orlando **40**

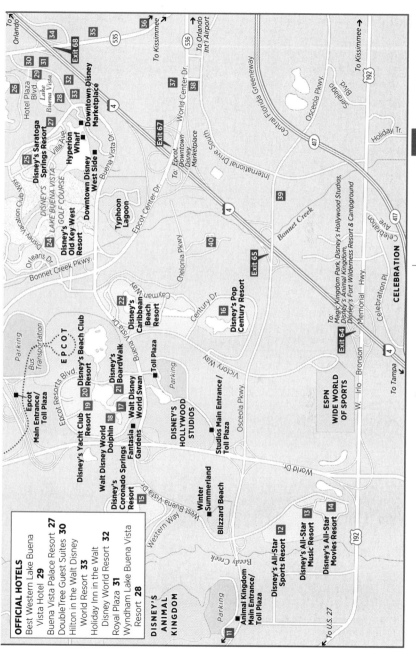

OFFICIAL HOTELS

Best Western Lake Buena Vista Hotel **29**
Buena Vista Palace Resort **27**
DoubleTree Guest Suites **30**
Hilton in the Walt Disney World Resort **33**
Holiday Inn in the Walt Disney World Resort **32**
Royal Plaza **31**
Wyndham Lake Buena Vista Resort **28**

DISNEY'S ANIMAL KINGDOM

Animal Kingdom Main Entrance/ Toll Plaza

Disney's All-Star Sports Resort **12**
Disney's All-Star Music Resort **13**
Disney's All-Star Movies Resort **14**

Disney's Coronado Springs Resort **15**

Winter Summerland

Blizzard Beach

DISNEY'S HOLLYWOOD STUDIOS

Studios Main Entrance/ Toll Plaza

Disney's Yacht Club Resort **19**
Disney's Beach Club Resort **20**
Disney's BoardWalk **21**
Walt Disney World Swan **17**
Walt Disney World Dolphin **18**

Fantasia Gardens

Toll Plaza

EPCOT

Epcot Main Entrance/ Toll Plaza

Disney's Old Key West Resort **24**

Disney's Caribbean Beach Resort **22**

Disney's Pop Century Resort **16**

Disney's Saratoga Springs Resort **25**

Hyperion Wharf **27**

Downtown Disney West Side **26**

Downtown Disney Marketplace

Typhoon Lagoon

ESPN WIDE WORLD OF SPORTS

CELEBRATION

To:
Magic Kingdom Park, Disney's Hollywood Studios,
Disney's Animal Kingdom,
Disney's Fort Wilderness Resort & Campground

THE perks OF STAYING WITH MICKEY

The decision of whether to bunk with the Mouse is one of the first you'll have to make when planning an Orlando vacation. In the sections "In & Around Walt Disney World" and "'Official' Hotels in Lake Buena Vista" of this chapter, you'll find information on the 36 hotels, resorts, villas, timeshares, and campsites that are owned by Disney or are "official" hotels—those that are privately owned but have earned Disney's seal of approval. All 36 are in WDW or Lake Buena Vista.

In addition to their proximity to the theme parks, there are other advantages to staying at a Disney property or one of the "official" hotels. The following amenities are included at all Disney resorts; some are offered by the "official" hotels, but be sure to ask when booking:

- Guests get free transportation from Orlando International Airport to their Disney resort using **Magical Express.** Not only does the shuttle service get Disney resort guests to their hotels, but it also delivers their luggage straight from the plane to their room, allowing them to bypass baggage claim! Guests can also check luggage and print boarding passes before leaving their Disney resort. Currently only select airlines participate in the program.
- Unlimited **free transportation** on the **WDW Transportation System**'s buses, monorails, ferries, or water taxis to and from the four WDW parks, from 2 hours prior to opening until 2 hours after closing. Free transportation is also provided to and from Downtown Disney, Typhoon Lagoon, Blizzard Beach, and the WDW resorts. Three of them—the Polynesian, Grand Floridian, and Contemporary resorts—are located on the monorail system. The transportation services offered can save money you might otherwise spend on a rental car, parking,

and shuttles. It also means you're guaranteed admission to all of the parks, even during peak times when parking lots sometimes fill to capacity.
- **Kids 17 and under stay free** in their parent's room, and reduced-price children's menus are available in most restaurants.
- Hotel guests have the option of adding the **Disney Dining Plan** (with three different plans designed to accommodate every budget and palate)—a definite money-saver when compared to dining a la carte.
- **Character breakfasts and/or dinners** at select restaurants.
- The **Extra Magic Hour** (see the box "The Early Bird . . ." below).
- TVs equipped with the Disney Channel, **nightly bedtime stories** (Channel 22, 7-10pm, audio only), and WDW information stations.
- A **Lobby Concierge** where you can buy tickets to all Disney parks and attractions—without standing in long lines at the parks—and get information on dining, recreation, and everything Disney.
- Playing privileges, **preferred tee times,** and, in some cases, free transportation to one of the Disney golf courses. (See "Hitting the Links," in chapter 6.)
- **Online check-in** within 10 days of arrival. Simply check in online, advise the resort of your arrival time, and provide a credit card to cover your charges—and you can skip the lengthy check-in line at the resort.
- WDW has some of the **best swimming pools** in Orlando and most are zero-entry or zero-grade pools, meaning there's a gradual slope into the water on at least one side rather than only a step down. These include pools at the

Grand Floridian, Animal Kingdom, and Polynesian resorts and others.

o On-premises **car rental** is available at the Magic Kingdom Auto Plaza through Alamo (© **407/824-3470**). There are also car-rental desks at the Walt Disney World Swan and Dolphin, as well as select Hotel Plaza Boulevard properties.

o Extensive **recreational options** (not including the parks), including fishing, tennis, boating, surfing, parasailing, horseback riding, golf, and more. Though many activities cost extra, they're all right at your fingertips and several offer experiences you won't find elsewhere.

o Disney's **refillable mug program** lets you buy—for around $13.50—a bottomless souvenir mug for soda, coffee, tea, and/or cocoa at its resorts. The offer is for the length of your stay, but it isn't transferable to the theme parks. You can use it only at the property at which it is bought, with two exceptions: Mugs are transferable between the Beach Club and Yacht Club resorts or among the three All-Star resorts. A similar program is available at Disney's two water parks, but again, they're not transferable beyond the park where they were purchased and these aren't valid beyond the day they are purchased.

o Resort guests can **charge most purchases** (including meals) made anywhere inside WDW to their room. In most cases, purchases made inside the theme parks can be delivered to your resort at no extra charge.

But there are also disadvantages to staying with the Mouse:

o The Transportation System can be *excruciatingly* time-consuming.

There are times when you have to take a ferry to catch a bus to get on the monorail to reach your hotel. It can take up to an hour or more to get to a place that's right across the lagoon from you.

o That free Magical Express shuttle system to and from the airport isn't perfect. Luggage delivery may take up to several hours. And departure shuttles (from your resort to the airport) are scheduled several hours in advance of your flight (thanks in part to the numerous resort stops it makes before getting on its way). Also note that though the Magical Express service is provided by Disney, the airlines still have a say in the matter. Changes to baggage policies (which vary by airline) have now spilled over to Magical Express. Though guests can still check their bags via the resort airline service, those with more than the allotted number of "free" bags (or those traveling via an airline that charges for each bag) will have to call ahead to the airline check-in service (© **407/824-1231**) to pay the additional fee (by credit card only) or else check in at the airport.

o Resort rates are around 20% to 30% higher than comparable hotels and motels away from the parks.

o Without a car or other means to get off the property, you'll be resigned to either paying Disney's higher prices or paying for shuttles to get to Orlando's other offerings.

o If you don't spend a little time away from Disney, the all-Mickey, all-the-time atmosphere can get overwhelming, and you'll miss out on the real Florida and all the other great attractions Orlando has to offer.

Disney's **Extra Magic Hour** lets resort guests into the parks either an hour before other guests, or allows them to stay and play up to 3 hours after everyone else has to head home. Many of the more popular rides and attractions are operational (pick up the latest schedule for a complete listing), as are some shops and restaurants. For more information on this program, see p. 192.

Very Expensive

3

WHERE TO STAY | **In & Around Walt Disney World**

Disney's Beach Club Resort ★★★ ☺ This property re-creates the grand turn-of-the-20th-century Victorian seaside resorts of Cape Cod but sports a more casual ambience than its sister, the Yacht Club (detailed below), with which it shares restaurants, shops, and numerous recreational activities. Wicker furnishings, seashells, and beach umbrellas adorn the hotel's casual beach house–inspired interior. From the Beach Club, it's an easy walk to Epcot's rear entrance, though most guests prefer to take the ferry (the parks are workout enough!). The shipwreck at Stormalong Bay (a sprawling 3-acre free-form swimming pool and water park) invites you to explore, climb around its decks, and slide into the water waiting below. It includes a stretch of sandy beach, sand-bottom pools, whirlpools, and water slides (including a toddler slide, so no one misses out). Room views range from the pool (more expensive) to the parking lot. Some units have balconies.

Note: Both the Beach Club and Yacht Club offer the chance to charter a reproduction of a 1930s mahogany runabout to **cruise Crescent Lake** or see Epcot's Illumi-Nations fireworks display (from $325 plus tax for up to six people for a 45-min. cruise to catch the fireworks). Daytime cruises ($90 for 30 min.) are available departing at 2:30 and 5:30pm (© **407/824-2621**). *Note:* At press time, the runabout was temporarily out of service, but guests can still catch the fireworks aboard a roomier, albeit less romantic, pontoon ($325 for up to 10 passengers).

1800 Epcot Resorts Blvd. (off Buena Vista Dr.; P.O. Box 10000), Lake Buena Vista, FL 32830. www.disneyworld.com. © **407/934-7639** or 407/934-8000. Fax 407/934-3850. 583 units. $335–$815 double; $475–$2,610 club; $620–$2,690 suite. Extra person $25. Children 17 and younger stay free in parent's room. AE, DC, DISC, MC, V. Valet parking $12; self-parking free. **Amenities:** 2 restaurants; grill; 4 lounges; babysitting; supervised children's program; concierge; concierge-level rooms; health club and small spa; Jacuzzi; 3-acre pool and play area; 2 outdoor heated pools; kids' pool; room service; 2 lighted tennis courts; watercraft/equipment rentals; WDW Transportation System; transportation to non-Disney theme parks for a fee; limited Wi-Fi (fee). *In room:* A/C, TV, fridge, hair dryer, Internet (fee), microwave (free, upon request).

Disney's BoardWalk Inn ★★★ Disney's plush 1940s-style "seaside" resort is worth a visit even if you don't stay here. The grounds encompass 45 acres along Crescent Lake, and it's just a ferry ride across the lake from Epcot. It's a great place to recapture a little bit of yesteryear, whether that means relaxing in a wooden rocker overlooking the courtyard or strolling along the many shops, restaurants, and clubs that line the resort's quarter-mile boardwalk. After the sun goes down, the boardwalk springs to life with street performers, food vendors, and midway games, reminiscent of the hustle and bustle of the Atlantic City Boardwalk in its heyday. (*Note:* The activity on the boardwalk sometimes reaches well into the late-evening hours, as does the noise, which carries to the rooms overlooking it.) Some of the Cape Cod–style rooms have balconies, and the corner units offer a bit more space. At night, the rooms overlooking the boardwalk, mostly those in the center, enjoy a view of Epcot's fireworks display. The more expensive rooms overlook the boardwalk or pool; the less expensive ones can't avoid a view of the parking lot but are sheltered from the boardwalk clamor. Hang on to your swimsuit if you hit the pool's famous—or infamous, depending on how you look at it—200-foot "keister coaster" water slide. See also the reviews for the **Flying Fish Café** (p. 126), **Kouzzinas** (p. 129), and **ESPN Club** (p. 131) restaurants.

2101 N. Epcot Resorts Blvd. (off Buena Vista Dr.; P.O. Box 10000), Lake Buena Vista, FL 32830. www. disneyworld.com. ℂ **407/934-7639** or 407/939-5100. Fax 407/934-5150. 372 units, 520 villas. $345–$885 double; $480–$2,865 club; $665–$2,865 suite. Extra person $25. Children 17 and younger stay free in parent's room. AE, DC, DISC, MC, V. Valet parking $12; self-parking free. **Amenities:** 4 restaurants; grill; 2 lounges; 3 clubs; babysitting; bike rentals; supervised children's program; concierge; concierge-level rooms; health club; Jacuzzi; 2 outdoor heated pools; kids' pool; room service; 2 lighted tennis courts; watercraft/equipment rental; WDW Transportation System; transportation to non-Disney parks for a fee; limited Wi-Fi (fee). *In room:* A/C, TV, fridge, hair dryer, Internet (fee), microwave (free, upon request).

Disney's BoardWalk Villas ★★★ Located on the same site as the BoardWalk Inn, and sharing its amenities and ambience, the villas are a great option for those traveling in larger groups. Sold as timeshares, they're also rented to traditional tourists. Rooms range from standard-size studios (with separate sleeping and living quarters) and villas to three-bedroom units with 2,100 square feet and beds for 12. Most have a balcony or patio and the same trimmings as the BoardWalk Inn. Studio rooms have kitchenettes, while the larger suite-style villas have full kitchens. The service is impeccable, and the location near Epcot is convenient as well (plus Disney's Hollywood Studios is just a hop, skip, and a jump behind it). The spacious accommodations are great for families traveling together.

2101 N. Epcot Resorts Blvd. (off Buena Vista Dr.; P.O. Box 10000), Lake Buena Vista, FL 32830. www. disneyworld.com. ℂ **407/934-7639** or 407/939-5100. Fax 407/934-5150. 520 units. $345–$555 studio; $480–$2,330 villa. Extra person $25. Children 17 and younger stay free in parent's room. AE, DC, DISC, MC, V. Valet parking $12; self-parking free. **Amenities:** 4 restaurants; grill; 2 lounges; 3 clubs; babysitting; bike rentals; supervised children's program; concierge; concierge-level rooms; health club; Jacuzzi; 2 outdoor heated pools; kids' pool; room service; 2 lighted tennis courts; WDW Transportation System; transportation to non-Disney parks for a fee. *In room:* A/C, TV/DVD, hair dryer, Internet (fee), kitchenette, full kitchen w/dishes (villa), washer and dryer (villa).

Disney's Contemporary Resort ★★ If location is one of your priorities, it's hard to beat this Disney resort, which is right beside the Magic Kingdom, and one of only four resorts **on the monorail system** (the Bay Lake Tower, Grand Floridian,

---

 The Beach Club's Baby Sister

Disney's **Beach Club Villas** (ℂ **407/ 934-7639** or 407/934-2175; www. disneyworld.com) are inspired by Cape May seaside homes of the early 20th century, with clapboard exteriors and intricate white-wood trim. The 280-room resort, opened in July 2002, is a member of the Disney Vacation Club that rents studios and one- and two-bedroom villas ($345–$555 studios, $480–$1,250 villas) to mainstream guests when their owners are not staying on the property. Amenities are shared with the Yacht Club and Beach Club resorts, with the exception of the Villa's quiet pool—which is only accessible to villa guests. It, too, is close to Epcot's International Gateway.

and Polynesian are the others). The Contemporary offers great views of the Magic Kingdom and Seven Seas Lagoon from its west side and Bay Lake on its east. This 15-story concrete A-frame (with a newer garden wing) dates to WDW's infancy, though it's been renovated to bring it into the modern era. Guest rooms were redecorated from top to bottom in 2006, and the resulting improvements brought the resort in line with the others in its class and category. The rooms reflect an upscale Asian/retro look that should appeal to adults (the flatscreen TVs are fabulous, and the color scheme is very appealing); those with kids in tow will appreciate the rounded corners, kid-proof locks on the sliding doors (remember how high up you are here), and breakables placed well above a little one's reach. Public areas were updated and renovated in 2008. Notable changes in recent years include the addition of the Wave of American Flavors, a full-service restaurant; and a high-tech (think touch-screen ordering) quick-service eatery. The pool is far less spectacular than most, though it is large and has a wading pool for toddlers and a small beach area. On the plus side, the rooms can fit up to five people instead of the usual four (though space will be tight). Kid-friendly facilities include a playground with a good-size sandbox and a pretty decent arcade (now located on the main concourse). The best views are from the upper floors of the tower (9th floor and up), where the rooms are a tad quieter than those on the lower floors, which are exposed to noisy public areas and the monorail (which runs right through the hotel). Come here for dinner at **Chef Mickey's** (p. 155) or the **California Grill** (p. 125), but if you have only very young kids, you may be better off checking into accommodations elsewhere.

Note: The **Bay Lake Tower,** the newest member of the Disney Vacation Club resorts and sibling to the Contemporary, opened in 2009. One-, two-, and three-bedroom villas (the largest with room for up to 12) feature full kitchens, washers and dryers, and unparalleled views of the Magic Kingdom. Connected by sky bridge to the existing resort (with its restaurants, shops, and the monorail), the Bay Lake Tower sports a swanky rooftop lounge, a viewing deck (think fireworks), and lakeside pool and water play area. Spacious public areas, modern artwork, trendy suite-style rooms, and an innovative contemporary design add up to Disney chic from top to bottom. Studios run $395 to $655, villas $490 to $2,550.

Note: Just at this guide was being written, Disney announced that rooms on the Contemporary Resort's 14th floor would soon be refit to follow a "health and wellness" theme. In-room amenities will include bamboo floors, low-allergen pillows, specially wrapped mattresses, 100% cotton linens, exercise equipment, and massage tables, while bathrooms will boast tea-tree oils and rainwater showers. Guests will have access to special menus offering organically grown and seasonal foods, and yoga classes (at private studios) and spa treatments at the wellness studio are in the works (at a date yet to be released).

4600 N. World Dr. (P.O. Box 10000), Lake Buena Vista, FL 32830. www.disneyworld.com. © **407/939-6244** or 407/824-1000. Fax 407/824-3539. 1,008 units. $300–$905 double; $555–$3,040 club; $645–$3,040 suite, $395–$2,550 villa. Extra person $25. Children 17 and younger stay free in parent's room. AE, DC, DISC, MC, V. Valet parking $12; self-parking free. **Amenities:** 3 restaurants; grill; 4 lounges; babysitting; concierge; concierge-level rooms; golf course (nearby); small health club and spa; Jacuzzi; 2 outdoor heated pools; kids' pool; watersports equipment/rentals; WDW Transportation System; transportation to non-Disney parks for a fee; limited Wi-Fi (fee). *In room:* A/C, TV, CD/DVD (concierge level), fridge, hair dryer, microwave (concierge level), Wi-Fi (fee).

Disney's Grand Floridian Resort & Spa ★★★ 📷   From the moment you step into the opulent five-story domed lobby, you'll feel as if you've slipped back to an era

A Piece of Yesterday, Today

The *Grand 1*, the Grand Floridian's 52-foot Sea Ray yacht, is available for hire for groups of up to 18. It cruises Seven Seas Lagoon and Bay Lake, where in the evenings you can see the Magic Kingdom's Fantasy in the Sky fireworks or arrange a gourmet-dinner cruise. Voyages cost $520 for an hour, $720 for 90 minutes, and $1,040 for 2 hours (dinner and a personal butler at an additional cost), including a captain and deck hand (✆ **407/824-2439** or **407/824-2682**).

that started with the late 19th century and lasted through the Roaring Twenties, when a guy named Gatsby was at the top of his game. Expect tea to be served in the afternoon (3–6pm daily), while a piano player runs the spectrum from lullabies to ragtime; then, as the evening arrives, a small, '40s-style band takes the helm upstairs. The Floridian has become the romantic choice for couples, especially honeymooners, who like luxuriating in the first-class spa and health club—one of the top two in WDW (the other is the one at Disney's Saratoga Springs Resort; see below). Families, however, will appreciate the extensive recreational facilities, including the large children's pool and play area, as well as the kids' programs (including a nightly campfire and movies under the stars) and character dining offered here. Virtually all of the inviting Victorian-style rooms overlook a garden, pool, courtyard, or the Seven Seas Lagoon; many have balconies, and the "dormer rooms" have vaulted ceilings (though they're smaller than standard rooms). It's one of three resorts located directly **on the monorail system** and near the Magic Kingdom. Top-end restaurants here include **Victoria & Albert's** (p. 127) and **Citricos** (p. 126), and there are also some **special programs** for pint-size princesses and young aspiring cooks (p. 128).

Note: Rumor has it that Disney plans to add to the Grand Floridian Resort—though no official plans have been announced, permits have been submitted for a six- to seven-story addition and covered walkway.

4401 Floridian Way (P.O. Box 10000), Lake Buena Vista, FL 32830. www.disneyworld.com. ✆ **407/934-7639** or 407/824-3000. Fax 407/824-3186. 900 units. $440–$1,145 double; $545–$3,145 club; $1,140–$3,145 suite. Extra person $25. Children 17 and younger stay free in parent's room. AE, DC, DISC, MC, V. Valet parking $12; self-parking free. **Amenities:** 5 restaurants; grill; 3 lounges; character meals; babysitting; supervised children's program; concierge; concierge-level rooms; golf course (nearby); health club and spa; Jacuzzi; heated outdoor pool; kids' pool; room service; 2 lighted tennis courts; watersports equipment/rentals; WDW Transportation System; transportation to non-Disney parks for a fee; limited Wi-Fi (fee). *In room:* A/C, TV/DVD, fridge, hair dryer, Internet (fee), microwave (free, upon request), minibar.

Disney's Old Key West Resort ★★★ Palms and pastels surround you with an understated theme (at least by Disney standards) at this beautiful resort, architecturally mirroring Key West at the turn of the 20th century. It's a good choice for those in search of a degree of separation from all the action. Located between Epcot and Downtown Disney West Side, it offers some of the quietest, homiest rooms on WDW property. Old Key West is affiliated with the Disney Vacation Club—a timeshare program—but many units are rented when not being used by their owners. The 156-acre complex sports 56 buildings on tree-lined brick walkways edged by white-picket fences. Two-bedroom villas have beds for eight; grand villas (2,202 sq. ft.) sleep 12. Villas have whirlpool tubs. All of the accommodations sport balconies or patios, and

All Disney resorts are wired for high-speed Internet access. A fee of $9.95 per 24-hour period applies to use the service. Be sure to check if your resort has a preselected "start" time, often the midafternoon, or you may find yourself being charged twice in a single day, depending on when you sign up for the service. Select Disney resorts (mostly in the very expensive range) offer limited Wi-Fi access (most only in public areas) for a 24-hour period at a rate of $9.95, or 60 minutes at $5. *Note:* At press time, Disney was in the midst of testing a free Wi-Fi pilot program at select resorts (Contemporary, Coronado Springs, and the Grand Floridian) to determine whether it should expand Wi-Fi to other areas of the hotels.

all have kitchens or kitchenettes. *Tip:* This resort is very spread out, and bus service can be sporadic, so a car is highly recommended if you choose to stay here.

1510 N. Cove Rd. (off Community Dr.; P.O. Box 10000), Lake Buena Vista, FL 32830. www.disneyworld. com. © **407/934-7639** or 407/827-7700. Fax 407/827-7710. 761 units. $305–$455 studio; $415–$1,780 villa. Children 17 and younger stay free in parent's room. AE, DC, DISC, MC, V. Self-parking free. **Amenities:** Restaurant; babysitting; bike rentals; children's activity center; concierge; exercise room and limited spa; Jacuzzi; 4 outdoor heated pools; kids' pool; room service; sauna; 3 tennis courts (2 lighted); extensive watercraft/equipment rentals; WDW Transportation System; transportation to non-Disney parks for a fee. *In room:* A/C, TV, DVD (villa), hair dryer, Internet (fee), kitchen (villa), kitchenette (studio), microwave, washer and dryer (villa).

Disney's Polynesian Resort ★★

One of only four resorts found **on the monorail line,** the 25-acre Polynesian is home to extensive recreational areas, including a stretch of beach along a lagoon dotted with hammocks and palm trees, a volcano-themed swimming pool, and watercraft rentals. An on-site child-care facility makes it a good choice for those traveling with kids. Its landscaped and torch-lit walkways, along with its longhouse-style thatched-roof buildings, give the resort a South Pacific ambience. The accommodations underwent extensive renovations a couple of years ago and include space-conscious furnishings, a muted earth-toned color scheme, and upscale amenities such as flatscreen TVs. Rooms can sleep up to five people; some have patios, while others have balconies. Many have views of the grounds or Seven Seas Lagoon; some lagoon-view rooms offer great views of Cinderella Castle (at a higher price, of course), so request your desired view when making your reservation. See the reviews of the 'Ohana restaurant (p. 130) and the **Spirit of Aloha Dinner Show** (p. 319).

1600 Seven Seas Dr. (P.O. Box 10000), Lake Buena Vista, FL 32830. www.disneyworld.com. © **407/939-6244** or 407/824-2000. Fax 407/824-3174. 853 units. $385–$1,020 double; $520–$3,120 club; $650–$3,120 suite. AE, DC, DISC, MC, V. Extra person $25. Children 17 and younger stay free in parent's room. Valet parking $12; self-parking free. **Amenities:** 3 restaurants; cafe; 2 lounges; dinner show; character meals; babysitting; bike rentals; supervised children's program; concierge; concierge-level rooms; golf course (nearby); health club and spa (at the nearby Grand Floridian); 2 heated outdoor pools; kids' pool; room service; watersports equipment/rentals; WDW Transportation System; transportation to non-Disney parks for a fee. *In room:* A/C, TV, DVD (select rooms), fridge, hair dryer, Internet (fee), microwave (free, upon request).

Disney's Saratoga Springs Resort & Spa ★★

The first phase of this Disney Vacation Club resort opened in 2004; its final phase—or so everyone thought—was completed in 2007. In 2009, however, after sitting idle for several years, Disney's

Treehouse Villas were resurrected—adding 60 new and very unique Vacation Club villas to Disney's lineup of ownership-based resorts. Saratoga Springs transports guests back in time to the heyday of upstate New York's 19th-century resorts. It resembles the resort town of Saratoga Springs, thus you'll find lavish gardens, Victorian-inspired architecture, and bubbling springs. The resort's main pool brings to mind its namesake's natural springs, with "healing" waters spilling over the rocky landscaping. The renowned spa offers a wide array of services and treatments meant to invoke the healing powers of Saratoga's springs themselves. Accommodations resemble those of the other Disney timeshare properties and range from studios that sleep 4 to grand villas that can sleep up to 12 more than comfortably. The **Treehouse Villas** are, however, quite unlike other Vacation Club villas—elevated some 10 feet off the ground by pedestals and beams in an effort to create the feeling of being nestled among the treetops. The three-bedroom "cabin casual" villas sleep up to nine and feature all the comforts and conveniences of home. Downtown Disney is a short ferry ride across the lake (or you can hoof it, if you so desire), but getting to the theme parks will require a bit more effort. This is another resort where a car would definitely come in handy. *Tip:* The accessible rooms at this resort are also equipped for the hearing impaired.

1960 Broadway St., Lake Buena Vista, FL 32830. www.disneyworld.com. ℂ **407/827-1100** or 407/934-3400. Fax 407/827-1151. 828 units. $305–$455 studio; $415–$965 villa; $1,280–$1,780 grand villa; $570–$965 Treehouse Villa. Children 17 and younger stay free in parent's room. AE, DC, DISC, MC, V. Self-parking free. **Amenities:** Restaurant; cafe; lounge; babysitting; bike rentals; concierge; concierge-level rooms; golf course; health club and spa; Jacuzzi; 4 heated outdoor pools; kids' interactive pool and play area; room service; sauna; 2 tennis courts; watersports equipment/rentals; free WDW Transportation System. *In room:* A/C, TV, DVD/VCR (villa), movie library, hair dryer, Internet (fee), kitchen (villa), kitchenette (studio), microwave, washer and dryer (villa).

Disney's Yacht Club Resort ★★ The Yacht Club has an atmosphere loaded with the posh elegance found in a turn-of-the-20th-century New England yacht club (as imagined by Disney). It is definitely more upscale than its sister resort, the Beach Club (reviewed above), as the rooms, views, service, and atmosphere (nautically themed, of course) are a grade or so better. Here you'll find fine leather furnishings,

---

 Taking Luxury to an All-New Level

The **Waldorf Astoria Orlando** (ℂ **800/925-3673** or 407/597-5500; www.waldorfastoriaorlando.com) opened its doors in 2010. The grandeur and elegance of the original Waldorf Astoria in New York City is not lost at this, the second of only four Waldorf Astoria resorts in the world (the others are located in Park City, Utah; Shanghai; and, of course, New York). The property boasts an impressive address, shared with the area's newest Hilton—the **Hilton Orlando Bonnet Creek** (ℂ **407/597-3600**; www.hiltonbonnetcreek.com). It's surrounded on three sides by Walt Disney World and nestled against the natural beauty of the Bonnet Creek Nature Preserve. The lavish hotel brings with it luxuriously appointed rooms and suites, unmatched personalized service (including an elite concierge team), a formal cabana-lined pool (with access to the lazy river and less formal family-friendly pool and play area at the neighboring Hilton), a Guerlain Spa, a championship golf course, a slew of dining options, and a children's program—oh, and did I mention private transportation to Disney?

antique glass chandeliers, and brass accents adorning the lobby. It's geared more toward adults and families with older children, though young kids are certainly catered to (this is Disney, after all). The Yacht Club and Beach Club resorts share a 25-acre lake, white-sand beaches, an extensive swimming area (with sand-bottom pools, water slides, and a life-size shipwreck), and magnificent landscaping, including a lighthouse to help you find your way back from the parks. Rooms have beds for up to five, and most have balconies. Views run from asphalt to Crescent Lake and the gardens; you would, however, have to be a contortionist to see the lake from some of the "water-view" rooms, so if this is a must, make sure that you request one with a direct view (as a bonus, you'll see Epcot in the distance). Epcot is a 10- to 15-minute walk from the front door, but save your energy for the parks and use the Disney ferry instead. Disney's BoardWalk, with its array of restaurants, shops, and entertainment options, is just a short ferry ride (or walk across the bridge) away, as are the WDW Swan and Dolphin resorts.

1700 Epcot Resorts Blvd. (off Buena Vista Dr.; P.O. Box 10000), Lake Buena Vista, FL 32830. www.disneyworld.com. © **407/934-7639** or 407/934-7000. Fax 407/924-3450. 630 units. $335–$990 double; $475–$2,875 club; $650–$2,875 suite. Extra person $25. Children 17 and younger stay free in parent's room. AE, DC, DISC, MC, V. Valet parking $12; self-parking free. **Amenities:** 3 restaurants; grill; lounge; babysitting; supervised children's program; concierge; concierge-level rooms; health club and small spa; Jacuzzi; 3-acre pool and play area; 2 outdoor heated pools; kids' pool; room service; 2 lighted tennis courts; watercraft/equipment rentals; WDW Transportation System; transportation to non-Disney theme parks for a fee; limited Wi-Fi (fee). *In room:* A/C, TV, fridge, hair dryer, Internet (fee), microwave (free, upon request).

Walt Disney World Dolphin ★★ If Antonio Gaudí and Dr. Seuss had teamed up on an architectural design, they might have created something like this Starwood resort and its sister, the Walt Disney World Swan (see below). This hotel centers on a 27-story pyramid with two 11-story wings crowned by 56-foot twin dolphin sculptures. Because it isn't as theme intensive as the other Disney resorts, it's popular with business travelers and those who prefer their accommodations a little less sugary. Rooms, after being redecorated in 2008, sport warm yet contemporary earth-tone color schemes, upgraded technology, and the usual array of amenities; all offer views of the grounds and other parts of Mickey's world. Public areas are a bit more avant-garde, thanks in part to dramatic lighting and upscale furnishings. The resort shares a grotto pool with waterfalls, water slide, and whirlpools, as well as a Body by Jake health club (for an extra fee) with the Swan. There's also a branch of the Mandara Spa. Camp Dolphin is a supervised children's program for kids ages 4 to 12, offering a variety of activities to keep the little ones busy while Mom and Dad enjoy some time alone. Epcot is the nearest park, just a short water-taxi ride away, and the BoardWalk and Beach and Yacht Club resorts are within walking distance, greatly expanding the dining and entertainment options within reach of your own two feet. That said, with **Todd English's bluezoo** (p. 127) heading up the resort's dining lineup, you won't need to go too far for a really good meal.

1500 Epcot Resorts Blvd. (off Buena Vista Dr.; P.O. Box 22653), Lake Buena Vista, FL 32830. www.swandolphin.com. © **800/227-1500** or 407/934-4000. Fax 407/934-4884. 1,509 units. $219–$579 double; $675–$4,300 suite. Extra person $25. Resort fee $12 per night. Children 17 and younger stay free in parent's room. AE, DC, DISC, MC, V. Valet parking $16; self-parking $12. **Amenities:** 4 restaurants; cafe; grill; 5 lounges; character meals; babysitting; supervised children's program; concierge; concierge-level rooms; health club and spa (fee); 5 heated outdoor pools; room service; 4 lighted tennis courts; watersports equipment/rentals; WDW Transportation System; transportation to non-Disney parks for a fee; limited Wi-Fi (fee). *In room:* A/C, TV, fridge (fee), hair dryer, Internet (included in resort fee), minibar.

When a WDW Property Is Not a WDW Property

As mentioned earlier, there are nine "official" Disney hotels that aren't owned by Disney itself. That's true. But there are a couple of asterisks. The Walt Disney World Swan and the Walt Disney World Dolphin have the Walt Disney name and are located right on the WDW resort property; they're not Disney-owned resorts, but are still considered "official" resorts.

Walt Disney World Swan ★ Not to be outdone by the huge dolphins at its sister property, this high-rise Starwood resort is topped with dual 45-foot swan statues and seashell fountains. It offers a good location, as it is close to Epcot, Disney's Hollywood Studios, Fantasia Gardens, and the nightlife of the BoardWalk. While the theme doesn't scream Mickey Mouse, the decor and atmosphere are inviting in both the public areas and the guest rooms. It shares a beach, health club, children's program, a number of restaurants, and other trimmings with the Dolphin (see above). The best room views are from the 11th and 12th floors' Royal Beach Club, the hotel's concierge level; the beach next to the pool offers a great view of Epcot's IllumiNations fireworks. Guest rooms here are just a tad smaller than those at the neighboring Dolphin.

1200 Epcot Resorts Blvd. (off Buena Vista Dr.; P.O. Box 22653), Lake Buena Vista, FL 32830. www.swandolphin.com. ✆ **800/248-7926** or 407/934-3000. Fax 407/934-4499. 756 units. $239–$505 double; $675–$4,300 suite. Extra person $25. Resort fee $12 per night. Children 17 and younger stay free in parent's room AE, DC, DISC, MC, V. Valet parking $16; self-parking $12. **Amenities:** 3 restaurants; grill; 5 lounges; character meals; babysitting; supervised children's program; concierge; concierge-level rooms; health club and spa (fee); 5 heated outdoor pools; room service; 4 lighted tennis courts; watersports equipment/rentals; WDW Transportation System; transportation to non-Disney parks for a fee; limited Wi-Fi (fee). *In room:* A/C, TV, fridge (fee), hair dryer, Internet (included in resort fee), minibar.

Expensive

Disney's Animal Kingdom Lodge ★★★ ☺ The feel of an African game-reserve lodge immediately surrounds you upon entering the grand stories-high lobby, which features a thatched roof and ornate shield chandeliers. The main resort's *kraal* design (a semi-circular layout) ensures most rooms overlook the 30-acre savanna, allowing guests an occasional view of the birds, giraffes, and array of other African animals that call the savanna home (rooms without the savanna view will save a few extra dollars; you can get the scenery for free through large picture windows in the lobby and from a nature trail set behind the pool area). Families will appreciate the animals and the array of unique activities, including storytelling by the fire, sing-alongs, and more. Those in the mood for romance will appreciate the remote setting and the more relaxed and sedate nature of the resort. Typical rooms are slightly smaller than those at Disney's other "Deluxe" resorts, but the distinctive theme and spectacular surroundings are unparalleled, making a stay here well worth the slightly tighter squeeze. Mosquito-netting curtains, balconies, and other neat detailing in the decor continue the theme. The 9,000-square-foot pool has a water slide, a wading area for young children, and a good view of the savanna. The lodge is adjacent to Animal Kingdom, but most everything else on WDW property is quite a distance away. **Boma** (p. 124) features a fabulous breakfast and dinner buffet. **Note:** The fifth and sixth floors of the main lodge (now referred to as Jambo House) are actually

Kidani Village, Also Known As the Villas at Disney's Animal Kingdom

Kidani Village, the second and final phase of the Disney's Animal Kingdom Villas, began welcoming its first guests in 2009 (with half of the village villas opening in May, the remaining villas in Oct). Built adjacent to Jambo House (the existing Animal Kingdom Lodge—which also houses two floors of Vacation Club villas), the Kidani Village, which shares amenities with the Lodge, also features its own full-service restaurant (Sanna—an artistically inspired eatery with an intimate atmosphere and a menu of African-inspired cuisine with an Indian twist), its own recreational facilities, a fitness center, and an extensive themed pool and water-play area. For all the details, or to book a room, go online to **www.disneyworld. com** or call ℂ **407/939-6244.**

Vacation Club villas—a great option for those needing additional room and homey amenities.

2901 Osceola Pkwy., Bay Lake, FL 32830. www.disneyworld.com. ℂ **407/934-7639** or 407/938-3000. Fax 407/939-4799. 1,293 units. $250–$615 double; $365–$2,990 club; $760–$2,990 suite; $280–$2,330 lodge villa. Extra person $25. Children 17 and younger stay free in parent's room. AE, DC, DISC, MC, V. Valet parking $12; self-parking free. **Amenities:** 2 restaurants; cafe; lounge; babysitting; supervised children's program; concierge; concierge-level rooms; health club and limited spa; heated outdoor pool; kids' pool; room service; WDW Transportation System; transportation to non-Disney parks for a fee. *In room:* A/C, TV, DVD (concierge level), fridge (free, upon request), hair dryer, Internet (fee), microwave (concierge level).

Disney's Wilderness Lodge ★★★ ☺ The geyser out back, the mammoth stone hearth in the lobby, and bunk beds for the kids are just a few reasons this resort is a favorite of families, though couples will find the surroundings to their liking as well. In keeping with the spirit of the great American Northwest, the lodge has the feel of a rustic national park lodge, as it is patterned after one in Yellowstone National Park. Surrounded by 56 acres of oaks and pines, it offers a woodsy and remote setting. That geyser mentioned above "spouts off" periodically throughout the day just to add to the authenticity, and the nightly electric water pageants can be viewed from the shores of Bay Lake. The lodge also has an immense swimming area, fed by a thundering water-fall whose water flows in from the "hot springs" in the lobby. The nearest park is the Magic Kingdom, but because the resort is in a remote area, it can take some time to get there. The main drawback is the difficulty in accessing other areas via the WDW Transportation System. See the review of the **Artist Point** restaurant on p. 128. *Note:* The lodge offers a free tour touting its architecture Wednesday through Saturday at 9am (kids will likely be bored), and each day a select family gets to traipse up to the roof to raise the resort's flag (if you're interested, ask at the front desk upon check-in).

The **Villas at Disney's Wilderness Lodge** is another Disney Vacation Club timeshare property that rents vacant rooms. It offers a more upscale mountain retreat experience and more spacious accommodations than at the Wilderness Lodge, though the properties share a grand lobby, amenities, and activities. The 181 one- and two-bedroom villas have 727 and 1,080 square feet, respectively.

901 W. Timberline Dr. (on the southwest shore of Bay Lake just east of the Magic Kingdom; P.O. Box 10000), Lake Buena Vista, FL 32830. www.disneyworld.com. ℂ **407/934-7639** or 407/938-4300. Fax 407/824-3232. 909 units. $250–$840 lodge; $425–$1,500 club; $875–$1,500 suite; $340–$520 studio; $340–$1,245 villa. Children 17 and younger stay free in parent's room. AE, DC, DISC, MC, V. Valet parking

$12; self-parking free. **Amenities:** 3 restaurants; 2 lounges; babysitting; bike rentals; concierge; concierge-level rooms; health club and limited spa; 2 Jacuzzis; 2 heated outdoor pools; kids' pool; room service; watersports equipment/rentals; WDW Transportation System; transportation to non-Disney parks for a fee. *In room:* A/C, TV, DVD (villa), fridge (villa; free, upon request at the lodge), hair dryer, Internet access (fee), microwave (villa).

Moderate

Disney's Caribbean Beach Resort ★★   Thanks to its moderate pricing scheme and recreational activities, the Caribbean Beach is a great choice for families. The resort's rooms are spread across five villages (all Disney "moderate" resorts share a similar general layout) of pastel-colored buildings, named for the islands of Aruba, Barbados, Jamaica, Martinique, and Trinidad (north and south). Try and snag a corner room if you can, as they let in more light, but don't bother springing for a pool view (those rooms can get noisy). In 2009, 384 rooms in Trinidad South were completely overhauled with a pirate theme (in this case, Pirates of the Caribbean), complete with ship-shaped beds and treasure-chest dressers. Disney expects to expand this type of "storybook" theming to other resorts sometime in the future. The lush tropical greenery adds a touch of island atmosphere. Parrot Cay, the resort's main pool area and playground, is themed as an old Spanish-style fort, complete with water cannons, water slides, and waterfalls. The closest park is Disney's Hollywood Studios, though it can take up to 45 minutes to get there using Disney transportation—it's best to rent a car if you stay here.

900 Cayman Way (off Buena Vista Dr.; P.O. Box 10000), Lake Buena Vista, FL 32830. www.disneyworld. com. **407/934-7639** or 407/934-3400. Fax 407/934-3288. 2,112 units. $154–$309 double. Extra person $15. Children 17 and younger stay free in parent's room. AE, DC, DISC, MC, V. Self-parking free. **Amenities:** Restaurant; food court; lounge; babysitting; bike rentals; Jacuzzi; large outdoor heated pool; 6 smaller pools in the villages; kids' pool; room service; watercraft/equipment rentals; WDW Transportation System; transportation to non-Disney parks for a fee. *In room:* A/C, TV, fridge (free, upon request), hair dryer, Internet (fee).

Disney's Coronado Springs Resort ★   An American Southwestern theme carries through four- and five-story hacienda-style buildings in shades of pink and desert-sand stucco, with terra-cotta tile roofs and shaded courtyards. The pool area, inspired by the Maya ruins of Mexico, sports a tremendous Mayan temple with cascading water and a twisting water slide. (Watch out for the spitting jaguar—he will likely surprise you as you pass by!) The rooms are identical in layout to those in the Caribbean Beach Resort, including the small bathrooms. Those located nearest the central public area, pool, and lobby tend to be a bit noisier—but if you stay in the outer buildings you might face an excruciatingly long walk to the pool or lobby area. Because it's a convention resort, you'll find extras—such as a barber and salon, a

Relax & Rejuvenate

If, after pounding the theme-park pavement, you find yourself in need of some R&R, Disney's got just the ticket. The Grand Floridian, Saratoga Springs, and Walt Disney World Dolphin each have a **full-service spa** offering services ranging from massage therapy to facials to full-body treatments—all designed to relax your mind, body, and soul. Small-scale spas (offering limited services) can be found at the Animal Kingdom, BoardWalk, Contemporary, Coronado, Wilderness Lodge, and Yacht Club resorts.

variety of suites, and Wi-Fi access (for a fee), among other perks—not found at Disney's other "moderate" resorts. The nearest park is Animal Kingdom, but the Coronado is at the southwest corner of WDW and a good distance from most other areas in the park; rent a car. See the review of the **Rix** lounge, Disney's newest and trendiest entry in its lineup of nightclubs, on p. 327.

1000 Buena Vista Dr. (near All-Star resorts and Blizzard Beach), Lake Buena Vista, FL 32830. www. disneyworld.com. ⓒ **407/934-7639** or 407/939-1000. Fax 407/939-1003. 1,921 units. $159–$284 double; $355–$1,320 suite. Extra person $15. Children 17 and younger stay free in parent's room. AE, DC, DISC, MC, V. Self-parking free. **Amenities:** Restaurant; grill/food court; 2 lounges; bike rentals; concierge; health club and limited spa; Jacuzzi; 4 outdoor heated pools; kids' pool; room service; sauna; watercraft equipment/rentals; WDW Transportation System; transportation to non-Disney parks for a fee; limited Wi-Fi (fee). *In room:* A/C, TV, fridge, hair dryer, Wi-Fi (fee).

Disney's Port Orleans Resort ★★ Port Orleans has the best location, landscaping, and perhaps the coziest atmosphere of the resorts in this class (and was renovated from top to bottom in recent years, so it's in great condition, too). This Southern-style property is really a combination of two distinct resorts: the French Quarter and Riverside. The French Quarter offers magnolia trees, wrought-iron railings, cobblestone streets, and an idealistic vision of New Orleans's famous French Quarter. Riverside transports you back to Louisiana's Mississippi River towns, its rooms housed in buildings resembling grand plantation homes and the "rustic" wooden shacks of the bayou. Overall, this resort offers some romantic spots and is relatively quiet, making it popular with couples. The pools, Tom Sawyer–style playgrounds, and array of activities (including a pirate-themed cruise that departs right from the resort) make it a favorite for families as well. The Doubloon Lagoon pool in the French Quarter is a family favorite, with a water slide that curves out of a Sea Serpent's mouth before entering the pool. The rooms and bathrooms (equivalent to all rooms at Disney's "moderate" resorts) are somewhat of a tight fit for four, though the Alligator Bayou rooms have a trundle bed that allows for an extra child, and the vanity areas have privacy curtains. Port Orleans is just east of Epcot and Disney's Hollywood Studios.

Note: Just as this book went to press, Disney announced that it would refit 512 of its rooms at Port Orleans Riverside with a princess theme (aptly naming them "Royal Rooms"), set for completion later this year. Expect to find Princess-and-the-Frog headboards (full-size mattresses replaced with queen-size ones), bathroom faucets that resemble Aladdin's lamp, golden accents, and more—oh, and don't be surprised to discover a premium price tag attached to the newest royal digs (pirate-themed rooms go for $30 more per night at Disney's Caribbean Resort).

2201 Orleans Dr. (off Bonnet Creek Pkwy.; P.O. Box 10000), Lake Buena Vista, FL 32830. www.disney world.com. ⓒ **407/934-7639** or 407/934-5000. Fax 407/934-5353. 3,056 units. $154–$269 double.

A Night Out

Several of the higher-priced Disney resorts—including Animal Kingdom Lodge, Beach Club, Grand Floridian Resort & Spa, and Wilderness Lodge, as well as the Polynesian Resort—have supervised kid care, usually from 4 or 4:30pm to midnight daily ($11.25 per child 4–12 per hour, dinner and activities included; ⓒ **407/939-3463**). Disney also offers in-room sitters through **Kid's Night Out** (ⓒ **407/827-5444**). The Walt Disney World Dolphin, an "official" resort, offers a supervised child-care program as well.

Disney's All-Star and Pop Century resorts charge a "preferred room" rate, but don't expect much for the top rate of $179. Guests who book it are paying for location: Preferred rooms are closer to the pools, food court, and/ or transportation. If you've got a rental car or don't mind walking, don't bother paying extra; some of the quietest rooms at the All-Stars are the standard ones (those farthest from the action).

Extra person $15. Children 17 and younger stay free in parent's room. AE, DC, DISC, MC, V. Self-parking free. **Amenities:** 2 restaurants; grill/food court; 2 lounges; babysitting; bike rentals; concierge; Jacuzzi; 6 heated outdoor pools; 2 kids' pools; room service; watersports equipment/rentals; WDW Transportation System; transportation to non-Disney parks for a fee. *In room:* A/C, TV, fridge, hair dryer, Internet (fee).

Shades of Green on Walt Disney World Resort ★ ✦ Shades of Green, nestled among three of Disney's golf courses near the Magic Kingdom, is open only to folks in the military and their spouses, military retirees and widows, veterans with 100% service-connected disabilities, and Medal of Honor recipients. If you qualify, don't think of staying anywhere else—it's the best bargain on WDW soil. A $92-million refit in 2004 doubled the room capacity of the resort and added fully ADA-compliant rooms with wide doorways and roll-in showers. In addition to the added rooms and suites (housing up to eight), existing rooms (among the largest in all of Disney, at just over 400 sq. ft.) were completely overhauled. All rooms offer TVs with wireless keyboards (access to the Internet is offered for a fee), balconies or patios, and pool or golf-course views. Transportation—though slow—is available to all of the Disney parks and attractions.

1950 Magnolia Palm Dr. (across from the Polynesian Resort), Lake Buena Vista, FL 32830. www. shadesofgreen.org. **⊘ 888/593-2242** or 407/824-3400. Fax 407/824-3665. 587 units. $93–$135 double (based on military rank); $250–$275 6- to 8-person suite (regardless of rank). Extra person $15. Children 17 and younger stay free in parent's room. Cribs $5 per night. AE, DC, DISC, MC, V. **Amenities:** 2 restaurants; cafe; 2 lounges; babysitting; concierge; health club; 2 heated outdoor pools; kids' pool; 2 lighted tennis courts; WDW Transportation System; transportation to non-Disney parks for a fee. *In room:* A/C, TV, fridge, hair dryer.

Inexpensive

Disney's All-Star Movies Resort Most kids love the larger-than-life themes at the three All-Star resorts; however, it can be Disney overload for many adults. Movies such as *Toy Story, 101 Dalmatians,* and *Fantasia* live on in a very big (and I mean BIG) way at this family-friendly resort. Gigantic larger-than-life characters such as Buzz Lightyear, Pongo, and even Mickey himself mark this resort's buildings. They add the only Disney flair to what is essentially a no-frills, budget motel with basic, tiny (260-sq.-ft.) rooms. Think old-school roadside motels, when all you expected was a clean bed and a bathroom (the ones here are positively Lilliputian). The soundproofing leaves something to be desired, especially with the number of children staying here. Like its two siblings (listed below), the All-Star Movies Resort is pretty isolated in WDW's southwest corner. If, like the White Rabbit, you're often "late for a very important date," renting a car is a far better choice than relying on the Disney Transportation System.

If you want to enjoy the amenities and service of a Disney resort but can't do without some beach time, the Disney Vacation Club offers visitors the option of renting a room just 2 hours south of WDW at its **Vero Beach Resort** (☏ **407 /939-7775; www.dvcresorts.com),** directly on the Atlantic Ocean, with sand, surf, and all the Disney trimmings included. Studios, standard rooms, one- and two-bedroom villas, and three-bedroom cottages are all available, ranging from about $190 to $1,175 per night. You will need to arrange your own transportation.

1991 W. Buena Vista Dr., Lake Buena Vista, FL 32830. www.disneyworld.com. ☏ **407/934-7639** or 407/939-7000. Fax 407/939-7111. 1,900 units. $82–$179 double. Extra person $10. Children 17 and younger stay free in parent's room. AE, DC, DISC, MC, V. Self-parking free. **Amenities:** Food court; lounge; babysitting; 2 outdoor heated pools; kids' pool; room service; WDW Transportation System; transportation to non-Disney parks for a fee. *In room:* A/C, TV, fridge (fee), hair dryer, Internet (fee).

Disney's All-Star Music Resort   Giant trombones and musical themes from jazz to calypso are the only things differentiating this from the other All-Star resorts (they're all clones of one another—including the microscopic bathrooms—except for the different themes). While the extra frills at the other Disney resorts won't be found at the All-Stars, the rooms do have a significant perk: They're the least expensive (by a large margin) of all the Disney resorts. Most people don't come to WDW to lounge in their rooms, so if you're only going to be here to sleep, the cramped quarters may not be so bad. The closest parks are Blizzard Beach and Animal Kingdom, which you can reach (not necessarily in an expedient manner) via the Disney Transportation System.

Tip: Larger families with smaller budgets can still stay at the Mouse's house thanks to a recent room redesign at this resort. The rehab brought with it the addition of larger, more comfortable family suites. At 550 square feet, the suites sleep up to six and feature two full bathrooms, a kitchenette, a separate bedroom and living area, and such upgraded amenities as flatscreen TVs.

1801 W. Buena Vista Dr. (at World Dr. and Osceola Pkwy.; P.O. Box 10000), Lake Buena Vista, FL 32830. www.disneyworld.com. ☏ **407/934-7639** or 407/939-6000. Fax 407/939-7222. 1,920 units. $82–$179 double; $194–$365 suite. Extra person $10. Children 17 and younger stay free in parent's room. AE, DC, DISC, MC, V. Self-parking free. **Amenities:** Food court; lounge; babysitting; 2 outdoor heated pools; kids' pool; room service; WDW Transportation System; transportation to non-Disney parks for a fee. *In room:* A/C, TV, fridge (fee), hair dryer, Internet (fee).

Disney's All-Star Sports Resort   It's an instant replay of the other All-Star resorts, including the tight quarters (if you aren't a team player, the togetherness may cause frayed tempers after awhile). The difference here is the decor, with buildings designed around football, baseball, basketball, tennis, and surfing themes. The turquoise surf buildings have huge waves along the roofs, colorful surfboards mounted on exterior walls, and pink fish swimming along balcony railings. Again, if your threshold for visual overload is low, you may want to choose a different resort. As mentioned above, the rates and themes draw mostly families with little kids, and the noise level can get quite high; if you're looking for a quiet vacation or romantic getaway, these resorts are out of bounds.

1701 W. Buena Vista Dr. (at World Dr. and Osceola Pkwy.; P.O. Box 10000), Lake Buena Vista, FL 32830. www.disneyworld.com. © **407/934-7639** or 407/939-5000. Fax 407/939-7333. 1,920 units. $82–$179 double. Extra person $10. Children 17 and younger stay free in parent's room. AE, DC, DISC, MC, V. Self-parking free. **Amenities:** Food court; lounge; babysitting; 2 outdoor heated pools; kids' pool; room service; WDW Transportation System; transportation to non-Disney parks for a fee. *In room:* A/C, TV, fridge (fee), hair dryer, Internet (fee).

Disney's Pop Century Resort 🛥 After numerous delays, the first phase of Disney's latest inexpensive resort debuted in 2003. Gigantic memorabilia representing the hottest fads of decades past—from Duncan Yo-Yos and the Rubik's Cube to flower power and eight-tracks—mark the exteriors of the Pop Century's buildings. Another clone of the All-Star school, you won't get a lot of frills, but the price is right for those on a budget. A family of four could, with a bit of effort, squeeze into the small, basic rooms. The resort is divided into decades, starting with the Legendary Years of the 1900s to 1940s (alas, there is no projected date for completion of this phase), and the Classic Years of the 1950s to 1990s (the only section currently operating). The resort is closest to the Wide World of Sports Complex but a bit of a ride from everything else (yes, you should definitely rent a car).

Note: In 2010, Disney announced that Pop Century's unfinished buildings were to become part of an all-new 2,000-room resort—the first new resort in just over 7 years. The **Art of Animation Resort,** another in Disney's lineup of "value" resorts, will be built on 65 acres (located across from the existing Pop Century Resort). The resort is scheduled to open just as this book hits the shelves, but is said to include family-size suites (boasting two bathrooms, a master bedroom, and a living area) along with a single building of standard rooms. The entire property will follow themes from Disney's most popular animated films (think *The Little Mermaid, The Lion King, Cars,* and *Finding Nemo*). Disney expects construction to be completed by the end of 2012.

1050 Century Drive Dr. (off the Osceola Pkwy.; P.O. Box 10000), Lake Buena Vista, FL 32830. www.disneyworld.com. © **407/938-4000** or 407/939-6000. Fax 407/938-4040. 2,880 units. $82–$179 double. Extra person $10. Children 17 and younger stay free in parent's room. AE, DC, DISC, MC, V. Self-parking free. **Amenities:** Food court; lounge; babysitting; 3 heated outdoor pools; kids' pool; room service; WDW Transportation System; transportation to non-Disney parks for a fee. *In room:* A/C, TV, fridge (fee), hair dryer, Internet (fee).

A Disney Campground

Disney's Fort Wilderness Resort & Campground ★ ☺ Pines, cypress trees, lakes, and streams surround this woodsy 780-acre resort. The only disadvantage of

---

In the Lineup at Priceline

For years Disney declined to peddle its unclaimed resort rooms alongside Priceline's lengthy list of participating hotels and resorts—but this is about to change. Beginning in November 2011, Disney will in fact list its hotel rooms on **Priceline.** Be aware, Disney is only taking baby steps—listing its rooms via the site's conventional booking engine rather than the "Name Your Own Price" service. Disney also lists rooms on **Travelocity** and **Orbitz.** *Note:* Disney involvement with Priceline does not extend to its European booking site (Booking.com).

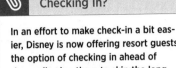

Checking In?

In an effort to make check-in a bit easier, Disney is now offering resort guests the option of checking in ahead of time—allowing them to skip the long lines often encountered upon arrival. Simply go online within 10 days of your arrival date, enter the requested check-in information, and advise the resort of your arrival time. You can also make room requests at this time, should you have any (keeping in mind that requests are not guaranteed). You'll need to register the names of all the people in your party and provide a credit card to cover any WDW resort charges. Upon arrival at the resort, simply head to the special welcome area, where you'll find your room keys and other registration material waiting for you.

staying here is the distance from Epcot, Disney's Hollywood Studios, and Animal Kingdom (it is close to Magic Kingdom). But if you're a true outdoors type, you may appreciate the feeling of being more sheltered from some of the Mickey madness. There are 784 campsites for RVs, pull-behind campers, and tents (110/220-volt outlets, grills, and comfort areas with showers and restrooms).

Some sites are open to pets (the ones with full hookups)—at an additional cost of $5 per site, not per pet, which is less expensive than using the WDW resort kennel, where you pay $10 to $69 per pet (nonresort guests add $2–$5 more per pet). The 408 wilderness cabins (actually trailers made to look like cabins) each offer 504 square feet of space, enough for six people once you pull down the Murphy beds, and they also feature kitchens and daily housekeeping service. Cabins also have an outside deck with grill. Roughing it Disney style isn't so rough, with all the comforts of home. Nearby Pioneer Hall is home to the popular **Hoop-Dee-Doo Musical Revue** (p. 319). In addition, there are plenty of outdoor recreational activities, including horseback riding, fishing, swimming, a petting farm, and playgrounds. The nightly campfire and marshmallow roast, followed by a Disney movie shown right in the great outdoors, is a big hit with families.

3520 N. Fort Wilderness Trail (P.O. Box 10000), Lake Buena Vista, FL 32830. www.disneyworld.com. © **407/934-7639** or 407/824-2900. Fax 407/824-3508. 784 campsites, 408 wilderness cabins. $46–$125 campsite double; $275–$450 wilderness cabin double. Extra person $2 campsites, $5 cabins. Children 17 and younger stay free in parent's room. AE, DC, DISC, MC, V. Self-parking free. Pets $5 (full hookup sites only), $10–$69 at the on-site kennel. **Amenities:** Restaurant; grill; lounge; dinner show; character dining (seasonal); babysitting; bike rentals; extensive outdoor activities (archery; fishing; horseback, pony, carriage, and hay rides; campfire programs; and more); 2 outdoor heated pools; kids' pool; 2 lighted tennis courts; watersports equipment/rentals; WDW Transportation System; transportation to non-Disney parks for a fee. *In room (cabins only):* A/C, TV/VCR, hair dryer, kitchen, outdoor grill.

"OFFICIAL" HOTELS IN LAKE BUENA VISTA

These properties, designated "official" Walt Disney World hotels, are located on and around Hotel Plaza Boulevard, which puts them at the northeast corner of WDW. They're close to Downtown Disney Marketplace, Downtown Disney West Side, and

Pleasure Island (soon to be Hyperion Wharf). The boulevard has been landscaped with enough greenery to make it a contestant for Main Street, U.S.A.

Guests at these hotels enjoy some WDW privileges (see "The Perks of Staying with Mickey," earlier in this chapter), including free bus service to the parks, but **be sure to ask when booking** which privileges you'll get, because they do vary from hotel to hotel. Their locations put you close to the parks, and even closer to the action of Downtown Disney, but, unlike the resorts on WDW property, which occupy their own completely separate areas, the hotels here are set along a tree-lined boulevard. Traffic can be a frustration, as the boulevard is a main access route to Downtown Disney from the outside world. Also note that the Walt Disney World Dolphin and Walt Disney World Swan (listed earlier) should be considered the eighth and ninth of the "official" hotels because they're not Disney-owned. The difference is they're located directly on WDW property.

Another perk of the "official" hotels is that they generally offer a less intense Mickey ambience, although some do offer character breakfasts a few days each week (call the reservations line for details and schedules). Decide for yourself if that's a plus or a minus.

You can make reservations for all of the properties below through the **CRO** (✆ **407/934-7639**) or through the direct hotel numbers included in the listings. To ensure you get the best rates, however, call the hotel or its parent chain directly to see if there are special rates or packages available.

You'll find all of these hotels located on the "Walt Disney World & Lake Buena Vista Hotels" map, earlier in this chapter.

Best for: Visitors who want to stay close to Disney (and take advantage of many of the perks associated with staying at one of Disney's resorts) without having to pay as high a price tag as those staying right on property, and those who prefer a more central location that ensures they can easily access Orlando's various offerings with ease and are not relegated to remaining solely at the Mouse's House.

Drawbacks: Its proximity to Downtown Disney (and all roads leading to Disney's theme parks and attractions) ensures that traffic is often very congested. Its popularity (rooms here book up well in advance) also ensures that area shops and restaurants remain busy from midafternoon (earlier if the weather is poor) until closing, which translates into a lengthy wait to dine (especially when staying here during peak season).

 Credit or Debit?

If you use your debit card (instead of a credit card) as collateral against any purchases you may make during your stay, your card may be charged anywhere from $50 to $250 (or more) *per day,* whether you actually charge anything to your room or not. This policy can seriously deplete your checking account, leaving you with far fewer funds than you might realize—and you won't see a credit back to your account until *up to 10 days after* you have checked out of your resort. Though WDW does not (at least for now) follow this practice, and no charges are applied to your account until you check out, other resorts in the area do. Be sure to ask exactly what your hotel's policy is regarding debit and credit charges the minute you check in (or before you arrive).

Expensive

Buena Vista Palace Resort ★★   The most upscale of the Hotel Plaza Boulevard–area properties, popular with business and leisure travelers alike (though businesspeople make up 75% of its guests), sports a chic and trendy look. Dramatic white walls, open spaces, stories-high curtains, and hints of silver and aqua welcome guests as they enter the lobby. Guest rooms feature an eclectic mix of stylish furnishings combined with a trendy color scheme of white, aqua, and brown (unfortunately, comfort, most notably in the living area, has been sacrificed for appearance's sake; the bedding, however, is quite cozy). Many of the upscale business-standard rooms, in addition to upgraded amenities, have balconies or patios; ask for one above the fifth floor with a "water view." That's the side facing the pools on Recreation Island, Downtown Disney, and, in the distance, Disney's Hollywood Studios' Tower of Terror. The "Disney view" offers distant views of Epcot's IllumiNations fireworks and a glimpse of Downtown Disney, but little else. Families will appreciate the Island Suites, with over 800 square feet of space, one-and-a-half bathrooms, microwave, fridge, and proximity to the pools and playgrounds. The resort is known for its spacious fitness center and full-service European-style spa, which are open to the public (for a fee). The recreational facilities are extensive, and one of the pools is situated partially indoors, providing cover from sun and rain. You'll find the best rates are offered in July and August, contrary to the mainstream tourist resorts—a bonus due to its popularity with the business set.

1900 Buena Vista Dr. (just north of Hotel Plaza Blvd.; P.O. Box 22206), Lake Buena Vista, FL 32830. www.buenavistapalace.com or www.downtowndisneyhotels.com. (C) **866/397-6516** or 407/827-3228. Fax 407/827-6034. 1,012 units. $89–$239 double; $142–$1,520 suite. Extra person $20. Daily resort fee $17. Children 17 and younger stay free in parent's room. AE, DC, DISC, MC, V. Valet parking $22; self-parking free. **Amenities:** 2 restaurants; grill; 2 lounges; character breakfast on Sun; babysitting; concierge; concierge-level rooms; health club; Jacuzzi; 3 heated outdoor pools; kids' pool; room service; sauna; spa; lighted tennis court; complimentary bus service to WDW parks; transportation to non-Disney parks for a fee; limited Wi-Fi (fee). *In room:* A/C, TV, fridge, hair dryer, Internet (fee), minibar, microwave (suite), Wi-Fi (fee).

Moderate

Best Western Lake Buena Vista Resort Hotel in the Walt Disney World Resort 🏅   This 12-acre lakefront hotel is reasonably modern, with nicer rooms and public areas than you might find in others within the chain (they were last renovated, to good effect, in 2008). Rooms, all with balconies, are located in an 18-story tower that is 100% nonsmoking. The views improve from the eighth floor up, and those on the west side have a better chance of seeing something Disney. Accommodations in this category are usually a step above the "moderates" inside WDW, and this one is no exception. You can reserve an oversize room (about 20% larger) or a WDW fireworks–view room for a few dollars more a night. *Note:* It definitely pays to surf the corporate website at **www.bestwestern.com** if you plan to stay here. It sometimes offers great deals and special rates for this hotel.

2000 Hotel Plaza Blvd. (btw. Buena Vista Dr. and Apopka–Vineland Rd./Hwy. 535), Lake Buena Vista, FL 32830. www.lakebuenavistaresorthotel.com or www.downtowndisneyhotels.com. (C) **800/348-3765** or 407/828-8933. 325 units. $79–$239 standard for 4; $299–$479 suite. 5th person $15. $8 daily resort fee. AE, DC, DISC, MC, V. Valet parking $10; self-parking free. **Amenities:** Restaurant; cafe; lounge; babysitting; concierge; fitness center; outdoor heated pool; kids' pool; room service; tennis courts; Wi-Fi (free); complimentary bus service to WDW parks; transportation to

Excess Charges

Several of the properties in this chapter add daily resort fees to their room rates. Though it's essentially a legal version of price gouging, charging for services that used to be included in the rates—such as use of the pool, admission to the health club, Internet access, self-parking, or in-room coffee or phones—has become a growing trend. Be sure to ask when you reserve to see if your hotel charges such a fee and, if so, exactly what's included (some may even be optional) so you're not blindsided at checkout.

non-Disney parks for a fee. *In room:* A/C, TV, fridge (fee, available upon request), game system (fee), hair dryer, Wi-Fi (free).

DoubleTree Guest Suites ★ Children have their own check-in desk and theater, and they get a gift upon arrival at this hotel, the best of the "official" hotels for families traveling with little ones (how can you not love a hotel that gives you freshly baked chocolate-chip cookies at check-in?). Adults may find some of the public areas lacking in personality, though the hand-painted mural that spans the lobby and large aviary is a nice touch. All of the accommodations in this seven-story hotel are two-room suites that offer 643 square feet—large by most standards—with space for up to six; none have balconies, but some have patios. This is the easternmost of the "official" resorts, which means it's farthest from the Disney action, but closest to (even within walking distance of) the shops, restaurants, and activities located in the Crossroads Shopping Center, or along Apopka–Vineland Road.

2305 Hotel Plaza Blvd. (just west of Hwy. 535/Apopka-Vineland Rd.), Lake Buena Vista, FL 32830. www.doubletreeguestsuites.com or www.downtowndisneyhotels.com. ✆ **800/222-8733** or 407/934-1000. Fax 407/934-1011. 229 units. $99–$289 double. Children 17 and younger stay free in parent's room. AE, DC, DISC, MC, V. Self-parking free. **Amenities:** Restaurant; 2 lounges; babysitting; concierge; health club; heated outdoor pool; kids' pool; limited room service; 2 lighted tennis courts; complimentary bus service to WDW parks; transportation to non-Disney parks for a fee. *In room:* A/C, 2 TVs, fridge, game system (fee), hair dryer, Internet, microwave.

Hilton in the Walt Disney World Resort ★★★ This upscale resort welcomes many a Disney vacationer, even though business travelers constitute the bulk of its clientele. Its major claim to fame: It's the only official resort on Hotel Plaza Boulevard to offer guests Disney's Extra Magic Hour option (p. 192). The lobby boasts a nautical flair, and public areas reflect a New England theme, sporting shingles, weathered-wood exteriors, and seafaring touches. The recently renovated rooms have an upscale and contemporary Shaker-style decor, as well as upgraded amenities, and they offer plenty of space in which to relax and unwind. Junior suites are the best choice for families. Rooms on the north and west sides of floors 6 though 10 offer a view of Downtown Disney (just a short walk away) and, in the distance, the Magic Kingdom fireworks. The resort offers a variety of recreational options, including a large pool area (with two pools and plenty of space to soak up the sun) and a game room for kids. Dining options are plentiful, too.

1751 Hotel Plaza Blvd., Lake Buena Vista, FL 32830. www.hilton.com or www.downtowndisneyhotels.com. ✆ **407/827-4000.** Fax 407/827-6369. 814 units. $89–$259 double; $359–$1,500 suite. Extra person $20. Children 17 and younger stay free in parent's room. AE, DC, DISC, MC, V. Valet parking $17; self-parking $10. **Amenities:** 4 restaurants; 2 cafes; 3 lounges; character breakfast (Sun); babysitting; concierge; concierge-level rooms; health club; 2 outdoor heated pools; room service; complimentary bus service to WDW parks; transportation to non-Disney parks for a fee. *In room:* A/C, TV, fridge (fee), hair dryer, Internet (fee), microwave (fee), minibar, MP3 docking station, Wi-Fi (fee).

Holiday Inn in the Walt Disney World Resort ★ After suffering extensive damage during the summer hurricanes of 2004—an unfortunate happenstance given that the hotel had just undergone a $6-million face-lift prior to the storms—this resort closed down for almost 5 years. In 2010, the $25-million reconstruction was finally complete and the resort reopened, bringing with it signature Holiday Inn amenities, a contemporary design, and a location that's hard to beat (within walking distance of Downtown Disney). Spacious, well-appointed rooms come with 32-inch HDTVs; an inviting zero-entry pool is connected to a lap pool; and the main restaurant features a Kids Eat Free program. Additional perks include complimentary Wi-Fi, package delivery for purchases made at Disney theme parks (a service usually offered only at official Disney resorts), preferred tee times at WDW golf courses, and free transportation to Disney parks (departing every 30 min.). The structure may seem familiar, but the bright decor is refreshing and the brand a welcome addition to the lineup of offerings along Hotel Plaza Boulevard.

1805 Hotel Plaza Blvd. (btw. Lake Buena Vista Dr. and Apopka–Vineland Rd./Hwy. 535), Lake Buena Vista, FL 32830. www.hiorlando.com or www.downtowndisneyhotels.com. © **800/223-9930** or 407/828-8888. Fax 407/827-4623. 323 units. $99–$279 double. Extra person $20. Children 17 and younger stay free in parent's room. AE, DC, DISC, MC, V. Self-parking free. **Amenities:** Restaurant; cafe; lounge; babysitting; concierge; health club; outdoor heated pool; room service; complimentary bus service to WDW parks; transportation to non-Disney parks for a fee. *In room:* A/C, TV, fridge, hair dryer, Wi-Fi (free).

Royal Plaza ★ The Plaza is one of the boulevard's originals, but renovations during its 25 years (including a multimillion-dollar makeover a couple of years ago) have kept it in quite good shape. A favorite with the budget-minded, its hallmark is a friendly staff (some of whom have been here since the hotel opened) who provide excellent service. The well-sized rooms offer quality furnishings and amenities (pullout sofas, plasma TVs, and more) and have enough space for five. Poolside rooms have balconies and patios; the tower rooms have separate sitting areas, and some offer whirlpool tubs in the bathrooms. If you want a view from up high, ask for a room facing west and WDW; the south and east sides keep a watchful eye on I-4 traffic. The inner courtyard offers a quiet escape where you can sit by the pool and soak up the Florida sunshine surrounded by scattered palm trees.

1905 Hotel Plaza Blvd. (btw. Buena Vista Dr. and Hwy. 535/Apopka–Vineland Rd.), Lake Buena Vista, FL 32830. www.royalplaza.com or www.downtowndisneyhotels.com. © **800/248-7890** or 407/828-2828. Fax 407/827-6338. 394 units. $69–$139 double; $189–$269 suite. Daily resort fee $8. Children 17 and younger stay free in parent's room. AE, DC, DISC, MC, V. Valet parking $16; self-parking $10. **Amenities:** Restaurant; lounge; Kids Eat Free program; babysitting; children's activity program; health club; heated outdoor pool; room service; 4 lighted tennis courts; complimentary bus service to WDW parks; transportation to non-Disney parks for a fee. *In room:* A/C, TV, game system, hair dryer, Internet (fee), minibar.

Wyndham Lake Buena Vista Resort ★ This lakeside resort (the Regal Sun in a previous life, and the Grosvenor before that) is within walking distance of Downtown Disney Marketplace's shops and restaurants. Thanks to a relatively recent top-to-bottom overhaul, guest rooms sport updated furnishings, cozy bedding, upgraded amenities (such as flatscreen TVs), and a stylish decor. Other notable features include an extensive zero-entry pool and aquatic playground, a children's lounge (with scheduled activities), and a completely redesigned lobby. Frequent package deals make it popular with budget travelers. Ask for a Tower Room on the west side (floors 9–19) for a limited view of Lake Buena Vista. A character breakfast is also offered 3 mornings a week.

1850 Hotel Plaza Blvd. (just east of Buena Vista Dr.), Lake Buena Vista, FL 32830. www.wyndham.com or www.downtowndisneyhotels.com. ✆ **800/624-4109** or 407/828-4444. Fax 407/828-8192. 626 units. $65–$199 double. Daily resort fee $16. Extra person $20. Children 17 and younger stay free in parent's room. AE, DC, DISC, MC, V. Valet parking $12; self-parking free. **Amenities:** Restaurant; 3 lounges; character breakfast (Tues, Thurs, Sat); babysitting; children's activity program; concierge; health club; Jacuzzi; 2 outdoor heated pools; 2 lighted tennis courts; complimentary bus service to WDW parks; transportation to non-Disney parks for a fee. *In room:* A/C, TV, fridge, MP3 docking station, Wi-Fi (fee).

AROUND LAKE BUENA VISTA

The hotels in this section are within a few minutes' drive of the WDW parks. They offer a great location but not the Disney-related privileges given to guests in the "official" hotels, such as Disney bus service and character breakfasts. On the flip side, because you're not paying for those privileges, hotels in this category are generally a shade less expensive for comparable rooms and services.

Note: These hotels are also listed on the "Walt Disney World & Lake Buena Vista Hotels" map, earlier in this chapter.

Best for: Visitors on a tighter budget will find that their choices are far greater the farther they venture from Disney. Those not concerned with financial constraints but who simply wish to remain farther away from all of the action (and traffic) associated with staying near Disney, or those who may only be spending a small amount of time with Mickey, will find an array of upscale, recreation-rich accommodations from which to choose.

Drawbacks: Staying farther away means having to either drive to the parks (and pay the hefty parking fees) or take a shuttle (which may or may not be free, but is definitely on a predetermined schedule that you will have to follow to the letter if you want to get back to your hotel).

Very Expensive

Hyatt Regency Grand Cypress Resort ★★★ 👜 After a $65-million renovation in 2009, the redesigned lobby, while still centered on an 18-story atrium, now sports a trendy updated decor with unique and inviting seating areas (perfect for small social or business gatherings) and an all-new Sushi Bar, where Chef Yoshi, a local celebrity of sorts, amazes onlookers and diners alike. The rooms (some renovated, others completely reconstructed) now feature a chic yet subtle decor with modernized amenities. A favorite of honeymooners and those seeking a luxurious adult oasis, there's plenty here for families as well. The west-side rooms on floors seven and up have a distant view of Cinderella Castle and the Magic Kingdom's fireworks. (This vantage point also shows how much of WDW and the surrounding area still remain wooded.) The Hyatt shares a golf club and academy, racquet club, and equestrian center (though at press time, the equestrian center had been closed indefinitely) with its sister property, Villas of Grand Cypress (see below); both offer excellent packages aimed at the sports set. The Hyatt's half-acre, 800,000-gallon pool is one of the best in Orlando and features caves, grottoes, waterfalls, a rope bridge, and a 45-foot water slide. A very nice child-care facility is also available.

Hemingway's, the resort's signature restaurant (p. 135), has a Key West theme and a menu featuring fresh and innovative seafood. At the **Chef's Table** (p. 136), guests can indulge in a unique and intimate dining experience—perfect for a special night out.

1 N. Jacaranda (off Hwy. 535/Apopka–Vineland Rd.), Orlando, FL 32836. www.hyattgrandcypress.com. ℂ **800/233-1234** or 407/239-1234. Fax 407/239-3800. 750 units. $149–$399 double; $599–$5,750 suite. Optional $20 daily resort fee (includes health club, local calls, daily newspaper, and in-room coffee). Extra person $25. Children 18 and younger stay free in parent's room. AE, DC, DISC, MC, V. Valet parking $23; self-parking $11. **Amenities:** 4 restaurants; 4 lounges; babysitting; supervised children's program; concierge; concierge-level rooms; 45 holes of golf; health club; large heated outdoor pool; room service; spa; 12 tennis courts (5 lighted); watersports equipment/rentals; free Disney shuttle; transportation to non-Disney parks for a fee. *In room:* A/C, TV, game system (fee), hair dryer, minibar, Wi-Fi (fee).

Villas of Grand Cypress ★★★ 🎎 This is an exceptional place to retreat to at the end of the day, though it's definitely a splurge in terms of budget. At its "modest" end, this Mediterranean-inspired resort starts with standard-size rooms with Roman tubs and patios, many of them backing up to ponds whose inhabitants include mallards, soft-shelled turtles, and largemouth bass eager for bread crusts or whatever else you can spare. Floor plans progress to elegant one- to four-bedroom villas that reach about 2,800 square feet at the top end. Some include kitchens, dining rooms, and patios. The resort shares a golf club and academy, racquet club, and equestrian center (at press time, this was closed indefinitely) with the Hyatt Regency Grand Cypress Resort (see above). Inside the resort, you're almost completely sheltered from Disney, which is situated only a few hundred yards away. Take some time to wander the lush grounds, which are dotted with lakes, bougainvillea, and hibiscus. There are also walking and jogging trails, biking trails, and a 24-foot rock-climbing wall. Shuttle buses allow you to park your car and get around the resort and to the nearby theme parks without driving. Unlike its sister Hyatt property, this resort caters primarily to adults, though guests with kids can use the Hyatt's child-care and other facilities—even the pool.

1 N. Jacaranda (off Hwy. 535/Apopka–Vineland Rd.), Orlando, FL 32836. www.grandcypress.com. ℂ **800/835-7377** or 407/239-4700. Fax 407/239-7219. 146 villas. $195–$575 club suite; $295–$2,000 1- to 4-bedroom villa. Resort fee $18. 1 extra person over the room limit stays free. Children 17 and younger stay free in parent's room. AE, DC, DISC, MC, V. Self-parking free. **Amenities:** 2 restaurants; 2 lounges; babysitting; supervised children's program (at the Hyatt); concierge; concierge-level rooms; 45 holes of golf; health club; 2 outdoor heated pools; room service; spa; 12 tennis courts (5 lighted); watersports equipment/rentals; free shuttle to WDW parks; transportation to non-Disney parks for a fee. *In room:* A/C, TV, hair dryer, full kitchens (some), minibar, washer and dryer (some; fee), Wi-Fi (free).

Expensive

Gaylord Palms ★★★ It's a convention center in disguise, but the Gaylord Palms appeals to vacationers, too, and is not your run-of-the-mill resort. It could be considered a destination unto itself, offering its own entertainment, fabulous dining, shops, and recreational facilities. The 4½-acre octagonal Grand Atrium topped by a glass dome surrounds a miniature version of the Castillo de San Marcos, the old fort at St. Augustine. Waterfalls, lush foliage, live alligators, and a rocky landscape complete the feel.

The resort and its rooms are divided into themes: Emerald Bay, a 362-room hotel within the hotel, has an elegant air; St. Augustine captures the essence of America's

A MARRIOTT montage

The December 2000 christening of the **Marriott Village at Lake Buena Vista,** 8623 Vineland Ave., Orlando, FL 32821 (**www.orlando2stay.com;** ✆ **877/682-8552** or 407/938-9001), brought together three of the flagship's properties in a cluster just east of Lake Buena Vista, 3 miles from WDW. In 2007, extensive renovations ensured the village remains appealing and up-to-date. The resort includes a 400-room Spring-Hill Suites ($116–$211 double; free continental breakfast), a 388-room Fairfield Inn ($107–$199 double; free continental breakfast), and a 312-room Courtyard by Marriott ($125–$224 double). Children younger than 17 stay free in a parent's room, and an extra person costs an additional $10.

Wi-Fi is available at all three resorts for an additional fee (in-room at the Fairfield; in the public areas at the Courtyard and Springhill Suites, and all rooms have free high-speed Internet access, PlayStations, and fridges (the SpringHill Suites also has microwaves, and the Fairfield features 48 bunk-bed suites for families). Each resort has its own pool and play area (the Courtyard features an indoor/outdoor pool with an interactive splash zone for the kids), though guests may use whichever pool they choose. The fitness center, Hertz rental-car desk (located at the Courtyard), arcade, and Marketplace are also shared. All offer transportation for a fee ($11–$30 per person per day) to Disney and non-Disney parks. There are three restaurants within walking distance, as well as an array of on-the-go and snack-style eateries located right in the village itself. To get here, take I-4, exit 68, Hwy. 535/Apopka–Vineland Road; head south to Vineland, and then go left for a half-mile to the village. There's free self-parking at this gated property.

oldest city; Key West delivers the laid-back ambience of Florida's southernmost city; and the Everglades uses a misty swamp, snarling faux gator, fiber-optic fireflies, and tin-roofed shanties to muster a wild-and-wooly air. The rooms are spacious, beautifully decorated, and well appointed (the soundproofing, though, could be a bit better); each has its own balcony. The kids' pool features a huge eight-legged octopus water slide, and cabanas at the adult pool have Internet access. If you need to unwind further, try the 20,000-square-foot **Relâche Spa.** As is befitting a luxury resort, the service is impeccable—yet it's also extremely friendly and welcoming, not standoffish, as is the case at many other resorts of this class.

Note: Just as this book was being written, Gaylord announced that DreamWorks characters (think *Shrek, Kung Fu Panda,* and *Madagascar*) will soon be arriving at the hotel. The "DreamWorks Experience" (details and pricing yet to be released) will roll out during the winter holidays later this year. Look for themed amenities (but not themed rooms), parades, meet-and-greet opportunities, and poolside activities to be part of the lineup.

6000 Osceola Pkwy., Kissimmee, FL 34747. www.gaylordpalms.com. ✆ **877/677-9352** or 407/586-2000. Fax 407/239-4822. 1,406 units. $139–$299 double; $635–$2,700 suite. Daily resort fee $15. Extra adult $20. Children 17 and younger stay free in parent's room. AE, DC, DISC, MC, V. Valet parking $20; self-parking $13. **Amenities:** 3 restaurants; 4 lounges; babysitting; supervised children's program; concierge; concierge-level rooms; health club; 2 outdoor heated pools; room service; spa; free transportation to Disney parks; transportation to non-Disney parks for a fee. *In room:* A/C, TV, CD player, computer (free), fridge, hair dryer, Wi-Fi (free).

Gooding's Supermarkets (☎ 407/827-1200; www.goodings.com or www.goodingsdelivers.com) offers grocery delivery service to theme-park area hotels in Lake Buena Vista, Disney, Celebration, I-Drive, and Kissimmee. There is a $50 minimum, and a $25 service charge is added to all orders. You can order groceries (but no alcohol) online up to 48 hours before your requested delivery date. Delivery hours are 4 to 7pm. For details, see the website or call ahead. This is a great service if you are staying in a hotel room with kitchen facilities or if you want to stock up on snacks and supplies.

3

Around Lake Buena Vista

WHERE TO STAY

Marriott Orlando World Center ★★★ This upscale resort caters to business and leisure travelers alike. Golf, tennis, and spa lovers will find plenty to do at the 230-acre property, as will families. The lobby's centerpiece is a 28-story tower, the decor contemporary and open with dramatic stories-high ceilings. The large, comfortable, and beautifully decorated rooms sleep four, and the higher poolside floors offer views of Disney. For a large-scale resort, it is surprisingly easy to get around, as it is not so much spread out as up. The largest of its five pools has water slides and waterfalls surrounded by plenty of space to relax among the palm trees and tropical plants. There's plenty of on-site dining, ranging from counter-service casual to gourmet cuisine; the **Mikado Japanese Steakhouse** (p. 136) headlines the hotel's four restaurants. The location, only 2 miles from the Disney parks, is a fabulous plus. Special offers (in the past, these have included getting a second room or an early booking bonus at a substantial savings) and vacation packages (often associated with area theme parks, most notably SeaWorld) are offered throughout the year, making the resort more affordable than you might think.

8701 World Center Dr. (on Hwy. 536 btw. I-4 and Hwy. 535/Apopka–Vineland Rd.), Orlando, FL 32821. www.marriott.com or www.marriottworldcenter.com. ☎ **800/621-0638** or 407/239-4200. Fax 407/238-8777. 2,111 units. $224–$399 for up to 5; $750–$1,600 suite. Children 17 and younger stay free in parent's room. AE, DC, DISC, MC, V. Valet parking $24; self-parking $14. **Amenities:** 4 restaurants; food court; 2 lounges; babysitting; concierge; concierge-level rooms; golf course (nearby); health club; 3 heated outdoor pools; heated indoor pool; kids' pool; room service; sauna; spa; 8 lighted tennis courts; transportation to all theme parks for a fee; limited Wi-Fi (fee). *In room:* A/C, TV, game system (fee), hair dryer, Internet (fee), minibar, MP3 docking station.

Moderate

Embassy Suites Lake Buena Vista ★ Set near the end of Palm Parkway, just off Apopka–Vineland Road, this fun and welcoming all-suite resort is close to all the action of Downtown Disney and the surrounding area, yet still remains a quiet retreat. Each suite sleeps five and includes a separate living area (with a pull-out sofa) and sleeping quarters. The roomy accommodations and on-site activities (including "dive-in" movies 4 nights a week) make it a great choice for families. Some of the other perks include a complimentary cooked-to-order breakfast, a nightly manager's reception, free transportation to Disney, and an indoor/outdoor pool.

8100 Lake St., Orlando, FL 32836. www.embassysuiteslbv.com or http://embassysuites1.hilton.com. ☎ **800/362-2779** or 407/239-1144. Fax 407/239-1718. 334 units. $109–$269 suite. Extra person $15. Rates include full breakfast and manager's reception. AE, DC, DISC, MC, V. Valet parking $12; self-parking free. **Amenities:** Restaurant; cafe; lounge; babysitting; concierge; health club; indoor and outdoor heated pools; kids' pool; room service; sauna; tennis court; free shuttle to Disney parks. *In room:* A/C, TV, fridge, hair dryer, kitchenette, microwave, Wi-Fi (fee).

Hawthorn Suites by Wyndham Lake Buena Vista ★   These moderately priced family suites are less than 2 miles from Disney, close to Downtown Disney. This hotel is a good choice if you want a little home-style comfort and the chance to perform do-it-yourself stuff in the fully equipped kitchen. The two-bedroom suites sleep up to eight and offer plenty of room to rest and relax. A complimentary buffet breakfast, free Wi-Fi, and evening receptions are just some of the perks you'll enjoy here. Special offers and packages can often save you a few more dollars; some include tickets to Disney. *Note:* The Hawthorn is a 100% smoke-free hotel.

8303 Palm Pkwy. (off S. Apopka–Vineland Rd./Hwy. 535), Orlando, FL 32836. www.hawthornlake buenavista.com or www.hawthorn.com. ✆ **800/337-0160,** 877/834-3613, or 407/597-5000. Fax 407/597-6000. 120 units. $89–$169 double. Extra person $15. Rates include continental breakfast. Children 18 and younger stay free in parent's room. AE, DC, DISC, MC, V. Self-parking free. **Amenities:** Health club; Jacuzzi, outdoor heated pool; free shuttle to Disney parks; transportation to non-Disney parks for a fee. *In room:* A/C, TV, hair dryer, fully equipped/stocked kitchen, microwave, Wi-Fi (free).

Holiday Inn Resort Lake Buena Vista ★ ☺   Just a mile from the Disney parks, this spruced-up inn caters to kids in a big way. They can check in at their own check-in desk (they'll even get a free goodie bag), watch a movie at the mini-theater in the lobby area, or have fun at the arcade. The hotel's 231 Kid Suites have beds for up to six; however, standard rooms (with separate kitchenettes) are also available. Top-to-bottom renovations were completed in 2010, adding a more stylish decor that, while still catering to the kid set in the way of amenities, is far more visually appealing to adults. The Kid Suites are now sans sugary themes and colorful characters—a welcome departure because you'll probably get your fill at the parks. If you like sleeping in, ask for a room that doesn't face the pool area. Kids younger than 12 eat free in their own restaurant, though fine dining it isn't (kids won't care about that anyway). The resort offers plenty of other dining options as well.

13351 Apopka–Vineland Rd./Hwy. 535 (btw. Hwy. 536 and I-4), Lake Buena Vista, FL 32821. www.hi resortlbv.com or www.ichotelsgroup.com. ✆ **877/272-9985** or 407/239-4500. Fax 407/239-7713. 507 units. $99–$159 standard for up to 4; $149–$219 Kid Suite. AE, DISC, MC, V. Self-parking free. Resort fee $9. Pets less than 30 lb. $40 for a 7-night stay, 2-pet maximum. **Amenities:** Restaurant; food court; Kids Eat Free program; babysitting; supervised children's program; health club; Jacuzzi; outdoor heated pool; kids' pool; room service; free shuttle to Disney parks; transportation to non-Disney parks for a fee. *In room:* A/C, TV, fridge, game system (fee), hair dryer, kitchenette, microwave, Wi-Fi (fee).

Lake Buena Vista Resort Village & Spa ★★★   Near the southern end of International Drive, within walking distance of the Lake Buena Vista Factory Stores (p. 312), this relatively new ownership-based resort offers spacious two-, three-, and four-bedroom apartment-style accommodations ranging in size from 1,080 square feet to 2,170 square feet, each tastefully decorated in tropical Tommy Bahama–style furnishings. Fully stocked full-size kitchens appointed with granite counters and rich dark-wood cabinetry, washers and dryers, plasma TVs, and master suites with Jacuzzis are the norm here. Kids and adults alike will love the 7,500-square-foot zero-entry lagoon-style pirate-themed pool (with a water slide that winds its way through a 70-ft.-long life-size pirate ship equipped with shooting water cannons). Swaying hammocks are scattered about the surrounding deck, while cabanas allow for a poolside massage. You can grab a bite to eat or sip on tropical concoctions poolside—a large entertainment deck provides a view of the entire pool. For those seeking a more relaxing experience, the Reflections Spa offers a tranquil undersea-inspired atmosphere

YOURS, MINE & ours...

With an ever-increasing number of condo-hotels springing up around the Orlando area, they're becoming more and more difficult to overlook. These properties rent rooms and suites to the general public as if the property were a mainstream hotel, but in this case the unit is either fully or partially owned by someone other than the hotelier. In the past, timeshares were notorious for their pushy sales tactics, luring mainstream guests to buy into their resorts by offering gimmicks and discounted attraction tickets. Nowadays, timeshares (or fractional ownerships, as they're usually called) are in the minority (and far less pushy) as wholly owned condos become more popular—in many cases, vacationers never even realize that the property is ownership based (especially as most condo-style resorts are completely sold out prior to completion—or at least prior to opening).

Among the newest (and nicest) to pop up in recent years are the **Westin Imagine** ★★ (✆ 888/822-3532; www.westin.com), a modern high-rise-style resort with standard rooms as well as one- and two-bedroom suites ($99–$309); and **Floridays Resort Orlando** ★★

(✆ 866/797-0022; www.floridaysresort orlando.com), a Mediterranean-inspired resort with two- and three-bedroom suites (around $150 to upwards of $450), plus extensive pool and play areas all in a villagelike setting. Each offers spacious and well-appointed accommodations, upscale amenities, inviting grounds, and locations close to the shops and restaurants that line I-Drive.

Several ownership-based properties cater to visitors planning an extended stay, offering extensive on-site amenities, spacious suite-style accommodations with full-fledged kitchens, and all the comforts of home (often at a more affordable rate—though in some cases in a location that's slightly more remote). **Lighthouse Key Resort & Spa** (✆ 877/463-4914; www.lighthousekeyresort orlando.com), an upscale Mediterranean-inspired resort, and **Runaway Beach Resort** (✆ 866/289-0238 or 407/997-1900; www.runawaybeachhotel. com), a Key West–inspired resort—both Mike Ditka resorts (www.mikeditka resorts.com)—rent one-, two-, and three-bedroom residences (Lighthouse Key also has four-bedroom residences) with landscaped grounds, extensive

with a slew of services guaranteed to rejuvenate even the most weary traveler. The resort's location—just off World Center Drive—allows for quick access to almost all the parks: Disney is less than 5 minutes by car and SeaWorld (Discovery Cove and Aquatica) is about 10 minutes away; Universal is more removed (approx. 20 min. from the resort). Complimentary shuttle service is available to all of the major theme parks.

8113 Resort Village Dr. (off S. Apopka–Vineland Rd./Hwy. 535), Lake Buena Vista, FL 32821. www.lbv orlandoresort.com. ✆ **866/401-2699** or 407/597-0214. Fax 407/597-1600. 498 units. $99–$499. Extra person $25. Children 17 and younger stay free in parent's room. AE, DC, DISC, MC, V. Self-parking free. **Amenities:** Restaurant; cafe; grill; 2 lounges; babysitting; supervised children's program; concierge; health club; Jacuzzi; 2 outdoor heated pools; children's water play area; room service; spa; transportation to all major theme parks at no charge. *In room:* A/C, multiple TVs, hair dryer, Internet (free), fully equipped and stocked full-size kitchen; washer and dryer.

Nickelodeon Family Suites ★★ 📷 ☺   This all-suite property, a former Holiday Inn transformed into the first ever Nickelodeon-branded resort, is one of the best recreational facilities, upscale amenities, grocery service, gated security, free shuttle service to Disney parks, and plenty more, all for a price that's hard to beat (approximately $129–$299). The **Cypress Pointe Resort & Grand Villas** (© **800/438-2929** or 407/238-2300; www.diamondresorts.com/cypress-pointe-grand-villas) can claim the most central location—close to Downtown Disney, the Crossroads Shopping Center, and a plethora of restaurants that line Apopka–Vineland Road ($159–$259).

The **Sheraton Vistana Resort** (© **407/239-3100;** www.starwood vacationownership.com/sheraton_ vistana_resort), in Lake Buena Vista, boasts a family-casual atmosphere with extensive recreational facilities ($139–$319), while the **Sheraton Vistana Villages** (© **407/238-5000;** www. starwoodvacationownership.com/ sheraton_vistana_villages) has a more upscale ambience (the stainless gas grills scattered about the meticulous grounds give you an idea of the added perks here) and a location on the southernmost end of I-Drive ($139–$379). Both feature extensive on-site amenities, spacious well-appointed accommodations, and locations near area theme parks, restaurants, and shops.

The **World Quest Resort** (© **407/ 387-3800;** www.worldquestorlando. com) and the **Regal Palms Resort** (© **877/477-2567;** www.regalpalms orlando.com) both feature a mix of townhomes, villas, and private homes set amid a sprawling gated vacation community with landscaped grounds, extensive recreational facilities, and homey accommodations.

Other options include the **Liki Tiki Village** (© **407/239-5000;** www.likitiki. com), **Bahama Bay Resort & Spa** (© **863/547-1200;** www.bahamabay. com), **Caribe Cove Resort Orlando** (© **877/291-4991;** www.caribecove. com), **Summer Bay Resort** (© **888/742-1100;** www.summerbayresort.com), and the newest Vacation Club property by Holiday Inn (one of only four in the country)—the **Holiday Inn Club Vacations at Orange Lake Resort** (© **877/ 863-4780** or 407/239-0000; www. holidayinn.com).

For reviews of the Lake Buena Vista Resort Village & Spa, Palisades Resort, and Grande Palisades, see the individual property listings in this chapter.

properties in the Orlando area for families. Its two-bedroom Kid Suites feature a kitchenette, a second bedroom for the kids with bunk or twin beds, and a pull-out sofa in the living area. Three-bedroom suites include a second bathroom, a full kitchen, upgraded amenities, and a trendy decor. One- and two-bedroom suites are themed with Nickelodeon colors; characters adorn the kids' rooms. The resort also has restaurants, an arcade, shops, a temporary tattoo and hair-wrap station (additional fees apply), and nightly entertainment (including Studio Nick). Its two pool areas (with lots of lifeguards) are veritable water parks, with extensive multilevel water slides, flumes, climbing nets, and water jets. Activities are scheduled poolside (including Slime Time), and the wide variety of recreational options includes a small minigolf course, playgrounds, and sand play areas. Required wristbands ensure that only resort guests can access the area. "Nick After Dark," a supervised activity program for kids ages 5 to 12, allows parents to take a night off. A daily character breakfast (SpongeBob SquarePants, Dora, and the Fairly Odd Parents oversaw things when I was last here) is offered in addition to the hotel's regular breakfast buffet (at the

On Request

Most hotels offer minifridges, microwaves, cribs, rollaways (or cots), and other similar items upon request—if they're not already located in your room, that is. Although some hotels offer these items at no additional charge, others may charge a nightly fee that can run anywhere from just a few dollars to a whopping $25—or more—per night, depending on the item and the resort. Be sure to ask which amenities are included in your room and which are not, as well as what the charges will be should you require such an item during your stay.

latter, kids eat free with paying adults). The only downside is that the resort's incredible popularity translates to an incredibly crowded, often overwhelming experience—combine this with a day at the theme parks, and parents may be in need of a vacation from their vacation. Discounted rates are available on off-peak nights and at select times throughout the year.

14500 Continental Gateway (off Hwy. 536), Lake Buena Vista, FL 32821. www.nickhotel.com. ✆ **877/642-5111,** 407/387-5437, or 866/NICK-KID (642-5543). Fax 407/387-1489. 777 units. $130–$552 suite. Daily resort fee $25. AE, DC, DISC, MC, V. Free self-parking. **Amenities:** Restaurant; food court; lounge; supervised children's program; extensive children's activities; 2 Jacuzzis; 2 water-park pools; free shuttle to Disney and non-Disney parks. *In room:* A/C, TV, fridge, game system, hair dryer, Internet (free), full kitchen (select suites), microwave.

Staybridge Suites Lake Buena Vista ★★ This chain hotel is ideally located just off Apopka–Vineland Road, close to the action of Downtown Disney and the theme parks, as well as area restaurants and shops. Spacious rooms, reasonable pricing, and a friendly staff make this an excellent choice for families. One- and two-bedroom suites (which sleep up to eight) all have full kitchens; two-bedroom suites have two full bathrooms. These suites offer large, comfortable, separate living areas when compared to other all-suite hotels. Stocking up on necessary supplies, snacks, and assorted sundries is much less of a hassle here, as a full-service grocer is located next door.

8751 Suiteside Dr., Orlando, FL 32836. www.sborlando.com. ✆ **800/866-4549** or 407/238-0777. Fax 407/238-2640. 150 units. $129–$289. Rates include full breakfast. Rollaway beds and cribs available at no charge. AE, DC, DISC, MC, V. **Amenities:** 24-hr. exercise room; Jacuzzi; outdoor heated pool; children's pool; free shuttle to WDW parks. *In room:* A/C, TV/VCR, hair dryer, free high-speed Internet access, kitchen.

Inexpensive

Hampton Inn Orlando/Lake Buena Vista Location rules at this modern property, which is only 1 mile from the entrance to Hotel Plaza Boulevard on the northeast corner of Disney. It's not fancy, but it's clean and comfortable, the price is right, and the perks include free high-speed Internet and a free, full, hot breakfast (at the hotel or on the go—packed in a grab-and-go bag for when you're in a hurry to get to the parks). Nearby are plenty of places to eat, shop, and party.

8150 Palm Pkwy., Orlando, FL 32836. www.orlandolakebuenavista.hamptoninn.com. ✆ **800/370-9259** or 407/465-8150. Fax 407/465-0150. 147 units. $69–$119 for up to 4. Extra person $10. Rates include a continental breakfast. Children 17 and younger stay free in parent's room. AE, DC, DISC, MC, V. Self-parking free. **Amenities:** Concierge; exercise room; Jacuzzi; outdoor heated pool; free shuttle to

Disney parks; transportation to non-Disney parks for a fee. *In room:* A/C, TV, fridge (select rooms), hair dryer, microwave (select rooms), Wi-Fi (free).

IN THE KISSIMMEE AREA

This stretch of highway—U.S. 192, also known as Irlo Bronson Memorial Highway—is within close proximity of the Disney parks. A revitalization of the area has added such features as extrawide sidewalks, streetlamps, highway markers, and widened roads to make it a more friendly and appealing area to stay and play. Traffic here can nevertheless be frustrating, especially when you are trying to cross the street. Budget hotels and restaurants abound, though a few higher-priced luxury resorts are starting to appear, albeit off the main drag. While Disney is close by, Universal and SeaWorld are not—the latter are a good 20-minute (or more) ride away. If you don't have a car, Mears Transportation (see "Getting Around," in chapter 10) is a good bet to take you there for about $15 to $18 per person per day, round-trip.

In addition to the hotels reviewed below, the **Saratoga Resort Villas,** 4787 W. Irlo Bronson Hwy. (© **407/397-0555;** www.saratogaresortvillas.com), offers spacious one-, two-, and three-bedroom town-house accommodations with full kitchens and extensive recreational facilities geared to families and larger groups. A recent redesign has brought the charm and elegance of the New Orleans French Quarter to the **Royale Parc Suites,** a Quality Suites Hotel (previously the Quality Suites Main Gate East), 5876 W. Irlo Bronson Hwy. (© **800/268-6048** or 407/396-8040; www.royaleparcsuitesorlando.com). The spacious suites have separate bedroom and living areas and fully stocked kitchens; perks include a complimentary hot and cold breakfast, free Wi-Fi, free transportation to the major theme parks, and a location that's hard to beat. And the **Radisson Resort Orlando–Celebration,** 2900 Parkway Blvd. (© **800/395-7046** or 407/396-7000; www.radisson.com), set back off the main drag, has stylish, well-appointed rooms; an inviting pool area with a water slide; several on-site dining options; beautifully landscaped grounds; and a location that's close to area shops, restaurants, and attractions.

Note: You'll find the hotels and motels described below on the "Kissimmee Hotels" map in this section.

Best for: Visitors who are on a tighter budget will find an array of accommodations (and restaurants) to choose from; a handful of high-end hotels have popped up, too. Vacation homes are also strewn throughout the area, making it an ideal location for larger families or groups.

Drawbacks: Only Disney is right nearby; if your itinerary includes Universal or SeaWorld, the drive to the parks will be lengthy—reaching upwards of 45 minutes during peak season, which translates to a painful (usually congested) drive home after park closing (yuck!). Because of its popularity, the area is also notorious for traffic jams, which can be an absolutely infuriating way to start off your day (or cap off your night).

Expensive

Bohemian Hotel Celebration ★ Once as picturesque as the Disney-created town that surrounds it, the Bohemian Hotel Celebration (previously the Celebration Hotel) no longer exudes its signature old-world Florida charm and elegance. Instead, it now reflects an artistic Bohemian-inspired ambience, the product of a recent renovation (though its transition seems somewhat incomplete and, in my opinion, misses the mark). The public areas, once elegant yet warm and inviting, are now accented with dramatic flowing curtains, trendy mismatched furnishings, and an eclectic collection of avant-garde artwork. Select areas, in fact, are quite stunning—in particular, the outdoor porch near the entryway, where white floor-to-ceiling draperies and chic sit-upons combine with brilliant red handcrafted chandeliers, and the back porch, where trendy sectional seating and unique light fixtures create an inviting space, with the lake as a backdrop. Rooms, which are stark and out of place by comparison, boast views of either the lakefront or the Marketplace—both of which are postcard perfect. Taken as a whole, however, the intended appeal is somewhat lost. By definition, the addition of "Bohemian" to the hotel's name is meant to evoke thoughts of an alternative, free-spirited, and unconventional atmosphere, but some tweaking is needed to better pull off the concept. The upscale ambience (which remains intact) continues to cater to adults, especially those seeking a quiet romantic getaway. Now part of Marriott's Autograph Collection, a portfolio of independently owned luxury hotels and resorts, the Bohemian offers guests the perks and privileges associated with the Marriott brand while maintaining its individuality and independence. One major drawback: You'll have to deal with the traffic on U.S. 192 to get almost anywhere.

700 Bloom St., Celebration, FL 34747. www.celebrationhotel.com. © **888/499-3800** or 407/566-6000. Fax 407/566-6001. 115 units. $169–$369 for up to 4; $299–$469 suite. Daily resort fee $12. Extra person $20. AE, DC, DISC, MC, V. Valet parking $15; no self-parking. **Amenities:** Restaurant; lounge; bike rentals; concierge; 18-hole golf course nearby; health club privileges (nearby, free shuttle); outdoor heated pool; spa privileges (nearby, free shuttle); free shuttle to WDW parks; transportation to non-Disney parks for a fee. *In room:* A/C, TV, CD player, hair dryer, game system (fee), Wi-Fi (fee).

Omni Orlando Resort at ChampionsGate ★★★ One of the newer luxury resorts to spring up just south of the Disney district in ChampionsGate, the Omni offers a comprehensive array of leisure facilities, including two championship golf courses designed by Greg Norman, a vast pool area with its very own lazy river, and a 10,000-square-foot spa. The beautifully decorated rooms feature 9-foot ceilings, free Wi-Fi, and plush amenities such as bathrobes. The service is as impressive as the facility itself; and there's a program especially geared to youngsters, so parents can get some relaxation time on their own.

1500 Masters Blvd., ChampionsGate, FL 33896. www.omnihotels.com. © **888/444-6664** or 407/390-6664. Fax 321/677-6600. 730 units. $109–$389 standard; $450–$2,500 suite. Extra person $30. Daily resort fee $16. AE, DC, DISC, MC, V. Valet parking $18; self-parking $14. Pets less than 25 lb. welcome ($50 fee). **Amenities:** 5 restaurants; grill; 3 lounges; supervised children's program; children's activities; concierge; 2 18-hole golf courses; 9-hole golf course; health club; 2 outdoor heated pools; room service; spa; 2 lighted tennis courts; free shuttle to WDW parks; transportation to non-Disney parks for a fee. *In room:* A/C, TV, CD player, game system (fee), fridge (free, upon request), hair dryer, microwave (free, upon request), minibar, Wi-Fi (free).

Reunion Resort Orlando ★★★ 📷 This luxury resort community, once planning to build on its existing inventory of villas, homes, and hotels (set to open in phases over a 10-year period), has halted construction—but is still worth seeking out. Currently, several different villas, a variety of vacation homes, and a luxury all-suites high-rise are available to rent as you would a hotel room. Several of the spectacular villas feature a rather unique layout—with bedrooms located on the ground level and the main living area, and additional bedrooms on the second level (making it less likely you'll have to drag your luggage up a flight of stairs). The villas' full kitchens have almost every gadget you could ask for, and the spacious bathrooms are loaded with upscale toiletries. Most villas have private patios or balconies; some of the

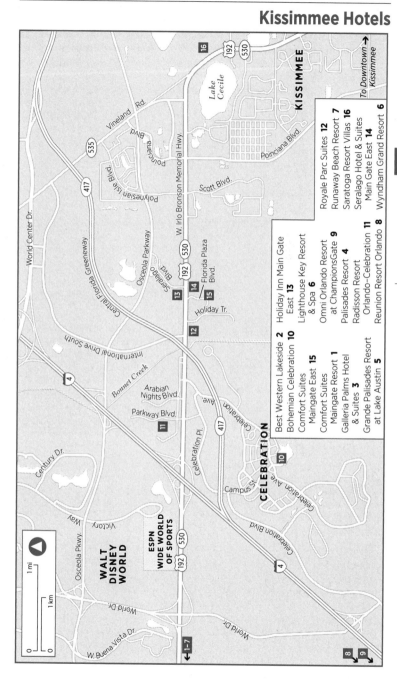

Best Western Lakeside 2
Bohemian Celebration 10
Comfort Suites
Maingate East 15
Comfort Suites
Maingate Resort 1
Galleria Palms Hotel
& Suites 3
Grande Palisades Resort
at Lake Austin 5

Holiday Inn Main Gate
East 13
Lighthouse Key Resort
& Spa 6
Omni Orlando Resort
at ChampionsGate 9
Palisades Resort 4
Radisson Resort
Orlando–Celebration 11
Reunion Resort Orlando 8

Royale Parc Suites 12
Runaway Beach Resort 7
Saratoga Resort Villas 16
Seralago Hotel & Suites
Main Gate East 14
Wyndham Grand Resort 6

vacation homes have their own private pools. Recent additions include the luxurious Wyndham Grand Resort, an extensive on-site water park (other resort pools are located throughout the property), a colonial-style spa, and a third championship golf course. There's also a comprehensive kids' program offering supervised activities. The downside: The property charges an exorbitantly high "gratuity" fee (though the staff is incredibly good).

1000 Reunion Way, Reunion, FL 34747. www.reunionresort.com. ☎ **888/418-9611** or 407/662-1000. Fax 407/662-1111. Eventually 8,000 units. $225–$545 villas; $495–$1,185 homes. 9.6% gratuity fee assessed on total bill. Self-parking free. **Amenities:** 3 restaurants; grill; lounge; bike rentals; supervised children's program; personal concierge; 3 golf courses; numerous pools; spa; 6 lighted tennis courts. *In room:* A/C, TV/DVD, CD player, hair dryer, Internet (free), fully equipped/stocked kitchen, washer and dryer.

Moderate

Comfort Suites Maingate East ★ 𝄞   Set back from the main drag, this welcoming hotel is one of the nicest in the area. The lobby and accommodations—consisting of studios and one-bedroom suites—are bright and inviting. The main pool and the children's pool, with an umbrella fountain to keep everyone cool, are open around the clock. For entertainment, Old Town (a small-scale shopping, dining, and entertainment complex) is next door, and a great miniature golf course is located just in front of the property.

2775 Florida Plaza Blvd., Kissimmee, FL 34746. www.comfortsuitesfl.com. ☎ **888/782-9772** or 407/397-7848. Fax 407/396-7045. 198 units. $79–$159 double. Extra person $10. Rates include continental breakfast. Children 17 and younger stay free in parent's room. AE, DC, DISC, MC, V. Self-parking free. **Amenities:** Concierge; health club; outdoor heated pool; kids' pool; free shuttle to Disney, Universal, and SeaWorld parks. *In room:* A/C, TV, fridge, Internet (free), microwave.

Holiday Inn Main Gate East ★ 𝄞   This Holiday Inn has the Mouse's "Good Neighbor" stamp of approval. An extensive redesign a couple of years ago gave it an updated contemporary look both inside and out, an inviting pool with a water slide and rocky waterfall, and all the hallmark amenities associated with this family-friendly chain. Younger guests will appreciate the children's theater, playground, and roomy Kid Suites—and parents will delight in the Kids Eat Free program. Shuttle service to WDW parks is free.

5711 W. Irlo Bronson Memorial Hwy., Kissimmee, FL 34746. www.holidayinnmge.com. ☎ **800/327-1128** or 407/396-4222. Fax 407/396-0570. 444 units. $79–$189 double; $159–$239 Kid Suite. Extra person $10. AE, DC, DISC, MC, V. Free self-parking. **Amenities:** Food court; lounge; Kids Eat Free program; health club; outdoor heated pool; kids' pool; room service; free shuttle to WDW parks; transportation to non-Disney parks for a fee. *In room:* A/C, TV, fridge (suites), game system, hair dryer, Internet (free), microwave (suites), Wi-Fi (fee).

Palisades Resort   Located off the beaten path, this all-suites resort isn't particularly lavish (it's pretty plain, actually), but does invite guests to experience a different side of Florida. Set against the backdrop of a 400-acre preserve, views include a lush green forest, a sparkling lake, and an array of local wildlife. Accommodations consist of spacious one-, two-, and three-bedroom suites filled with all the comforts of home (including fully equipped kitchens, two full-size bathrooms, washers and dryers, and private screened-in balconies)—all at a price that won't put a hole in your pocketbook. Flatscreen TVs in every room ensure that no one will fight over what to watch, though the view of the lake from your balcony is far better than any show you'll find on television. In the morning, the lobby lounge serves up a complimentary continental

Scheduled to open by the end of 2012 (possibly early 2013—a snafu in a recent refinancing has set back construction and caused a delayed debut) is the new **Grande Palisades Resort at Lake Austin** (✆ 866/455-4062; www. grandepalisadesresort.com), a full-service luxury resort and sibling to the Palisades Resort. When completed, it will feature 800 luxuriously appointed suites ranging from 1,263 to 1,504 square feet, most with views of the lake and conservation area. Distinguishing the Grande Palisades from its sibling will be extensive on-site amenities, including numerous pools and Jacuzzis; saunas; children's play areas; tennis courts; a full-service spa; a full-service restaurant, cafe, grill, and lounge; an Internet cafe; shops and boutiques; and boating and water-related activities. Palisades Resort guests will be able to access these amenities via complimentary transportation. Think Universal's Portofino Bay (p. 86) with a Mediterranean twist, but on a slightly less luxurious scale.

breakfast, after which it becomes an ideal spot to sit, relax, have a drink, or check your e-mail. Movies are shown in the mini-theater off the lobby. There's an on-site minimart (and I do mean mini), but if stocking up is what you have in mind, the full-service grocery store just down the road is a far better option. A sprawling, brick-lined sun deck running the length of the resort sports plentiful seating and grills for barbecuing. *Note:* A new roadway is scheduled to open (though an official date has yet to be set for its completion) that will connect the resort directly to Disney property, allowing guests to skip the traffic jams that often plague the main thoroughfare when heading to the parks.

14200 Avalon Rd. (off U.S. 192), Kissimmee, FL 34787. www.palisadesresortorlando.com or www.stay sky.com. ✆ **866/455-4062,** 321/250-3030, or 407/597-0370. Fax 321/250-3031. 99 units. $79–$399. Extra person $25. Children 17 and younger stay free in parent's room. Rates include continental breakfast. AE, DC, DISC, MC, V. Self-parking (covered) free. **Amenities:** Cafe; lounge; babysitting; supervised children's program; children's activities; health club; Jacuzzi; outdoor pool; sauna; free transportation to all major theme parks. *In room:* A/C, TV, hair dryer, Internet (free), fully equipped and stocked kitchen, washer and dryer.

Inexpensive

In addition to the accommodations described here, there are scores of other inexpensive but serviceable motels, including chains. Most are within a few miles of Disney, have rooms in the 300-square-foot range, and arrange transportation to the parks. Many sell attractions tickets, but be careful: Some people land at the parks with *invalid tickets* or waste a half-day or more listening to a timeshare pitch to get 30% to 40% off the regular price (single-day Disney park tickets are $82 for adults, $74 for kids 3–9). If a discount is more than $2 to $5 per ticket, it's probably too good to be true. Stick to buying tickets through the parks, or accept the modest discounts offered by such groups as AAA, AARP, and the visitor information centers listed under "Visitor Information," in chapter 2.

Best Western Lakeside ★★ ☺ ⚑   The hand-painted exteriors, lobby, and common areas of this property give it a unique charm not found in its hotel brethren. Just up the road from the Disney entrance, this 24-acre resort looks deceptively small when you first pull up (most of the accommodations are hidden behind the lobby area), but amenities include numerous recreational options (pools, playgrounds, and so on), a food court, a good-size convenience store, and more. Rooms are standard in size and offerings, but are nicely decorated and will comfortably sleep four. Other pluses include a child-care facility and free transport to *all* the major theme parks. A small "Pooch Park" was recently added to accommodate four-legged guests, and a small number of pet-friendly rooms comes complete with mats and bowls to accommodate Fifi and Fido (the general store is now stocked with a selection of pet supplies). *Note:* The Lakeside is another of the many area hotels to go 100% smoke-free.

7769 Irlo Bronson Memorial Hwy. (U.S. 192), Kissimmee, FL 34747. www.bestwesternlakeside.com. ☏ **800/848-0801** or 407/396-2222. Fax 407/997-1171. 651 units. $59–$129 double. Extra person $10. Daily resort fee $7.50. Children 17 and younger stay free in parent's room. Pets less than 80 lb. $10 per pet per night (2-pet maximum). AE, DC, DISC, MC, V. Self-parking free. **Amenities:** Restaurant; grill; food court; supervised children's program; children's activities; exercise room; small minigolf course; 3 outdoor heated pools; 2 kids' pools; 2 tennis courts; free bus to WDW, Universal, and SeaWorld parks. *In room:* A/C, TV, fridge, hair dryer, Internet (free).

Comfort Suites Maingate Resort ★ 🏷

Just across the street from the Best Western Lakeside (see above) and up the road from WDW, this clean, comfortable place to stay has kept itself modern and in good shape. The "suites" have a small dividing wall slightly separating the living area from the sleeping quarters, but the illusion of privacy is there. Accommodations are a bit bigger than most and can squeeze in up to six. A bit of tropical landscaping gives it an inviting atmosphere and shelters guests from busy U.S. 192. At least 10 restaurants and a small shopping plaza are within walking distance, and there's a miniature golf course right across the street. A free expanded continental breakfast will start off your day, and there's free transportation to Disney, Universal, and SeaWorld to boot.

7888 W. Irlo Bronson Memorial Hwy. (U.S. 192), Kissimmee, FL 34747. www.comfortsuiteskissimmee. com. ☏ **888/390-9888** or 407/390-9888. Fax 407/390-0981. 150 units. $59–$199. Rates include continental breakfast. Children 17 and younger stay free in parent's room. AE, DC, DISC, MC, V. Self-parking free. **Amenities:** Lounge; concierge; Jacuzzi; outdoor heated pool; kids' pool; free shuttle to WDW, Universal, SeaWorld, and Wet 'n Wild parks. *In room:* A/C, TV, fridge, hair dryer, Internet (free), microwave.

Galleria Palms Hotel & Suites ★

Just 1½ miles west of WDW, this welcoming hotel is a good choice for the budget-conscious vacationer. The rooms are nicely decorated and sport a modern, upscale look, but are a bit on the small side, making them a snug fit for four. The property is well maintained and provides a bit beyond the basics with good taste; frills include flatscreen TVs, pillow-top mattresses, and rain-shower shower heads. There's no restaurant, but a free breakfast is served in the lobby, and there are more than enough dining choices just a minute or two away to keep you from going hungry.

3000 Maingate Lane, Kissimmee, FL 34747. www.galleriapalmsorlando.com. ☏ **800/391-7909** or 407/396-6300. Fax 407/396-8989. 118 units. $60–$110 double. Extra person $10. Rates include continental breakfast. Children 17 and younger stay free in parent's room. AE, DC, DISC, MC, V. Self-parking free. **Amenities:** Concierge; outdoor heated pool; free shuttle to WDW, Universal, and SeaWorld parks. *In room:* A/C, TV, fridge, hair dryer, Internet (free), microwave.

Seralago Hotel & Suites Main Gate East ★ 😊 🏷

Location (it's just down the road from Disney) and price are some of the perks at this former Holiday Inn. The hotel is bright and colorful, and still features themed Kid Suites with separate sleeping

homes AWAY FROM HOME

Some travelers—especially those who like all the comforts of home, prefer quiet privacy, or are traveling in groups of five or more—bypass motels in favor of rental condos or homes. Rates vary widely depending on quality and location; some may require at least a 2- or 3-night minimum. Many of these properties are 3 to 15 miles from the theme parks and offer no transportation, so a car is a necessity.

On the plus side, most have two to six bedrooms and a convertible couch, two or more bathrooms, a full kitchen, multiple TVs and phones, and irons. Some have washers and dryers. Homes often have their own private screen-enclosed pool, while condos generally have a common pool and a clubhouse.

On the minus side, they can be lacking in services. Most don't have daily maid service, and restaurants can be as far away as the parks. (That's another reason you'll need a car.) And unless a condo or home is in a gated community, don't expect on-site security. Some properties offer dinnerware, utensils, and salt-and-pepper shakers; others are fully stocked with pots, pans, and every gadget imaginable—check when you book, as amenities vary widely.

Rates range from about $129 to $979 per night ($903–$6,853 per week).

All Star Vacation Homes ★★★ (✆ **800/592-5568** or 407/997-0733; www.allstarvacationhomes.com) is the cream of the city's home and condo rental crop, with a wide variety of properties to choose from—all of them within a 4-mile radius of Disney. Many of the homes feature such amenities as pool tables, personal home theaters, and Jacuzzi tubs along with private pools. Do check out the website—you will be able to see the exact home you are renting, as opposed to a "typical" room—but be sure to call if you have special requirements, want a specific theme (there's a Disney-themed home if you don't want to give up Mickey while sleeping), or need help selecting the home that meets your needs. The staff is exceptionally cordial and well informed; and when you are on-site, there's always someone on-call should you encounter any issues or need assistance.

Other popular players include **Villa Direct** (✆ **877/259-9908** or 407/397-9818; www.villadirect.com), **Holiday Villas** (✆ **800/344-3959;** www.holidayvillas.com), **Global Resort Homes** (✆ **866/921-1167** or 407/387-3030; www.globalresorthomes.com), and **Elite Vacation Homes** (✆ **888/510-6679;** www.elitevacationhomes.com), among others.

areas for your tots, as well as standard rooms and regular two-room suites. The rooms provide a reasonable amount of space for a family of five, with the two-room unit sleeping up to eight. There are plenty of recreational activities, from swimming to tennis, and the hotel's movie theater shows free family films nightly. There's a family-friendly food court, and kids 12 and younger eat breakfast for free in the hotel's cafe.

5678 Irlo Bronson Memorial Hwy. (U.S. 192), Kissimmee, FL 34746. www.seralagohotel.com. ✆ **800/411-3457** or 407/396-4488. Fax 407/396-8915. 614 units. $45–$89 double. Extra person $10. Children 18 and younger stay free in parent's room. AE, DC, DISC, MC, V. Self-parking free. **Amenities:** Restaurant; food court; lounge; Kids Eat Free program; exercise room; Jacuzzi; 2 outdoor heated pools; kids' pool; room service; 2 tennis courts; free shuttle to WDW parks; transportation to non-Disney parks for a fee. *In room:* A/C, TV, CD players (select rooms), fridge, game system, hair dryer, microwave, Wi-Fi (select rooms, free).

IN THE INTERNATIONAL DRIVE AREA

The hotels and resorts listed here are 7 to 10 miles north of Walt Disney World (via I-4) and 1 to 5 miles from Universal Orlando and SeaWorld. The advantages of staying on I-Drive: It's a destination unto itself, filled with accommodations, restaurants, and small attractions; it has its own inexpensive trolley service (see "Getting Around," in chapter 2); and it's centrally located for those who want to visit Disney, Universal, SeaWorld, *and* the downtown area. The disadvantages: The north end of I-Drive is badly congested; the shops, motels, eateries, and attractions along this stretch can be tacky; and some of the motels and hotels don't offer free transportation to the parks (the going rate is $15–$18 round-trip).

You'll find these places located on the "International Drive Area Hotels" map in this section.

Best for: Visitors heading to Universal or SeaWorld will discover that I-Drive is the best location to call home base (the northern end closest to Universal, the southern end closest to SeaWorld), no matter their budget. The area is chock-full of both affordable and high-end hotels.

Drawbacks: I-Drive is excruciatingly busy no matter the time of year (or time of day), thanks in part to the convention crowd (the Convention Center is located near the south end). Driving here can be frustrating and terribly time consuming—even dangerous, with all of the tourists reading maps or watching their GPS unit while driving. Pedestrians should never cross from one side to the other unless absolutely necessary, using extreme caution if they do. The dense population of hotels also ensures that restaurants and smaller attractions here fill quickly (and remain busy throughout the evening), making dining out or playing miniature golf more of an adventure than an enjoyable experience at times.

Very Expensive

The Peabody Orlando ★★★ 📷 The five Peabody mallards continue to march into the main lobby fountain each and every morning at 11am and then back out at 5pm, accompanied by John Philip Sousa's "King Cotton March," and are only a small unique part of the appeal of this very upscale and service-oriented hotel. If your budget allows, you won't be disappointed with a stay here. Primarily a business and convention destination, the Peabody also appeals to adults looking for an ultraclassy hotel that provides top-of-the-line service, amenities, and atmosphere (though families with older children accustomed to the finer things in life will find the array of recreational offerings and spacious accommodations to their liking as well). Combining with the main hotel's classical elegance and sophisticated decor is the visually stunning Peabody Tower (a $450-million addition that added 870 guest rooms and suites in late 2010), the transition between the two buildings surprisingly seamless—a particularly impressive feat given the Tower's chic retro-inspired decor and Sinatra-esque ambience. In addition, the tower brings with it a full-service spa and athletic club, salon (yet to open at press time), gourmet deli, coffee bar, Napa restaurant and bar (with patios overlooking the meticulously landscaped grotto-style pool below), and sophisticated piano lounge (the Rocks, which evokes the Rat Pack days). Rooms sleep up to five (though suites are available) and are especially well appointed with high-tech luxe amenities such as 42-inch LCD TVs and mini LCD TVs in the

International Drive Area Hotels

Crowne Plaza Universal **8**

DoubleTree by Hilton at the Entrance to Universal Orlando **2**

DoubleTree by Hilton Orlando at SeaWorld **15**

Embassy Suites Orlando **10**

Fairfield Inn & Suites Orlando at SeaWorld **17**

Grande Lakes Orlando **18**

Hampton Inn at Universal Studios **1**

Hard Rock Hotel **5**

Hyatt Place Universal **3**

JW Marriott Orlando **18**

Lake Eve Resort **19**

La Quinta Inn & Suites Convention Center **11**

Marriott Lakeshore Reserve **18**

The Peabody Orlando **13**

Point Orlando Resort **7**

Portofino Bay Hotel **4**

Renaissance Orlando Resort at SeaWorld **20**

Ritz-Carlton Orlando **18**

Rosen Shingle Creek **14**

Royal Pacific Resort **6**

Sheraton Vistana Villages **19**

SpringHill Suites Orlando at SeaWorld **16**

Staybridge Suites **9**

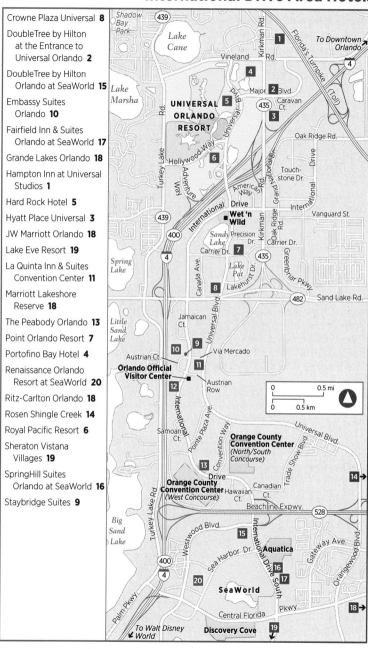

Several area timeshare resorts rent rooms or apartments to tourists when the owners aren't using them. The **Disney Vacation Club** (📞 407/939-7775; www.dvcresorts.com) offers studios and one- to three-bedroom villas at its timeshare resorts. Some have small fridges and microwaves; others have full kitchens. Rates start at about $275 per night and can run up to $2,260 per night.

Outside Disney World, rates begin at around $189 per night for one- and two-bedroom apartments with kitchens. As with hotel rooms, you can get major discounts off the rack rates (as low as $79 a night) if you do your homework. An especially nice choice is **Sheraton's** **Vistana Resort** (📞 407/239-3100; www.sheraton.com/vistanaresort) and **Vistana Villas** (📞 407/238-5000; www.sheraton.com/vistanavillages). Other good places to look include the **Marriott Vacation Club** (📞 800/845-5279; www.marriottvacationclub.com) and the **Hilton Grand Vacations Club** (📞 800/448-2736 or 407/239-0100 for the SeaWorld location, 407/465-2600 for the International Drive location, or 407/465-4000 for the Lake Buena Vista location; www.hiltongrandvacations.com).

One minor caveat: Because each room and apartment that's rented is individually owned, quality can vary, so be sure to specify your exact requirements when booking.

bathroom mirrors. Those on the west side of the main hotel (sixth floor and higher) and the west end of the Tower offer distant views of Disney and its fireworks displays, while the remaining tower rooms (10th floor and higher) offer impressive after-dark views of International Drive. *Note:* Dux (once the hotel's signature restaurant) is now used only for private dining, and the B-Line Diner (p. 145) now sports a more contemporary yet diner-inspired decor. Self-parking is once again available, in the new multi-story parking garage.

9801 International Dr. (btw. Beachline Expwy. and Sand Lake Rd.), Orlando, FL 32819. www.peabody orlando.com. 📞 **800/732-2639** or 407/352-4000. Fax 407/354-1424. 1,641 units. $150–$495 standard room for up to 3; $575–$1,875 suite. Extra person $25. Daily resort fee $15. Children 17 and younger stay free in parent's room. AE, DC, DISC, MC, V. Valet parking $20; self-parking $12. **Amenities:** 3 restaurants; 3 grills; 2 cafes; 4 lounges; babysitting; concierge; concierge-level rooms; health club; Jacuzzi; 4 outdoor heated pools; kids' pool; room service; 4 lighted tennis courts, instruction available (fee); shuttle to WDW and other parks for a fee. *In room:* A/C, TV, WebTV (fee), fridge (select suites), hair dryer, Internet (fee), minibar.

Portofino Bay Hotel ★★★ 🎁 Universal's first hotel is as grand as Disney's Grand Floridian and makes a perfect getaway for couples and adults seeking a romantic, upscale atmosphere. This resort is a replica of the village of Portofino, Italy, complete with a harbor and canals on which boats travel to the theme parks. Old-world ambience is carried throughout the public areas, restaurants, and rooms. The luxurious accommodations are large (sleeping up to five), and hypoallergenic rooms are available. The beds have Egyptian-cotton sheets, the pillows are so soft you'll want to take them home, and the amenities are top-notch. Ask for a view overlooking the piazza and "bay" area. The Portofino doesn't just have swimming pools; its beach pool has a fort with a water slide, and the villa pool rents several private cabanas. The resort's privately run Mandara Spa (www.mandaraspa.com) features a state-of-the-art fitness center and full-service spa. The drawbacks: There are stairs everywhere you

3

In the International Drive Area

WHERE TO STAY

turn (be prepared for some exercise), and the sheer size of the resort can make it difficult to find your way around. It also remains the least kid-friendly resort in Universal's collection of upscale offerings, despite the small number of Seussian-themed suites added in 2008. Look for a review of the resort's premier restaurant, **Bice,** on p. 137. *Note:* Guests enjoy special privileges at the Universal Orlando theme parks, including Express-line access to rides, preferred seating at shows and restaurants, and early access to the Wizarding World of Harry Potter—a full hour prior to the official park opening.

Warning: The Universal hotels (Portofino, Hard Rock, and Royal Pacific) inexcusably gouge customers in the parking department. Self-parking (almost always free at most Orlando hotels, including the Disney ones) at all of the Universal properties is a steep $15 per day.

5601 Universal Blvd., Orlando, FL 32819. www.loewshotels.com/hotels/Orlando or www.universal orlando.com. ℂ **888/322-5541** or 407/503-1000. Fax 407/224-7118. 750 units. $284–$564 double; $574–$2,500 suites and villas. Extra person $25. Children 17 and younger stay free in parent's room. AE, DC, DISC, MC, V. Valet parking $22; self-parking $15. Small pets welcome ($25). **Amenities:** 4 restaurants; deli; 3 lounges; babysitting; supervised children's program; concierge; concierge-level rooms; health club; 3 outdoor heated pools (1 for concierge-level and suite guests only); kids' pool; room service; spa; watersports equipment/rentals; free water-taxi and bus transportation to Universal Studios, Islands of Adventure, and CityWalk; free shuttle to SeaWorld; transportation to WDW parks for a fee; limited Wi-Fi (free). *In room:* A/C, TV, CD player, fridge (suites; otherwise upon request for a fee), game system, hair dryer, Internet (free), microwave (suites; otherwise upon request for a fee), minibar.

Expensive

Grande Lakes Orlando ★★★ 🏨 This development is home to two (soon to be three) top-level properties. Debuting back in 2003, the **Ritz-Carlton Orlando** has fast become one of the city's best destinations for deep-pocketed travelers. The posh 584-room luxury hotel features exquisitely manicured grounds, a lobby designed after an Italian palazzo, and a 40,000-square-foot, three-level spa with 40 treatment rooms. The spacious rooms at this smoke-free hotel have balconies, flatscreen TVs, hand-painted Italian furniture, and lots of other luxury perks. The level of service is exceptional.

Sharing quarters (and most recreational facilities, from pools to an 18-hole golf course to several child-care programs) with the Ritz is the less expensive, slightly more casual 1,000-room **JW Marriott Orlando.** The smoke-free resort (with rooms ranging in price from $199–$359 for up to four people, and $399–$4,500 for suites) has a fabulous 24,000-square-foot zero-entry lazy river pool that winds through rock formations and small waterfalls (depth 3–5 ft.). The tiptop rooms at the Moorish-themed resort are on par with those in Disney's "moderate" class. Ask for a west-facing room for the best views.

In late 2010, the **Lakeshore Reserve,** a Marriott Vacation Club property with 340 villas and town homes was added to the Grande Lakes lineup. Sharing facilities with the JW Marriott, and connected by a waterside walkway, the Lakeshore Reserve features casual dining options, a marketplace, two pool and play areas of its own, a children's maze, and other recreational facilities.

A recent addition to the Grande Lakes resort's outdoor activities is a zipline adventure, with two separate courses to choose from, each with multilevel structures, poles, cables, platforms, and unique climbing elements. Prices starts at $60 for adults, $45 for kids 10 and up; a complimentary shuttle to and from the course is provided. The major drawback to staying here: Grande Lakes is outside of the main tourist areas, a 7- or 8-mile drive southeast of SeaWorld and about the same distance east of Walt Disney World. Free transportation is provided to Universal Orlando, Wet 'n Wild, and SeaWorld's various parks, but for Disney parks, you're on your own.

4012–4040 Central Florida Pkwy., Orlando, FL 32819. www.grandelakes.com. (ℂ) **800/576-5760** or 407/206-2400 for the Ritz; (ℂ) **800/576-5750** or 407/206-2300 for the JW Marriott; (ℂ) **407/393-6410** for the Lakeshore Reserve. 584 units. $199–$599 double; $599–$6,500 suite. AE, DC, DISC, MC, V. Valet parking $23; self-parking $17 (JW Marriott only). **Amenities:** 8 restaurants; 3 lounges; babysitting; concierge; health club; golf course; Jacuzzi; 2 outdoor heated pools; kids' pool; 3 tennis courts; transportation to non-Disney parks for a fee. *In room:* A/C, TV, DVD/VCR (suite), CD player, fridge (suite), game system, microwave, Wi-Fi (fee).

Hard Rock Hotel ★★★ ☺ You can't get any closer than this to Universal Studios Florida. Opened in 2001, this California mission–style resort sports a rock-'n'-roll theme with rates a shade less expensive than the Portofino (see above). The atmosphere here is also more casual (though with an air of sophistication) and teen-friendly (thanks to its "coolness" quotient) than that of its Universal Orlando sisters. The collection of rock memorabilia scattered throughout the public areas is impressive. The pool area, however, takes center stage: A tremendous oasis of palm trees and rocky landscaping surrounds a large free-form pool whose most unique feature is a first-rate underwater sound system that makes sure you won't miss a beat. The rooms and amenities at the Hard Rock are a cut above some of Disney's comparable properties, even the Animal Kingdom Lodge (p. 57). Accommodations are very comfortable, with a sophisticated modern decor. Thanks to a relatively recent multimillion-dollar renovation, rooms now have flatscreen TVs, MP3 docking stations, and upgraded bedding. Unfortunately, though the walls are fairly soundproof, a few notes still seep through, so you may want to ask for a room that's away from the lobby area. *Tip:* One of the biggest perks of staying on Universal property is that guests get Express-line access to almost every ride at Universal's theme parks, plus preferred seating privileges for shows and restaurants. Universal resort guests now have early access to the Wizarding World of Harry Potter, a full hour prior to the official park opening.

5000 Universal Blvd., Orlando, FL 32819. www.loewshotels.com/hotels/Orlando or www.universal orlando.com. (ℂ) **888/430-4999** or 407/503-2000. Fax 407/224-7118. 650 units. $244–$524 double; $479–$2,020 suite. Extra person $25. Children 17 and younger stay free in parent's room. AE, DC, DISC, MC, V. Valet parking $22; self-parking $15. Small pets welcome ($25). **Amenities:** 3 restaurants; grill; 2 lounges; babysitting; supervised children's program; concierge; concierge-level rooms; health club; outdoor heated pool; kids' pool; room service; limited spa; free water-taxi or bus transportation to Universal Studios, Islands of Adventure, and CityWalk; free shuttle to SeaWorld; transportation to WDW parks for a fee; limited Wi-Fi (free). *In room:* A/C, TV, CD player, CD library (concierge-level), fridge (suites; otherwise upon request for a fee), game system, hair dryer, Internet (fee), microwave (suites; otherwise upon request for a fee), minibar, MP3 docking station.

Renaissance Orlando Resort at SeaWorld ★★ You can't beat the location if you're a fan of SeaWorld—the park is just across from the resort. What appears to be a rather simple-looking hotel from the exterior gives way to an inviting and modern interior, with trendy touches throughout. A glass-covered atrium rises high above a stunning indoor courtyard, where you'll find lush foliage, cascading waterfalls, a chic lounge, the Boardwalk sports bar, and Mist Sushi and Spirits (each of which features a distinctive open concept within the courtyard). The tastefully decorated rooms, all recently revamped, are oversized, providing plenty of space to spread out and relax. After extensive renovations to the pool area in 2006, 2007 saw a $20-million makeover that included the addition of an 8,000-square-foot full-service spa. New in the summer of 2011, just as this book goes to print, is an extensive pool and play area (aptly named the "Splash Zone") filled with water slides, water jets, spinners, water cannons, and an area dedicated to tinier tots, too. **Note:** This is now an official "on-site" SeaWorld hotel, with added benefits such as complimentary transportation to SeaWorld, Aquatica, and Discovery Cove (as well as Universal Orlando); complimentary quick queue passes (limited to a daily allotment); early entry at both SeaWorld and Aquatica; and discounts at select shops and eateries on select days of the week.

6677 Sea Harbor Dr., Orlando, FL 32821. www.renaissanceseaworld.com. ☏ **800/327-6677** or 407/351-5555. Fax 407/351-1991. 778 units. $129–$286 double. Extra person no charge. Daily resort fee $15. Children 17 and younger stay free in parent's room. AE, DC, DISC, MC, V. Valet parking $20; self-parking $15. **Amenities:** 2 restaurants; cafe; grill; 2 lounges; babysitting; concierge; concierge-level rooms; golf course (nearby); putting area; health club; 2 Jacuzzis; outdoor heated pool; kids' pool; room service; 2 lighted tennis courts; sauna; spa; free transportation to SeaWorld parks and Universal Orlando parks; transportation to other theme parks for a fee; limited Wi-Fi (fee). *In room:* A/C, TV, fridge (upon request), game system, hair dryer, high- speed Internet (free), minibar, MP3 docking station.

Rosen Shingle Creek ★★★   The flagship of the Rosen group of upscale hotels, this magnificent Mediterranean-inspired resort evokes thoughts of a bygone era when Florida's legendary grand hotels were bastions of high style. Striking architecture (both inside and out), lavishly appointed rooms, and exceptional service are signatures of this fabulous resort. While luxurious by design, the lush natural grounds have been preserved, and references throughout the property recall both the historical and natural significance of the area, with rooms named for Florida's lakes, rivers, and historical landmarks—even the resort itself, the Shingle Creek, is named for the waterway that winds alongside the property, the headwater to the Florida Everglades. The extensive array of recreational facilities includes a championship golf course and golf academy, a full-service spa, two pools (one for families), lighted tennis courts, nature trails, and a playground. Dining options are just as varied, ranging from elegant to on-the-go. And though it may have old-world style, modern conveniences, including an on-site airline check-in and bag-check service, cater to guests' needs. Because it's a distance from the mainstream tourist district, a car is a must. Shuttle service to Universal Orlando is complimentary, and available, for a fee, to other parks. **Note:** The resort recently announced its purchase of additional acreage adjacent to the existing property, making way for the addition of up to 500 villas, along with a separate check-in area, pool, restaurant, and clubhouse, though additional details have yet to be released (and construction has yet to begin).

9939 Universal Blvd. (just east of International Dr., beyond the Convention Center), Orlando, FL 32819. www.rosenshinglecreek.com. ☏ **866/996-6338** or 407/996-9933. Fax: 407/996-9932. 1,501 units. $129–$349 double. Extra person $20. Children 17 and younger stay free in parent's room. AE, DC, DISC, MC, V. Valet parking $20; self-parking $12. **Amenities:** 5 restaurants; 2 grills; 3 lounges; babysitting; supervised children's program; concierge; concierge-level rooms; health club; golf club and academy; 2 Jacuzzis; 2 outdoor heated pools; kid's pool; room service; spa; 2 lighted tennis courts; free transportation to Universal Orlando; transportation to other parks for a fee. *In room:* A/C, TV w/NXTV technology and connectivity panel for laptops and MP3 players, fridge, hair dryer, Internet (fee).

Royal Pacific Resort ★★ ☺   The third of Universal Orlando's three resorts features a spectacular beachfront lagoon-style pool with an interactive water play area right nearby. It's lined with palm trees, winding walkways, waterfalls, and an exquisite orchid garden, all giving it a remote island feel (though admittedly the screams emanating from the nearby Islands of Adventure may remind you that you're not so isolated). The abandoned floatplane (a scene reminiscent of *Gilligan's Island*) makes a great backdrop. The rooms, smaller than those at other Universal resorts, are more reflective of the island theme thanks to the recent addition of bamboo accents, a warm yet muted color scheme, and upgraded technology (including flatscreen TVs and Wi-Fi). The decor, however, is rather understated when compared to that of equivalent Disney resorts. The public areas (whether inside or out), however, are very impressive and well worth exploring. The addition of the Wantilan Luau Pavilion ensures that the resort's weekly luau is now held rain or shine. If you're traveling with children ages 6 and younger, the Royal Pacific is the best choice at Universal; the eight Jurassic Park–themed Kid Suites are sure to be a hit. *The big plus:* Guests get Express-line access to almost every ride at Universal Studios Florida and Islands of Adventure, plus preferred seating privileges for shows and restaurants. And Universal resort guests now have early access to the Wizarding World of Harry Potter, a full hour prior to the official park opening.

6300 Hollywood Way, Orlando, FL 32819. www.loewshotels.com/hotels/Orlando or www.universal orlando.com. ⓒ **800/232-7827** or 407/503-3000. Fax 407/503-3202. 1,000 units. $229–$479 double; $339–$1,950 suite. Extra person $25. Children 17 and younger stay free in parent's room. AE, DC, DISC, MC, V. Valet parking $22; self-parking $15. Small pets welcome ($25). **Amenities:** 2 restaurants; 3 lounges; babysitting; supervised children's program; concierge; concierge-level rooms; Jacuzzi; outdoor heated pool; kids' pool; sauna; small spa; free water-taxi and bus transportation to Universal Orlando; free shuttle to SeaWorld; transportation to WDW parks for a fee; limited Wi-Fi (free). *In room:* A/C, TV, DVD (suites), fridge (suites; otherwise upon request for a fee), hair dryer, Internet (fee), microwave (suites; otherwise upon request for a fee), minibar, MP3 docking station.

Staybridge Suites ★ Like its Lake Buena Vista cousin (p. 76), this hotel is friendly, well run, and neat as a pin, attracting both leisure and business travelers. Its price and its spacious one- and two-bedroom suites (the latter are 550 sq. ft., with enough beds for eight) are two of its biggest pluses. Courtyard rooms have balconies. The property is just up the road from Pointe Orlando and its various shopping and dining options.

8480 International Dr. (btw. Beachline Expwy. and Sand Lake Rd.), Orlando, FL 32819. www.sborlando. com or www.staybridgesuites.com. ⓒ **800/866-4549** or 407/352-2400. Fax 407/352-4631. 146 units. $129–$289 suite. Rates include continental breakfast and manager's reception on select nights. AE, DC, DISC, MC, V. Self-parking free. **Amenities:** Exercise room; Jacuzzi; outdoor heated pool; kids' pool; free transportation to all major theme parks. *In room:* A/C, TV/DVD/VCR, movie library (free), CD player, fridge, hair dryer, Internet (free), fully equipped kitchen.

Moderate

Crowne Plaza Universal ★ This sleek, 15-story high-rise is conveniently located a block east of I-Drive and caters primarily to business travelers. Although it's closer to Universal Orlando and SeaWorld (about midway between them) than to WDW, getting to Disney is no problem because the hotel offers free shuttles to the major parks. It's also close to the I-Ride Trolley, which saves shoe leather for those interested in exploring International Drive. The subdued rooms (most inside the Crowne Wing, along with the hotel's meeting space) are well appointed and offer floor-to-ceiling windows. Some of the pricier rooms (with Jacuzzi tubs) are in the circular Atrium Tower, where you can climb to the top in high-speed glass elevators. Facilities include a state-of-the-art fitness center.

7800 Universal Blvd., Orlando, FL 32819. www.cporlando.com. ⓒ **866/864-8627** or 407/355-0519. Fax 407/355-0504. 400 units. $99–$199 double. Extra person $20. Children 17 and younger stay free in parent's room. AE, DISC, MC, V. Valet parking $17; free self-parking. **Amenities:** Restaurant; cafe; lounge; babysitting; concierge; health club; outdoor heated pool; room service; limited spa services; free transportation to WDW, Universal, SeaWorld and Wet 'n Wild; Wi-Fi (free). *In room:* A/C, TV, CD player, fridge (select rooms; suites), game system, hair dryer, Internet (fee), microwave (select rooms).

DoubleTree Hotel by Hilton at the Entrance to Universal Orlando ★
Location alone—right across the street from Universal Orlando—earns this hotel a star. Built for the convention trade, this former Radisson has reasonably nice accommodations. Rooms on the west side of floors 6 through 18 offer views of the Universal parks and CityWalk. DoubleTree's famous chocolate-chip cookies are complimentary upon check-in (though you may want to buy some to take home because they're *that* good).

5780 Major Blvd., Orlando, FL 32819. www.doubletreeorlando.com. © **800/327-2110** or 407/351-1000. Fax 407/363-0106. 742 units. $89–$169 double. Extra person $10. Children 17 and younger stay free in parent's room. AE, DC, DISC, MC, V. Valet parking $16; self-parking $12. **Amenities:** 2 restaurants; food court; lounge; exercise room; Jacuzzi; outdoor heated pool; kids' pool; room service; free transportation to Universal, SeaWorld and Wet 'n Wild parks; transportation to WDW parks for a fee; Wi-Fi (free). *In room:* A/C, TV, fridge, hair dryer, MP3 docking station, Wi-Fi (fee).

DoubleTree by Hilton Orlando at SeaWorld Extensive renovations have brought this nicely landscaped 28-acre resort back to life—the grounds filled with flowing fountains, waterfalls, and gardens blooming with color. Located just feet from SeaWorld (and its sibling parks) and minutes from I-Drive, it's a good option for guests who plan on venturing beyond Disney. Rooms, redesigned to include a sliding partition that can close off the vanity from the main room, are more sophisticated now—some even border on chic and trendy with splashes of color. Select rooms sport laminate-wood floors, while others are carpeted; views range from the pool (interior) to the parking lot (exterior). Palm-lined pools (including three main pools and two attended kids' pools), a small minigolf course, a kids' club, and a full-service spa are just a sampling of what you'll find to keep you busy here. On-site dining options are plentiful and varied, though a slew of restaurants line nearby I-Drive for those who prefer to venture out.

10100 International Dr. (near the Beachline Expwy./S.R. 528), Orlando, Florida 32831. www.double treeorlandoidrive.com or www.doubletree.com. © **800/327-0363** or 407/352-1100. Fax 407/354-4007. 1,100 units. $89–$239 double; $279–$430 suite. Extra person $25. Children 17 and younger stay free in parent's room. Pets allowed (1 pet under 25 lbs.) at a one-time fee of $75. AE, DC, DISC, MC, V. Valet parking $18; self-parking $10. **Amenities:** Restaurant; cafe; 2 lounges; babysitting; children's activities; health club; Jacuzzi; 3 outdoor pools including 2 kids' pools; free transportation to all major theme parks. *In room:* A/C, TV, fridge (select rooms), game system, hair dryer, microwave (select rooms), MP3 docking station, Wi-Fi (fee).

Embassy Suites Orlando ★ This hotel's run-of-the-mill exterior hides an impressive interior atrium highlighted by brick and wrought-iron accents, palm trees, and lush foliage. Renovations have kept the property in good condition. Eight floors of suites surround the atrium, some with balconies overlooking the courtyard below. Suites are fairly spacious, with separate living and sleeping areas. It's one of the few hotels to offer both indoor and outdoor pools. Another big advantage: the proximity to I-Drive's nightlife, restaurants, and shops. A complimentary cooked-to-order breakfast and evening reception are a few of the perks of staying here.

8978 International Dr., Orlando, FL 32819. www.embassysuitesorlando.com. © **800/EMBASSY** (362-2779) or 407/352-1400. Fax 407/363-1120. 244 units. $109–$229 suite. Extra person $10. Rates include full breakfast and nightly manager's reception. AE, DC, DISC, MC, V. Valet parking $12; self-parking free. **Amenities:** Restaurant; lounge; health club; 2 heated pools (1 indoor, 1 outdoor); kids' pool; room service; free transportation to WDW parks; Wi-Fi. *In room:* A/C, TV, CD players (select rooms), fridge, hair dryer, Internet access (fee), microwave, MP3 docking station.

If you're coming into town during peak season and having trouble finding a room, the 1,052-unit **Wyndham Orlando Resort**, 8001 International Dr. (© **877/ 999-3223** or 407/351-2420; www. wyndham.com), is an impeccably landscaped property that's good for families and features numerous pools, playgrounds, and a kids' club for children 4 to 12. Rates run between $113 and $194. The 1,338-unit **Caribe Royale Orlando All-Suites Hotel & Convention** **Center**, 8101 World Center Dr. (© **800/ 823-8300** or 407/238-8000; www. cariberoyale.com), has spacious one-bedroom suites (with kitchenettes) and two-bedroom villas (with Jacuzzis and full kitchens). The grounds are beautifully landscaped, the pool has cascading waterfalls and a 75-foot water slide, there's a playground nearby, and the service is tops. Rates run between $109 and $209.

Hampton Inn at Universal Studios   There's nothing fancy about this simple hotel, but it's in a good location if you plan to spend most of your time at Universal Orlando, which is only 2 blocks away. It's also relatively close to SeaWorld and among the closest to downtown Orlando, but a 10-mile haul from Disney. Although there's no restaurant on the premises, there are plenty within walking distance. A complimentary continental breakfast is included—if you're in a hurry to get to the parks, just pick up a bagged grab-and-go breakfast on your way out the door.

5621 Windhover Dr., Orlando, FL 32819. www.hamptoninn.com. © **800/426-7866**, 800/231-8395, or 407/351-6716. Fax 407/363-1711. 120 units. $89–$125 double. Extra person $10. Rates include continental breakfast. Children 17 and younger stay free in parent's room. AE, DC, DISC, MC, V. Self-parking free. **Amenities:** Exercise room; outdoor heated pool; free transportation to Universal and SeaWorld parks; transportation to WDW parks for a fee. *In room:* A/C, TV, fridge (select rooms), hair dryer, Internet (free), microwave (select rooms).

Hyatt Place Universal   If your goal is to be very close to the Universal theme parks without having to pay the heftier rates that come with staying on park property, this stylish and modern hotel is the place for you. The lobby sports a cafe, TV den, and e-room (with free access to public computers and a printer) all amid a chic and upscale decor. Self-service check-in and checkout kiosks offer an efficient alternative to standing in line at the front desk, and rooms feature comfy bedding, sleeper sofas, 42-inch flatscreen TVs, and more space for stretching out than in standard hotel/ motel accommodations. Complimentary Wi-Fi, available throughout the hotel, keeps you connected without costing you a bundle. A free continental breakfast is also part of the package, but for those with a heartier appetite, hot breakfast entrees are available (they'll cost you extra).

5895 Caravan Court, Orlando, FL 32819. www.orlandouniversal.place.hyatt.com. © **800/833-1516** or 407/351-0627. Fax 407/331-3317. 151 units. $79–$229 for up to 4. Rates include full breakfast. Children 17 and younger stay free in parent's room. AE, DC, DISC, MC, V. Self-parking free. **Amenities:** Exercise room; outdoor heated pool; free transportation to all major theme parks. *In room:* A/C, TV w/connectivity panel for laptops, DVD players and game systems, fridge, hair dryer, MP3 players, Wi-Fi (free).

Lake Eve Resort ★★   One of the newest additions to the collection of Sky Hotels and Resorts, Lake Eve features one-, two-, and three-bedroom suites (the latter sleep up to 10), each with a direct view of (surprise!) Lake Eve. Flatscreen TVs (in the living area as well as every bedroom), well-equipped gourmet kitchens (with stainless-steel appliances and granite countertops), washers and dryers, and a stylish modern decor are staples in every suite. The free-form pool is particularly inviting, with the lake making a spectacular backdrop. Kids will appreciate the wading pool, water play area, and Sky Kids Club; parents will appreciate the many conveniences, including a complimentary grocery shopping service (the service is free—the groceries are not), restaurant delivery service (for a small fee), complimentary transportation to area theme parks, and the stress-free atmosphere.

12388 International Dr. (the southernmost end of I-Dr.), Orlando, FL 32819. www.lakeeveresort.com or www.staysky.com. ✆ **866/999-5383** or 407/597-0370. Fax 407/597-0371. 176 units. $99–$309 suite. Extra person $25. Children 17 and younger stay free in parent's room. AE, DC, DISC, MC, V. Self-parking free. **Amenities:** Restaurant; lounge; supervised children's program; children's activities; concierge; health club; Jacuzzi; outdoor pool (heated seasonally); kids' pool and water play area; room service; sauna; free transportation to all major theme parks. *In room:* A/C, TV, DVD player (upon request; fee), hair dryer, fully equipped and stocked kitchen, washer and dryer, Wi-Fi (free).

Point Orlando Resort   This all-suite boutique hotel is one of the newest ownership resorts to spring up along International Drive in one of Orlando's busiest tourist districts. Each of the junior suites (385 sq. ft.), one-bedroom executive suites (716 sq. ft.), and two-bedroom family suites (1,056 sq. ft.) has a private balcony that overlooks the courtyard below, tasteful contemporary decor, full-size kitchen, flatscreen TV, and soothing whirlpool tub. Take a refreshing dip in the pool, lounge around the spacious deck, or rejuvenate in the poolside Jacuzzi. Though on-site dining options are minimal, a vast array of restaurants is within minutes of the resort's door (some just a short walk away). A daily continental breakfast and in-room Internet access (wired) are just two of the complimentary perks when staying here. While already a good value, the resort offers an ever-changing array of packages that should entice even the most budget-conscious traveler.

6039 Carrier Dr. (off I-Dr. at the corner of Carrier Dr. and Universal Blvd.), Orlando, FL 32819. www.thepointorlando.com. ✆ **866/956-2015** or 407/956-2020. Fax 407/956-2001. 144 units. $89–$279. Extra person $25. Children 17 and younger stay free in parent's room. Rates include continental breakfast. Daily resort fee $9.95. AE, DC, DISC, MC, V. Self-parking free. **Amenities:** Cafe; lounge; health club; Jacuzzi; 2 outdoor heated pools. *In room:* A/C, TV, fridge, hair dryer, Internet (free), fully equipped and stocked kitchen, washer and dryer.

SpringHill Suites Orlando at SeaWorld ⚐   This all-suites property offers guests a chance to stay near SeaWorld (and I-Drive's numerous restaurants, shops, and attractions) without the congestion that plagues areas north of the convention center. A chic decor, spacious suites (about 700 sq. ft., with beds enough for five and a separate living area), a themed pool and play area (albeit small), reasonable rates, and a handful of perks (such as a complimentary breakfast buffet and free Internet access) make this all-new property worth considering.

10801 International Dr., Orlando, FL 32821. www.springhillsuites.com. ✆ **866/468-4651** or 407/354-1176. Fax 407/354-1182. 200 units. $107–$174 double. Extra person $10. Rates include hot breakfast buffet. Children 17 and younger stay free in parent's room. AE, DC, DISC, MC, V. Self-parking free. **Amenities:** Restaurant; room service; concierge; exercise room; outdoor heated pool; free transportation to SeaWorld parks; transportation to WDW and Universal for a fee; Wi-Fi (fee). *In room:* A/C, TV, fridge, hair dryer, Internet (free), microwave.

Inexpensive

Fairfield Inn & Suites Orlando at SeaWorld ★ ⚐   If you're looking for I-Drive's best value, it's hard to beat this one. This all-new Fairfield combines a trendy decor, quiet location (south of the convention center), down-to-earth rates, and a small themed pool all in one package. It's not only the best in this category, but is arguably a step above even a handful of moderate properties in the area. The rooms are quite comfortable, the staff is friendly, and a number of restaurants are located within minutes of the hotel (plus a Friday's is right on site). SeaWorld is just across the street, and Aquatica is next door.

10815 International Dr., Orlando, FL 32819. www.fairfieldinn.com. © **888/468-3870** or 407/354-1139. Fax 407/354-1151. 152 units. $89–$149 double. Rates include continental breakfast. AE, DC, DISC, MC, V. Self-parking free. **Amenities:** Restaurant; room service; outdoor heated pool; free transportation to SeaWorld parks, transportation to WDW and Universal for a fee. *In room:* A/C, TV, fridge (select rooms), hair dryer, Internet (free), microwave (select rooms).

La Quinta Inn & Suites Convention Center 🏌️ Opened in 1998, this is one of a handful of moderately priced motels on Universal Boulevard, which runs parallel to (but isn't as congested as) I-Drive. The hotel is aimed at business travelers, but this is Orlando, so families traveling with kids are welcomed with open arms. King rooms are designed for extended stays and have a fridge and microwave. A limited number of two-room suites offering separate living and sleeping areas is available.

8504 Universal Blvd., Orlando, FL 32819. www.lq.com. © **800/753-3757,** 407/345-1365, or 407/654-0209. Fax 407/345-5586. 184 units. $69–$109 double; $79–$129 suite. Extra person $10. Rates include continental breakfast. Children 18 and younger stay free in parent's room. AE, DC, DISC, MC, V. Self-parking free. Small pets accepted. **Amenities:** Exercise room; Jacuzzi; outdoor heated pool; transportation to all theme parks for a fee; Wi-Fi (free). *In room:* A/C, TV, fridge (some rooms), game system, hair dryer, Internet (free), microwave (some rooms).

IN DOWNTOWN ORLANDO

The main reason travelers usually give for staying in downtown Orlando is to avoid the hustle and bustle (and crowds) of the theme-park zone. One other plus: Those traveling without children may greatly appreciate the lack of them in the downtown hotels, which generally cater to business travelers.

But if you're traveling in the middle of peak season, including summer or around the December holidays, you'll likely find yourself bumping into other people no matter where you go. And in my opinion, unless you're getting a really fabulous discount at one of downtown's many business hotels, there's only one property that really stands out in the area and is worth the schlep (see below).

Best for: The business set traveling to the city proper, as well as visitors who prefer to avoid the theme parks altogether, will find an array of upscale boutique hotels set amid a trendy cityscape—with its own eclectic array of shops, restaurants, clubs, and recreational and entertainment venues that, while aimed at locals, are worth experiencing if the theme parks aren't really your thing.

Drawbacks: If you plan to spend most of your days in the theme parks and nights at CityWalk, then you're better off staying in the thick of things. Unless you avoid driving during rush hour from 7 to 9am and 4 to 6pm, you'll likely spend a lot more vacation time on I-4 and in its traffic than you'd like. It will also be harder to escape back to your hotel for an afternoon swim or a nap.

Expensive

Grand Bohemian Hotel Orlando ★★ 👜 Part of the upscale Kessler Collection and Marriott's Autograph Collection, downtown Orlando's jewel opened in 2001 with an early-20th-century Euro-Bohemian theme. It caters almost exclusively to the business and romance crowds, which means—much to the satisfaction of the adult guests here—you'll find almost no children on the premises. The comfortable and plush rooms have an Art Deco look, with plenty of chrome and shades of reds and purples. The upper floors on the east side overlook the pool; those on the north side face downtown. The classy hotel, which is entirely smoke-free, has more than 100 pieces of 19th- and 20th-century American fine art, and its lounge features a rare Imperial Grand Bösendorfer piano—one of only two in the world and valued at a cool quarter of a million. The downside: You'll have to pay for transportation to all of the theme parks.

Check out the hotel's location on the "Hotels & Restaurants Elsewhere in Orlando" map, on p. 151.

325 S. Orange Ave. (across from City Hall). www.grandbohemianhotel.com. © **866/663-0024** or 407/313-9000. Fax 407/313-6001. 250 units. $224–$374 for up to 4; $279–$619 suite. Extra person $25. AE, DC, DISC, MC, V. Valet parking $22. The garage is 2 blocks west on Jackson St. **Amenities:** Restaurant; 2 lounges; concierge; concierge-level rooms; health club; heated outdoor pool; room service; shuttle to the theme parks for a fee. *In room:* A/C, TV, CD player, game system, hair dryer, minibar, Wi-Fi (fee).

ORLANDO BED & BREAKFASTS

Although most of the properties in Orlando are resorts or chains, there are a few good bed-and-breakfast options. These properties offer a respite from the crowded, run-and-gun world of the theme parks, and they're ideal for couples looking for a little quiet time or romance. Note that most of the inns and B&Bs in Orlando do not accept children—a major selling point for some visitors. If you choose to stay at one of these properties, you'll need a car or some other kind of transportation, because these inns do not provide it. Unless otherwise noted, all B&Bs in this section can be found on the "Hotels & Restaurants Elsewhere in Orlando" map, on p. 151. You can find other options in the area through **Florida Bed & Breakfast Inns** (© **800/524-1880;** www.florida-inns.com).

Expensive

The Courtyard at Lake Lucerne ★ 🏛 You might feel the sting of Cupid's arrows in this downtown hideaway, where each of the buildings is historic. The Art Deco Wellborn, a late bloomer that arrived in 1946, offers 14 one-bedroom apartments and a honeymoon suite (styles range from Thai to the Fab '50s). The Norment–Parry Inn is an 1883 Victorian-style home with six rooms decorated with English and American antiques; four have sitting rooms, and all have private bathrooms. It, too, has a honeymoon suite, highlighted by a walnut bed and a Victorian fireplace. The I. W. Phillips House, built in 1919, is reminiscent of old Southern homes with large verandas. There are three suites upstairs, one with a whirlpool, all with verandas overlooking the gardens and fountain. Finally, the Dr. Phillips House, built in 1893, made its bed-and-breakfast debut on Valentine's Day 1999 with six impeccably furnished, antiques-laden rooms. A carafe of wine awaits guests upon check-in.

211 N. Lucerne Circle E., Orlando, FL 32801. www.orlandohistoricinn.com. © **800/444-5289** or 407/648-5188. Fax 407/246-1368. 30 units. $100–$225 double. Rates include continental breakfast and evening cocktails. AE, DC, MC, V. Self-parking free. Children permitted only in the Wellborn suites. Take Orange Ave. south; immediately following City Hall (dome building with fountains and glass sculpture),

turn left onto Anderson. After 2 lights, at Delaney Ave., turn right. Take first right onto Lucerne Circle. Be aware of one-way streets. Follow the brown "historic inn" signs. *In room:* A/C, TV, Wi-Fi (free).

Moderate

The Veranda Bed & Breakfast 🎁   Located in Thornton Park, this inn near scenic Lake Eola is another option if you want to stay near downtown. Its four buildings date back to the early 1900s. All units (studios to suites) include private bathrooms and entrances; some have garden tubs, balconies, kitchenettes, and four-poster beds. A few of the nicer options include the Washington Suite, which sports a four-poster bed and a Jacuzzi, and the romantic Carriage Suite, which has a four-poster bed and an antique claw-foot tub. The two-bedroom, two-bathroom Keylime Cottage ($169) sleeps four and has a full kitchen. Complimentary Wi-Fi is included if you can't resist connecting with the outside world.

115 N. Summerlin Ave., Orlando, FL 32801. www.theverandabandb.com. ✆ **800/420-6822** or 407/849-0321. Fax 407/849-0321, ext. 24. 12 units. $109–$189 double; $269 2-bedroom suite; $209 cottage. Rates include continental breakfast and Wi-Fi. AE, DC, DISC, MC, V. Self-parking free. Children are not permitted. From I-4, take exit 84, Hwy. 50/Colonial Dr.; go left 1 mile to Summerlin, turn right, and go 1 mile, crossing Robinson St. The inn is 1 block up on the left. **Amenities:** Jacuzzi; outdoor pool. *In room:* A/C, TV, fridge, hair dryer.

PRACTICAL INFORMATION

The Big Picture

Beautifully landscaped grounds are the rule at properties in WDW, neighboring Lake Buena Vista, Universal Orlando, and on the mid- and southern portions of I-Drive. But the beauty of the area is often offset by the beast of heavier traffic and, at times, higher prices. No matter what your budget or crowd tolerance, there is something for everyone. If you're looking for an inexpensive or moderately priced motel, check out the options in Kissimmee (though that area is no longer limited only to the budget conscious) and, to a lesser degree, on the northern end of International Drive.

Once you've decided on your vacation dates, book your accommodations as soon as possible, especially if you want to stay on Disney or Universal property. Advance reservations are an absolute necessity if you're planning on staying at any of the preferred resorts in town, whether on theme-park property or in Orlando proper.

How to Choose a Hotel & Save Money

You can almost always negotiate a better price by purchasing a package deal, by assuring the reservationist that he or she can do better, or by mentioning that you belong to one of several organizations that receive a discount (such as AARP, AAA, the armed services, or a labor union). The **Orlando Magicard** can save you plenty of cash as well (this discount card is available through the Orlando CVB at www.visitorlando.com). Even the type of **credit card** you use could get you a 5% to 10% discount at some of the larger chains. Any discount you get will help ease the impact of local resort taxes, which aren't included in the quoted rates. *These taxes will add as much as 14.5% to your bill, depending on where you're staying.*

The **average, undiscounted hotel rate** for the Orlando area is currently about $92 per night double, and that rate in good times can climb up by 5% to 9% a year. The lowest rates at WDW are at the Pop Century and the three All-Star resorts, which, depending on the season, can run from $82 to $179. They're pricier than comparable rooms in the outside world; though they're small and basic, they're still Disney owned and offer the same on-property advantages as Disney's more expensive resorts.

WDW's 2011 value seasons or lowest rates fell from January 2 to February 16, and August 14 to September 29. Regular season rates were in effect from February 27 to March 10 and May 1 to June 24. Easter rates ran from April 17 to 30. Summer rates (only at Disney's "value" and "moderate" resorts) ran from June 3 to August 13. Fall rates were generally scheduled from September 30 to November 18 and November 26 to December 22. Peak rates applied from February 17 to February 26 and from March 11 to April 16. Holiday rates were scheduled from November 19 to November 25 and December 23 through December 31. The same general time periods, give or take a day or two here and there, should also apply in 2012. Be aware, however, that Disney's new pricing schedule breaks down seasonal rates even further to include specific weekends and holidays such as New Year's Day, Presidents' Day, Independence Day, MLK Day, and Disney's marathon weekend, among others (none of which are listed above). Although the actual dates will shift a little (and will also change depending on the level of hotel you choose—Disney's deluxe and villa resorts follow a rate schedule that is slightly skewed from what is listed), the same general periods should apply in 2012.

If you're not renting a car or staying at a Walt Disney World or Universal resort, be sure to ask when booking your room if the hotel or motel offers **transportation to the theme parks** and, if so, whether there's a charge and exactly what it is. Some hotels and motels offer free service with their own shuttles (listed in the reviews in this chapter). Others use Mears Transportation (see "Getting Around," in chapter 10), and rates can be as high as $18 per person round-trip (some hotels make these arrangements for you; others require you to do it). On the other hand, if you have a vehicle, expect to pay $14 a day to park it at Disney or SeaWorld, and $15 at Universal (with same-day in/out privileges at all parks).

If you stay at a WDW resort or one of Disney's "official" hotels, transportation is complimentary within WDW. For more information on this and the other advantages of staying at Disney properties, see "The Perks of Staying with Mickey," earlier in this chapter.

In or out of Walt Disney World, if you book your hotel as part of a **package** (see "Vacation & Cruise Packages" on p. 37 for more details), you'll likely enjoy some type of savings. The **Walt Disney Travel Company** (© **407/934-7806**) offers a number of Disney resort packages.

Outside Disney, you'll probably be quoted a rate better than the rack rates contained in this chapter's listings, but you should try to bargain even further to ensure you get the best rates possible. If any apply to you, ask about discounts for students, government employees, seniors, military, firefighters, police, AFL-CIO members,

---

 Tight Squeeze

An average hotel or motel room in the Orlando area has about 325 to 400 square feet and beds for four. Although hardly a castle, most travelers find it adequate for a short stay. I've made a special note in the listings of properties where the rooms are substantially larger or smaller than the average.

corporate clients, and, again, AARP or AAA, holders of the Orlando Magicard, even frequent-traveler programs for hotel chains or airlines. Special Internet-only discounts and packages may also be featured on hotel websites, especially those of the larger chains. No matter where you end up staying, always ask again when you arrive if there are any additional discounts or promotions available. But never come to Orlando without a reservation: Taking chances on your negotiating skills is one thing; taking chances on room availability is quite another. Orlando is a year-round destination, with a heavy convention and business trade, and international vacationers flock here during periods when domestic travelers don't. If you come without a reservation, you may find yourself extremely disappointed—or completely out of luck.

In the "Amenities" section of the accommodations listings in this chapter, I mention **concierge levels** where available. In these hotels within a hotel, guests pay more to enjoy a luxurious private lounge (sometimes with great views), free continental or full breakfast, hot and cold hors d'oeuvres served at cocktail hour, and/or late-night cordials and pastries. Rooms are usually on higher floors, and guests are pampered with additional special services (including private registration and check-out, a personal concierge, and nightly bed turndown) and amenities (such as upgraded toiletries, terry robes, hair dryers, and more). Ask for the specifics when you reserve a room.

You'll also find counselor-supervised **child care** or **activity centers** at some hotels. Very popular in Orlando, these can be marvelous, creatively run facilities that might offer movies, video games, arts and crafts, storytelling, puppet shows, indoor and outdoor activities, and more. Some provide meals and/or have beds where a child can sleep while you're out on the town. Check individual hotel listings for these facilities.

Reservation Services

Many of the Kissimmee hotels listed under "In the Kissimmee Area," earlier in this chapter, can be booked through the **Kissimmee Convention & Visitors Bureau** (© **407/742-8200;** www.visitkissimmee.com). The same goes for Orlando and the **Orlando/Orange County Convention & Visitors Bureau** (© **800/972-3304** or 407/363-5872; www.visitorlando.com).

Florida Hotel Network (© **800/293-2419;** www.floridahotels.com), **Central Reservation Service** (© **800/555-7555** or 407/740-6442; www.crshotels.com), and **Hotels.com** (© **800/246-8357;** www.hotels.com) are three other services that can help with hotel and other kinds of reservations in Central Florida. **Hotel Kingdom.com** (© **877/766-6787** or 407/294-9600; www.hotelkingdom.com) is also a good source of hotel and vacation-rental bargains.

You can also book Disney World hotels directly by calling © **407/934-7639** or visiting **www.disneyworld.com**; Universal Orlando properties can be booked by calling © **888/430-7333** or 888/273-1311, or by visiting **www.universalorlando.com**.

Walt Disney World Central Reservations Office (CRO) & Walt Disney Travel Company

To book a room or package at Disney's resorts, campgrounds, and "official" hotels through the **Walt Disney World Travel Company,** contact the **Central Reservations Office (CRO),** P.O. Box 10000, Lake Buena Vista, FL 32830 (© **407/934-7639;** www.disneyworld.com).

Special Treatment

AAA (© 800/732-1991; www.aaa.com) members can take advantage of special lodging programs at select WDW resorts and preferred parking at the theme parks if they purchase an AAA Disney vacation package or prepurchase their park tickets at participating AAA locations. *Note:* These cannot be purchased at the parks!

CRO can recommend accommodations suited to your price range and specific needs, such as a location near a particular park, facilities that offer supervised child-care centers, or a pool large enough to swim laps. But the staffers who answer the phones usually don't volunteer information about a better deal or the latest special offer *unless you ask.*

Be sure to inquire about Disney's numerous package plans, which can include meals, tickets, recreation, and other features. The right package can save you money and time if you use all of its features (there's no sense in paying for something you won't use); having a comprehensive game plan in place is helpful in computing the cost of your vacation in advance.

CRO can also give you information about various theme-park ticket options, the airlines, and car rentals. It can even make dinner-show reservations for you at the resort of your choice.

Other Sources for Orlando Hotel Packages

In addition to the Disney sources above, several other travel companies offer packages utilizing Disney resorts. **AAA** (© 800/732-1991; www.aaa.com), **American Express Vacations** (© 800/346-3607; http://travel.americanexpress.com/travel/personal), and nearly all of the major airlines offer vacation packages to Orlando. See "Vacation & Cruise Packages" on p. 37 for more options. Give each source a call, ask for brochures, and compare offerings to find the best package for you.

On a slightly smaller scale than Disney, **Universal Orlando** offers several travel packages that can include resort stays (both on and off property), VIP access to the parks, discounts to other Orlando attractions, and cruises. Airfare and car rentals are also available. You can book a package by calling © **800/711-0800** or 877/801-9720. On the Internet, visit **www.univacations.com** or **www.universalorlando.com**.

SeaWorld offers vacation packages that include stays at nearby resorts and park tickets. These can be booked by calling © **800/423-8368** or visiting www.seaworld.com.

3

WHERE TO STAY

Practical Information

WHERE TO EAT

I t should come as no surprise that Orlando has something for everybody when it comes to pleasing the palate, ranging from fast food to five-star restaurants and everything in between. The Mouse's arrival launched an invasion of fast-food joints, a response to the number of families flocking to see Mickey, while theme restaurants, focusing on everything from race cars and rainforests to superheroes and sporting goods, weren't far behind. Today, the city overflows with more than 5,000 dining options, and while renowned for its numerous theme and chain restaurants (some admittedly more upscale than others), a small number of noteworthy eateries has managed to enter Orlando's dining scene in recent years.

The local dining scene doesn't compare to that found in such metropolitan foodie hot spots as New York, San Francisco, or Las Vegas, but there are certainly more than a few places here that could easily hold their own against the competition (disbelievers can grab a chair at **Emeril's** at City-Walk, **Victoria & Albert's** at Disney's Grand Floridian Resort & Spa, or **Norman's** at the Grande Lakes, among others). That said, keep in mind that Orlando is the undisputed king of U.S. family destinations, and restaurants generally do their darnedest to cater to their target audience.

As so many Central Florida visitors spend the biggest chunk of their time at Disney, a good deal of this chapter deals with the restaurants at Disney. For those of you who find yourselves beyond the boundaries of Mickey's doorstep, there's no need to worry: I also cover what's cooking at Universal Orlando's best restaurants, the hottest dining spots on International Drive, and a fair share of other area dining rooms.

Note to parents: Keep in mind that most moderate to inexpensive restaurants have kids' menus ($5–$9), and many offer distractions, such as coloring books and crayons, in the hopes it will keep your little ones otherwise occupied until their dinner arrives. If you go to a place catering to children, expect the noise level to be high. They don't take a vacation from squeals of joy or fits of temper, so you shouldn't expect to, either. On the plus side, if it's your kids who tend to turn up the volume, it's far more likely that their antics will go unnoticed when there are others around doing the very same things.

If dining with kids isn't your cup of tea, steer clear of any restaurant where Mickey and Minnie stop by to say hello during the meal. Character meals, no matter what restaurant they are in, are guaranteed to be filled with families, making them, at times, excruciatingly loud and almost unnerving to those not used to dining in a room full of children. As a general rule, the more expensive your meal, the less likely you'll be dining with a lot of little ones around. So if you prefer to dine in peace—and can afford it—consider a meal at some of the more expensive restaurants in the resorts, on International Drive, or around Orlando proper. *Tip:* Parents in need of a night off from the kids can arrange for in-room babysitting or supervised child care (p. 368) so they, too, can indulge in one of the area's finer dining options.

For additional information about area restaurants, visit **www.visitorlando.com**, **www.go2orlando.com**, or the websites in the listings that follow.

Advance Reservations at WDW Restaurants

Walt Disney World's Advance Reservations system, while similar to a reservation, is not nearly as rigid. Essentially, the system guarantees that you will get the next available table that will accommodate your party *after* you've arrived at a restaurant (which should be 5–10 min. prior to the time you've reserved). In other words, a table isn't kept empty while the restaurant waits for you. As such, it's likely that you'll end up waiting anywhere from 15 to 30 minutes, even if you arrive at the time you scheduled your meal. You can arrange Advance Reservations 180 days in advance at most full-service restaurants in the Magic Kingdom, Epcot, Disney's Hollywood Studios, Animal Kingdom, Disney resorts, and Downtown Disney. Advance Reservations can also be made for character meals (p. 153) and dinner shows throughout the World. To make arrangements, call ✆ **407/939-3463**; groups of eight or more can also call ✆ **407/939-7707**. Disney also takes Advance Reservations online at **www.disney world.com/dining**.

Nighttime dinner-theater shows (see chapter 8, "Walt Disney World & Orlando After Dark") can be booked up to 180 days in advance as well. Be aware, however, that these dinner shows (along with select character dining experiences) require full payment in advance and that cancellations must be made at least 48 hours prior to the time of the show to avoid penalties.

Note: Since the Advance Reservations phone number was instituted in 1994, it has become much more difficult to obtain a table as a walk-in at the resorts' more popular restaurants. I *strongly* advise you to call as far ahead as possible, especially if you're traveling during the peak seasons. It wouldn't hurt to mark your calendar and enter the phone number into your speed dial either. Amazingly, some restaurants, especially the dinner shows and character meals, can book up quite literally within only a minute or two of the phone lines' opening (7am EST) on that 180th day out.

If you don't make your dining plans in advance, you can take your chances by making your Advance Reservations in person once you have arrived in the parks. You can make reservations right from your smartphone at **www.disneyworld.com/dining**, head directly to your desired restaurant to see what's available, or stop by one of the following places:

- **In Epcot** at Guest Relations on the east side of Spaceship Earth.
- **In the Magic Kingdom** via the telephones at several locations, including the Walt Disney World Railroad station just inside the entrance and at City Hall near the front of Main Street, U.S.A.
- **In Disney's Hollywood Studios** via the telephones just inside the entrance or at Guest Relations near Hollywood Junction.
- **In Animal Kingdom** at Guest Relations on the left near the entrance. (Note that Rainforest Cafe here is a *verrry* popular place, so the sooner you call for Advance Reservations, the better.)
- **In Downtown Disney** at Guest Services in the Marketplace and at West Side.

Also, keep these restaurant facts in mind:

- *All* Florida restaurants and bars that serve food are **smoke free.**
- The Magic Kingdom (including its restaurants) serves no alcoholic beverages, but liquor is available at Animal Kingdom, Epcot, and Disney's Hollywood Studios restaurants and elsewhere in the WDW complex. And the selection of liquors and wines available at many of the hotels is both varied and extensive; Disney World, the largest single-site purveyor of wine in the world, employs more sommeliers than any other organization on the planet—more than 700 of them, including one advanced sommelier.
- All sit-down restaurants in Walt Disney World take American Express, Diners Club, Discover, MasterCard, Visa, and the Disney Visa Card.
- Unless otherwise noted, restaurants in the parks **require park admission.**
- Guests staying at Disney resorts and official properties can make Advance Reservations through Guest Services or the concierge.
- Nearly all WDW restaurants with sit-down or counter service offer children's menus with items ranging from $5 to $9, though in a few cases they're $10 to $14. Some include beverages and sides.

4 | A Palatable Perk: The Disney Dining Plan

Over the years, Disney has dished up a number of changes to its popular dining plan, which first debuted in 2005. What was once a relatively simple system, aimed at making the Disney dining experience less complicated and more financially palatable to its guests, has since evolved into a diverse lineup of customized dining plans with a broader appeal than ever before.

For those of you who may already be familiar with Disney's dining program, be advised of these changes worth noting: (1) Refillable mugs are now included in the basic Disney Dining Plan. Each person in your party receives a single mug that can be refilled unlimited times with soda, coffee, tea, or hot chocolate at quick-service establishments *only* at the Disney resort hotel where you're staying. (2) The Disney Quick-Service Dining Plan now allows for only one snack per day, rather than the original allotment of two snacks per day.

For those of you not yet familiar with Disney's dining program, here's the lowdown. The Disney Dining Plan (or plans, as there are currently five from which to choose) is an option available exclusively to guests of the official WDW hotels who book a Magic Your Way vacation package. When you book your package, you can choose one of the five add-on dining plans and then enjoy the convenience and savings during the duration of your Disney vacation. Each person in your party is allotted a certain number of credits for a select number of meals and snacks (depending on which plan you choose) that can be redeemed at any of the participating WDW restaurants (there are over 100 to choose from throughout the theme parks and Disney resorts). When you've finished your meal or are ready to purchase a snack, you simply present your key card and let the cashier or server know how many meals (or snacks) you would like to redeem (and for what age—this is important, as each member of your party is allotted meal credits based on his or her age). Your key card keeps an electronic record of how many meals and snacks you are allotted per adult and per child, along with how many you have already redeemed. Your receipt will include a printout of your remaining balance—in other words, the number of meals and snacks you have left.

THE DINING PLANS

Disney offers five different dining plans; which one is right for you depends on the type of meals you prefer to eat, the type of establishments you prefer to frequent (quick counter-service eateries and snack spots, casual sit-down restaurants, or fine-dining establishments), the amount of money you wish to spend on dining out (with prices ranging from $35 to $230 per adult per night, and from $12 to $161 per child ages 3 to 9 per night), and how many meals you actually intend on eating at a restaurant (as opposed to in your room or possibly elsewhere).

The **Disney Quick-Service Dining Plan** ($34.99 per night per adult, $11.99 per night per child) includes two quick-service meals and one snack per person, per night (based on the length of stay, for everyone in your party ages 3 and up). Also included is a single refillable mug for each person in your party (good only at quick-service establishments located at your resort hotel).

The basic **Disney Dining Plan** ($51.54 per night per adult, $15.02 per night per child) includes one quick-service meal, one snack, and one table-service meal per person, per night (based on the length of stay, for everyone in your party ages 3 and up), plus a single refillable mug for each person in your party.

The **Disney Deluxe Dining Plan** ($85.52 per night per adult, $23.79 per night per child) includes three meals and two snacks per person, per night (based on the length of stay, for everyone in your party ages 3 and up), plus a single refillable mug for each person in your party.

The **Disney Premium Plan** ($169.99 per night per adult, $119.99 per night per child) includes breakfast, lunch, dinner, and two snacks per person, per night, plus a single refillable mug for each person in your party. In addition, guests may participate in unlimited recreational activities, take in a Cirque du Soleil show, enjoy unlimited admittance to Disney's supervised child-care centers, and opt to join select WDW tours.

The **Disney Platinum Plan** ($229.99 per night per adult, $160.99 per night per child) includes breakfast, lunch, dinner, and two snacks per person, per night, plus a single refillable mug for each person in your party. In addition to enjoying all of the perks included in the Disney Premium Plan (above), guests can sit in reserved seating at Fantasmic!, take a fireworks cruise (either Wishes or IllumiNations), indulge in a single spa treatment, and get personal itinerary planning.

ADDITIONAL DETAILS

To help you decide which plan is best for you and your family, keep in mind that a **quick-service meal** includes an entree and a nonalcoholic drink at breakfast, or an entree or combo meal, a dessert, and a nonalcoholic drink at lunch or dinner.

A **table-service meal** includes an entree and a nonalcoholic drink, or a full buffet, at breakfast; and an appetizer (for children ages 3–9 only), an entree or combo meal, a dessert, and a nonalcoholic drink, or a full buffet, at lunch or dinner.

Snacks are defined as a novelty ice-cream bar, ice pop, fruit bar, single-serving box of popcorn, single piece of fruit, single-serving bag of snacks, a 20-ounce bottle of soda or water, a 22-ounce fountain drink, a single-serving carton of milk or juice, and a 12-ounce cup of coffee or hot chocolate or tea.

The dining plan can be used for **character dining** experiences, which count as one table-service meal per person (gratuities not included). One exception to the rule: Dining at Cinderella's Royal Table counts as two table-service meals per person—and in this case, gratuities *are* included.

The dining plan is also applicable to **signature dining** and **dinner shows,** but note that a single signature meal counts as two table-service credits. A signature meal consists of an appetizer (for children ages 3–9 only), an entree, a dessert, and a non-alcoholic drink. Gratuities are not included.

If you feel like staying in, the dining plan includes the option of **in-room dining** and **pizza delivery.** An in-room dining meal, which counts as two table-service credits, includes an appetizer (for children ages 3–9 only), an entree, a dessert, and a nonalcoholic drink. Pizza delivery, which also counts as two table-service credits, includes two nonalcoholic drinks, a pizza, and two desserts.

The dining plan is not available to guests under the age of 3. However, tinier tots are allowed to share from an adult plate without incurring an extra charge. Or, if you prefer, you may simply purchase a separate meal outright, with the price of the meal added to your bill. Guests between the ages of 3 and 9 who are on the dining plan are required to order from the children's menu when one is available.

Gratuities are generally not included (unless otherwise indicated). For parties of six or more people, an automatic 18% gratuity will be added to your bill. An automatic gratuity charge may also be added to your bill for items that are not included in the dining plan (alcoholic beverages, appetizers, and so on).

If you are unsure whether a given restaurant, quick-service eatery, or snack cart participates in the plan, simply look for the Disney Dining Plan symbol. You can also consult your Disney Dining Plan brochure, check the official WDW website, or ask the Disney dining agent when you book Advance Dining reservations.

FOOD FOR THOUGHT

So now that you have the facts, here's the real question: Is it worth it? In most cases, the answer is yes. The cost of any given plan is less than you would pay if you purchased all meals on your own, but to determine whether it is truly cost-effective, you need to consider the following:

How many meals do you actually plan on eating out each day? If you plan on dining out only a few times during your vacation, then the dining plan probably isn't for you. If, however, you plan on dining out most, if not all, of the time, the dining plan will definitely save you money in the end.

Will you actually eat three meals a day, or some days will you want only two meals? Do you prefer to eat breakfast in your hotel room (stocking the room with cereal and other breakfast items) on most days (or only some days)? Choosing the right dining plan—one that includes only the number of meals you plan on actually using—is the key to saving money. If you know that you will dine out only twice a day, purchase a plan that includes only two meals. Spending on a plan that includes meals that will go to waste defeats the entire purpose.

Also keep in mind that the biggest perks included in the Premium and Platinum plans are not even related to dining; they are reflective of the vacation package rather than the actual dining plan. Consider these only if the added perks are of interest to you. The average guest will generally find the Disney Quick-Service Dining Plan and the basic Disney Dining Plan more than adequate; those who enjoy dining out for all three meals should also consider the Disney Deluxe Plan.

When comparing the price of any given dining plan to the amount you would pay at restaurants on your own, the dining plan comes out ahead every time—but only if you use all your credits.

UNIVERSAL & SEAWORLD OPTIONS

Universal and SeaWorld have also tossed meal plans into the mix of offerings (albeit rather abridged versions when compared to the Disney Dining Plan).

The **Universal Meal Deal** (good at only a very select number of theme-park restaurants) allows you an unlimited number of trips through the line at participating restaurants, at a cost of $20.99 for adults and $9.99 for children 3 to 9 for 1 day at a single park, $24.99 for adults and $11.99 for children 3 to 9 for 1 day at both parks. A single entree and a dessert are included in each trip through the line. Drinks are not included, but you can add on a Meal Deal Sipper Cup, allowing 1 day of unlimited fountain drinks at participating restaurants, for a price of $8.99. Although the amount of food can make this a cost-effective option, the limited number of participating restaurants makes it far less appealing.

SeaWorld's All-Day Dining Deal costs $29.99 per adult, $14.99 per child ages 3 to 9. The deal includes an entree, a nonalcoholic drink, and either a side or a dessert each time you pass through the restaurant line (which you can do an unlimited number of times per visit). The dining deal is not valid at snack carts or signature dining experiences (Sharks Underwater Grill or the Makahiki Luau); however, for the average guest, it can be a cost-effective option as long as you plan on eating at least two meals at the park.

THE best DINING BETS

It may not have the lineup or caliber of restaurants of, say, New York or San Francisco, but Orlando's diverse dining scene offers an array of eateries that will please the palate of even finicky foodies. That said, keep in mind that for the most part Orlando is a family destination first and foremost—and therefore caters mostly to the masses. Here are my picks for the best eating in town.

○ **Best for Kids:** Kids adore the meals served up with Disney characters bounding about, and there are plenty to choose from throughout the **Walt Disney World** resorts and theme parks. (For the scoop, see "Only in Orlando: Dining with Disney Characters," p. 153.) They also love the eclectic atmosphere, sounds, and visuals of the jungle-themed **Rainforest Cafe** (𝄢 407/827-8500) and the **T-Rex Cafe** (𝄢 **407/828-8739**), its prehistoric-themed sibling—both located at the **Downtown Disney Marketplace** (a second Rainforest Cafe can be found at Disney's Animal Kingdom; 𝄢 **407/938-9100**). If horsing around is more your style, try dining at the **Whispering Canyon Café** (𝄢 **407/939-3463**), inside Disney's Wilderness Lodge, for some foot-stomping fun.

○ **Best Character Meal:** It doesn't get any better than **Chef Mickey's** breakfasts and dinners at the Contemporary Resort (𝄢 **407/939-3463**). These "events" have their respective namesake and other characters, but a word of warning: They also attract *up to 1,600 guests* each morning. A close second is a meal at the **Crystal Palace Buffet** (𝄢 **407/939-3463**), located in the Magic Kingdom. You will not see Mickey and Minnie, but your kids will be greeted at your table by Winnie the Pooh, Tigger, and some of their pals. For additional options, check out "Only in Orlando: Dining with Disney Characters," p. 153.

○ **Best Spot for a Romantic Dinner: Victoria & Albert's** (𝄢 **407/939-3463**) will spoil you with superior service and lavish surroundings. Dinner in the main dining room is an intimate seven-course meal offering some of the finest food around, the experience topped only by the 10-course meal offered in the new and very intimate Queen Victoria's Room, with only four tables.

○ **Best View:** The **California Grill** (𝄢 **407/939-3463**), high atop Disney's Contemporary Resort, offers a spectacular view of the Magic Kingdom, as well as a front-row seat for the park's nightly fireworks display through its immense floor-to-ceiling windows.

- **Best Wine List:** For something a bit out of the ordinary, try **Jiko—The Cooking Place** (✆ **407/939-3463**), at Disney's Animal Kingdom Lodge; it features one of the most extensive collections (65 vintages) of South African wines in the country.

- **Best Value:** At **Taverna Opa** (✆ **407/351-8660**), in the Pointe Orlando complex, the casual yet lively ambience and the Mediterranean cuisine score very high, and prices are low, low, low.

- **Best Asian Cuisine:** The **Mikado Japanese Steakhouse** (✆ **407/239-4200**), in Marriott Orlando World Center, offers a tastier meal and a more intimate atmosphere than other Japanese steakhouses in the area. For Chinese cuisine, head to **Ming Court** (✆ **407/351-9988**), which offers a menu as impressive as its elaborate surroundings. **Emeril's Tchoup Chop** (✆ **407/503-2467**) takes your taste buds on a tour of the Pacific Rim islands, while its chic and trendy decor is among the most inviting around.

- **Best Barbecue:** Follow your nose to **Bubbalou's Bodacious BBQ** (✆ **407/295-1212**) after catching a whiff of the tangy hickory smoke. It tastes as good as it smells.

- **Best Italian Cuisine:** It's a toss-up between **Bice** (✆ **407/503-1415**), at Universal's Portofino Bay Hotel, with its chic yet elegant atmosphere, and the more casual **Portobello,** in Downtown Disney's Marketplace (✆ **407/934-8888**).

- **Best Seafood:** Of the area's many seafood restaurants, the best around is **Ocean Prime** (✆ **407/781-4880**), which combines a lively Sinatra-inspired supper-club atmosphere with a menu filled with fresh ocean fare and service that is simply unsurpassed. **Fulton's Crab House** (✆ **407/934-2628**) offers a creative menu and a rich wine list. **Todd English's bluezoo** (✆ **407/934-1111**) blends a unique atmosphere with creative seafood dishes to great success.

- **Best Tapas:** **Café Tu Tu Tango** (✆ **407/248-2222**) takes the tapas concept to another dimension, serving items ranging from Cajun egg rolls with blackened chicken to alligator bites in a fabulous artist-loft atmosphere.

- **Best Steakhouse:** The **Capital Grille** (✆ **407/370-4392**) serves up a menu of dry-aged steaks, chops, and seafood (all prepared to perfection) combined with an award-winning collection of over 400 wines in an elegant upscale atmosphere. Dining at **Texas de Brazil Churrascaria** (✆ **407/355-0355**) is an experience not to be missed, as melt-in-your-mouth cuts of beef, pork, lamb, and chicken are served up tableside at this upscale eatery.

- **Best Late-Night Dining:** The trendy **B-Line Diner** (✆ **407/345-4460**), at the Peabody Orlando, is open around-the-clock for eclectic fare ranging from steaks to falafel sandwiches to grits and eggs. You won't be able to pass up one of the decadent desserts.

- **Best Spot for Celebrating:** **Emeril's** (✆ **407/224-2424**), at Universal's CityWalk, and **Tchoup Chop** (✆ **407/503-2467**), at Universal's Royal Pacific Resort, are great choices for a high-end special occasion. For the pure party factor, you can't beat **Jimmy Buffett's Margaritaville** (✆ **407/224-2155**), at CityWalk.

- **Best Outdoor Dining:** The terrace at **Artist Point** (✆ **407/939-3463**), the premier restaurant at Disney's Wilderness Lodge, overlooks a lake, waterfall, and scenery evocative of America's national parks. The **Rose & Crown Pub & Dining Room** (✆ **407/939-3463**) and **La Cantina de San Angel** (✆ **407/939-3463**) deliver a front-row seat for Epcot's IllumiNations fireworks display.

o **Best Sunday Brunch:** The champagne brunch at **La Coquina** (*©* **407/239-3853**), at the Hyatt Regency Grand Cypress Resort, is served in a sun-drenched atmosphere overlooking a lake. The menu usually features such treats as quail, duck, lamb chops, Cornish hen, clams, mussels, snapper, sea bass, sushi, a selection of breakfast favorites, and much more. For a themed brunch, the **House of Blues** (*©* **407/934-2583**), at Disney's West Side, has a down-home gospel brunch featuring live foot-stomping music and an array of Southern/Creole vittles. The food is so-so—the same quality as at a dinner show, which this is, morning style—but the entertainment makes it a certifiable winner.

IN WALT DISNEY WORLD

From fast food on the fly to fine-dining establishments, there are literally hundreds of restaurants scattered throughout Walt Disney World, including those at the theme parks (Epcot, Magic Kingdom, Disney's Hollywood Studios, and Animal Kingdom), the Disney resorts, and the "official" hotels. And those totals don't include restaurants located throughout the Downtown Disney areas of Pleasure Island (soon to be Hyperion Wharf), the West Side, and the Marketplace, some of which are listed in the Lake Buena Vista section later in this chapter. As a general rule, the food at Disney is decent enough, though only a small handful of the restaurants truly qualifies as gourmet. Portions are generally large, practically ensuring that you'll never walk away hungry, though prices match portion sizes accordingly. Be prepared to spend a rather hefty amount each day for just a few meals, a snack, and a drink (or two). If you have kids, sharing may be a good option, especially with very young children who tend not to eat so much when on the go. For those unwilling to share, sit-down and counter-service eateries, at least in the theme parks, do offer pint-size platters in the $4-to-$9 range (though some may cost up to $12 or $14). Another option is to order a la carte, but don't expect to see this listed as an option on the restaurant menus—you have to ask.

The prices for meals at Orlando restaurants—except at theme parks and other attractions—are no more exorbitant than you'd find anywhere else. The better the restaurant, the higher the price you can expect to pay (though you shouldn't necessarily consider a restaurant's pricing a benchmark of its quality). To help you out a bit, the restaurants in this chapter have been categorized by the price of an average entree per person. In this chapter, restaurants in the **inexpensive** category charge less than $10 for an entree; those in the **moderate** category charge anywhere from $11 to $20. **Expensive** restaurants will set you back $21 to $30, and **very expensive** restaurants will top that, sometimes by a rather large margin. Do note that when you toss in drinks, appetizers, side dishes, desserts, and the tip, the final tally at even a moderate restaurant can get rather high. Be sure to budget accordingly.

One last note: The restaurants listed in this chapter occasionally change menus (sometimes seasonally, occasionally weekly, in some cases even daily). So items I feature here may not necessarily be on the menu when you visit. And, as entrees vary, so do prices.

That said, it's time to divide and conquer.

Special Tastes

When it comes to eating at Disney, just because something's not on the menu doesn't mean it's not available. Looking for kosher food? Worried WDW can't entertain your vegetarian taste buds? What about low-sodium, low-sugar, or fat-free diets? Disney can usually handle these and other lifestyle diets as well as other special dietary requirements (meals for those with allergies or lactose intolerance) at any of its full-service restaurants as long as guests give advance notice—3 days is suggested to accommodate special dietary needs, while at least 24 hours is necessary for lifestyle diets (48 hr. if you are dining at the WDW Swan & Dolphin, Yak & Yeti, Rainforest Cafe, or T-Rex). This holds true for other dining requests, too. If you are headed to one of the resort's restaurants and know your kids may have a tough time with the menu, chicken nuggets and some other kid-friendly items can be requested in advance. (*Note:* Kosher meals are not available at Teppan Edo or Tokyo Dining.) It's easiest to make special requests when you make your Advance Reservations (✆ 407/939-3463) or, if you're staying at a Disney resort, by stopping by the lobby concierge desk.

In Epcot

The world is at your feet at Epcot, quite literally. In addition to the restaurants found at Future World, the World Showcase features several ethnic cuisines from around the globe, all served in some rather impressive settings. Though dining at one of the World Showcase pavilions is a traditional part of the Epcot experience, I remind you that many of the following establishments are rather overpriced when compared to an equivalent restaurant beyond the park's boundaries. Unless your budget is unlimited, you may want to consider the more casual counter-service eateries located throughout the park and save the sit-down service for somewhere else. These informal dining spots don't require Advance Reservations (for details, check the Epcot guide map that you picked up upon entering the park) and often go overlooked. If you simply can't resist a more formal meal (and it is difficult at times), try the full-service restaurants at lunchtime, when the price for a meal is much lower than at dinner. Almost all of the establishments listed here serve lunch and dinner daily (hours vary with park hours), and, unless otherwise noted, they offer children's meals. All require theme-park admission and the $14 parking fee. These restaurants are located on the "Epcot Restaurants" map, on p. 109.

Note: Because the clientele at even the fanciest Epcot World Showcase restaurant comes directly from the park, you don't have to dress up for dinner, but do bring along a sweater or sweatshirt to ward off the sometimes chilly indoor temperatures. **Advance Reservations** (✆ **407/939-3463**), which reserve your place but not a specific table, are available at all WDW sit-down restaurants and are strongly recommended. Otherwise, the chances of getting a table without a wait—often a long wait—are pretty slim (and you run the risk of not getting a table at all).

EXPENSIVE

Biergarten GERMAN   The Biergarten, with its festive atmosphere, feels like a Bavarian village at Oktoberfest. A working water wheel and geranium-filled flower

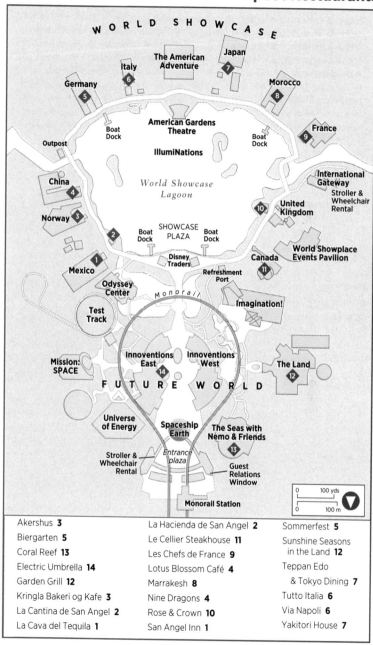

Akershus **3**

Biergarten **5**

Coral Reef **13**

Electric Umbrella **14**

Garden Grill **12**

Kringla Bakeri og Kafe **3**

La Cantina de San Angel **2**

La Cava del Tequila **1**

La Hacienda de San Angel **2**

Le Cellier Steakhouse **11**

Les Chefs de France **9**

Lotus Blossom Café **4**

Marrakesh **8**

Nine Dragons **4**

Rose & Crown **10**

San Angel Inn **1**

Sommerfest **5**

Sunshine Seasons
in the Land **12**

Teppan Edo
& Tokyo Dining **7**

Tutto Italia **6**

Via Napoli **6**

Yakitori House **7**

4

In Walt Disney World

WHERE TO EAT

boxes adorn the Tudor-style houses that line the dining area. An oompah band entertains with accordions and cowbells, and guests are encouraged to dance and sing along. The all-you-can-eat buffet is filled with Bavarian fare (assorted sausages, pork schnitzel, sauerbraten, spaetzle, and sauerkraut), as well as rotisserie chicken, pork, and salmon. Beck's and Kirschwasser—served in immense steins—are both on tap for adults.

Germany Pavilion, World Showcase. ☎ **407/939-3463.** www.disneyworld.com. Advance Reservations recommended. Lunch buffet $20 adults, $11 kids; dinner buffet $33 adults, $14 kids. AE, DC, DISC, MC, V. Daily noon–3:10pm and 4–8:50pm (last show at 8–8:15pm). Parking $14.

Coral Reef SEAFOOD   All of the seating at this aptly named establishment surrounds a 5.6-million-gallon aquarium filled with tropical fish and a coral reef. While some of Disney's denizens swim by, songs such as Debussy's "La Mer" and Handel's "Water Music" softly play in the background. Tiered seating, mainly in semicircular booths, allows everyone a good view. You'll be provided with pictorial fish listings so you can put names on the faces swimming by your table. This is one of the most popular restaurants in all of the parks, especially with kids—what could be better than a fish tank of tremendous proportions to entertain tinier tots while you eat? The menu primarily features fresh seafood and shellfish, including grilled mahimahi, roasted Scottish salmon, and jumbo sea scallops. A selection of landlubber fare is available as well. Wine is available by the glass.

Living Seas Pavilion, Future World. ☎ **407/939-3463.** www.disneyworld.com. Advance Reservations recommended. Main courses $15–$29 lunch, $19–$32 dinner, $9 kids. AE, DC, DISC, MC, V. Daily 11:30am–3pm and 4:30pm–park closing. Parking $14.

Le Cellier Steakhouse CANADIAN/STEAK   This restaurant's French Gothic facade and steeply pitched copper roofs lend it a castlelike ambience. The lantern-lit dining room resembles a wine cellar, and you'll sit in tapestry-upholstered chairs under vaulted stone arches. If you're in the mood for steak, this is the right place; offerings include the usual range of cuts (though a new menu—and a new chef—made a debut in 2011). Options beyond beef include roasted duck with cheddar-bread pudding, Swiss chard, and pepper jelly (adding just the right kick); Pacific king salmon with parsnip purée and braised greens; and seared gooseberry cod accompanied by braised oxtail ravioli. New to the menu are an artisanal spicy chicken served with chipotle sausage and roasted corn polenta, and a tasty black-and-blue beef steak tartare with grilled jumbo asparagus gratin drizzled in a creamy Hollandaise. The lunch menu features lighter fare, including sandwiches and salads, along with a selection of meatier meals. Wash down your meal with a Canadian wine or choose from a selection of Canadian beers; for an after-dinner treat, try a Canadian ice wine.

Canada Pavilion, World Showcase. ℂ **407/939-3463.** www.disneyworld.com. Advance Reservations recommended. Main courses $15–$32 lunch, $21–$42 dinner, $9 kids. AE, DC, DISC, MC, V. Daily noon–3pm and 3:30pm to park closing. Parking $14.

Les Chefs de France NOUVELLE FRENCH   Focusing on nouvelle cuisine, Les Chefs de France is one of the most expensive restaurants at Epcot, but not without good reason. An eye-catching, domed-glass exterior hides an intimate Art Nouveau interior, filled with candelabras and glass-and-brass partitions. An outdoor dining area adds to the authentic brasserie atmosphere. You can credit three internationally acclaimed chefs—Paul Bocuse, Roger Verge, and Gaston LeNotre—with the menu here, which combines fresh Florida ingredients with a good dose of French imports. Light sauces (when compared to more traditional French cooking, that is) complement such tasty entrees as grilled tenderloin of beef with a black-pepper sauce, potato gratin, and green beans; or broiled salmon served with tomato Béarnaise and ratatouille. A substantial wine list complements the menu, and the desserts and pastries are among the best in the World. The service, however, can get a bit lackluster when the restaurant is busy. If a slightly more formal setting (and a pricier dinner) is what you're seeking, try the **Bistro de Paris,** just upstairs.

France Pavilion, World Showcase. ℂ **407/939-3463.** www.disneyworld.com. Advance Reservations recommended. Main courses $16–$23 lunch, $19–$35 dinner; $37 prix fixe. AE, DC, DISC, MC, V. Daily noon–3pm and 5pm to 1 hr. before park closes. Parking $14.

Marrakesh ★ MOROCCAN   This unique dining spot exemplifies the spirit of Epcot more than any other restaurant. The hand-set mosaic tiles, latticed shutters,

---

No Italian? No Way!

Longtime Epcot dining fixture L'Originale Alfredo di Roma is no longer on Epcot's menu of dining options. It's been replaced, by **Tutto Italia ★★**. Set inside one of the most beautiful of the world pavilions, the replacement retains its spot as one of Epcot's most popular restaurants, thanks to its fabulous food and noticeably friendly service. The elegant establishment features a menu filled with traditional pastas, fish, chicken, and pork; kids will find a small selection of familiar favorites. If you want a quieter setting, ask for a seat on the veranda overlooking the center courtyard. Lunch costs $15 to $28; dinner runs $22 to $36, with sides priced separately (about $8 a pop). Kids' meals run just under $10.

Via Napoli ★★, an authentic Neapolitan pizzeria—featuring a mouth-watering menu of handcrafted pizzas, pastas, sandwiches, and Italian wines—opened in 2010. The decor is upscale yet casual, with hand-painted murals along the seemingly aged walls, brick ovens surrounded by tremendous stone faces, and an eclectic collection of light fixtures accenting the entire establishment like artwork. The open kitchen along the perimeter gives way to tables that run the length of the room, with smaller, more intimate tables set along the edges. The menu at lunch and dinner is the same and runs $17 to $26 for entrees, $16 for an individual pizza, and upwards of $39 for a 12-slice pie. Seating for up to 300 (both indoor and outdoor) is available.

Traveling with less-than-adventurous eaters? WDW has plenty of familiar favorites for little ones more willing to ride the roller coasters than try unfamiliar foods (though pint-size portions of more adventurous items such as mahimahi, salmon, and steak, among others, are available, too). Topping the menus are PB&J, pizza, chicken strips, grilled chicken, grilled cheese sandwiches, turkey sandwiches, macaroni and cheese, burgers, hot dogs, pizzas, pastas, and french fries (now available only upon request), among others.

The **Electric Umbrella,** for example, is a counter-service eatery located near Innoventions in Epcot. It serves up familiar fare including burgers and chicken nuggets, making it especially popular with younger kids with picky palates. Note that because it is one of only two quick-service eateries located in Future World (the third option, Coral Reef, is a full-service sit-down restaurant), expect the lines to be long and the tables to be filled no matter the time of day. Try upstairs first, as the lower level is often filled with families toting strollers.

4

In Walt Disney World

WHERE TO EAT

and painted ceiling represent some 12 centuries of Arabic design. Exquisitely carved faux-ivory archways frame the dining area. Unfortunately, many guests shy away, mistakenly thinking the cuisine's just too exotic—but don't be put off. The menu features marinated beef and chicken shish kabobs; braised chicken with green olives, garlic, and lemon; and a medley of seafood, chicken, and lamb. Most entrees come with the national dish, couscous (steamed semolina with veggies). If you can't decide what you want, sampler platters featuring a taste of everything are available. Belly dancers and musicians entertain while you dine. There's a small selection of wine and beer.

Morocco Pavilion, World Showcase. ✆ **407/939-3463.** www.disneyworld.com. Advance Reservations recommended. Main courses $15–$28 lunch, $21–$29 dinner, $5–$8 kids; $42–$45 prix fixe. AE, DC, DISC, MC, V. Daily noon to park closing. Parking $14.

San Angel Inn ★ MEXICAN It's always nighttime at the San Angel, where you can dine under starry skies (a la Disney) and feast on some of the best south-of-the-border cuisine in all of the theme parks. The restaurant offers one of the best (and most romantic) atmospheres around. Against the backdrop of the marketplace, candlelit tables set the mood, and the menu delivers reasonably authentic food—don't expect to find Americanized hard-shell tacos and nachos here. *Mole poblano* (chicken simmered in a combination of chili, green tomatoes, ground tortillas, 11 spices, and a hint of chocolate) is a popular choice. Another favorite is *sirloin con chili relleno* (grilled sirloin served with a spicy *chili ancho* sauce and accompanied by black beans, cheese-stuffed pepper strips, and fried plantains). The occasional rumble of a volcano and the sounds of the distant songbirds can be heard as you wait for your dinner—you may find yourself singing right along if you've tried too many margaritas or had more than your limit of Dos Equis. **La Cava del Tequila,** a new tequila bar, now serves up some 70 types of tequila alongside a selection of tasty tapas-style treats (inside the pavilion).

Note: If the restaurant is booked (as it often is), head to **La Hacienda de San Angel** (located just across from the San Angel Inn, and adjacent to the recently refurbished Cantina)—Epcot's newest addition to its lineup of sit-down eateries, with room for up to 250 guests. Slightly more casual than its older sibling, La Hacienda serves up a menu of authentic Mexican dishes in an architecturally inviting atmosphere. The delectable entrees here might include flank steak served with spring onions, tamal with rajas, cactus leaves, and beans; a roast pork tenderloin with mole negro sauce, roasted corn, and sweet potato mash; or grilled tilapia served with roasted corn, cactus leaves, and a sweet mango chutney—all running about $25. Kids will appreciate familiar favorites such as tacos, nachos, and chicken tenders. Dinner service begins at 4pm daily.

Mexico Pavilion, World Showcase. ⓒ **407/939-3463.** www.disneyworld.com. Advance Reservations recommended. Main courses $15–$25 lunch, $23–$30 dinner. AE, DC, DISC, MC, V. Daily 11:30am to park closing. Parking $14.

Teppan Edo JAPANESE   After extensive renovations a few years back, the old Teppanyaki Dining reopened as Teppan Edo. While retaining its original appeal—chefs expertly slicing, dicing, and preparing your meal right before your eyes—the restaurant now features a chic upscale interior. The culinary acrobatics here are a sight to see, though the cuisine is only average. Expect entrees that include chicken, steak, shrimp, scallops, lobster, or a combination. Miso soup, a small salad with ginger dressing, stir-fried veggies, and white rice accompany every meal. Next door you'll find **Tokyo Dining** (replacing the Matsunoma Lounge and Tempura Kiku), where the menu may side on the traditional (with an emphasis on sushi), but the atmosphere is trendy with an Asian touch. Sit near the windows for great views of Illumi-Nations. Entrees run $15 to $30; kids can dine for $11 to $12.

Japan Pavilion, World Showcase. ⓒ **407/939-3463.** www.disneyworld.com. Advance Reservations recommended. Main courses $20–$30 lunch, $20–$30 dinner, $11–$12 kids. AE, DC, DISC, MC, V. Daily 11am to 1 hr. before park closes. Parking $14.

MODERATE

Nine Dragons CHINESE   After extensive renovations in recent years, the Nine Dragons shines with brightly colored lanterns and silk hangings accenting a now simplified modern decor (with the servers sporting modernized attire to match the new look). Brightened by numerous windows overlooking the lagoon, the restaurant is airy and open. But (is there an echo?) the food, while tasty and artistically presented, doesn't quite match its surroundings. Main courses cover a variety of Chinese regional cuisines, but portions are quite small and prices are high, especially when compared to Chinese restaurants elsewhere. The selection of hot and cold appetizers is the highlight of the now-shortened menu: The Dioa Yu Tai cucumber salad is lightly spiced and has a sweetly sour bite, the spicy beef is sliced paper thin and accompanied by a cilantro-chili dressing that packs a bit of a kick, and the shrimp summer rolls—stuffed with fresh Asian veggies and wrapped in rice paper—include a rich peanut dipping sauce. Boxed lunches, family dinners, and appetizer samplers offer a chance to try a bit of everything. Chinese and California wines are offered.

China Pavilion, World Showcase. ⓒ **407/939-3463.** www.disneyworld.com. Advance Reservations recommended. Main courses $13–$22 lunch, $13–$26 dinner, $8–10 kids. AE, DC, DISC, MC, V. Daily 11:30am to park closing. Parking $14.

Rose & Crown Pub & Dining Room ENGLISH   Visitors from the U.K. flock to this spot, where English folk music and the occasionally saucy server entertain as you feast your eyes and palate on a short but traditional menu. It beckons with cod and chips wrapped in newspaper, bangers and mash, grilled steak, cottage pie, and warm bread pudding. The interior has dark-oak wainscoting, beamed Tudor ceilings, and a

A Balancing Act

In an effort to promote better eating habits, Disney kids' menus have been revised over the past few years and now feature healthy options including low-fat milk, 100% fruit juice, water, and sides such as unsweetened applesauce, veggies, and fresh fruit. Soda pop and french fries are still available, but only upon request.

All of the WDW restaurants (in the theme parks and at the resorts) are also currently wrapping up the transition to become entirely trans-fat-free (a trend that is just beginning to take hold at other area theme parks).

belly-up bar. Speaking of the bar, it features slightly lighter fare including corned beef sandwiches, fish and chips, a fried hard-boiled egg wrapped in sausage and mustard sauce, and a Stilton cheese and fruit plate. Wash it down with a pint of Irish lager, Bass Ale, or Guinness Stout (the pub has an ale warmer to make sure Guinness is served at 55°F/13°C, just like its British guests prefer). If you only want to grab a pint or a snack at the bar, you don't need Advance Reservations. *Note:* The outdoor tables, weather permitting, offer a fantastic view of IllumiNations. These seats are first-come, first-served, so ask the hostess when you arrive if a patio table is available (an expansion of the patio is coming soon).

Tip: If you're in a hurry, you can grab some tasty fish and chips to go at the **Yorkshire County Fish Shop,** a small quick-service kiosk adjoining the pub.

United Kingdom Pavilion, World Showcase. ✆ **407/939-3463.** www.disneyworld.com. Advance Reservations recommended for dining room, not necessary for pub. Main courses $11–$18 lunch, $15–$25 dinner, $9 kids; pub food $7–$12. AE, DC, DISC, MC, V. Daily 11am to 1 hr. before park closes. Parking $14.

INEXPENSIVE

Kringla Bakeri og Kafe NORWEGIAN   The lunch-pail crowd loves this combination cafe/bakery. Grab-and-go options include a plate of smoked salmon and scrambled eggs, or smoked ham and Jarlsberg cheese sandwiches, but it's the array of tempting pastries, cakes, cookies, and waffles with strawberry preserves that bring in the majority. Sit in the small, open-air seating area (just beyond the door, adjacent to the Stave Church and the replica Viking ship). Wine is sold by the glass.

Norway Pavilion, World Showcase. ✆ **407/939-3463.** www.disneyworld.com. Advance Reservations not accepted. Sandwiches and salads $4–$10; baked treats $2–$6. AE, DC, DISC, MC, V. Daily 11am to park closing. Parking $14.

La Cantina de San Angel MEXICAN   Counter-service eateries are the most common places to grab a bite in the parks, and this one's no exception (though its waterside location ensures that it is one of the park's most popular). Located directly across from the San Angel Inn, the newly renovated cantina features a menu of tacos, empanadas, nachos, guacamole, and other assorted items. You can also grab a Dos Equis or frozen margarita—the large semicovered patio (a result of a recent refit) overlooking the lagoon is the perfect spot to sit and sip your drink (and if you time it right, a great spot to catch IllumiNations). Extensive refurbishments also included the addition of a new indoor table-service establishment (with a separate menu and family casual atmosphere).

Mexico Pavilion, World Showcase. ✆ **407/939-3463.** www.disneyworld.com. Advance Reservations not accepted. Meals $9–$12. AE, DC, DISC, MC, V. Daily 11:30am to 1 hr. before park closes. Parking $14.

Lotus Blossom Café CHINESE   If you're in a hurry but still in the mood for some good Chinese, this recently renovated counter-service stop offers a tasty beef noodle soup bowl, sesame-chicken salad, and fast-food favorites including egg rolls, pot stickers, stir-fry, and fried rice. A covered outdoor patio provides respite from the sun and views of the pavilion. Chinese beer and wine are available.

China Pavilion, World Showcase. ℂ **407/939-3463.** www.disneyworld.com. Advance Reservations not accepted. Meals $4–$8.50. AE, DC, DISC, MC, V. Daily 11am to park closing. Parking $14.

Sommerfest GERMAN   At the rear of the Germany Pavilion, this outdoor eatery's quick-bite menu includes bratwurst and frankfurter sandwiches (one is still a hot dog) with sauerkraut. The apple strudel goes nicely with a glass of German wine or a Beck's beer.

Germany Pavilion, World Showcase. ℂ **407/939-3463.** www.disneyworld.com. Advance Reservations not accepted. All meals less than $7. AE, DC, DISC, MC, V. Daily 11am to park closing. Parking $14.

Sunshine Seasons in the Land 🍴 FOOD COURT   This moderately upscale food court has a very contemporary earthy decor, continuing the look and feel of the intricate mosaic leading to its entrance. The large, open seating area is separated into smaller sections by decorative partitions; open to the second story, it retains an airy feel. The food isn't gourmet, but of all the cafeterias and counter-service stops in the World, Sunshine Seasons has the most diversity because it is five walk-ups in one. It's especially good if you're traveling with kids who possess finicky (and varied) palates; it's often crowded with families for that very reason. There's an Asian Wok shop (stir-fry and barbecue), a wood-fired grill (grilled chicken, pork, and fish), a sandwich shop (grilled veggie flatbread, Reuben panini, turkey and Monterey jack on focaccia), a soup-and-salad counter (with veggies from the Land's own gardens), and a small bakery. An open kitchen allows everyone to watch the behind-the-scenes action. Wine by the glass, frosty drafts, and bottled beer are available.

Land Pavilion, Future World. ℂ **407/939-3463.** www.disneyworld.com. Advance Reservations not accepted. Meals $7–$11. AE, DC, DISC, MC, V. 11am to park closing. Parking $14.

Yakitori House JAPANESE   Resembling the teahouse of the Imperial Summer Palace, this small eatery offers a menu of teriyaki chicken, salmon, and beef; Japanese curry rice; sushi; tempura shrimp; and chicken ginger salad, among other light delights. The food is reasonably good, with an updated menu replacing what was a somewhat blah selection (though it's still not particularly stellar), but portions are smaller than at many other Disney restaurants. There's seating both indoors and out, but no matter where you dine, you'll be overlooking tranquil Japanese gardens and a gentle waterfall.

Japan Pavilion, World Showcase. ℂ **407/939-3463.** www.disneyworld.com. Advance Reservations not accepted. Meals $9–$13. AE, DC, DISC, MC, V. 11am to park closing. Parking $14.

In the Magic Kingdom

In addition to the restaurants mentioned below, there are plenty of fast-food outlets located throughout the park. You may find, however, that a quiet sit-down meal is an essential but all-too-brief way to get away from the day's activities. The restaurants listed below can all be found on the "Walt Disney World & Lake Buena Vista Restaurants" map, on p. 118. See also "The Magic Kingdom" map, on p. 176. And remember—Magic Kingdom restaurants *don't serve alcohol.*

For information on Magic Kingdom's Crystal Palace restaurant, see "Only in Orlando: Dining with Disney Characters," at the end of this chapter.

VERY EXPENSIVE

Cinderella's Royal Table ★ AMERICAN   You'll be greeted by none other than Cinderella herself before making your way inside this royal restaurant—by far the most popular place to dine in the Magic Kingdom. Those who enter are usually swept off their feet as they're transported back to a time when medieval kings and queens reigned (a feeling that's helped along by the Gothic interior, which includes leaded-glass windows, stone floors, and high-beamed ceilings). Upon your arrival, the royal photographer will snap a few photos of your group to be delivered during your meal (and are included in the price). The servers treat you like a lord or lady (I'm not kidding; that's how they'll address you), and the menu has fetching names, but the fine print reveals traditional entrees. Braised cobia, duck confit, and roasted beef tenderloin are just a sampling of the choices.

The restaurant recently expanded its character dining experience to include not only breakfast but lunch and dinner as well. Breakfast remains an all-you-can-eat affair (served tableside), while lunch and dinner offer a selection of appetizers, entrees, and desserts to choose from (basic beverages are included; specialty coffees and smoothies will cost a bit extra). Disney princesses (and other members of the royal family) are on hand during breakfast, lunch, and dinner.

Note: Because of its location and ambience, a meal here is sought by everyone from little girls who dream of Prince Charming to romantics seeking a more intimate meal. The problem: This is actually one of the smallest dining rooms in the World, making Advance Reservations a must. And you'll have your work cut out for you to get one—it may very well take several calls (and a lot of flexibility on your part) to ensure a spot.

Cinderella Castle, Fantasyland. ✆ **407/939-3463.** www.disneyworld.com. Advance Reservations recommended. Character breakfast $47 adults, $31 kids; character lunch $51 adults, $32 kids; character dinner $57 adult, $35 kids. AE, DC, DISC, MC, V. Daily 8–11:15am, noon–3pm, and 4pm to 1 hr. before park closing. Parking $14.

EXPENSIVE

Tony's Town Square Restaurant ITALIAN   Inspired by the cafe in *Lady and the Tramp,* Tony's dishes up pastas and pizzas in a pleasant if somewhat harried dining room featuring etched glass and ornate gingerbread trim. The lunch menu includes sandwiches, salads, and pizzas, along with such entrees as pasta primavera, spaghetti and meatballs, and the catch of the day. Evening fare might include chicken Florentine, seafood in a spicy tomato sauce, or a New York strip steak. Kids will enjoy the pizzas and plainer pastas. Original cels from the movie (including the film's famous spaghetti smooch) line the walls. Additional seating is available in a sunny, plant-filled solarium that offers a view out over Main Street. *Tip:* Dinner is by far the busiest time to dine here, but if you time it just right, you can see the Wishes fireworks display after your meal while remaining close enough to the park exit to make a quicker getaway than most.

Main St. ✆ **407/939-3463.** www.disneyworld.com. Advance Reservations recommended. Main courses $12–$17 lunch, $17–$29 dinner, $9 kids. AE, DC, DISC, MC, V. Daily 11:30am–3pm and 4:30pm to park closing. Parking $14.

MODERATE

Liberty Tree Tavern AMERICAN   Step into a replica of an 18th-century Colonial pub and its historic atmosphere, including oak-plank floors, pewterware-stocked hutches, and a big brick fireplace hung with copper pots. The background music suits the period. Lunch includes sandwiches, seafood (such as cured salmon and crab cakes), salads, soups, burgers, roast turkey, and pot roast. Dinner is a set family-style meal (now sans the characters) that includes salad, roast turkey, carved beef, and smoked pork loin, with mashed potatoes, stuffing, and macaroni and cheese. Cherry cobbler and vanilla ice cream top it all off. While the fare's not that interesting, it is appropriate to the early-American setting.

Note: If you're looking for a buffet with a bit more to offer than just the usual fare, you could try Epcot's **Akershus Royal Banquet Hall** (p. 154) or Animal Kingdom Lodge's **Boma** (p. 124); if you don't want to venture outside the Magic Kingdom, this is your best option.

Liberty Sq. ℂ **407/939-3463.** www.disneyworld.com. Advance Reservations recommended. Main courses $13–$18 lunch; dinner buffet $32 adults, $15 kids. AE, DC, DISC, MC, V. Daily 11:30am–3pm and 4pm to park closing. Parking $14.

Plaza Restaurant AMERICAN   It shouldn't be confused with the nearby Plaza Ice Cream Parlor, but the sundaes, banana splits, and other ice-cream creations at this popular dining spot are arguably the best in WDW. This 19th-century-inspired restaurant features tasty if expensive sandwiches (turkey, Reuben, cheese-steak, chicken, vegetarian, tuna, and burgers) that come with fries or potato salad. You can eat indoors, in an intimate Art Nouveau dining room filled with glass and brass accents, or outdoors at umbrella-shaded tables on a veranda overlooking Cinderella Castle.

Main St. ℂ **407/939-3463.** www.disneyworld.com. Advance Reservations recommended. Meals $11–$15; ice cream $4.50–$9. AE, DC, DISC, MC, V. Daily 11am to park closing. Parking $14.

INEXPENSIVE

Columbia Harbour House ★ AMERICAN/SEAFOOD   This small restaurant often goes overlooked because of its location (across from the Haunted Mansion) and size—it features only a handful of cozy little rooms, all nautically themed—but it does offer some rather decent light fare. The menu features battered fish and chicken (far meatier than most), tasty tuna sandwiches, a BLT salad (with chicken, bacon, egg, and tomato), a hummus-and-tomato sandwich served up with a side of broccoli slaw, a harvest salad (with chicken, veggies, cheese, and sunflower seeds), clam chowder, and fruit.

Liberty Sq. ℂ **407/939-3643.** www.disneyworld.com. Advance Reservations not accepted. All items $8–$10, $5 kids. AE, DC, DISC, MC, V. Daily 11am to park closing. Parking $14.

Cosmic Ray's Starlight Café AMERICAN   The largest of the park's fast-food spots, this cafe features an appropriately huge menu. Three separate counters, similar to a food court, serve a variety of chicken options (whole- or half-rotisserie, dark meat, white meat, fried, or grilled), ribs, sandwiches, burgers, hot dogs, veggie wraps, soups, and salads. The casual atmosphere and varied menu make Ray's a great choice for those with kids (who also enjoy the occasional mealtime entertainment by "alien" Sonny Eclipse). Do note, however, that you may have to wait in more than one line here, as each station offers a different selection. Other minuses: The large dining area fills up quickly at lunch and dinner, and the noise level is generally high. **Tip:** Kosher meals are available here for direct purchase (though they're pricey and not particularly noteworthy in the taste department).

Main St. ℂ **407/939-3463.** www.disneyworld.com. Advance Reservations not accepted. All items $7–$14. AE, DC, DISC, MC, V. Daily 11am to park closing. Parking $14.

4

WHERE TO EAT

In Walt Disney World

Walt Disney World & Lake Buena Vista Restaurants

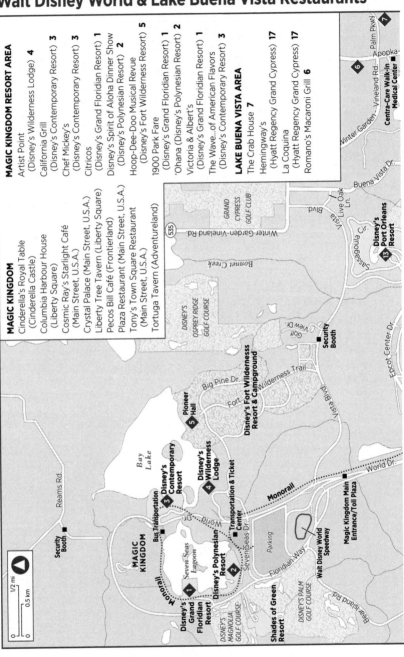

MAGIC KINGDOM

Cinderella's Royal Table
(Cinderella Castle)

Columbia Harbour House
(Liberty Square)

Cosmic Ray's Starlight Café
(Main Street, U.S.A.)

Crystal Palace (Main Street, U.S.A.)

Liberty Tree Tavern (Liberty Square)

Pecos Bill Café (Frontierland)

Plaza Restaurant (Main Street, U.S.A.)

Tony's Town Square Restaurant
(Main Street, U.S.A.)

Tortuga Tavern (Adventureland)

MAGIC KINGDOM RESORT AREA

Artist Point
(Disney's Wilderness Lodge) **4**

California Grill
(Disney's Contemporary Resort) **3**

Chef Mickey's
(Disney's Contemporary Resort) **3**

Citricos
(Disney's Grand Floridian Resort) **1**

Disney's Spirit of Aloha Dinner Show
(Disney's Polynesian Resort) **2**

Hoop-Dee-Doo Musical Revue
(Disney's Fort Wilderness Resort) **5**

1900 Park Fare
(Disney's Grand Floridian Resort) **1**

'Ohana (Disney's Polynesian Resort) **2**

Victoria & Albert's
(Disney's Grand Floridian Resort) **1**

The Wave...of American Flavors
(Disney's Contemporary Resort) **3**

LAKE BUENA VISTA AREA

The Crab House **7**

Hemingway's
(Hyatt Regency Grand Cypress) **17**

La Coquina
(Hyatt Regency Grand Cypress) **17**

Romano's Macaroni Grill **6**

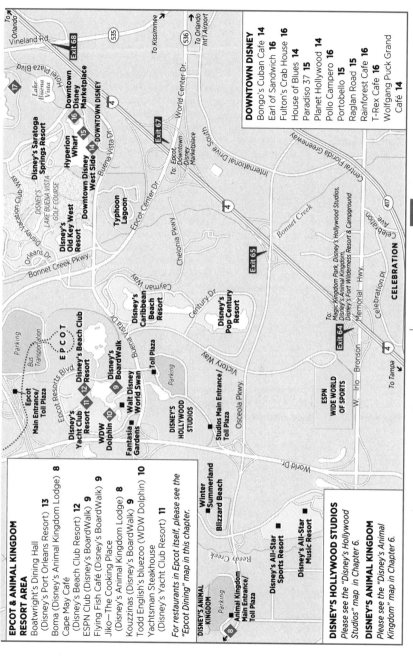

EPCOT & ANIMAL KINGDOM RESORT AREA

Boatwright's Dining Hall
(Disney's Port Orleans Resort) **13**
Boma (Disney's Animal Kingdom Lodge) **8**
Cape May Café
(Disney's Beach Club Resort) **12**
ESPN Club (Disney's BoardWalk) **9**
Flying Fish Café (Disney's BoardWalk) **9**
Jiko—The Cooking Place
(Disney's Animal Kingdom Lodge) **8**
Kouzzinas (Disney's BoardWalk) **9**
Todd English's bluezoo (WDW Dolphin) **10**
Yachtsman Steakhouse
(Disney's Yacht Club Resort) **11**

For restaurants in Epcot itself, please see the "Epcot Dining" map in this chapter.

DISNEY'S ANIMAL KINGDOM

Please see the "Disney's Animal Kingdom" map in Chapter 6.

DISNEY'S HOLLYWOOD STUDIOS

Please see the "Disney's Hollywood Studios" map in Chapter 6.

DOWNTOWN DISNEY

Bongo's Cuban Cafe **14**
Earl of Sandwich **16**
Fulton's Crab House **16**
House of Blues **14**
Paradiso 37 **15**
Planet Hollywood **14**
Pollo Campero **16**
Portobello **15**
Raglan Road **15**
Rainforest Cafe **16**
T-Rex Cafe **16**
Wolfgang Puck Grand Café **14**

The menu at **Tomorrowland Terrace** includes a potpourri of quick dishes such as cheeseburgers, fried chicken sandwiches, pasta primavera and pasta Alfredo, lobster rolls, beef and blue salad, chicken nuggets, and assorted desserts. Kids' meals include familiar favorites such as PB&J, macaroni and cheese, and chicken nuggets. It's one of the prettiest and largest outdoor seating areas in the park; you can eat out in the fresh air even as you get a respite from the hot Florida sun. And as an added bonus, you get a great view of the gardens, waterways, and Cinderella Castle. If you've picked up a sweet treat along one of Main Street's eateries and can't find a place to sit down (often the case), this is the perfect place to head, as it's often overlooked by visitors. *Note:* The Terrace is a seasonal eatery that closes sporadically, so be sure to check your guide map to see if it's open when you're visiting. All items cost $7 to $9.

Another on-again/off-again eatery at the Magic Kingdom is the **Diamond Horseshoe.** This saloon-themed space functions as a counter-service spot only when the park is in need of an additional dining venue for visitors. Check your *Times Guide* to see if it's open when you're here—in the past it has served up sandwiches during lunch and full-fledged all-you-can-eat family-style dinners during the holidays and peak travel seasons (lunch runs $7–$9; dinner, $15 for kids and $28 for adults). Because it's not well publicized, it's often a quieter and less crowded option than the usual hot spots.

Pecos Bill Café ★ AMERICAN   Set in an old-time saloon of sorts, with ornate wrought-iron accents, tile work, heavy flamelike chandeliers, and a golden stucco interior, this sit-and-go fast-food joint serves up burgers, salads (taco and chicken Caesar), a barbecued pork sandwich, and a great chicken wrap. There's also a fixin's bar full of extras. Portions are large, and like all other park dining options, so are the prices. Its good location—just between Frontierland and Adventureland—means that those traveling clockwise through the park will probably hit the area just in time for lunch. It can get very crowded at peak meal times, though there is quite a bit of indoor and outdoor seating. If you want to save time and avoid waiting in line, self-service kiosks (located to the far left of the counter) now allow you to place and pay (credit cards only) for your order yourself.

Tip: If your cravings run more toward Mexican than American, head through the indoor seating area in the back to the seasonal **Tortuga Tavern** (El Pirata y Perico in a previous life), a covered outdoor snack spot featuring tacos, burritos, chips, and taco salad (all under $8). It's located in Adventureland, just across from Pirates of the Caribbean.

Frontierland. ℂ **407/939-3643.** www.disneyworld.com. Advance Reservations not accepted. All items $7–$9, $5 kids. AE, DC, DISC, MC, V. Daily 11am to park closing. Parking $14.

At Disney's Hollywood Studios

Some of the one-of-a-kind themed restaurants in all of WDW are set among the movie sets, action-packed shows, and wild rides of Disney's Hollywood Studios. That fact, in turn, makes them some of the most difficult to get into. Be sure to make Advance Reservations if you want to eat at any full-service restaurant here. Listed below are the best of the bunch. They're located on two maps, "Walt Disney World & Lake Buena Vista Restaurants" (p. 118) and "Disney's Hollywood Studios" (p. 215).

VERY EXPENSIVE

Hollywood Brown Derby AMERICAN   This elegant restaurant is modeled after the famed Los Angeles celebrity haunt where Louella Parsons and Hedda Hopper once held court. It features some of the finest food and the fanciest surroundings in the park—along with some of the highest prices. White linens top dark-wood tables, chandeliers and amber lighting set the mood, and potted palms add to the upscale atmosphere. Lining the walls are more than 1,500 caricatures of its most famous patrons through the years, including Lucille Ball, Bette Davis, and Clark Gable. Owner Bob Cobb created the original restaurant's signature Cobb salad in the 1930s. (It's so popular that this Derby serves more than 31,000 of them a year.) Dinner entrees at Disney's version include pan-fried grouper with balsamic roasted asparagus; sesame-seared ahi tuna with honey-gingered spaghetti squash, shiitake broth, and wasabi oil; and roasted pork rib chop with smoked cheese–tomato fondue. The Derby's signature dessert, grapefruit cake with cream-cheese icing, is the perfect way to end your meal. The Derby features a full bar and a modest selection of California wines.

Hollywood Blvd. ✆ **407/939-3463.** www.disneyworld.com. Advance Reservations recommended. Main courses $28–$40 lunch and dinner; $6–$9 kids; Fantasmic! package varies (a la carte pricing). AE, DC, DISC, MC, V. Daily 11:30am to park closing. Parking $14.

MODERATE

50's Prime Time Café ☺ AMERICAN   Ever want to go back to when life was simpler? Well, you can here, even if it's just for a meal. Several homey dining rooms, separated by knickknack-lined shelves and curtained windows, look just like Mom's kitchen did back in the 1950s, complete with Formica countertops, stove, fridge, and black-and-white TVs showing clips from classics such as *My Little Margie*. The servers add to the fun, greeting diners with such lines as, "Hi Sis, I'll go tell Mom you're home," and they may threaten to withhold dessert if you don't eat all your food or catch you with your elbows on the table. Kids love it. The entrees—fried chicken, meatloaf (ask for extra catsup), pot roast, tuna casserole, open-faced sandwiches—aren't quite as good as Mom used to make, but are decent nonetheless. The desserts,

 A Royal Dining Affair

The **Earl of Sandwich** (the famous edible was allegedly invented by said earl in 1762, when he was too busy playing cards to eat a real meal—and found that putting meat between two slices of bread allowed for both) made its debut in Downtown Disney in 2004. The casual eatery offers a great selection of hot and cold sandwiches, including a variety of breakfast sandwiches to start your day off right, French roast beef with cheddar and horseradish sauce, turkey with apple bacon and Swiss cheese, Caribbean jerk chicken, Caprese, Hawaiian BBQ, and several others. A variety of salads—Cobb, Chinese chicken, chicken Caesar, Mediterranean, house, Caprese—are available as well. There's some indoor seating, though most diners head for the benches outside. If you're looking for a quick, light meal at a decent price (sandwiches and salads are all under $6), this is the place.

Studio Dining Alternative

If you forgot to make Advance Reservations or couldn't get a table at your chosen restaurant, try the Sci-Fi Dine-In Theater Restaurant's next-door neighbor, the **ABC Commissary**. While not a themed restaurant per se, it offers a reasonably diverse menu, featuring items such as Asian salad, fish and chips, curry chicken, burgers, and more. It has rather good desserts as well. Most items cost $7 to $9. Plainer than most Disney eateries, it really does resemble a commissary, and TVs lining the walls play commercials for the latest and greatest shows running on Disney-owned ABC. *Note:* Kosher meals are readily available here.

viewed via a View-Master, include s'mores, sundaes, and cakes; they're all definitely worth the wait. Beer and a varied list of specialty drinks (try the mean margarita) are served. Kids will get a kick out of the glowing "electric" ice cubes in their drinks.

Near the Indiana Jones Epic Stunt Spectacular. ✆ **407/939-3463.** www.disneyworld.com. Advance Reservations recommended. Main courses $12–$17 lunch, $15–$21 dinner. AE, DC, DISC, MC, V. Daily 11am to park closing. Parking $14.

Mama Melrose's Ristorante Italiano ITALIAN   Found along the "movie" set of a New York street, this large neighborhood eatery welcomes diners with checked tablecloths, wood floors, and red-vinyl booths. The best bets here are the wood-fired flatbreads (grilled pepperoni, four-cheese, vine-ripened tomato, and others) offered at both lunch and dinner. Also on the menu are a mouthwatering charred strip steak accompanied by roasted potatoes, onions, and balsamic-shallot butter, and topped off with a Chianti wine reduction; wood-grilled tuna served over a vegetable risotto and olive-caper butter; and wood-grilled chicken tossed with pipette pasta and veggies and topped with a rich and creamy basil and four-cheese sauce.

Near the Backlot Tour. ✆ **407/939-3463.** www.disneyworld.com. Advance Reservations recommended. Main courses $12–$29 lunch, $12–$29 dinner; Fantasmic! dinner package $33 adults, $12 kids. AE, DC, DISC, MC, V. Daily noon to park closing. Parking $14.

Sci-Fi Dine-In Theater Restaurant ☺ AMERICAN   This restaurant's simulated nighttime sky is filled with fiber-optic twinkling stars that look down on you as you sit in a chrome "convertible" watching a giant screen showing '50s and '60s sci-fi flicks, zany newsreels, cartoons, and B-horror-movie clips, such as *Frankenstein Meets the Space Monster*. Fun-loving carhops deliver free popcorn along with your meal. I'm disappointed that the menu, which was almost as fun to read as the movies are to watch, is far less cosmic than it used to be. Entrees once listed as the Attack of the Killer Club Sandwich, the Beach Party Panic, and the Red Planet now require little translation as they sport names that are far more down-to-earth (sure, they're more recognizable, but the fun factor ain't there). The menu includes a selection of sandwiches, ribs, burgers, seafood, pasta, steak, and salads. Drinks are served with souvenir glow-in-the-dark ice cubes. The food is average; it's the atmosphere that keeps the crowds coming.

Near Indiana Jones Epic Stunt Spectacular. ✆ **407/939-3463.** www.disneyworld.com. Advance Reservations recommended. Main courses $13–$23 lunch and dinner. AE, DC, DISC, MC, V. Daily 11am to park closing. Parking $14.

INEXPENSIVE

Toy Story Pizza Planet AMERICAN   The menu here is far from original, but it will satisfy some of the younger (and pickier) eaters in your family with pizza, salad, drinks, and desserts. It's a big favorite of kids, thanks to the array of arcade games located right next door—just remember to bring plenty of change.

In the Muppet Courtyard. ℂ **407/939-3463.** www.disneyworld.com. Advance Reservations not accepted. All meals $6–$9. AE, DC, DISC, MC, V. Daily 11am to park closing. Parking $14.

In the Animal Kingdom

There are few restaurants in the newest of Disney's parks, and most that exist are counter-service or grab-and-go places (of these, the Flame Tree Barbecue is the best). Nevertheless, there are three notable enough to list.

EXPENSIVE

Tusker House AFRICAN/AMERICAN   The thatched-roof Tusker House in Harambe village now features a bountiful buffet with a definite culinary flair. Several stations, each with a different selection of African-inspired items, are located throughout the inviting open-air market-style interior. Blatjang chutneys with South African preserves, sambals tabbouleh, hummus and baba ghanoush, curried rice salad, couscous with roasted vegetables, vegetable samosas, seafood stew, roasted chicken, and a variety of other offerings are all on the menu. Kids will find a selection of familiar favorites (including PB&J, chicken drumsticks, mac 'n' cheese, and corn-dog nuggets) to please their pint-size palates. A character breakfast (Donald's Safari Breakfast) is offered in the morning. A slightly shaded stone patio out back, with a view over the trees, allows you to relax and enjoy your meal tucked away from the crowds. Out front, the pavilion offers shade and—if timed right—a view of the live entertainment. Beer and wine are served. *Note:* Reserved seating for the 3:15pm showing of Finding Nemo–The Musical is available for guests who book advance lunch reservations (btw. 1 and 1:40 pm).

In Africa, near entrance. ℂ **407/939-3463.** www.disneyworld.com. Advance Reservations suggested for breakfast. Breakfast $25 adults, $11 kids 3–9; lunch $21 adults, $12 kids; dinner $29 adults, $14 kids. AE, DC, DISC, MC, V. Daily 8–10:30am, 11:30am–3:30 or 4pm, and 4–6pm. Parking $14.

MODERATE

Rainforest Cafe ★ ☺ CALIFORNIAN   Expect California fare with an island spin at this Rainforest and its cousin (p. 133). Menu offerings tend to be tasty and somewhat creative, with far more choices than most can contend with. That said, the cafe, like other Disney restaurants, tends to fall on the pricier side. Fun dishes include Monsoon Grill (macadamia-crusted snapper with shrimp scampi and Caribbean coconut shrimp), Rumble in the Jungle Turkey Wrap (with romaine, tomatoes, and bacon), and Mojo Bones (slow-roasted St. Louis–style spareribs with safari fries). Tables situated among the dining room's dense vines and generally inanimate animals are usually packed; that's partially due to the lack of other full-service dining options at Animal Kingdom, but also due to the actual popularity of this loud (thanks in part to the cracks of thunder and chatter of animals) and lively establishment. Beer, wine, and other alcoholic concoctions are served.

Just outside Animal Kingdom entrance. *Park admission not required* (though there is an entrance from inside the park, too). ℂ **407/938-9100.** www.rainforestcafe.com. Advance Reservations strongly recommended. Main courses $9–$14 breakfast, $13–$31 (most under $25) lunch and dinner. AE, DC, DISC, MC, V. Daily 8:30am–6 or 7pm. Parking $14.

If you want to take in one of Disney's many popular character-dining experiences or dinner shows, plan on paying a bit extra if you find yourself dining during the holidays. Disney has added an extra $5 (or so) to the price of character meals and dinner shows during select times throughout the year—including, but not limited to, the days and sometimes weeks surrounding New Year's, Easter, Memorial Day, the 4th of July, Labor Day, Thanksgiving, and Christmas. For details (including the exact dates that Disney's holiday pricing is in effect), check out www.disney world.com or call ✆ 407/939-3463.

Yak & Yeti ★ ASIAN FUSION/PACIFIC RIM   Animal Kingdom's newest dining spot opened in Asia (near Expedition Everest) in the fall of 2007. This Pan-Asian restaurant offers both sit-down and counter-service dining in a uniquely eclectic and meticulously detailed setting that blends seamlessly into the Himalayan village surrounding it. The menu features such specialties as crispy wok-fried green beans (even the kids will love these); lettuce cups filled with minced chicken, chopped veggies, and a yummy maple tamarind sauce; seared miso salmon; crispy mahimahi; and maple tamarind chicken. Be sure to leave room for dessert—the mango pie and fried wontons (filled with cream cheese and served with skewers of fresh pineapple, vanilla ice cream, and a sweet honey-vanilla drizzle) are simply delish. Kids will appreciate the miniburgers, veggie lo mein, egg rolls, and chicken bites. An outdoor counter-service outpost (offering many, but not all, of the items from the main restaurant menu) is located just to the right of the entrance—it makes a great alternative for those who prefer to dine outdoors in the village-like setting.

In Asia, near Expedition Everest. ✆ **407/939-3463.** www.disneyworld.com. Advance Reservations suggested. Main courses $17–$24 lunch and dinner; $8–$11 kids. AE, DC, DISC, MC, V. Daily 11am to park closing. Parking $14.

In the Walt Disney World Resorts

Most restaurants in this category continue the Disney trend of being above market price. On the flip side, many offer food and atmosphere that far exceed what you'll find in the theme parks. The quality level means that even those not staying at Disney resorts like to dine at these restaurants, so Advance Reservations are a must. **Note:** Valet parking at any of the Disney resorts runs $12 (plus tip), unless otherwise noted.

All the restaurants in this section are shown on the "Walt Disney World & Lake Buena Vista Restaurants" map, on p. 118.

VERY EXPENSIVE

Boma ★★★ 📷 AFRICAN   Here's a truly unique and worthwhile dining experience. This restaurant's warm and welcoming atmosphere, evoking an African marketplace, is enhanced by colorful banners hanging from high above. A thatched roof and large wooden tabletops made from tree trunks add to the impressive decor. In front of the open kitchen is an incredible buffet of international cuisine, featuring authentic dishes from more than 50 African nations. A wood-burning grill sends delicious aromas wafting throughout the room, enticing diners to try some of the more diverse delicacies. Adventurous eaters can expect such treats as Moroccan seafood salad (mussels, scallops, shrimp, and couscous); curried coconut seafood stew; chicken pepper pot soup; and much more. The watermelon rind salad, a specialty, is both delicious and refreshing—just don't forget to save room for the yummy desserts. Kids with less sophisticated taste buds can dine on traditional American favorites. There's also a breakfast buffet (try the specialty juices—they're delicious).

Tip no. 1: If there's something you particularly like, ask for the recipe—Disney is surprisingly good about sharing culinary secrets. *Tip no. 2:* Most tables here seat larger parties, so couples or single diners may end up waiting longer for a table.

2901 Osceola Pkwy., at Disney's Animal Kingdom Lodge. ℂ **407/939-3463.** www.disneyworld.com. Advance Reservations recommended. Breakfast buffet $24 adults, $13 kids 3-9; dinner buffet $39 adults, $19 kids. AE, DC, DISC, MC, V. Daily 7-11am and 5-10pm. Valet or free self-parking.

California Grill ★★★ CALIFORNIAN   Located on the Contemporary Resort's 15th floor, this stunning restaurant offers views of the Magic Kingdom and lagoon below while your eyes and mouth feast on an eclectic menu. A Wolfgang Puck–ish interior incorporates Art Deco elements (curved pearwood walls, vivid splashes of color, polished black-granite surfaces) with a charged and upbeat atmosphere, but the central focus is an exhibition kitchen with a wood-burning oven and rotisserie. The menu's headliners change to take advantage of fresh market fare, but may include pan-seared arctic char with spring pea risotto, buttered carrots, and a pinot noir glaze, or an oak-fired filet of beef with Gruyere-potato pave, broccoli, and teriyaki barbecue sauce. The Grill also has a nice sushi and sashimi menu (tuna, crab, shrimp, and others) ranging from appetizers to large platters. The servers are exceptionally attentive. This is one of the few spots in WDW that isn't inundated with kids. The list of California wines complements the meal and views.

Note: It can be tough to get a table at the Grill, especially on weekends and during Disney fireworks hours, so make a reservation as early as possible. Also be aware that a business-casual dress code is required.

4600 N. World Dr., at Disney's Contemporary Resort. ℂ **407/939-3463.** www.disneyworld.com. Advance Reservations are required and need a credit card guarantee. Main courses $28-$44; sushi and sashimi $21-$26; $8-$13 kids. AE, DC, DISC, MC, V. Daily 5:30-10pm. Valet or free self-parking.

 Picnicking in the Park

In 2009, Disney's Animal Kingdom introduced a new dining option. Visitors who prefer the spectacular surroundings of the park can now **"Picnic in the Park"** rather than heading indoors to dine. Meals (for two to six guests) include a choice of gourmet sandwich, a side dish, a dessert, and bottled water (referred to as tier 1); or a choice of meatier entree (rotisserie chicken or ham), a side dish, a dessert, and bottled water (referred to as tier 2). Tier 1 meals are available for pick-up at Dinobites; tier 2 meals are available for pick-up at the Kusafiri Coffee Shop. All meals are bagged (along with plates and utensils) in eco-friendly bags, and it's off to the picnic spot of your choice. Locations are scattered throughout the park and marked on park maps. Prices start at $18 (for two guests) and, depending on which meal you choose, can reach as high as $57 (for six). Orders must be placed at least 2 hours in advance at the Picnic in the Park podium, located near Guest Relations, or at the podium outside the Island Mercantile, between 8:30am and 2:30pm. Payment is due when you pick up your meal. For details, check out **www.disneyworld.com** or call ℂ **407/939-3463.**

THE BEST tables IN THE WORLD

There are two special dining options at **Victoria & Albert's.** Reserve the **Chef's Table** (far, far in advance) and dine in a charming alcove hung with copper pots and dried flower wreaths at an elegantly appointed candlelit table—in the heart of the kitchen! You'll begin by sipping bubbly with the chef while discussing your food preferences for a menu (up to 13 courses) created especially for you. There's a cooking-seminar element to this experience: Diners get to tour the kitchen and observe the artistry of the chefs at work. The Chef's Table can accommodate up to 10 people a night. It's a leisurely affair, lasting 3 or 4 hours. The price is $200 per person without wine, $295 with five wines. This is so popular that Disney takes Advance Reservations (180 days out for both the main dining room and the Chef's Table), so reserve *early* by calling 𝄢 407/939-3463.

Disney's newest and most exclusive dining experience to date is **Queen Victoria's Room.** Here, at just four tables behind closed doors (right off the main dining room), discerning diners will experience a sumptuous 10-course meal with authentic French gueridon service and unsurpassed personalized attention. The price tag is $200 per person; add an additional $95 per person for wine pairings. To reserve a table (a single seating is offered nightly), call the restaurant's private line (𝄢 **407/939-3862**) up to 180 days in advance.

For additional details and sample menus, check out www.victoria-alberts.com.

Citricos ★ CONTEMPORARY FRENCH Located on the second floor of the Grand Floridian, Citricos features a fusion menu of French and Mediterranean cuisine with a Florida twist. Items change regularly, but you might find yummy grilled lamb chops with crispy polenta and puttanesca sauce, or sautéed salmon with roasted fennel and gold potatoes. The old-world decor features warm hues of yellows and oranges, wrought-iron railings, mosaic-tile floors, flickering lights, a show kitchen, and a view of the Seven Seas Lagoon and Magic Kingdom fireworks. Add a three-course wine pairing for $30. The Chef's Domain, at $85 per person, offers an experience similar to the Chef's Table at Victoria & Albert's for up to four guests.

4401 Floridian Way, in Disney's Grand Floridian Resort & Spa. 𝄢 **407/939-3463.** www.disneyworld.com. Advance Reservations recommended. Main courses $23–$46. AE, DC, DISC, MC, V. Wed-Sun 5-10pm; Chef's Domain Wed-Sat 6 and 8:30pm. Valet or free self-parking.

Flying Fish Café ★★ SEAFOOD Chefs at this upscale Coney Island–inspired restaurant take the stage in a show kitchen that turns out entrees such as potato-wrapped red snapper with a creamy leek fondue; or citrus, sesame, and Szechuan pepper-crusted yellowfin tuna with bok choy and snap peas. The food is far better than what you'll find at the Coral Reef (p. 110) and Cape May Café (p. 129), but not quite in the same league as Todd English's bluezoo (p. 127). Vibrantly colored tile floors, lily pads, accents of shimmering fish scales, and golden fish, along with delicate jellyfish-like lighting hanging by fish hooks from high above, combine to create an undersea ambience. A whimsical Ferris wheel and hand-painted murals conjure thoughts of the boardwalk. ***Note:*** If you can't get a table here, ask to sit at the counter—you'll get a great view of the exhibition kitchen.

2101 N. Epcot Resorts Blvd., at Disney's BoardWalk. (©) **407/939-3463.** www.disneyworld.com. Advance Reservations recommended. Main courses $28–$42; $7–$12 kids. AE, DC, DISC, MC, V. Daily 5:30–10pm. Valet or free self-parking.

Todd English's bluezoo ★★ SEAFOOD   This is still one of the hippest, hottest, most happening places to dine in town. Acclaimed chef Todd English has created a menu of fresh seafood and coastal dishes that are served with creative flair (possibly a bit too creative at times) in an artsy undersea setting. An exhibition kitchen showcases the chefs at work, and the dining areas feature a contemporary (and very blue) decor designed to evoke the ocean. Appetizers include the amazing "Olive's" classico flatbread, a roasted beet salad, and teppan-seared sea scallops. Melt-in-your-mouth entrees include Cantonese lobster, miso-glazed black cod, rubbed swordfish, and the daily "Dancing Fish" (slowly spinning over the grill at the far end of the exhibition kitchen for all to see). Worth noting, however, is the fact that several dishes (and even a few of the signature drinks) have become overly complicated, some created from upwards of 14 ingredients. While a true foodie might find this to his liking, many find it a bit off-putting (costing this establishment a star). Thankfully, a selection of fresh grilled fish (aptly named "simply fish"), complemented by several unique sauces, helps to offset the number of overly complex entrees. Unlike the portions at many upscale restaurants of this caliber, those here are meal worthy, not minuscule. That said, the prices are hefty and do not include side dishes, which will run you an extra $7 to $11. Dress is casual (this is Disney), though the atmosphere is definitely adult and upscale.

Tip: The front of the restaurant has a bar and lounge where live music is often featured or a DJ spins a selection of today's hottest tunes.

1500 Epcot Resort Blvd., at the WDW Dolphin. (©) **407/934-1111.** www.disneyworld.com. Advance Reservations highly recommended. Main courses $27–$60. AE, DC, DISC, MC, V. Daily 3:30–11pm. Free self- and validated valet parking (validate ticket on your way out).

Victoria & Albert's ★★★ 🍴 INTERNATIONAL   It's not often that I can describe dinner as "an event," but Disney's most elegant restaurant deserves that distinction. Dinner is next to perfect—if the portions seem small, they're designed that way to ensure you get through all seven courses—and the setting is exceptionally romantic. The fare changes nightly, but expect a feast fit for royalty (and costing a royal fortune). You might begin with roasted duck with candy-striped and golden beets, followed by Monterey abalone with lemon and baby spinach. Then, pheasant consommé might precede an entree such as tamari-glazed bluefin tuna over bok choy stir-fry or veal tenderloin; pheasant with porcini pasta and truffle foam; or Australian Kobe beef tenderloin. English Stilton served with a burgundy-poached pear sets up desserts such as vanilla-bean crème brûlée and Kona chocolate soufflé. The intimate dining room (with seating for only 65) is crowned by a domed, chapel-style ceiling. Victorian lamps softly light 18 exquisitely appointed tables; a harp plays softly in the background, and your servers (always named Victoria and Albert) provide service that is unmatched anywhere else in Orlando. The luxurious experience ends as a personalized menu is presented to you and a rose given to all the ladies in your party. *Tip:* Wine pairings, an extra $60 per person, are a great way to enhance the dinner experience.

4401 Floridian Way, in Disney's Grand Floridian Resort & Spa. (©) **407/939-3463.** www.disneyworld. com. Advance Reservations required. Jackets required for men. Not recommended for children. Prix

Cooking for Kids

Disney's Grand Floridian Resort & Spa offers a special cooking program for children. The **Wonderland Tea Party** gives kids ages 4 to 10 a 1-hour primer in cupcake decorating—with their fingers! They also feast on sandwiches (turkey or berry) or chicken nuggets and sip apple-juice "tea" while they play with Alice and the Mad Hatter ($40 per child). Call © **407/824-3000** or 407/939-3463 for details.

fixe $125 per person, $185 with wine pairing; $200 Chef's Table, $295 with wine. AE, DC, DISC, MC, V. 2 dinner seatings daily Sept–June 5:45-6:30pm and 9-9:45pm; 1 dinner seating July–Aug 6:45-8pm. Chef's Table 6pm only. Free self- and validated valet parking.

Yachtsman Steakhouse ★ SEAFOOD/STEAK   It is somewhat of a backhanded compliment to name this the best steakhouse in Disney—there are only two true steakhouses on property. Even so, when you compare it to similar spots in the outside world, the Yachtsman still earns high grades. Its grain-fed, Western beef is aged, cured, and cut here. You can see the cuts in a glass-enclosed aging room, and the exhibition kitchen provides a tantalizing glimpse of steaks, chops, and seafood being grilled over oak and hickory. Steak options range from an 8-ounce filet to a 12-ounce strip to a belly-busting 24-ounce porterhouse. If you're not in the mood for beef, the Yachtsman also serves free-range chicken, stone bass, braised beef ravioli, roasted rack of lamb, and gnocchi. The decor includes knotty-pine beams, plank floors, and leather-and-oak chairs, though unlike most steakhouses it sports a lighter, nautical New England feel. The staff is very cordial. The Yachtsman has an extensive wine list, though it's not in the same league as the other contestants in this category.

1700 Epcot Resorts Blvd., in Disney's Yacht Club Resort. © **407/939-3463.** Advance Reservations recommended. Main courses $24-$44. AE, DC, DISC, MC, V. Daily 5:30-10pm. Valet or free self-parking.

EXPENSIVE

Artist Point ★★ 🍴 SEAFOOD/STEAK   Enjoy a grand view of Disney's Wilderness Lodge and tasty cuisine at this rustically elegant establishment. Hand-painted murals of Pacific Northwest scenery adorn the impressive two-story center ceiling, and ornate iron lanterns hang from tremendous timber columns. Immense windows overlook the waterfalls, rocky landscaping, and the resort's own Fire Rock geyser. The menu changes seasonally and might feature grilled buffalo strip loin or crispy-seared Pacific ruby Onaga snapper, but the restaurant's signature is the cedar plank–roasted king salmon. There's terrace seating for fair-weather dining. Expect a reasonably extensive wine list that now exclusively features wines from the Pacific Northwest. *Note:* Artist Point has a much more relaxed atmosphere than some of the busier WDW resort restaurants.

Tip: If you're looking for more family-oriented dining at the Wilderness Lodge, try the **Whispering Canyon Café,** where a decor dedicated to cowboys and Indians is warm and welcoming. Kids can horse-race on broomsticks, and everyone gets a whoopin' and a hollerin' at dinner. Meals are served family style (though a la carte service is available if you so desire). It's open for breakfast, lunch, and dinner. Entrees run from $13 to $18 at lunch ($19 for the buffet), $19 to $32 at dinner ($29 for the buffet).

901 W. Timberline Dr., in Disney's Wilderness Lodge. © **407/939-3463.** www.disneyworld.com. Advance Reservations recommended. Dinner $27-$48, wine pairing $28 additional. AE, DC, DISC, MC, V. Daily 5:30-10pm. Valet or free self-parking.

Cape May Café SEAFOOD/STEAK   This New England–style clambake offers a selection of oysters, clams, mussels, baked fish, and small peel-and-eat shrimp. Accompaniments include corn on the cob, potatoes, and other assorted veggies. Landlubbers, fear not; the not-so-fishy fare includes barbecued pork ribs and prime rib. The casual nautical theme carries into the restaurant from the surrounding Beach Club resort. The Cape May Café also offers a character breakfast buffet every morning (p. 154).

1800 Epcot Resorts Blvd., at Disney's Beach Club Resort. ℂ **407/939-3463.** www.disneyworld.com. Advance Reservations recommended. Character breakfast $27 adults, $13 kids 3–9; dinner buffet $37 adults, $16 kids. AE, DC, DISC, MC, V. Daily 7:30–11am and 5:30–9:30pm. Valet or free self-parking.

Jiko—The Cooking Place ★★ AFRICAN   The Animal Kingdom Lodge's signature restaurant offers a nice diversion from Disney's more conventional offerings and a complementary addition to the multicultural dining rooms at Epcot's World Showcase. Jiko's show kitchen, sporting two wood-burning ovens, turns out an innovative menu of international cuisine with African overtones. Dishes, depending on the season, might include Durban shrimp curry, maize-crusted wrekfish with seasonal veggies and a tasty tomato-butter sauce, or oak-grilled filet mignon. An impressive wine list features South African vintages exclusively. Warm colors and diffuse lighting add to the sophisticated atmosphere.

2901 Osceola Pkwy., at Disney's Animal Kingdom Lodge. ℂ **407/939-3463.** www.disneyworld.com. Advance Reservations recommended. Main courses $26–$41. AE, DC, DISC, MC, V. Daily 5:30–10pm. Valet or free self-parking.

Kouzzinas MEDITERRANEAN   Replacing Spoodles is Kouzzinas, run by celebrity Iron Chef Cat Cora. While changes to the restaurant's decor have been minimal—its warm golden hues, wrought-iron accents, tremendous wood beams, old-world murals, and show kitchen remain intact, albeit in updated form—the menu is now filled with authentic family recipes with a Mediterranean flavor. Simple yet creative dishes might include cinnamon stewed chicken, chargrilled lamb burgers, or fishermen's stew, with sides ranging from smashed garlic fried potatoes to chilled salt-roasted beets. The pizza window, a popular late-night stop, is open for business until midnight—you can pick up a slice ($3.50–$4) or order an entire pie to go (starting at $18, plus $1.50 for each topping).

2101 N. Epcot Resorts Blvd., at Disney's BoardWalk. ℂ **407/939-3463.** www.disneyworld.com. Advance reservations recommended. Main courses $16–$28. AE, DC, DISC, MC, V. Daily 5:30–10pm. Pizza Window 5pm–midnight. Valet or free self-parking.

 For Smaller Stomachs

If your kids aren't satisfied with the offerings on the kids' menu (though many feature pint-size portions of more adult options along with plenty of familiar favorites), try the appetizer menu. They'll have more to choose from, and the price is right. Also, ask if half-portions are available; they are generally not advertised, though some restaurants offer them upon request. The same applies when requesting items a la carte. Disney's menus (even at quick-service restaurants) won't always reflect a la carte items, though they are often available if you ask.

If your kids are adventurous in the dining department but can't handle adult-size portions, several Disney restaurants allow children to sample dishes geared to adult tastes but served in portion sizes suited to smaller stomachs (and at smaller prices, too). Options include (but are not limited to):

- **Artist Point** (Wilderness Lodge): Baked salmon with mashed potatoes and veggies ($11)
- **California Grill** (Contemporary): Oak-fired steak or roasted salmon with mashed potatoes and veggies ($12–$13)
- **Citricos** (Grand Floridian): Chicken noodle soup ($3), oak-grilled filet of beef ($13)
- **Coral Reef** (Epcot): Seared mahimahi ($9)
- **Flying Fish Café** (BoardWalk): Lettuce salad ($4), Florida coast fish sticks with roasted potatoes and veggies ($11)
- **Rose & Crown** (Epcot): Bangers and mash or shepherd's pie ($9)

'Ohana ★ ☺ PACIFIC RIM   Its star is earned on the fun front, but the decibel level here can get a bit overwhelming, especially for those looking for a relaxing evening out. Inside, you're welcomed as a "cousin," which fits because 'Ohana means "family" in Hawaiian. As your food is being prepared over an 18-foot fire pit, the staff keeps your eyes and ears filled with all sorts of shenanigans. The blowing of a conch shell summons a storyteller, coconut races get underway in the center aisle, and you can shed your inhibitions and shake it at the hula lessons. When it starts, the meal is served rapid-fire (ask your waiter to slow the pace if it's too fast). The edibles include a variety of skewers (think shish kabob), including oak-grilled chicken, marinated steak, Asian barbecue pork, and spicy shrimp. Trimmings include stir-fried veggies, pineapple-coconut bread, pork fried dumplings, mixed greens with mango poppy-seed dressing, and coriander chicken wings, all served up family style. A full bar offers limited wine selections (tropical alcoholic drinks are available for an added fee). **Note:** Ask for a seat in the main dining room, or you won't get a good view of the entertainment.

1600 Seven Seas Dr., at Disney's Polynesian Resort. ☏ **407/939-3463.** www.disneyworld.com. Advance Reservations strongly recommended. Character breakfast $21 adults, $12 kids 3–9 (p. 156); family-style dinner $33 adults, $16 kids. AE, DC, DISC, MC, V. Daily 7:30–11am and 5–10pm. Valet or free self-parking.

MODERATE

Boatwright's Dining Hall ☺ SOUTHERN/CREOLE   A family atmosphere (noisy), good food (by Disney standards), and reasonable prices (ditto) make Boatwright's a hit with Port Orleans Resort guests, if not outsiders. The jambalaya is sans seafood, but is filled with vegetables, rice, chicken, and sausage—all rather spicy and giving it quite a kick. Other dinner items include andouille-crusted catfish, slow-roasted prime rib, voodoo chicken, and blackened fish. Boatwright's is modeled after a 19th-century boat factory, complete with the wooden hull of a Louisiana fishing boat suspended from its lofty beamed ceiling. Most kids like the wooden toolboxes on every table; each contains a salt shaker that doubles as a level, a wood-clamp sugar dispenser, a pepper-grinder-cum-ruler, a jar of unmatched utensils, shop rags (to be used as napkins), and a little metal pail of crayons. **Note:** Breakfast is no longer served.

2201 Orleans Dr., in Disney's Port Orleans Resort. ☏ **407/939-3463.** www.disneyworld.com. Advance Reservations recommended. Main courses $16–$28. AE, DC, DISC, MC, V. Daily 5–10pm. Free self-parking.

ESPN Club ★ AMERICAN   If you're a sports enthusiast, this is *the* place for you. Sports memorabilia hangs from every wall, and TV screens (all 71 of them) surround you at every turn—ensuring you won't miss a minute of the big game. The all-American fare includes such choices as "Boo-Yeah" chili, hot wings, and burgers. Heartier entrees include a center-cut sirloin, barbecued ribs, and grilled salmon. Sandwiches and salads are available as well. The service is impeccable—never have I had a waiter so quick on his feet. While the food is quite good, it's the upbeat action-packed atmosphere that draws the crowds here.

2101 N. Epcot Resorts Blvd., at Disney's BoardWalk. ☏ **407/939-1177.** www.disneyworld.com. Advance Reservations not needed. Main courses $11–$15 lunch, $11–$21 dinner. AE, DC, DISC, MC, V. Mon–Thurs 11:30am–1am; Fri–Sat 11:30am–2am. Valet or free self-parking.

The Wave . . . of American Flavors ★ AMERICAN   The Contemporary's newest restaurant (opened in 2008) lures diners with a modern but welcoming atmosphere and seasonal menus of fresh and healthy American fare accented with flavors from around the world. Dishes are prepared with local and regional products whenever possible, and entrees might include whole-wheat linguine with clams, rock shrimp, and fresh thyme in a chunky tomato broth; or a scrumptious braised lamb shank smothered in a bulgur lentil stew and red-wine sauce. You'll also find a selection of organic beers and trendy cocktails, including an antioxidant cosmo (with wildberry vodka, black-raspberry liqueur, açai juice with agave, lychee, aloe juice, and freshly squeezed lemon juice), as well as an extensive and innovative wine list from around the globe (though, quirkily, they all have screw caps). *Note:* The Wave is now open for breakfast. The buffet ($19 for adults, $11 for children 3–9) is lined with made-to-order eggs and omelets, grits, pancakes, hash browns, quiche, and bacon, among other familiar morning fuel.

4600 N. World Dr., in Disney's Contemporary Resort. ☏ **407/939-3463.** www.disneyworld.com. Advance Reservations recommended. Breakfast $10–$12; lunch $12–$21; dinner $18–$30. AE, DC, DISC, MC, V. Daily 7:30–11am, noon–2pm, and 5:30–11pm. Valet or free self-parking.

IN LAKE BUENA VISTA

In this section, I list restaurants located in Downtown Disney and the Lake Buena Vista area. Many eateries included below can be found on the "Walt Disney World & Lake Buena Vista Restaurants" map, on p. 118. Downtown Disney is located 2½

Hidden Mickey?

All over the Walt Disney World Resort, you will find Mickey Mouse popping up in some rather interesting places. You had better take a good look at your food before you take a bite—you might be surprised to find him staring back at you. Mickey can be found in pancakes, waffles, muffins, pastas, and pats of butter. He can be seen in fruits and cheeses, sandwiches, and sundaes. There are Mickey mashed potatoes, ice-cream bars, cookies, and cakes. Even cucumbers are grown (with a little help from a plastic mold) to look like the famous mouse.

miles from Epcot off Buena Vista Drive. It encompasses the Downtown Disney Marketplace, a complex chock-full of cedar-shingled shops and themed restaurants overlooking a scenic lagoon; the adjoining Pleasure Island (soon to be Hyperion Wharf), a lively entertainment venue full of shops and restaurants of its own; and Downtown Disney West Side, a slightly more upscale collection of shops, restaurants, the Cirque du Soleil (p. 324), and a multiplex. The restaurants below have kids' menus, usually in the $5-to-$10 range, though sometimes higher.

Pleasure Island (Hyperion Wharf)

EXPENSIVE

Portobello ★★ SOUTHERN ITALIAN/MEDITERRANEAN Along with the name change (once the Portobello Yacht Club) comes an updated menu of truly authentic, regional Italian fare and a reinvigorated wine list. The pizzas here go beyond the routine to *quattro formaggi* (mozzarella, Gorgonzola, Fontina, and Parmesan, with sun-dried tomatoes) and *margherita* (Italian sausage, plum tomatoes, and mozzarella). But it's the less casual entrees that pack people into this place. The menu changes from time to time. Start off with the mozzarella-stuffed rice balls (perfection in a tasty little package); the portobello mushrooms stuffed with Gorgonzola, polenta, and drizzled with a rosemary sauce; or the Sambuca shrimp—or choose a few and share, as each offers a unique explosion of tastes and textures not to be missed. Pastas might include bucatini, with tomato, guanciale, garlic, chili pepper, and olive oil; or black linguine, with Florida rock shrimp, garlic, tomatoes, and asparagus. You'll also find offerings such as mahimahi, *osso buco,* and grilled chicken as well as a small selection of steaks (the filet simply melts in your mouth). The Mediterranean-inspired decor, now more inviting, is accented by terra-cotta tiles and rustic iron set against warm earth tones and amber lighting. The Portobello's awning-covered patio overlooks Lake Buena Vista. Its cellar is small, but there's a nice selection of wine to match the meals.

1650 Buena Vista Dr., at Pleasure Island. ⓒ **407/934-8888.** www.levyrestaurants.com. Advance Reservations recommended. Lunch $10–$24; dinner $18–$40; pizzas $10–$13. AE, DC, DISC, MC, V. Daily 11:30am–3pm and 5–11pm. Free self-parking.

MODERATE

Planet Hollywood AMERICAN Those who flock to this restaurant come for the unique surroundings, movie memorabilia, and scenery from some of Hollywood's hottest hits, much like those who head to the Hard Rock (a far better choice) at CityWalk (p. 139) to check out its musical montage. Diners, however, are doomed to be disappointed. Though the atmosphere is fairly neat (including a planetarium-like ceiling), the Planet's servers can cop an attitude, and the food is at best blasé. If you must, you'll find the usual suspects: wings, salads, sandwiches, big burgers, ribs, pasta, steaks, and seafood. Even with a less-than-stellar lineup on the menu, the lines to get in can at times be excruciatingly long.

1506 Buena Vista Dr., at Pleasure Island (look for the big globe). ⓒ **407/827-7827.** www.planethollywood.com. Limited Advance Reservations accepted. Main courses $12–$27 (most less than $19). AE, DC, DISC, MC, V. Daily 11am–1am. Free self-parking.

Downtown Disney Marketplace

VERY EXPENSIVE

Fulton's Crab House ★★ SEAFOOD Lobster (Maine and Australian) and crab (stone, king, and Dungeness) continue to dominate the menu at this upscale eatery, which is housed in a replica of an elegant (albeit permanently moored) 19th-century Mississippi riverboat. It's one of the area's best seafood houses—and your bill will reflect that. The casual yet elegant decor, recently refreshed in 2010, is accented with folk art, nautical brass, and seafaring paraphernalia scattered throughout its various rooms (the Market Room, Trophy Room, Industry Room, and Constellation Room, each boasting its own unique decor dedicated to the denizens of the deep). The menu changes often, but with more than 50 fresh seafood selections to choose from, you won't be disappointed. The seared tuna (served rare) and blue crab cakes are delicious. There's a scattering of Florida seafood, including black grouper and red snapper. In mild weather, consider dining on one of the three outdoor decks for a more panoramic view. Be prepared for a long wait (even with Advance Reservations); try having a late lunch here to shorten your waiting time. Fulton's has one of Lake Buena Vista's better wine lists. And though you may not see many of them, kids are welcomed here.

1670 Buena Vista Dr., aboard the riverboat docked at Downtown Disney. ✆ **407/934-2628.** www. levyrestaurants.com. Advance Reservations recommended. Main courses $11–$18 lunch, $20–$52 dinner. AE, DC, DISC, MC, V. Daily 11:30am–4pm and 5–11pm. Free self-parking.

MODERATE

Rainforest Cafe ☺ CALIFORNIAN   Don't arrive starving unless you have Advance Reservations. Without them, waits average 2 hours, although even with them, you'll wait longer here than at Animal Kingdom's Rainforest Cafe (p. 123). Expect fare with an island spin at this Rainforest. The menu can be tasty and creative, though somewhat overpriced. Fun dishes include Caribbean Coconut Shrimp (with a sweet mango sauce) and Maya's Mixed Grill (ribs, chicken breast, and shrimp), but the menu goes on and on (and on) with an extensive variety of salads, pastas, pizzas, burgers, sandwiches, seafood, beef, chicken, and pork. The setting is its biggest draw (though the food is pretty good), filled with jungles, waterfalls, and animatronic animals—and the occasional clap of thunder in the background, so don't expect a quiet evening out. Kids are thoroughly entertained by all the action; adults can calm their nerves with the beer, wine, and other alcoholic mixers.

Downtown Disney Marketplace, near the smoking volcano. ✆ **407/827-8500.** www.rainforestcafe. com. Advance Reservations recommended. Main courses $13–$31 lunch and dinner (most less than $25). AE, DISC, MC, V. Sun–Thurs 10:30am–11pm; Fri–Sat 10:30am–midnight. Free self-parking.

T-Rex Cafe ☺ AMERICAN   Families will find this paleontologist's paradise a fun diversion thanks to its prehistoric environment—think Rainforest Cafe, only several thousand or so years earlier. The menu, while varied, is filled with familiar favorites (rotisserie chicken, ribs, salads, and the like) but with a slightly creative twist (and fun names). The Footprints Flatbread is topped with melted cheddar, mozzarella, Parmesan, and goat cheeses; rotisserie chicken; and caramelized onions drizzled with a balsamic glaze—a tasty way to start off your meal (and large enough to share). It may take the entire family to finish the Chocolate Extinction, a decadent dessert that's got it all: vanilla ice cream, chocolate fudge cake, whipped cream, and caramel drizzle. A thematic decor inspired by water, fire, and ice combines with animatronic dinosaurs, bubbling geysers, meteor showers, and a slew of other prehistoric special effects to create this unique Disney dining experience. Waits can average around 2 hours, unless you've made Advance Reservations.

Downtown Disney Marketplace, near Pollo Campero. ✆ **407/828-8739.** www.trexcafe.com. Advance Reservations recommended. Main courses $14–$32 lunch and dinner (most less than $20). AE, DC, DISC, MC, V. Sun–Thurs 10:30am–11pm; Fri–Sat 10:30am–midnight. Free self-parking.

4

WHERE TO EAT

In Lake Buena Vista

Disney recently opened its newest full-service restaurant at Downtown Disney: **Paradiso 37.** The first new dining option to open for business at the newly re-imagined Pleasure Island (a project slated to open in stages over a 2-year period—the end result of which will soon become Disney's Hyperion Wharf), Paradiso 37 features a menu that is representative of the 37 countries throughout the Americas—North, Central, and South—in keeping with its name. In addition, an international bar features 50 or so tequilas and a varied selection of signature frozen margaritas. Menu items might include North American Sliders (blackened mahimahi, grilled barbecued chicken, or barbecued pulled pork); Colombian-style whole crispy hen marinated with onions, garlic, lemon, and cilantro; Chilean salmon, skewered and served with a tomato vinaigrette; or an Argentinean skirt steak topped with caramelized onions and chimichurri sauce. The waterfront location offers an unparalleled view of the entire Downtown Disney skyline. Open daily from 11am until late at night.

Downtown Disney also welcomed **Pollo Campero** in late 2010, a quick-service eatery with a flavorful menu of Latin dishes such as Campero Latin chicken, yucca fries, sweet plantains, and others ($5–$8). Pollo Campero replaces McDonald's, which closed in April 2010. Look for additional eateries to debut in upcoming months as the reimagined Hyperion Wharf begins to take shape.

Disney's West Side

EXPENSIVE

Wolfgang Puck Grand Café ★★ CALIFORNIAN   The wait can be distressing, but the energized atmosphere and eclectic menu make it well worth the effort. In the more casual downstairs cafe, colorful tiles accent practically everything, and an eye-catching exhibition kitchen allows you to watch as your food is prepared. A favorite stop is the sushi bar, a copper-and-terrazzo masterpiece that delivers some of the best sushi in Orlando. The upstairs, with tables that are available only with Advance Reservations, offers a more refined atmosphere, with a separate menu and service to match. Floor-to-ceiling windows allow for a fabulous view over the lake and a glimpse of the fireworks, if you time it right. The seasonally changing menu might feature butternut-squash risotto with roasted apples, seasonal vegetables, fried basil, Parmesan cheese, and poached lobster; or seared salmon with sunchoke purée, seasonal veggies, and lobster nage. Desserts include a triple-chocolate mousse tower with chocolate gelato, a chocolate phantom cookie, and a fudge brownie (a chocolate lover's dream come true). Puck's is noisy, making conversation difficult no matter which level you choose. **Note:** If you're in a hurry or on the go, you'll find a **Wolfgang Puck Express,** offering sandwiches, pizzas, desserts, and more, at both the West Side and the Marketplace.

1482 Buena Vista Dr., at Disney's West Side. ✆ **407/938-9653.** www.wolfgangpuck.com or www.levyrestaurants.com. Reservations not accepted on lower level; Advance Reservations recommended for upstairs dining room. Main courses $27–$41 upstairs, $18–$26 cafe; pizza and sushi $13–$18; Express $10–$16. AE, DC, DISC, MC, V. Daily 11am–4pm; Sun–Mon 6–10pm, Tues–Thurs 6–10:30pm, Fri–Sat 6–11:30pm. Free self-parking.

MODERATE

Bongo's Cuban Cafe ♨ CUBAN   Singer Gloria Estefan and her husband, Emilio, created this restaurant with high expectations. Its exterior, with a giant pineapple standing tall against the Downtown Disney skyline, is hard to miss. The interior is Art Deco with a Havana flavor and includes colorful tile mosaics and hand-painted murals of Cuba in its heyday. A Desi Arnaz impersonator gets things going every night as the restaurant fills with loud Latin music. Alas, while visually appealing, the food isn't great. The *churrasco* (a thin, tenderized steak) can't match what you find at Rolando's (p. 150). The *ropa vieja* (shredded beef) is tasty but dry, and the *arroz con pollo* (chicken with yellow rice) would be a highlight if the portion matched the price. The best bet: the Cuban sandwich—thin, toasted Cuban bread with ham, pork, and cheese—is safe and sanely priced. For a more relaxing experience, grab a drink at the bar (just know that the bongo-shaped barstools can be difficult to manage after a few drinks), or sit a spell out in the patio lounge upstairs.

1498 Buena Vista Dr., in Disney's West Side. ✆ **407/828-0999.** www.bongoscubancafe.com. Reservations not accepted. Dinner main courses $14–$29 (many less than $20); walk-up window $7–$9. AE, DC, DISC, MC, V. Sun–Thurs 11am–10:30pm, Fri–Sat 11am–11:30pm (dancing till 2am). Free self-parking.

House of Blues SOUTHERN/CREOLE   Most folks come for the blues bands and Sunday's gospel brunch, a foot-tapping, thigh-slapping musical affair worth high marks on the entertainment side. (The omelets are good, and there are enough fillers—bacon, salads, dessert, and bread—that few leave hungry.) The average food has a New Orleans flavor and includes such offerings as pan-seared voodoo shrimp; gumbo with smoked turkey and shrimp; and Creole jambalaya with shrimp, chicken, ham, andouille sausage, and roasted green onions. The rustic backwater bayou interior has a Cajun voodooish sort of feel and is by far the most interesting in Downtown Disney, filled (literally) with bottle caps and buttons, skeletal etchings, and hand-painted folk art. Do check out the restrooms; they're decorated with that diamond plating seen on the beds of some pickup trucks, especially in the South.

1490 Buena Vista Dr., at Disney's West Side, beneath water tower. ✆ **407/934-2583.** www.hob.com. Reservations not accepted (except brunch). Main courses $14–$28; sandwiches $11–$13; brunch $34 adults, $17 children 3–9. AE, DC, DISC, MC, V. Daily 11:30am–2am; brunch 10:30am and 1pm. Free self-parking.

Elsewhere in Lake Buena Vista

VERY EXPENSIVE

Hemingway's ★★ SEAFOOD   The interior of Hemingway's has an upscale Key West air, and the walls are hung with sepia photos of the author and his fishing trophies. The restaurant has a romantic indoor dining room lit by hurricane lamps, while the outdoor wooden deck overlooks a waterfall. Several smaller rooms add to the intimate atmosphere, and the tall picture windows allow for plenty of natural light and some beautiful views. Several of the restaurant's dishes are displayed in a glass case near the entry, so if you have any questions, the chefs are there to answer. Highlights include the beer-battered coconut shrimp with horseradish sauce and orange marmalade, the Mediterranean sea bass, and the jumbo lump crab–crusted mahimahi. The wine list is decent, but to stay in the spirit of the experience, order the Papa Dobles, a potent rum concoction invented by Hemingway, who, according to legend, once downed 16 at one sitting! It's usually pretty child-free here, though there is a kids' menu.

1 Grand Cypress Blvd., in the Hyatt Regency Grand Cypress Resort. ☎ **407/239-3854.** www.hyatt grandcypress.com. Reservations recommended. Main courses $27–$49. AE, DC, DISC, MC, V. Daily 6–10pm. Free self- and validated valet parking. Take I-4 exit 68, Hwy. 535/Apopka–Vineland Rd., north to Winter Garden–Vineland Rd./Hwy. 535, and then left.

La Coquina ★ INTERNATIONAL   Expect an imaginative menu from the most acclaimed of the Hyatt Regency's five restaurants. The **Chef's Table ★★★**, available Thursday through Saturday evenings (seasonally Sept–June), allows guests the unique experience of dining right in the kitchen (completely transformed by ambient lighting and a chic contemporary decor into an intimate and upscale private dining room). Guests are invited and encouraged to come right into the exhibition kitchen as their dinner is prepared. Chef Orlando personally brings each of the five tantalizing courses to your table. You might be lucky enough to enjoy lavender-honey-glazed rack of lamb, Hawaiian tuna tartare, buffalo tenderloin, or confit Chilean poached sea bass. A personalized menu signed by the chef and a Grand Cypress apron are given to each guest at the end of the evening. Even at $95 per person ($120 with wine pairings), this unique dining experience is well worth the splurge. Make the very-hard-to-obtain reservations as far in advance as possible. The Sunday brunch (Sept–June) also allows diners to try out the intimate setting of the kitchen, though most opt to sit in the main dining room.

1 Grand Cypress Blvd., in the Hyatt Regency Grand Cypress Resort. ☎ **407/239-3853.** www.grand cypress.com. Reservations recommended. Jackets suggested for men. Chef's table $95; Sun brunch $69 adults ($75 holidays), $34 children; no kids' menu. AE, DC, DISC, MC, V. Thurs–Sat 6:30–10pm; Sun brunch 10:30am–2pm. Free self- and validated valet parking. Take I-4 exit 68, Hwy. 535/Apopka–Vineland Rd., north to Winter Garden–Vineland Rd./Hwy. 535, and then left.

Mikado Japanese Steakhouse ★★ JAPANESE   This restaurant offers a tastier meal and a more intimate atmosphere than the other Japanese steakhouses in the area. The sushi menu is one of the area's best, as is its *teppanyaki*. Here the chefs slice, dice, and send the occasional piece of chicken, seafood, and beef from their grill to your plate, and the chef's addition of a few extra special spices make it the best *teppanyaki* around. Shoji screens lend intimacy to a dining area where windows overlook rock gardens, reflecting pools, and a palm-fringed pond. Sake, from the restaurant lounge, is the recommended mood enhancer.

8701 World Center Dr. (off Hwy. 536), in Marriott Orlando World Center. ☎ **407/239-4200.** Reservations recommended. Main courses $29–$48, $12–$14 kids. AE, DC, DISC, MC, V. Thurs–Tues 6–10pm. Free self- and validated valet parking. Take I-4 exit 67/Hwy. 536 east to the Marriott World Center.

MODERATE

The Crab House SEAFOOD   Even if it is a chain, this casual restaurant offers a good variety of seafood (and a handful of options for landlubbers) at satisfactory prices. The all-you-can-eat seafood and salad bar is great for those who like variety; it has lots of tasty dishes. The regular menu features a variety of fish dishes, seafood, Maine lobster, and, of course, crabs—from Alaskan and king to Maryland blue. The service is friendly and relatively prompt. Fishing gear and lobster traps are spread about the casual dining room, strands of lights are strewn across exposed ceilings, and brown paper (good for kids to draw on) lines the tables. *Note:* The chain has several other branches in the Orlando area.

8496 Palm Pkwy. (just off Apopka–Vineland across and up from Hotel Plaza Blvd.). ☎ **407/239-1888.** www.crabhouseseafood.com. Reservations accepted. Lunch $9–$24; dinner $14–$36; lobster varies according to market. AE, DC, DISC, MC, V. Daily 11:30am–11pm. Free self-parking. Take I-4 to exit 68

(Hwy. 535/Apopka–Vineland), turn right, follow past the Crossroads to Palm Pkwy., turn right. The restaurant is back a bit on the right.

Romano's Macaroni Grill 🍴 NORTHERN ITALIAN Though it's part of a multistate chain, Romano's has the down-to-earth cheerfulness of a mom-and-pop joint. The laid-back atmosphere makes it a good place for families or those looking for a casual dinner at a good price. The menu offers thin-crust pizzas made in a wood-burning oven and topped with such items as barbecued chicken. The grilled chicken portobello—simmering between smoked mozzarella and spinach orzo pasta—is worth a visit. Equally good is an entree of grilled salmon with a teriyaki glaze, also with spinach orzo. Premium wines are served by the glass.

12148 Apopka–Vineland Rd. (just north of Hwy. 535/Palm Pkwy.). ℃ **407/239-6676.** www.macaroni grill.com. Main courses $7–$16 lunch, $12–$26 dinner (most less than $20). AE, DC, DISC, MC, V. Sun-Thurs 11am–10pm; Fri-Sat 11am–11pm. Free self-parking. Take I-4 exit 68, Hwy. 535/Apopka–Vineland Rd. north and continue straight when Hwy. 535 goes to the right. Romano's is about 2 blocks up on the left.

IN UNIVERSAL ORLANDO

Universal Orlando stormed onto the restaurant scene with the 1999 opening of its dining and entertainment venue, CityWalk, which is between and in front of its two parks, Universal Studios Florida and Islands of Adventure. But Universal's sudden entry onto the food front doesn't mean quality was lost in the rush. In fact, some of the best dining options around can be found here—even inside the theme parks (and most especially at Islands of Adventure). Several of Universal's restaurants offer cuisine ranging from respectable light bites to dependable dinners (a few even border on fine dining), with most offering unique and casual atmospheres. Do note, of course, that the better-than-average food and surroundings come with higher-than-average prices.

Universal takes "Priority Seating" arrangements for its park and CityWalk restaurants, which can be made up to 30 days in advance by calling ℃ **407/224-3613** for USF restaurants, **407/224-4012** for IOA restaurants, and **407/224-3663** for City-Walk dining spots (except Margaritaville and NBA City). Actual reservations are available only for **Mythos** (℃ **407/224-4534**) and **Emeril's** (℃ **407/503-2467**). For more information on dining at Universal, call ℃ **407/224-9255.**

Note: Most of the restaurants below can be found on the "CityWalk" map, on p. 325. All of the hotel restaurants listed can be found on the "International Drive Area Restaurants" map, on p. 143.

Very Expensive

Bice ★ ITALIAN Universal Orlando's top Italian restaurant is appropriately located in the romantic and spectacular Italian setting of the Portofino Bay Hotel. The family-owned and -operated restaurant, part of a Milan-based international chain, serves creative cuisine in a sophisticated atmosphere. The extensive menu includes items such as a Belgian endive salad in a light Dijon dressing with Gorgonzola cheese and toasted walnuts; spaghetti with Maine lobster and cherry tomatoes in a tomato bisque; and veal chops with sautéed mushrooms, potatoes, and spinach. The dining room overlooks the waters along the piazza of the hotel, itself a beautiful and romantic setting—and a table on the patio, if timed right, may allow you to enjoy the music of the strolling musicians performing just below along the piazza. The interior is elegant, accented by a beautiful muted fresco of the Italian countryside and soft, subdued lighting. The lounge has a more contemporary feel (though the flatscreen TV above the bar detracts greatly from the otherwise exceptional ambience). If there's a disappointment to be found at this restaurant, it's the air of aloofness created by the servers and staff.

5601 Universal Studios Blvd., in the Portofino Bay Hotel. © **407/503-3463** or 407/503-1415. Reservations recommended. Main courses $18–$45. AE, MC, V. Daily 5:30–10:30pm. Free validated self-parking; valet parking $5. From I-4, take exit 75B, Kirkman Rd./Hwy. 435, and follow the signs to Universal.

Emeril's ★★ SOUTHERN/CREOLE   It's next to impossible to get short-term reservations for dinner at Emeril's (less than 3–4 weeks in advance) unless your stars are aligned or you come at the opening bell and take your chances with no-shows (highly unlikely). If you do get in, you'll find the dynamic cuisine is worth the struggle. The Creole-inspired, seasonally changing menu is varied and might include such dishes as a grilled double-cut pork chop with caramelized sweet potatoes, or perhaps andouille-crusted Texas redfish with a grilled vegetable relish, Creole meunière sauce, toasted pecans, and shoestring potatoes. If you want some *vino* with your meal, the back half of the building houses a glass-walled, 12,000-bottle, above-ground wine cellar. The warehouse-style decor is casual and inviting yet still upscale; original artwork, much of it by New Orleans artists, lines the walls, and arched lighting spans the two-story ceilings. If you want a show, I highly recommend you try for one of eight counter seats where you can watch chefs working their magic, but to get one, reservations are required *excruciatingly* early (2–3 months in advance, especially during holidays, in summer, and on weekends).

Note: Lunch costs about half what you'll spend on dinner, and the menu has many of the same entrees. It's also easier to get a reservation, and the dress code is more casual—jackets are recommended for the guys at dinner, although that goes against the grain after a long day in the parks. No matter when you come, leave the kids at home—this restaurant caters to adults.

6000 Universal Studios Blvd., in CityWalk. © **407/224-2424.** www.emerils.com. Reservations necessary. Main courses $21–$32 lunch, $28–$42 dinner. Daily 11:30am–3pm; Sun–Thurs 5–10pm; Fri–Sat 5–10:30pm. AE, DISC, MC, V. Parking $15 (free 2-hr. valet parking at lunch), $3 after 6pm. From I-4, take exit 75B, Kirkman Rd./Hwy. 435, and follow the signs to Universal.

The Palm SEAFOOD/STEAK   This upscale restaurant is the 23rd member of a chain started more than 75 years ago in New York. The food is good, although somewhat overpriced for the value received (as is the case with most Disney and Universal restaurants). Beef and seafood rule a menu headlined by a 36-ounce prime aged double-cut New York strip steak for two ($92) and a 3-pound Nova Scotia lobster (market price). There are, however, plenty of steaks, pasta, seafood, and salads to please every palate. There are even a few options for those on smaller budgets. The decor harkens back to the upscale supper club of the '30s and '40s, and the walls are lined with caricatures of celebrities and stars.

5800 Universal Blvd., in the Hard Rock Hotel. © **407/503-7256.** www.thepalm.com. Reservations recommended. Main courses $29–$58 dinner. AE, DC, DISC, MC, V. Mon–Thurs 5–10pm; Fri–Sat 5–11pm; Sun 5–9pm. Validated valet parking. From I-4, take exit 75B, Kirkman Rd./Hwy. 435, and follow the signs to Universal.

Expensive

Emeril's Tchoup Chop ★★★ PACIFIC RIM   Perfection is pronounced "chop chop." Emeril Lagasse's second restaurant in Orlando is named for the location of his original restaurant, Tchoupitoulas Street in New Orleans. Think Todd English's bluezoo (p. 127) with an Asian Pacific twist—very chic, very contemporary, very cool. The upbeat yet relaxing atmosphere, visually stunning surroundings, and excellent food will ensure the experience is unmatched. The exotic decor features glass flower chandeliers and a grand stone wall that reaches high above an exhibition kitchen (a seat at the counter allows for quite an impressive show). Polynesian- and Asian-influenced dishes such as macadamia-encrusted Atlantic salmon, crab cakes with mango-habanero-butter sauce and papaya salsa, and crunchy shrimp drizzled with a hot-and-sour chili glaze are just a sampling of the tasty offerings found here. Mains range from Mongolian barbecue grilled pork tenderloin to seared yellowfin tuna—but the sake-braised short ribs simply melt in your mouth. Not one but several waiters will impeccably cater to your every need, serving meals as if they were in a perfectly choreographed production. In 2010, a Sunday brunch was added to the lineup. Served up between 10:30am and 2pm, the prix-fixe menu offers a choice of starter, soup or salad, and entree. While too extensive to list in full, expect to find a mix of traditional offerings (but with Emeril's signature culinary kick) alongside a varied selection of Asian-inspired dishes. *Note:* The dress code here is more casual than at Emeril's (listed above), but it's still pretty upscale, so leave the T-shirts and tanks at home.

6300 Hollywood Way, in Universal's Royal Pacific Resort. (C) **407/503-2467.** www.emerils.com or www. universalorlando.com. Reservations strongly recommended. Main courses $16–$38; Sun brunch $22–$28. AE, DISC, MC, V. Daily 11:30am–2:30pm; Sun–Thurs 5:30–10pm; Fri–Sat 5:30–11pm; Sun brunch 10:30am–2pm. Valet parking (near the restaurant at the Convention Center entrance, not the hotel lot) $5. From I-4, take the Kirkman Rd./Hwy. 435 exit, and follow the signs to Universal.

Moderate

Bubba Gump Shrimp Company SEAFOOD   This casual family-friendly eatery, based on the blockbuster film *Forrest Gump,* features a diverse menu likely to please almost every palate—don't let the name fool you, it's not just for seafood lovers. Entrees run the gamut from the eponymous shrimp to fried chicken to T-bone steaks. There's also a wide array of salads and sandwiches. Spilling over with movie memorabilia, it's a perfect addition to a trip to the movie-themed Universal theme parks.

6000 Universal Studios Blvd., at Universal CityWalk. (C) **407/903-0044.** www.bubbagump.com or www.universalorlando.com. Reservations not accepted. Main courses $10–$23. AE, MC, V. Daily 11am–midnight. Parking $15 ($3 after 6pm). From I-4, take exit 75B, Kirkman Rd./Hwy. 435, and follow the signs to Universal.

Hard Rock Cafe AMERICAN   The largest Hard Rock Cafe on the planet features a 1959 pink Cadillac spinning above the bar. With its size, however, comes that much more noise—and the sound levels are loud. Kids love it, but adults shouldn't even think about having a conversation here. The menu is the same found at Hard Rocks around the world: burgers, chicken, okay steaks, and fried this-and-that. And, of course, it has its very own souvenir shop, too. The food is average American fare; it's the experience that draws people in. *Note:* The adjacent Hard Rock Live is a huge venue for concerts.

6000 Universal Studios Blvd., near Universal CityWalk. (C) **407/351-7625.** www.hardrock.com. Reservations not accepted. Main courses $10–$35. AE, MC, V. Daily 11am–midnight. Parking $15 ($3 after 6pm). From I-4, take exit 75B, Kirkman Rd./Hwy. 435, and follow the signs to Universal.

Jimmy Buffett's Margaritaville CARIBBEAN   The laid-back atmosphere may take you away to paradise, but the noise level after 4pm makes it futile for Parrot Heads and plain folk alike to try to talk with their table-mates. But most people come to Margaritaville in the evenings to party, not to participate in deep conversation. Come for lunch if you want to actually speak with your fellow diners during your meal. The back "Porch of Indecision" offers the quietest spot in the place to dine. Despite the Cheeseburgers in Paradise (yes, they're on the menu at $8–$9), the menu has Caribbean leanings and includes jerk salmon and Jimmy's Jammin' Jambalaya. While it's not contending for a critic's choice award, it's fairly tasty grub. But watch the tab: At $7 to $9 a pop for margaritas, the bill can climb to $50 or more per person for a routine meal that includes the jerk chicken or crab cakes. If you don't hanker for margaritas, the drink menu is almost as long as the main menu and features domestic and imported beer, as well as some unique tropical concoctions.

1000 Universal Studios Plaza, in CityWalk. ✆ **407/224-2155.** www.margaritavilleorlando.com or www.universalorlando.com. Reservations not accepted. Main courses $10–$25 (most less than $17). AE, DISC, MC, V. Daily 11:30am–2am. Parking $15 ($3 after 6pm). From I-4, take exit 75B, Kirkman Rd./Hwy. 435, and follow the signs to Universal.

Mythos ★ AMERICAN/SEAFOOD/STEAK   If you've ever wanted to dine inside a volcano covered in cascading waterfalls and images of Greek Titans, then here's the place for you. Actually, this upscale restaurant, which overlooks Islands of Adventure's Inland Sea, is quite classy. Diners are transported to a mythical underwater world upon entering the restaurant's cavernous interior, where low lighting and eerie music help set the atmosphere. The menu features salads, ranging from a simple bowl of greens to a full-fledged meal, and elaborate entrees of fish, chicken, seafood, pasta, and steaks. Simpler fare is available as well, including artistically presented burgers and sandwiches.

1000 Universal Studios Plaza, in Islands of Adventure. ✆ **407/224-9255** or 407/224-4534. Reservations recommended. Main courses $10–$18. AE, DISC, MC, V. Daily 11am to park closing. Parking $15 ($3 after 6pm). From I-4, take exit 75B, Kirkman Rd./Hwy. 435, and follow the signs to Universal.

Pastamoré Ristorante & Market SOUTHERN ITALIAN   This family-style restaurant greets you with display cases brimming with mozzarella and other goodies on the menu. The Antipasto Amore is a meal unto itself, including bruschetta, melon with prosciutto, olives, a medley of Italian cold cuts, fresh mozzarella, and more. The menu also features such traditional offerings as veal Marsala, chicken piccata, shrimp scampi, fettuccine Alfredo, lasagna, and pizza. Kids will appreciate an "all-you-will-allow" menu of familiar favorites (chicken fingers, pizzas, pastas, mac 'n' cheese, fries, veggies, and pudding), while parents will appreciate the price ($10). The food is actually pretty interesting, and the presentation isn't bad either. There's an open kitchen that lets you see the chefs in action, and the atmosphere is pleasant and lively. Pastamoré has a basic beer and wine menu. You can also eat in the **Market Cafe,** where a lighter menu—breakfast fare and sandwiches—is served from 8am to 2am. *Note:* If you're looking for a more intimate experience (and if Emeril's and Tchoup Chop are booked), Pastamoré's **Chef's Table** offers seating for up to six adults, private service, and a personalized menu; the required reservations must be made at least 48 hours in advance.

1000 Universal Studios Plaza, in CityWalk. ✆ **407/363-8000.** www.universalorlando.com. Reservations accepted. Main courses $11–$23. AE, DISC, MC, V. Daily 5–10pm; Market Cafe 8am–2am. Parking $15 ($3 after 6pm). From I-4, take exit 75B, Kirkman Rd./Hwy. 435, and follow the signs to Universal.

A Not-So-Grand Reopening

Originally named for the Peabody's resident ducks, who parade ceremoniously along the red carpet in and out of the lobby each and every day (p. 294), **Dux** (℃ **407/345-4550**; www.peabody orlando.com) had become one of the area's most popular upscale eateries, thanks to its unparalleled service and ever-changing menu. Upon completion of the new Peabody Tower, the hotel's signature restaurant reopened—well, sort of. The once-popular restaurant is now open only for private dining.

IN THE INTERNATIONAL DRIVE AREA

International Drive has one of the area's larger collections of fast-food joints, but mixed in around its midsection and southern end are some of the region's better restaurants. South I-Drive is 10 minutes by auto from the Walt Disney World parks. Restaurant Row, located in a small area just above I-Drive along Dr. Phillips Boulevard and Sand Lake Road, is currently the hottest dining area in Orlando. Most of the restaurants listed here are shown on the "International Drive Area Restaurants" map in this section.

Very Expensive

Texas de Brazil Churrascaria ★ BRAZILIAN   The decor (high ceilings, crimson walls, and abstract art) at this Brazilian churrascaria is dramatic, but the atmosphere is casual, upbeat, and welcoming. Upon being seated, you'll be directed to the extensive seasonal salad bar, filled with a variety of more than 40 salads, roasted vegetables, and soups. After filling your plate, head back to your seat, where you'll find a coaster-like disc—one side red, the other green. When you're ready for your main course, just flip your disc to green. Immediately a troop of carvers will show up, offering a variety of grilled and roasted meats, including garlic-marinated *picanha* (rump steak), Brazilian sausage, pork ribs, and chicken breast from their skewers. The bacon-wrapped filet is to die for—it simply melts in your mouth. When you've had your fill, simply turn your disc back to red. Assorted side dishes (served tableside) are available to complement your meal (if you actually have any room for them). A handful of a la carte items, including Australian lobster tail and shrimp cocktail, are available as well (at an additional cost). Drinks and desserts are extra, too. *Tip:* Kids ages 7 to 12 eat half price here, and kids 6 and younger eat for free.

5259 International Dr. ℃ **407/355-0355.** www.texasdebrazil.com. Reservations accepted. Fixed-price meals $48. AE, MC, V. Sun noon–3pm and 4–9:30pm; Mon–Thurs 5–10pm; Fri 5–10:30pm; Sat noon–3pm and 4–10:30pm. Free self-parking. From I-4, take exit 74A, turn right onto Sand Lake Rd., and then left onto International Dr.; the restaurant will be on the left.

Expensive

Ocean Prime ★★★ SEAFOOD/STEAK   This elegant and sophisticated establishment—a welcome addition to the Dr. Phillips dining scene—combines a menu of

DINING ON restaurant row

In the past few years, just east of I-4 along a stretch of Sand Lake Road, in the swanky suburb of Dr. Phillips, several very chic, very trendy, and very hip eateries have popped up. This high concentration of upscale (and, at times, ethnic) eateries, now known as **Restaurant Row,** is home to some of Orlando's best eating opportunities. In addition to the restaurants already listed in this guide (including **Roy's, Ocean Prime,** and the **Samba Room**), there are lots of others worth noting.

- **Seasons 52 ★**, 7700 W. Sand Lake Rd. (© **407/354-5212;** www.seasons52.com). Enter this combination grill and wine bar and you'll feel as if you've stepped onto the set of a Rock Hudson movie thanks to the '50s-style Art Deco architecture and an interior accented with stacked stone walls. The menu, which changes weekly, is both sophisticated and designed to be healthy, so it's relatively easy on the waistline and the palate.

- **City Fire American Oven & Bar,** 7958 Via Dellagio Way, off Sand Lake Road (© **407/722-8888;** www.cityfirerestaurants.com). Heating up the Orlando dining scene is City Fire, the latest addition to Restaurant Row's lineup. Although upscale, a homey and comfortable atmosphere is what sets this place apart. The restaurant is lined with photos and antiques dating back to the early 1900s; the lighting (an eclectic mix of mismatched fixtures) gives off a warm glow; and the tremendous stone wood oven stands before a shining copper wall. The menu offers a selection of signature flatbreads, seafood, and steaks.

A patio overlooking Sand Lake Road allows for outdoor dining in good weather.

- **Cedars of Orlando,** 7732 W. Sand Lake Rd. (© **407/351-6000**). A simple yet elegant atmosphere featuring Ottoman arches and columns, white table linens, and a roof-topped terrace for outdoor dining combine with a selection of more than 50 Lebanese specialties (and a bit of belly dancing) to make this Middle Eastern restaurant a very attractive package.

- **Amura ★**, 7786 Sand Lake Rd. (© **407/370-0007**). One of the city's best Asian restaurants features a contemporary decor that runs throughout its three unique dining areas, which include a sushi counter, performance grills, and a more intimate dining room. The main menu tilts toward a fusion of Japanese and European cuisines.

- **Timpano Italian Chophouse ★**, 7488 W. Sand Lake Rd. (© **407/248-0249;** www.timpanochophouse.net). Classic, sophisticated styling (think old New York supper club) is the signature of this Italian steakhouse, which features fabulous aged steaks and impeccable service. Large booths, chandeliers, an indoor fireplace, and a baby grand piano add to the ambience, while the sounds of Sinatra, swing, and jazz play in the background.

To get to Restaurant Row: From I-4 E., take exit 74A, and turn left onto Sand Lake Road. From I-Drive, turn left onto Sand Lake Road. Restaurants run along both sides of the road in the Fountains, Rialto, and Venezia plazas, as well as the Marketplace.

4

In the International Drive Area

WHERE TO EAT

International Drive Area Restaurants

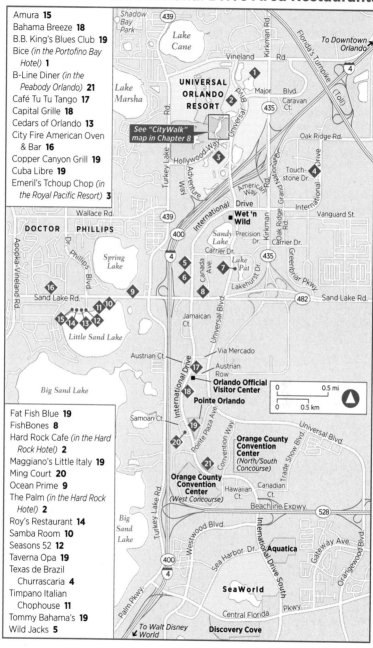

Amura **15**
Bahama Breeze **18**
B.B. King's Blues Club **19**
Bice *(in the Portofino Bay Hotel)* **1**
B-Line Diner *(in the Peabody Orlando)* **21**
Café Tu Tu Tango **17**
Capital Grille **18**
Cedars of Orlando **13**
City Fire American Oven & Bar **16**
Copper Canyon Grill **19**
Cuba Libre **19**
Emeril's Tchoup Chop *(in the Royal Pacific Resort)* **3**

Fat Fish Blue **19**
FishBones **8**
Hard Rock Cafe *(in the Hard Rock Hotel)* **2**
Maggiano's Little Italy **19**
Ming Court **20**
Ocean Prime **9**
The Palm *(in the Hard Rock Hotel)* **2**
Roy's Restaurant **14**
Samba Room **10**
Seasons 52 **12**
Taverna Opa **19**
Texas de Brazil Churrascaria **4**
Timpano Italian Chophouse **11**
Tommy Bahama's **19**
Wild Jacks **5**

If you're on a tight budget and your room has a kitchen or a spot to sit and enjoy a bite, consider dining in a night or two and saving a few bucks. Area grocers, many with delis that turn out ready-to-eat treats, include **Publix,** near Universal (Venezia Shopping Plaza, 7640 Sand Lake Rd.; ✆ **407/226-3315;** and 4606 S. Kirkman Rd.; ✆ **407/293-7673;** www.publix.com), along I-Drive near SeaWorld (Regency Shopping Village, 8145 Vineland Ave.; ✆ **407/238-9924),** and in Kissimmee near Disney (Xentury City Shopping Center, 2925 International Dr. S.; ✆ **407/397-1711);** and **Gooding's,** in Lake Buena Vista (Crossroads Shopping Plaza, 12521 Hwy. 535/Apopka–Vineland Ave.; ✆ **407/827-1200;** www.goodings.com) and along I-Drive (8255 International Dr.; ✆ **407/352-4215).** You can find more options in the Orlando Yellow Pages under "Grocers."

fresh seafood and prime steaks, unique hand-crafted cocktails (I highly recommend the Berries and Bubbles—it's served tableside, but you'll have to order one for yourself to see why!), an extensive wine list, and an unbeatable Sinatra-esque atmosphere reminiscent of a 1930s supper club (albeit an updated version of one). Start off with the Sonoma goat-cheese ravioli (simply delish) and move on to the ginger salmon with soy-butter sauce or the seared arctic char; both are light yet very flavorful. In addition to an array of signature dishes, you'll find an assortment of seafood and steaks along with a medley of tasty and creative sauces to complement your selection. Sides are offered separately ($7–$10 extra). An incredibly knowledgeable and attentive staff top off the exceptional experience here—it's a must for discerning diners!

7339 W. Sand Lake Rd. ✆ **407/781-4880.** www.ocean-prime.com. Reservations suggested. Main courses $19–$48. AE, DC, DISC, MC, V. Mon–Thurs 4–10pm; Fri–Sat 4–11pm; Sun 4–9pm. Valet parking free. Take I-4 exit 74A, Sand Lake Rd./Hwy. 528, and go west 1 mile. Restaurant is on the right in the Rialto Plaza.

Roy's Restaurant ★ PACIFIC RIM   Created in Hawaii in 1988 by Roy Yamaguchi, this small chain made its Orlando debut in 2001. The restaurant has an island theme and, unlike the nearby Samba Room (see below), an atmosphere that allows for intimate conversation. The main dining area has a large open exhibition kitchen, offering quite a show for those seated at the surrounding counter. The emphasis is on fresh seafood (though other items are offered as well), prepared with a variety of sauces and imaginatively presented with an Asian-style flair. Menus change weekly (classic dishes remain a constant), but entrees might include Hawaiian Island blackened ahi with spicy soy-mustard butter, roasted macadamia-crusted mahimahi with a lobster-butter sauce, and hibachi-style grilled salmon with Japanese vegetables and citrus-ponzu sauce. Roy's also has a reasonably deep wine list.

7760 W. Sand Lake Rd. ✆ **407/352-4844.** www.roysrestaurant.com. Reservations suggested. Main courses $25–$40; fixed-price menu $35. AE, DC, DISC, MC, V. Sun–Thurs 5:30–10pm; Fri–Sat 5:30–10:30pm. Take I-4 exit 74A, Sand Lake Rd./Hwy. 528, and go west 1 mile. Restaurant is on left.

Moderate

Bahama Breeze ★ CARIBBEAN   This chain restaurant sports a creative menu that offers a variety of delicious sandwiches and chicken, fish, and pasta entrees with Caribbean twists. Try starting with the Creole baked goat cheese before moving on to the Cuban sandwich, one of the most authentic around. If that's not to your liking, go for the pan-seared pork or Bahamian chicken kabobs. The atmosphere is island casual, with rich wood and wicker throughout. On a warm evening, ask to eat outside. Live music (offered nightly) adds to the ambience. Once famous for its long waits, the restaurant now accepts call-ahead reservations—be sure and make one. *Note:* A second branch is located in Lake Buena Vista at 8735 Vineland Ave., near the I-4 intersection (© **407/938-9010**).

8849 International Dr. © **407/248-2499.** www.bahamabreeze.com. Call-ahead reservations available. Lunch and dinner $9–$26. AE, DISC, MC, V. Sun–Thurs 11am–1am; Fri–Sat 11am–1:30am. Free self-parking. From I-4, take exit 74A; follow I-Drive 1 mile south.

B-Line Diner AMERICAN   Retaining slightly more than a smidgen of its original Art Deco diner-inspired feel, recent refurbishments have transformed the B-Line into a more sophisticated establishment (albeit updated, rather than completely redone). Diners can still sink into upholstered booths or belly up to the counter in this casual upscale eatery, but rather than red upholstery and neon lights, expect the '50s-style flair to be less evident than before (chrome accents, trendier lighting, and so on). The round-the-clock menu has expanded to match the newer concept—alongside comfort foods such as chicken potpie, mouthwatering smoked bacon meatloaf, and pot roast smothered in a creamy stout gravy, expect to find items such as Moroccan spiced Atlantic salmon and mini crab rolls with spicy coconut and a yummy curry dipping mayo. The portions are hearty, but so are the prices. And although it is a diner-style restaurant, it is not particularly kid-friendly, unless your children are exceptionally well behaved.

9801 International Dr., in the Peabody Orlando. © **407/345-4460.** www.peabodyorlando.com. Reservations not accepted. Main courses $4–$17 breakfast, $12–$26 lunch and dinner (most less than $18). AE, DC, DISC, MC, V. Daily 24-hr., B-Line Express daily 6am–11pm. Free validated valet parking. From I-4, take exit 74A, Sand Lake Rd./Hwy. 528, east to International Dr., and then south. Hotel is on the left across from the Convention Center.

Café Tu Tu Tango ★★ 👔 INTERNATIONAL/TAPAS   Authentic cuisine and the eclectic atmosphere of a Mediterranean artist's loft—complete with working artist—are the main draws at this interesting tapas bar. The portions are small, but the tastes are big. The roasted pears on pecan crisps—topped with Spanish blue cheese and a balsamic reduction—are a must. The staff is fabulous, and your server will be happy to educate you about the menu or make suggestions. Wine is available by the glass or bottle.

8625 International Dr. © **407/248-2222.** www.cafetututango.com. Reservations accepted but not required. Tapas (small plates) $5–$12. AE, DC, DISC, MC, V. Sun–Thurs 11:30am–11pm; Fri–Sat 11:30am–2am. Free self-parking. From I-4, take exit 74A, Sand Lake Rd./Hwy 528, east to International Dr., and then south. It is on the left.

FishBones SEAFOOD   The fish at this Key West–themed restaurant is hand-picked daily to ensure freshness and taste. You can create your own meal by mixing and matching sauces and salsas to enhance your selection. If fish isn't your dish, other offerings include rack of lamb, prime rib, and duck. You can dine in one of two distinctive seating areas: one sporting a classic steakhouse decor, the other a more casual space that's evocative of an outdoor porch.

6707 Sand Lake Rd., off International Dr. © **407/352-0135.** www.talkofthetownrestaurants.com/fishbones_orlando.html. Main courses $13–$40 (most less than $25). AE, MC, V. Sun–Thurs 4:30–10:30pm; Fri–Sat 4:30–11pm. Free self-parking. From I-4 take exit 74A, go ½-mile east on S.R. 482 (Sand Lake Rd.).

4

WHERE TO EAT

In the International Drive Area

For those of you who would rather take a break from eating out, there are several Orlando restaurants that are more than willing to come to you. A local delivery service, **Room Service Orlando** (formerly Take Out Express), will deliver takeout from a number of area restaurants (even more than one at a time, for an extra charge) right to your hotel room. The delivery cost is $6 per restaurant ($5 if ordering online), plus a 15% gratuity automatically added for the driver. Check out **www.roomservice orlando.com**, or call © **407/352-1170** for details.

Ming Court ★★ CHINESE   Local patronage and a diverse menu make this one of Orlando's most popular Chinese restaurants; it has racked up awards and praise from a host of respected international food critics. Start off with the duck lettuce cup before going on to the lightly battered, deep-fried chicken breast—it's got plenty of zip from a delicate lemon-tangerine sauce. If you're in the mood for beef, there's a grilled filet mignon that's seasoned Szechuan style (the topping has toasted onions, garlic, and chili). The mildly innovative menu is extensive and features the freshest ingredients (there's not a freezer in sight). Portions are sufficient, there's a moderate wine list, and the service is quite good. The romantic candlelit interior is decorated in soft earth tones, glass-walled terrace rooms overlook lotus ponds filled with colorful koi, and a plant-filled area sits under a lofty skylight ceiling. A musician plays classical Chinese music on a *zheng* (a long zither) at dinner. The children's menu features a boxed meal with a choice of Oriental-style shrimp, pork, beef, or chicken (and french fries!), and comes with a story for kids to read along with their dinner. *Tip:* The restaurant's extensive website features lots of information on and photos of individual dishes.

9188 International Dr., btw. Sand Lake Rd. and Beachline Expwy. © **407/351-9988.** www.ming-court. com. Reservations recommended. Main courses $6–$28 lunch, $11–$43 dinner; dim sum mostly $3–$5. AE, DC, DISC, MC, V. Daily 11am–3pm and 4:30–11pm. Free self-parking. From I-4, take exit 74A, Sand Lake Rd./Hwy. 528, east to International Dr., and then south. It's on the right.

Samba Room ★ CUBAN   Don't count on intimate conversation, because the Cuban and Brazilian music here is loud, *loud,* LOUD (and the regulars like it that way). The atmosphere is upbeat and sophisticated, enhanced by contemporary artwork and vividly colorful murals. The kitchen turns out an enterprising menu that includes rum teriyaki–glazed salmon with stir-fried veggies, soba noodles, and Kaffir lime sauce; Spanish paella (chicken, mussels, shrimp, calamari, and lobster over saffron rice); and pork *barbacoa* (marinated in beer and slow-roasted in banana leaves) with gringo rice and Asian barbecue sauce. If you're worried about saving room for dessert (portions are large), the restaurant offers downsized versions of decadent desserts that won't bust your buttons. Alfresco dining is available on the patio and is especially enjoyable in milder weather. *Tip:* Fridays feature late-night samba lessons, while live Latin bands play to the Saturday-night crowds.

7468 W. Sand Lake Rd. © **407/226-0550.** www.sambaroom.net. Reservations recommended. Main courses $17–$25. AE, DC, DISC, MC, V. Sun 5–10pm; Mon–Wed 4–10pm; Fri 4–11pm; Sat 5–11pm. Free self-parking. Take I-4 exit 74A, Sand Lake Rd./Hwy. 528, west 1 mile. Restaurant is on the left.

Wild Jacks BARBECUE/STEAK   Come hankering for red meat or don't come at all to this chuck wagon–style eatery. Jacks serves Texas-size (and sometimes Texas-tough) hunks of cow grilled on an open pit and served with jalapeño smashed potatoes and corn on the cob. The ribs are generally moist and tender, but at crowded times, when the kitchen gets backed up, they may be dry and chewy. The menu also has chicken, salmon, and pork, but it's not a good idea to experiment in a beef house. To add to the mood, you'll be treated to mounted buffalo heads; long-stuffed jackalopes; and more dying-calf-in-a-hailstorm, twitch-and-twang country-western music than a city slicker can endure in a lifetime. Wash the meal down with an icy longneck (there is a wine list, but it's very basic).

7364 International Dr., btw. Sand Lake Rd. and Carrier Dr. ✆ **407/352-4407.** Reservations accepted. AE, DC, DISC, MC, V. Main courses $14–$23. Daily 4–10pm. Free self-parking. From I-4, take exit 74A, Sand Lake Rd./Hwy. 528, east to International Dr., and then go south. It's on the right.

ELSEWHERE IN ORLANDO

There's life beyond the main tourist areas, as a lot of locals and some enterprising visitors discover. The restaurants listed below are found on the "Hotels & Restaurants Elsewhere in Orlando" map in this section.

Very Expensive

Chalet Suzanne ★ AMERICAN   Though located quite a distance from Orlando's main tourist districts, this charming family-owned inn, established some 80 years ago, offers a romantic fairytale-style ambience that could easily rival that of Cinderella Castle (sans the characters). The five intimate and inviting dining rooms are each filled with an eclectic collection of mismatched dinnerware (which only

---

A Reason to Celebrate

An eclectic array of upscale eateries lines the streets along Market Square in the Disney-built town of Celebration (www.celebrationfl.com). From the **Market Street Café** (✆ 407/566-1144), an updated '50s-style diner, to **Shannon's of Celebration,** an authentic Irish pub (✆ 407/566-8733; www.shannons ofcelebration.com), to the shabby-chic surroundings of **Imperium Food & Wine** (✆ 407/566-9044; www.imperium foodandwine.com), those in search of stylish surroundings and creative cuisine won't be disappointed. An ornate old-world Spanish decor and Cuban-influenced cuisine are the signature of the **Columbia Restaurant** (✆ 407/566-1505; www.columbiarestaurant.com), while **Café D'Antonio Ristorante** (✆ 407/566-2233; www.antonios online.com) serves up tasty Italian cuisine in a warm and welcoming atmosphere. You'll feel as if you've traveled halfway across the world at **Thai Thani** (✆ 407/566-9444; www.thaithani orlando.net), where an endless menu of authentic dishes, an ornate decor, and friendly service await. The **Seito Sushi Japanese Restaurant** (✆ 407/566-1899; www.seitosushi.com) is known for its fresh sushi, fusion-style cuisine, and stylish atmosphere. And finally, the **Celebration Town Tavern** (✆ 407/566-2526; www.thecelebrationtowntavern. com) is a more casual alternative that sports a nautical theme and fresh seafood.

GET THE pointe?

Pointe Orlando, 9101 International Dr. (📞 **407/248-2838;** www.pointeorlando.com), has evolved, thanks to a multi-million-dollar redevelopment a few years ago, into an upscale collection of outdoor shops and trendy eateries. In addition to the restaurants already listed in this guide, there are others here worth noting, including:

○ **Cuba Libre Restaurant & Rum Bar** (📞 **407/226-2481;** www.cubalibrerestaurant.com). This exotic addition to the lineup of upscale eateries located at Pointe Orlando features contemporary Cuban cuisine, lively Latin music, professional salsa floorshows, and an open-air tropical ambience with outdoor dining—and did I mention the extensive rum selection?

○ **Capital Grille** ★ (📞 **407/370-4392;** www.capitalgrille.com). The menu at this reputable establishment is filled with tempting appetizers, dry-aged steaks, hand-carved chops, fresh seafood, and decadent desserts. An extensive wine list (400-plus selections) and impeccable service are two other hallmarks. Discerning diners will appreciate not only a mouthwatering meal (with options that include a dry-aged sirloin rubbed with black peppercorns and served in a rich cognac cream–and–peppercorn sauce), but also the relaxed yet sophisticated atmosphere.

○ **Maggiano's Little Italy** (📞 **407/241-8650;** www.maggianos.com). You'll find a taste of New York's Little Italy, Chicago's Taylor Street, Boston's North End, and South Philly on Maggiano's menu. It's filled with authentic home-cooked Italian fare, including such specialties as lobster ravioli, braised beef cannelloni (with Asiago and Parmesan cheeses), and chicken cacciatore. The warm and inviting atmosphere is casual and relaxed, making you feel as if you've stepped into the neighborhood Italian kitchen.

○ **Copper Canyon Grill** (📞 **407/363-3933;** www.ccgrill.com). The Southwest-inspired decor spills over to the menu, with specialties that range from fire-grilled

adds to the charm), stained-glass windows, and antique lamps. Best known for its traditional prix-fixe dinner (broiled grapefruit topped with chicken liver, homemade romaine sour, and a Caesar salad start things off, followed by your choice of either roasted chicken, buffalo filet, or crab cakes, and ending with dessert), Chalet Suzanne now offers an a la carte menu for guests who prefer a less intensive dining experience. Entrees include duck confit a l'orange, black angus filet, and lobster Newburg. The fare here leans to the traditional side, though it's the atmosphere, not the food, that brings diners this far out. An award-winning wine list ensures you'll find an appropriate wine to complement your meal. Brunch is a casual affair, but dinner is a bit more formal (jackets are the norm for men).

3800 Chalet Suzanne Dr., Lake Wales. 📞 **800/433-6011.** www.chaletsuzanne.com. Reservations recommended. Main courses $28–$42; 5-course prix-fixe dinner $59–$78. AE, DC, DISC, MC, V. Tues–Sun 10am–2pm; Tues–Thurs 5–8pm; Fri–Sat 5–9pm. Free self-parking.

chicken to smoked Atlantic salmon. Comfort foods (with a creative culinary twist), hearty salads, and a selection of steak and seafood are the norm at this casual yet upscale eatery. Portions are large and filling, so come hungry.

o **Tommy Bahama's Tropical Café & Emporium** (© 321/281-5888; www.tommybahama.com). The eclectic yet elegant decor here invokes thoughts of the Pacific Rim, with accents of bamboo, palm leaves, beads, and island-inspired artwork lining the walls. Those looking for fresh seafood won't be disappointed by signature dishes such as macadamia-encrusted pink snapper or sautéed jumbo shrimp and scallops in a curry-coconut sauce. If you prefer to dine outdoors, the patio is the place to be—and thanks to a partition, you'll be able to enjoy a bit of privacy along with your meal.

o **Taverna Opa** (© 407/351-8660; www.opaorlando.com). Diners will appreciate the authentic Greek fare, casual atmosphere, and down-to-earth prices here. For a more celebratory experience, head to Taverna later in the evening, when a far more festive atmosphere prevails as plate breaking and napkin throwing are common occurrences.

o **B.B. King's Blues Club** (© 407/370-4550; www.bbkingclubs.com). Southern cuisine, ranging from barbecued ribs to Carolina glazed salmon, is served amid live music and four full-service bars. An inviting open-air patio allows for outdoor dining.

Note: Additional restaurants, other than the ones listed above, have opened at Pointe Orlando in recent months—including the **Funky Monkey Wine Company** (© 407/418-9463; www.funkymonkeywine.com), with its eclectic menu of Asian-American dishes served up alongside a vast selection of wines, and **Fat Fish Blue** (407/480-2000; www.orlandofatfishblue.com), featuring live entertainment and casual American fare with a New Orleans twist. Be sure to check out **www.pointeorlando.com** before your visit for up-to-the-minute developments.

Moderate

Carrabba's ★ ITALIAN   Here's yet another chain, but one that is well run with above-average food. The menu features such specialties as *tagliarini picchi pacchiu* (a fine pasta with crushed tomatoes, garlic, olive oil, and basil served with either chicken or shrimp) and *pollo Rosa Maria* (fire-roasted chicken stuffed with fontina cheese and prosciutto, and topped with mushrooms and a basil–lemon butter sauce). Also available are wood-fired pizzas, an array of soups and salads, pastas, and other Italian classics. The atmosphere is casual but lively; the interior features a show kitchen and lots of exposed brick. Save room for dessert—they're large enough to share (though you may not want to!). **Note:** A second location has recently opened in Lake Buena Vista, on Vineland Road between the Orlando Premium Outlets and S.R. 535.

Downtown Delights

Orlando's revitalized downtown area is now home to some chic clubs and trendy upscale restaurants well worth a second look—and the 20-minute drive. **Hue ★★**, 629 E. Central Blvd. (🕾 **407/849-1800; www.huerestaurant. com**), recognized in 2003 by *Condé Nast Traveler* as "one of the best new restaurants in the world," lives up to its reputation, thanks to creative American cuisine and a sophisticated urban loft atmosphere. **Kres Chophouse ★**, 17 W. Church St. (🕾 **407/447-7950; www. kresrestaurant.com**), a not-so-distant relative of Hue, offers an ever-changing menu of traditional yet exceptional steakhouse fare, as well as an extensive wine list. **Citrus Restaurant ★**, 821 N. Orange Ave. (🕾 **407/373-0622; www. citrusorlando.com**), features fresh American cuisine with a definitive Latin influence in a contemporary atmosphere. Blue-crab cakes, marinated skirt steak, bacon-wrapped Maine scallops, and yellowfin tuna are just a sampling of what you'll find on the menu. **Ceviche Tapas Bar & Restaurant,** 125 W. Church St. (🕾 **321/281-8140; www. ceviche.com**), serves up over 100 different tapas, each created from recipes and ingredients imported directly from northern Spain and Catalan to ensure an authentic flavor.

7890 Irlo Bronson Memorial Hwy. (U.S. 192), in the Formosa Gardens Plaza, Kissimmee. 🕾 **407/390-9600.** www.carrabbas.com. Main courses $10–$24 dinner only. AE, DC, DISC, MC, V. Sun–Thurs 4–10pm; Fri–Sat 4–11pm. Free self-parking. From I-4 take exit 64 for U.S. 192, continue on, and it is on the left in the Formosa Gardens Plaza.

Pacino's Italian Ristorante ★ NORTHERN ITALIAN The house specialty, *osso buco,* is a delicious collision of pork shank, mushrooms, Barolo wine, herbs, and mushrooms. The 18-ounce rib-eye, while not quite a belly buster, is more than filling, and the house's *frutti di mare* has shrimp, calamari, clams, and scallops sautéed with white wine and herbs and heaped onto a mound of linguine. The open two-story interior is filled with exposed brick, wrought-iron accents, and a ceiling with fiber optics that creates the illusion of dining under the stars. The second story offers more intimate seating overlooking the interior courtyard below. Grape vines are strewn throughout for an authentic feel. Outdoor seating is available on the patio.

5795 W. Irlo Bronson Memorial Hwy./U.S. 192, Kissimmee. 🕾 **407/396-8022.** www.pacinos.com. Reservations accepted. Main courses $15–$27 (most less than $20). AE, MC, V. Daily 4–11pm. Free self-parking. From I-4, take exit 64A/U.S. 192 east 1 mile.

Rolando's ★ CUBAN If you like neighborhood-style Cuban cuisine, you won't be disappointed here. This mom-and-pop restaurant serves large portions of traditional Cuban fare, such as *arroz con pollo* (chicken with yellow rice), *ropa vieja* (shredded beef), and, if you call a few hours or a day in advance, paella (fish and shellfish served on a bed of rice). Entrees come with a side of yucca (a chewy root) or plantains (a banana-like fruit). The plain dining room has Formica tables, old photographs of Cuba, and potted philodendrons suspended from the ceiling. Soft lighting adds a smidgen of ambience, and there's a very limited beer and wine list.

870 E. Hwy. 436/Semoran Blvd., Casselberry. 🕾 **407/767-9677.** Reservations accepted. Main courses $4–$6 lunch, $10–$18 dinner. AE, DC, DISC, MC, V. Tues–Thurs 11am–3pm and 5–9pm; Fri 11am–3pm and

4

Elsewhere in Orlando WHERE TO EAT

Hotels & Restaurants Elsewhere in Orlando

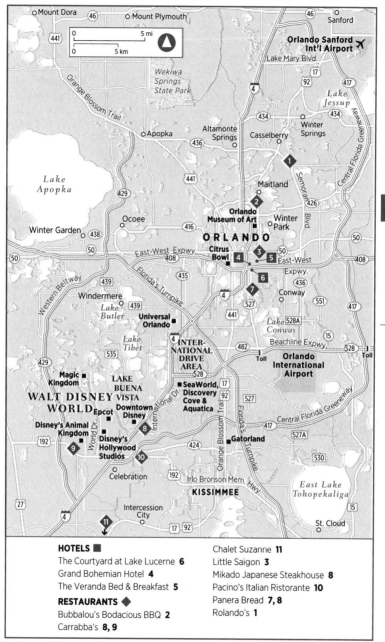

HOTELS ■
The Courtyard at Lake Lucerne **6**
Grand Bohemian Hotel **4**
The Veranda Bed & Breakfast **5**

RESTAURANTS ◆
Bubbalou's Bodacious BBQ **2**
Carrabba's **8, 9**

Chalet Suzanne **11**
Little Saigon **3**
Mikado Japanese Steakhouse **8**
Pacino's Italian Ristorante **10**
Panera Bread **7, 8**
Rolando's **1**

I won't list them all, but if you spend time on International Drive or U.S. 192/ Irlo Bronson Memorial Highway between Kissimmee and Disney, you'll see billboards peddling all-you-can-eat breakfast buffets for $5 to $8. This is a good way to fill your tank early and skip (or at least go easy on) lunch, especially if your day is in the theme parks, where lunches are overpriced. Note that you won't find award-winning cuisine here, except perhaps for the highest concentration of grease! Those with kids, however, will appreciate the inexpensive and kid-friendly fare— especially over some of the high-priced restaurants at the resorts.

Breakfast buffets are served by **Golden Corral,** 8033 International Dr. (✆ **407/352-6606); Ponderosa Steak House,** 6362 International Dr. (✆ **407/ 352-9343),** and 7598 U.S. 192 W. (✆ **407/396-7721);** and **Sizzler Restaurant,** 9142 International Dr. (✆ **407/ 351-5369),** and 7602 U.S. 192 W. (✆ **407/397-0997).** The latter two are the better bets.

5–10pm; Sat noon–10pm; Sun noon–8pm. Free self-parking. From I-4, take exit 82A, Hwy. 408/East-West Expwy., head east, and make a left on Hwy. 436.

Inexpensive

Bubbalou's Bodacious BBQ ★ 🔥 BARBECUE   You can smell the hickory smoke emerging from this restaurant for blocks, the tangy scent cutting through the humid Florida air. This is, hands down, some of the best barbecue you'll find anywhere. And, if nothing else, you have to love the name. If you can eat the night or day away, go for "The Big-Big Pig" platter (beef, sliced pork, and turkey with fixin's). There are also several barbecue baskets, combos, dinners, and sandwiches, as well as sides ranging from fried pickles and okra to collard greens and black-eyed peas. The uninitiated should stay away from the "Killer" sauce, which can render your taste buds useless, likely for hours; you might even taste-test the mild before moving up to the hot. The beans are the perfect side dish. Only the sometimes-soggy garlic bread brings the meal down, but not too far. Beer is available.

5818 Conroy Rd. (near Universal Orlando). ✆ **407/295-1212.** www.bubbalous.com. Reservations not accepted. Main courses $4–$15, with larger sizes available for takeout up to $25. AE, MC, V. Mon–Thurs 10am–9:30pm; Fri–Sat 10am–10:30pm; Sun 11am–9pm. Free self-parking. Take I-4 exit 75B, head east on Kirkman, and follow your nose; Bubbalou's is at the intersection of Kirkman and Conroy.

Little Saigon ★ 🍴 VIETNAMESE   Asian immigrants created the demand for Vietnamese cuisine in Orlando, and this noisy little restaurant is one of the best. Better yet, it doesn't attract many tourists, as it's located a bit off the beaten path, and was slightly off the radar without a presence on the Internet until recently. Try the summer rolls—a soft wrap filled with rice, shrimp, and pork, served with a delicious peanut sauce. Head next for the grilled pork and egg over rice and noodles, or barbecued beef with fried egg and rice. If your appetite is larger than average, try one of the traditional soups with noodles, rice, vegetables, and either chicken, beef, or seafood. The numbered menu is now translated in a way that allows diners to know what they're eating—you no longer need to ask your server exactly what goes into no. 86 (and given that some of the servers don't speak English, this is a plus). As a testament to the restaurant's authenticity, tables here are usually filled with members of the local Vietnamese community. There are very limited wine and beer choices.

1106 E. Colonial Dr./Hwy. 50 (near downtown Orlando). ☎ **407/423-8539.** www.littlesaigonrestaurant. com. Reservations not accepted. Main courses $7–$9. AE, DISC, MC, V. Daily 10am–9pm. Free self-parking. Take exit 83B, Colonial Dr./Hwy. 50, off I-4 and head east. Turn right on Thornton Ave. The parking lot is immediately to the left.

ONLY IN ORLANDO: DINING WITH DISNEY CHARACTERS

Dining with your favorite costumed characters is a treat for many Disney fans, but it's a truly special occasion for those younger than 10. Some of the most beloved movie characters seemingly come to life: shaking hands, hugging, signing autographs, and posing for family photos (most never speak, with the exception of the princesses and a very small handful of others, so forget about conversation). These are huge events—it's not uncommon for Chef Mickey's, listed below, to have **1,600 or more guests on a weekend morning**—so make your Advance Reservations (a must!!!!!) as far in advance as possible (when you book your room, if not earlier). Don't expect more than

NOT JUST fries ANYMORE

Some of you may not be able to go your entire vacation without a trip to McDonald's for a Big Mac. If you just can't pass up a trip to Mickie D's for a fast-food fix, the good news is that Orlando has a handful of uniquely themed McDonald's unlike any you'll find in your neighborhood. All of them sport unique and eclectic menus, which, in addition to the usual fare, add (among other items) pizzas, turkey wraps, portobello and eggplant panini, and crème brûlée cheesecake.

The 24-hour McDonald's **European Café,** 7344 Sand Lake Rd. (☎ 407/264-0776), boasts two levels with plenty of glass to allow sunlight to pour in. You won't mistake it for a European cafe (it's still a McDonald's, so don't get too carried away), but neat features include a pool table and arcade games on the second level, plus fabulous views of the sand lakes.

The **Ancient Ruins** branch, 5401 Altamira Dr. (☎ 407/345-9477), is themed (wonder of wonders) to the ancient ruins of Greece, complete with broken columns, stone walls, and frieze-style moldings.

The **Club Safari** location, 2944 S. Kirkman Rd. (☎ 407/296-6265), boasts an African safari theme complete with rich wooden fixtures, African masks and artwork, crystal chandeliers, and animal prints galore. Animatronic toucan and Tiki figures sing jungle jingles, and you can't help but take note of the 13-foot bronze giraffe and two bronze tigers keeping watch.

Chrome shines everywhere you turn at the **Motorcycle McDonald's,** 5400 S. Kirkman Rd. (☎ 407/352-1526). Tail pipes, shocks, and various other bike parts adorn the restaurant's walls.

Finally, the **world's largest McDonald's** can also be found in Orlando, right on 6875 Sand Lake Rd. (☎ 407/351-2185). The location boasts a huge tubular maze with 25,000 feet of twists, turns, and sliding, crawling, and jumping space for kids to play in. Another unique feature: You can book hotels and transportation, buy attraction tickets, and get daily park information, all while enjoying your fries and a Coke (or, in this case, maybe a gourmet coffee).

For a complete list of themed McDonald's throughout the Orlando area (there are several), head to **www. mcfun.com/restaurants.**

just a few moments of one-on-one, but what time there is will be sure to bring a big smile to your little ones' faces.

The prices for character meals are much the same, no matter where you're dining (with one exception: Cinderella's Royal Table). Breakfast (most serve it) runs $20 to $36 for adults and $11 to $24 for children 3 to 9; those that serve dinner charge $28 to $56 for adults and $14 to $28 for kids. The prices vary a bit, though, from location to location. Note that for character meals inside the theme parks, you'll also have to pay park admission fees and will be subject to the $14 parking charge.

To make reservations for WDW character meals, call ✆ **407/939-3463.** American Express, Diners Club, Discover, MasterCard, Visa, and the Disney Visa Card are accepted at all character meals.

You'll find all of the restaurants mentioned in this section on the "Walt Disney World & Lake Buena Vista Restaurants" map, on p. 118. For online information, go to **www.disneyworld.com**.

Note: Although the character appearances below were accurate when this book went to press, lineups and booking requirements change frequently (as do menus and prices). I strongly recommend against promising children they will meet a specific character at a meal. And never mention dining with the characters unless your Advance Reservations are confirmed first; character meals book up quickly, and trying to make Advance Reservations too late in the game (or worse, attempting to walk in) will mostly likely result in disappointment. If you have your heart set on meeting a certain character, call to confirm his or her appearance when making your Advance Reservations.

Akershus Royal Banquet Hall NORWEGIAN   This restaurant, set inside a re-created 14th-century castle, now features **Princess Storybook** character meals for breakfast, lunch, and dinner. Here you can sample from an all-you-can-eat feast of traditional Norwegian fare, making it a bargain for big eaters. It is also reasonably good food, though some diners will find it difficult to adapt to Scandinavian tastes. An impressive smorgasbord of *smavarmt* (hot) and *koldtbord* (cold) dishes, including mustard-glazed salmon, citrus-marinated mahimahi, a grilled venison sandwich, and traditional *kjottkake* (beef and pork dumplings), is served up family style during lunch and dinner. Kids can stick to more familiar options such as grilled chicken, cheese ravioli with meatballs, hot dogs, and pizza. Breakfast features traditional American fare (scrambled eggs, French toast, sausage, bacon, and potatoes). The biggest draws are the Disney princesses (excluding Cinderella) who make their way around the hall, stopping at each table to say hello. The staff is friendly, and the white-stone interior, beamed ceilings, leaded-glass windows, and archways add to the authentic atmosphere. Norwegian beer and aquavit complement a list of French and California wines.

Norway Pavilion, World Showcase, in Epcot. Character breakfast $40 adults, $24 kids; character lunch $42 adults, $25 kids; character dinner $47 adults, $26 kids. Daily 8:30–10am, 11:40am–3pm, and 4:20–8:30pm. Theme-park admission required.

Cape May Café   This delightful New England–themed dining room serves lavish buffet breakfasts (eggs, pancakes, bacon, pastries) hosted by **Admiral Goofy** and his crew—**Chip 'n' Dale** and **Pluto** (characters may vary). Its location at the Beach Club Resort makes it a great way to start the day when you're on your way to nearby Epcot.

1800 Epcot Resorts Blvd., at Disney's Beach Club Resort. Character breakfast $27 adults, $13 kids. Daily 7:30–11am.

Chef Mickey's ★★   The whimsical Chef Mickey's offers buffet breakfasts (eggs, bacon, sausage, pancakes, fruit) and dinners (entrees change daily; plus salad bar, soups, vegetables, and ice cream with toppings). Aside from the characters, kids will also enjoy watching the monorail go by overhead as it passes through the Contemporary Resort. **Mickey** and **Minnie** and various pals make their way to every table while meeting and mingling with guests. While this is one of the largest restaurants offering character dining, if you plan on eating here during spring break or around the holidays, it's best to make Advance Reservations well ahead of time.

4600 N. World Dr., at Disney's Contemporary Resort. Character breakfast $27 adults, $14 kids; character dinner $34 adults, $17 kids. Daily 7–11:30am and 5–9:30pm.

Cinderella's Royal Table ★   Cinderella Castle—the most recognized icon in all of the WDW resort, not to mention the center of the Magic Kingdom—serves character breakfast buffets daily (a variety of breakfast favorites including scrambled eggs, bacon, and Danishes) and recently began serving a character lunch and dinner (with a choice of appetizer, entree, salad, and dessert from a fixed menu) as well. Princess hosts vary, but **Cinderella** always puts in an appearance, welcoming guests to the castle before they go upstairs to dine. This is one of the most popular character meals in the park and the hardest to get into, so **reserve far, far in advance** (reservations are taken 180 days in advance, and you must pay in full at the time you book). To have the best shot at getting in, be flexible about your seating arrangements and dining times, and call Disney exactly at 7am EST on your first date of reservations eligibility (if you aren't sure what date that is, call Disney and they'll help you figure it out). If you get through on your first try (lucky you!), tell the reservations clerk you want Cinderella's Table for whatever date you've picked. Don't even think about requesting a specific time—take whatever you can get (most reservations will be gone by 7:15am).

Cinderella Castle, in the Magic Kingdom. Character breakfast $45 adults, $30 kids; character lunch $49 adults, $31 kids; character dinner $55 adults, $34 kids. Daily 8–10:20am, noon–3pm, and 4pm to park closing. Theme-park admission required.

Crystal Palace Buffet ★   The prettiest of the Magic Kingdom's restaurants, the Crystal Palace features a glass exterior that glimmers in sunlight. **Winnie the Pooh** and pals hold court here throughout the day. The restaurant serves breakfast (eggs, French toast, pancakes, bacon, and more), lunch, and dinner. The latter features a long list of hot and cold entrees that usually include some type of poultry, beef, seafood, an array of veggies, salads, and kid-friendly favorites. The dessert buffet includes a make-your-own-sundae bar.

Crystal Palace, in the Magic Kingdom. Character breakfast $23 adults, $13 kids; character lunch $25 adults, $14 kids; character dinner $37 adults, $18 kids. Daily 8–10:30am, 11:30am–3pm, and 4pm to park closing. Theme-park admission required.

Donald's Safari Breakfast ★   **Donald, Goofy,** and **Pluto** host a safari-themed buffet breakfast (eggs, bacon, French toast, and more) in Africa's Tusker House.

Africa, at Disney's Animal Kingdom. Character breakfast $25 adults, $11 kids. Daily park opening to 10:30am. Theme-park admission required.

Garden Grill ★   There's a "Harvest Feast" theme at this revolving restaurant, where hearty family-style meals are hosted by **Mickey** and **Chip 'n' Dale.** (Mickey sure gets around, eh?) Dinner, featuring chicken, fish, steak, vegetables, and potatoes, is the only meal served.

Land Pavilion, in Epcot. Character dinner $35 adults, $17 kids. Daily 4:30pm to park closing. Theme-park admission required.

OTHER CASTS OF characters

Not wanting to feel left out, Universal Orlando has instituted its own character dining experiences. Like Disney's meals, these are very popular, so be sure to reserve your spot as far in advance as possible.

At Islands of Adventure, the **Confisco Grill** is home to a character breakfast buffet where Spider-Man, Captain America, the Cat in the Hat, and Thing 1 and Thing 2 all join in the fun. It runs Thursday and Sunday from 9 to 10:30am. The cost is $18 for adults, $12 for kids 3 to 9, plus the required park admission. Call 🕿 **407/224-4012** for information or reservations.

Universal characters also make an appearance at the **Kitchen** (Sat 6–9pm at the Hard Rock Hotel), **Trattoria del Porto** (Fri 6–9pm at the Portofino Bay Hotel), and the **Islands Dining Room** (Wed and Sat 6:30–9:30pm at the Royal Pacific Resort).

1900 Park Fare ★   The elegant Grand Floridian offers breakfast (eggs, French toast, bacon, pancakes) and dinner buffets (steak, pork, fish) at the exposition-themed 1900 Park Fare. Big Bertha—a French band organ that plays pipes, drums, bells, cymbals, castanets, and xylophone—provides the music. **Mary Poppins, Alice in Wonderland,** and their pals appear at breakfast; **Cinderella** and friends show up for Cinderella's Gala Feast at dinner.

4401 Floridian Way, at Disney's Grand Floridian Resort & Spa. Character breakfast $23 adults, $13 kids; character dinner $36 adults, $18 kids. Daily 8–11:10am and 4:30–8:20pm.

'Ohana Character Breakfast   Traditional breakfasts (eggs, pancakes, bacon) are prepared in an 18-foot fire pit and served family style. **Mickey, Stitch, Lilo,** and **Pluto** appear, and children are given the chance to parade around with Polynesian musical instruments.

1600 Seven Seas Dr., in 'Ohana at Disney's Polynesian Resort. Character breakfast $21 adults, $12 kids. Daily 7:30–11am.

RESTAURANTS BY CUISINE

AFRICAN

Boma ★★★ (Animal Kingdom Lodge, $$$$, p. 124)

Jiko—The Cooking Place ★★ (Animal Kingdom Lodge, $$$, p. 129)

Tusker House (Animal Kingdom, $–$$$, p. 123)

AMERICAN

ABC Commissary (Disney's Hollywood Studios, $, p. 122)

B.B. King's Blues Club (Pointe Orlando, $$, p. 149)

B-Line Diner (International Dr. Area, $$, p. 145)

Celebration Town Tavern (Celebration, $$, p. 147)

Chalet Suzanne ★ (Lake Wales, $$$$, p. 147)

Cinderella's Royal Table ★ (Magic Kingdom, $$$$, p. 116)

Citrus Restaurant ★ (Downtown Orlando, $$$, p. 150)

City Fire American Oven & Bar (Sand Lake Rd., $$$, p. 142)

KEY TO ABBREVIATIONS:
$$$$** = Very Expensive   **$$$** = Expensive   **$$** = Moderate   **$ = Inexpensive

Columbia Harbour House ★ (Magic Kingdom, $, p. 117)

Copper Canyon Grill (Pointe Orlando, $$, p. 148)

Cosmic Ray's Starlight Café (Magic Kingdom, $, p. 117)

Diamond Horseshoe (Magic Kingdom, $, p. 120)

Earl of Sandwich (Downtown Disney, $, p. 121)

ESPN Club ★ (Disney's BoardWalk, $$, p. 131)

Fat Fish Blue (Pointe Orlando, $$, p. 149)

50's Prime Time Café (Disney's Hollywood Studios, $$, p. 121)

Funky Monkey Wine Company (Pointe Orlando, $$, p. 149)

Hard Rock Cafe (Universal CityWalk, $$, p. 139)

Hollywood Brown Derby (Disney's Hollywood Studios, $$$$, p. 121)

Hue ★★ (Downtown Orlando, $$$, p. 150)

Liberty Tree Tavern (Magic Kingdom, $$, p. 116)

Market Street Café (Celebration, $$, p. 147)

Mythos ★ (Islands of Adventure, $$, p. 140)

Paradiso 37 (Pleasure Island, $$–$$$, p. 134)

Pecos Bill Café ★ (Magic Kingdom, $, p. 120)

Planet Hollywood (Pleasure Island, $$, p. 132)

Plaza Restaurant (Magic Kingdom, $$, p. 117)

Seasons 52 ★ (Sand Lake Rd., $$$, p. 142)

Sci-Fi Dine-In Theater Restaurant (Disney's Hollywood Studios, $$, p. 122)

Tomorrowland Terrace (Magic Kingdom, $, p. 120)

Toy Story Pizza Planet (Disney's Hollywood Studios, $, p. 123)

T-Rex Cafe (Downtown Disney Marketplace, $$, p. 133)

Tusker House (Animal Kingdom, $$$, p. 123)

The Wave . . . of American Flavors ★ (Contemporary Resort, $$–$$$, p. 131)

Whispering Canyon Café (Wilderness Lodge, $$$, p. 128)

ASIAN FUSION

Yak & Yeti ★ (Animal Kingdom, $$, p. 124)

BARBECUE

Bubbalou's Bodacious BBQ ★ (Casselberry, $, p. 152)

Wild Jacks (International Dr. Area, $$, p. 147)

BRAZILIAN

Texas de Brazil Churrascaria ★ (International Dr. Area, $$$$, p. 141)

CALIFORNIAN

California Grill ★★★ (Disney's Contemporary Resort, $$$$, p. 125)

Rainforest Cafe ★ (Downtown Disney Marketplace & Animal Kingdom, $$, p. 133 and 123)

Wolfgang Puck Grand Café ★★ (Disney's West Side, $$$, p. 134)

CANADIAN

Le Cellier Steakhouse (Epcot, $$$, p. 110)

CARIBBEAN

Bahama Breeze ★ (International Dr. Area & Lake Buena Vista, $$, p. 144)

Jimmy Buffett's Margaritaville (Universal CityWalk, $$, p. 139)

CHARACTER MEALS

Akershus Royal Banquet Hall (Epcot, $$$, p. 154)

Cape May Café (Disney's Beach Club Resort, $$$, p. 154)

Chef Mickey's ★★ (Disney's Contemporary Resort, $$$, p. 155)

Cinderella's Royal Table ★ (Magic Kingdom, $$$$, p. 155)

Confisco Grill (Islands of Adventure, $$, p. 156)

Crystal Palace Buffet ★ (Magic Kingdom, $$$, p. 155)

Donald's Safari Breakfast ★ (Animal Kingdom, $$, p. 155)

Garden Grill ★ (Epcot, $$$, p. 155)
1900 Park Fare ★ (Disney's Grand
    Floridian Resort & Spa, $$$, p. 156)
'Ohana Character Breakfast (Disney's
    Polynesian Resort, $$, p. 156)

CHINESE
Lotus Blossom Café (Epcot, $, p. 115)
Ming Court ★★ (International Dr. Area,
    $$, p. 146)
Nine Dragons (Epcot, $$, p. 113)

CUBAN
Bongo's Cuban Cafe (Disney's West
    Side, $$, p. 135)
Columbia Restaurant (Celebration, $$,
    p. 147)
Cuba Libre Restaurant & Rum Bar
    (Pointe Orlando, $$, p. 148)
Rolando's ★ (Casselberry, $$, p. 150)
Samba Room ★ (Sand Lake Rd., $$,
    p. 146)

ENGLISH
Rose & Crown Pub & Dining Room
    (Epcot, $$, p. 113)

FOOD COURT
Sunshine Seasons in the Land (Epcot,
    $, p. 115)

FRENCH
Citricos ★ (Disney's Grand Floridian
    Resort & Spa, $$$$, p. 126)
Les Chefs de France (Epcot, $$$, p. 111)

GERMAN
Biergarten (Epcot, $$$, p. 108)
Sommerfest (Epcot, $, p. 115)

GREEK
Taverna Opa (Pointe Orlando, $$,
    p. 149)

INTERNATIONAL
Café Tu Tu Tango ★★ (International
    Dr. Area, $$, p. 145)
Imperium Food & Wine (Celebration,
    $$, p. 147)
La Coquina ★ (Lake Buena Vista, $$$$,
    p. 136)

Victoria & Albert's ★★★ (Disney's
    Grand Floridian Resort & Spa, $$$$,
    p. 127)

IRISH
Shannon's of Celebration (Celebration,
    $$, p. 147)

ITALIAN
Bice ★ (Universal's Portofino Bay
    Hotel, $$$$, p. 137)
Café D'Antonio Ristorante (Celebration,
    $$$, p. 147)
Carrabba's ★ (Kissimmee, $$, p. 149)
Maggiano's Little Italy (Pointe Orlando,
    $$$, p. 148)
Mama Melrose's Ristorante Italiano
    (Disney's Hollywood Studios, $$,
    p. 122)
Pacino's Italian Ristorante ★ (Kissim-
    mee, $$, p. 150)
Pastamoré Ristorante & Market (Univer-
    sal CityWalk, $$, p. 140)
Portobello ★★ (Pleasure Island, $$$,
    p. 132)
Romano's Macaroni Grill (Lake Buena
    Vista, $$, p. 137)
Tony's Town Square Restaurant (Magic
    Kingdom, $$$, p. 116)
Tutto Italia ★★ (Epcot, $$, p. 111)
Via Napoli ★★ (Epcot, $$, p. 111)

JAPANESE
Amura ★ (Sand Lake Rd., $$$, p. 142)
Mikado Japanese Steakhouse ★★
    (Marriott Orlando World Center,
    $$$$, p. 136)
Seito Sushi Japanese Restaurant (Cele-
    bration, $$$, p. 147)
Teppan Edo (Epcot, $$$, p. 113)
Yakitori House (Epcot, $, p. 115)

LATIN AMERICAN
Pollo Campero (Downtown Disney Mar-
    ketplace, $, p. 134)

MEDITERRANEAN
Kouzzinas (Disney's BoardWalk, $$$,
    p. 129)
Portobello ★★ (Pleasure Island, $$$,
    p. 132)

MEXICAN

La Cantina de San Angel (Epcot, $, p. 114)

La Hacienda de San Angel (Epcot, $$$, p. 112)

San Angel Inn ★ (Epcot, $$$, p. 112)

MIDDLE EASTERN

Cedars of Orlando (Sand Lake Rd., $$$, p. 142)

MOROCCAN

Marrakesh ★ (Epcot, $$$, p. 111)

NORWEGIAN

Akershus Royal Banquet Hall (Epcot, $$$, p. 154)

Kringla Bakeri og Kafe (Epcot, $, p. 114)

PACIFIC RIM

Emeril's Tchoup Chop ★★★ (Universal's Royal Pacific Resort, $$$, p. 138)

'Ohana ★ (Disney's Polynesian Resort, $$$, p. 130)

Roy's Restaurant ★ (Sand Lake Rd., $$$, p. 144)

Tommy Bahama's Tropical Café & Emporium (Pointe Orlando, $$$, p. 149)

Yak & Yeti ★ (Disney's Animal Kingdom, $$, p. 124)

SEAFOOD/STEAK

Artist Point ★★ (Disney's Wilderness Lodge, $$$, p. 128)

Bubba Gump Shrimp Company (Universal CityWalk, $$, p. 139)

Cape May Café (Disney's Beach Club Resort, $$$, p. 129)

Capital Grille ★ (Pointe Orlando, $$$, p. 148)

Columbia Harbour House ★ (Magic Kingdom, $, p. 117)

Coral Reef (Epcot, $$$, p. 110)

The Crab House (Lake Buena Vista, $$, p. 136)

FishBones (International Dr. Area, $$, p. 145)

Flying Fish Café ★★ (Disney's Board-Walk, $$$$, p. 126)

Fulton's Crab House ★★ (Downtown Disney Marketplace, $$$$, p. 132)

Hemingway's ★★ (Lake Buena Vista, $$$$, p. 135)

Kres Chophouse ★ (Downtown Orlando, $$$, p. 150)

Le Cellier Steakhouse (Epcot, $$$, p. 110)

Mythos ★ (Islands of Adventure, $$, p. 140)

Ocean Prime ★★★ (Sand Lake Rd., $$$, p. 141)

The Palm (Universal's Hard Rock Hotel, $$$$, p. 138)

Timpano Italian Chophouse ★ (Sand Lake Rd., $$$, p. 142)

Todd English's bluezoo ★★ (WDW Dolphin, $$$$, p. 127)

Wild Jacks (International Dr. Area, $$, p. 147)

Yachtsman Steakhouse ★ (Disney's Yacht Club Resort, $$$$, p. 128)

SOUTHERN/CREOLE

B.B. King's Blues Club (Pointe Orlando, $$, p. 149)

Boatwright's Dining Hall (Disney's Port Orleans Resort, $$, p. 130)

Emeril's ★★ (Universal CityWalk, $$$$, p. 138)

House of Blues (Disney's West Side, $$, p. 135)

TAPAS

Café Tu Tu Tango ★★ (International Dr. Area, $$, p. 145)

Ceviche Tapas Bar & Restaurant (Downtown Orlando, $$$, p. 150)

THAI

Thai Thani (Celebration, $$, p. 147)

VIETNAMESE

Little Saigon ★ (Downtown Orlando, $, p. 152)

EXPLORING WALT DISNEY WORLD

T he land of pixie dust and fairytales . . . the "Happiest Place on Earth" . . . and that mouse—Walt Disney World is all this and more to the over 50 million visitors who pour through its gates every year. Prices may be high and the lines long, but you can learn to love Disney with a little know-how. When you see kids' eyes light up as they meet Mickey or glimpse Cinderella Castle on the horizon, you'll no longer able be able to say that you don't like Disney without your nose growing an inch or two.

5

Attractions & Rides   Disney-savvy travelers obtain the FASTPASS to skip the lines at popular rides. Tots in tow? Take them to the **Magic Kingdom** to ride on Dumbo and meet princesses. Adults can travel the globe at **Epcot**'s World Showcase or spot rhinos on an **Animal Kingdom** safari. For the ultimate adrenaline rush, ride **Hollywood Studios**' 13-story Twilight Zone. When Florida heats up, cool off on water slides at the snow-capped **Blizzard Beach** or snorkel with sharks (yes, real ones) at **Typhoon Lagoon.**

Restaurants & Dining   Kids won't want to miss **character dining,** from buffet breakfasts with Mickey to princess banquets at **Cinderella's Royal Table.** For sit-down dining, tuck into Maine lobster as fish swim by in Epcot's **Coral Reef,** order a sizzling steak in the Hollywood Studios' wood-paneled **Hollywood Brown Derby,** or eat in the jungle at Animal Kingdom's **Rainforest Cafe.** The themed restaurants at **Downtown Disney** dish up everything from Cuban food to Creole—they're sure to please every palate (and pocketbook).

Nightlife & Entertainment   The 21-plus set can sip handcrafted cocktails at Disney's more sophisticated (translation: less sugary) lounges, like the popular **Rix** (at Disney's Coronado Resort) and the **Outer Rim** (at Disney's Contemporary Resort). At **Downtown Disney,** a 24-screen dine-in cinema shows the latest blockbuster hits, while bendy acrobats wow the crowds at Cirque du Soleil's **La Nouba.** By nightfall, street performers appear to entertain the crowds strolling Disney's **BoardWalk,** furthering the Coney Island feel.

Characters & Parades   For kids, what's magical is catching the parades and getting a hug (and an illegible autograph) from favorite characters.

Check the *Times Guide* so you can plan around the classic **Celebrate a Dream Come True Parade,** the dazzling **SpectroMagic Parade,** and the fireworks at **Wishes Nighttime Spectacular.** Arrive early for a spot in front of Cinderella Castle for the best view. At Epcot, **IllumiNations** lights up the lagoon with its laser and light show, while Hollywood Studios' **Fantasmic!** is worth staying up late for.

ESSENTIALS

Getting Information in Advance

Before leaving home, call or write to the Walt Disney World Co., Box 10000, Lake Buena Vista, FL 32830-1000 (© **407/934-7639**), for a vacation CD and the *Walt Disney World Vacations* brochure; both are valuable planning aids. Both can also be ordered (and even viewed) online at **www.disneyworld.com.** When you call, also ask about special events that will be going on during your visit. Though I list some of the annual events under "When to Go," on p. 25, there are many other events that may be of interest to you.

Once you've arrived at your hotel, Guest Services and the concierge desks (especially at the Disney properties and "official" hotels) will have up-to-the-minute information about happenings in the parks. Stop by to ask questions and get literature, including a schedule of park hours and events. If you have questions your hotel's personnel can't answer, call Disney at © **407/824-4321.**

There are also information areas at City Hall in the Magic Kingdom and Guest Relations at Epcot, Disney's Hollywood Studios, and Animal Kingdom.

For online information, try **www.disneyworld.com,** which features extensive, entertaining, and regularly updated information on the parks. The website will also let you design customized park itinerary maps that Disney will mail to you (though you'll have to do these several weeks in advance if you want them in time for your trip).

Also try the Orlando/Orange County Convention & Visitors Bureau site at **www.visitorlando.com.** Another good site, **www.visitkissimmee.com,** is sponsored by the Kissimmee Convention & Visitors Bureau.

Getting to WDW by Car

The interstate exits to all Disney parks and resorts are well marked. Once you're off I-4, there are signs directing you to individual destinations. If you miss your exit, *don't panic.* Simply get off at the next one and turn around. It may take a little more time, but it's safer than cutting across five lanes of traffic to make the off ramp, or worse—risking a fender bender. Drive with extra caution in the attractions area. Disney drivers are divided into two categories: workers in a hurry to make their shift and tourists in a hurry to get to the parks before anyone else (and trying to drive while looking at a map).

Upon entering WDW grounds, you can tune your radio to 1030 AM when approaching the Magic Kingdom, or 850 AM when approaching Epcot, for park information. Tune to 1200 AM when departing the Magic Kingdom, or 910 AM when departing Epcot. TVs in all Disney resorts and "official" hotels also have park information channels.

Parking

All WDW lots are tightly controlled; the Disney folks have parking down to a science. You park where they tell you to park—and there's no room for discussion. *Remember to write down your parking place (lot and row number) so you can find your vehicle later.* Parking attendants won't be there to direct you to it when you leave the park, and, at the end of the day, you'd be surprised how many cars look alike through tired eyes. And though you might think that catchy character name on the pole above your car will ring a bell when you return to your vehicle, what will really be ringing will be your ears with all of the names you've heard so many times throughout the day—was it Minnie . . . Donald . . . Goofy . . . Pluto?

Visitors should generally ride the free trams that travel the massive Magic Kingdom lots, but it's often easier to skip them and walk to the gates at Epcot, Disney's Hollywood Studios, and Animal Kingdom. You may not even have a choice: Disney has cut service to some parking areas near the entrances to its parks. Guests who can't make the hike have to park in special lots for travelers with disabilities (see below) or have a driver drop them at special unloading areas outside the entrances. If you're walking, *be careful!* These lots aren't designed for pedestrians, so if you hear a tram coming, move out of the way—and quickly.

Parking costs $14 at the four major WDW attractions ($15 for RVs). Parking is free to those staying at Disney-owned resorts. There are special lots for travelers with disabilities; a valid disabled parking permit is required (call ℂ **407/824-4321** for details). Those who have booked their Disney vacation through AAA can access a special lot close to the entrance.

Tickets

Disney's ticketing structure (called **Magic Your Way**) gives visitors who stay here for a few days far better deals than those who come for just a day. The system allows guests to customize their tickets by first purchasing a Base Ticket for a set fee, and then allowing them to purchase add-ons, including a Park Hopper option, a no-expiration option, and the option to include admission to some of Disney's smaller venues, such as Pleasure Island, the water parks, and DisneyQuest (the latter is known as the Water Park Fun & More option).

 Buy Ahead of Time

Purchasing multiday tickets (from 4 days and up) ahead of time—through AAA or the **Orlando/Orange County Convention & Visitors Bureau**—can result in substantial savings (up to $12 per adult and $8 per child ages 3–9, depending on the type of ticket). The savings for a family of four can easily add up to $40—that's worth a lunch (well, at least a snack in Mickeyville).

Walt Disney World Parks & Attractions

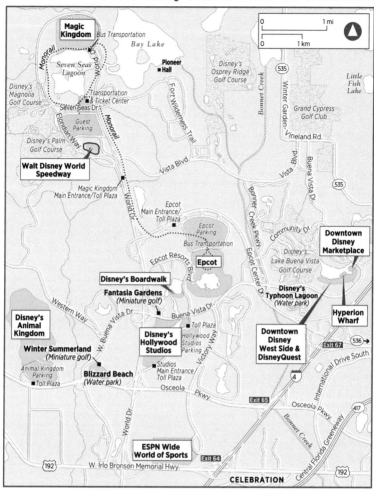

You can purchase your Base Tickets for durations running from a single day to several days, with the latter being the most cost effective; the longer you stay, the less you'll pay per day. If you crunch the numbers, tickets good for at least 4 days will cost at least $25 less per day than a single-day ticket would; buy a 6-day ticket and your per-day price drops by just under 50%. Do note, however, that under the new system, tickets now expire 14 days from the first day of use unless you add on a no-expiration feature (however, you don't have to use the tickets on consecutive days within that 14-day period).

Unless noted, the following prices do not include the **6% to 7.5% sales tax** (Disney actually falls in two different counties). ***Note:*** Price hikes are frequent

Shorter Days, Fewer Shows

Although attendance has been steadily climbing back to where it had been before the hurricane season of 2004, the theme parks—like everyone else—are still feeling the financial crunch (though that didn't stop them from raising ticket prices by significant percentages in 2010—and again in 2011). Given recent history, increases should be expected again in 2012—they usually take effect in mid-August. If you haven't been to Disney in several years, you may notice that, in many cases, the parks **close earlier** than in previous years, and some areas **open later**. Additionally, select shows and parades are offered less often or only on certain days. The hours and shows listed in this chapter generally apply, but in order to avoid being disappointed, call ✆ **407/824-4321** or go to **www.disneyworld.com** for up-to-the-minute information.

occurrences (and usually come about in mid-August), so call ✆ **407/824-4321** or visit www.disneyworld.com for the most up-to-the-minute pricing.

Note: All tickets include unlimited use of the WDW transportation system. Bear in mind that Disney considers children 10 and older to be adults for pricing purposes, and children younger than 3 aren't charged admission.

One-day/one-park Base Tickets, for admission to the Magic Kingdom, Epcot, Animal Kingdom, or Disney's Hollywood Studios, are $85 for adults, $79 for children ages 3 to 9. Ouch! **Four-day Base Tickets** (one park per day) are $243 adults, $224 children ages 3 to 9. **Seven-day Base Tickets** (one park per day) cost $267 for adults (just over $38 a day), $248 for kids ages 3 to 9 ($36 a day).

Adding on a **Park Hopper** option to your ticket allows you unlimited admission to the Magic Kingdom, Epcot, Disney's Hollywood Studios, and Animal Kingdom for the duration of your Base Ticket. Pricing for the Park Hopper is the same for adults and children and costs $55 above the price of your Base Ticket (added to multiday park tickets valid for 2 or more days). Single-day Base Tickets add $35 for the privilege to hop between parks—a slight drop in price from previous years (but still adding up to a whopping $120 for an adult—not a cost-effective option), but if you purchase any multiday Base Ticket (even a 7-day Base Ticket), the option will still only cost you $55 (for a total of $322—a good deal).

If you add a **Water Park Fun & More** option to your Base Ticket, you'll get several admissions to some of WDW's smaller attractions: Blizzard Beach, Typhoon Lagoon, DisneyQuest, Disney's Oak Trail Golf Course, and the ESPN Wide World of Sports Complex (Disney's Wide World of Sports in a past life). The number of visits allowed depends on the number of days your Base Ticket is good for (two visits for Base Tickets good for either 1 or 2 days, three visits for a 3-day Base Ticket, four visits for a 4-day Base Ticket, and so on; the number of visits equals the number of days your Base Ticket is good for). This option adds an additional $55 to the cost of your Base Ticket, and, like the Park Hopper, the longer you stay at Disney, the more cost-effective the option becomes. If you plan on visiting only one smaller attraction (visiting only once) while at WDW, paying the separate admission fee is cheaper and smarter than opting for the Water Park Fun & More add-on.

A 1-day ticket to **Typhoon Lagoon** or **Blizzard Beach** is $49 for adults, $41 for children. A 1-day ticket to DisneyQuest is $43 for adults, $37 for children.

If you're planning an extended stay or going to visit Walt Disney World more than once during the year, **annual passes** ($519–$649 adults, $478–$598 children) are another great option (Florida residents catch a slight break: $389–$509 adults, $358–$469 children).

Operating Hours

Hours of operation vary throughout the year and are often influenced by special events, so it's a good idea to call to check opening/closing times.

The **Magic Kingdom** and **Disney's Hollywood Studios** are generally open from 9am to 7 or 8pm, with hours often extended to 9pm and sometimes as late as midnight—even 1am during major holidays and summer. **Animal Kingdom** is usually open from 9am to 5 or 6pm but sometimes closes as late as 8pm.

Epcot's Future World is generally open from 9am to 7pm and occasionally later. **Epcot's World Showcase** usually opens at 11am and closes at 9pm. Once again, there are extended holiday and summer hours.

Typhoon Lagoon and **Blizzard Beach** are open from 10am to 5pm most of the year (with slightly extended hours during summer and some holidays). Both are closed on a rotating basis during part of the winter for maintenance; be sure to check ahead if they're on your to-do list.

MAKING YOUR VISIT MORE ENJOYABLE

How This Chapter Is Useful to Parents

Before every listing in the major parks, you'll note the **"Recommended Ages"** entry that lists which ages will most appreciate that ride or show (though you should keep in mind your child's personality and maturity when evaluating these recommendations). Though most families want to do everything, these guidelines are helpful in planning your daily itinerary. In my ride ratings, I indicate whether a ride will be more enjoyable for kids than for adults. Many, even a couple in the Magic Kingdom, are too intense for young kids; all it takes is one bad experience, and the rest of your day will be ruined. You'll also find any **height** and **health restrictions** noted in the listings.

Price Alert

Single- and multiday admission prices don't include Florida's 6% to 7.5% sales tax and are subject to change. Annual price increases are normal, so, although the prices listed on these pages were accurate when this book went to press, they may be higher at the time you actually visit.

Best Time of Year to Visit

Because of the large number of international visitors, there's really no off season at Disney, but during the winter months, usually mid-January through March, crowds are smaller (except on weekends), and the weather can be mild (though at times it can get quite cool). The crowds also thin from mid-September until the week before Thanksgiving, and in May, before Memorial Day weekend. (Again, weekends tend to be clogged with locals.) Summer is when the masses throng to the parks. It's also very humid and hot, *Hot,* HOT. If you can skip a summer visit, you also won't have to worry much about the possibility of a hurricane (admittedly rare, but as the summer of 2004 proved, not unheard of) or an electrical storm (an almost daily occurrence).

Best Days to Visit

The busiest days at all parks are generally Saturday and Sunday. Seven-day guests usually arrive and depart on one of these days, so fewer of them turn the turnstiles; but weekends are when locals and Florida commuters come to play. Beyond that: Monday, Thursday, and Saturday are pretty frantic in the Magic Kingdom; Tuesday and Friday are hectic at Epcot; Sunday and Wednesday are crazy at Disney's Hollywood Studios; and Monday, Tuesday, and Wednesday are a zoo (forgive the pun) at the Animal Kingdom. Periods around major holidays also attract throngs—mid-December through the first weekend in January is busy beyond belief. Crowds tend to thin later in the day, so if you're going to visit during the busy season and have included the Park Hopper option on your ticket, you'll bump into fewer guests the later you visit. This also applies to the water parks.

The big attractions at Animal Kingdom are, obviously, the animals, and the best time to see them is early in the day or late in the afternoon or evening, when things are cooler. You'll also get a decent midday glimpse of some of them during the cooler months. *Note:* If the forecast for the day calls for extended rain, you should save Animal Kingdom for another time because many of the primo attractions are outdoors.

Plan Your Visit

How you plan your time at Walt Disney World will depend on a number of factors. These include the ages of any children in your party; what, if anything, you've seen on previous visits; your interests; and whether you're traveling at peak time or off season. Preplanning is always essential. So is choosing age-appropriate activities.

Nothing can spoil a day in the parks more than a child devastated because he or she can't do something that was promised. Before you get to the park, review this book and the suggested ages for children, including **height restrictions.** The WDW staff won't bend the rules despite the pitiful wails of your little ones. *Note:* Many rides that have minimum heights also have enough turbulence to make them unsuitable for folks with neck, back, or heart problems; those prone to motion sickness; or pregnant women.

Unless you're staying for more than a week or two, you won't be able to experience all of the rides, shows, or attractions included in this chapter. A ride may last only 5 minutes, but you may have to wait an hour or so, even with FASTPASS (detailed shortly). You'll wear yourself to a frazzle trying to hit everything. It's better to follow a relaxed itinerary, including leisurely meals and some recreational activities, than to make a demanding job out of trying to see everything—think less is more and you'll get the idea. Your vacation is supposed to be fun, not frenzied.

Create an Itinerary for Each Day

Read the previously mentioned *Walt Disney World Vacations* brochure and the detailed descriptions in this book, and then create your own "must-see" list, including all the shows and attractions that you absolutely have to experience. After that, you can sort out just where to go, when to go, and what you would like to do while you're there.

At the same time, consider your loyalties. My younger kids could spend all day in Tomorrowland spinning around like space rangers with Woody and Buzz Lightyear, but touring Fantasyland is of far less interest to them. Put the ride featuring your

FASTPASS

"Get a time—why wait in line . . ." says Disney. If lines aren't your thing—well, you had better turn back now. Lines are a part of the deal at Disney (and the other parks, too, for that matter). On the other hand, if you're savvy, you can usually avoid the worst of them if you take advantage of Disney's FASTPASS. The free system allows you to wait in a far shorter line at some of the park's most popular attractions. Seems easy enough, right? Well, it is. There is, however, a small price to be paid for skipping the big lines. Here's the drill:

Hang on to your ticket stub when you enter and head to the hottest ride on your list. If it's a FASTPASS attraction (they're noted in the guide map you get when you enter), you'll see a sign marking the FASTPASS kiosk just near the entrance. Feed your ticket into the ticket taker. *Note:* Every member of your group must get an individual FASTPASS. Retrieve both your ticket and your FASTPASS slip. Printed on the slip are two times. You can return anytime during that 1-hour window and enter the ride (there's a much shorter and faster line for FASTPASS holders). Be sure to keep your slip handy, as you'll need it to get in the right line.

Note II: Early in the day, your 1-hour window may begin as soon as 40 minutes after you feed the FASTPASS machine, but later in the day it may be hours later. Initially, Disney only allowed you to do this on one ride at a time. Now, your FASTPASS ticket has a time printed when you can get a second FASTPASS, usually about 2 hours after you got the first one, though it can sometimes be as soon as 45 minutes later, even if you haven't used the first pass yet.

Note III: Don't think you can fool Disney by feeding your ticket stub in multiple times, figuring you can hit the jackpot for multiple rides or help others in your group who lost their tickets. These "smart" stubs will reject your attempts by spitting out a coupon that says "Not a valid FASTPASS."

Note IV: FASTPASS slips can run out. So if you have your heart set on a ride and it's the middle of the peak season, be sure to head to your chosen attraction's FASTPASS machine as soon as you can. Tickets for top rides often run out by the early afternoon, sometimes even earlier.

Note V: Word has it that Disney's tinkering with new FASTPASS options that may or may not be implemented in the future (including the possibility of a central FASTPASS distribution center), so be sure to pick up a park map when you arrive—it lists which rides are FASTPASS rides and the location of FASTPASS kiosks.

favorite character, or theirs, at the top of your list. Sketch out a daily itinerary that includes your must-see attractions and shows; it's almost certain to change once you get to the parks, but will at least provide you with a good starting point. With a plan in mind and a map in hand (park maps can be found in this guide, but be sure to grab the free maps distributed as you enter each theme park), touring the parks will be that much easier. Understand that rides and exhibits nearest an entrance are usually the busiest when the gates open because a lot of people visit the first thing they see, even if the more popular attractions tend to be found deeper into the park.

I repeat this advice: Schedule sit-down shows, recreational activities (a boat ride or a refreshing swim late in the afternoon), and at least some unhurried meals where time permits. This will save you from exhaustion and aggravation. The suggested itineraries (see below) allow you to see a great deal of the parks as efficiently as possible. If you have the luxury of a multiday pass, you can divide and conquer at a slower pace and can even repeat some favorites.

Suggested Itineraries

My suggested itineraries will allow you to cover most of the ground in each park as efficiently as possible. Note, though, that using FASTPASS may require you to double back to a land you've already covered.

There are a ton of ways to see the parks. Time and budget permitting, it's often better to do it in limited doses—where you spend 2 or more days in a park at a casual pace. My suggested itineraries are options for those on a tighter schedule, organized to get the most out of the least amount of time. Where appropriate, I break things into one game plan for families with kids and another for teens and adults. With few exceptions (noted later), Disney World doesn't have enough true stomach-turning thrill rides to warrant a special itinerary for teens or take-no-prisoners adults. Frankly, the only Orlando park in that class is Universal's Islands of Adventure, which I tackle in chapter 6, "Exploring Beyond Disney: Universal Orlando, SeaWorld & Other Attractions."

A DAY IN THE MAGIC KINGDOM WITH KIDS

Consider making Advance Reservations for dinner at **Cinderella's Royal Table** (📞 **407/939-3463**), located inside Cinderella Castle.

If you have preschoolers, stop at the **Town Square Theater** to start off the day meeting Mickey (as well as Disney's most popular princesses); then make your way down Main Street and head straight to **Fantasyland.** Tots will be wowed when they ride the **Prince Charming Regal Carrousel, Dumbo the Flying Elephant,** and the **Many Adventures of Winnie the Pooh.** Kids under the age of 8 will want to take a spin on the **Mad Tea Party,** catch **Mickey's PhilharMagic,** and fly over London on **Peter Pan's Flight** before heading elsewhere.

If your kids are 6 or older, start the day at **Tomorrowland** and brave **Buzz Lightyear's Space Ranger Spin** (younger kids will love this one, too) and **Space Mountain.** Then cool off a bit and catch the show at the **Monsters, Inc. Laugh Floor.** (Littler tykes like the **Tomorrowland Indy Speedway,** but there's not much else for them here, so skip it if you don't have a lot of time.)

Grab lunch at Cosmic Ray's Starlight Café in **Tomorrowland** or the Columbia Harbour House in **Liberty Square.**

Next, head west to **Liberty Square.** Most kids 10 and older will like the animatronic history lesson in the **Hall of Presidents** show. Before leaving, visit the **Haunted Mansion** and then move to **Frontierland. Splash Mountain** and **Big Thunder Mountain Railroad** are best suited for those 8 and older, while the **Country Bear Jamboree** and **Tom Sawyer Island** are fun for the younger set and parents looking to get off their feet.

Go to **Adventureland** next. Ride the **Magic Carpets of Aladdin, Pirates of the Caribbean** (and check the schedule for **Captain Jack's Pirate Tutorial**—a must for pint-size pirates), and **Jungle Cruise,** and then let the kids burn some energy in the **Swiss Family Treehouse.** Younger kids (ages 4–8) will appreciate the **Enchanted Tiki Room.**

Check the board on Main Street for showtimes—**Dream Along with Mickey** (Fantasyland) and the **Pirate Tutorial** (Adventureland) are entertaining—and then consult the daily *Times Guide.* If the **Wishes** fireworks display, **SpectroMagic** parade, or **Electrical Parade** (summers only) are scheduled, be sure to stick around to watch them, too.

Note: Be aware that some attractions in Fantasyland may be closed due to construction as the area continues to undergo an expansion slated for completion in 2013 (with select areas opening in phases beginning in late 2012).

A DAY IN THE MAGIC KINGDOM FOR TEENAGERS & ADULTS

Consider making Advance Reservations at **Cinderella's Royal Table** (☎ **407/939-3463**) if you want a sit-down dinner.

From Main Street, cut through the center of the park to Frontierland, challenge **Splash Mountain,** and then ride **Big Thunder Mountain Railroad.** If you need to rest your feet or escape the heat, the **Country Bear Jamboree** is the place for it—adults will find it an amusing throwback, though teens may think it's too corny.

Next, go to Liberty Square and visit the **Haunted Mansion** and **Hall of Presidents;** then have lunch at the Liberty Tree Tavern.

Now cut diagonally through the park, past Cinderella Castle, and into Tomorrowland to **Space Mountain, Buzz Lightyear's Space Ranger Spin,** and **Monsters, Inc. Laugh Floor.**

If time permits, head to Adventureland for the **Jungle Cruise** and **Pirates of the Caribbean;** then, if it's scheduled, end the day with the **Wishes** fireworks display.

IF YOU CAN SPEND ONLY 1 DAY AT EPCOT

Epcot deserves at least 2 days, so this is a barnstorming highlight tour. Remember to make **Advance Reservations** if you want to eat in the park (call ☎ **407/939-3463** before you arrive). I suggest the **Coral Reef** restaurant in the Seas with Nemo & Friends or the **San Angel Inn** in the World Showcase's Mexico exhibit for lunch, and **Marrakesh** in Morocco or **Akershus** in Norway for dinner. See other options in chapter 4, "Where to Eat."

While additions and refurbishments over the years have improved the kid-friendliness of this park, it remains the **least desirable of the parks for tinier tots.** Even some tweens and teens may not enjoy the heavy educational and technology themes, though there are more tot-friendly rides, attractions, and characters to entertain the younger set than ever before.

As you enter, go to any of your favorite rides that have FASTPASS (they're noted in the handout guide map). If the lines are short, don't bother with the pass. If the fast track isn't in your itinerary, take the *other* strategic approach:

Future World, near the front of the park, is the first of Epcot's two areas to open, so start there. Skip **Spaceship Earth** for now (save it for the end of the day as you make your way out of the park, when lines are at their shortest—or if you're staying until park closing, make time to ride before IllumiNations). Go straight to **Mission: Space,** where you can train as the astronauts do. Follow up with next-door-neighbor **Test Track.** Then cut to the west to **Imagination!** and its two great shows: **Journey into Imagination with Figment** and **Honey, I Shrunk the Audience** (which has been temporarily replaced with Michael Jackson's **Captain EO,** but is slated to return at an unspecified date). Next up is the **Seas with Nemo & Friends,** for a quick conversation with Crush and a "clamobile" ride under the sea, before heading on to the **Land,** where **Soarin'** takes riders on a high-flying adventure over California.

If time permits before a late lunch, visit **Innoventions.** On its East Side, all but the smallest kids will like seeing some of today's and tomorrow's high-tech gadgets, while future Imagineers can design and then ride their very own thrill ride at the **Sum of All Thrills.** Over on the West Side, kids and adults find it hard to leave **Video Games of Tomorrow.**

Unless your feet could use a rest, bypass Spaceship Earth and proceed to the **World Showcase** in midafternoon. For me, this is the best part of Epcot—the pavilions of 11 nations surround a big lagoon that you can cross by boat. But, again, kids (especially small ones) and teens may get the itch to leave. To keep them entertained, play the new **Kim Possible Adventure** (an interactive spy-adventure where you, alongside Kim Possible, help to save the world from supervillains as you make your way around the World Showcase).

Norway delivers a history lesson and boat ride called **Maelstrom,** while **China** and **Canada** have fabulous 360-degree movies; **France** has a magnificent large-screen production, too. Don't leave without taking in the show and concerts at **U.S.A.—The American Adventure.** And don't miss the taiko drum show at **Japan.**

After dinner, be sure to watch **IllumiNations** (and before the show, catch a ride on **Spaceship Earth,** if you skipped it earlier in the day).

IF YOU CAN SPEND 2 DAYS AT EPCOT

Ignore the 1-day itinerary, but consider my earlier advice about Advance Reservations and choice of restaurants.

The basic plan of attack here is to hit Future World and all of its rides and exhibits on your first day, and then cruise the World Showcase the next day. (Because the showcase opens later, you can hit any missed areas or go back for seconds in Future World early on Day 2.) Remember to go straight to FASTPASS rides that appeal to you (check your guide map).

Day 1 If you want to eat in the park, book **Advance Reservations** for lunch and dinner if you haven't already. Skip **Spaceship Earth** because that's where a lot of the park's visitors go first (do that before you leave the park for the day). Instead, take a spin on **Test Track,** in the southeast corner of Future World; if it's crowded, use FAST-PASS and come back later. Blast off as the astronauts do on **Mission: Space,** and then double back to **Ellen's Energy Adventure** in the Universe of Energy before grabbing lunch.

Next, spend time in **Innoventions East,** where you'll get a whirlwind lesson on hurricanes and other wild weather at **Storm Struck.** At **Innoventions West,** try your luck at the **Video Games of Tomorrow** exhibit. Before you call it a day, enjoy the peaceful exhibits in the **Seas with Nemo & Friends** (including Turtle Talk with Crush, the Seas with Nemo & Friends, and Bruce's

Shark World) and the **Land** (be sure to check out **Soarin',**), and then cut to **Imagination!** for the **Journey into Imagination with Figment** and **Honey, I Shrunk the Audience** (or **Captain EO**) shows. Younger kids will appreciate the dancing fountains (next to Imagination! and between Innoventions East and West); parents will appreciate the break from walking.

Day 2 If you arrive when the park opens, go to any **Future World** rides or shows that you missed or want to repeat. Or sleep a little later and arrive for the opening of **World Showcase.**

Start in **Canada,** to the far right of the entrance. The movie here is uplifting and entertaining. Then continue counterclockwise to the **United Kingdom** for street shows, people-watching, and a real pub. **France** has a captivating film and a wonderful pastry shop; **Morocco** has a colorful casbah with merchants, Moorish tile and art, and little passages that put you in Bogartville. (For some, this is better than the real Casablanca, which is actually dirty and run-down.)

Japan has a store packed with enticements and grand architecture, while **U.S.A.—The American Adventure** is a patriotic triumph of audio-animated characters. This is a large theater, so waits are rarely long. Next, head to **Italy** and St. Mark's Square, which comes complete with a 105-foot bell tower.

Germany's Biergarten has oompah bands, beer, and wursts. Don't miss the model railway and the Bavarian-looking shops. Then steer yourself to **China,** which offers food, bargain buys, gardens and ponds, and a 360-degree movie. Continuing counterclockwise, **Norway** features the **Maelstrom** ride. **Mexico** completes the World Showcase semicircle with a boat ride through the country that features a new animated element including Donald Duck and the Three Caballeros.

End your day with the **IllumiNations** fireworks display.

A DAY AT DISNEY'S HOLLYWOOD STUDIOS THEME PARK

Here's a park that's easier to manage in 1 day.

Remember my advice on making **Advance Reservations** (☎ **407/939-3463**) if you want to eat in the park. The **Hollywood Brown Derby** is a decent sit-down restaurant. See chapter 4, "Where to Eat," for more information on dining options in the park.

Head directly to the **Twilight Zone Tower of Terror.** The high-voltage ride is not for the very young or faint of heart. The same goes for the **Rock 'n' Roller Coaster,** which blends incredible takeoff speed with three inversions. The park is small, so backtracking isn't as much of a concern here. Consider passing up attractions that have long lines, or use FAST-PASS where you can. Lines also can be long at **Star Tours** (especially after the recent upgrade), the **Indiana Jones Epic Stunt Spectacular,** and the **Lights, Motors, Action! Extreme Stunt Show.**

Voyage of the Little Mermaid is a must for the young (in years or yearnings); the same goes for **Jim Henson's Muppet*Vision 3-D,** a truly fun show for all ages.

With luck, you'll make it through most of the above before a late lunch at the **50's Prime Time Café,** where the food is so-so, but the experience is . . . well, surreal.

Afterward, take the ton-of-fun **Studio Backlot Tour** and try your luck at the family-friendly **Toy Story Mania** ride.

Check your show schedule for favorites such as **Disney Junior—Live on Stage!** (which is great for little kids), **Beauty and the Beast, Pixar Pals Countdown to Fun** (the park's all-new Pixar-themed parade), and the **American Idol Experience.** At night, do *not* miss **Fantasmic!**

A DAY AT ANIMAL KINGDOM

Be here when the gates open, usually around 8 or 9am. (Call Disney information at ☎ **407/824-4321** to check the time.) This will give you the best chance of seeing animals—they're most active in the morning air (the next best is late in the afternoon, although some can be seen throughout the day in cooler months). If you want to eat at **Yak & Yeti** or the **Rainforest Cafe,** make Advance Reservations by calling ☎ **407/939-3463.**

The size of the park (500 acres) means a lot of travel once you pass through the gates. Don't linger in the **Oasis** area or around the **Tree of Life;** instead, head directly to the back of the park, grab a FASTPASS for **Expedition Everest** (in Asia), and then go immediately back to Africa to be first in line for **Kilimanjaro Safaris.** This will allow you to see animals before it gets hot and the lines become monstrous.

Work your way back through Africa, visiting **Pangani Forest Exploration Trail** and its lowland gorillas, and then head to the Flame Tree Barbecue for a quick bite to eat, though kids may prefer the Restaurantosaurus just inside DinoLand. After lunch, head to the **Tree of Life** on Discovery Island for **It's Tough to Be a Bug.** If you want a bird-show fix, see **Flights of Wonder,** and then go on the **Maharajah Jungle Trek,** both in Asia. **Expedition Everest** will thrill older kids and teens (adults, too). Then you're off to tackle **Kali River Rapids,** a great way to cool off in the midday heat (some of you might even get soaked).

Older kids, teens, and adults can ride **Dinosaur** and **Primeval Whirl** in DinoLand U.S.A.; both are good choices if you get there before lines form or if you use FAST-PASS. Younger kids deserve some time at the **Boneyard** and on **TriceraTop Spin** in DinoLand. Visitors of all ages will be entranced by **Finding Nemo–The Musical** (be sure to check the *Times Guide* for showtimes).

Make time in your day for the **Festival of the Lion King,** over in Camp Minnie-Mickey; it's a must-see (again, check the *Times Guide* to see which showing fits in best with your schedule).

Services & Facilities in the Parks

ATMS   Cash machines are available near the entrances to all parks and usually at least one other place inside (see the guide map as you enter the park). They honor cards from banks using the Cirrus, Honor, and PLUS systems.

BABY CARE   All parks have a Baby Care Center that's equipped with private breast-feeding rooms and sells baby-care basics, which are also available at Guest Relations. All women's restrooms, and some men's, are equipped with changing tables.

Smoking Alert

Disney prohibits smoking in its shops, attractions, restaurants, and ride lines (even its resorts). There are, however, a few designated outdoor smoking areas in the park if you feel the urge to light up.

CAMERAS & FILM   Film and Kodak disposable cameras are sold at various locations in all parks (at much higher prices than in the free world), as are limited digital supplies. Services, including CD burning, film developing, and minor repairs, vary from location to location.

CAR ASSISTANCE   If you need a battery jump or other assistance, raise the hood of your vehicle and wait for security to arrive. When necessary, AAA provides free towing from the parks during park operating hours.

FIRST AID   All parks have stations marked on the handout guide maps.

INTERNET ACCESS   Disney has installed phones with large touch screens and Internet access capabilities at several locations in the theme parks, resorts, and other locations (locations are marked on park guide maps). For 25¢ a minute, with a 4-minute minimum, you can access the Internet or check your e-mail.

LOST CHILDREN   Every park has a designated spot for lost children to be reunited with their families. In the Magic Kingdom, it's City Hall or the Baby Care Center; in Epcot, the Earth Center or the Baby Care Center; in Disney's Hollywood Studios, Guest Relations; and in Animal Kingdom, Discovery Island. *Children younger than 7 should wear name-tags inside their clothing; older children and adults should have a prearranged meeting place in case your group gets separated.* If someone gets lost, tell the first park employee you see—many wear the same type of clothing and all have special name-tags.

PACKAGE PICKUP   Nearly all WDW stores can arrange for packages to be sent to the front of the park. Allow at least 3 hours for delivery. If you're staying at a Disney resort, you can also have all packages purchased by 7pm sent to your hotel (they will be delivered by noon the next day).

PARKING   At press time, Disney charged $14 for car, light truck, and van parking, and $15 for RVs.

PET CARE   It's illegal to leave yours in a parked car, even with a window cracked open; cars become ovenlike death traps in Florida's sun. Only service animals are permitted in the parks, but Disney recently opened a new luxury facility, the Best Friends Pet Care Center, at WDW (© **877/493-9738;** $10–$76 per day, depending on whether your pet is staying overnight, the type of pet you have, the accommodations and extras you choose, and whether you are a Disney resort guest), with posh accommodations for around 270 dogs and 30 cats. The center offers both day care

5

EXPLORING WALT DISNEY WORLD | Making Your Visit More Enjoyable and overnight boarding as well as numerous services aimed at the pampered pet set. The pet centers located at Disney's Transportation and Ticket Center, Epcot, and Disney's Fort Wilderness Campground have closed for good (though pets are still welcome to stay with their owners at select campsites at Disney's Fort Wilderness Campground at a rate of $5 per night). *Proof of vaccination is required.* For more information, see "Fast Facts: Orlando," beginning on p. 367.

SHOPS In addition to the ones listed in the following pages, many of Disney's attractions feature small gift shops filled with merchandise and souvenirs based on that attraction's theme.

STROLLER RENTAL Strollers are available near all of the park entrances. The cost is $15 for a single and $31 for a double. Length-of-stay rentals are available at a rate of $13 per day for a single and $27 per day for a double. Full payment is expected upfront for length-of-stay rentals.

TIP BOARDS Each park has a tip board that tells visitors the approximate waiting time at all of the major rides and attractions. In Magic Kingdom, it's at the end of Main Street on the left as you face the castle; in Epcot, the digital board is in Inno-ventions Plaza; at Hollywood Studios, it's at the intersection of Hollywood and Sunset boulevards; and inside Animal Kingdom, you'll find it just over the bridge to Discovery Island.

WHEELCHAIR RENTAL A wheelchair is $12 per day. Length-of-stay rentals are available for $10 per day. Electric wheelchairs rent for $50, with a $20 refundable deposit.

For Travelers with Special Needs

WDW does a lot to assist guests with disabilities. Its services are detailed in the *Guidebook for Guests with Disabilities,* available from Guest Relations in the parks, other information areas, Disney resorts, or online at **www.disneyworld.com** and **www.disney.go.com/disabilities**. You can also call ✆ **407/824-4321** with questions regarding special needs. Some examples of other services: Almost all Disney resorts have rooms for those with disabilities, and there are Braille directories inside the Magic Kingdom—in the front of the Main Street train station, and in a gazebo in front of the Crystal Palace restaurant. There are special parking lots at all parks. Complimentary guided-tour audiocassette tapes and players are available at Guest

 All Aboard

If your kids appreciate experiences a bit out of the ordinary, ask if you can co-pilot the Disney monorail for a spin around the kingdom. Being a **monorail pilot** doesn't mean that you get to drive the train, but your family will get to ride up front with the *real* pilot. It requires a little patience because no more than four or five people can do it per ride, so ask a cast member at the monorail stations at the Grand Floridian, Polynesian, Contemporary, or Bay Lake Tower resorts if there's room for you in the cockpit. You may not have much luck during peak seasons or busier times of the day (at park opening and closing), or if there's a pilot trainee on board. But at other times, especially if you're patient enough to wait for the next train, you may be treated to the best seats aboard. Best of all: It's free.

Relations to assist visually impaired guests, and a new audio description service (added in 2010) now offers guests (via a handheld wireless device also available at Guest Relations) a detailed narrative of the rides and attractions as they move through the ride and as their experience unfolds (rather than a simple description). The new service is also available for those with hearing impairments. Personal translator units are available to amplify the audio at some Epcot attractions (inquire at Earth Station). For hearing-impaired information, call ☏ **407/939-7670;** for information regarding Telecommunications Devices for the Deaf (TDDs), call ☏ **407/827-5141** **(TTY)** or the main number listed above.

THE MAGIC KINGDOM

The Magic Kingdom still attracts millions from around the world, drawn here by the opportunity to experience the fun and fantasy that only Disney can deliver. Attendance, at slightly more than 17 million, makes this America's most popular theme park. The 107-acre Magic Kingdom is filled with more than 40 attractions (with new experiences added almost yearly), unique shops, and themed restaurants. Its most recognizable feature is Cinderella Castle, the park's icon and centerpiece. And surrounding the castle are the park's **six themed lands,** stretching out like the spokes of a wheel.

ARRIVING   The parking lot here is huge—so big, in fact, that it's necessary to take a tram just to get to the **Transportation and Ticket Center** (more commonly known as the TTC), where you can buy your park tickets. Each of the parking lot's sections is named for Disney characters (Goofy, Pluto, Minnie, and so on), and aisles are numbered. I can't stress enough just how important it is to *write down where you left your vehicle*—you would be amazed at how many white minivans look just like yours. Once you have your tickets in hand (or if you've arrived with them—the best route), you'll need to make your first decision of the day—do you take the ferry or the monorail to the park from the TTC? The ferry offers a more leisurely (and windy) ride, while the monorail is the speedier of the two.

Upon arriving at the park entrance, you must pass through security and have your bags inspected. All told, the time it takes to get from your car to Main Street, U.S.A., is somewhere around **35 to 45 minutes,** sometimes longer. And that total doesn't include the time spent in lines if you have to stop at Guest Relations or rent a stroller. You'll face the same agony (complicated by escaping crowds) on the way out, so relax. This is one of the most crowded parks, so plan to arrive an hour before the opening bell or an hour or two after.

The most important thing you can do upon arriving at the park is to pick up a copy (or two) of the Magic Kingdom **guide map** (if you can't find one at the turnstiles, stop at City Hall or the nearest shop). It provides an array of detailed information about available services, restaurants, and attractions. The *Times Guide* (separate from the guide map) will be your key to the daily schedules for showtimes, parades, fireworks, character meet-and-greets, and park and restaurant hours.

If you have questions, all park employees are very knowledgeable, and City Hall, on your left as you enter, is the park's main information center. To the right is a center of a different sort, the Town Square Theater—now the place to meet and greet Disney's favorite costumed characters. Character greeting places are also featured on the guide map.

HOURS   The park is usually open from at least 9am to 6 or 7pm, sometimes later—as late as midnight during major holidays and summer.

TICKET PRICES Ticket prices are $85 for adults, $79 for children 3 to 9. Kids younger than 3 get in free. See "Tickets," on p. 162, for information on the Magic Your Way ticketing scheme.

Services & Facilities in the Magic Kingdom

Most of the following are noted on the handout guide maps in the park.

ATMS Machines inside the park honor cards from banks using the Cirrus, Honor, and PLUS systems. They're located near the main entrance; in Frontierland, near the Shootin' Gallery; and in Tomorrowland, next to Space Mountain.

BABY CARE Located next to the Crystal Palace at the end of Main Street, the Baby Care Center is furnished with a nursing room with rocking chairs and toddler-size toilets. Disposable diapers, formula, baby food, and pacifiers are sold at a premium (bring your own or pay the price). There are changing tables here as well as in all women's restrooms and some men's.

CAMERAS & FILM Film and Kodak disposable cameras are available throughout the park, but digital camera equipment is in far shorter supply. Services, which vary from location to location, include CD burning, film developing, and minor repairs.

FIRST AID It's located beside the Crystal Palace next to the Baby Care Center and staffed by registered nurses.

LOCKERS Lockers are located in the arcade below the Main Street Railroad Station. The cost is $7 to $9 (depending on size), plus a $5 refundable deposit.

LOST CHILDREN Lost children in the Magic Kingdom are usually taken to City Hall or the Baby Care Center. *Children younger than 7 should wear name-tags inside their clothing.*

PACKAGE PICKUP Any package can be sent by a shop clerk to Guest Relations in the Entrance Plaza; allow at least 3 hours for delivery. If you're staying overnight at a Disney resort, you can also have all packages purchased by 7pm sent to your hotel (they will be delivered by noon the next day).

PET CARE Boarding is available at the Best Friends Pet Care Center, located on the Bonnet Creek Parkway (✆ **407/824-6568**), for $10 to $76 per day. Proof of vaccination is required.

STROLLERS They can be rented at the Stroller Shop near the entrance to the Magic Kingdom. The cost is $15 for a single and $31 for a double, with length-of-stay rentals available for $13 per day for a single and $27 per day for a double. Full payment is required upfront for a length-of-stay rental.

WHEELCHAIR RENTAL For wheelchairs, go to the gift shop to the left of the ticket booths at the Transportation and Ticket Center, or to the Stroller and Wheelchair Shop inside the main entrance to your right. The cost is $12 for a regular wheelchair, or $50, plus a $20 refundable deposit, for electric convenience vehicles.

Main Street, U.S.A.

Designed to model a turn-of-the-20th-century American street (though it ends in a 13th-c. European castle), this is the gateway to the Kingdom. Don't dawdle on Main Street (it's filled mostly with shops and restaurants) when you enter; leave it for the end of the day when you're heading back to your hotel.

The Magic Kingdom

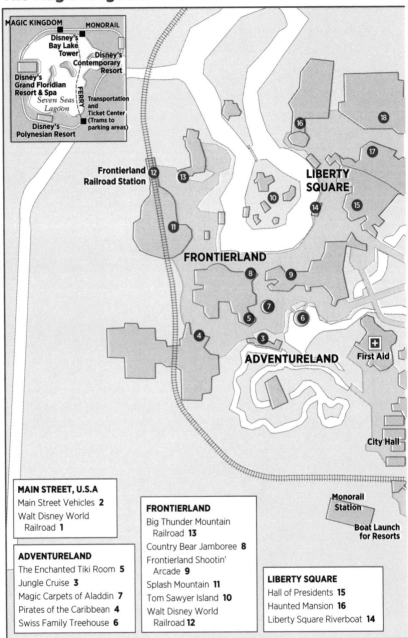

MAIN STREET, U.S.A

Main Street Vehicles **2**

Walt Disney World
Railroad **1**

ADVENTURELAND

The Enchanted Tiki Room **5**

Jungle Cruise **3**

Magic Carpets of Aladdin **7**

Pirates of the Caribbean **4**

Swiss Family Treehouse **6**

FRONTIERLAND

Big Thunder Mountain
Railroad **13**

Country Bear Jamboree **8**

Frontierland Shootin'
Arcade **9**

Splash Mountain **11**

Tom Sawyer Island **10**

Walt Disney World
Railroad **12**

LIBERTY SQUARE

Hall of Presidents **15**

Haunted Mansion **16**

Liberty Square Riverboat **14**

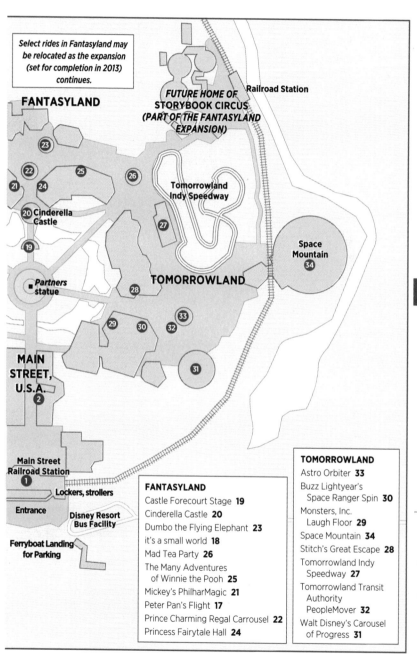

Select rides in Fantasyland may be relocated as the expansion (set for completion in 2013) continues.

FANTASYLAND

FUTURE HOME OF STORYBOOK CIRCUS (PART OF THE FANTASYLAND EXPANSION)

Railroad Station

Tomorrowland Indy Speedway

Cinderella Castle

Space Mountain 34

Partners statue

TOMORROWLAND

MAIN STREET, U.S.A.

Main Street Railroad Station

Lockers, strollers

Entrance

Disney Resort Bus Facility

Ferryboat Landing for Parking

FANTASYLAND

Castle Forecourt Stage **19**
Cinderella Castle **20**
Dumbo the Flying Elephant **23**
it's a small world **18**
Mad Tea Party **26**
The Many Adventures
  of Winnie the Pooh **25**
Mickey's PhilharMagic **21**
Peter Pan's Flight **17**
Prince Charming Regal Carrousel **22**
Princess Fairytale Hall **24**

TOMORROWLAND

Astro Orbiter **33**
Buzz Lightyear's
  Space Ranger Spin **30**
Monsters, Inc.
  Laugh Floor **29**
Space Mountain **34**
Stitch's Great Escape **28**
Tomorrowland Indy
  Speedway **27**
Tomorrowland Transit
  Authority
  PeopleMover **32**
Walt Disney's Carousel
  of Progress **31**

FROMMER'S RATES THE rides

Because there's so much to do, we're shifting from the star-rating system used for rooms and restaurants to one that has a bit more range. You'll notice most of the grades below are *As, Bs,* and *Cs.* That's because Disney designers have done a reasonably good job on the attractions front. But occasionally our ratings show *Ds* for Duds.

Here's what **Frommer's Ratings** mean:

A+ = Your trip wouldn't be complete without it.

A = Put it at the top of your "to-do" list.

B+ = Make a real effort to see or do it.

B = It's fun but not a "must-see."

C+ = A nice diversion; see it if you have time.

C = Go if there's no wait and you can walk right in.

D = Don't bother.

Main Street Vehicles
Frommer's Rating: C
Recommended Ages: Mainly nostalgic adults or toddlers

Ride a horse-drawn trolley, jitney, vintage fire engine, or horseless carriage *only* if you don't mind waiting around for a bit. While a nice little diversion, there are far more interesting things to see and do throughout the realm.

Walt Disney World Railroad
Frommer's Rating: B
Recommended Ages: All ages

Climb aboard an authentic 1928 steam-powered train for a relaxing 15-minute tour of the perimeter of the park. This is a great way to entertain the younger kids in your family while the older ones are off taking in some of Disney's more thrilling attractions. It's also a good way for kids and adults alike to rest for a brief moment while taking in the surrounding sights. There are currently two stations: one at the park entrance, the other at Frontierland; the status of the third station remains unknown (as Mickey's Toontown Fair is permanently closed due to the Fantasyland expansion).

While you're cruising down Main Street, be on the lookout for the **Dapper Dans,** a lively barbershop quartet that harmonizes its way up and down the boulevard.

SHOPPING ON MAIN STREET

Shopping at Disney has almost become a pastime in and of itself, and the largest collection of shops in the Kingdom is located right along Main Street, U.S.A. If you find you've forgotten something or just need a present for the neighbor who's taking care of your plants, you'll likely be able to find it here. The **Emporium,** in Town Square, has the park's largest selection of Disneyana, with everything from T-shirts to picture frames to cookie jars. Stop by and pick up some of the more unique sweets and treats at the **Main Street Confectionary** or shiny baubles at **Uptown Jewelers.** Many of the street's stores are interconnected, pretty much allowing you to shop from one end of Main Street to the other without ever having to walk outside.

Adventureland

Cross a bridge marked by tikis and torches as the rhythm of beating drums sounds in the distance. As you make your way through lush jungle foliage, trees hung with

Spanish moss, dense vines, and stands of palm and bamboo, you are transported to an exotic locale where swashbuckling adventures await.

The Enchanted Tiki Room

Frommer's Rating: B for kids, C for adults in need of an amusing break
Recommended Ages: 2–10 and older adults

The large Tiki Room serves up a Polynesian atmosphere, with its thatched roof, bamboo beams, tapa-bark murals, and torches. Inside, guests are entertained by the likes of Jose, Fritz, Michael, and Pierre—the attraction's original animatronic hosts—as well as an ensemble of boisterous tropical birds (more than 200 of them, in fact), chanting totem poles, and singing flowers that whistle, warble, and tweet. "New Management" (Iago and Zazu) has flown the coop (the reference now dropped from the attraction's name), having been replaced after recent renovations and the storyline tweaked. The result is more reminiscent of the attraction's original show, Tropical Serenade. Overall, it's good family fun, but be aware that it's rather loud, and a brief simulated tropical storm, with crackling thunder and flashes of lightning, combined with the multitude of audio and visual effects, may be a bit too overwhelming for very young children.

Jungle Cruise

Frommer's Rating: C+ (B for the foot-weary)
Recommended Ages: 4–adult

This 10-minute ride's slower pace is a yawner for many older kids and teens, but it's a nice break from the madness if the line isn't long or you use FASTPASS. You'll sail through the African veldt in the Congo, an Amazon rainforest, and along the Nile in Egypt as your boat captain offers somewhat corny but humorous commentary on your travels. You'll encounter dozens of exotic animatronic animals, ranging from playful elephants to lions and tigers, as you sail through dense tropical and subtropical foliage (most of it is real). You'll pass a Cambodian temple guarded by snakes, a rhino chasing terrified African singers and drummers as they clamor up a totem pole for safety, and

 Mickey's Disappearing Act

The **Town Square Theater** (located on Main Street, U.S.A.) is now the Mouse's new house in the Magic Kingdom. After recent refurbishments, what was once the Town Square Exposition Hall has been re-imagined to resemble a lavish turn-of-the-20th-century theater. The queue, winding along what appears to be a series of backstage corridors, leads to a rehearsal room lined with steamer trunks and stage props; it is here that Mickey (decked out in magician's attire) meets and greets his anxiously awaiting guests. And there's a bonus: Mickey's meet-and-greet is now a FASTPASS attraction. Keep in mind that FASTPASSES can (and most likely will) run out, often early in the day.

Note: In February 2011, Toontown permanently closed due to the ongoing expansion of Fantasyland. As a result, Disney's princess meet-and-greets (along with Tinker Bell's Pixie Hollow) have also been displaced. Until their permanent home is complete (the Princess Fairytale Hall, set to open at a later date where Snow White's Scary Adventure now stands), Disney princesses will meet and greet guests at the Town Square Theater (alongside Mickey), while Pixie Hollow (its status still uncertain) is slated to move to Epcot.

A Cut Above

The **Harmony Barber Shop**, its entrance on Main Street marked by signature candy-striped poles, is a real working barbershop. It's open daily from 9am to 5pm and gives hundreds of haircuts each week. If your child gets his or her first cut here, Disney throws in several extras—bubbles, stickers, a special set of mouse ears, and a certificate—to mark the occasion ($18). Kids 12 and younger can get a cut for about $15; cuts for adults cost around $19. To jazz up the experience, kids and adults can add some color to their coif (thanks to a special colored hair gel) for just $7.50.

a jungle camp taken over by apes. While you're waiting to board, read the prop menu; it includes fricassee of giant stag beetle and barbecued three-toed skink.

Magic Carpets of Aladdin
Frommer's Rating: A for tykes and parents
Recommended Ages: 2–8
Younger kids will appreciate this ride's gentle ups and downs as they fly through the sky on colorful magic carpets. The view of Agrabah from above is impressive, but be prepared as you make your way around the genie's giant bottle—the spitting camels have pretty good aim, making it likely that you'll get squirted with water (similar to One Fish, Two Fish, Red Fish, Blue Fish at Universal Orlando's Islands of Adventure; p. 267). There are only 16 four-passenger fiberglass carpets on the ride, which can make for extremely long lines (though not nearly as unbearable as some you'll encounter in Fantasyland).

Pirates of the Caribbean
Frommer's Rating: A
Recommended Ages: 6–adult
The release of *Pirates of the Caribbean: On Stranger Tides* (along with the earlier films in the series, *The Curse of the Black Pearl, Dead Man's Chest,* and *At World's End*) has once again revitalized the popularity of this oldie but goodie. The series also inspired the recent renovations that now have Jack Sparrow and Barbossa joining the original set of swashbucklers. A tweak in the storyline to better mirror the movie and a mix of new and updated special effects have been added, too. Still, the ride might be a bit scary for kids younger than 5 due to an unexpected yet small waterfall and moments of darkness.

After making their way through dark and dank dungeons, guests board a boat and set sail for a small Caribbean town, its shores teeming with pillaging animatronic pirates who carouse, chase wenches, and wreak general havoc, all as Jack and Barbossa race to reach the pirates' treasure. There's plenty of gunfire, and cannonballs fly through the air as the marauders battle each other, with you, of course, caught in the middle. The effects are great, as is the yo-ho-ho music of "A Pirate's Life for Me" that plays in the background (you won't be able to stop yourself from humming along). The bonus here is an immense covered queue area that will protect you and your stroller-bound children from both sun and rain (this ride offers the only covered stroller parking in the park). **Tip:** Nod hello to the parrot (Peg-legged Pete) above the entrance plaza and he may offer you his own greeting.

Swiss Family Treehouse
Frommer's Rating: C
Recommended Ages: 4–12

This attraction, based on the 1960 Disney movie version of *Swiss Family Robinson,* includes a few more comforts from home than did the original. After climbing its many, many steps, you'll finally reach the treehouse, its rooms filled with mahogany furnishings, decorative accents, and running water. If you're nervous about heights, this one's not for you—visitors will find themselves walking along a rope-suspended bridge high above the ground, not to mention the climbing that's required to make it up and down all the stairs that lead around this 50-foot banyan tree. The "tree," designed by Disney Imagineers, has 330,000 polyethylene leaves sprouting from a 90-foot span of branches; although it isn't real, it's draped with actual Spanish moss. It's a good place for kids to work off some excess energy, though things can get crowded up there. *Note:* People with limited mobility, beware—this attraction requires a lot of climbing.

SHOPPING IN ADVENTURELAND

Located at the Pirates of the Caribbean exit, the **Pirates Bazaar** is filled with everything a child needs to play pirate, from hats to hooks and everything in between. There are also muskets, toy swords, and loads of other pirate booty, as well as a small selection of island wear and costume jewels. If it's the pirate life you prefer, head to the **Pirates League** (p. 187), where buccaneer wannabes (of all ages) are transformed into swaggering swashbucklers.

Frontierland

From Adventureland, you'll step into the wild and woolly past of the American frontier, where the sidewalks are wooden, rough-and-tumble architecture runs to log cabins and rustic saloons, and the landscape is Southwestern scrubby with mesquite, cactus, yucca, and prickly pear.

Big Thunder Mountain Railroad
Frommer's Rating: A
Recommended Ages: 8–adult

This roller coaster earns high marks for what it is—a ride designed for those not quite up to the lunch-losing thrills of the Rock 'n' Roller Coaster at Disney's Hollywood Studios (p. 222). Think of Big Thunder as Roller Coasters 101. (Survive and graduate to the next level.) It sports fun hairpin turns and dark descents rather than sudden,

---

 Earning Your Ears

Mouse ears are practically a staple at Disney, but for those who prefer something a bit more unique, the **Chapeau Hat Shoppe** on Main Street features a "create your own" twist on the classic headwear. Starting with a base ($9.95), you simply add on the pieces you like, choosing from 19 different ears, various colors, and trims (about $4 for a pack of lettering; $3 for stickers sealed with a hot press)—you can even have your name embroidered on it ($3). If, however, you prefer the original version, they're available, too, for $11.95. *Note:* A second "create your own" mouse ears station is open at Disney's Wonderful World of Memories (Downtown Disney Marketplace).

A (BAKER'S) DOZEN suggestions FOR FEWER HEADACHES

1. **Be a leader, not a follower:** Try going against the grain and head left toward Adventureland to begin your day (most visitors sprint for Tomorrowland). If you have the time and aren't a slave to the compressed itinerary of a 1-day visit, make your way to one (maybe two) major attractions early on; then save the others for early on your second day when crowds are lightest. Pick up a FASTPASS when and wherever you can. And try and make mealtimes a bit earlier or later than usual—11am or 2pm for lunch and 4 or 7pm for dinner. Even a few minutes can make all the difference in the restaurant lines.

2. **Note your car's location:** That bright yellow Hummer in the next space may not be there when you get out. Write your lot and row number on something with ink that won't run if it gets wet.

3. **Avoid the rush:** I-4 can get horribly crowded at times, so be ready for bumper-to-bumper traffic from 7 to 9am, 4 to 7pm, and often in between. Check your map for secondary roads and alternate routes, and try to leave the parks a half-hour before closing, to avoid the crowds disbursing in droves.

4. **Be realistic:** You aren't going to be able to do everything in every park (believe me, I've tried). As a group, list three or four "must-do" things each day. If you can, consider splitting up, with each adult taking one or more kids—one heading for the thrill rides, the other for the tamer, tot-friendly attractions. If time allows, you can always backtrack later, and this way no one really misses out on the fun.

5. **Timing is everything:** I often laugh when I see people racing to make a tram, and then gunning for the turnstiles. Relax—the park isn't going anywhere. And rushing just to wait in line seems rather silly, doesn't it? Once inside the park, mix it up a bit; stagger the attraction lines with indoor shows or even breaks on a shady bench.

6. **Call ahead:** If a sit-down dinner in a special restaurant is important to you, be sure to make Advance Reservations (✆ **407/939-3463**) before your visit.

7. **Set a spending limit:** Kids should know they have a set amount to spend on take-home trinkets (if they do, they generally spend more wisely). You should, too. Sticking to your budget

---

steep drops and near collisions. Your runaway train covers 2,780 feet of track and careens through the ribs of a dinosaur, under a thundering waterfall, past spewing geysers, and over a bottomless volcanic pool. Animatronic characters (such as a long john–clad fellow in a bathtub) and critters (goats, chickens, donkeys) enhance the scenic backdrop, along with several hundred thousand dollars' worth of authentic antique mining equipment. ***Note:*** You must be at least 40 inches tall to ride, and Disney discourages expectant mothers, people prone to motion sickness, or those with heart, neck, or back problems from riding.

Country Bear Jamboree
Frommer's Rating: B+

Recommended Ages: 3–adult, though the younger the child, the better

This is a foot-stomping hoot! It opened as one of the park's original attractions wayback-when in 1971, a time when entertainment was more low-tech but fun just the same. The 15-minute show stars a backwoods troupe of fiddlin', strummin',

will be beneficial in the end, but building in a small contingency "fun" fund for emergencies is also a good idea.

8. **Take a break:** If you're staying at a WDW property, spend midafternoon napping (don't laugh, you may need it) or unwinding in your resort's pool. Return to the parks for a few more attractions and the closing shows. (Get your hand stamped when you leave, and you'll be readmitted without charge.)

9. **Dress comfortably:** This may seem like common sense, but judging by the limping, blistered crowds trudging the parks, most people don't understand the immeasurable amount of walking they'll be doing. Wear comfortable, broken-in walking shoes or sneakers (you know, the ones that won't give you blisters because you just bought them) and skip the sandals and mules that can fall off or cause you to trip.

10. **Don't skimp on the sunscreen:** The Florida sun can be relentless, even in the shade, under the clouds, or in the cooler months. A bad first-day burn can ruin your trip, not to mention your skin. Dress appropriately—wear lightweight, light-colored clothing, and bring along hats (especially for toddlers and infants, even if they'll be in a stroller). If you must show off your skin, slather it in sunscreen (with at least a 30 SPF). This is especially important for children. Make sure that you and your kids drink plenty of water in summer to avoid dehydration. Bringing a pair of sunglasses is a smart move, too.

11. **Travel light:** Don't carry large amounts of cash. The Pirates of the Caribbean aren't the only thieves in WDW. There are ATMs in the parks and most resorts if you run short.

12. **Get a little goofy:** Relax, put on those mouse ears, eat that extra piece of fudge, and sing along at the shows. Don't worry about what the staff thinks; they've seen it all (and they're dressed pretty goofily, too).

13. **Take measure of your kids:** This guide, park maps, and information boards outside the more adventurous rides list minimum heights. If you know the restrictions early, you can avoid disappointment in the parks. Trust me—WDW won't budge because of sad faces or temper tantrums when your safety is involved.

harmonica-playin' bears (all audio-animatronic, of course) belting out lively tunes and woeful love songs. The chubby Trixie, decked out in a satiny skirt, laments lost love as she sings "Tears Will Be the Chaser for Your Wine." Teddi Barra descends from the ceiling in a swing to perform "Heart, We Did All That We Could." Big Al moans through "Blood in the Saddle." In the finale, the cast joins in a rousing sing-along. *Blue-light bonus:* The jamboree is a great summertime place to cool your heels in the A/C.

Frontierland Shootin' Arcade
Frommer's Rating: C
Recommended Ages: 8–adult

Combining state-of-the-art electronics with a traditional shooting-gallery format, this arcade presents an array of targets (slow-moving ore cars, buzzards, and gravediggers) in an 1850s boomtown scenario. Fog creeps across the graveyard, and the setting changes as a calm, starlit night turns stormy with flashes of lightning and claps of

Riding the Rails

Although it's an oldie, Big Thunder Mountain Railroad is still a magnet for the masses. If a FASTPASS isn't available (and that can happen), try riding it late in the day (coaster veterans swear the ride is even better after dark) or during one of the parades that draw visitors away from the attractions.

thunder. Coyotes howl, bridges creak, and skeletal arms reach out from the grave. If you hit a tombstone, it might spin around and mysteriously change its epitaph. To keep things authentic, newfangled electronic firing mechanisms loaded with infrared bullets are concealed in vintage buffalo rifles. A dollar buys you 35 shots. Though it's a pretty cool arcade, there are far better ways to spend your time in the Magic Kingdom.

Splash Mountain
Frommer's Rating: A+
Recommended Ages: 8–adult

If you need a quick cooling off, this is the place to go—because you will get wet (though it's hit or miss whether you get damp or drenched)! Based on Disney's 1946 film *Song of the South*, Splash Mountain takes you flume-style down a flooded mountain, past 26 colorful scenes that include backwoods swamps, bayous, spooky caves, and waterfalls. Riders are caught in the bumbling schemes of Brer Fox and Brer Bear as they chase the ever-wily Brer Rabbit, who, against the advice of Mr. Bluebird, leaves his briar-patch home in search of fortune and the "laughing place." The music from the film forms a delightful audio backdrop. Your hollow-log vehicle (now equipped with lap bars for added safety) twists, turns, and splashes, sometimes plummeting in darkness as the ride leads to a 52-foot, 45-degree, 40-mph splashdown in a briar-filled pond (you'll feel the drop!). And that's not the end. The ride keeps going until it's a Zip-A-Dee-Doo-Dah kind of day. **Note:** You must be at least 40 inches tall to ride. Also, expectant mothers and people prone to motion sickness or those with heart, neck, or back problems shouldn't climb aboard.

Tom Sawyer Island
Frommer's Rating: C for most, B+ for energetic kids who need a release
Recommended Ages: 4–12

Huck Finn's raft will take you on a 2-minute journey across the Rivers of America to the densely forested Tom Sawyer Island, where kids can explore the narrow passages of Injun Joe's cave (complete with such scary sound effects as whistling winds), walk through a windmill, examine a serpentine abandoned mine, and investigate Fort Longhorn. The island's two bridges—one a suspension bridge, the other made of barrels floating on top of the water—create quite a challenge for anyone trying to cross. Maintaining your balance is difficult at best, if (or should I say when) the other guests are jumping up and down—but that's half the fun. Narrow, winding dirt paths lined with oaks, pines, and sycamores create an authentic backwoods atmosphere. It's easy to get briefly lost and stumble upon some unexpected adventure, but for younger children, the woods and caves can pose a real problem—toddlers who can't easily find their way back to you or who may get scared by darkness and eerie noises should be watched very carefully.

SHOPPING IN FRONTIERLAND

Mosey into the **Frontier Trading Post** for the latest and greatest in cowboy wear. The **Prairie Outpost and Supply** is your best bet for sweets and treats.

Liberty Square

Unlike the other lands in Magic Kingdom, Liberty Square doesn't have clearly delineated boundaries. Pass through Frontierland into this small area, and you'll suddenly find yourself in the middle of Colonial America. Before you can say "George Washington," you'll be standing in front of the Liberty Tree, an immense live oak decorated with 13 lanterns symbolizing the first 13 colonies. The entire area has an 18th-century, early American feel, complete with Federal and Georgian architecture, quaint shops, and flowerbeds bordering manicured lawns. You may even encounter a fife-and-drum corps marching along the cobblestone streets. The **Liberty Tree Tavern** (p. 116) is one of the better Magic Kingdom restaurants.

Hall of Presidents
Frommer's Rating: B+
Recommended Ages: 8–adult

American presidents from George Washington to Barack Obama are represented by lifelike audio-animatronic figures (arguably the best in WDW). If you look closely, you'll see them fidget and whisper during the performance. The show begins with a film projected on a 180-degree, 70mm screen. It talks about the importance of the Constitution; then the curtain rises on America's leaders, and, as each comes into the spotlight, he nods or waves with presidential dignity. Lincoln then rises and speaks, occasionally referring to his notes. In a tribute to Disney thoroughness, painstaking research was done in creating the figures and scenery, with each president's costume reflecting period fashion, fabrics, and tailoring techniques.

Haunted Mansion
Frommer's Rating: A
Recommended Ages: 6–adult

What better way to show off Disney's eye for detailed special effects than through this oldie but goodie (Walt had a hand in its development), where "Grim Grinning Ghosts" come out to socialize—or so the ride's theme song goes? The queue here is one of the most amusing in the park, the recently re-imagined path now winding its way through a graveyard filled with tombstones boasting extraordinary interactive elements (the high-tech special effects giving guests a first-hand glimpse at Disney's

---

 Parental Touring Tip

Many of the attractions at Walt Disney World offer a **Parent Switch program,** designed for parents traveling with small children. While one parent rides an attraction, the other stays with kids not quite ready to handle the experience; then the adults switch places without having to stand in line again. The bonus (beyond the obvious) is that the kids able to ride the attraction will get to ride again, too. Notify a cast member if you wish to participate when you get in line. Most other Orlando theme parks offer this option, too.

It's a Dirty Job . . .

The Disney parks are usually fairly clean, but there's one notable spot in the Magic Kingdom that takes pride in its dreary image. In order to maintain the Haunted Mansion's weathered and worn appearance, employees spread large amounts of dust over the home's interior and also string up plenty of real-looking cobwebs. It takes a lot of effort to keep the place looking bedraggled, which may explain why your haunted hosts are only a handful of Disney cast members without smiles plastered on their faces.

impressive NextGen technology); the epitaphs and effects are sure to make you chuckle. Upon entering the mansion, you're greeted by a ghostly host, who encloses you in a windowless portrait gallery (are those eyes following you?) where the floor seems to descend (actually, it's the ceiling that's rising) and the room goes dark (the only truly scary moment). Darkness, spooky music, eerie howling, and mysterious screams and rappings enhance the ambience. Your vehicle—er, Doom Buggy—takes you past a ghostly banquet and ball, a graveyard band, a suit of armor that comes alive, cobweb-draped chandeliers, a ghostly talking head in a crystal ball, and more. Keep your eyes on the mirror you pass at the end of your ride, as you may find another passenger atop your buggy—or that your head's gone missing—boo! Thanks to a rather lengthy rehab in 2010 (complementing the overhaul completed back in 2007), the ghosts are even ghoulier, the spectral special effects more spectacular, and the sinister silliness . . . well, you get the picture. Overall, the experience is more amusing than terrifying; most children 6 and older will be fine, but those younger (and even some of the older ones) may not be so amused.

Liberty Square Riverboat 🖐

Frommer's Rating: C

Recommended Ages: All ages

The *Liberty Belle*, a grand steam-powered riverboat (recently refurbished in order to retain its stature as such), offers lazy 17-minute cruises along the Rivers of America, allowing thrill-ride-weary passengers the chance to relax. As you pass along the shores of Frontierland, the Indian camp, wildlife, and wilderness cabin, it seems as if you're traveling through the wild and woolly West. It's generally a pleasant ride that offers tired feet a chance to gear up for trekking through the remainder of the park, but all in all the experience is rather blah and uneventful, and the scenery not nearly as impressive as it could be.

SHOPPING IN LIBERTY SQUARE

The **Heritage House** is filled with replicas of famous documents (they're great for school projects), including the Declaration of Independence; miniature models of the Statue of Liberty; and everything Americana, from souvenir spoons and campaign buttons to flags and red-white-and-blue T-shirts. **Ye Olde Christmas Shoppe,** stocked with decorations and Disney ornaments galore, celebrates Christmas every day of the year.

Fantasyland

The most fanciful land in the park, Fantasyland features attractions that bring classic Disney characters to life. It is by far the most popular land in the park for young children, who can sail over Merry Ole' London and Never Never Land, ride in a honey pot through the Hundred-Acre Wood, and fly with Dumbo. If your kids are younger than 8, you'll find yourself spending a lot of your time here.

Note: At press time, construction was underway on what is being touted as the largest expansion in the history of the Magic Kingdom—the expansion of Fantasyland. Over the next year or so (with a completion date set for 2013), new rides, attractions, character experiences, and restaurants will be added (rolled out in phases beginning in late 2012). Select Disney princesses will get their own themed villages within the newly created Fantasyland Forest, where guests will soon be able to journey under the sea with Ariel, take a first-of-its-kind train ride through the Seven

A SWISH OF THE wand & A SWOOSH OF THE sword

As you walk around Disney lately, it might be difficult not to notice the ever-increasing number of pint-size princesses (often decked out from head to toe) wandering about the World. These magical makeovers (for kids ages 3 and up) are all the rage thanks to Disney's new **Bibbidi Bobbidi Boutique** (the original boutique is located in Downtown Disney, the second located in Cinderella Castle at the Magic Kingdom). The boutique, run by Fairy Godmothers in training, is open daily from 9am to 5pm, and reservations are practically a must (☎ **407/939-7895**).

Princess package options include the **Coach** (hair styling, shimmering makeup, and a princess sash for $49.95 plus tax); the **Crown** (hair styling, shimmering makeup, nails, and a princess sash for $54.95 plus tax); and the **Castle** (hair styling, shimmering makeup, nails, a princess sash, and an entire princess costume complete with shoes, crown, magic wand, and photos for $189.95–$249.95 plus tax). The **Knight** package, great for little brothers who have to wait it out with sis, includes hair styling, sword, and shield for $14.95. The Downtown Disney boutique offers, in addition to the princess packages, a **Secret Star** makeover ($109.95, not available at the Magic Kingdom location) that includes a wig, microphone headset, guitar bag,

jeans, and a T-shirt to complete the look.

In addition to pop stars and princesses, pint-size pirates are also popping up around Disney thanks to the opening of the **Pirates League** in Adventureland. Similar to the Bibbidi Bobbidi Boutique, the Pirates League transforms pint-size pirate wannabes into swashbuckling buccaneers complete with all the trimmings. Pirate packages include the **First Mate** (bandana; facial effects including scars, tattoos, fake teeth, earring, and eye patch; a sword and sheath; a pirate coin necklace; a personalized pirate oath; and a 5×7 photo, all for $29.95 plus tax) and the **Empress** (bandanna; shimmering makeup including face gems, tattoos, nail polish, earring, and eye patch; sword and sheath; pirate coin necklace; a personalized pirate oath; and a 5×7 photo, for $29.95 plus tax). Costumes, wigs, photo packages, and additional accessories are available for an extra fee. Reservations, which are highly recommended, can be made by calling ☎ **407/WDW-CREW** (407/939-2739). A $10 cancellation fee will be charged to your credit card (required when making reservations) for no-shows and cancellations less than 24 hours in advance. Kids must be at least 3 years old and accompanied by an adult at all times.

5

EXPLORING WALT DISNEY WORLD

The Magic Kingdom

Dwarfs Mine, and dine at the Beast's Castle. Enhancements to existing rides and attractions are also in the works: Dumbo will practically double in size, and the Barnstormer will return with a bolder, brighter look. During the construction, select rides and attractions within Fantasyland may be affected (some temporarily shut down, others permanently closed). At this writing, Pooh's Playful Spot had been disassembled, the honey tree integrated into the new interactive queue leading up to the Many Adventures of Winnie the Pooh (also featuring a slew of new special effects), and Toontown had closed for good (the character meet-and-greets relocated to the recently revamped Town Square Theater near the park entrance). Ariel's Grotto and Snow White's Scary Adventure (soon to be replaced by Princess Fairytale Hall, a royal princess meet-and-greet) are also among the attractions currently affected.

Cinderella Castle 📷

Frommer's Rating: A (for visuals)
Recommended Ages: All ages

There's actually not a lot to do here, but it's the Magic Kingdom's most widely recognized symbol, and I guarantee that you won't be able to pass it by without a look. It's not as if you could miss it anyway. The fairy-tale castle looms over Main Street, U.S.A., its 189-foot-high Gothic spires taking center stage from the minute you enter the park.

Set inside the castle is one of the most popular restaurants in the park, **Cinderella's Royal Table** (p. 116), along with the **Bibbidi Bobbidi Boutique.** Elaborate mosaic murals depict the Cinderella story in the castle's archway, and Disney family coats of arms are displayed over a fireplace. An actress portraying Cinderella, dressed for the ball, often makes appearances in the lobby. The Castle Forecourt Stage features live shows daily, so be sure to check the *Times Guide* for the **Dream Along with Mickey** schedule. Disney's latest outdoor stage show is an entertainer that features singing and dancing by Mickey, Peter Pan, Captain Hook, and plenty of other familiar favorites (both good and evil).

Dumbo the Flying Elephant

Frommer's Rating: B+ for younger kids and parents
Recommended Ages: 2–6

This is a favorite of the preschool set, a fact that will quickly become apparent when you see the line wrapping around, and around, and around. Much like Magic Carpets of Aladdin (p. 180), the Dumbo vehicles fly around in a circle, gently rising and dipping as you control them from inside the elephant. If you can stand the brutal lines—extending well beyond the barely covered queue (there are gigantic fans, though I have yet to see them actually running) and out into the blazing sun—this ride is almost sure to make your little one's day. **Note:** Be aware that Dumbo is slated for a major overhaul (doubling its size) during the Fantasyland expansion. Be sure to check the *Times Guide* upon entering at the park (or check online before you arrive) to see if it will be operational during your visit.

it's a small world

Frommer's Rating: B+ for youngsters and first-timers
Recommended Ages: 2–8

Recently refurbished to spruce up some of its older displays, it's a small world is one of those rides that you just have to do because it's been there since the beginning—it's a classic (built for the 1964 World's Fair before being transplanted to Disney), and in this day and age it's nice to see that some things don't change (or at least not too much). Besides, it's a big favorite of younger kids. And as much as some adults pooh-pooh it, I'd take bets they come out smiling and singing right along with their kids. If you don't know the song, you will by the end of the ride (and probably ever after), as the hard part is trying to get it *out* of your head. As you sail along, you'll pass through the countries of the world, each filled with appropriately costumed audio-animatronic dolls greeting you by singing "It's a Small World" in tiny Munchkin voices. The cast of thousands includes Chinese acrobats, Russian kazachok dancers, Indian snake charmers, French cancan girls, and, well, you get the picture. To truly experience everything Disney, this one's a must.

Mad Tea Party

Frommer's Rating: C+
Recommended Ages: 4–adult

Traditional amusement park ride it may be, but it's still a family favorite—maybe because it is so simple. The mad tea party scene in *Alice in Wonderland* was the inspiration for this one, and riders sit in giant pastel-colored teacups set on saucers that careen around a circular platform while the cup, saucer, and platform all spin round and round. Occasionally, the woozy Dormouse pops out of a big central teapot to see what's going on. Tame as it may appear, this can be a pretty active, even nauseating, ride, depending on how much you spin your teacup's wheel. Adolescents seem to consider it a badge of honor if they can turn the unsuspecting adults in their cup green—you have been warned!

 PLAYING THE part

Immersive entertainment experiences continue to be added to the already impressive lineup of street-style shows in the Magic Kingdom.

In **Captain Jack Sparrow's Pirate Tutorial (Adventureland),** the great Captain himself, along with his mate Mack, take on a pint-size crew of pirates in training, teaching them the art of swordplay and other silly swashbuckling fun. Upon completion, the little pirates are sworn in as official swashbucklers as they say the pirate's oath and become honorary buccaneers and part of Captain Jack's crew.

During the **Move It Shake It Celebrate It Parade (Main Street, U.S.A.),** guests are invited to join in and dance down Main Street right along with their favorite Disney characters, floats, and stilt walkers during this high-energy street celebration.

Disney rides sometimes break down or need routine maintenance that can take them out of commission for a few hours, a day, a week, or sometimes months. Test Track at Epcot, for example, occasionally experiences technical difficulties. The Hall of Presidents (2009), Space Mountain (2010), the Haunted Mansion (2010), and Star Tours (2011) have all closed for several weeks at a time (some for several months) in order to complete scheduled renovations. Many, but not all, of the ride rehabs are listed on the Disney website (www.disneyworld.com). Deb's Unofficial Walt Disney World Information Guide (www.allearsnet.com) and A Parent's Guide to Walt Disney World, Orlando, and More (www.mouseearsandmore.com) list most ride rehabs as well. The moral of the story: Err on the side of caution and don't make promises to kids about specific rides just in case something happens (especially given the ongoing construction at the Magic Kingdom, with the Fantasyland expansion affecting existing rides and attractions). Note that refurbishments and technical difficulties are unfortunate but part of the deal—neither Disney nor Universal will discount or refund any tickets when rehabs occur.

The Many Adventures of Winnie the Pooh
Frommer's Rating: B
Recommended Ages: 2–8

When this replaced Mr. Toad's Wild Ride over a decade ago, it drew a small storm of protest from Toad lovers, but things have quieted since then. This fun ride features the cute and cuddly little fellow along with Eeyore, Piglet, and Tigger. You board a golden honey pot and ride through a storybook version of the Hundred-Acre Wood, keeping an eye out for Heffalumps, Woozles, Blustery Days, and the Floody Place. Young kids absolutely love it, but be prepared to brave some *very* long lines if you don't use FASTPASS. **Note:** Pooh's Playful Spot had permanently closed at press time due to ongoing construction and the expansion of Fantasyland. The honey tree has since been integrated into the recently re-created queue, now filled with interactive elements (such as oversized vegetable drums and touch screens dripping with virtual honey) aimed at entertaining tinier tots.

Mickey's PhilharMagic
Frommer's Rating: A+
Recommended Ages: All ages

This is by far the most amazing 3-D movie production I've ever laid eyes on and is a must-see for everyone. Popular Disney characters—including Ariel, Simba, and Aladdin—are brought to 3-D life on a 150-foot screen (the largest wraparound screen on the planet) as they try to help (or in some cases hinder) the attempts of Donald Duck to retrieve Mickey's magical sorcerer's hat before the Mouse discovers it's missing. It's the first time the classic Disney characters have ever been rendered in 3-D. Even if you're not a big fan of shows, this is one you should see. Like (but far better than) the whimsical **Jim Henson's Muppet*Vision 3-D** (p. 219) at Disney's Hollywood Studios, the show combines music, animated film, puppetry, and special effects that tickle several of your senses. The kids will love the animation and effects, and parents will enjoy the nostalgia factor.

Peter Pan's Flight
Frommer's Rating: A for kids and parents
Recommended Ages: 3–8

Another of Disney's simple pleasures, this is a classic ride that's fun for the whole family. You'll fly through the sky in your very own ship (much like that of Captain Hook), gliding over familiar scenes from the adventures of Peter Pan. Your adventure begins in the Darlings' nursery and includes a flight over an elaborate nighttime cityscape of Merry Ole' London, before you move on to Never Land. There you encounter mermaids, Indians, Tick Tock the Croc, the Lost Boys, Princess Tiger Lilly, Tinker Bell, Hook, and Smee, all while listening to the theme, "You Can Fly, You Can Fly, You Can Fly." It's *very* tame fun for the young and young at heart. It's also another one where the long lines could inspire the theme "you can wait, you can wait, you can wait." *Tip:* The lines here often shrink to manageable proportions around the evening parade times, so if you can hold out until later in the day, you might save yourself some aggravation.

Prince Charming Regal Carrousel 📷
Frommer's Rating: B+ for younger kids, A for carousel fans
Recommended Ages: All ages

One of the most beautiful attractions at Disney—and known until 2010 as **Cinderella's Golden Carrousel**—this one is as enchanting to look at as it is to ride. Originally built by the Philadelphia Toboggan Co. in 1917, the carousel toured many an amusement park in the Midwest long before Walt Disney bought it and brought it to Orlando 5 years before the Magic Kingdom opened. Disney artisans meticulously refurbished it, adding 18 hand-painted scenes from Cinderella on a wooden canopy above the horses. Its organ plays Disney classics such as "When You Wish Upon a Star." Adults and children alike adore riding the ornate horses round and round; there are even a few benches for the littlest tykes in the family. The ride is longer than you might expect, but the lines can get lengthy as well, so check back a bit later if your timing is off the first time around.

Snow White's Scary Adventures
Frommer's Rating: C
Recommended Ages: 4–8

Though Disney has changed this ride a bit since its debut, attempting to make it less scary for the small children that it was intended for, it still features the wicked witch rather predominantly (though Snow White appears far more often than before). Many of the scenes are now more pleasant, including such happier moments from the movie as the scenes at the wishing well and Snow White riding away with the prince to live happily ever after. There are new audio-animatronic dwarfs, and the colors have been brightened and made less menacing. Even so, this ride still has plenty of scary moments if your child is younger than 5 (and those much older likely won't even want to ride), so if the lines are long, think about passing this one up. *Note:* Alas, Snow White's Scary Adventure will soon be part of Disney's past—a casualty of the Fantasyland expansion (a closing date yet to be announced). Replacing the ride will be a princess meet-and-greet aptly named **Princess Fairytale Hall.**

SHOPPING IN FANTASYLAND

Fantasy Faire is filled with plenty of items for your little prince or princess to play with, including costumes, swords, and much more. Little girls adore **Tinker Bell's**

EXTRA MAGIC—extra time

The free **Extra Magic Hour** program allows Disney resort guests (as well as those staying at the WDW Swan, the WDW Dolphin, and the Hilton at the Walt Disney World Resort) some extra playtime in the parks (even the water parks). Under the program, a select number of attractions, shops, and restaurants at one of the four major Disney parks (or one of its two water parks) open an hour early on scheduled mornings, and those at another park remain open up to 3 hours after official closing on scheduled evenings. And because only resort guests can participate in the Extra Magic Hour, crowds are almost nonexistent, and lines are much shorter—not to mention that the temperatures are usually a lot more agreeable early in the morning and later in the evening.

To enter a park for the morning Extra Magic Hour, you must present your Disney resort room key and park ticket. For the evening Extra Magic Hour, your room key, park ticket, and a special wristband (for every member in your group) are required. You can obtain the wristband at the park scheduled to remain open that evening, but no earlier than 1 hour prior to park closing.

Warning: If you hold a ticket with a Park Hopper add-on (see p. 162 for information on Disney ticketing options), then you can attend any Extra Magic Hour at any park. But, if you hold a Base Ticket with no park-hopping privileges, then you can only attend the Extra Magic Hour at the park where you're spending your day. So, if you have only a Base Ticket and go to the morning Magic Hour at Epcot and spend the day there, you cannot head over to Magic Kingdom's evening Magic Hour on the same day. Call ✆ **407/824-4321,** or visit **www.disneyworld.com** for details.

Treasures, its wares comprising Peter Pan merchandise, costumes (Tinker Bell, Snow White, Cinderella, Pocahontas, and others), and collector dolls. **Pooh's Thotful Shop** is filled with T-shirts and toys featuring those cuddly characters from the Hundred-Acre Wood for kids and adults alike.

Mickey's Toontown Fair

Note: In February 2011, Toontown closed down for good due to the ongoing expansion of Fantasyland. Mickey has since moved to a new home at the recently revamped Town Square Theater on Main Street U.S.A. (described earlier in this chapter). The Disney princesses have relocated there as well, albeit only temporarily—the Princess Fairytale Hall, their permanent home, will be opening at a later date. Tinker Bell, meanwhile, is rumored to be moving to Epcot.

Tomorrowland

This land was originally designed to focus on the future, but in 1994, the WDW folks decided Tomorrowland (originally designed in the 1970s) was beginning to look a lot like "Yesteryear." So it was revamped to show the future as envisioned in the '20s and '30s—a galactic, sci-fi-inspired community inhabited by humans, aliens, and robots. A video-game arcade also was added.

Astro Orbiter

Frommer's Rating: C+

Recommended Ages: 4–10

Although touted as a tame ride much like the ones you might have ridden when you were a child and the carnivals came to town, it does offer a bit of unexpected uneasiness. Its "rockets" are on arms attached to "the center of the galaxy," and move up and down while orbiting the planets, but they also tilt to the side—and when you're on top of a two-story tower, looking down from your perch can make you rather anxious. Because of its limited capacity, the line tends to move at a snail's pace, so unless it's short, skip this one.

Buzz Lightyear's Space Ranger Spin

Frommer's Rating: A+ for kids and parents

Recommended Ages: 3 and up

Recruits stand ready as Buzz Lightyear briefs you on your mission. The evil emperor Zurg is once again up to no good, and Buzz needs your help to save the Universe. As you cruise through "space," you'll pass through scenes filled with brightly colored aliens, most of whom are marked with a big "Z," so you know where to shoot. Kids love using the dashboard-mounted laser cannons as they spin through the sky (filled with gigantic toys instead of stars). If they're good shots, they can set off sight and sound gags with a direct hit from their lasers (when my youngest was only 4 years old, he aimed just about everywhere but at the target and still had loads of fun; now, at the age of 8, he has far better aim and still has fun). A display in the car keeps score, so take multiple cars if you have more than one child. This ride uses the same technology as Universal Studios Florida's Men in Black Alien Attack (p. 257), but it's aimed at a younger audience, and therefore it's far tamer.

Monsters, Inc. Laugh Floor

Frommer's Rating: B+

Recommended Ages: 4 and up

Taking its cue from the hit Disney/Pixar flick *Monsters, Inc.*, Mike, along with an entire cast of monster comedians, pokes fun at audience members in hopes of getting enough laughs to fill the gigantic laugh canister. This relatively new immersive experience is live and unscripted, using real-time animation, digital projection, sophisticated voice-activated animation, and a tremendous cast of talented improv comedians. Text your favorite jokes to the show from your cellphone (just prior to showtimes)—and you may find yourself laughing at a joke or two of your own! The number is available near the attraction's entrance (and works only within a very short radius).

Space Mountain

Frommer's Rating: B+

Recommended Ages: 10–adult

This cosmic roller coaster usually has *long* lines—especially after undergoing a lengthy refurbishment in 2010—but thankfully it has FASTPASS. Disney has added 87 high-tech video-game stations (each themed around space travel) and updated the special effects (space-age music and exhibits—think meteorites, shooting stars, and space debris whizzing past overhead) throughout the queue in an effort to revive the coaster's futuristic appeal. Once aboard your rocket, you'll climb and dive through the inky, starlit blackness of outer space (the interior darkened in an effort to better hide what twists and turns lie ahead). The hairpin turns and plunges make it seem as if you're going at breakneck speed (thanks in part to a recalibrated track), but your car doesn't go any faster than 28 mph. As on many coasters, the front seat of the train offers the biggest thrills and is the best place to maintain the illusion of flying through space. While no longer outdated when compared to other rides out there, the coaster retains much of its original classic appeal, as the refurbishment was meant to enhance the experience rather than to replace it (the changes are modest when compared to the rehab recently completed at its California counterpart). All in all, it's a good coming-of-age test for future thrill-ride junkies; so if your kids are just starting out on the coasters and don't mind a spin in the dark, this is a good place to begin. **Note:** Riders must be at least 44 inches tall. Also, expectant moms and people prone to motion sickness or those with heart, neck, or back problems shouldn't climb aboard.

Stitch's Great Escape
Frommer's Rating: D
Recommended Ages: 6–10

In 2003, the scarier **ExtraTERRORestrial Alien Encounter** was closed permanently to make way for this newer and (allegedly) more family-friendly attraction. Unfortunately, Disney missed the mark on this one. Even though it features the mischievous experiment 626, otherwise known as Stitch—a favorite of many younger kids—the ride isn't really that child-friendly (at least not for the young set). It's not particularly exciting, either. Upon entering the attraction, guests are briefed on their responsibilities as newly recruited alien prison guards. Suddenly an alarm sounds—a new prisoner is arriving, and the pandemonium begins. Stitch, after appearing by teleportation, is confined in the middle of the room, but only momentarily—the ride isn't called Stitch's Great Escape for nothing. Guests are seated around the center stage, overhead restraints on their shoulders (which are slightly uncomfortable unless you're sitting straight up when they are lowered) allowing them to "feel" special sensory effects. It's the attraction's long periods of darkness and silence that make this one inappropriate for younger children—a fact made apparent by some of the screams you'll hear from the audience (I've seen at least one 5-year-old walk out somewhat traumatized). **Note:** There's a 40-inch height requirement to experience the attraction, though this may change—it's already been adjusted twice since the ride first debuted.

> ## Snacking in the Parks
>
> For my money, you can't beat the smoked turkey drumsticks sold for about $8 in WDW parks (they're called "Galactic Gobblers" at the Lunching Pad in Tomorrowland). How popular are they? Each year, Disney guests gobble-gobble 1.6 million of them.

Tomorrowland Indy Speedway
Frommer's Rating: B+ for kids; D for tweens, teens, and childless adults
Recommended Ages: 4–10

Younger kids love this ride, especially if they get the chance to drive one of the gas-powered miniature sportscars—though they may need the help of a parent's foot to push down on the gas pedal—for a 4-minute spin around the track. Tweens and teens, however, hate it: Speeds reach a mere 7 mph, which for most is *incredibly* slow, and the steering is atrocious (you can't control the cars without bumping the rail that it follows). The slow speed seems to work well for young kids (who also think the bumping around is fun). The long lines move even more slowly than the ride does, so

Where to Find Characters

The **Town Square Theater** (on Main Street, U.S.A.) was recently re-imagined as a place where kids can meet and mingle one on one with Disney's most famous character: Mickey Mouse. Disney princesses, temporarily displaced during the Fantasyland expansion, can also be found in residence (their permanent home—as well as a slew of all-new meet-and-greet opportunities, is scheduled to open in Fantasyland as the first phases of the expansion begin to roll out). **Adventureland** (at Pirates of the Caribbean and near Magic Carpets of Aladdin), **Tomorrowland** (near the Space Ranger Spin), and **Frontierland** (near the Diamond Horseshoe) are other hot spots for character sightings. Be sure to have your camera ready and waiting, and autograph book and pen in hand, if you want to capture the moment before it's gone.

Tip: If you're willing to spend money to avoid waiting in line, character meals at restaurants such as the **Crystal Palace** and **Cinderella's Royal Table** (as well as at select WDW resorts) all offer the opportunity to meet your favorite characters. Just don't forget to make Advance Reservations if you go the dining route.

be prepared to wait this one out. There's a 52-inch height minimum to take a lap without an older rider along with you. *Note:* It carries Disney's warning that expectant mothers and people with heart, neck, or back problems shouldn't climb aboard, likely because of the potential for getting bumped as you try to board or disembark.

Tomorrowland Transit Authority PeopleMover
Frommer's Rating: C, B+ for tired adults and toddlers
Recommended Ages: All ages

After making your way up a moving walkway, you'll spot the futuristic train cars that will take you on a tour of Tomorrowland from high above the ground. The engineless train runs on a track and is powered by electromagnets, creating no pollution, little noise, and using little power. Narrated by a computer guide named Horack I, TTAP offers an overhead view of Tomorrowland, including a brief interior look at Space Mountain (though extremely rare, I've actually caught a glimpse of the coaster with the lights up—impressive!). Lines are often nonexistent, as most riders are parents awaiting the return of their children from Space Mountain, or those with tired toddlers in need of a brief respite from the activity below. The view of the park is especially impressive after dark, when the streets and attractions are lit up.

Walt Disney's Carousel of Progress 👋
Frommer's Rating: C
Recommended Ages: 5–10

Only open seasonally, when crowds are at their peak, the Carousel of Progress offers more of a respite from the hustle and bustle of the crowds than it does an interesting experience. It first debuted at the 1964 World's Fair before Disney decided to include it in his collection. The ride emigrated from Disneyland to Disney World in 1975 and was refurbished to its original state a little more than 10 years ago. The entire show rotates through scenes illustrating the state of technology from the 1900s to the 1940s. Most adults find it rather boring, but kids willing to sit still for a few minutes may actually learn a thing or two.

5

EXPLORING WALT DISNEY WORLD

The Magic Kingdom

SHOPPING IN TOMORROWLAND

Mickey's Star Traders is a large shop filled from top to bottom with Disneyana; it's probably the best place to shop in the Magic Kingdom after Main Street.

Parades, Fireworks & More

Pick up a guide map (or two) and a *Times Guide* (or three) when you enter the park. The information includes the day's **entertainment schedule,** listing all the special goings-on for the day. Included are concerts, encounters with characters, holiday events, parades, fireworks, restaurant hours, and the major happenings. *Tip:* There's also an all-parks guide that includes much of the same information and is well worth picking up, too.

Celebrate a Dream Come True Parade

Frommer's Rating: B

Recommended Ages: All ages

Floats filled with Disney characters make their way through the park and up Main Street on a daily basis. Each features a different theme ("imagination" at the heart of each); one stars Pinocchio, another Snow White. Even Disney's more sinister characters, including the evil queen, Maleficent, and Cruella De Vil, have their place in the parade.

Main Street Electrical Parade 📷

Frommer's Rating: A

Recommended Ages: All ages

After a 10-year hiatus, this popular parade has once again been brought back to life (albeit only seasonally). Fanciful floats adorned with thousands of sparkling lights and a cast of colorful characters, led by none other than Disney's most popular pixie (Tinker Bell, of course), entrance onlookers of all ages as the parade makes its way along Main Street, U.S.A. While I may not remember every last detail about my first trip to Disney (in this instance, Disneyland), the Electrical Parade left a lasting impression—so you can only imagine how impressive the parade is today (some 39 years later).

SpectroMagic 📷

Frommer's Rating: A

Recommended Ages: All ages

In April 2001, this after-dark display returned for a second engagement at WDW, replacing the Main Street Electrical Parade, a Disney classic that ran from 1976 to 1991, and again from 1996 to 2001 at the Magic Kingdom (see above for details on the current incarnation). *SpectroMagic is only held on a limited number of nights.* The 20-minute parade combines fiber optics, holographic images, clouds of liquid nitrogen, old-fashioned twinkling lights, and a soundtrack featuring classic Disney tunes. Mickey, dressed in an amber and purple grand magician's cape, makes an appearance in a confetti of light. You'll also see the SpectroMen atop the title float, and Chernabog, *Fantasia's* monstrous demon, who unfolds his 38-foot wingspan. It takes the electrical equivalent of seven lightning bolts (enough to power a fleet of 2,000 over-the-road trucks) to bring the show to life. See your entertainment schedule for availability. *Tip:* On some nights, during busy periods, SpectroMagic runs twice. If your party consists of adults or kids old enough to stay up late, the second running is almost always less crowded than the first. As an added benefit, catching the late parade lets you take advantage of shorter lines at the major rides during the first running.

Wishes

Frommer's Rating: A+

Recommended Ages: All ages

Wishes, Disney's breathtaking 12-minute fireworks display, replaced the old **Fantasy in the Sky** fireworks in October 2003. The show, narrated by Jiminy Cricket and with background music from several Disney classics, is the story of a wish coming true, and it borrows one element from the old one—Tinker Bell still flies overhead. The fireworks go off nightly during summer and holidays, and on selected nights (usually Mon and Wed–Sat) the rest of the year. See your entertainment schedule for details. Numerous good views of the action are available, so long as you're standing on the front side of the castle—get too far off to the side or behind the display, and it loses much of its impressive and meticulously choreographed visual effect. Disney hotels close to the park (Grand Floridian, Polynesian, Contemporary, and Wilderness Lodge) also offer excellent views.

EPCOT

Epcot is an acronym for *Experimental Prototype Community of Tomorrow,* and it was Walt Disney's dream for a planned city. Alas, after his death, it became a theme park—Central Florida's second major one, which opened in 1982. Its aims are described in a dedication plaque: "May Epcot entertain, inform, and inspire. And, above all . . . instill a new sense of belief and pride in man's ability to shape a world that offers hope to people everywhere."

Ever growing and changing, Epcot occupies 300 vibrantly landscaped acres. If you can spare it, take a little time to stop and smell the roses on your way to and through the two major sections: **Future World** and **World Showcase.**

Epcot is so big that hiking the World Showcase end to end (1⅓ miles from the Canada pavilion on one side to Mexico on the other) can be an exhausting experience. That's why some folks are certain Epcot stands for "Every Person Comes Out Tired." Depending on how long you intend to linger at each country in World Showcase, this part of the park can be experienced in 1 day (though you can easily spend 2). Most visitors simply make a leisurely loop, working clockwise or counterclockwise from one side of the Showcase to the other.

Unlike Magic Kingdom, much of Epcot's parking lot is close to the gate. Parking sections are named for themes (Harvest, Energy, and so forth), and the aisles are numbered. While some guests are happy to walk to the gate from nearer areas, trams are available, but these days mainly to and from the outer areas. If you're a guest of the Epcot-area resorts including the BoardWalk, the Swan and Dolphin, or the Beach and Yacht Club resorts, you'll have an easier time of it. Simply hop aboard the water taxi (one services each resort) and you'll be transported directly to the International Gateway—Epcot's back entrance. If you're feeling really energetic, you can even walk.

Be sure to pick up a guide map and entertainment schedule as you enter the park. The guide uses a white κ in a red square to note "Kidcot" stops. These play and learning stations are for the younger set and allow them to stop at various World Showcase countries, do crafts, get autographs, have their Kidcot passports stamped (these are available for purchase in most Epcot stores and make a great souvenir), and chat with cast members native to those countries. They generally open at 1pm daily.

If you plan to eat lunch or dinner here and haven't already made Advance Reservations (☎ **407/939-3463**), you can make them at the restaurants themselves or at

Guest Relations (near Spaceship Earth)—here you'll find a board that posts which restaurants still have space (including for which meal) and those that don't. Many Epcot restaurants are described in chapter 4, "Where to Eat."

Before you get underway, check the *Times Guide* for show schedules and incorporate any shows you want to see into your itinerary.

HOURS   Future World is usually open from 9am to 7pm, but sometimes closes as late as midnight during major holidays and in summer. World Showcase doesn't open until 11am, and it usually closes at 9pm, but, like Future World, it sometimes has longer hours on holidays and in summer.

TICKET PRICES   Ticket prices are $85 for adults, $79 for children 3 to 9, and free for children younger than 3. See "Tickets," on p. 162, for information on the Magic Your Way ticketing system.

Services & Facilities in Epcot

ATMS   The machines here accept cards issued by banks using the Cirrus, Honor, and PLUS systems and are located at the front of the park, in Italy, and near the bridge between World Showcase and Future World.

BABY CARE   Epcot's Baby Care Center is by the First Aid station near the Odyssey Center in Future World. It's furnished with a nursing room with rocking chairs; disposable diapers, formula, baby food, and pacifiers are for sale. There are also changing tables in all women's restrooms as well as in some of the men's restrooms. Disposable diapers are also available at Guest Relations.

CAMERAS & FILM   Kodak disposable cameras are available throughout the park, including at the Kodak Camera Center at the Entrance Plaza; digital supplies are limited. Services, varying from location to location, include CD burning, film processing, and minor repairs.

FIRST AID   The First Aid station, staffed by registered nurses, is located near the Odyssey Center in Future World.

LOCKERS   Attended lockers are to the west of Spaceship Earth as you enter the park; unattended lockers are located at the International Gateway. The cost is $7 to $9 a day, plus a $5 deposit.

LOST CHILDREN   Lost children in Epcot are usually taken to Earth Center or the Baby Care Center, where lost-children logbooks are kept. *Children younger than 7 should wear name-tags inside their clothing.*

PACKAGE PICKUP   Any package you purchase can be sent by the shop clerk to Guest Relations at the Entrance Plaza. Allow at least 3 hours for delivery. There's another package pickup location at the International Gateway entrance in the World Showcase. If you're staying overnight at a Disney resort, you can also have all packages purchased by 7pm sent to your hotel room (they will be delivered by noon the next day).

PARKING   It's $14 for cars, light trucks, and vans, and $15 for RVs.

PET CARE   Accommodations are offered at Disney's new luxury pet facility, the Best Friends Pet Care Center (© **877/493-9738**), for $10 to $76 per day, depending on whether your pet is staying overnight, the type of pet you have, the accommodations and extras you choose, and whether you are a Disney resort guest. Proof of

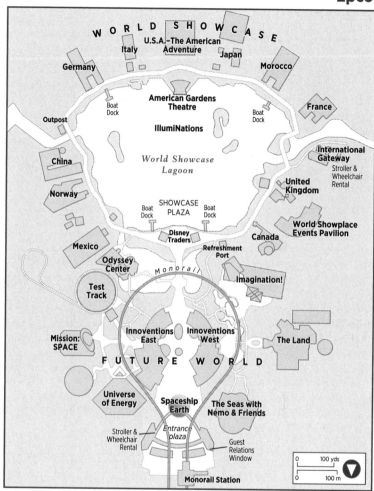

vaccination is required. For more information, see "Fast Facts: Orlando," beginning on p. 367.

STROLLERS These can be rented from special stands on the east side of the Entrance Plaza and at World Showcase's International Gateway. The cost is $15 for a single and $31 for a double. Length-of-stay rentals are available at $13 per day for a single and $27 per day for a double. Full payment is required upfront for length-of-stay rentals.

WHEELCHAIR RENTAL Rent wheelchairs inside the Entrance Plaza to your left, to the right of the ticket booths at the Gift Shop, and at World Showcase's International Gateway. The cost for regular chairs is $12. Electric wheelchairs cost $50 a day, plus a $20 refundable deposit.

TOP 10 ORLANDO-AREA ACTIVITIES
FOR grown-ups

1. **Spa Treatments:** First-rate spas such as those at Disney's Grand Floridian Resort & Spa, the Saratoga Springs Resort & Spa, the WDW Dolphin, the Buena Vista Palace Resort, the Peabody, the Portofino Bay Hotel, the Renaissance Orlando Resort at SeaWorld, the Lake Buena Vista Village Resort & Spa, and the Gaylord Palms provide heavenly pampering and relief for the sore muscles and tired feet caused by the parks (see chapters 1 and 3).

2. **World Showcase Pavilions:** Experience a 'round-the-world journey, visiting 11 "nations" with authentically reproduced architectural highlights, restaurants (many of which have recently been updated), shops, and cultural performances (see later in this chapter).

3. **Cirque du Soleil:** This no-animals circus (p. 324) is compelling for most anyone older than the age of 6, but its intensity and choreography make it a real winner for adults.

4. **The City's Nightlife:** Pleasure Island (soon to be Hyperion Wharf) and CityWalk, entertainment and restaurant districts located respectively at WDW and Universal Orlando (see chapter 8), provide nonstop fun for the wine-dine-and-dance set. Lounges and clubs, often more upscale than those you'll find in the entertainment districts, can be found at select resorts throughout Orlando—a particular standout at Disney is Rix, which opened a few years back in Disney's Coronado Springs Resort.

5. **A Romantic Dinner at Victoria & Albert's:** Loving couples cherish the intimate evening and scrumptious seven-course dinner at the headline restaurant in Disney's Grand Floridian Resort & Spa—especially with the addition of Queen Victoria's Room (p. 126).

6. **Discovery Cove:** SeaWorld's sister park offers guests a chance to rest, relax, and swim with the dolphins in a remote island atmosphere. It's an expensive but ultimately satisfying retreat (see chapter 6).

7. **Richard Petty Driving Experience** and the **Indy Racing Experience:** *Vrr-rooooommmmmm!* If you're 18 or older and have the courage, try driving or at least riding in a real NASCAR rocket at speeds significantly above the legal limit (p. 242).

8. **The *Grand 1:*** Take another break from the Mickey madness and cruise Disney's Seven Seas Lagoon (perhaps catching a glimpse of Wishes fireworks) aboard this vintage 45-foot yacht (p. 53).

9. **Innoventions:** Epcot is generally geared more to adults than the other WDW parks, and this display of future technologies is especially intriguing, providing a preview of life well into the 21st century (p. 201).

10. **Tee Time:** Orlando is home to some of the country's best golf courses—Walt Disney World alone offers 99 holes, including one with a sand trap shaped like Mickey Mouse—so enthusiasts will find plenty of places to tee up (see "Hitting the Links," in chapter 6).

Future World

Future World is in the northern section of Epcot, the first area mainstream guests see after entering the park. Its icon is a huge geosphere known as Spaceship Earth—also known as that giant golf ball. Major corporations sponsor Future World's 10 themed areas (that means they're making pricey investments, such as the $100 million that

Hewlett-Packard dropped on the Mission: Space ride, described a little later in this chapter). The focus here is on discovery, scientific achievements, and tomorrow's technologies in areas running from energy to undersea exploration.

Here are the main attractions:

Imagination
Frommer's Rating: B+
Recommended Ages: 6–adult

In this pavilion, even the fountains are magical. "Water snakes" arc in the air, offering kids a chance to dare them to "bite." This pavilion was upgraded in 2001 to include more high-tech gadgets, and a year later Figment, the pavilion's much-loved mascot, returned (see below).

The **Honey, I Shrunk the Audience** 3-D ride is the big attraction here, deserving of an **"A" rating** by itself. Based on the Disney hit film *Honey, I Shrunk the Kids*, you're terrorized by mice and, once you're shrunk, by a large cat; then you're given a good shaking by a gigantic 5-year-old. Vibrating seats and creepy tactile effects enhance dramatic 3-D action. Finally, everyone returns to proper size—except the family dog, which creates the final surprise. *Note:* At press time, Honey, I Shrunk the Audience had been temporarily replaced by **Captain EO,** a futuristic 3-D flick starring Michael Jackson, first shown some 25 years ago (1986–94). Brought back by popular demand (in the wake of Jackson's untimely death), this musical adventure through space (the special effects tweaked a bit to bring it up-to-date) makes a surprisingly appropriate addition to Epcot's lineup of techy attractions. How long EO will actually run remains unknown—the official line stating that it will run for an indefinite time, but that Honey, I Shrunk the Audience will eventually return.

Figment, the crazy but lovable dragon mascot of the park when it opened, was resurrected in the **Journey into Your Imagination** ride in 2002. Things begin with an open house at the Imagination Institute, with Dr. Nigel Channing taking you on a tour of labs that demonstrate how the five senses capture and control one's imagination, except you never get to touch and taste once Figment arrives to prove it's far, far better to set your imagination free. He invites you to his upside-down house, where a new perspective enhances your imagination. "One Little Spark," an upbeat ditty that debuted when the attraction opened in 1983, has also been brought back.

Once you disembark from the ride, head for the **"What If"** labs, where your kids can burn lots of energy while exercising their imagination at a number of interactive stations that allow them to conduct music and experiment with video.

Innoventions East and West
Frommer's Rating: B+ for hungry minds and game junkies
Recommended Ages: 8–adult

Innoventions East, behind Spaceship Earth and to the left as you enter the park, features the **Sum of All Thrills,** where budding Imagineers can create (and ride) their own simulated coaster, while **Don't Waste It** is filled with edu-taining games about garbage—and how we can reduce what we produce. Across the plaza at **Innoventions West,** crowds flock to **Video Games of Tomorrow,** which has nearly three dozen game stations. **Where's the Fire,** geared to smaller kids, teaches the basics of fire safety and demonstrates how firefighters fight fires with the help of a pump truck. At **Storm Struck,** the focus is on wild weather, as hurricanes, tornados, and other storms are explored in a 3-D theater. Strangely enough, the next exhibit planned for the area revolves around financial planning—talk about timing!

Club Cool offers complimentary Coke products to everyone who enters. Just don't expect to completely quench your thirst—drinks are served up in sample sizes here. And don't expect to find the same flavors you would in your local grocery, either—the products served here come from all over the world, and flavors are often unique. If, however, you're truly in need of a drink, full-size servings (in familiar flavors only) are available for purchase—the oversized "build your own" character cups make a great souvenir (and this is the only spot in Mickeyville that I've come across them). In addition, you'll find an assortment of Coca-Cola merchandise. The club is located just outside Innoventions West, on your left as you exit the walkway heading to the plaza outside Mission: Space and Test Track.

Note: The Underwriters Laboratories exhibit at Innoventions East, the **Test the Limits Lab,** has six kiosks that let kids and fun-loving adults try out a variety of products. In one, you can pull a rope attached to a hammer that crashes into a TV screen to see if it's shatter resistant. In another, you can push a button that releases a magnet that falls onto a firefighter's helmet.

The Land

Frommer's Rating: B+ for environmentalists, gardeners; C+ for others

Recommended Ages: 8–adult

The largest of Future World's pavilions highlights food and nature. **Living with the Land** is a 13-minute boat ride through three ecological environments (a rainforest, an African desert, and the windswept American plains), each populated by appropriate audio-animatronic denizens. New farming methods and experiments ranging from hydroponics to plants growing in simulated Martian soil are showcased in real gardens. If you'd like a more serious overview, take the 45-minute **Behind the Seeds** guided walking tour of the growing areas, offered daily. Sign up at the Green Thumb Emporium shop on the ground floor near the Sunshine Season Food Festival. The cost is $16 for adults, $12 for children 3 to 9. *Note:* It's really geared to children.

Circle of Life combines spectacular live-action footage with animation in a 15-minute motion picture based on *The Lion King.* In this cautionary environmental tale, Timon and Pumba are building a monument to the good life called Hakuna Matata Lakeside Village, but their project, as Simba points out, is damaging the savanna for other animals. The message: Everything is connected in the great circle of life.

Soarin' is a copy of a popular attraction at Disney's California Adventure theme park. Guests are seated in giant hang gliders and surrounded by a tremendous projection-screen dome. After being lifted up more than 40 feet into the air, you'll fly through the sky over the landscapes of California. This amazing adventure is enhanced by sensory effects as guests are treated to the sights, sounds, and even smells (think orange blossoms and pine trees) of a dozen locations in California, including the Golden Gate Bridge, the redwood forests, Napa Valley, Yosemite, and more. You really will feel almost as if you're flying through the sky. The ride carries a 40-inch height minimum. For the best experience, try to get seated in the first row; if you're not sanguine about heights, the third row works best.

Mission: Space

Frommer's Rating: A+

Recommended Ages: 10–adult

This $100-million attraction, developed in partnership with Hewlett-Packard and NASA, seats up to four riders at a time in a simulated flight to the Red Planet. You'll assume the role of commander, pilot, navigator, or engineer, depending on where you sit, and must complete related jobs vital to the mission (don't worry if you miss your cue; you won't crash). The ride uses a combination of visuals, sound, and centrifugal force to create the illusion of a launch and trip to Mars. Even veteran roller-coaster riders who tried the simulator said the sensation mimics a liftoff, as riders are pressed into their seats and the roar and vibration trick the brain during the launch portion of the 4-minute adventure. As one of only two real thrillers in the park, this one often has incredibly long lines, so get here early or FASTPASS it. A second, less intense version of the ride is available, the spinning sensation removed all together. The original, or orange, version is definitely not for the faint at heart—the green, however, is far less intense and allows astronauts-in-training (those not ready for G-forces and spinning simulators) the chance to experience space travel. If the lines are unbearably long for the green ride, head back later or pick up a FASTPASS—some may not find it worth the excruciating wait. **Note:** Riders must be at least 44 inches tall. If you're claustrophobic, have a low tolerance for loud noises, or have stuffy sinuses, you should avoid the ride entirely. If spinning causes you to get dizzy or motion sick, simply avoid the orange version and head directly for the line marked in green. Speaking from experience, taller guests may have difficulties seeing the screen the way it was meant to be viewed; shorter guests may have trouble reaching some of the gear.

The Seas with Nemo & Friends

Frommer's Rating: B+

Recommended Ages: 3–adult

This recently transformed pavilion is still home to a signature aquarium filled with 5.7 million gallons of saltwater and coral reefs inhabited by some 4,000 sharks, barracudas, parrotfish, rays, dolphins, and other critters. Now, however, instead of exhibits tracing the history of undersea exploration and a 7-minute edu-flick, you'll pass through a serene undersea setting before climbing aboard a "clamobile" to ride **The Seas with Nemo & Friends.** Guests join in on an undersea field trip led by Mr. Ray, who eventually discovers that Nemo's gone missing and it's up to everyone

 Where's Mickey?

Although I've mentioned on more than one occasion that Epcot is the least tot-friendly of the Disney parks, I have to admit, Disney's made a concerted effort to change (or at least better) its image. Rides and attractions have been revamped (becoming far more kid-friendly), Kidcot stations can now be found at almost every World Showcase pavilion (there are even a few in Future World), characters walk the park on a daily basis—there's even an indoor meet-and-greet spot (aptly named the Character Connection) located next to the Fountainview Café—and an interactive superspy secret-agent-style adventure (Disney's Kim Possible World Showcase Adventure) has been added. For the preschool set, kid-friendly maps (that include all the Disney parks—even the water parks) are available at guest relations.

BEHIND THE SCENES: special tours
IN WALT DISNEY WORLD

In addition to the greenhouse tour in Epcot's Land pavilion (see below), the Disney parks offer a number of walking tours and learning programs (keep in mind that not all are listed below). The tours are subject to change, but those listed here represent a sampling of the most recent ones available at press time. Times, days, and prices also change. It's best to call ahead to Disney's tour line (✆ **407/939-8687**) to make reservations or get additional information. *Tip:* **Custom Guided Tours** (✆ **407/560-4033**) are available at $175 per hour with a 6-hour minimum.

o Epcot's **Seas Aqua Tour** lends you a wet suit and then takes you on a 2½-hour journey that includes a 30-minute swim in the 5.7-million gallon Seas with Nemo & Friends Aquarium, home to some 65 marine species. The tour includes a souvenir T-shirt, refreshments, and group photo. The cost is $140, park admission is not required, and it's open to guests 8 and older (those 12 and younger must be accompanied by a participating adult). It's offered daily at 12:30pm.

o The **Family Magic Tour** explores the nooks and crannies of the Magic Kingdom in the form of a 2-hour scavenger hunt. You meet and greet characters at the end. It costs $34 per adult or child 3 and older. You must also buy admission tickets to the park and book in advance. If you have young kids and want to do a special tour, this is the one to take. It begins daily at 10am outside City Hall.

o The 3-hour **Magic Behind Our Steam Trains Tour** (ages 10 and up) is a fun one for locomotive buffs. A pair of veteran conductors gives you insight, which other guests don't get, into the history and present operations of the little engines that could. It's offered Monday, Tuesday, Thursday, and Saturday at 7:30am; the cost is $49 per person, plus park admission.

The following tours are for those 16 and older:

o The 4½- to 5-hour **Keys to the Kingdom Tour** provides an orientation to the Magic Kingdom and a glimpse into the high-tech systems behind the magic.

to find him. This family-friendly ride slowly moves riders past several stunning undersea scenes in search of everyone's favorite clownfish. Thanks to new animation technology, Marlin, Dory, Mr. Ray, Bruce, and other familiar finned friends seemingly swim right along with the live inhabitants of the aquarium.

You can journey through rooms and more rooms for close-up views of the denizens of the deep, including manatees and other marine life. Be sure to check out the adorable **Turtle Talk with Crush.** Crush from *Finding Nemo* chitchats with the audience from behind his undersea movie screen, engaging them in conversation and telling a joke or two. This is a first-of-its-kind attraction using digital projection and voice-activated animation to create a real-time experience. Your kids will get a huge kick out of it; you will, too.

Bruce's Shark World, a small interactive play area, is the perfect spot to let little ones run around, climb, and work off excess energy—not to mention snap a photo or two.

It's $70 (mandatory park admission not included) and includes lunch at Colombia Harbor House. Tours are held daily at 8:30, 9, and 9:30am.

o At the top of the price chain ($224 per person) is **Backstage Magic,** a 7-hour, self-propelled bus tour through areas of Epcot, the Magic Kingdom, and Disney's Hollywood Studios that aren't seen by mainstream guests. The 10am tour (Mon–Fri only) is limited to 20 adults, and you might have trouble getting a date unless you book early. Some will find this one isn't worth the price, but if you have a brain that must know how things work or simply want to know more than your family or friends, you might find it's worth the cost. You'll see WDW mechanics and engineers repairing and building animatronic beings from it's a small world and other attractions. You'll peek over the shoulders of cast members who watch closed-circuit TVs to make sure visitors are surviving the harrowing rides. And at the Magic Kingdom, you'll venture into the tunnels used for work areas as well as corridors for the cast to get from one area to the others without fighting tourist crowds. It's not unusual for tour takers to see Snow White enjoying a Snickers bar, find Cinderella having her locks touched up at an underground salon, or view woodworkers as they restore the hard maple muscles of the carousel horses. Park admission *isn't* required. Lunch is included.

o **Backstage Safari** at Animal Kingdom ($72 per person, plus park admission) offers a 3-hour look at the park's veterinary hospital as well as lessons in conservation, animal nutrition, and medicine (Mon and Wed–Fri). ***Note:*** You won't see many animals.

o **Yuletide Fantasy,** available from November 30 to December 24 (Mon–Sat) each year, gives visitors a 3½-hour front-row look at how Disney creates a winter wonderland to get visitors in the holiday spirit. It costs $84 per person, and theme-park admission *isn't* required.

Note: The **Epcot DiveQuest** enables certified divers (ages 10–16 must have a scuba-certified adult accompany them, ages 10–17 must have a signed parental waiver) to participate in a 3-hour program that includes a 40-minute dive in the Living Seas aquarium. The program costs $175 and is offered Tuesday through Saturday. Call ✆ **407/939-8687** for more information. Keep in mind, however, that you get far more for your money at Discovery Cove (p. 288) if you want to swim with dolphins.

Spaceship Earth ✋
Frommer's Rating: C
Recommended Ages: All ages

This massive, silvery geosphere symbolizes Epcot and is probably the most recognizable Disney icon next to Cinderella Castle (and those mouse ears, of course). That

Many an ordinary item at Disney World has hidden entertainment value. Take a drink at the water fountain in Innoventions Plaza (the one right next to MouseGear) and it may beg you not to drink it dry. No, you haven't gotten too much sun—the fountain actually talks (much to the delight of kids and the surprise of unsuspecting adults). A few more talking fountains are scattered around Epcot. And the fountains aren't the only items at WDW that talk. I've kibitzed with a walking and talking garbage can (named PUSH) in Magic Kingdom, and a personable palm tree (who goes by Wes Palm) at Animal Kingdom. Ask a Disney employee to direct you if you want to meet one of these chatty contraptions.

makes it a must-do for many, though it's something of a yawner for others. The 15-minute show/ride takes visitors to the distant past, where an audio-animatronic Cro-Magnon shaman recounts the story of a hunt while others record it on cave walls. You advance thousands of years to ancient Egypt, where hieroglyphics adorn temple walls and writing is recorded on papyrus scrolls. You'll progress through the Phoenician and Greek alphabets, the Gutenberg printing press, and the Renaissance. Technologies develop at a rapid pace, through the telegraph, telephone, radio, movies, and TV. Then it's on to the age of electronic communications before catapulting into outer space. While the premise remains the same, recent (and long overdue) updates have brought this adventure through time more in line with the park's other edu-taining offerings. New scenes have been added, existing scenes enhanced, and the special effects spiffed up, the result of which is a greatly improved experience. Judi Dench now narrates as you move slowly along the track (which at times is rather steep), tracing the progress of communications. Touch screens add an interactive element (and do a good job keeping you distracted as you move backwards down through the giant sphere at the end of the ride). **"Project Tomorrow: Inventing the World of Tomorrow"** is a hands-on postshow exhibit filled with futuristic games focusing on such themes as medicine, transportation, and energy management.

Test Track

Frommer's Rating: A+

Recommended Ages: 8–adult

Test Track is a $60-million (the figure once raised eyebrows, but is now considered mere peanuts next to HP's $100 million for Mission: Space) marvel that combines GM engineering and Disney Imagineering. Most of you will have a blast. The line can be more than an hour long in peak periods, so consider the FASTPASS option (but remember to get one early before they run out). The last part of the line snakes through displays about corrosion, crash tests, and other things from the GM proving grounds (you can linger long enough to see them even with FASTPASS). The 5-minute ride follows what looks to be an actual highway. It includes braking tests, a hill climb, and tight S-curves in a six-passenger convertible. The left front seat offers the most thrills as the vehicle moves through the curves. There's also a 12-second burst of speed that reaches 65 mph on the straightaway (no traffic!). **Note:** Signs of GM's economic woes are visibly apparent as several brands (including the Hummer, Saturn, Saab, and Pontiac) are not only missing from GM's lineup, but also missing from the Test Track showroom—replaced with core brands such as GMC, Chevy, Buick, and Cadillac.

Note II: Riders must be at least 40 inches tall. Also, expectant mothers and people prone to motion sickness or those with heart, neck, or back problems shouldn't test the track.

Note III: This is the only attraction in Epcot that has a single-rider line, which allows singles to fill in vacant spots in select cars. If you're part of a group that doesn't mind splitting up and riding in singles, you can shave off some serious waiting time by taking advantage of this option. FASTPASS offers the same time savings without the break-up, but Test Track is in such demand that the last FASTPASS for the *day* is often gone by 11am, so if you don't catch it early enough, the single-rider line is the only option you'll have.

Note IV: Test Track often experiences technical difficulties and, to add insult to injury, it's one of the few rides in Epcot that closes due to inclement weather. If you know a storm's brewing in the afternoon, be sure to head here early in the day.

Universe of Energy
Frommer's Rating: B+
Recommended Ages: 6–adult

Sponsored by Exxon, this pavilion has a roof full of solar panels and a goal of bettering your understanding of America's energy problems and potential solutions. Its 32-minute ride, **Ellen's Energy Adventure,** features comedian Ellen DeGeneres being tutored (by Bill Nye the Science Guy) to be a *Jeopardy!* contestant. On a massive screen in Theater I, an animated motion picture depicts the earth's molten beginnings, its cooling process, and the formation of fossil fuels. You move back in time 275 million years into an eerie, storm-wracked landscape of the Mesozoic Era, a time of violent geological activity. Here, giant audio-animatronic dragonflies, earthquakes, and streams of molten lava threaten you before you enter a steam-filled tunnel deep in the bowels of a volcano. When you emerge, you're in Theater II and the present. In this new setting, which looks like a NASA Mission Control room, a 70mm film projected on a massive 210-foot wraparound screen depicts the challenges of the world's increasing energy demands and the emerging technologies that will help meet them. Your moving seats now return to Theater I, where swirling special effects herald a film about how energy impacts our lives. It ends on an upbeat note, with a vision of an energy-abundant future, and Ellen as a new *Jeopardy!* champion. **Note:** I've taken kids as young as 2 on this ride with no problems, but recommend that children be at least 6 or they won't get much out of the experience beyond flashing lights and sounds.

SHOPPING IN FUTURE WORLD

Most of Epcot's more unique shopping lies just ahead in World Showcase, but there are a few places in this part of the park that offer special souvenirs. You can browse through cels and other collectibles at the **Art of Disney** in Innoventions West (how about an $8,800, 5-ft. wooden Mickey watch?), purchase almost anything imaginable at **MouseGear** in Innoventions East (one of the best and most comprehensive shops in all of WDW), and find gardening and other gifts in the **Land.**

World Showcase

You can tour the world in a day at this community of 11 miniaturized nations, which line the 40-acre World Showcase Lagoon on the park's southern side. All of the

In early October, Epcot's 6-week-long **International Food & Wine Festival** adds 25 booths to the park's 1⅓-mile World Showcase promenade. Here's your chance to walk off some calories while you sip and savor the cuisine and beverages of several of the world's cultures. On the food front, the appetizer-size temptations might include burgundy escargot, seared alligator medallions, green mussels, shrimp on the barbie, octopus on purple potato salad, chicken *sa cha,* and much more ($3–$8). You can also sample wine and beer from more than 100 wineries and breweries. Tickets for the dinner-and-concert series, select wine tastings, and specialty dining experiences (some offered at Disney's signature resort restaurants) run from $45 to $450 including tip, but you can cruise the festival for standard park admission ($82 adults, $74 kids 3–9). Call ℂ 407/ 939-3378 for details, or go to www. disneyworld.com.

showcase's countries have authentic architecture, landscaping, background music, restaurants, and shops. The nations' cultural facets are explored in art exhibits, song and dance performances, and innovative rides, films, and attractions. And all of the employees in each pavilion are natives of the country represented.

All pavilions offer some kind of live entertainment throughout the day. Times and performances change, but they're listed in the guide map and the *Times Guide.* World Showcase opens between 11am and noon daily, so there's time for a Future World excursion if you arrive earlier. *Note:* There are **regular appearances by characters** at Showcase Plaza (consult the daily schedule for times).

Canada
Frommer's Rating: A
Recommended Ages: 8–adult

Our neighbors to the north are represented by architecture ranging from a mansard-roofed replica of Ottawa's 19th-century French-style Château Laurier (here called Hôtel du Canada) to a British-influenced stone building modeled after a famous landmark near Niagara Falls. An Indian village, complete with a rough-hewn log trading post and 30-foot replicas of Ojibwa totem poles, signifies the culture of the Northwest. The Canadian wilderness is reflected by a rocky mountain; a waterfall cascading into a white-water stream; and a miniforest of evergreens, stately cedars, maples, and birch trees. Don't miss the stunning floral displays of azaleas, roses, zinnias, chrysanthemums, petunias, and patches of wildflowers inspired by the Butchart Gardens just outside of Victoria, British Columbia.

The pavilion's highlight attraction is **O Canada!**—a dazzling (and recently updated) 18-minute, 360-degree CircleVision film that shows Canada's scenic splendor, from a dogsled race to the thundering flight of thousands of snow geese departing an autumn stopover near the St. Lawrence River to its modern cities and diverse people. If you're looking for foot-tapping live entertainment, **Off Kilter** raises the roof with New Age Celtic music as well as some get-down country music. Days and times vary.

Northwest Mercantile carries sandstone and soapstone carvings, fringed leather vests, duck decoys, moccasins, an array of stuffed animals, Native American dolls, Native American spirit stones, rabbit-skin caps, heavy knitted sweaters, and, of course, maple syrup.

China
Frommer's Rating: A
Recommended Ages: 10–adult

Bounded by a serpentine wall that snakes around its perimeter, the China Pavilion is entered via a triple-arched ceremonial gate inspired by the Temple of Heaven in Beijing, a summer retreat for Chinese emperors. Passing through the gate, you'll see a half-size replica of this ornately embellished red-and-gold circular temple, built in 1420 during the Ming dynasty. Chinese tomb sculptures, similar to those recently unearthed near Xian, were recently added. Gardens simulate those in Suzhou, with miniature waterfalls, fragrant lotus ponds, and groves of bamboo, corkscrew willows, and weeping mulberry trees.

Reflections of China ★★ is a 20-minute movie that explores the culture and landscapes in and around seven Chinese cities. Shot during a 2-month period in 2002, it visits Hong Kong, Beijing, Shanghai, and the Great Wall (begun 24 c. ago!), among other places. **Land of Many Faces** is an exhibit that introduces China's ethnic peoples, and entertainment is provided daily (the amazing Dragon Legend Acrobats recently ended their run, with a replacement yet to be named).

The **Yong Feng Shangdian Shopping Gallery** features silk robes, lacquer and inlaid mother-of-pearl furniture, jade figures, cloisonné vases, Yixing teapots, brocade pajamas, silk rugs and embroideries, wind chimes, and Chinese clothing. Artisans occasionally demonstrate Chinese calligraphy.

France
Frommer's Rating: B
Recommended Ages: 8–adult

This pavilion focuses on La Belle Epoque, a period from 1870 to 1910 in which French art, literature, and architecture flourished. It's entered via a replica of the beautiful cast-iron Pont des Arts footbridge over the Seine. It leads to a park with bleached sycamores, Bradford pear trees, flowering crape myrtle, and sculptured parterre flower gardens inspired by Seurat's painting *A Sunday Afternoon on the Island of La Grande Jatte.* A one-tenth-scale replica of the Eiffel Tower constructed from Gustave Eiffel's original blueprints looms above *les grands boulevards.*

The highlight is **Impressions de France.** Shown in a palatial sit-down theater a la Fontainebleau, this 18-minute film is a scenic journey through diverse French landscapes projected on a vast 200-degree wraparound screen and enhanced by the music of French composers. The antics of **Serveur Amusant,** a comedic waiter, delight children and adults, as do the yummy pastries at **Boulangerie Patisserie.**

The covered arcade has shops selling French prints and original art, cookbooks, wines (there's a tasting counter), French food, Babar books, perfumes, and original letters of famous Frenchmen ranging from Jean Cocteau to Napoleon. Another marketplace/tourism center revives the defunct Les Halles, where Parisians used to sip onion soup in the wee hours.

Germany
Frommer's Rating: B
Recommended Ages: 8–adult

Enclosed by castle walls and towers, this festive pavilion is centered on a cobblestone *platz* (square) with pots of colorful flowers girding a fountain statue of St. George and the Dragon. An adjacent clock tower is embellished with whimsical glockenspiel figures that herald each hour with quaint melodies. The pavilion's **Biergarten** (p. 108) was inspired by medieval Rothenberg and features a year-round Oktoberfest

Sure, *you* want to be educated about the cultures of the world, but for most, the two big attractions at the World Showcase are eating and shopping. Dining options are explained in chapter 4. This list gives you an idea of additional items available for purchase.

If you'd like to check out the amazing scope of Disney merchandise at home, everything from furniture to bath toys, you can order a catalog by calling ℂ **800/237-5751** or surfing the Web at **www.disneystore.com**. (Just be aware that the selection is different from what you'll find at the parks.)

○ The silver jewelry in **Mexico** is beautiful. Choose from a range of merchandise that goes from a simple flowered hair clip to a kidney-shaped stone-and-silver bracelet. Soccer fans will find plenty to choose from, as the outdoor outpost is filled top to bottom with Mexico's national team merchandise.

○ There are lots of great sweaters available in the shops of **Norway,** and it's really tough to resist the Scandinavian trolls. They're so ugly, you have to love them.

○ Forget about all those knockoff products stamped "Made in China." The merchandise in **China** is among the more expensive to be found in Epcot, from jade teardrop earrings to multicolored bracelets to Disney art.

○ Porcelain and cuckoo clocks are the things to look at in **Germany.** You might find a Goebel collectible Winnie the Pooh or a handcrafted Pooh cuckoo clock. Of course, Hummel figurines and stuffed Steiffs are big sellers, too.

○ In **Italy,** look for 100% silk scarves in a variety of patterns, as well as fine silk ties and crystal.

○ Your funky teenager might like the Taquia knit cap, a colorful fezlike chapeau, that's available in **Morocco.** There's also a variety of celestial-patterned pottery available in vases and platters.

○ Tennis fans may be interested in the Wimbledon shirts, shorts, and skirts available in the **United Kingdom.** There's also a nice assortment of rose-patterned tea accessories, Shetland sweaters, tartans, pub accessories, and loads of other stuff from the U.K.

and its music. And 16th-century facades replicate a merchant's hall in the Black Forest and the town hall in Römerberg Square.

The shops here carry Hummel figurines, crystal, glassware, cookware, Anton Schneider cuckoos, cowbells, Alpine hats, German wines (there's a tasting counter), specialty foods, toys (German Disneyana, teddy bears, dolls, and puppets), and books. An artisan demonstrates the molding and painting of Hummel figures; another paints detailed scenes on eggs. Background music runs from oompah bands to Mozart symphonies.

Model-train enthusiasts and kids enjoy the exquisitely detailed miniature version of a small Bavarian town, complete with working train station.

Italy

Frommer's Rating: B

Recommended Ages: 10–adult

One of the prettiest World Showcase pavilions, Italy lures visitors over an arched stone footbridge to a replica of Venice's intricately ornamented pink-and-white Doge's

Palace. Other architectural highlights include the 83-foot Campanile (bell tower) of St. Mark's Square, Venetian bridges, and a piazza enclosing a version of Bernini's Neptune Fountain. A garden wall suggests a backdrop of provincial countryside, and citrus, cypress, pine, and olive trees frame a formal garden. Gondolas are moored on the lagoon.

Shops carry cameo and filigree jewelry, Armani figurines, kitchenware, Italian wines and foods, Murano and other Venetian glass, alabaster figurines, and inlaid wooden music boxes.

In the street-entertainment department, the **World Showcase Players,** a talented group of actors, can often be seen performing skits in the pavilion's courtyard.

Japan
Frommer's Rating: A
Recommended Ages: 8–adult

A flaming red *torii* (gate of honor) on the banks of the lagoon and the graceful blue-roofed Goju No To pagoda, inspired by a shrine built at Nara in A.D. 700, welcome you to this pavilion, which focuses on Japan's ancient culture. In a traditional Japanese garden, cedars, yews, bamboo, "cloud-pruned" evergreens, willows, and flowering shrubs frame a contemplative setting of pebbled footpaths, rustic bridges, waterfalls, exquisite rock landscaping, and a pond of golden koi. It's a haven of tranquillity in a park that's anything but. The **Yakitori House** is based on the renowned 16th-century Katsura Imperial Villa in Kyoto, designed as a royal summer residence and considered by many to be the crowning achievement of Japanese architecture. The moated **White Heron Castle** is a replica of the Shirasagi-Jo, a 17th-century fortress overlooking the city of Himeji. The **Bijutsu-kan Gallery** displays changing exhibits on various aspects of Japanese culture (for example, a past exhibit focused on Japanese tin toys).

The **Mitsukoshi Department Store** (Japan's answer to Macy's) is housed in a replica of the Shishinden (Hall of Ceremonies) of the Gosho Imperial Palace, built in Kyoto in A.D. 794. It sells lacquerware, kimonos, kites, fans, dolls in traditional costumes, origami books, samurai swords, Japanese Disneyana, bonsai trees, Japanese foods, netsuke carvings, pottery, and modern electronics.

The drums of **Matsuriza**—one of the best performances in the World Showcase—entertain guests daily.

Mexico
Frommer's Rating: A
Recommended Ages: 8–adult

You'll hear the music of marimbas and mariachi bands as you approach the festive showcase of Mexico, fronted by a towering Mayan pyramid modeled on the Aztec temple of Quetzalcoatl (God of Life) and surrounded by dense Yucatán jungle landscaping. Upon entering the pavilion, you'll be in a museum of pre-Columbian art and artifacts.

Down a ramp, a small lagoon is the setting for the **Gran Fiesta Tour Starring the Three Caballeros,** where visitors board boats for an 8-minute cruise through Mexico. A new animated overlay (along with refurbished backdrops and sound) features José and Panchito as they search the Mexican countryside for Donald Duck before finally reuniting in Mexico City. Passengers get a close-up look at the Mayan pyramid. **Mariachi Cobre,** a 12-piece band, plays Tuesday through Saturday.

Shops in and around the **Plaza de Los Amigos**—a "moonlit" Mexican *mercado* (market) with a tiered fountain and street lamps—display an array of leather goods,

Disney recently added an interactive experience to Epcot aimed at entertaining the kid set. Inspired by the Disney Channel's popular animated series, Disney's Kim Possible World Showcase Adventure allows guests the chance to become supersleuth secret agents—albeit temporarily. Using a handheld device aptly named a Kimunicator (obtained by swiping your park ticket at one of the five designated Kim Possible locations marked on your Epcot guide map), guests team up with Kim Possible characters to save the world (in this case, the World Showcase) in a high-tech 'round-the-world spy-venture. Mexico, China, Norway, Germany, Japan, France, and the U.K. pavilions each feature a different mission that takes approximately 30 minutes to complete. Instructions and clues are texted to guests via the Kimunicator—simply follow them in order to complete your mission.

baskets, sombreros, piñatas, pottery, embroidered dresses and blouses, maracas, jewelry, serapes, colorful papier-mâché birds, and blown-glass objects (an artisan occasionally gives demonstrations). The Mexican Tourist Office also provides travel information.

Morocco
Frommer's Rating: A
Recommended Ages: 10–adult

This exotic pavilion has architecture embellished with geometrically patterned tile work, minarets, hand-painted wood ceilings, and brass lighting fixtures (the king of Morocco sent his own royal artisans to work on the pavilion). It's headlined by a replica of the Koutoubia Minaret, the prayer tower of a 12th-century mosque in Marrakesh. Note the imperfections in each mosaic tile; they were put there on purpose in accordance with the Muslim belief that only Allah is perfect.

The Medina (old city), entered via a replica of an arched gateway in Fez, leads to **Fez House** (a traditional Moroccan home) and the narrow, winding streets of the **souk,** a bustling marketplace where all manner of authentic handcrafted merchandise is on display. Here you can browse or purchase pottery, brassware, hand-knotted Berber or colorful Rabat carpets, ornate silver and camel-bone boxes, straw baskets, and prayer rugs. There are weaving demonstrations in the souk periodically during the day. The Medina's rectangular courtyard centers on a replica of the ornately tiled Najjarine Fountain in Fez, the setting for musical entertainment.

Treasures of Morocco is a three-times-per-day 45-minute guided tour (1–5pm) that highlights this country's culture, architecture, and history. The pavilion's **Gallery of Arts and History** contains an ever-changing exhibit of Moroccan art, and the Center of Tourism offers a continuous three-screen slide show. Morocco's landscaping includes a formal garden, citrus and olive trees, date palms, and banana plants. On the entertainment side, **Mo'Rockin'** plays Arabian rock music on traditional instruments daily.

Norway
Frommer's Rating: B+
Recommended Ages: 10–adult

This pavilion is centered on a picturesque cobblestone courtyard. A *stavekirke* (stave church), styled after the 13th-century Gol Church of Hallingdal, has changing exhibits. A replica of Oslo's 14th-century **Akershus Castle,** next to a cascading woodland waterfall, is the setting for the featured restaurant (p. 154). Other buildings simulate the red-roofed cottages of Bergen and the timber-sided farm buildings of the Nordic woodlands.

There's a two-part attraction here. **Maelstrom,** a boat ride in a dragon-headed Viking vessel, traverses Norway's fjords and mythical forests to the music of *Peer Gynt.* (It's the only attraction in World Showcase that offers FASTPASS.) Along the way, you'll see images of polar bears prowling the shore, and then trolls cast a spell on the boat. The watercraft crashes through a narrow gorge and spins into the North Sea, where a storm is in progress. (This is a relatively calm ride, though it's not recommended for expectant mothers or folks with heart, neck, or back problems.) The storm abates, and passengers disembark safely to a 10th-century Viking village to view the 5-minute 70mm film **Norway,** which documents 1,000 years of history. **Spelmanns Gledje** entertains with Norwegian folk music.

Shops sell hand-knit wool hats and authentic (and expensive) Scandinavian sweaters, troll dolls, toys (there's a LEGO table where kids can play), woodcarvings, Scandinavian foods, pewterware, and jewelry.

United Kingdom
Frommer's Rating: B
Recommended Ages: 8–adult

The U.K. pavilion takes you to Merry Olde England through **Britannia Square,** a formal London-style park complete with a copper-roofed gazebo bandstand, a typical red phone booth, and a statue of the Bard. Four centuries of architecture are represented along quaint cobblestone streets; there's a traditional British pub and a formal garden with low box hedges in geometric patterns, flagstone paths, and a stone fountain that replicates the landscaping of 16th- and 17th-century palaces.

The **British Invasion,** a popular rock group that impersonated the Beatles, ended their run at Epcot in early 2011 (after 15 years); at press time, their replacement had yet to be named. High Street and Tudor Lane shops display a broad sampling of British merchandise, including toy soldiers, Paddington bears, personalized coats of arms, Scottish clothing (cashmere and Shetland sweaters, golf wear, tams, and tartans), English china, Waterford crystal, and pub items such as tankards, dartboards, and the like. A tea shop occupies a replica of Anne Hathaway's thatched-roof 16th-century cottage in Stratford-on-Avon. Other emporia represent the Georgian, Victorian, Queen Anne, and Tudor periods. Background music ranges from "Greensleeves" to the Beatles.

U.S.A.—The American Adventure
Frommer's Rating: A
Recommended Ages: 8–adult

Housed in a vast Georgian-style structure, the **American Adventure** is a 29-minute dramatization of U.S. history, utilizing a 72-foot rear-projection screen, rousing music, and a large cast of lifelike audio-animatronic figures, including narrators Mark Twain and Ben Franklin. The adventure begins with the voyage of the *Mayflower* and encompasses major historic events. You'll view Jefferson writing the Declaration of Independence, Matthew Brady photographing a family about to be divided by the Civil War, the stock market crash of 1929 (but not the crash of Disney stock in 1999 and 2000), Pearl Harbor, and the *Eagle* heading toward the moon. Teddy Roosevelt discusses the need for national parks. Susan B. Anthony speaks out on women's rights; Frederick Douglass, on slavery; and Chief Joseph, on the plight of Native

Watching Epcot's IllumiNations fireworks display (see below) from the World Showcase Lagoon can make for a magical evening. You can charter a pontoon for a lagoon cruise lasting 45 to 50 minutes; you must rent the entire boat for your group or else find your own boat mates ($325 for up to 10 people, soda and bagged snacks included). For information or to make reservations, call ☎ **407/939-7529.** You can make arrangements for additional food and beverages to be served on your cruise, though only through Disney, by calling ☎ **407/934-3160.** *Note:* At press time, the vintage speedboat *Breathless II* was listed as unavailable until further notice due to maintenance difficulties, with no official word regarding its future status.

Americans. It's one of Disney's best historical productions. Formal gardens shaded by live oaks, sycamores, elms, and holly complement the 18th-century architecture.

Entertainment includes the **Spirit of America Fife & Drum Corps** and the **Voices of Liberty,** an a cappella group that sings patriotic songs.

Heritage Manor Gifts sells autographed presidential photographs, needlepoint samplers, quilts, pottery, candles, Davy Crockett hats, books on American history, historically costumed dolls, classic political campaign buttons, and vintage newspapers with banner headlines such as "Nixon Resigns!"

Other Shows

IllumiNations 📷
Frommer's Rating: A+
Recommended Ages: 3–adult
Little has changed since Epcot's millennium version of IllumiNations ended on January 1, 2001. This 13-minute grand nightcap continues to be a blend of fireworks, lasers, and fountains in a display that's signature Disney. The show is worth braving the crowds that flock to the parking lot when it's over (just be sure to keep a firm grip on young kids). *Tip:* Stake your claim to your favorite viewing area a half-hour before showtime (listed in your entertainment schedule). The ones near Showcase Plaza offer a head start for the exits. Another good place for viewing the show is the terrace at the Rose & Crown Pub in the United Kingdom (p. 113) and the patio at the Cantina de San Angel (p. 114).

DISNEY'S HOLLYWOOD STUDIOS

You'll probably see the Tower of Terror and the Earrfel Tower, a water tank with mouse ears, even before you enter this park (formerly the Disney–MGM Studios), which Disney bills as "the Hollywood that never was and always will be." Once inside, you'll find pulse-quickening rides such as **Rock 'n' Roller Coaster,** movie- and TV-themed shows such as **Voyage of the Little Mermaid** and the **American Idol Experience,** and a spectacular laser-light show called **Fantasmic!** The main streets include Hollywood and Sunset boulevards, where Art Deco movie sets remember the golden age of Hollywood. The Streets of America sets include New York, lined with

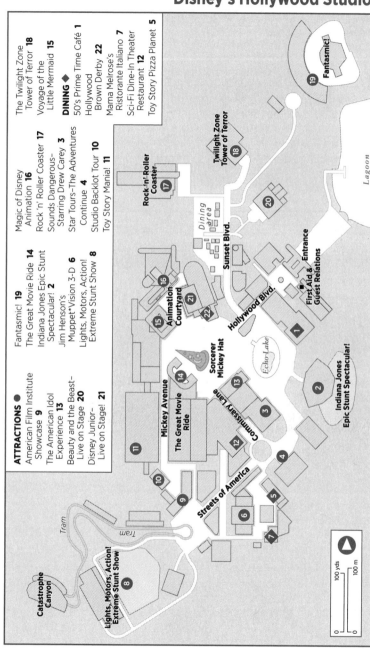

ATTRACTIONS ●

American Film Institute Showcase **9**
The American Idol Experience **13**
Beauty and the Beast-Live on Stage **20**
Disney Junior-Live on Stage! **21**

Fantasmic! **19**
The Great Movie Ride **14**
Indiana Jones Epic Stunt Spectacular! **2**
Jim Henson's Muppet*Vision 3-D **6**
Lights, Motors, Action! Extreme Stunt Show **8**

Magic of Disney Animation **16**
Rock 'n' Roller Coaster **17**
Sounds Dangerous-Starring Drew Carey **3**
Star Tours-The Adventures Continue **4**
Studio Backlot Tour **10**
Toy Story Mania! **11**

The Twilight Zone Tower of Terror **18**
Voyage of the Little Mermaid **15**

DINING ◆

50's Prime Time Café **1**
Hollywood Brown Derby **22**
Mama Melrose's Ristorante Italiano **7**
Sci-Fi Dine-In Theater Restaurant **12**
Toy Story Pizza Planet **5**

miniature renditions of Gotham's landmarks (the Empire State, Flatiron, and Chrysler buildings); as well as San Francisco, Chicago, and others. Pixar Place (formerly part of Mickey Ave.) is home to **Toy Story Mania.** You'll find some of the best street performers in the Disney parks here.

Arrive at the park early. Unlike Epcot, the Studios' 154 acres of attractions can pretty much be seen in a day. The parking lot reaches to the gate, with trams serving the outlying areas. Pay attention to your parking location; this lot isn't as well marked as the Magic Kingdom's. Again, write your lot and row number on something you'll be able to find at the end of the day.

If you don't get a *Hollywood Studios Guide Map* and entertainment schedule as you enter the park, you can pick one up at Guest Relations or most shops. First things first—check showtimes, and then sketch out a plan for your day, because many of the of the park's best offerings are its shows. Schedule your rides around the shows that interest you most and go from there. My favorite Hollywood Studios restaurants are described in chapter 4, "Where to Eat."

There's a tip board listing the day's shows, ride closings, and other information at the corner of Hollywood and Sunset boulevards.

HOURS   The park is usually open from 9am to at least 6 or 7pm, with extended hours sometimes as late as midnight during holidays and summer.

TICKET PRICES   A 1-day park ticket is $85 for adults, $79 for children 3 to 9. Kids younger than 3 get in free.

Services & Facilities in Disney's Hollywood Studios

ATMS   Cash machines accept cards from banks using the Cirrus, Honor, and PLUS systems; they're located on the right side of the main entrance and near Toy Story Pizza Planet.

BABY CARE   A small Baby Care Center, to the left of the main entrance, has facilities for nursing and changing. Disposable diapers, formula, baby food, and pacifiers are for sale. Changing tables are also in all women's restrooms and some men's restrooms.

CAMERAS & FILM   Film and Kodak disposable cameras are available throughout the park. Digital supplies, however, are limited. Services, varying from location to location, include CD burning, film developing, and minor repairs.

FIRST AID   The First Aid station, staffed by registered nurses, is in the Entrance Plaza adjoining Guest Relations and the Baby Care Center.

LOCKERS   Lockers are located alongside Oscar's Classic Car Souvenirs, to the right of the Entrance Plaza after you pass through the turnstiles. The cost is $7 to $9, plus a $5 deposit.

LOST CHILDREN   Lost children at Disney's Hollywood Studios are taken to Guest Relations, where lost-children logbooks are kept. *Children younger than 7 should wear name-tags inside their clothes.*

PACKAGE PICKUP   Any purchase can be sent to Guest Relations in the Entrance Plaza; allow at least 3 hours for delivery. If you're staying overnight at a Disney resort, you can also have all packages purchased by 7pm sent to your hotel (they will be delivered by noon the next day).

Rock Out!

With the popularity of Disney Channel's hit TV shows, movies, and music videos (think *High School Musical, Camp Rock,* and *StarStruck*—or *Jonas Brothers, Hannah Montana,* and *Wizards of Waverly Place*—and you'll get the idea), it shouldn't surprise anyone that a bit of Disney's musical screen magic has made its way to the streets of Disney's Hollywood Studios. **Disney Channel Rocks!** (replacing High School Musical 3: Senior Year—Right Here! Right Now!) has guests joining in on the dancing and singing as the mobile movie stage makes its way down Hollywood Boulevard (before stopping at the Sorcerer's Hat for the final act).

PARKING   It's $14 a day for cars, light trucks, and vans, and $15 for RVs.

PET CARE   Accommodations are offered at Disney's new luxury pet facility, the Best Friends Pet Care Center (☎ **877/493-9738**), for $10 to $76 per day, depending on whether your pet is staying overnight, the type of pet you have, the accommodations and extras you choose, and whether you are a Disney resort guest. Proof of vaccination is required. For more information, see "Fast Facts: Orlando," beginning on p. 367.

STROLLERS   Strollers can be rented at Oscar's Super Service, inside the main entrance, for $15 for a single and $31 for a double. Length-of-stay rentals are available at $13 per day for a single and $27 per day for a double. Full payment is expected upfront for length-of-stay rentals.

WHEELCHAIR RENTAL   Wheelchairs are rented at Oscar's Super Service inside the main entrance. The cost for regular chairs is $12 a day. Electric wheelchairs rent for $50, plus a $20 refundable deposit.

Major Attractions & Shows

American Film Institute Showcase
Frommer's Rating: C
Recommended Ages: 10–adult
This shop and exhibit area is the final stop on the Studio Backlot Tour (see below) and looks at the efforts of the editors, cinematographers, producers, and directors whose names roll by in the blur of credits. It also showcases the work of the American Film Institute's Lifetime Achievement Award winners, including Bette Davis, Jack Nicholson, and Elizabeth Taylor. A special exhibit here, **"Villains: Movie Characters You Love to Hate,"** features the costumes and props of several notable bad guys, including Davy Jones, Darth Vader, and King Miraz.

Beauty and the Beast Live on Stage
Frommer's Rating: B+
Recommended Ages: All ages
A 1,500-seat covered amphitheater is the home of this 30-minute live Broadway-style production of Beauty and the Beast that's adapted from the movie. Musical highlights from the show include the rousing "Be Our Guest" opening number and the poignant title song featured in the romantic waltz scene finale. The sets and costumes are lavish, and the production numbers are pretty spectacular. There are usually four or five shows a day.

At press time, Disney was offering preferred seating at the end-of-the-day spectacular, **Fantasmic!**, along with a fixed-price dinner at one of Disney's Hollywood Studios' sit-down restaurants. All you need to do is make Advance Reservations (📞 **407/939-3463**) and request the Fantasmic! Dinner Package (a credit card guarantee is required) for the Hollywood Brown Derby (prices vary, as you can now order a la carte), Mama Melrose's Ristorante Italiano ($33 adults, $12 kids 3–11), or Hollywood & Vine ($27 adults, $14 kids). You'll get your line pass at the restaurant and instructions on getting to the special entrance to the preferred seating area of the show. Lunch packages are also available (good for the first Fantasmic! show when two are scheduled on a single night).

Note: The prices above are for a fixed-price meal (except for at Hollywood Brown Derby) and do not include sales tax, tip, or alcoholic beverages; if you order off the menu, you'll pay more. The prices also don't include a reserved seat at Fantasmic!, only a pass that will get you into the preferred seating area. You must arrive at least 30 to 45 minutes in advance—still a much shorter wait than usual for good seats.

5

Disney Junior—Live on Stage!
Frommer's Rating: B
Recommended Ages: 2–5

Recently updated, this 22-minute show is a hit with younger audiences, who will surely love being encouraged to dance, sing, and play along with characters from *Jake and the Never Land Pirates* (Disney's latest preschool production), *Little Einsteins*, *Mickey Mouse Clubhouse*, *Handy Manny*, and other popular preschool favorites. Check the show schedule as this one's offered several times a day.

Fantasmic! 📷
Frommer's Rating: A+
Recommended Ages: All ages

Disney mixes heroes, villains, stunt performers, choreography, laser lights, and fireworks into a spectacular end-of-the-day extravaganza. This is a 25-minute visual feast where the Magic Mickey comes to life in a show featuring shooting comets, great balls of fire (my apologies to Jerry Lee), and animated fountains that really charge the audience. The cast includes 50 performers, a giant dragon, a king cobra, and 1 million gallons of water, just about all of which are orchestrated by a sorcerer mouse that looks more than remotely familiar. You'll probably recognize other characters as well as musical scores from Disney movie classics such as *Fantasia, Pinocchio, Snow White and the Seven Dwarfs, The Little Mermaid,* and *The Lion King*. You'll also shudder at the animated villainy of Jafar, Cruella De Vil, and Maleficent in the battle of good versus evil, part of which is projected onto huge water-mist screens. The amphitheater holds 9,000 souls, including standing room, and during busy periods (holidays and summers) it's often standing room only, so arrive at least 30 to 60 minutes early (if you don't mind a late dinner, you can pick up food from a fast-food counter on Sunset Blvd. and picnic in the stands while you wait). There is sometimes an additional show earlier in the evening. *Note:* The show's loud pyrotechnics may frighten younger children, and earplugs aren't a bad idea for anyone with ears sensitive to very loud noises.

The Great Movie Ride
Frommer's Rating: C for most, B+ for adults who love classics
Recommended Ages: 8–adult

Film footage and 50 audio-animatronic replicas of movie stars are used to re-create some of the most famous scenes in filmdom on this 22-minute ride through movie history. You'll relive magic moments from the 1930s through the present: the classic airport farewell scene by Bergman and Bogart in *Casablanca*; Brando bellowing "Stellaaaaa"; Harrison Ford in full Indiana Jones mode while facing all of those snakes; Sigourney Weaver fending off slimy aliens; Gene Kelly singin' in the rain; and arguably the best Tarzan, Johnny Weissmuller, giving his trademark yell while swinging across the jungle. The action is enhanced by special effects, and outlaws hijack your tram en route. So pay attention when the conductor warns, "Fasten your seat belts. It's going to be a bumpy night." The setting is a full-scale reproduction of Hollywood's famous Mann's Chinese Theatre, complete with handprints of the stars out front. **Note:** Though it's a classic, the ride is somewhat dated and is often the target of rumors claiming it will be replaced or upgraded (Disney remains closemouthed on the matter).

Indiana Jones Epic Stunt Spectacular
Frommer's Rating: A+
Recommended Ages: 6–adult

Visitors get a peek into the world of movie stunts in this dramatic 30-minute show, which re-creates major scenes from the Indiana Jones series. The show opens on an elaborate Mayan temple backdrop. Indy crashes onto the set via a rope, and, as he searches with a torch for the golden idol, he encounters booby traps, fire, and steam. Then a boulder straight out of *Raiders of the Lost Ark* chases him! The set is dismantled to reveal a colorful Cairo marketplace where a sword fight ensues, and the action includes virtuoso bullwhip maneuvers, gunfire, and a truck bursting into flames. An explosive finale takes place in a desert scenario. Theme music and an entertaining narrative enhance the action. Throughout this, guests get to see how elaborate stunts are pulled off. Arrive early and sit near the stage if you want a shot at being picked as an audience participant. Alas, it's a job for adults only. Younger kids may prefer a seat a bit farther away from all the action, and I've found that the mid- to upper rows offer the best views. It's one of the most popular shows in the park, so try and arrive a bit before showtime in order to get a better choice of seating.

 Water World

The large moat surrounding the Fantasmic! stage at Disney's Hollywood Studios contains 1.9 million gallons of water. More than 80,000 gallons of that are needed every minute to create the three mist screens used to project video portions of the show.

Jim Henson's Muppet*Vision 3-D
Frommer's Rating: A+
Recommended Ages: All ages

This must-see film stars Kermit and Miss Piggy in a delightful marriage of Jim Henson's puppets and Disney audio-animatronics, special-effects wizardry, 70mm film, and cutting-edge 3-D technology. The coming-right-at-you action includes flying Muppets, cream pies, and cannonballs, plus high winds, fiber-optic fireworks, bubble

FIND THE hidden MICKEYS

Hidden Mickeys started as an inside joke among early Disney Imagineers and soon became a park tradition (I'm not kidding—the entire Disney's Hollywood Studios layout when viewed from the sky is one giant Hidden Mickey!). Today, dozens of subtle Mickey images—usually silhouettes of his world-famous ears, profile, or full figure—are hidden (more or less) in attractions and resorts throughout the Walt Disney empire. No one knows how many, because sometimes they exist only in the eye of the beholder. But there's a semiofficial, maybe-you-agree-maybe-you-don't list. See how many HMs (Hidden Mickeys) you can locate during your visit. And be sharp-eyed about it: Those bubbles on your souvenir mug might be forming one. Here are a few to get you started:

IN THE MAGIC KINGDOM

- In the Haunted Mansion banquet scene, check out the arrangement of the plate and adjoining saucers on the table.

- In the Africa scene of it's a small world, note the purple flowers on a vine on the elephant's left side.

- While riding Splash Mountain, look for Mickey lying on his back in the pink clouds to the right of the *Zip-A-Dee Lady* paddle-wheeler.

AT EPCOT

- In Imagination, check out the little girl's dress in the lobby film of Honey, I Shrunk the Audience, one of five HMs in this pavilion.

- There are three HMs on the wall surrounding Mission: Space.

- As you enter the Mexico Pavilion, check out the large block statue on your right as you climb the stairs—the Hidden Mickey is right at the top.

- In Maelstrom in the Norway Pavilion, a Viking wears Mickey ears in the wall mural facing the loading dock.

- There are four HMs inside Spaceship Earth, one of them in the

showers, even an actual spray of water. Kermit is the host; Miss Piggy sings "Dream a Little Dream of Me"; Statler and Waldorf critique the action (which includes numerous mishaps and disasters) from a balcony; and Nicki Napoleon and his Emperor Penguins (a full Muppet orchestra) provide music from the pit. In the pre-show area, guests view an entertaining Muppet video on overhead monitors. Note the cute Muppet fountain out front and the Muppet version of a Rousseau painting inside. The 25-minute show, including the 12-minute video preshow, runs continuously.

Tip: Sweetums, the giant but friendly Muppet monster, usually interacts with a few kids sitting in the front rows during the show. If you want to sit up front, move to the leftmost theater door in the preshow area.

Lights, Motors, Action! Extreme Stunt Show
Frommer's Rating: B+
Recommended Ages: 5–adult
The Studios' latest action-packed addition debuted in mid-2005—and it's a biggie. Taking its cue from the original show at Disneyland Resort Paris, this stunt show features high-flying, high-speed movie stunts full of pyrotechnic effects and more. Like the **Indiana Jones Epic Stunt Spectacular** (p. 219), the storyline has the

Renaissance scene, on the page of a book behind the sleeping monk. Try to find the other three.

AT DISNEY'S HOLLYWOOD STUDIOS

o On the Great Movie Ride, there's an HM on the window above the bank in the gangster scene.

o At Jim Henson's Muppet*Vision 3-D, take a good look at the top of the sign listing five reasons for turning in your 3-D glasses, and note the balloons in the film's final scene.

o In the Twilight Zone Tower of Terror, note the bell for the elevator behind Rod Serling in the film. There are more than eight HMs in this attraction.

o Outside Rock 'n' Roller Coaster, look for two HMs in the rotunda area's tile floor. (Reportedly, the entire coaster is one giant HM.)

o By the way, the park's least Hidden Mickey is what's called the Earrfel

Tower, Disney's Hollywood Studios' tall water tower, which is fitted with a huge pair of Mouseket-"ears."

IN ANIMAL KINGDOM

o Look at the Boneyard in Dino-Land U.S.A., where a fan and two hard hats form an HM.

o There are 25 Hidden Mickeys at Rafiki's Planet Watch, where Mickey lurks in the murals, tree trunks, and paintings of animals.

IN THE RESORT AREAS

o HMs are on the weather vane atop the Grand Floridian Resort & Spa's convention center, in the interactive fountains at the entrance to Downtown Disney Marketplace, and one forms a giant sand trap next to the green at the Magnolia Golf Course's 6th hole.

For more information on the plethora of HMs at WDW, check out **www.hidden mickeys.org.**

audience following the filming of an action-packed movie (in this case, a spy thriller set in a Mediterranean village). More than 40 vehicles are used in the show, including cars, motorcycles, and watercraft—each modified to perform the rather spectacular stunts. It's entertaining and certainly offers its share of thrills, but it's not as engaging as the Indiana Jones production unless you're a car buff. Although the outdoor stadium seating is set back from the action, the noise level is extremely high—and completely unavoidable, no matter where you sit. Very young children may find it overwhelming. The show is part of the redevelopment of the Studios' backlot area that's also seen the addition of cityscapes of San Francisco and Chicago, among others. Check the entertainment schedule for showtimes. **Note:** Herbie the Lovebug, though appearing only briefly, has been replaced with Lightning McQueen, his debut at the park timed perfectly with the release of *Cars 2* (a sequel to *Cars* and yet another wildly popular Pixar production).

Magic of Disney Animation

Frommer's Rating: B

Recommended Ages: 8–adult

Once hosted by the late Walter Cronkite and Robin Williams, the current version of Magic of Disney Animation features Mushu, the dragon from Disney's *Mulan,* as he

Fit for Royalty

Over at soundstage 4, on Mickey Avenue (a small section remains after the addition of Pixar Place), **Journey into Narnia** was transformed in order to keep pace with the release of *The Chronicles of Narnia: Prince Caspian.* Rather than venturing through a gigantic wardrobe into the wintry white world, guests explore Aslan's Stone Chamber, re-created from the mold used to create the original—alas, the meet-and-greet with Prince Caspian is no longer available. Filling the gallery just beyond the set are elaborate creatures, along with actual costumes, armory, and props used in the making of the film. *Note:* Although another film in the Narnia series has hit the big screen *(The Voyage of the Dawn Treader),* there is no word on whether or not the attraction will receive yet another update.

co-hosts a theater presentation where some of Disney's animation secrets are revealed. The Q&A session that follows allows guests to ask questions about the animation process before attempting their own Disney character drawings while under the supervision of a working animator (a big hit with adults—don't miss it!). Currently joining in on the fun for a meet-and-greet opportunity is Winnie the Pooh—even Mickey makes an occasional appearance. Keep in mind, however, that the lineup has changed several times in the past few years and will likely change again.

Rock 'n' Roller Coaster
Frommer's Rating: A+
Recommended Ages: 10–adult

Some say this is one of Disney's attempts to go head-to-head with Universal Orlando's Islands of Adventure. True or not, this inverted roller coaster is one of the best and definitely the hippest of the thrill rides at WDW. It's a fast-and-furious indoor ride in semidarkness. You sit in a 24-passenger "stretch limo" outfitted with 120 speakers that blare Aerosmith at 32,000 watts! Flashing lights deliver a variety of messages and warnings, including "prepare to merge as you've never merged before." Then, faster than you can scream "I want to live!" (around 2.8 sec., actually), you shoot from 0 to 60 mph and into the first gut-tightening inversion at 5Gs. It's a real launch (sometimes of lunch), followed by a wild ride through a make-believe California freeway system. One of three inversions cuts through an "O" in the Hollywood sign, but you don't feel you're going to be thrown out—it's too fast for that. So fast, the Disney hype says, it's similar to sitting atop an F-14 Tomcat. (I've never been in an F-14, so I can't argue.) The smooth ride lasts 3 minutes, 12 seconds, the running time of Aerosmith's hit "Sweet Emotion." Like Space Mountain, all of the ride action takes place indoors, but this one kicks it up a few notches. *Note:* Riders must be at least 48 inches tall. Expectant moms and people prone to motion sickness or those with heart, neck, or back problems shouldn't try to tackle this ride.

Sounds Dangerous Starring Drew Carey
Frommer's Rating: C
Recommended Ages: 8–Adult

Drew Carey provides laughs while dual audio technology provides some hair-raising effects during this 12-minute show at ABC Sound Studios. You'll feel like you're right in the middle of the action of a TV pilot featuring undercover police work and plenty of mishaps. Even when the picture disappears and the theater is plunged into darkness (an effect that will likely turn off younger audience members), you continue on Detective Charlie Foster's chase via headphones that show off "3-D" sound effects.

Tip: After the show is over, check out **Sound Works,** which offers interactive activities that allow you to experiment with different sound effects. If you skipped the show, you can enter from the street.

Star Tours—The Adventures Continue
Frommer's Rating: B+
Recommended Ages: 8–adult

The power of the force remains strong as Star Tours immerses riders in a completely re-imagined 3-D experience (slated to debut just as this book goes to print). After making their way through the bustling spaceport, riders board the Starspeeder 1000, embarking on an ever-changing adventure across the galaxy (with some 50 or so scenarios, each randomly selected at the launch—taking a cue from the Twilight Zone Tower of Terror). With C3PO at the helm (inadvertently piloting the Starspeeder after a series of mishaps), you're off with a whoosh, speeding across the galaxy on a journey full of sudden drops, crashes, and oncoming laser blasts—with destinations that may include the icy planet of Hoth or the lush jungles of Kashyyk, the underwater Gungan world of Naboo, Coruscant or Tatooine (for the Boonta Eve Podrace), among other locations made famous in the *Star Wars* series. **Note:** The virtual-simulator may go nowhere at all, but it sure feels like you do. Riders must be at least 40 inches tall. Also, expectant mothers and people with neck, back, and heart problems or those prone to motion sickness shouldn't ride. There are, however, plenty of places

Idol, a la Disney

Disney's version of *American Idol*—aptly dubbed the **American Idol Experience**—made its debut in the spring of 2009. Based on the wildly popular TV show of the same name, the American Idol Experience brings with it an exciting new element to the park's existing lineup of spectacular shows and experiences. Guests are invited to audition, perform, and even compete live on stage—a stage that practically mimics the original (audition slots are open to guests ages 14 and up; space, however, is very limited—and only those who pass this phase are selected to actually compete on stage). Each seat is equipped with buttons for voting, with your votes determining the winner. If you can, avoid sitting in the very first few rows, as the cameramen can be somewhat distracting and at times can (and will) block your view. The entire production, as impressive and exciting as its namesake thanks to the extraordinary special effects, takes about a half-hour (not counting the wait in line). Though not quite as popular as the televised version, it's close enough, so arrive at least a half-hour early or you could miss out. Check the park's *Times Guide* for the current show schedule. **Note:** Outside, near the entrance, a large video screen simultaneously broadcasts the action happening on stage. If you caught one of the earlier shows, it's especially fun to watch the last show of the day, when the winning contestants from that day compete for a chance to audition for the actual *American Idol.*

to focus your vision other than the screen (unlike some of the newer simulator rides) if you begin to feel a bit green.

Studio Backlot Tour
Frommer's Rating: B+
Recommended Ages: 6–adult

This 35-minute tram tour takes you behind the scenes for a close-up look at the vehicles, props, costumes, sets, and special effects used in your favorite movies and TV shows. On many days, you'll see costume makers at work in the wardrobe department (Disney has around two million garments here). But the real fun begins when the tram heads for **Catastrophe Canyon,** where an earthquake in the heart of oil country causes canyon walls to rumble. A raging oil fire, massive explosions, torrents of rain, and flash floods threaten you and the other riders before you're taken behind the scenes to see how filmmakers use special effects to make such disasters. The preshow is almost as interesting. While waiting in line, you can watch entertaining videos hosted by several TV and movie stars. The Backlot Tour is a solid ride that's of the same type as Universal Studios' Disaster! A Major Motion Picture Ride . . . Starring You! (p. 255).

Tune Time

Weekdays from noon to 4pm, you can watch B. B. Good broadcast her Radio Disney show live from a studio next to Sounds Dangerous Starring Drew Carey. You can tune into the show and others on Radio Disney at 990 on your AM dial.

The Twilight Zone Tower of Terror 📷
Frommer's Rating: A+
Recommended Ages: 10–adult

This is a truly stomach-lifting (and dropping) ride, and Disney continues to fine-tune it to make it even better. The legend says that during a violent storm on Halloween night 1939, lightning struck the Hollywood Tower Hotel, causing an entire wing and an elevator full of people to disappear. And you're about to meet them as you become the star in a special episode of . . . *The Twilight Zone.* En route to this formerly grand hotel, guests walk past overgrown landscaping and faded signs that once pointed the way to stables and tennis courts. The vines over the entrance trellis are dead, and the hotel is a crumbling ruin. Eerie corridors lead to a dimly lit library, where you can hear a storm raging outside. After various spooky adventures, the ride ends in a dramatic climax: a 13-story free-fall in stages. The ride features random drop sequences, allowing for a real sense of the unknown (and a different experience every time you ride), and visual, audio, and olfactory effects make the experience even more frightening. Because it's a different experience every time you dare to ride, it's far better than any other ride of its kind. Some believe this rivals (even exceeds) Rock 'n' Roller Coaster in the thrill department; one of the Imagineers who designed the tower admitted that he's too scared to ride his own creation. At 199 feet, it's the tallest ride in WDW, and it's a grade above Dr. Doom's Fearfall at Islands of Adventure (and has far better atmosphere—it's one of Walt Disney World's best attractions in the theme department). **Note:** You must be at least 40 inches tall to ride, and expectant moms and people prone to motion sickness or those with heart, neck, or back problems shouldn't try to tackle it. Your stomach may need a few minutes to find its way back to where it belongs after it's all over.

Voyage of the Little Mermaid
Frommer's Rating: B+
Recommended Ages: 4–adult

Hazy lighting creates an underwater effect in a reef-walled theater and helps set the mood for this charming musical based on the Disney feature film. The show combines live performers with more than 100 puppets, movie clips, and innovative special effects. Sebastian sings the movie's Academy Award–winning song, "Under the Sea"; the ethereal Ariel shares her dream of becoming human in a live performance of "Part of Your World"; and the evil Ursula, 12 feet tall and 10 feet wide, belts out "Poor Unfortunate Soul." It has a happy ending, as most of the young audience knows it will; they've seen the movie. This 17-minute show is a great place to rest your feet on a hot day, and you get misted inside the theater to further cool you off.

Parades, Playgrounds & More

Pixar Pals Countdown to Fun!, the Studios' big parade, made its debut in early 2011, replacing Disney's Block Party Bash (which had only recently replaced the Disney Stars and Motor Cars parade in 2008). Unlike its predecessors, where guests were encouraged to sing and dance along with the characters, dancers, and acrobats, the new Pixar parade is far more procession-like, with fan favorites from Disney/Pixar flicks such as *Finding Nemo, Toy Story 2, Monsters, Inc., The Incredibles,* and *A Bug's Life* (and others) simply strolling past park-goers.

Aside from the parades, there are character-greeting hot spots at the **Animation Courtyard,** on the north and south ends of the **Streets of America,** at **Pixar Place** near Toy Story Mania, at the **Magic of Disney Imagination,** and at the **Sorcerer's Hat.** The list of characters changes from time to time, but expect to find favorites from *Cars* (and the recently released *Cars 2*), the *Toy Story* trilogy, *Phineas and Ferb,*

 Buzz & Woody Are Back in Action

Disney's **Toy Story Mania ★★★** made its debut in 2008. This interactive attraction, based on the popular Disney/Pixar *Toy Story* movies, features several classic midway-style games, each with a *Toy Story*—and technological—twist. Shrunk to the size of a toy and sporting 3-D glasses, guests attempt to score points at the various booths that line the midway. Similar to Buzz Lightyear's Space Ranger Spin at the Magic Kingdom (p. 193), onboard cannons will fire at the targets (the old-fashioned way—by hand, not via electronic wizardry) as characters, including Buzz, Bo Peep, Woody, and even the little green men, cheer everyone on as they play. Hidden targets will earn you extra points and lead to different levels of play, ensuring that each experience will be different than the last—and that you'll want to come back for more (but you may need to rest your hands between rides—they really get a workout). Characters from the recently released *Toy Story 3* have been added to the experience, along with an entirely new midway game and a character meet-and-greet opportunity with Lots-O-Huggin' Bear. *Note:* If you've got little ones (or even if you don't), be sure everyone hits the restrooms before getting in line here. I've waited for well over an hour or more on more than one occasion, and it wasn't during peak season; though you are able to leave if need be, don't expect to get back in line at the point you departed from.

Disney's Hollywood Studios is home to some of Disney World's most unique restaurants (see chapter 4 for more details). If you plan to dine in any of them, be sure to make Advance Reservations (preferably before you leave home, but if not, then the minute you arrive at your hotel or in the park). Waiting until lunchtime or dinnertime will almost assure that you'll miss out, especially at the Sci-Fi Dine-In Theater Restaurant and 50's Prime Time Café.

and a handful of other popular Pixar flicks. See the *Times Guide* handout for the schedule.

Shopping at Disney's Hollywood Studios

With more than 20 shops in the park, I can't list them all, but some of the Studios' more unique offerings include the following:

The **Animation Courtyard Shops** carry collectible cels, costumes from Disney classic films, and pins.

Sid Cahuenga's One-of-a-Kind sells autographed photos of the stars, original movie posters, and star-touched items such as canceled checks signed by Judy Garland and others.

Celebrity 5 & 10, modeled after a 1940s Woolworth's, has movie-related merchandise: *Gone With the Wind* memorabilia, Hollywood Studios T-shirts, movie posters, Elvis mugs, and more.

The major park attractions also have their own shops selling Indiana Jones adventure clothing, Little Mermaid stuffed characters, *Star Wars* souvenirs, and so on.

ANIMAL KINGDOM

Disney's fourth major park opened in 1998 and combines exotic animals, the elaborate landscapes of Asia and Africa, and the prehistoric lands of the dinosaur. Animals, architecture, and lush surroundings take center stage here, with a handful of rides thrown in for good measure.

A conservation venue as much as an attraction, Animal Kingdom ensures that you won't find the animals blatantly displayed throughout the 500-acre park; instead, naturalistic habitats blend seamlessly into the spectacular surroundings. This unfortunately means that, at times, you'll have to search a bit to find the inhabitants. Expect your experience here to be quite different from that at Disney's other parks. It's the spectacular surroundings, meticulously re-created architecture, and intricate detailing, not so much the attractions sprinkled throughout (even though **Expedition Everest** is pretty impressive), that make the park so unique and so interesting. First bonus: Because this is one of Disney's less ride-intensive parks, it's easily enjoyed in a single day, usually less, making it a good choice when you need to cut back and take it a bit slower and easier. Second bonus: The best shows in all of Disney can be found here: **Finding Nemo–The Musical** and the **Festival of the Lion King** should definitely be on your to-do list.

Animal Kingdom is divided into the **Oasis,** a shopping area near the entrance that offers limited animal viewing; **Discovery Island,** home of the Tree of Life, the park's unique icon; **Camp Minnie-Mickey,** the Animal Kingdom equivalent of Mickey's

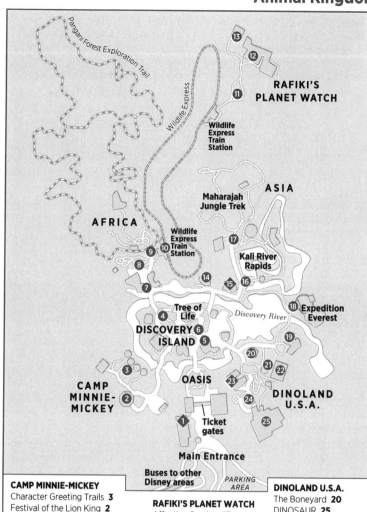

CAMP MINNIE-MICKEY
Character Greeting Trails **3**
Festival of the Lion King **2**

DISCOVERY ISLAND
Discovery Island Trails **4**
Guest Information Board **5**
It's Tough to Be a Bug! **6**

AFRICA
Harambe Village **7**
Kilimanjaro Safaris **8**
Pangani Forest Exploration Trail **9**
Wildlife Express Train station
for Rafiki's Planet Watch **10**

RAFIKI'S PLANET WATCH
Affection Section **13**
Conservation Station **12**
Habitat Habit! **11**

ASIA
Expedition Everest **18**
Flights of Wonder **14**
Kali River Rapids **16**
Maharajah Jungle Trek **17**

DINOLAND U.S.A.
The Boneyard **20**
DINOSAUR **25**
Dino-Sue **24**
Finding Nemo–
The Musical **19**
Primeval Whirl **22**
TriceraTop Spin **21**

DINING ◆
Rainforest Cafe **1**
Restaurantosaurus **23**
Tusker House **7**
Yak & Yeti **15**

Animal Kingdom (and the other parks, too) can get very hot, especially during summer, and despite all the foliage, shade can sometimes be hard to come by. Bring bottled water (freeze it the night before to keep it cold), refilling at the fountains inside the park. Remember to bring sunscreen and wide-brimmed hats *for the whole family,* and plan to ride Kali River Rapids during the hottest part of the day (be sure to bring a change of clothes, as you will get wet . . . and possibly soaked).

Toontown Fair in the Magic Kingdom but without any of the fun little rides; **Africa,** where you can wander the village streets and head out on safari (you'll find the largest concentration of animals here); **Asia,** with Mt. Everest looming on the horizon (within it, the coolest thrill ride in the park), plus a raging river ride, exotic animal exhibits (including Bengal tigers and giant fruit bats), and a bird show; and **Dino-Land U.S.A.,** filled with carnival-style rides and games, a large play area, and a herky-jerky thrill ride that transports you back in time.

The park covers more than 500 acres, and your feet will tell you that you've covered the territory at the end of the day.

Most of the rides are accessible to guests with disabilities, but the hilly terrain, large crowds, narrow passages, and long hikes can make for a strenuous day if there's a wheelchair-bound person in your party. Anyone with neck or back problems, as well as pregnant women, may not be able to enjoy rides such as **Expedition Everest, Kali River Rapids,** and **Dinosaur.**

The 145-foot-tall **Tree of Life** is in the center of the park. It's an intricately carved free-form representation of animals, handcrafted by a team of artists over the period of a year. It's not nearly as tall or imposing as Spaceship Earth, which has come to symbolize Epcot, or Cinderella Castle in the Magic Kingdom. The tree is impressive, though, with 8,000 limbs, 103,000 leaves, and 325 mammals, reptiles, bugs, birds, dinosaurs, and Mickeys in its trunk, limbs, and roots. For more on the tree, see "Discovery Island," below.

ARRIVING   From the parking lot, walk or (where available) ride one of the trams to the entrance. If you do walk, watch out for the trams and autos—the lot isn't designed for pedestrians. Also, make certain to note where you parked (section and row). Lot signs aren't as prominent as in the Magic Kingdom, and the rows will look alike when you come back out. Upon entering the park, consult the handout guide map for special events or entertainment. If you have questions, ask park staffers.

HOURS   Animal Kingdom is open from at least 9am to 5pm, but it sometimes opens an hour earlier and stays open an hour or so later.

TICKET PRICES   Ticket prices are $85 for adults, $79 for children 3 to 9. See "Tickets," on p. 162, for information on the Magic Your Way ticketing scheme.

Services & Facilities in Animal Kingdom

ATMS   Animal Kingdom has an ATM near Garden Gate Gifts to the right of the entrance, as well as in DinoLand across from the Primeval Whirl. It accepts cards from banks using the Cirrus, Honor, and PLUS systems.

BABY CARE   The Baby Care Center is located near the Creature Comforts gift shop on the west side of the Tree of Life. As in the other Disney parks, you'll also find changing tables in restrooms, and you can buy disposable diapers at Guest Relations.

CAMERAS & FILM   You can drop off film for same-day developing at the Kodak Kiosk in Africa and Garden Gate Gifts near the park entrances. Cameras and film are available in Disney Outfitters in Safari Village; at the Kodak Kiosk in Africa, near the entrance to the Kilimanjaro Safari; and in Garden Gate Gifts.

FIRST AID   The First Aid station, staffed by registered nurses, is located near the Creature Comforts gift shop on the west side of the Tree of Life.

LOCKERS   Lockers ($7–$9, plus a $5 refundable deposit) are located in Garden Gate Gifts to your right as you enter the park. They're also located to the left, near Rainforest Cafe.

LOST CHILDREN   A center for lost children is located near Creature Comforts at the Baby Care Center on the west side of the Tree of Life. This is also the site of same-day lost and found. At the risk of repeating myself, *make your younger kids wear name-tags inside their clothing.*

PACKAGE PICKUP   Any purchases can be sent to the front of the park at Garden Gate Gifts. Allow at least 3 hours for delivery. WDW resort guests can have their purchases delivered directly to their hotel; if purchased by 7pm, the item will be delivered by noon the next day.

PARKING   The cost is $14 a day for cars, light trucks, and vans, and $15 for RVs.

PET CARE   Accommodations are offered at Disney's new luxury pet facility, the Best Friends Pet Care Center (✆ **877/493-9738**), for $10 to $76 per day, depending on whether your pet is staying overnight, the type of pet you have, the accommodations and extras you choose, and whether you are a Disney resort guest. Proof of vaccination is required. For more information, see "Fast Facts: Orlando," beginning on p. 367.

STROLLERS   Stroller rentals are available at Garden Gate Gifts to the right as you enter the park ($15 for a single, $31 for a double). Length-of-stay rentals are available at $13 per day for a single, $27 per day for a double; payment in full is expected at time of rental. There are also satellite locations throughout the park; ask a Disney employee to steer you.

WHEELCHAIR RENTAL   You can rent wheelchairs at Garden Gate Gifts to the right as you enter the park. Rentals are $12 for a standard wheelchair, $50 for an electric wheelchair (plus a $20 refundable deposit). Ask Disney employees for other rental locations throughout the park.

The Oasis

This painstakingly designed landscape of streams, grottoes, and miniwaterfalls sets the tone for the rest of the park. This is a good place to see wallabies, tiny deer, giant anteaters, sloths, iguanas, tree kangaroos, otters, and macaws (*if,* I remind you ad nauseum, you get here early or stay late). But the thick cover provides a camouflage for the animals and sometimes makes seeing them difficult. There are no rides in this area, and, aside from the animals, it's mainly a pass-through zone. Those guests traveling with eager children will probably have more time to enjoy these exhibits on the way out.

ANIMAL KINGDOM tip sheet

1. Arrive at opening or stay until near closing for the best view of the animals.
2. **Expedition Everest** offers the biggest thrills in the park, and a FAST-PASS may be your only ticket to avoiding the ride's excruciatingly long lines.
3. **Kilimanjaro Safaris** is one of the most popular rides and the best place to see a lot of animals in one sitting. But in summer, the animals can be scarce during the midday heat. If you can hoof it there first thing, do it. If not, try late in the day. The same applies to viewing the gorillas on the **Pangani Forest Exploration Trail.**
4. **Finding Nemo–The Musical** and the **Festival of the Lion King** shows are a must.
5. Looking for Disney characters? Go to the Character Greeting Trails in **Camp Minnie-Mickey.**
6. Make Advance Reservations for a meal at **Yak & Yeti,** the park's newest themed full-service restaurant.

Discovery Island

Like Cinderella Castle in the Magic Kingdom and Spaceship Earth in Epcot, the 14-story **Tree of Life** located here has been designed to be the park's central landmark. The man-made tree and its carved animals are the work of Disney artists. Teams of them worked for a whole year creating the various sculptures, and it's worth a stroll on the walks around its roots; most folks are smart to save it for the end of the day. (Much of it can be seen while you're in line for **It's Tough to Be a Bug!** or on the **Discovery Island Trails.**) The intricate design makes it seem as if a different animal appears from every angle. One of the creators says he expects it to become one of the most photographed works of art in the world. (He's probably a Disney shareholder.) There's a wading pond directly in front of the tree that often features flamingos.

Discovery Island Trails

Frommer's Rating: B

Recommended Ages: All ages

The old, pre-FASTPASS queue for It's Tough to Be a Bug! provides a leisurely path through the root system of the Tree of Life and a chance to see real, not-so-rare critters, such as axis deer, red kangaroos, otters, flamingos, lemurs, Galápagos tortoises, ducks, storks, and cockatoos. Again, the best viewing times are early or late in the day.

It's Tough to Be a Bug!

Frommer's Rating: A, C for young ones scared silly from sensory effects

Recommended Ages: 5–adult

This show's cuteness quotient is enough to earn it a B+. But it goes a rung higher thanks to the preshow: To get to the theater, you have to wind around the Tree of Life's 50-foot base, giving you a front-row look at this man-made marvel. After you've passed that, grab your 3-D glasses and settle into a sometimes creepy-crawly seat. Based on the film *A Bug's Life,* the special effects in this multimedia show are pretty impressive. It's not a good one for very young kids (it's dark and loud) or bug haters (though my bug-phobic editor loves it), but for others it's a fun, sometimes poignant look at life from a smaller perspective. Flick, Hopper, and the rest of the cast—ants, beetles, spiders, and, ugh, a stink bug—awaken your senses with, literally, some in-your-face action. And the show's finale always leaves the crowd buzzing.

Dinoland U.S.A.

Enter by passing under Olden Gate Bridge, a 40-foot Brachiosaurus reassembled from excavated fossils. Speaking of which, until late summer 1999, this land had three paleontologists working on the very real skeleton of Sue, a monstrously big *Tyrannosaurus rex* unearthed 9 years earlier in the Black Hills of South Dakota. They patched and assembled the bones here because Disney helped pay for the work. Alas, Sue's permanent home is at Chicago's Field Museum, but DinoLand U.S.A. has a replica cast from her 67-million-year-old bones. It's marked as **Dino-Sue** on park guide maps.

The Boneyard
Frommer's Rating: B+ for children, B for parents who need to rest their feet
Recommended Ages: 3–12
Kids love the chance to slip, slither, slide, and slink through this giant playground and dig site where they can discover the real-looking remains of triceratops, *T. rex*, and other vanished giants. Contained within a latticework of metal bars and netting, this area is popular, but not as inviting as the Honey, I Shrunk the Kids play area in Disney's Hollywood Studios.

Dinosaur
Frommer's Rating: B
Recommended Ages: 8–adult
This ride hurls you through the darkness in CTX Rover "time machines" back to the time when dinosaurs ruled the earth. The expedition takes you past an array of snarling and particularly ferocious-looking dinosaurs, one of whom decides you would make a great munchie. What started out as a journey back through time becomes a race to escape the jaws of an irritated and rather ugly carnotaurus. Young children may find the large lizards and the darkness a bit frightening, while everyone will find the ride a bit jarring. *Note:* You must be 40 inches or taller to climb aboard. Also, expectant mothers and people with neck, back, and heart problems or those prone to motion sickness shouldn't ride.

It Costs to Recycle

The animals here deposit more than 1,600 tons of dung a year. Disney pays a company to haul it away, and then buys some of it back as compost for landscaping.

Finding Nemo—The Musical
Frommer's Rating: A+
Recommended Ages: All ages
Disney's new, live stage production is simply enchanting. Nemo, Marlin, Dory, Crush, and Bruce (among other film favorites) come to life before your eyes. Live actors, in creatively designed puppetlike costumes, work together to re-create the undersea adventure made popular by the hit Disney/Pixar film *Finding Nemo*. Stunning special effects (making this one of the best and most unique stage productions in all of Disney) and a moving musical score (written especially for the show by the composers of the Tony Award–winning *Avenue Q*) complete the experience. Even with a slight tweak in the storyline, you'll find yourself thoroughly engrossed from start to finish, thanks to the absolutely entrancing performances that,

Pin buying, collecting, and trading can reach frenzied proportions among Disney fans, including many cast members. All of the theme parks have special locations set aside for the fun, which are marked on the handout guide maps. There are, however, a few rules of pin-trading etiquette that must be followed. You can learn more about the madness on the Internet at **www.dizpins.com** and **www.officialdisney pintrading.com**.

at times, spill into the entire theater. Even the squirmiest toddler will sit mesmerized through this 30-minute show—it's a must-see for the entire family.

Primeval Whirl

Frommer's Rating: B+

Recommended Ages: 8–adult

Disney introduced this spinning, free-style twin roller coaster in 2002 in an effort to broaden the park's appeal to young kids (odd, as this ride has a pretty tall height minimum). You control the action through its wacky maze of curves, peaks, and dippity-do-dahs, encountering faux asteroids and hokey cutouts of dinosaurs. This is a cross between those old carnival coasters of the '50s and '60s and an expanded version of the old Barnstormer at Goofy's Wiseacre Farm (which is currently closed as part of the Fantasyland expansion). **Note:** The ride carries a 48-inch height minimum, and expectant moms as well as those with neck, back, or heart problems and folks prone to motion sickness should stay planted on firm ground.

TriceraTop Spin

Frommer's Rating: B+ for tykes and parents

Recommended Ages: 2–7

Cut from the same cloth as the Magic Carpets of Aladdin at WDW's Magic Kingdom, this is another minithrill for youngsters. In this case, the cars look like cartoon dinosaurs. They circle the hub while gently moving up and down and all around. This ride, Primeval Whirl, and an arcade-game area make up the DinoLand U.S.A. miniland called Chester & Hester's Dino-Rama.

Camp Minnie-Mickey

Disney characters are the main attraction in this land designed in the same vein as an Adirondack resort. Aside from those characters, however, this zone for the younger set isn't nearly as kid-friendly as Woody Woodpecker's KidZone in Universal Studios Florida (see "Universal Studios Florida," in chapter 6).

Character Greeting Trails 📷

Frommer's Rating: A for kids, D for waiting parents

Recommended Ages: 2–12

Some say this is a must-do for people traveling with children; I say run the other way—quickly. If, however, your kids are hooked on getting every character autograph possible, this is the place to go. A variety of Disney characters, from Winnie the Pooh and Pocahontas to Timon and Baloo, have separate trails where you can meet and mingle, snap photos, and get those autographs. Mickey, Minnie, Goofy, and Pluto make periodic appearances. Be aware, however, that the lines for these meet-and-greet opportunities are at times excruciatingly long, so unless your kids are really gung ho on collecting the characters' signatures, don't even think of coming here. **Note:** Disney introduced a new character experience in 2009—each and every evening at closing time (near the park exit), Mickey, Minnie, and Goofy wave good night to their guests as they head back to their hotels for the night. While not a meet-and-greet, the kids will likely get a kick out of seeing their favorite characters on their way out of the park, even if just for a quick wave.

Festival of the Lion King

Frommer's Rating: A+

Recommended Ages: All ages

Almost everyone in the audience comes alive when the music starts in this rousing 28-minute show in the Lion King Theater. It's one of the top three theme-park shows in Central Florida. The production celebrates nature's diversity with a talented, colorfully attired cast of singers, dancers, and life-size critters leading the way to an inspiring sing-along that gets the entire audience caught up in the fun. Based loosely on the animated film, this stage show blends the pageantry of a parade with a tribal celebration. The action is on stage as well as moving around the audience. Even though the pavilion has 1,000 seats, it's best to arrive at least 20 minutes early.

Africa

Enter through the town of Harambe, a worn and weathered African coastal village poised on the edge of the 21st century. (It actually took a great deal of effort to create the run-down appearance.) Costumed employees will greet you as you enter the buildings. The whitewashed structures, built of coral stone and thatched with reed by African craftspeople, surround a central marketplace rich with local wares and colors.

Kilimanjaro Safaris

Frommer's Rating: A+ early or late, B+ other times

Recommended Ages: All ages

Animal Kingdom doesn't have many rides, but the animals you'll see on this one make it a winner as long as your timing is right. They're scarce at midday during most times of year (cooler months being the exception), so I recommend you ride it as close to park opening or closing as possible. If you don't make it in time for one of the first or last journeys, the lines can be horrific, so a FASTPASS is almost a must.

A large, rugged truck takes you through the African landscape (though a decade ago it was a cow pasture). The animals usually seen along the way include giraffes, black rhinos, hippos, antelopes, Nile crocodiles, zebras, wildebeests, cheetahs, and a pair of lions that may offer half-hearted roars toward some gazelles that are safely out of reach. Early on, a shifting bridge gives riders a brief thrill; later, you get a bit of drama (a la Disney) as you help catch some poachers. While everyone has a good view, photographers may get a few more shots when sitting on the left side of their row.

Did You Know?

Tobacco products aren't the only things unavailable in the theme parks. You can't buy chewing or bubble gum, either. It seems too many guests stuck it under tables, benches, and chairs—or tossed it on sidewalks, where it often hitched a ride on the soles of the unsuspecting.

Adventurous guests (with plenty of pocket change) can now book a trek through the Harambe Wildlife Reserve, navigate the bushwalk, cross the rope bridges hanging precariously above the Safi River (all the while tethered to a safety line—the bridge, of course, is actually well secured), hang over the cliffs above pools filled with hippo and crocodiles, and experience, first hand, remote areas of the reserve via open-air vehicle. The adventure ends at a private safari camp elevated above the savanna for optimal wildlife viewing, with a sampling of African fare and refreshing beverages ready and waiting. Limited to 12 guests, the **Wild Africa Trek** currently costs $129 per person (though expect this to increase as time goes on). Call Disney's tour line (☎ **407/939-8687**) to make reservations or get additional information.

Pangani Forest Exploration Trail 👫

Frommer's Rating: B+, A if you're lucky enough to see the gorillas

Recommended Ages: All ages

The hippos put on quite a display (and draw a riotous crowd reaction) when they do what comes naturally and use their tails to scatter it over everything above and below the surface. There are other animals here, including ever-active mole rats, but the **lowland gorillas** are the main event. The trail has two gorilla-viewing areas: One sports a family, including a 500-pound silverback, his ladies, and his children; the other has bachelors. Guests who are unaware of the treasures that lie herein often skip or rush through it, missing a chance to see some magnificent creatures. That said, the gorillas are not always cooperative, especially in hot weather, when they spend most of the day in shady areas out of view. There's also an Endangered Animal Rehabilitation Centre with colobus and mona monkeys.

Rafiki's Planet Watch ✋

Frommer's Rating: C

Recommended Ages: All ages

Board an open-sided train (the Wildlife Express) near Pangani Forest Exploration Trail for a trip to the back edge of the park, which has three attractions. **Conservation Station** offers a behind-the-scenes look at how Disney cares for animals (the entrance mural is loaded with Hidden Mickeys). You'll pass nurseries and veterinarian stations— but these facilities need to be staffed to be interesting, and that's not always the case. Older kids and adults will find the audio presentations at the sound booths pretty neat. **Habitat Habit!** is a trail with small animals such as cotton-top tamarins. The **Affection Section** has a petting zoo with rare goats and potbelly pigs, but not much more.

Asia

Disney's Imagineers have outdone themselves in creating the kingdom of **Anandapur.** The intricately painted artwork and detailed carvings are very appealing—they even seem to make the lines move a tad faster.

Expedition Everest

Frommer's Rating: A+

Recommended Ages: 8–adult

If there's a knock against Animal Kingdom, it's that it doesn't pack a lot of punch in the adrenaline department due to its lack of thrill rides. But naysayers have been quieted by the 2006 addition of Expedition Everest, Animal Kingdom's first true thrill ride. Your journey begins in the small Himalayan village of Serka Zong, where guests board the Anandapur Rail Service for a seemingly casual trek to the snowcapped peak of Mount Everest. Upon departing, you'll pass through an Asian mountain range and dense bamboo forests, and then move past glacier fields and pounding waterfalls. But your journey will quickly get off track (almost literally) and become an out-of-control high-speed train ride that sends you careening along rough and rugged terrain, moving backward and forward along icy mountain ledges and through darkened caves—only to end up confronting the legendary Yeti. Bet your adrenaline is running already. The meticulous and painstaking detail is some of the most impressive in all of WDW. Prayer flags are strung between the aged and distressed buildings, while intricately carved totems, stone carvings, and some 2,000 authentic handcrafted Asian objects are scattered throughout the village.

Flights of Wonder
Frommer's Rating: C+
Recommended Ages: All ages
This live-animal action show has undergone several transformations since the park opened. It's still a low-key break from the madness and has a few laughs, including Groucho the African yellow-nape, who entertains the audience with his op-*parrot*-ic a cappella solos. For thrills, there's the just-above-your-head soaring of a Harris hawk and a Eurasian eagle owl. To entertain guests waiting in line for the show, trainers will often bring out an owl or hawk, allowing for an up-close look and the opportunity to learn some interesting facts about the stars of the show.

Kali River Rapids
Frommer's Rating: B+
Recommended Ages: 6–adult
Its roiling water mimics real rapids, and the ride's optical illusions will have you wondering if you're about to go over churning falls. The ride begins with a peaceful tour of lush foliage, but soon you're dipping and dripping as your tiny craft is tossed and turned. The snowcapped peak of Expedition Everest makes a brief but impressive appearance along the way. If the rapids themselves don't drench you, the kids manning water cannons along the route will ensure you get wet—sometimes even soaked—hence the cart selling oversize towels and socks just beyond the ride's exit. (Bring a plastic bag for your valuables. The rafts' center storage areas alone likely won't keep them dry.) The lines can be long, but keep your head up and enjoy the marvelous art overhead and on beautiful murals. It's not nearly as wild as the water rides at Universal Orlando, so even the younger kids will be able to handle this one. **Note:** There's a 38-inch height minimum, and expectant moms and people with neck, back, and heart problems or those prone to motion sickness shouldn't ride it.

Cool Trivia

Two things you might hear during your day in the park: Bugs make up 80% of the real animal kingdom, and cheetahs are the only great cats that purr. Both are true.

Maharajah Jungle Trek
Frommer's Rating: B
Recommended Ages: 6–adult
Disney keeps its promise to provide up-close views of animals with this exhibit. If you don't show up in the midday heat, you may see Bengal tigers through a wall of thick

glass, while nothing but air separates you from dozens of giant fruit bats hanging in what appears to be a courtyard. Some have wingspans of 6 feet. (If you have a phobia, you can bypass this, though the bats are harmless.) Guides are on hand to answer questions, and you can also check a brochure that lists the animals you may spot; it's available on your right as you enter. You'll be asked to "recycle" it as you exit.

Parades

Mickey's Jammin' Jungle Parade at Animal Kingdom is an interactive street party featuring whimsical, colorful animals and characters on expedition. The music and overall atmosphere are lively, and the one-of-a-kind visuals are some of the best in all the parks.

DISNEY WATER PARKS

Note: All of the attractions mentioned in this section can be found on the "Walt Disney World Parks & Attractions" map, on p. 163.

Typhoon Lagoon

Ahoy swimmers, floaters, run-aground boaters!

A furious storm once roared 'cross the sea

Catching ships in its path, helpless to flee . . .

Instead of a certain and watery doom

The winds swept them here to TYPHOON LAGOON.

Such is the Disney legend relating to **Typhoon Lagoon ★★★**, which you'll see posted on consecutive signs as you enter the park. Located off Buena Vista Drive between the Downtown Disney Marketplace and Disney's Hollywood Studios, this is the ultimate in themed water parks. Its fantasy setting is a palm-fringed island village of ramshackle, tin-roofed structures, strewn with cargo, surfboards, and other marine wreckage left by the "great typhoon." A storm-stranded fishing boat (the *Miss Tilly*) dangles precariously atop 95-foot Mount Mayday, the steep setting for several attractions. Every half-hour, the boat's smokestack erupts, shooting a 50-foot geyser of water into the air.

ESSENTIALS

HOURS The park is open from at least 10am to 5pm, with extended hours during some holiday periods and summer (✆ **407/560-4141;** www.disneyworld.com).

ENTRANCE FEES A 1-day ticket to Typhoon Lagoon is $49 for adults, $41 for kids 3 to 9, plus tax.

HELPFUL HINTS In summer, arrive no later than 9am to avoid long lines. The park is often filled to capacity by 10am, and then closed to later arrivals. Beach towels ($2.50 per towel) and lockers ($8–$10) can be rented, and beachwear can be purchased at **Singapore Sal's.** Light fare is available at two eateries, **Leaning Palms** and **Typhoon Tillie's.** A beach bar called **Let's Go Slurpin'** sells beer and soft drinks, and **Lowtide Lou's** sells ice cream and soft drinks. There are picnic tables, so consider bringing picnic fare (you can keep it in your locker until lunch).

Guests aren't permitted to bring their own flotation devices, and glass bottles are prohibited.

ATTRACTIONS IN THE PARK

Castaway Creek   Hop onto a raft or an inner tube and meander along this 2,100-foot lazy river that circles most of the park. It tumbles through a misty rainforest, then by caves and secluded grottoes and on into the sunshine, all the while passing along some of Disney's meticulously maintained tropical foliage. Tubes are included in the admission price.

Crush 'n' Gusher   The last new thrill to splash onto the scene is a first-of-its-kind water coaster featuring three separate experiences to choose from. The **Banana Blaster, Coconut Crusher,** and **Pineapple Plunger** each offer steep drops, twists, and turns of varying degrees as you're sent careening through an old, rusted-out fruit factory. Intense jets of water actually propel riders back uphill at one point. Recently replacing the original rafts are new two-person rafts with padded bottoms (similar to those used at the AquaDuck slide on the *Disney Dream* cruise ship), making for a more comfortable ride.

Ketchakiddie Creek   Many of the park's other attractions require guests to be older children, teens, or adults, but this section is a **kiddie area** exclusively for 2- to 5-year-olds. An innovative water playground, it has bubbling fountains to frolic in, miniature water slides, a pint-size "white-water" tubing run, spouting whales and squirting seals, rubbery crocodiles to climb on, grottoes to explore, and waterfalls to loll under. It's also small enough for you to take good home videos or photographs.

Closed for the Winter

Both Disney water parks are refurbished annually on a rotating basis. That means if you're traveling in fall or winter, it is likely that one of the parks will be closed for a month or more. So if a water park is on your itinerary, ask in advance about closings.

Shark Reef   Guests are given free equipment (and instruction) for a 15-minute swim through this very small snorkeling area that includes a simulated coral reef populated by about 4,000 parrotfish, angelfish, yellowtail damselfish, and other cuties including small rays and sharks. If you don't want to get in, you can observe the fish via port-holes in a walk-through viewing area.

Typhoon Lagoon Surf Pool   This large (2.75-million gal.) and lovely lagoon is the size of two football fields and surrounded by a white sandy beach. It's the park's main swimming area. The chlorinated water has a turquoise hue much like the Caribbean. **Large waves** roll through the deeper areas every 90 seconds. A foghorn sounds to warn you when one is coming. Young children can wade in the lagoon's more peaceful tidal pools—**Blustery Bay** or **Whitecap Cove.** The lagoon is also home to a special early-morning surfing program provided by the **Ron Jon Surf School** (see "Staying Active," in chapter 6).

Water Slides   **Humunga Kowabunga** consists of three 214-foot Mount Mayday slides that propel you down the mountain on a serpentine route through waterfalls and bat caves and past nautical wreckage before depositing you into a bubbling catch pool; each offers slightly different views and 30-mph thrills. There's seating for non-Kowabunga folks whose kids have commissioned them to "watch me." Women should

1. Go in the afternoons, about 2pm, even in summer, if you can stand the heat that long and want to avoid crowds. The early birds usually are gone by then.
2. Go early in the week, when most of the weeklong guests are filling the lines at the theme parks.
3. Kids can get lost just as easily at a water park as at the other parks, and the consequences can be tragic. All Disney parks have lifeguards, usually wearing bright red suits, but, to be safe, make sure *you* are the first line of safety for the kids in your crew.
4. Women should remember the one-piece bathing-suit rule mentioned under "Water Slides," above. And all bathers should remember the **"wedgie" rule** on the more extreme rides, such as Summit Plummet (at Blizzard Beach, below). What's the "wedgie" rule? It's a principle of physics that causes you to start out wearing baggies and end up in a thong.
5. Use a waterproof sunscreen with an SPF of at least 30 and drink plenty of fluids. Despite all that water, it's easy to get dehydrated in summer.

wear a one-piece swimsuit on the slides (except those who don't mind putting on a show for gawkers). *Note:* You must be 48 inches or taller to ride. **Storm Slides** offer a tamer course through the park's man-made caves.

White-Water Rides Mount Mayday is the setting for three white-water rafting adventures—**Keelhaul Falls, Mayday Falls,** and **Gangplank Falls**—all offering steep drops coursing through caves and passing lush scenery. Keelhaul Falls has the most winding route, Mayday Falls has the steepest drops and fastest water, and the slightly tamer Gangplank Falls uses large tubes so that the whole family can pile on.

Blizzard Beach

Blizzard Beach ★★★ is the younger of Disney's water parks, a 66-acre "ski resort" in the midst of a tropical lagoon centering on the 90-foot—uh-oh—Mount Gushmore. There's a legend for this one as well. Apparently a freak snowstorm dumped tons of snow on Walt Disney World, leading to the creation of Florida's first—and, so far, only—mountain ski resort (complete with Ice Gator, the park's mascot). Naturally, when temperatures returned to their normal broiling range, the snow bunnies prepared to close up shop, when they realized—this is Disney, happy endings are a must—that what remained of their snow resort could be turned into a water park featuring the fastest and tallest waterlogged "ski" runs in the country. The base of Mount Gushmore has a sand beach with several other attractions, including a wave pool and a smaller version of the mount for younger children. The park is located off World Drive, just north of the All-Star Movie, Music, and Sports resorts.

ESSENTIALS

HOURS It's open from at least 10am to 5pm, with extended hours during holiday periods and summer (℃ **407/560-3400;** www.disneyworld.com).

ENTRANCE FEES A 1-day ticket to Blizzard Beach is $49 for adults, $41 for children 3 to 9, plus tax.

HELPFUL HINTS Arrive at or before opening to avoid long lines and to be sure you get in. Both beach towels ($2.50 per towel) and lockers ($8–$10) can be rented for the day, and you can buy any beachwear you forgot to bring at the **Beach Haus.** Grab something to eat at **Avalunch,** the **Warming Hut,** or **Lattawatta Lodge** (burgers, hot dogs, nachos, pizza, and sandwiches).

MAJOR ATTRACTIONS IN THE PARK

Cross Country Creek   Inner-tubers can float lazily along this park-circling 2,900-foot creek, but beware of the mysterious Polar Caves, where you'll get splashed with melting ice.

Melt-Away Bay   This 1-acre bobbing wave pool is fed by waterfalls of melting "snow" and features relatively calm waves.

Runoff Rapids   Another tube job, this one lets you careen down any of three twisting-turning runs, one of which sends you through darkness.

Ski-Patrol Training Camp   Designed for tweens and teens, it features a rope swing, a T-bar drop over water, slides like the wet and slippery **Mogul Mania** from the Mount, and a challenging ice-floe walk along slippery floating icebergs.

Slush Gusher   This superspeed slide travels along a snow-banked gully. *Note:* It has a 48-inch height minimum.

Snow Stormers   These three flumes descend from the top of Mount Gushmore and follow a switchback course through ski-type slalom gates.

Summit Plummet   Read *every* speed, motion, vertical-dip, wedgie, and hold-onto-your-breast-plate warning in this guide. Then, test your bravado in a bullring, a space shuttle, or dozens of other death-defying hobbies as a warm-up. This puppy starts pretty slowly, with a lift ride to the 120-foot summit. Then . . . well . . . kiss any kids

5

EXPLORING WALT DISNEY WORLD

Disney Water Parks

💬 DID YOU KNOW?

o Walt Disney World employs 60,000 cast members, making it the largest single-site employer in the United States.

o Mickey Mouse has more than 175 outfits, ranging from scuba gear to formal wear. But he's second banana to Minnie, who has 200.

o The number of Disney T-shirts sold by the parks each year could plaster the image of Mickey Mouse on the chest of every Chicagoan.

o Since 1971, the total miles logged by Walt Disney World monorail trains would be equal to more than 30 round-trips to the moon.

o Mowing the lawn at WDW is no joke. The staff mows 450,000 miles each year—the equivalent

of 18 trips around the Earth's equator.

o The WDW Laundry handles 240,000 pounds of laundry *a day!* To get the equivalent, you'd have to wash and dry a load every day for 44 years.

o More than a million pounds of watermelon are served every year at Walt Disney World Resort (watch out for flying seeds!).

o Walt Disney World gift shops sell about 500,000 character watches annually. Not surprisingly, most of them are Mickeys.

o According to Kodak estimates, about 4% of the amateur photographs snapped in the U.S. are taken at Walt Disney World.

or religious medal you may be carrying. Because, if you board, you *will enter* the self-proclaimed world's fastest body slide (I believe it!), a test of your courage and swimsuit that virtually goes straight down and has you moving *sans* vehicle at 60 mph by the catch pool (also known as the stop zone). Even the hardiest rider may find this one hard to handle; a veteran thrill-seeker described the experience as "15 seconds of paralyzing fear." *Note:* It has a 48-inch height minimum. Also, expectant mothers and people with neck, back, and heart problems shouldn't ride.

Teamboat Springs   On the World's longest white-water raft ride, your six-passenger raft twists down a 1,200-foot series of rushing waterfalls.

Tike's Peak   This kid-size version of Mount Gushmore offers short water slides, rideable animals, a snow castle, a squirting ice pond, and a fountain play area for young guests.

Toboggan Racers   Here's an eight-lane slide that sends you racing headfirst over exhilarating dips into a "snowy slope." (If you've ever been on one of those tall superslides at amusement parks, imagine doing it headfirst, on your belly, on a raft. This baby can pack a lot of zip by the end.)

OTHER WDW ATTRACTIONS

Note: All of the attractions mentioned in this section can be found on the "Walt Disney World Parks & Attractions" map, on p. 163.

Fantasia Gardens & Winter Summerland

Fantasia Gardens Miniature Golf ★★, located off Buena Vista Drive across from Disney's Hollywood Studios, offers two 18-hole miniature courses drawing inspiration from the Walt Disney classic cartoon of the same name. You'll find hippos, ostriches, and alligators on the **Fantasia Gardens** course, where the Sorcerer's Apprentice presides over the final hole. It's a good bet for beginners and kids. Seasoned minigolfers will probably prefer **Fantasia Fairways,** which is a scaled-down golf course complete with sand traps, water hazards, tricky putting greens, and holes ranging from 40 to 75 feet.

Santa Claus and his elves provide the theme for **Winter Summerland ★★**, which has two 18-hole miniature courses across from Blizzard Beach on Buena Vista Drive. The **Winter** course takes you from an ice castle to a snowman to the North Pole. The **Summer** course is pure Florida, from sandcastles to surfboards to a visit with Santa on the "Winternet."

Tickets at both venues are $12.78 for adults and $10.65 for children 3 to 9 (including tax). Both are open from 10am to 10 or 11pm daily. For information about Fantasia Gardens, call ✆ **407/560-4582.** For information about Winter Summerland, call ✆ **407/560-3000.** You can find both on the Internet at **www.disneyworld.com**.

ESPN Wide World of Sports Complex

The 200-acre ESPN Wide World of Sports Complex—known until 2009 as **Disney's Wide World of Sports**—has a 7,500-seat professional baseball stadium, 10 other baseball and softball fields, six basketball courts, 12 lighted tennis courts, a track-and-field complex, a golf driving range, and six sand volleyball courts. It's a haven for sports fans and wannabe athletes.

Note: The **Hess Sports Field North,** opened in the spring of 2005, is the first expansion of the sports venue since its opening in 1997. The addition features 20

DISNEYQUEST

The reaction that visitors have upon experiencing this popular attraction is often the same. No matter if it's from kids just reaching the video-game age, teens who are firmly hooked, or adults who never outgrew *Pong,* they leave saying: "Awesome!"

Four separate zones—**explore zone,** a virtual adventure land; **score zone,** a superhero competition city; **create zone,** where imagination and invention rule; and **replay zone,** filled with classic games but in a futuristic setting—ensure that everybody will be entertained . . . and likely for hours.

The five-level virtual-video arcade has everything from nearly old-fashioned pinball to virtual games and rides. Want appetizers?

Aladdin's Magic Carpet Ride puts you astride a motorcycle-like seat and flies through the 3-D Cave of Wonders. **Invasion! An ExtraTERRORestrial Alien Encounter** has the same kind of intensity. Your mission is to save colonists from intergalactic bad guys. One player flies the virtual module while others fire weapons.

Pirates of the Caribbean: Battle for Buccaneer Gold puts you and three mates in 3-D helmets so that you can battle pirate ships, virtual-reality style. One plays captain, steering your ship, while the others assume positions behind cannons to blast the black hearts into oblivion. Each time you do, you're rewarded with some doubloons, but

beware of the sea monsters that can gobble you and your treasure. In the final moments, you come face to face with a ghost ship, which can send you to Davy Jones's locker.

Try the **Mighty Ducks Pinball Slam** if you're a pinball fan. It's an interactive life-size game where you ride platforms and use body English to score points.

If you have an inventive mind, stop in at **CyberSpace Mountain** ★★, where Bill Nye the Science-Turned-Roller-Coaster-Guy helps you create the ultimate loop-and-dipster, which you can then ride in a simulator (yes, you'll actually turn upside down). It's a major hit with the coaster-crazy crowd.

Finally, if you need some quiet time, sign up at **Animation Academy** for a minicourse in Disney cartooning (a drawback, however, is that you'll have to fork out yet more bucks just to keep your artwork). There are also snack and food areas for those who need something more tangible than virtual refreshment.

DisneyQuest (✆ **407/828-4600;** www.disneyquest.com) is located in Downtown Disney West Side on Buena Vista Drive. The admission ($43 for adults, $37 for kids 3–9, plus 6.5% sales tax) allows you unlimited play from 11:30am to 11pm (until midnight Fri–Sat). Unfortunately, heavy crowds tend to gather here after 1pm, which can cut into your fun and patience.

acres of playing fields, with space for four football/soccer fields and four baseball/softball diamonds.

The complex is located on Victory Way, just north of U.S. 192 and west of I-4 (✆ **407/939-1500;** www.disneyworldsports.com). It's open daily from 10am to 5pm; the cost is $13.55 for adults, $9.34 for kids 3 to 9. Organized programs and events include the following:

○ The **Multi-Sports Experience** challenges guests with a variety of activities, covering many sports: football, baseball, basketball, hockey, soccer, and volleyball. It's open only on select days.

- The **Atlanta Braves** play 16 spring-training games during a 1-month season that begins in early March. Tickets cost $15 to $28 through Ticketmaster (📞 **407/939-4263**).
- The **NFL, NBA, NCAA, PGA,** and **Harlem Globetrotters** also host events, sometimes annually and sometimes more frequently, at the complex. Admission varies by event.

Richard Petty Driving Experience & Indy Racing Experience

Test Track is for sissies. The **Richard Petty Driving Experience,** and now the **Indy Racing Experience,** both located at the WDW Speedway, give you a chance to do the real thing in a 600-horsepower NASCAR car. How real is it? Expect to sign a two-page waiver that features words like *dangerous* and *calculated risk* before you climb in. At one end of the spectrum, you can ride shotgun for a couple of laps at 145 mph ($116.09, including tax, at the Richard Petty Experience; $109 at the Indy Experience). At the other, spend from 3 hours to 2 days learning how to drive the car yourself and race fellow daredevils in 8 to 30 laps of excitement ($478.19–$1,383.44, including tax, at the Richard Petty Experience; $399 for 8 laps at the Indy Experience). *Note:* You must be at least 18 years old to do this. Richard Petty operates daily from 9am until 4pm, the Indy Experience daily from 4pm until dusk. For reservations at Richard Petty Driving Experience, call 📞 **800/237-3889** or go to **www.1800 bepetty.com**. For reservations at the Indy Racing Experience, call 📞 **888/357-5002,** or head to **www.indyracingexperience.com**.

EXPLORING BEYOND DISNEY: UNIVERSAL ORLANDO, SEAWORLD & OTHER ATTRACTIONS

"Anything you can do, we can do better." This seems to be the Orlando motto. Every time one park adds an attraction, the next park feels the need to add two attractions (or at least one that's far more impressive), and so on, and so on, and so on. This has been going on since Mickey first arrived in town. The game of cat and mouse between Disney and its top-ranked challenger Universal Orlando, which each year since 1999 has chipped away at what was once WDW's virtual monopoly, however, is all good—at least for you and me. Each time one park tries to outdo the other, we reap the benefits of their additions. Still, make no mistake: Disney is king, leading in theme parks (4:2) and smaller attractions (9:1). Disney may have lost its edge in nightclub venues when it closed the clubs on Pleasure Island, but it retains a huge lead in restaurants, and, when it comes to hotel rooms, its lead is insurmountable.

Nevertheless, Universal is trying. It had a substantial growth spurt in 1999, bolstering its original park, **Universal Studios Florida,** with a second theme park, **Islands of Adventure;** a nightclub and restaurant complex, **CityWalk;** and its first resort, **Portofino Bay,** a 750-room Loews hotel. In 2001, it opened a second resort, the **Hard Rock Hotel;** and, in 2002, it followed up with the **Royal Pacific Resort.** In 2009, **Hollywood Rip Ride Rockit,** an interactive musically themed mega-coaster, made its debut. Universal then sent J. K. Rowling fans into a tizzy when it announced it would open the **Wizarding World of Harry Potter** in Islands of Adventure. Universal Orlando still has plenty of room for expansion beyond that, and, while the company's lips are sealed, it's known there are plans for at least two more hotels (but even though signs of an economic upswing are beginning to surface, I wouldn't expect to see any construction just yet). In the meantime, they've partnered with several area hotels in an effort to broaden their offerings. A golf course and acres of additional rides and attractions, while not likely for several years to come, are not inconceivable in the future.

A few miles south, **SeaWorld** and its sister park, **Discovery Cove,** also grab a share of the Orlando action. In 2004, SeaWorld added a 5-acre shopping and dining area, appropriately named the Waterfront, and in 2007 expanded the children's area (now double its original size), adding six kid-friendly ocean-themed rides. In 2009, Manta, SeaWorld's single most expensive (not to mention ambitious) attraction to date, was making waves, while just across the street, Discovery Cove carved out the Grand Reef in 2011 (bringing with it a unique underwater walking tour), expanding its islandlike offerings. **Aquatica,** an innovative eco-edutainment themed water park (and the first new park to open in Orlando in over 8 years), made a splashy debut in 2008 (and Omaka Rocka, a surf-inspired slide, was added to its lineup in 2010), taking its own bite out of the city's ever-changing market.

Aside from greater variety, these players mean more multiday packages and special deals for you. To compete with Disney, SeaWorld and Universal Orlando teamed up on multiday pass options a few years back. They currently offer a **FlexTicket** that also includes admission to **Wet 'n Wild** (a Universal-owned water park) and has an optional add-on that includes **Busch Gardens** in Tampa (p. 337).

While the wars rage on in the traditional tourist areas, it has finally dawned on the rest of Orlando that Central Florida is one of the world's favorite vacation destinations. Since the early 1990s, and most notably in the past few years, downtown Orlando has undergone a transformation in hopes of wooing tourists to its own set of attractions, nightclubs, and restaurants. Expansions at the Orlando Museum of Art and the Orlando Science Center, combined with a number of upscale dining options and trendy clubs, shows the city is trying to grab back a share of tourist dollars. This expansion means visitors can enjoy the spoils: more variety, greater opportunities, and a world beyond the theme parks.

THE FLEXTICKET The most economical way to see the various "other-than-Disney" parks is with a multiday pass that counters Disney's Park Hopper add-on. With the **FlexTicket,** you pay one price to visit any of the participating parks as many times as you want during a 14-day period. A five-park pass to Universal Studios Florida, Islands of Adventure, Wet 'n Wild, Aquatica, and SeaWorld is $274.95 for adults and $254.95 for children 3 to 9. A six-park pass, which adds Busch Gardens in Tampa, is $314.95 for adults and $294.95 for kids. Both passes also include entrance to Universal CityWalk. The FlexTicket can be ordered through Universal (© **407/363-8000;** www.universalorlando.com), SeaWorld (© **407/351-3600;** www.seaworld.com), Aquatica (© **800/363-2559**; www.aquaticabyseaworld.com), or Wet 'n Wild (© **800/992-9453** or 407/351-1800; www.wetnwild.com). *Note:* There's a round-trip shuttle available to Busch Gardens (p. 337) that's free for Flex-Ticket buyers (it's $10 for other guests).

UNIVERSAL EXPRESS PLUS PASS This is Universal's answer to Disney's FASTPASS; however, at Universal, you'll pay a price (literally) to skip the long lines. Single-day and multiday ticket buyers not staying at a Universal resort can purchase

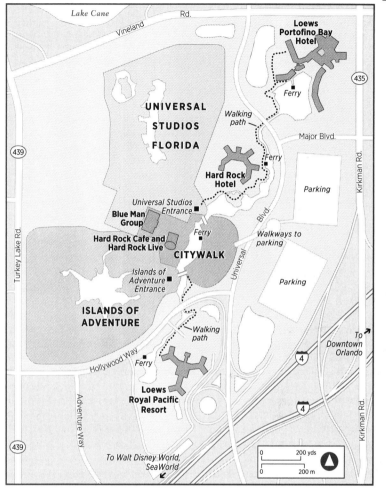

an Express Plus Pass that's good for either 1 day at one park ($19.99–$59.99) or 1 day at two parks ($25.99–$69.99). The downside (other than having to fork out the extra cash): Express Plus Passes are good only on select dates during the year (for a complete list, see Universal's website), and they are only valid for a single entry to each ride featuring an express line. In other words, you can only wait in the express line for the Hulk once; if you want to ride a second (or third, or fourth) time, you'll have to head to the regular line with everyone else. And if you are a multiday ticket holder, the Express Plus Pass is only good for a single day—you'll have to purchase an additional Express Plus Pass if you want to skip the long lines for more than just a single day. Another option (albeit far more pricy than the first) is to purchase the 2-Park Express VIP Pass (good for btw. 1 and 4 days during a consecutive 14-day period) that allows unlimited express access at both parks for as long as the ticket is valid. A 4-day VIP ticket costs between $285.99 and $365.99 for adults (depending on the season), and between $269.99 and $349.99 for kids 3 to 9. The 1-day option costs between $169.99 and $209.99 for adults and between $159.99 and $199.99 for kids.

The plus in Express Plus: Waits are usually 15 minutes or less. Be aware, however, that passes are not unlimited and can run out during busier times (especially as they are now available ahead of time online). If you're at the parks during peak season (when lines grow even more intolerable, as those who have purchased Express Plus back things up even more), really can't stand waiting in line, and have plenty of cash to spare, the pass may be worth your while (but it's not likely); otherwise, don't bother.

A family of four would be far better off spending the extra bucks ($80–$260 for Express Plus Passes, $620–$780 for Express VIP Passes—and that's only for single-day access) to stay at one of Universal's resorts (even if only for a portion of your vacation). Guests of the Portofino Bay, Hard Rock, and Royal Pacific hotels (see chapter 3, "Where to Stay") need only show their room key to skip the long lines. And the best part: Resort guests are allowed unlimited express-line access for the length of their stay. Call ✆ **407/363-8000** or go to **www.universalorlando.com** for more information.

UNIVERSAL STUDIOS FLORIDA

Fast-paced thrill rides, edgy themes, and meticulously detailed movie-style sets are a signature of this popular theme park. Here, the hottest blockbuster films come to life, jumping off the screen and right into the theme park—and park-goers are immersed in all the action. In addition to its lineup of adrenaline-boosting rides, grown-up shows, and smattering of kid-friendly attractions, USF is also a working production studio, so on occasion you might get a chance to catch live filming as it's taking place.

Attractions & Rides   Coaster-junkies should head straight for **Hollywood Rip Ride Rockit** and **Revenge of the Mummy.** Tweens and teens (and even adults) with a taste for action and adventure can shoot it out with alien invaders on **Men in Black Alien Attack,** take on a great white on **Jaws,** survive a Richter-rocking earthquake on **Disaster!,** or experience a swirling storm on **Twister.** The touchy-feely effects of **Shrek 4-D** amuse crowds of all ages (though its humor is a bit beyond younger riders).

Restaurants & Dining   For sit-down dining, **Lombard's** serves up a waterside view and a menu of seafood, pasta, and salads. Taste a slice of the Big Apple at **Louie's Italian Restaurant.** Fifties buffs should head to **Mel's Diner,** inspired by the likes of *American Graffiti* and complete with neon signage and a lot filled with classic cars; its burgers are among the best in the park.

Nightlife & Entertainment   After-dark laser-light productions and plenty of edgy action-packed shows, including **Fear Factor Live!, Total Nonstop Action Wrestling–Impact,** and **Blue Man Group** (a separately ticketed show, and one of the park's most recent additions) round out the offerings. **Universal 360: A Cinesphere Spectacular** projects images of blockbuster hits across four tremendous cinespheres in the park's central lagoon, with 300 outdoor speakers, lasers, and pyrotechnic effects adding to the spectacle.

Special Events   Past lineups of the **Summer Concert Series** have featured Third Eye Blind, Nelly, the Go-Go's, and Boys Like Girls. You're in for the scare of a lifetime during the frightfully haunting **Halloween Horror Nights** (the annual nightmarish event strictly geared towards older teens and adults). Ring in the holidays watching the **Macy's Holiday Parade** as it marches its way through the park, complete with several floats and gigantic balloons from the original Macy's Thanksgiving Day Parade in New York.

Essentials

GETTING TO UNIVERSAL BY CAR   Universal Orlando is a half-mile north of I-4 exit 75B, Kirkman Road/Highway 435. There may be construction in the area, so follow the signs directing you to the parks.

PARKING   If you park in the multilevel garages, write down the theme and row in your area to help you find your car later. Parking costs $15 for cars, light trucks, and vans; spots closest to the entranceway cost $20. Valet parking is $25. Universal's garages are connected to its parks and have moving sidewalks, but it's still a long walk.

TICKET PRICES   In advance of the Wizarding World's grand opening (back in 2010), Universal decided it would be in its best interest to overhaul its entire ticketing schedule; the result is a ticketing system similar to (but not exactly like) Disney's, with single-park tickets and multipark tickets good for between 1 and 7 days. Currently a **1-day, one-park ticket** costs $85 for adults, $79 for children 3 to 9. A **2-day, one-park-per-day ticket,** good for admission to either of Universal's major theme parks (Universal Studios or Islands of Adventure) on each day your ticket is valid, runs $115.99 for adults, $105.99 for children. As the number of days increases, so does the ticket price. A **1-day park-to-park access ticket** (allowing you to park-hop between Universal Studios and Islands of Adventure) costs $120.99 for adults, $114.99 for children 3 to 9. A **2-day park-to-park ticket** costs $135.99 for adults, $125.99 for children; again, as the number of days increases, so does the ticket price (up to a 4-day park-to-park access ticket at a cost of $155.99 for adults, $142.99 for children)—but the bonus is the cost per day goes down substantially as the number of days your ticket is good for increases (a 4-day park-to-park access ticket averaging less than $40 per day). Tickets purchased at the gate cost an extra $20 each. A **two-park premier annual pass** runs $349.99 (any age). The latter includes unlimited admission to the parks (no blackout dates), free self-parking, free valet parking on most days, Universal Express Plus privileges after 4pm, all-club access at CityWalk, and a slew of discounts good at Universal parks and resorts. A **two-park preferred annual pass** is less expensive at $229.99 (any age) and includes unlimited admission to the parks (no blackout dates), free self-parking, and numerous discounts good at Universal parks and resorts.

Like Disney, Universal offers savings on tickets if you purchase them before you leave home. Buy your park tickets online (single or park-to-park), and you'll save $20 per ticket, adding up to a substantial savings for families. You can pick up your tickets at the front gate of either park or have them sent (for a delivery charge) to your home. Using the print-at-home option, while adding $2.15 to your ticket, can be a real timesaver. Note that the type of tickets offered (and the various special offers associated with them) often come and go, so be sure to check Universal's website at **www.universalorlando.com** when planning your vacation and your budget.

All multiday passes let you move between Universal Studios Florida and Islands of Adventure. *Multiday passes also give you free access to the CityWalk clubs at night.* Because the parks are within walking distance of each other, you won't lose much time jockeying back and forth, which is not the case at Disney. Nevertheless, it's a long walk for tykes and people with limited mobility, so consider a stroller or wheelchair.

Universal Studios Florida

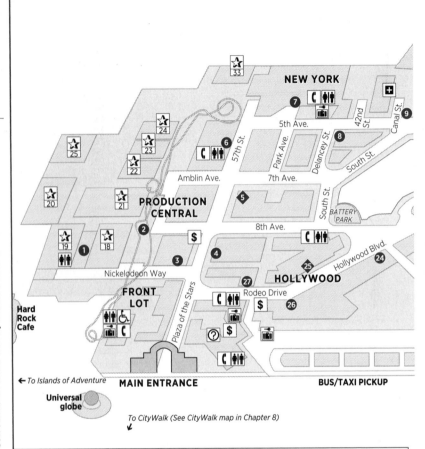

← To Islands of Adventure **MAIN ENTRANCE** **BUS/TAXI PICKUP**

Universal globe

To CityWalk (See CityWalk map in Chapter 8)
↓

PRODUCTION CENTRAL
Blue Man Group **1**
Despicable Me
 (opening in 2012) **3**
Hollywood Rip Ride Rockit **2**
Shrek 4-D **4**

NEW YORK
The Blues Brothers **8**
Revenge of the Mummy **7**
Twister...Ride It Out **6**

SAN FRANCISCO/AMITY
Beetlejuice's Graveyard Revue **9**
Disaster! A Major Motion Picture
 Ride...Starring You **11**
Fear Factor Live! **14**
JAWS **13**
Universal 360: A Cinesphere
 Spectacular **10**

WORLD EXPO
Men in Black: Alien Attack **15**
The Simpsons **16**

WOODY WOODPECKER'S KIDZONE
Animal Actors
 on Location! **18**
Curious George
 Goes to Town **20**
A Day in the Park
 with Barney **19**
E.T. Adventure **23**
Fievel's Playland **22**
Woody Woodpecker's
 Nuthouse Coaster **21**

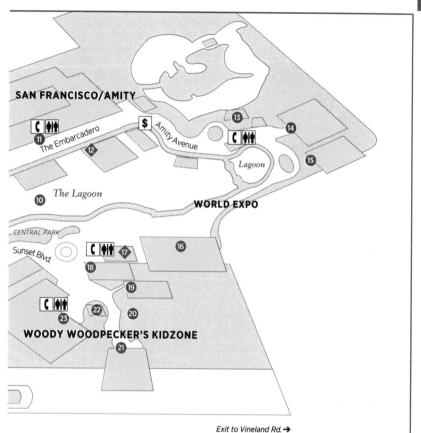

SAN FRANCISCO/AMITY

The Embarcadero 11

Amity Avenue

12

13

14

Lagoon

15

The Lagoon 10

WORLD EXPO

CENTRAL PARK

Sunset Blvd.

16

17

18

19

22

23

20

WOODY WOODPECKER'S KIDZONE

21

Exit to Vineland Rd. →

HOLLYWOOD
Lucy, A Tribute **27**
Terminator 2: 3-D Battle
 Across Time **26**
Universal Horror
 Make-Up Show **24**

DINING ◆
Classic Monsters Cafe **5**
International Food
 and Film Festival **17**
Lombard's Seafood Grille **12**
Schwab's Pharmacy **25**

☆	Film & TV Production Stage
$	Banking
✚	First Aid
🛅	Lockers
�	Restrooms
☎	Telephones
?	Guest Services
♿	Wheelchair & Stroller Rental

Like Disney, Universal juggles park hours to adjust for varying attendance due to seasonal shifts and holidays. The hours listed in this chapter are generally accurate, but sometimes the parks close earlier, or some rides or shows open later. To avoid disappointment, check the park's website at **www.universal orlando.com**, or call ✆ **407/363-8000** for up-to-the-minute schedules.

See the beginning of this chapter for information on the **FlexTicket,** which provides multiday admission to Universal Studios Florida, Islands of Adventure, SeaWorld, and Wet 'n Wild.

There are also 5-hour **VIP tours** at either Universal Studios Florida or Islands of Adventure, which include a guided tour, free valet parking, refreshments, and line-cutting privileges at a number of high-profile attractions, among other perks, for $150 per person. A 7-hour, two-park VIP tour covers both parks and costs $185 per person. Prices for both tours do not include 6.5% tax and *do not include admission to the parks!* For more information on the VIP tour, call ✆ **407/363-8295,** or send an e-mail to **viptours@universalorlando.com**. Tours start at 10am and noon daily. Anyone 17 and under must be accompanied by a paying adult. If you plan on visiting during peak season, if money isn't an issue, and if you aren't staying at one of the Universal resorts, this is a good way to experience the best of the park without having to spend most of your day in lines.

HOURS   The park is open 365 days a year, usually at least from 9am to 6pm, though it's open as late as 8 or 9pm, sometimes later, in summer and around holidays. The best bet is to call before you go so that you're not caught by surprise.

Making Your Visit More Enjoyable
PLANNING YOUR VISIT
You can get information before you leave home by calling **Universal Orlando Guest Services** at ✆ **877/801-9720** or 407/363-8000. Ask about travel packages as well as theme-park information. Universal sometimes offers a promotion that adds additional days free or at a deeply discounted price. You can also write to Guest Services, 1000 Universal Studios Plaza, Orlando, FL 32819-7601.

Online, you can find information about Universal Orlando at **www.universal orlando.com**. Orlando's daily newspaper, the *Orlando Sentinel,* also produces **OrlandoSentinel.com.** Additionally, there's a lot of information about the parks, hotels, restaurants, and more at the Orlando/Orange County Convention & Visitors Bureau site at **www.visitorlando.com**. Two unofficial but thorough sites worth a peek are **www.mouseearsandmore.com** and **www.allearsnet.com.**

FOR VISITORS WITH SPECIAL NEEDS
Guests with disabilities should go to **Guest Services,** located just inside the main entrance, for a *Rider's Guide for Rider Safety & Guests with Disabilities,* a Telecommunications Device for the Deaf (TDD), or other special assistance. You can rent a standard wheelchair for $12 or an electric one for $50 (both require a signed rental agreement and a $50 deposit). You can reserve them a week or more in advance by calling ✆ **407/224-6350.** You can arrange for sign language interpreting services at no charge by calling ✆ **888/519-4899** (toll-free TDD), 407/224-4414 (local TDD), or

407/224-5929 (voice). Make arrangements for an appointment with an interpreter 1 to 2 weeks in advance. Information is also available at **www.universalorlando.com**.

Tip: The *Rider's Guide* is also a great tool for parents, as it describes in detail the various rides' special effects, warnings, and height requirements, plus general guest services information at both Universal parks.

Note that some of the park's best rides are action-based thrill rides, so your options are limited if you are pregnant, are prone to motion sickness, or have heart, neck, or back problems. The same applies to smaller children. Review the rides and restrictions on the following pages or when you enter the park so that you don't stand in line for something you're unable to enjoy. (There are stationary areas available at some moving rides. Check your park guide under "expectant mothers," as well as the boards in front of each ride, and then ask the attendants for help as you enter.) A child-swap program (allowing parents to switch off on rides without having to stand in line twice) is available at the rides as well.

BEST TIME OF YEAR TO VISIT

As at Disney World, there's really no off season for Universal, but the week after Labor Day until mid-December (excluding Thanksgiving week) and January to mid-May (excluding spring break) are known for smaller crowds, cooler weather, and less humid air. And you won't have to worry about the daily thunderstorms that often plague Orlando during the warmer months. The summer months, when the masses throng to the parks, are the worst time for crowds and feature hot, sticky, humid days.

BEST DAYS TO VISIT

Go near the end of the week, on a Thursday or Friday. The pace is somewhat fast Monday through Wednesday, with the heaviest crowds on weekends and during summers and holidays. If you do end up visiting during peak seasons or on holidays (when the parks are open late), consider waiting until late afternoon and staying until closing time—after the dinner hour the parks are generally much less crowded.

Note: Universal Studios Florida is probably the best of all the major theme parks to visit when the weather is bleak simply because the majority of its rides and attractions are indoors (there's still a ton of walking outdoors, but at least you don't have to worry about many of the attractions closing because of lightning or heavy rain). A shower or two is almost inevitable in Central Florida on a summer afternoon, but if the forecast for the day calls for a sustained downpour, then USF is a great bet.

AGE-APPROPRIATE RIDES/SHOWS

Here, as in Walt Disney World, height and age restrictions aren't bent to accommodate a screaming child. Even where restrictions don't exist, some shows have loud music and pyrotechnics that can scare young kids. Check the attraction descriptions that follow to make sure your child won't be unduly disappointed or frightened.

 Universal Has a Few 'Toons, Too

While the options pale in comparison to Disney, Universal has character meet-and-greets on a rotating basis. At **Universal Studios Florida,** you may run into the Simpsons, Scooby-Doo, SpongeBob SquarePants, Shrek, the Rugrats, and Jimmy Neutron, among others. At **Islands of Adventure,** the cast may include Spider-Man, Captain America, the X-Men, Popeye and Olive Oyl, the Cat in the Hat, Betty Boop, or Boris and Natasha.

Universal Studios Florida

Universal Orlando announced the addition of two themed miniature golf courses soon to be built at the City-Walk entertainment complex. They'll be located next to the AMC Universal Cineplex movie theater, attracting the attention of park-goers as they make their way along the walkway leading to CityWalk from the parking garage. Slated to open in summer 2012,

Hollywood Drive-In Golf will have guests putting their way through haunted graveyards, flying saucers, and spider-infested basements. In line with the park's edgy themes and signature attention to detail, the 1950s sci-fi-inspired courses (aptly named "The Haunting of Ghostly Green" and "Invaders from Planet Putt") will surely be an out-of-this-world experience.

Overall, Universal Studios does a much better job in the way of entertaining its guests while they wait in line for the attractions (though recent upgrades at Disney have ensured there are a few notable exceptions). Many have preshows or TV screens with previews or introductions to the attractions. They've also got it all over the House of Mouse when it comes to beating the sun—many of the attractions here have waiting areas under some sort of cover or, in some cases, indoors (unless the line is so long that it extends beyond these areas, which it sometimes does in the busiest seasons). It is also exponentially easier to get from your car (or resort) to the parks. From the parking lot, if you have kids and all of the gear that comes with them, pack your stroller and bring it along—you will be able to walk directly to the parks, though it can be a long haul for small feet (and there are no trams from the parking decks to the theme parks). Elevators, moving sidewalks, and covered walkways will take you up to the entrance of CityWalk. And, if you're staying at a Universal resort, you'll be glad to know that all three resorts are relatively close by and are serviced by a water taxi that'll drop you off in CityWalk (and the Hard Rock is within walking distance). I'm not saying that you will not have to wait at all—it can take several minutes—but not nearly as long as some trips at Disney can.

Suggested Itineraries

Pick three or four things that you must see or do and plan your day along a rough geographical guide. Universal Studios Florida and Islands of Adventure are both relatively small, so walking from one end of the park to the other isn't as daunting as it is at some of the Disney parks.

FOR FAMILIES WITH YOUNG CHILDREN

Waste no time: Hoof it to **Woody Woodpecker's KidZone,** where you and your kids can spend most of the day. If they're 36 inches or taller, don't miss multiple rides on **Woody Woodpecker's Nuthouse Coaster.** Try to make an early pit stop at **Fievel's Playland** (especially its water slide, which is slow-moving and has longer lines after 10:30am). Then adopt a leisurely pace to see **E.T. Adventure, A Day in the Park with Barney,** and, if you can squeeze it in, **Animal Actors on Location!**

Take a stroll down Hollywood Boulevard to **Mel's Diner** for a burger and a shake (and a brief reprieve from the chaos) before heading back and letting the kids loose at the wet-and-wild **Curious George Goes to Town.** After your kids have run down their batteries a bit, you can rest your feet at an afternoon showing of **Animal Actors on Location!** (if you didn't catch it before lunch).

FOR OLDER CHILDREN, TEENS & ADULTS

A single day is usually sufficient to see the park if you arrive early and keep a fairly brisk pace. Skip the city sidewalks of the main gate and Terminator 2: 3-D Battle Across Time until later. Go to the right and tackle the **Simpsons** and **Men in Black Alien Attack,** and then make a counterclockwise loop to catch **Fear Factor Live!, Jaws, Disaster! A Major Motion Picture Ride . . . Starring You!, Revenge of the Mummy,** and **Twister . . . Ride It Out.** Break for lunch at some point in the midst of that quartet (there are plenty of eateries along the route), and then tackle the **Shrek 4-D** adventure, before catching the fun in **Terminator 2: 3-D Battle Across Time.** If you can manage to wait, save **Hollywood Rip Ride Rockit** (which debuted in mid-2009) for last, as lines will be longest early in the day.

A second day lets you revisit some of your favorites or see those you missed. With the pressure to hit all the major rides lessened, you can take on the park in a more leisurely fashion, ensuring a more enjoyable experience. You can also visit the **Universal Horror Make-up Show** and **Beetlejuice's Graveyard Revue.**

Money Saver

You can save 10% off your purchases at many Universal Orlando gift shops and restaurants by showing your AAA card. Note that this discount isn't available at food and merchandise carts or on tobacco, candy, film, collectibles, and sundry items.

Services & Facilities in Universal Studios Florida

ATMS Machines accepting cards from banks using the Cirrus, Honor, and PLUS systems are to the right of the main entrance (outside and inside the park) and in San Francisco/Amity near Lombard's Landing restaurant.

BABY CARE Changing tables are in men's and women's restrooms; there are nursing facilities at Family Services, just inside the main entrance and to the right. A very limited amount of baby supplies is sold at select stores on the premises, so come prepared if you have little ones.

CAMERAS & FILM Film and disposable cameras are available at the On Location shop in the Front Lot, just inside the main entrance. One-hour photo developing is available, though I don't recommend paying park prices.

CAR ASSISTANCE Battery jumps are provided. If you need assistance with your car, raise the hood and use the call boxes located throughout the garage to call for security.

FIRST AID The First Aid station is located between New York and San Francisco, next to Louie's Italian Restaurant on Canal Street. There's also one just inside the main entrance next to Guest Services.

LOCKERS Lockers are across from Guest Services near the main entrance and cost $8 or $10 a day, depending on the size.

LOST CHILDREN If you lose a child, go to Guest Services near the main entrance or contact any park employee for assistance. *Children younger than 7 should wear name-tags inside their clothing.*

PET CARE A kennel is available ($15 a day) near the parking lot. Ask the parking attendant for directions upon entering the toll plaza. Overnight boarding is not permitted. Owners are responsible for walking and feeding their pets during their stay.

FROMMER'S RATES THE rides

As I do for the Disney parks in chapter 5, "Exploring Walt Disney World," I use a grading system to score the Universal Orlando and SeaWorld rides in this chapter. (I return to the star-rating system toward the end of the chapter, where I explore some of Orlando's smaller attractions.) Most of the grades below are *As*, *Bs*, and *Cs*. That's because the major parks' designers have done a pretty good job on the attractions. But you'll also find a few *Ds* for Duds.

Here's what the Frommer's ratings mean:

A+ = Your trip wouldn't be complete without it.

A = Put it at the top of your to-do list.

B+ = Make a real effort to see or do it.

B = It's fun but not a must-see.

C+ = A nice diversion; see it if you have time.

C = Go if it appeals to you but not if there's a wait.

D = Don't waste your time.

STROLLER RENTAL Strollers can be rented in Amity and at Guest Services just inside the entrance to the right. The cost (including tax) is $15 to $18 for a single, $25 to $28 for a double.

WHEELCHAIR RENTAL Regular wheelchairs can be rented for $12 in the central hub of the walkway between the parking complex and CityWalk or at Guest Services just inside the main gate. Electric wheelchairs are $50. Both require a $50 deposit and a signed rental contract.

Major Attractions at Universal Studios Florida

Rides and attractions here combine technology and special effects to produce excellent entertainment. While waiting in line, you'll be entertained by excellent pre-shows—far better than those at the Disney parks (some are as entertaining as the attractions themselves). Universal, as a whole, takes itself less seriously than the Mouse, and the atmosphere is peppered by subtle reminders that in the competitive theme-park industry, it's really not such a small world after all.

Animal Actors on Location!
Frommer's Rating: B+ for young kids and parents
Recommended Ages: All ages
Get an up-close look at Hollywood's hottest animal actors as they entertain audience members in a 20-minute multimedia show that combines video clips and lots of live action.

Beetlejuice's Graveyard Revue
Frommer's Rating: C+ for classic rock fans, C for others
Recommended Ages: 10–adult
This rock musical stars Dracula, Wolfman, the Phantom of the Opera, Frankenstein and his bride, and Beetlejuice. The fun includes pyrotechnic special effects, some adult jokes, and MTV-style choreography. It's loud and lively enough to scare some small children and frazzle some older adults. It carries Universal's PG-13 rating, meaning it may not be suitable for preteens.

A Day in the Park with Barney
Frommer's Rating: A+ for tiny tots and parents, D for almost everyone else

Recommended Ages: 2–6

Set in a parklike theater-in-the-round, this 25-minute musical stars the Purple One, Baby Bop, and BJ. It uses song, dance, and interactive play to entertain the kids. This could be the highlight of the day for preschoolers (parents can console themselves with their kids' happiness). The playground adjacent to the theater has chimes to ring, treehouses to explore, and lots to intrigue wee ones. The theater is air-conditioned, so if you must endure this one, you'll at least be comfortable.

Disaster! A Major Motion Picture Ride . . . Starring You!

Frommer's Rating: A

Recommended Ages: 6–adult

Replacing the popular (albeit dated) Earthquake, Disaster! still rocks the Richter scale. While the ride itself remains relatively identical to its predecessor, tweaks to the storyline (placing you smack in the middle of filming for *Mutha Nature*, a fictitious action adventure flick) and updated high-tech special effects add a unique interactive element to the revamped experience. That said, you still climb aboard an underground train, when suddenly an earthquake hits—and a big one, at 8.3 on the Richter scale! As you sit helplessly trapped, slabs of concrete collapse around you, a propane truck bursts into flames, a runaway train hurtles your way, and the station floods, with 65,000 gallons of water cascading down the steps. A tongue-in-cheek trailer, created from clips filmed during the ride, caps off the experience. **Note:** Universal says expectant moms should skip this one.

E.T. Adventure

Frommer's Rating: B for preteens and their families

Recommended Ages: All ages

You'll soar with E.T. on a mission to save his ailing planet, through the forest and into space aboard a bicycle. Along the way, you'll also meet some of the characters created by Steven Spielberg for the ride, including Botanicus, Tickli Moot Moot, Horn Flowers, and Tympani Tremblies. This family favorite is definitely a charmer. If there is a knock, it's that there are two waiting areas—inside and outside. And wait you will.

Fear Factor Live!

Frommer's Rating: B for most, D for those who can't stomach the stunts

Recommended Ages: 8 and older

Having debuted in the spring of 2005, Fear Factor Live! is the first reality show (based on NBC's blockbuster hit *Fear Factor*) to become a theme-park attraction. Audience members willing to sign up perform stunts that test their courage, strength, and, at times, their stomach—similar to the stuff seen on the TV show, but live in Orlando. You can catch the show in the venue set between Jaws and Men in Black. **Note:** At press time, Fear Factor Live! was operating only seasonally.

 Quiet on the Set!

The comedy, music, and multimedia theatrics of **Blue Man Group** have taken up residence in Orlando. This highly dynamic and unique group of wild and (at times) wacky performers wows audiences nightly at Universal Studios Florida at the Sharp Aquos Theater (previously Nickelodeon Studios), accessible from both Universal Studios and CityWalk. Park admission is not required for this separately ticketed show, which features two daily performances. Tickets for the show start at $74 for adults, $25 for children ages 3 to 9.

Survey Says!

In summer 2010, the **Family Feud** game show began taping at Universal Studios in front of a live studio audience. Taping is scheduled to run through the 2011 season (before moving to Atlanta in 2012). Park admission is not required, and seating is on a first-come, first-served basis. For schedule details, call ✆ **407/224-6000**.

Hollywood Rip Ride Rockit
Frommer's Rating: A
Recommended Ages: 10–adult

In 2009, Universal opened a new anchor attraction at Universal Studios Florida (a welcome departure from the recent onslaught of refits and replacement rides). Hollywood Rip Ride Rockit sports speeds of 65 mph, wild corkscrew turns, several near misses, and an incredible record-breaking noninverting loop that could turn the stomach of even hard-core coaster crazies. Suspended high above the walkways of Universal Studios and CityWalk, this all-new megacoaster takes riders on an interactive musical multisensory experience. The bonus, thanks to a sophisticated on- and off-board video system, is that riders get to piece together their own take-home music video from footage taken during the ride (for a fee, of course). **Note:** Like Universal's other top-notch thrillers, this ride touts the usual slew of warnings for riders who may be pregnant or have neck, back, or heart conditions (or any other medical condition that may be aggravated by riding). There is also a height restriction of between 51 and 79 inches.

Jaws
Frommer's Rating: B+
Recommended Ages: 6–adult

As your boat heads into the 7-acre, 5-million-gallon lagoon, a dorsal fin appears on the surface. Then, what goes with the fin—a 3-ton, 32-foot, mechanical great white shark—tries to sink its urethane teeth into your hide (or at least your boat's). A 30-foot wall of flame that surrounds the vessel truly causes you to feel the heat in this $45-million attraction. I won't tell you exactly how it ends, but in spite of a captain who can't hit the broad side of a dock with his grenade launcher, some lucky Orlando restaurant will be serving blackened shark tonight. **Tip:** The effects of this ride are far more spectacular after dark. **Note:** While it lacks a height requirement, the shark may be too intense for some kids younger than age 6, and Universal recommends that expectant mothers avoid it.

Jimmy Neutron's Nicktoon Blast
Frommer's Rating: A
Recommended Ages: 6–adult

At press time, Jimmy Neutron had hurtled through hyperspace and taken on the evil Yokians for the last time. A new ride will soon take its place, and though Universal has released few details, the rumor that it will be based on the blockbuster hit film *Despicable Me* has been officially confirmed. Rather than mimicking the original storyline, the all-new attraction will take riders alongside Gru and his three adorable little girls on an all-new adventure (with riders turned into minions sporting goofy goggles in order to help him deploy his latest wacky invention).

Men in Black Alien Attack

Frommer's Rating: A+

Recommended Ages: 6–adult

Armageddon may be upon us—unless you and your mates fly to the rescue and destroy the alien menace. Once on board your six-passenger cruiser, you'll buzz the streets of New York, using your "zapper" to splatter up to 120 bug-eyed targets. You have to contend with return fire and distractions such as light, noise, and clouds of liquid nitrogen (also known as fog), any of which can spin you out of control. Your laser tag–style gun fires infrared bullets. Earn a bonus by hitting Frank the Pug (to the right, just past the alien shipwreck). The 4-minute ride relies on 360-degree spins rather than speed for its thrill factor. At the conclusion, you're swallowed by a giant roach (it's 30 ft. tall with 8-ft. fangs and 20-ft. claws) that explodes, spraying you with bug guts—okay, it's just warm water—as you blast your way to safety and into the pest-control hall of fame—maybe. When you exit, Will Smith rates you anywhere from galaxy defender to bug bait. (There are 38 possible scores; those assigned to less than full cars suffer the scoring consequences.) Guests must be at least 42 inches tall to climb aboard this $70-million ride.

Note: Men in Black often has a *much* shorter line for single riders. Even if you're not alone but are willing to be split up, get in this line and hop right on a vehicle that has fewer than six passengers.

Revenge of the Mummy

Frommer's Ratings: A+

Recommended Ages: 10 and older

Ten years in the making, the $40-million Revenge of the Mummy made its debut in 2004. The indoor roller coaster uses a sophisticated propulsion system to hurtle riders through the shadowy, darkened tombs of ancient Egypt (all spectacularly re-created) while trying to escape the curse of the Mummy. The sound system—enhanced by 200 speakers and surround-sound technology in the coaster cars—will spook you, too. Highly advanced robotics are used to bring to life some pretty scary-looking skeletal warriors, one of whom jumps aboard your car; even Imhotep makes an appearance. Overhead flames, fireballs, and creepy creatures all combine with surprising twists, turns, stops, and starts to make for a thrill like no other in the park. And just when you think it's over . . . well, I have to leave some surprises for you.

Shrek 4-D

Frommer's Rating: B+

Recommended Ages: All ages

Still listed among the "newest" rides at Universal (although I think that's stretching it just a bit), this 20-minute show can be seen, heard, felt, and smelled thanks to film, motion simulators, OgreVision glasses, and other special effects, such as water spritzers. The attraction picks up where the original movie left off—allowing you to join Shrek and Princess Fiona on their honeymoon (at least the G-rated portions of it). After one of the most amusing preshows in the park—featuring a ghostly Lord Farquaad, the Three Little Pigs, Pinocchio, and the Magic Mirror—you're settled into specially designed seats in the main auditorium and then transported to the fairy-tale realm of Duloc as the screen comes alive. The theater's seats are pneumatic air-propulsion nodules that are capable of turning and tilting (though not dramatically). Again, if your kids don't like touchy-feely special effects, they may get upset at certain points while experiencing this attraction.

Guests holding multipark passes or annual passes purchased with an **American Express** card (either at the front gate or online at www.universalorlando.com) now have a place to sit, relax, and recharge (literally—the lounge features recharging stations for cameras and cellphones) before heading back out to the park to fight off aliens, tackle a twister, and survive a shark attack (not to mention those lengthy lines). The American Express Lounge opened in summer 2011 and can be found along the side street between Shrek 4-D and the Classic Monster Cafe. Complimentary beverages and light refreshments are available in air-conditioned comfort, with a concierge staff available to help with dining reservations and similar services. The lounge is open 7 days a week from noon to 5pm.

The Simpsons
Frommer's Rating: A+
Recommended Ages: 10 and up

Universal's *Back to the Future* ride, suffering from the ravages of time, went the way of the DeLorean and closed its doors for good in 2006. But with Universal real estate at a premium, the Simpsons wasted no time moving in, back in 2008. Homer, Marge, Bart, Lisa, and Maggie join in on all the fun and excitement, riding along (at top speed, I might add) on a hysterical adventure through a wild and wacky Krusty the Clown–created carnival.

An over-the-top Krustyland exterior gives way to the signature Universal queue hidden inside (an appropriate prelude of what's to come, filled with oversized attraction posters, video screens, and animated elements that hint at its predecessor). Krusty himself makes an appearance, taunting guests before entering the Fun House (okay, it's really just the small waiting area that opens onto the ride). From here, it becomes a bit more familiar as you board one of several elevated cars, each facing the gargantuan screen—though instead of time travel, you're off on a wild ride through Krustyland. Although a tweak to the motion simulator's mechanics has smoothed out the ride, expect to be bounced around just the same—the special effects, however, are enough to make you hold on for dear life. The cartoon's creator Matt Groening claims "the ride is designed to duplicate the *Simpsons* home-viewing experience, only at high speed and with lots of screaming." He's right!

Terminator 2: 3-D Battle Across Time
Frommer's Rating: A
Recommended Ages: 10–adult

This is billed as "the quintessential sight and sound experience for the 21st century!" The same director who made the movie, Jim Cameron, supervised this $60-million production. After a slow start, it builds into an impressive experience featuring the Governator (on film), along with other original cast members. It combines 70mm 3-D film (utilizing three 23×50-ft. screens) with thrilling technical effects and live stage action that includes a custom-built Harley-Davidson "Fat Boy" and six 8-foot-tall cyberbots. **Note:** The crisp 3-D effects are among the best in any Orlando park, but Universal has given this show a PG-13 rating, meaning the violence and loud noise may be too intense for preteens. That may be a little too cautious, but some kids younger than 10 may be frightened.

Twister . . . Ride It Out

Frommer's Rating: B+

Recommended Ages: 10–adult

Visitors from the twister-prone Midwest may find this re-creation a little too close to the real thing. An ominous funnel cloud, five stories tall, is created by swirling 2 million cubic feet of air per minute (that's enough to fill four full-size blimps), and the sound of a freight train fills the theater at rock-concert level as cars, trucks, and a cow fly about while the audience stands just 20 feet away. It's the windy version of the old *Earthquake* and packs quite a wallop. Crowds have been known to applaud when it's over. **Note:** This show, too, comes with a PG-13 rating. Its loudness and intensity certainly can be too much for children younger than 8.

Woody Woodpecker's Nuthouse Coaster ☺

Frommer's Rating: A+ for kids and parents, B+ for others

Recommended Ages: 5–adult

This is the top attraction in Woody Woodpecker's KidZone, an 8-acre concession Universal Studios made a while back after being criticized for having too little for young visitors. This ride is a kiddie coaster that will thrill some moms and dads, too. While only 30 feet at its peak, it offers quick, spiraling turns while you sit in a miniature steam train. The ride lasts only 55 seconds, and waits can be 30 minutes or more, but few kids will want to miss it. It's very much like the Barnstormer at Goofy's Wiseacre Farm in the Magic Kingdom (currently closed due to the Fantasyland expansion). **Note:** Its height minimum is 36 inches.

Additional Attractions

The somewhat corny **Universal Horror Make-Up Show** gives behind-the-scene looks at what goes into (and oozes out of) some of Hollywood's most frightening monsters (PG-13, shows from 11am). **Lucy, A Tribute** is a remembrance of America's queen of comedy, and the **Blues Brothers** launch their foot-stomping revue several times a day on Delancey Street.

Back at Woody Woodpecker's KidZone, **Fievel's Playland** is a wet, western-themed playground with a house to climb and a water slide for small fry. **Curious George Goes to Town** is filled with whimsical watery fun, from fountains to ball-shooting cannons—bring a change of clothes.

Shopping at Universal Studios Florida

Every major attraction has a theme store attached, many of them selling unique merchandise. Although the prices are high when you consider you're just buying a souvenir, the **Hard Rock Cafe** shop in adjacent CityWalk is extremely popular and has a small but diverse selection of Hard Rock everything (including memorabilia with astronomical sticker prices). For just about everything else a la Universal, the **Universal Studios Store** carries a decent selection of toys, T-shirts, and souvenirs.

More than two dozen other shops in the park sell collectibles. Be warned, though, that unlike Walt Disney World, where Mickey is everywhere, Universal's shops are specific to individual attractions. If you see something you like, buy it; you probably won't find it in another store. If you did forget to pick something up, there's a shop-by-phone service—call ✆ **407/224-5800,** describe the item and where you think you saw it, and the likelihood is they'll be able to help you out. There is also a Universal store at Orlando International Airport, but it mainly carries the usual souvenirs.

UNIVERSAL STUDIOS cuisine

The best restaurants here are just outside the main gates at CityWalk (p. 324), Universal's restaurant and nightclub venue. But there are more than a dozen places to eat inside the park. Here are my favorites:

Best Sit-Down Meal: Head to **Lombard's Seafood Grille** for a hearty fried shrimp basket, as well as a selection of seafood, pasta, salads, and sandwiches ($11–$13) in slightly more upscale surroundings. It's located across from the Disaster! ride.

Best Counter Service: Try **Universal Studios' Classic Monster Cafe** for salads, pizza, pasta, and rotisserie chicken ($8–$11) with a side of classic and creepy creatures. It's off 7th Avenue, near Shrek 4-D. *Note:* The cafe, of late, has only been open seasonally.

Best Place for Hungry Families: Similar to a mall food court, the **International Food and Film Festival** offers a variety of foods in a single location. With options ranging from stir-fry to chicken Parmesan, families can easily please all palates (even the pickier ones) under one roof. There are kids' meals for less than $7 at most locations. The fare is far from gourmet, but it is a cut above regular fast food ($8–$11). It's located near the back of Animal Actors on Location!

Best Snack: Milkshakes ($4–$5) and ice-cream sundaes ($5–$6) at **Schwab's Pharmacy** make perfect pick-me-ups. It's located across the street from Terminator 2: 3-D Battle Across Time.

Note: Universal has a service similar to Disney's in which you can have your purchases delivered to **It's a Wrap** at the front of the park so you don't have to schlep that 5-foot-tall E.T. around the park with you. Allow at least 3 hours for delivery.

GREAT BUYS AT UNIVERSAL STUDIOS FLORIDA

Here's a sampling of the more unusual gifts available at some of the Universal stores. Of course, in addition to these options, you can find the standard tourist fare, with a staggering array of mugs, key chains, T-shirts, and the like. I've tried to include things you wouldn't find (or consider buying) anywhere else.

- **E.T.'s Toy Closet and Photo Spot**   This is the place for plush stuffed animals, including a replica of the alien namesake.
- **MIB Gear**   If you find yourself in need of a ray gun or alien blaster, this is the place to buy everything out of this world.
- **Quint's Surf Shack**   This is the place to go for a different kind of T-shirt. Tropical colors with subtle Universal logos and island wear are the thing here.
- **Silver Screen Collectibles**   Fans of *I Love Lucy* will adore the collectible dolls. There's also a Betty Boop line. For an interesting, practical, and inexpensive little something to take home, check out the Woody Woodpecker back-scratcher.
- **Universal Studios Store**   This store, near the entrance, sells just about everything when it comes to Universal apparel, and there are plenty of toys and trinkets as well. Logo blankets (made of supersoft jersey—think comfy sweatshirt) are one of the more useful souvenirs sold here.

ISLANDS OF ADVENTURE

Universal's second theme park opened in 1999 with a vibrantly colored, cleverly themed collection of fast and sometimes furious rides. At just over 120 acres, it's now, thanks to the addition of the Wizarding World, slightly larger in size than its big brother, Universal Studios Florida, and it's definitely *the* Orlando park for thrill-ride junkies. Roller coasters roar above pedestrian walkways, and water rides slice through the park. The trade-off: Far fewer shows.

Expect total immersion in the park's various "island" sights, sounds, and surroundings. From the wobbly angles and Day-Glo colors in **Seuss Landing** to the lush foliage of **Jurassic Park** to the magical mystical world of witchcraft and wizardry in the **Wizarding World of Harry Potter,** Universal has done an amazing job of differentiating the various sections of this $1-billion-plus park (unlike Universal Studios Florida, where you ease into the next area and all of a sudden you realize that you're in San Francisco, not New York anymore). They've also done an outstanding job of differentiating Islands from Disney or any other Orlando park. In Florida, the closest competitor (and that's a stretch) is Busch Gardens in Tampa, but this park clearly has the edge on the ride front—and most definitely in the atmosphere department.

The adventure is spread across seven very different islands: the **Port of Entry,** a pass-through zone themed to resemble an exotic open-air bazaar and lined with a collection of shops and restaurants, and six themed islands—**Seuss Landing,** the **Lost Continent,** the **Wizarding World of Harry Potter, Jurassic Park, Toon Lagoon,** and **Marvel Super Hero Island.** The park offers a concentration of thrill rides and coasters, but there are plenty of places to play for young kids, too.

Essentials

GETTING TO ISLANDS OF ADVENTURE BY CAR   Universal Orlando is a half-mile north of I-4 exit 75B, Kirkman Road/Highway 435. There may be construction in the area, so follow the signs directing you to the park.

PARKING   If you park in the multilevel garage, write down the row and theme in your area to help you find your car later. Parking costs $15 for cars, light trucks, and vans; preferred spots cost $20. Valet parking is available for $25.

TICKET PRICES   Currently a **1-day, one-park ticket** costs $85 for adults, $79 for children 3 to 9. A **2-day, one-park-per-day ticket,** good for admission to either of Universal's major theme parks (either Universal Studios or Islands of Adventure) on each day your ticket is valid, runs $115.99 for adults, $105.99 for children. As the number of days increases, so does the ticket price. A **1-day park-to-park access ticket** (allowing you to park-hop between Universal Studios and Islands of Adventure) costs $120.99 for adults, $114.99 for children 3 to 9. A **2-day park-to-park ticket** costs $135.99 for adults, $125.99 for children; again, as the number of days increases, so does the ticket price (up to a 4-day park-to-park access ticket at a cost

---

   A Night at the Movies

Universal 360: A Cinesphere Spectacular, Universal Orlando's seasonal nighttime show, made its debut in the summer of 2006. This spectacular after-dark production immerses guests in the movie experience, projecting images from Hollywood's hottest hits across four tremendous "cinespheres" in the park's central lagoon. The scenes and images appear and change throughout the show, while 300 outdoor speakers ensure that the accompanying music is heard by everyone who's even remotely nearby. Lasers and special pyrotechnic effects add to the already amazing visuals.

of $155.99 for adults, $142.99 for children)—but the bonus is the cost per day goes down substantially as the number of days your ticket is good for increases (a 4-day park-to-park access ticket averaging less than $40 per day). Tickets purchased at the gate run $20 higher.

For details on VIP tours at Islands of Adventure, see "Ticket Prices" in the "Universal Studios Florida" section, earlier in this chapter.

HOURS The park is open 365 days a year, generally from 9am to 6pm, though often later, especially in summer and around holidays, when it's frequently open until 9pm, sometimes later. Also, during Mardi Gras and Halloween Horror Nights, the park closes around 5pm, reopens at 7pm (with a new admission), and remains open until at least midnight. The best bet is to call before you go so that you're not caught by surprise.

Making Your Visit More Enjoyable
PLANNING YOUR VISIT
You can get information before you leave by calling ☏ **407/224-4233** or 407/363-8000. Ask for information about travel packages, as well as theme-park information and discounts; Universal sometimes offers additional days free or at a deeply discounted price. You can also write to Guest Services, 1000 Universal Studios Plaza, Orlando, FL 32819-7601.

Online, you can find information about Islands of Adventure at **www.universal orlando.com**. Orlando's daily newspaper, the *Orlando Sentinel*, also produces **OrlandoSentinel.com.** Additionally, there's a lot of information about the parks, hotels, restaurants, and more at the Orlando/Orange County Convention & Visitors Bureau's website, **www.visitorlando.com**. Additional sites worth searching through include **www.mouseearsandmore.com** and **www.allearsnet.com**.

FOR VISITORS WITH SPECIAL NEEDS
Those with disabilities should stop by **Guest Services,** located just inside the main entrance, for a *Rider's Guide for Rider Safety & Guests with Disabilities*, a Telecommunications Device for the Deaf (TDD), or other special assistance. You can rent a standard wheelchair for $12 or an electric one for $50 (both require a $50 deposit and a signed rental contract). You can reserve them a week or more in advance by calling ☏ **407/224-6350.** You can arrange for sign language interpreting services at no charge by calling ☏ **888/519-4899** (toll-free TDD), 407/224-4414 (local TDD), or 407/224-5929 (voice). Make arrangements for an appointment with an interpreter 1 to 2 weeks in advance. Check **www.universalorlando.com** for more information.

BEST DAYS TO VISIT
Like Universal Studios Florida, it's best to visit Islands near the end of the week, on a Thursday or Friday. The pace is somewhat fast Monday through Wednesday, with the heaviest crowds on weekends and during summer and holidays.

RIDE RESTRICTIONS
Note that many of the park's attractions have minimum height requirements; see the listings that follow for details. Universal also recommends that expectant mothers steer clear of some rides (also noted in the listings).

Suggested Itineraries
FOR FAMILIES WITH YOUNG CHILDREN
If you have kids 8 and younger, enter the park and go to the right to **Seuss Landing,** an island where everything is geared to the young and young at heart. You'll easily

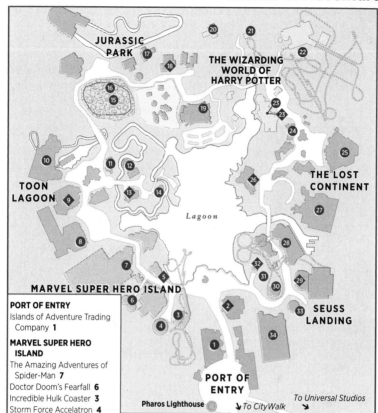

PORT OF ENTRY
Islands of Adventure Trading
Company **1**

**MARVEL SUPER HERO
ISLAND**
The Amazing Adventures of
Spider-Man **7**
Doctor Doom's Fearfall **6**
Incredible Hulk Coaster **3**
Storm Force Accelatron **4**

TOON LAGOON
Dudley Do-Right's Ripsaw
Falls **10**
King's Row & Comic Strip
Lane **11**
Me Ship, The Olive **14**
Performance Stage **8**
Popeye & Bluto's Bilge-Rat
Barges **12**

JURASSIC PARK
Camp Jurassic **16**
Jurassic Park Discovery
Center **19**
Jurassic Park River
Adventure **17**
Pteranodon Flyers **15**

**THE WIZARDING WORLD
OF HARRY POTTER**
Dervish and Banges **23**

Dragon Challenge **22**
Filch's Emporium of
Confiscated Goods **20**
Flight of the Hippogriff **21**
Harry Potter and the Forbidden
Journey **20**
Hogsmeade Village **23**
Hogwarts Castle **20**
Honeydukes **23**
Ollivander's **23**
Owl Post **23**
Zonko's Joke Shop **23**

THE LOST CONTINENT
Eighth Voyage of Sindbad **25**
Mystic Fountain **24**
Poseidon's Fury **27**

SEUSS LANDING
Caro-Seuss-El **30**

The Cat in the Hat **34**
High in the Sky Seuss Trolley
Train Ride **28**
If I Ran the Zoo **31**
One Fish, Two Fish, Red Fish,
Blue Fish **33**

DINING ◆
Captain America Diner **5**
Circus McGurkus Cafe
Stoo-pendous **29**
Comic Strip Cafe **9**
Confisco Grille **2**
Green Eggs and Ham Cafe **32**
Hog's Head **23**
Mythos **26**
Three Broomsticks **23**
Thunder Falls Terrace **18**
Wimpy's **13**

SOME practical advice FOR ISLAND ADVENTURERS

1. The Shorter They Are . . . : Currently some 13 of the 15 major rides at Islands of Adventure (including those in the Wizarding World) have height restrictions. The Dragon Challenge and the Incredible Hulk Coaster, for instance, deny access to anyone shorter than 54 inches, and unless you're at least 48 inches tall you can forget about Harry Potter and the Forbidden Journey. For those who want to ride but have come with kids, there's a baby or child swap at all of the major attractions, allowing one parent to ride while the other watches the tykes. But sitting in a waiting room isn't much fun for the little ones. So take your child's height into consideration before coming to the park or at least to some of the islands. Think about splitting up for a while, and then meeting up again a bit later.

2. Cruising the Islands: If you hauled your stroller with you on your vacation, bring it with you to the park. It's a very long walk from your car, through the massive parking garage and the nighttime entertainment district, CityWalk, before you get to the fun. (Universal, however, does a good job of disguising just how long it is thanks to all of the covered walkways near the parking area.) Carrying a young child and the accompanying paraphernalia, even with a series of moving sidewalks, can make the long

trek seem even longer—especially at the end of the day.

3. The Faint of Heart: Even if you don't have children, make sure you consider all of the ride restrictions. Expectant mothers, anyone prone to motion sickness, and those with heart, neck, or back trouble will be discouraged—with good reason—from riding most primo attractions. There's still plenty to see and do, but without the roller coasters, Islands of Adventure is far less adventurous.

4. Beat the Heat: Some rides require that you wait outside without any cover to protect you from the sizzling Florida sun, so bring some bottled water (freeze it the night before) for the long waits (a $1.25 free-world bottle costs $2.50 or more if you buy it here), or take a sip or two from the fountains placed in the waiting areas. Also, beer, wine, and liquor are more available at the Universal parks than the Disney ones, but booze, roller coasters, and hot weather can make for a messy mix.

5. Cash in on Your Card: You can save 10% on your purchases at any gift shop or on a meal at Islands of Adventure by showing your AAA card. This discount isn't available at food or merchandise carts. And tobacco, candy, film, collectibles, and sundry items aren't included.

spend the morning or longer exploring real-life interpretations of the wacky, colorful world of Dr. Seuss. (The wild colors make for some good photographs.) Be sure to ride the **Cat in the Hat; One Fish, Two Fish, Red Fish, Blue Fish;** the **High in the Sky Seuss Trolley Train Ride!;** and **Caro-Seuss-El.** After all that waiting in line, let the little ones burn some energy playing in **If I Ran the Zoo.**

Grab lunch at the **Green Eggs and Ham Cafe,** or **Circus McGurkus Cafe Stoo-pendous** if you prefer to eat indoors. Next, head to the **Lost Continent** to talk to the **Mystic Fountain;** then let them play in **Camp Jurassic** (many could stay here for hours if you let them) or watch a "hatching" at the **Discovery Center** in

Jurassic Park. They can have some more interactive fun in **Toon Lagoon** aboard **Me Ship, The Olive,** and grab autographs at the **King's Row & Comic Strip Lane.** Those 40 inches or taller—and a bit braver—can end the day in **Marvel Super Hero Island** by riding the **Amazing Adventures of Spider-Man.**

FOR TEENS & ADULTS

Save the Wizarding World for later in the day when wait times (which remain excruciatingly long during peak season) may be shorter (albeit only slightly). Instead, head left from Port of Entry to **Marvel Super Hero Island** and ride the **Incredible Hulk Coaster,** the **Amazing Adventures of Spider-Man,** and **Doctor Doom's Fearfall.** (If you arrive early, the line will be short for your first choice, but you'll likely have to wait—unless you have an Express Plus Pass—for the others.) There should be time to squeeze in **Dudley Do-Right's Ripsaw Falls** in **Toon Lagoon** before you break for lunch (a full stomach isn't recommended) at **Comic Strip Café** or **Blondie's.**

Now that you're fully refueled, ride **Popeye & Bluto's Bilge-Rat Barges,** and then move to **Jurassic Park,** where you can ride **Jurassic Park River Adventure** and visit the **Discovery Center.** Make your way through the **Lost Continent,** where you can catch the show in **Poseidon's Fury.** End your day in the **Wizarding World of Harry Potter,** where you can test your courage aboard the **Dragon Challenge** and the **Forbidden Journey,** take in a street show or two (the **Triwizard Spirit Rally** and **Hogwarts Frog Choir**), and experience **Ollivander's,** where the wand (and the wandmaker) chooses the wizard. If you haven't already, grab a bite—and a butterbeer—at the **Three Broomsticks.**

Services & Facilities at Islands of Adventure

ATMS Machines accepting cards from banks using the Cirrus, Honor, and PLUS systems are located outside and to the right of the main entrance and in the Lost Continent near the bridge to Jurassic Park.

BABY CARE Nursing facilities are located at Family Services near the First Aid station in the Port of Entry. Look for the FAMILY SERVICES sign. Changing tables are available in both the men's and women's restrooms throughout the park. Diapers and baby food are not sold in the park, so be sure to come prepared with a supply of diapers, food, and other necessities. There are baby-swap stations at all of the major attractions, allowing one parent to wait while the other rides.

CAMERAS & FILM Film and disposable cameras are available at De Foto's Expedition Photography, to the right just inside the main entrance.

CAR ASSISTANCE Battery jumps are provided. If you need assistance with your car, raise the hood and use the call boxes located throughout the garage to call for security.

FIRST AID There's one station just inside and to the right of the main entrance and another in the Lost Continent, near the Mystic Fountain.

LOCKERS Lockers are across from Guest Services near the main entrance and cost $8 a day (no oversize lockers here). There are also lockers near the Incredible Hulk Coaster in Marvel Super Hero Island, the Jurassic Park River Adventure in Jurassic Park, and Dragon Challenge in the Wizarding World. The lockers at Dragon Challenge and the Incredible Hulk Coaster are free for the first 45 minutes. Thereafter, and at the Jurassic Park River Adventure, they're $2 per hour up to a maximum of $14 per day. You're not supposed to—and shouldn't—take things on these rides, so put them in a locker or give them to a nonrider.

LOST CHILDREN If you lose a child, head to Guest Services near the main entrance, or go to the first park employee you see. *Children younger than 7 should wear name-tags inside their clothing.*

PET CARE You can board your small animals at the kennel in the parking garages for $15 a day (no overnight stays), but you'll have to feed and walk them during your visit. Ask the parking attendant for directions upon entering the toll plaza.

STROLLER RENTAL Look to your left as you enter through the turnstiles. The cost (including tax) is $15 to $18 for a single, $25 to $28 for a double.

WHEELCHAIR RENTAL Regular wheelchairs can be rented for $12 in the center concourse of the parking garage or to your left as you enter the turnstiles of the main entrance. Electric wheelchairs are $50. Both require a $50 deposit and a rental contract.

Port of Entry

This marketplace of sorts is filled with six shops and four different places to grab a bite, as well as many of the park's more mundane but necessary guest services (mostly near the very front of the Port). If you plan to save shopping for the end of the day, return to **Islands of Adventure Trading Company,** which offers a variety of merchandise linked to attractions throughout the park—from Jurassic T-shirts to stuffed Cat in the Hat dolls.

Seuss Landing

This 10-acre island, inspired by the works of the late Theodore Seuss Geisel, is awash in Day-Glo colors, whimsical architecture, and curved trees (the latter were downed and bent by Hurricane Andrew before the park acquired them). Needless to say, the main attractions here are aimed at the younger set, though anyone who loved the good Doctor as a child will enjoy some nostalgic fun on these rides. And those who aren't familiar with his work will enjoy the visuals—Seussian art is like Dalí for kids.

Caro-Seuss-El

Frommer's Rating: A+ for young kids, parents, and carousel lovers
Recommended Ages: All ages

Forget tradition. This not-so-average carousel gives you a chance to ride seven whimsical characters of Dr. Seuss (a total of 54 mounts), including cowfish, elephant birds, and mulligatawnies. They move up and down as well as in and out. Their eyes blink and heads bob as you twirl through the riot of color surrounding the ride. *Note:* A special ride platform lets guests in wheelchairs experience the up-and-down motion of the ride, making this a great stop for visitors with disabilities.

The Cat in the Hat

Frommer's Rating: A for the under-10 set, C+ for teens and adults
Recommended Ages: All ages

Any Seuss fan will recognize the giant candy-striped hat looming over the entrance to this ride and probably the chaotic journey. Comparable to (but spunkier than) it's a small world at Magic Kingdom (p. 189), the Cat in the Hat is among the signature children's experiences at Islands of Adventure. Love or hate the idea, *do it* and earn your stripes. Your couch travels through 18 scenes retelling the Cat in the Hat's tale of a day gone very much awry. You, meanwhile, spin about and meet Thing 1 and

After years of klonking, bonking, jerking, and berking, the miniature monorail that hangs high over Seuss Landing (which had gone riderless for what seemed an eternity) now runs from morning till night. The **High in the Sky Seuss Trolley Train Ride** is a whimsical kid-friendly ride that runs along two separate tracks. Traveling in individual "cars," you'll pass classic Seussian scenes and colorful characters—with an occasional view of Seuss Landing below. Lines can be excruciatingly long, but high-power fans will keep you cool while you wait.

Note: Each day, one child is picked to be the "Conductor of the Day." As honorary conductor, the child is decked out in a trolley hat, red leather gloves, blue bandanna, and sticker before getting to announce that boarding is about to begin. Front-row seating on the trolley, as well as Universal Express Passes for the child's family (good for a single attraction at either Universal park), are part of the package.

Thing 2 in addition to other characters. The highlight is a revolving 24-foot tunnel that alters your perceptions and leaves your head with a feeling oddly reminiscent of a hangover. *Note:* Pop-up characters may be scary for riders younger than 5, and expectant moms are discouraged from riding the Cat.

If I Ran the Zoo ☺
Frommer's Rating: A for the very young
Recommended Ages: 2–6
This 19-station interactive play land features flying water snakes and a chance to tickle the toes of a Seussian animal. Kids can also spin wheels, explore caves, fire water cannons, climb, slide, and otherwise burn off some excess energy.

One Fish, Two Fish, Red Fish, Blue Fish
Frommer's Rating: B+ for kids and parents
Recommended Ages: 2–7
This kiddie charmer is similar to the Dumbo and Magic Carpets of Aladdin rides at Magic Kingdom (including the ridiculously long line, though this ride's waiting area is covered), but this one has a few added features. Your controls allow you to move your funky fish up or down 15 feet as you spin around on an arm attached to a hub. All the while, a song belts out rhyming flight instructions. Watch out for "squirt posts," which spray unsuspecting riders who don't follow the rhyme. Actually, even the most careful driver is likely to get a little wet.

Marvel Super Hero Island

Thrill junkies love the twisting, turning, stomach-churning rides on this island filled with building-tall murals of Marvel Super Heroes. Fans can **Meet the Marvel Super Heroes** across from the Amazing Adventures of Spider-Man (for times, check your adventure map, handed out when you enter, or grab a copy at Guest Services). And the munch crowd can dig into sandwiches and burgers at **Captain America Diner** (in the $9–$12 range) or hit **Café 4** for pizza, pasta, and sandwiches (around $6–$20, most less than $12).

The Amazing Adventures of Spider-Man 🎁
Frommer's Rating: A+
Recommended Ages: 8–adult

The original Web Master stars in this exceptional show/ride (arguably, one of the best in town—second only to the Forbidden Journey), which features 3-D action and special effects. The story line: You're on a tour of the *Daily Bugle* when—yikes!—something goes horribly wrong. Peter Parker suddenly encounters evil villains and becomes Spider-Man. This high-tech ride isn't stationary—cars twist and spin, plunge and soar through a comic-book universe. Passengers wearing 3-D glasses squeal as computer-generated objects fly at their 12-person cars. There's a simulated 400-foot drop that feels an awful lot like the real thing. If you want the biggest thrills, try to get a seat in the front row of your vehicle. ***Note:*** At press time, Universal announced that the ride was being reanimated in high definition—while the storyline will remain untouched, the visuals will be enhanced to such a degree that every last detail will be vividly apparent (and the new Spidey-Vision glasses might help a bit, too). ***Note:*** There's a 40-inch height minimum. Expectant mothers or those with heart, neck, or back problems shouldn't ride.

Tip: Waits can be 45 minutes or longer even on an off day. Unless you have an Express Plus Pass, heading to the single-rider line is the only way to drastically reduce your waiting time. So if it's an option on the day you're here and your party doesn't mind splitting up, take advantage of it.

Doctor Doom's Fearfall
Frommer's Rating: C+
Recommended Ages: 8–adult

Look! Up in the sky! It's a bird, it's a plane . . . uh, it's you falling 150 feet, if you're courageous enough to climb aboard this towering metal skeleton. The screams that can be heard at the ride's entrance add to the anticipation of a big plunge followed by smaller ones. The plot? You're touring a lab when—are you sensing a recurring theme here?—something goes wrong as Doctor Doom tries to cure you of fear. You're fired to the top, with feet dangling, and dropped in intervals, feet first, leaving your stomach at several levels. The thrills and the atmosphere aren't nearly as good as those of the Tower of Terror (p. 224), but it's still frightful (and you do get a neat view of the entire park). ***Note:*** Expectant mothers and those with heart, neck, or back problems shouldn't ride. Minimum height is 52 inches.

Incredible Hulk Coaster 🏦
Frommer's Rating: A+
Recommended Ages: 10–adult

Bruce Banner is working in his lab when—yes, again—something goes wrong. But this rocking rocket of a ride makes everything oh so right, except maybe your heartbeat and stomach. From a dark tunnel, you burst into the sunlight while accelerating from 0 to 40 mph in 2 seconds. While that's only two-thirds the speed of the Rock 'n' Roller Coaster (p. 222) at Disney's Hollywood Studios, this is in broad daylight, there's a lot more motion still to come, and you can *see* the asphalt! From there, you spin upside-down 128 feet from the ground, feel weightless, and careen through the center of the park over the heads of other visitors. Coaster lovers will be pleased to know that this ride, which lasts 2 minutes and 15 seconds, includes seven inversions and two steep drops. The ride is extremely smooth, however, making it one of the better coaster experiences for all types of riders. Sunglasses, change, and an occasional set of car keys lie in a mesh net beneath the ride—proof of its motion and the fact that most folks don't heed the warnings to stash their stuff in the nearby lockers (you should). As a nice touch, the 32-passenger metal coaster glows green at night (riders who ignore all the warnings occasionally turn green as well). **Note:** Expectant mothers and those with heart, neck, or back problems should skip this one. Riders must be at least 54 inches tall.

Storm Force Accelatron
Frommer's Rating: C+
Recommended Ages: 4–adult

Despite the exotic name, this ride is little more than a spin-off of the Magic Kingdom's Mad Tea Party (p. 189)—spinning teacups that, in this case, have a 22nd-century design. While aboard, you and the X-Men's superheroine, Storm, try to defeat the evil Magneto by converting human energy into electrical forces. To do that, you need to spin faster and faster. In addition to some upset stomachs, the spiraling creates a thunderstorm of sound and light that gives Storm all the power she needs to blast Magneto into the ever-after (or until the next riders arrive). This ride is sometimes closed during off-peak periods. **Note:** Expectant moms are advised not to ride this ride.

Toon Lagoon

More than 150 life-size sculpted cartoon images—ranging from Betty Boop and Flash Gordon to Bullwinkle and Cathy—let you know you've entered an island dedicated to your favorites from the Sunday funnies.

Dudley Do-Right's Ripsaw Falls
Frommer's Rating: A
Recommended Ages: 8–adult

The setting and effects at WDW's Splash Mountain (p. 184) are better, but the adrenaline rush here is higher (and so is the splash factor). The staid red hat of the heroic Dudley can be deceiving: The ride that lies under it has a lot more speed and drop than onlookers suspect. Six-passenger logs (they're pretty uncomfortable, especially if you have long legs) take you around a 400,000-gallon lagoon before launching you into a 75-foot drop at 50 mph. At one point, you're 15 feet below the surface. Though the water is contained on either side of you, you *will* get wet. **Note:** Once again, expectant mothers and folks with heart, neck, or back problems should do something else. Riders must be at least 44 inches tall.

King's Row & Comic Strip Lane
Frommer's Rating: C+
Recommended Ages: All ages

Dudley Do-Right, Woody Woodpecker, Popeye, and other favorites from the Sunday comics will have you rockin' and rollin' in the streets as they sing and make you laugh during this several-times-a-day show. It's one to skip if you're on a tight schedule, but it's a nice respite from the madness.

Me Ship, The Olive
Frommer's Rating: B+
Recommended Ages: 4–adult

This three-story boat is a family-friendly play land with dozens of interactive activities from bow to stern. Kids can toot whistles, clang bells, or play the organ. Sweet Pea's Playpen is a favorite of younger guests. Kids 6 and older as well as adults will love Cargo Crane, where they can drench riders on Popeye & Bluto's Bilge-Rat Barges (see below). **Tip:** The second and third decks of the good ship offer great views and photo ops of the Incredible Hulk Coaster and some of the rest of Islands of Adventure.

Popeye & Bluto's Bilge-Rat Barges

Frommer's Rating: A

Recommended Ages: 6–adult

This is the same kind of ride with the same kind of raft as Kali River Rapids at WDW's Animal Kingdom (p. 235), but it's a bit faster and bouncier. You'll be squirted by mechanical devices as well as the water cannons fired by guests at Me Ship, The Olive (see above), and the water is *c-c-cold,* a blessing on hot summer days but less so in January. The 12-passenger rafts bump, churn, and dip (14 ft. at one point) along a white-water course lined with Bluto, Sea Hag, and other villains. You will get *s-s-soaked.* **Note:** Yes, once again, expectant mothers and people with heart, neck, or back problems shouldn't ride this one. Riders must be at least 42 inches tall.

Jurassic Park

All of the basics and some of the high-tech wizardry from Steven Spielberg's wildly successful films are incorporated in this lushly landscaped tropical locale that includes a replica of the visitor center from the movie. Expect long lines at the River Adventure and pleasant surprises at the Discovery Center.

Camp Jurassic ☺

Frommer's Rating: A+ for young children

Recommended Ages: 2–12

This play area, similar in theme but even better than the Boneyard at Animal Kingdom (p. 231), has everything from lava pits with dinosaur bones to a rainforest. Watch out for the spitters that lurk in dark caves. The multilevel play area has plenty of places for kids to crawl, explore, and expend energy. Young kids need close supervision, though. It's easy to get turned around inside the caverns, and some of the areas enhanced with sound effects may be a bit too frightening for the very young. Be prepared for your kids to get soaked—you will be too if you have to retrieve them (very likely).

Jurassic Park Discovery Center

Frommer's Rating: B+

Recommended Ages: All ages

Here's an amusing, educational pit stop that has life-size dinosaur replicas and some interactive games, including a sequencer that pretends to combine your DNA with a dinosaur's. The "Beasaur" exhibit allows you to see and hear as the huge reptiles did. You can play the game show *You Bet Jurassic* (grin) and scan the walls for fossils. The highlight is watching a Velociraptor "hatch" in the lab. Because there are a limited number of interactive stations, this can consume a lot of time on busy days. Be sure to enter from the lower level—the view is spectacular and there's an elaborate stone plaza—which is far more impressive than the doors upstairs. Also come equipped with a camera—if you want your photo snapped with a dinosaur, this spot is a great place to do it.

Jurassic Park River Adventure

Frommer's Rating: A

Recommended Ages: 8–adult

A leisurely raft tour along a river is interrupted when some raptors, who could hop aboard your boat at any moment, escape. The ride lets you literally come face-to-face with "breathing" inhabitants of Jurassic Park. At one point, a *Tyrannosaurus rex*

Strength and fitness folks can get a little extra workout at the small rock-climbing venue (for an additional fee) outside the Thunder Falls Terrace restaurant in Jurassic Park. If you or the kids are looking for a more economical and less strenuous option, try walking the elevated trails and climbing the net ladders beneath the Pteranodon Flyers attraction, also in Jurassic Park.

decides you look like a tasty morsel, and at another point, spitters launch venomous saliva your way. The only way out: an 85-foot plunge in your log-style life raft. It's steep and quick enough to lift your fanny out of the seat. (When Spielberg rode it, he made them stop the ride and let him out before the plunge.) Expect to get wet (how wet depends on the individual experience—I've seen some people get soaked and some emerge barely damp). If your stomach can take only one flume ride, this one's a lot more comfortable than Dudley Do-Right (see above), and the atmosphere is better. **Note:** Expectant mothers and those with heart, neck, or back problems shouldn't ride. Guests must be at least 42 inches tall.

Pteranodon Flyers ☺
Frommer's Rating: C+
Recommended Ages: All ages
The 10-foot metal frames and simple seats are flimsy, but this quick spin around Jurassic Park offers a great bird's-eye view. The landing is bumpy, and you'll swing side to side throughout, which makes some riders queasy. Unlike the traditional gondolas in the sky rides, on this one your feet hang free from the two-seat skeletal flyer, and there's little but a restraining belt between you and the ground. **Note:** That said, this is a child's ride—single passengers must be between 36 and 56 inches tall; adults can climb aboard *only* when accompanying someone that size. And, because this ride launches only two passengers every 30 to 40 seconds, it can consume an hour of your day, even in the off season. So, although it is nice, pass it up if you're pressed for time.

The Lost Continent

Although they've mixed their millennia—ancient Greece with a medieval forest—Universal has done a good job creating a foreboding mood in this section of the park, whose entrance is marked by menacing stone griffins. **As a note:** The **Wizarding World of Harry Potter** has officially opened—splashing over into the Lost Continent, which is now significantly smaller in size, its borders realigned to accommodate the addition. Obvious signs of the intrusion include the demolition of the Enchanted Oak Tavern; the re-theming of what was, in a past life, Dueling Dragons (now the Dragon Challenge, and part of the Wizarding World rather than the Lost Continent); and the addition of a large stone archway marking the Wizarding World's entrance. The temporary bridge (built during the construction) connecting the Lost Continent to Jurassic Park remains in place; whether or not it will become permanent has yet to be determined. This, however, may not be the end of the changes and intrusions, as rumors continue to fly regarding a second phase of Wizarding World in the works (which means several Lost Continent attractions may be reworked and refit to accommodate the changes).

Eighth Voyage of Sindbad ✋
Frommer's Rating: C+
Recommended Ages: 6–adult

The mythical sailor is the star of a stunt demonstration that takes place in a 1,700-seat theater decorated with blue stalagmites and eerie, gloomy shipwrecks. The show has water explosions and dozens of pyrotechnic effects, including a 10-foot circle of flames. Younger kids may find some of the characters too scary, so a seat in the back may be in order if you have tots in tow. Although it offers a rest for park-weary feet, it doesn't come close to the quality of the Indiana Jones stunt show at Disney's Hollywood Studios (p. 219).

Mystic Fountain ☺
Frommer's Rating: B+ for kids
Recommended Ages: 3–8

Located just outside Sindbad's theater, this interactive "smart" fountain delights younger guests (and often amuses adults, too). It can see and hear, leading to a lot of kibitzing with those who stand before it. But if you want to stay dry, don't get too close when it starts "spouting" its wet wisdom. On the other hand, if you need a quick cool-off—go for it.

Poseidon's Fury
Frommer's Rating: B+
Recommended Ages: 6–adult

This is the park's best show—though with a lack of competition (there are only two productions at Islands), that's something of a backhanded compliment. The story line revolves around a battle between Poseidon, god of the sea, and the evil Darkenon. The highlight is when you pass through a small room with a 42-foot vortex where 17,500 gallons of water swirl around you, barrel-roll style. (If you wear glasses, note that they will fog up completely when passing through the vortex—take them off if you can.) Unfortunately, as well done as the queue, the preshow, and vortex are, it's downhill from there. In the battle royal (its special effects, in my opinion, not at all up to Universal's usually high standards), the gods hurl 25-foot fireballs at each other. It's more interesting than frightening, but it's not worth the long lines that often plague it, so if you're on a tight schedule, skip it unless you have express-line privileges. *Note:* The fireballs, explosive sounds, and rushing water (not to mention the dark and eerie passageways of the queue area) may be too intense for children younger than 6.

The Wizarding World of Harry Potter

In June 2010, the **Wizarding World of Harry Potter,** after 3 years of watching and waiting, finally cast its magical spell. Based on the wildly popular book series by J. K. Rowling (as well as the blockbuster movies), the Wizarding World brings to life the adventures of the young wizard through immersive rides and next-generation interactive attractions—including meticulous re-creations of Hogwarts Castle and the village of Hogsmeade—plus an array of shops and restaurants (think Diagon Alley, albeit on a much smaller scale) created from areas within the Lost Continent, extending beyond to land that had, until now, remained undeveloped.

The entrance (there are two—one at the north end, near Hogwarts Castle, that leads into Hogsmeade from Jurassic Park, and the other, far more impressive entrance at the south end, leading into the village from the Lost Continent) is marked by an immense stone archway, from which hangs a sign reading PLEASE RESPECT THE SPELL LIMITS, and offers the most impressive view of the snow-capped village and Hogwarts Castle as it looms in the distance. Beyond the entrance, the Hogwarts Express stands waiting at Hogsmeade station as if it had only just arrived (steam occasionally billowing from the engine while the whistle blows), welcoming each and every muggle who enters. The incredible attention to detail is simply beyond description, as crooked chimneys, jagged snow-topped rooflines, and wildly imaginative storefronts crowd along the street, all leading to the magnificent edifice of Hogwarts Castle on the horizon.

Thrill seekers will find the **Dragon Challenge** (Dueling Dragons in a past life) to their liking, while families with younger kids may find the **Flight of the Hippogriff** (previously Flying Unicorn) a tamer option. **Harry Potter and the Forbidden Journey,** located in the iconic Hogwarts Castle, takes riders soaring over Hogwarts grounds, through the Forbidden Forest, alongside a fire-breathing dragon, and into the middle of a Quidditch match—it's by far the best ride in the park.

The Wizarding World, while impressive in the daylight, is even more so after dark, when torches and lanterns light up the village and illuminate the castle. Check the show schedule to ensure you catch the **Triwizard Spirit Rally** and the **Hogwarts Frog Choir,** both thoroughly entertaining street shows that take place just below Hogwarts Castle.

Dragon Challenge 🎁

Frommer's Rating: A+

Recommended Ages: 10–adult

The entrance, marked by an ominous, albeit somewhat unremarkable, stone archway and flanked by flags and Triwizard Tournament banners (rather than the magnificent intertwining dragons, which, to be perfectly honest, were far more eye-catching), leads to the ride's lengthy queue. A stone path winds along the edge of the Forbidden Forest, the Weasleys' flying car plunked amid the trees near the castle entrance—the interior of which has been re-themed to resemble the Triwizard champions' tent, with the Goblet of Fire prominently displayed in the center. Just beyond lies the Triwizard Cup. The ride itself remains much the same (though the Hungarian Horntail and the Chinese Fireball now await you rather than Fire and Ice). There's no doubt that maniacal minds created this thrill ride—sending two roller coasters right at each other at high speeds. True coaster crazies will love the intertwined set of leg-dangling racers that climb to 125 feet, invert five times, and three times come within 12 inches of each other as the two dragons battle. This coaster sports a tighter track with quick banking turns and sharp twists, making the ride somewhat jerky—far from the smooth and fluid experience of the Hulk. But the roughness may be part of its charm—a couple of thrill junkies revealed to me that this is where they head when they want the city's ultimate adrenaline rush. For the best ride, try to get one of the two outside seats in each of the eight rows. If you want to get into the front seat (for that extra jolt), there's a special line near the loading dock so that daredevils can claim the first car. *Note:* Expectant mothers and those with heart, neck, or back problems shouldn't ride. Riders must be at least 54 inches tall.

Flight of the Hippogriff 😊

Frommer's Rating: B

Recommended Ages: 6–10

This repurposed roller coaster, previously known as the Flying Unicorn, offers those who aren't quite up to the Dragon Challenge a little zip and zing as it twists and turns along the kid-friendly track. Before boarding the wicker-fronted cars for your training flight, riders are instructed on how to properly approach (and bow before) a

Hippogriff as they pass by Hagrid's Hut (visible only from the queue). If you look carefully, you can catch a glimpse of a Hippogriff in its nest.

Harry Potter and the Forbidden Journey

Frommer's Rating: A+

Recommended Ages: 8–adult

Set within the walls of Hogwarts Castle, the Forbidden Journey is by far the best ride in the park (if not Orlando). The queue, as much a part of the experience as the ride itself, is signature Universal. Even if you decide not to ride, make your way through the queue at least once—it's well worth the wait, especially for true Potter fans. After reaching the castle entrance, you'll continue through passageways filled with familiar objects. You'll wind your way back outside, through the greenhouses (look for the mandrakes) to the portrait hall, on to Dumbledore's office and the Defense Against the Dark Arts classroom (where Harry, Ron, and Hermione invite those in line to ditch class and join them for a bit of flying). Then it's on to the Gryffindor Common Room and the ride itself. Without giving everything away, the key here is to take your time and really look around—at everything. The theming is simply unparalleled and the special effects unrivaled.

The ride's all-new robotic technology, special effects, and spherical screen create an immersive experience like no other. After boarding the four-seat bench in the Great Hall (complete with floating candles—or so you think), riders travel by Floo Network, soar over Hogwarts, narrowly escape a dragon attack, encounter a Whomping Willow, get pulled into a game of Quidditch, and come face to face (so to speak) with Dementors and gigantic spiders, before returning safely to the castle. While not one of Universal's corkscrew-style coasters, the ride is far from timid. A robotic arm, on which the four-seat bench is situated, allows for a wide range of movement (at one point it verges on tipping backwards, with riders lying beyond a perpendicular position). As expected, this ride carries every warning imaginable along with a 48-inch height requirement. The intensity, combined with some scary scenes and periods of darkness, will keep younger fans from riding—but all is not lost, since anyone can walk through the queue and exit before boarding. **Note:** Tempted as you may be to sit forward, sitting back against the bench will ensure that the soundtrack comes through clearly—and if you do not know the storyline, you may very well be lost without the commentary.

Keep your eyes wide open from start to finish, as even the most minute detail shouldn't be overlooked. Look for the statue of the one-eyed witch, the Mirror of Erised, and the hall of paintings (where the heads of the four Hogwarts houses can be seen moving within their frames and heard talking not only to one another but also

---

Paying the Price

The Wizarding World is a boon for fans, as a plethora of Potter paraphernalia can be found lining the shelves of Universal shops. Here, and only here (save Universal's new online store, created because of the onslaught of souvenir seekers), is where you can purchase magic wands ($25–$30), robes from each of the four Hogwarts houses ($100), Sneakoscopes ($15), Golden Snitches ($15), and butterbeer in a souvenir mug ($9). In addition, you'll find brooms, Sorting Hats, an array of plush toys, pins, hats, bags, scarves, stationery, and more.

Could Have, Should Have

6

While living up to expectations, and in many cases far exceeding them (which is saying a lot, given all the secrecy and hype leading up to its opening), bear in mind that the Wizarding World is, in reality, simply another island. As such, it is not nearly as large you might initially think. The village and castle, each meticulously re-created, are spectacular, but the disappointingly small number of attractions leaves park-goers and Potter fans wanting more—much more. In fact, a great many opportunities for expansion remain. Here are a few thoughts:

Why not make the Hogwarts Express a working train? It would offer another distraction for those not quite tall enough (or brave enough) to take on the Dragon Challenge or the Forbidden Journey. Why not expand upon the popularity of the wizarding shops?

Flourish & Blotts, Gringotts, and Madam Malkin's (among others) would make fabulous additions to the existing lineup (and reduce the number of faux facades mixed in amid the working storefronts). Why not add the Shrieking Shack, Hagrid's Hut, and even Azkaban as walk-through attractions (providing another great "downtime" distraction and crowd-control measure)? Don't get me wrong, I'm not knocking what Universal's done thus far—it's unrivaled and quite spectacular—but am just thinking out loud about the endless possibilities that present themselves.

Note: At press time, rumors were flying about like broomsticks regarding a second phase of attractions that would further expand the Wizarding World (though Universal has yet to release any official confirmation).

EXPLORING BEYOND DISNEY: UNIVERSAL ORLANDO, SEAWORLD & OTHER ATTRACTIONS

Islands of Adventure

to passersby). Watch for Dumbledore, the Pensieve, and the Sorting Hat (listen carefully—the poem, written by J. K. Rowling, was created specifically for the attraction).

As a note: If you're unsure whether you'll fit in the rather snug seats (an issue that caused Universal to almost immediately tweak the size of the seats in an effort to accommodate park-goers with fuller figures), a test seat is located near the castle gate, and a second one is just inside the castle doors (to the left). Lockers, free while you ride, are available inside the castle doors (go to your right and head to the back—there's usually a crowd at the touch screens located close to the entry). Carefully read the instructions; like Universal's other lockers, these use fingerprint recognition and allow only a single entry.

Ollivander's 🎁
Frommer's Rating: A+
Recommended Ages: 8–adult

More an experience than an actual attraction, Ollivander's is not to be missed. Small groups of 25 to 30 people are led into the dimly lit shop, where shelves upon shelves (most set slightly askew and scattered with dust) are filled with muted colored boxes—each containing a wand. It takes a minute to take it all in, but do look around. A glass case (on the back wall) displays the various wands available at the shop, but unfortunately the tight quarters don't allow for much moving about. Once the door is shut, the show begins. From behind the counter, the wand-maker emerges to pick a *single* person from the group. It is that person who will be given several wands to try until, finally, one chooses him as its owner. With each flick of the wand comes a flurry of special effects (and while not nearly as dramatic as the effects seen onscreen, they are impressive nonetheless). Once the wand has chosen the wizard, the group then

275

moves through the door and into the wand shop next door. Here anyone who wishes to purchase a wand (or other wizarding items) may do so.

Shopping at Islands of Adventure

There are more than 25 shops within the park, offering a variety of theme merchandise. You may want to check out **Cats, Hats & Things** and **Mulberry Street** for special Seussian souvenirs. **Jurassic Outfitters** and **Dinostore** feature a variety of stuffed and plastic dinosaurs, plus safari-themed clothing. Superhero fans should check out the **Marvel Alterniverse Store** and the **Spider-Man Shop.** Stop by **Toon Extra** for the largest selection of souvenirs in Toon Lagoon. **Islands of Adventure Trading Company** is a good stop on the way out if you're still searching for something that will help you or the folks back home remember your visit.

Over in the Wizarding World, options include **Zonko's Joke Shop,** for Extendable Ears, Sneakoscopes, Nose-Biting Teacups, and Pink Pygmy Puffs; and **Honeydukes,** with an array of candy treats from Chocolate Frogs to Bertie Bott's Every-Flavour Beans. At the **Owlery,** roosting owls await their next delivery (high above in the rafters) while weary muggles rest in the shade of the grand Owlery roof. The **Owl Post** is an actual working post office where you can mail letters to the muggle world with a certified Hogsmeade postmark. Wands are available at **Ollivander's** (see above), but **Dervish and Banges** is the place to pick up the latest Quidditch gear, Triwizard apparel, and Spectrespecs (space here is limited, but the shop is worth a look). **Filch's Emporium of Confiscated Goods** (located in Hogwarts Castle at the exit to the Forbidden Journey, but shoppers can enter from the outside door as well) stocks the largest array of magical merchandise in the Wizarding World: journals, T-shirts, pins, sweatshirts, scarves, Golden Snitches, and more. *Warning:* Most of the shops are excruciatingly small, making them difficult to maneuver when crowds are at their worst. Wait times—yes, you have to wait in line just to shop—can be downright disturbing, at times reaching 2 hours or more just to enter Dervish and Banges.

Note: Universal has a service similar to Disney's in which you can have your purchases delivered to the front of the park; allow 3 hours. Universal also has a shop-by-phone service—call © **407/224-5800,** describe the item and where you think you saw it, and the likelihood is they'll be able to help you out and have it shipped to you.

Dining at Islands of Adventure

Islands offers some of the best theme-park dining in town, with a number of stands where you can get a quick bite to eat, plus a handful of full-service restaurants. The park's creators have taken some extra care to tie in restaurant offerings with the theme. In the Wizarding World, dining options include the **Three Broomsticks** and the **Hog's Head,** where traditional British fare is offered alongside pumpkin juice, butterbeer (a delightfully creamy concoction that comes either frozen or chilled and is nonalcoholic, of course—think cream soda mixed with root beer and a touch of whipped cream), and Hog's Head Brew (available only at the Hog's Head Pub). A wood-beamed vaulted ceiling, wooden benches, and wrought-iron accents create a rustic feel at the Three Broomsticks, while next door at the smaller Hog's Head, the atmosphere is more intimate thanks to lower ceilings and dim lighting.

Elsewhere in the park, the **Green Eggs and Ham Cafe** may be one of the few places on earth where you'd be willing to eat tinted huevos. (They sell as an egg-and-ham sandwich for about $8.) No matter which Island you're on, each offers a selection of sit-down restaurants, eateries, and snack carts. To save money, look for

Here's a sampling of some of the more unusual wares available at Islands of Adventure. It represents a cross-section of tastes.

Jurassic Outfitters: There are plenty of T-shirts with slogans such as "I Survived the [whatever ride]."

Spider-Man Shop: This stop specializes in its namesake's paraphernalia, including red Spidey caps covered with black webs and denim jackets with logos.

Toon Extra: Where else can you buy a miniature stuffed Mr. Peanut beanbag, an Olive Oyl and Popeye frame, or a

stuffed Beetle Bailey? Life doesn't get any better for some of us.

For those who prefer to shop from home (or haven't found the perfect souvenir while at the park—especially because larger-than-average crowds have left store shelves sparsely stocked at times), Universal has launched an online store that includes a slew of **Wizarding World** merchandise. Simply head to **www.universalorlando.com** and click on the "shop" link at the top of the page. For additional Wizarding World merchandise, please see above.

the kiddie menus, offering a children's meal and a small beverage for $7 to $9. Also consider combo meals (good for sharing), which usually offer a slight price break. **Thunder Falls Terrace** in Jurassic Park, for instance, offers a rib-and-chicken combo as well as other options in the $11-to-$16 range.

Here are some of my other favorites at Islands:

o **Best Sit-Down Restaurant** At **Mythos** (p. 140) on the Lost Continent, choose from main courses such as cedar-planked salmon, balsamic chicken, or a selection of sandwiches and pastas. The atmospheric undersea setting is pleasant. This is best suited to adults and children older than 10. Entrees cost $12 to $18. Coming in a close second is the **Three Broomsticks,** its less varied menu the sole reason it doesn't take the top spot.

o **Best Atmosphere for Adults** The **Hog's Head** offers an intimate atmosphere, dim lighting, and a selection of brews. What sets it apart is the animatronic hog's head behind the bar and the delightfully creamy, ever-popular butterbeer.

o **Best Atmosphere for Kids** The fun never stops under the big top at **Circus McGurkus Cafe Stoo-pendous** in Seuss Landing, where animated trapeze artists swing from the ceiling. Kids' meals, including a souvenir cup, are $6 to $8. The adults' menu features fried chicken, chicken sandwiches, cheeseburgers, spaghetti, and pizza. Try the fried chicken platter or the spaghetti for around $8.

o **Best Diversity** **Comic Strip Cafe,** located in Toon Lagoon, is a four-in-one counter-service-style eatery offering burgers, pizza and pasta, chicken and fish, and even Chinese (entrees run $8–$12).

There are also several restaurants (see chapter 4, "Where to Eat") and clubs (see chapter 8, "Walt Disney World & Orlando After Dark") that are just a short walk from the park in Universal's entertainment complex, CityWalk.

SEAWORLD

Cleverly disguised as a theme park—or as SeaWorld likes to call it, an adventure park—this popular 200-acre marine park lets guests explore the mysteries of the deep

SeaWorld

and learn about the oceans and their inhabitants, all while having tons of fun. Sea-World combines wildlife conservation awareness, actual marine life care, and plain old fun all in one fell swoop (a concept it calls "edutainment"). While that's what Disney is attempting at Animal Kingdom, the message here is subtle and a more inherent part of the experience.

SeaWorld's beautifully landscaped grounds center on a 17-acre lagoon and include flamingo and pelican ponds and a lush tropical rainforest. Shamu, a killer whale, is the star of the park along with his expanding family, which includes baby whales. The pace is much more laid-back than at either Universal or Disney, and it's a good way to break up a long week trudging through the other parks. Close encounters at feeding pools are among the real attractions (so be sure to budget a few extra dollars to buy fishy handouts for the sea lions and dolphins, who make begging an art form).

SeaWorld manages a few thrills and chills. **Journey to Atlantis** is a high-tech water ride similar to Splash Mountain at Disney's Magic Kingdom. **Kraken** is a floorless roller coaster that sports seven inversions, much like coasters such as Montu and Kumba at SeaWorld's sister, Busch Gardens in Tampa (p. 337). In 2009, **Manta,** the park's most ambitious (and expensive) thrill ride to date, splashed onto the SeaWorld scene. But this park doesn't try to compete with the wonders of WDW or Universal. Instead it lets you discover the crushed-velvet texture of a stingray or the song of seals.

Essentials

GETTING TO SEAWORLD BY CAR   The marine park is south of Orlando and Universal, north of Disney. From I-4, take exit 72, Beachline (previously Bee Line) Expressway/Highway 528, and follow the signs.

PARKING   Parking costs $12 for cars, light trucks, and vans; it's $20 for preferred parking closer to the park entrance. The lots aren't huge, and most folks can walk to the entrance; trams also run. Note the location of your car—SeaWorld characters such as Wally Walrus mark sections, but at the end of a long day it's easy to forget where you parked.

TICKET PRICES   A **1-day ticket** at the gate costs $79.99 for adults, $69.99 for children 3 to 9, plus 6.5% sales tax. The park's online ticketing system allows you to go to **www.seaworld.com**, buy your ticket over the Internet (saving about $8 on an adult ticket), print it out, and take the printout right to the turnstiles. *Note:* SeaWorld also offers multipark passes and, at times, free days, discounted pricing, and other money-saving promotions, so be sure to check online for the most up-to-date offers.

See the beginning of this chapter for information on the **FlexTicket,** a multiday ticket that provides admission to SeaWorld, Universal Orlando, Wet 'n Wild, and Busch Gardens.

SeaWorld's **VIP Tour** ($125 adults, $100 kids 3–9, *plus mandatory park admission*) is a 7-hour guided excursion that includes front-of-the-line access to Journey to Atlantis, Kraken, Manta, and Wild Arctic; reserved seating at the shows; lunch at Shamu Stadium (Dine with Shamu); and a chance to touch or feed penguins, dolphins, stingrays, and sea lions (© **800/327-2424**). It's one of only two ways to dodge park lines, though these usually aren't as long as at Disney or Universal. Here, however, the pass allows unlimited front-of-the-line access. The second way to avoid lines is via the park's new seasonal **Quick Queue** pass—starting at $14.95 and topping off

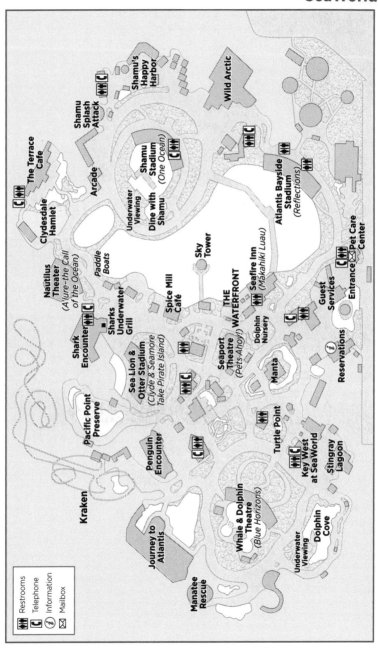

Restrooms
Telephone
Information
Mailbox

Shamu's Happy Harbor
Wild Arctic
Shamu Splash Attack
The Terrace Café
Arcade
Shamu Stadium (One Ocean)
Underwater Viewing
Dine with Shamu
Clydesdale Hamlet
Atlantis Bayside Stadium (Reflections)
Paddle Boats
Sky Tower
Nautilus Theater (Azure—the Call of the Ocean)
Spice Mill Café
Seafire Inn (Makahiki Luau)
THE WATERFRONT
Sharks Underwater Grill
Pet Care Center
Shark Encounter
Seaport Theatre (Pets-Ahoy!)
Guest Services
Entrance
Sea Lion & Otter Stadium (Clyde & Seamore Take Pirate Island)
Dolphin Nursery
Pacific Point Preserve
Manta
Reservations
Penguin Encounter
Turtle Point
Kraken
Key West at SeaWorld
Stingray Lagoon
Whale & Dolphin Theatre (Blue Horizons)
Underwater Viewing
Dolphin Cove
Journey to Atlantis
Manatee Rescue

Shuttle Service

SeaWorld and Busch Gardens in Tampa, both owned by Blackstone, have a shuttle service that offers $10 round-trip tickets to get you from Orlando to Tampa and back. The 1½- to 2-hour each-way shuttle runs daily and has five pickup locations in Orlando, including at Universal and on I-Drive (✆ **800/221-1339**). The schedule allows about 7 hours at Busch Gardens. The service is free if you have a Flex-Ticket.

at $24.95 for one-time access, $19.95 to $34.95 for unlimited access—which is similar to Universal's fee-based Express Pass program.

HOURS The park is usually open from 9am to 7pm (later during the summer and around holidays), 365 days a year. Call ✆ **800/327-2424** or 407/351-3600 for more information.

Making Your Visit More Enjoyable
PLANNING YOUR VISIT
Get information before you leave by writing to **SeaWorld Guest Services,** 7007 SeaWorld Dr., Orlando, FL 32801, or by calling ✆ **407/351-3600.**

Online, official SeaWorld information is available at **www.seaworldorlando. com**. The *Orlando Sentinel* newspaper produces **OrlandoSentinel.com,** which features a Theme Park Rangers and Tourism Central blog as well as an array of local coverage. You can also get a ton of information from the Orlando/Orange County Convention & Visitors Bureau website at **www.visitorlando.com**. Additional information, much of it aimed at the family set, can be found at **www.wdworldoand more.com**.

FOR VISITORS WITH SPECIAL NEEDS
The park publishes an accessibility guide for guests with disabilities, although most of its attractions are easily accessible to those in wheelchairs. SeaWorld also provides a Braille guide for the visually impaired. For the hearing impaired, there's a very brief synopsis of shows. Sign-language interpreting services are available at no charge, but must be reserved by calling ✆ **407/363-2414** at least a week in advance of your visit. Assisted-listening devices are available at select attractions for a $20 refundable deposit. For a complete rundown on all of your options, head to Guest Services when you enter the park; you can also call ✆ **407/351-3600** or go online to download the park accessibility guide in PDF format.

BEST TIME OF YEAR TO VISIT
Because this is a mostly outdoor, water-related park, you may want to keep in mind that even Florida gets a tad nippy during January and February. The months of January through April are when crowds are smallest.

BEST DAYS TO VISIT
Weekends, Thursday, and Friday are busy days at this park. Monday through Wednesday are usually better days to visit because tourists coming for a week in Orlando go to the Disney and Universal parks early in their stays, saving SeaWorld for the end, if at all. *Tip:* Be advised that if the weather report for the day calls for sustained rain, save SeaWorld for another time. Many attractions here are outdoors or involve—surprise!—water

and animals, a combination that can be lethal in a lightning storm. These close down at the merest hint of storm activity in the area, which will leave you with a whole lot less to do for your money.

AGE-APPROPRIATE ACTIVITIES

Because it has few thrill rides, SeaWorld has few restrictions, but you may want to check out the special tour programs offered through the education department. Sea-World lives up to its reputation for making education fun. The **Behind the Scenes Tour** offers a 90-minute glimpse into how SeaWorld cares for the animals it rescues (manatees and sea turtles in particular). The cost is $30 for adults and $10 for children 3 to 9, plus park admission. Highlights of the 4-hour **Family Fun Tour** include touching a penguin, feeding the dolphins and sea lions, reserved seating at One Ocean (the park's newest whale show), a light lunch, and front-of-the-line access to select kid-friendly rides at Shamu's Happy Harbor. The price tag is $75 for adults, $55 for children 3 to 9, plus park admission. The 2-hour **Sea Lion Up Close Tour** takes you behind the scenes at the sea-lion stadium to find out what it takes to care for the park's sea lions and harbor seals. Included in the tour are an opportunity to feed the sea lions and harbor seals at the Pacific Point Reserve, reserved seats at the sea-lion show (Clyde & Seamore Take Pirate Island), and a photo-op with the stars of the show. The cost is $40 for adults and $20 for children 3 to 9, plus park admission. The **Dolphin Up Close Tour** takes you backstage at the whale-and-dolphin stadium and behind the scenes at Dolphin Cove for an hour-long tour, where you'll find out just what's involved in training and caring for the park's bottlenose dolphins. The cost is $50 for adults and $30 for children 3 to 9, plus park admission. The **Penguin Up Close Tour** takes you backstage at the Penguin Encounter. The cost is $40 for adults and $20 for children 3 to 9, plus park admission. Call ℂ **407/363-2380** for information or ℂ **800/406-2244** for reservations.

BUDGETING YOUR TIME

SeaWorld has a leisurely pace, in part because its biggest attractions are up-close encounters with the animals. Don't be in a rush—you won't have to hurry everywhere, for a change. This park can easily be enjoyed in a day. Its layout, lush landscaping, and many outdoor exhibits give it an open feel. Because of the large capacity and walk-through nature of many of the attractions, crowds generally aren't a concern except at Journey to Atlantis, Kraken, and Manta. You also need to be in Shamu Stadium in plenty of time for the show. Wild Arctic, at times, can draw a sizable crowd, but the lines here don't come close to reaching Disney's proportions, so relax. Isn't that what a vacation is supposed to be about?

Services & Facilities at SeaWorld

ATMS   An ATM is located at the front of the park. It accepts Cirrus-, Honor-, and PLUS-affiliated cards.

BABY CARE   Changing tables are in or near most women's restrooms, and in the men's restroom at the front entrance near Shamu's Emporium. You can buy diapers in machines located near changing areas and at Shamu's Emporium. There's a special area for nursing mothers near the women's restroom at Friends of the Wild gift shop, near the center of the park.

CAMERAS & FILM   Film and disposable cameras are available at stores throughout the park.

DINING WITH THE wildlife

SeaWorld dives into the dining experience scene, offering an ask-the-expert dining opportunity aptly named **Breakfast with Jack Hanna,** which includes reserved seating at Jungle Jack's first show of the day ($18 adults, $16 kids 3–9). In addition to your meal, **Dinner with Jack Hanna** includes up-close encounters with endangered and exotic birds, mammals and reptiles; a copy of Jack's book (*Passport into the Wild*); a photo with your host; and priority reserved seating at *One Ocean* ($80 adults; $40 kids 3–9).

At **Sharks Underwater Grill** (☎ **407/351-3600** for reservations),

diners can dig into pretty sophisticated Floridian and Caribbean treats while watching denizens of the deep swim by in the Shark Encounter exhibit. It's not unlike the Coral Reef restaurant at Disney (p. 110), though here you view fish that would just as easily turn *you* into lunch. Menu prices run $18 to $32 for adults and $6 to $12 for kids (pasta, hot dogs, chicken breast, chicken tenders, and popcorn shrimp); theme-park admission is required. Special dining needs (vegetarian, kosher, and so on) can be accommodated with advance notice.

FIRST AID   First Aid stations, staffed with registered nurses, are behind Stingray Lagoon and near Shamu's Happy Harbor.

LOCKERS   Lockers are located next to Shamu's Emporium, just inside the park entrance. The cost is $7 for small lockers, $10 for larger ones. There are also short-term lockers located near Journey to Atlantis, Manta, and Kraken; the cost is 50¢ for small lockers, $1 for larger ones.

LOST CHILDREN   Lost children are taken to the Information Center. A parkwide paging system helps reunite guests. *Children younger than 7 should wear name-tags inside their clothing.*

PET CARE   A kennel is available between the parking lot and the main gate. The cost is $15 a day (no overnight stays). Owners are responsible for walking and feeding their pets during their visits.

STROLLER RENTAL   Fabric joggerlike strollers (replacing the old hard plastic dolphin-shaped ones) can be rented at the Information Center near the entrance. The cost is $13 for a single, $18 for a double. You can also purchase an umbrella stroller for around $30.

WHEELCHAIR RENTAL   Regular wheelchairs are available at the Information Center for $12; electric wheelchairs are $45.

Major Attractions at SeaWorld

A'lure—The Call of the Ocean
Frommer's Rating: B+
Recommended Ages: All ages

Replacing Odyssea, this 30-minute Cirque du Soleil–style production takes guests on a journey through the depths of the ocean by combining music, special effects, colorful projections, circus acrobatics, aerialists, and dancers (among other performers) to create a new, mythically inspired undersea-themed show. Performances are held daily at the park's Nautilus Theater. The special effects outshine those of its predecessor, as do the acrobatic stunts. And because it's completely indoors, it's a good place to escape one of the brief showers that usually spring up in Orlando on summer afternoons.

Blue Horizons
Frommer's Rating: A
Recommended Ages: All ages
At the partially covered, open-air Key West Dolphin Stadium, Blue Horizons combines elements of the sea and sky with a storyline that follows the dream of a young girl in this dolphin spectacular. Though it starts off a bit slowly as the little girl's dream begins, it's not long before the action kicks in. Everything from high dives to incredible aerial acrobatics take place above the water, while dolphins and whales show off their talents below in this action-packed production filled with colorful costumes and an upbeat musical score.

Clyde & Seamore Take Pirate Island
Frommer's Rating: A
Recommended Ages: All ages
A lovable sea lion and otter, with a supporting cast of walruses and harbor seals, plus a few quick-witted trainers, appear in this fish-breath comedy with a swashbuckling conservation theme. It's corny, but don't hold it against the animal stars. With all those high-tech rides at the other parks, you need a break, and this one delivers some laughs. Watch out if you enter late—the mime entertaining the audience may make you part of the preshow.

Journey to Atlantis
Frommer's Rating: A
Recommended Ages: 8–adult
Taking a cue from Disney Imagineers, SeaWorld has created a storyline to go with this $30-million water coaster. It's pretty thin and has to do with a Greek fisherman and ancient Sirens in a battle between good and evil. But what really matters is the drop—a wild plunge from an altitude of 60 feet, in addition to lugelike curves and a shorter drop. Journey to Atlantis breaks from SeaWorld's edutainment formula and offers good old-fashioned fun. There's no hidden lesson, just a splashy thrill when you least expect it. It's nearly as good as Jurassic Park River Adventure at Islands of Adventure (p. 270)—the thrills are equal (or maybe just a wee bit more exciting) at SeaWorld, but the thematic detailing on the Universal ride is better. **Note:** Riders must be at least 42 inches tall. Expectant moms, as well as folks with heart, neck, or back problems, should find some other way to pass the time.

A Whale of a Good Time, Part I

Shamu Underwater Viewing is an exhibit that adjoins *One Ocean* and lets you get close to killer whales and learn about breeding programs. The underwater viewing area allows a great close-up look at the tremendous creatures. You may even get to see a mother with her baby: The newest calf made his debut in October 2010.

Key West at SeaWorld

Frommer's Rating: A+ for kids, B+ for adults

Recommended Ages: All ages

This Caribbean-style village has island food, entertainers, and street vendors. But the big attractions are the hands-on encounters with harmless Southern diamond and cownose rays at Stingray Lagoon; Sea Turtle Point, the home of threatened and endangered species; and Dolphin Cove, where you can feed smelt to the namesakes. *Warning:* If you have a soft heart, it's easy to spend $20 feeding them.

Kraken

Frommer's Rating: A+

Recommended Ages: 10–adult

Like many coasters, Kraken starts off a bit slow, but it ends with pure speed. Kraken is named for a massive, mythological underwater beast. This 21st-century version offers floorless and open-sided 32-passenger trains that plant you on a pedestal high above the track. When the monster breaks loose, you climb 151 feet, fall 144 feet, hit speeds of 65 mph, go underground three times (spraying bystanders with water), and make seven loops during a 4,177-foot course. It may be the longest 3 minutes, 39 seconds of your life. *Note:* Kraken carries a 54-inch height minimum. Expectant moms as well as folks with heart, neck, or back problems should skip this one.

Manatee Rescue

Frommer's Rating: B+

Recommended Ages: All ages

The West Indian manatee is an endangered species, with as few as 3,200 remaining in the wild. Underwater viewing stations, innovative cinema techniques, and interactive displays combine here for a tribute to these gentle marine mammals. While this isn't as good as seeing them in the great outdoors, it's as close as most folks get, and it's a much roomier habitat than the tight quarters their kin have at the Seas with Nemo & Friends at Epcot.

Marine Mammal Keeper Experience

Frommer's Rating: A for trainer wannabes

Recommended Ages: 13–adult

This 9-hour program (starting bright and early at 6:30am) allows guests to work side by side with a trainer, preparing meals, feeding the animals, and learning how to care for and interact with dolphins, beluga whales, sea lions, and walruses. The cost is $399 (with tax), which includes 7 days of consecutive park admission, lunch, a DVD on conservation careers, and a T-shirt. *Note:* You must be at least 13 years old and able to climb, as well as able to lift and carry 15 pounds of critter cuisine. To reserve, call © **800/432-1178** (hit "5," when prompted).

One Ocean

Frommer's Rating: A+

Recommended Ages: All ages

Replacing Believe in 2011, just as this book goes to press, SeaWorld's newest killer-whale show highlights the park's most popular inhabitants in a freer, less choreographed way—the whales able to interact with one another more as they would in the wild, with a degree of unpredictability that translates to a different experience with each and every show. Certain elements, in particular the big splash (where guests sitting in the first several rows are completely doused in bone-chilling water), have been retained, while others (including the set, which is now far more vibrant, while

In 2009, **Manta,** SeaWorld's newest thrill-a-minute megacoaster, made a splashy debut. Touted as an experience unlike any other, the manta-inspired flying coaster takes riders soaring as high as the sky before diving as deep as the ocean depths—and all at speeds of up to 60 mph past some of the largest underwater habitats in the park. Oh, and did I mention that riders will be face-down, headfirst, and in a prone horizontal position? Don't let the name—or its appearance from the ground—fool you: Mantas may be graceful creatures that effortlessly glide through the ocean depths, but Sea-World's newest signature ride is wild from beginning to end. At times riders will find themselves within inches of the sea—at others skimming the sky, twisting through four inversions and several near misses, the wildly twisted tracks disorienting (albeit temporarily) even the most veteran coaster crazies. This one's definitely not for the faint of heart.

still featuring the tremendous whale tail and video screens) have changed. An exciting musical score helps create a rather impressive production. ***Note:*** One noticeable difference is that the trainers are no longer in the water during the show (although they are back in the water with the whales in smaller pools, now equipped with specially designed safety floors).

Note: On summer nights, when the park is open late, the last Shamu show of the day is Shamu Rocks instead of One Ocean. You don't really need to see both, as the acrobatics and tricks aren't all that different, though the music most definitely is.

Penguin Encounter ✋ ☺
Frommer's Rating: C for most, B for young kids
Recommended Ages: All ages
Here you are transported by moving sidewalk through Arctic and Antarctic displays. You'll get a glimpse of penguins as they preen, socialize, and swim at bullet speed in their 22°F (–6°C) habitat. You'll also see puffins and murres in a similar, separate area. While it gives you a nice view of the penguins (and they are always a hit with the kids), the surroundings around the viewing area leave a bit to be desired, especially among so many other elaborate and well-done exhibits.

Pets Ahoy!
Frommer's Rating: B
Recommended Ages: All ages
Eighteen cats, 12 dogs, three pot-bellied pigs, and a horse are joined by birds and rats to perform comic relief in a 25-minute show held several times a day. Almost all of the stars were rescued from animal shelters.

Shamu's Happy Harbor ☺
Frommer's Rating: A for kids
Recommended Ages: 3–12
This 4-acre play area has a four-story net tower with a 35-foot crow's-nest lookout, water cannons, remote-controlled vehicles, nine slides, a submarine, and a water maze. It's one of the most extensive play areas at any park and a great place for kids to unwind. Bring extra clothes for the kids (and maybe for yourself, too) because it's not designed to keep you dry. Smaller kids will require close supervision, however, as

In addition to the 9-hour **Marine Mammal Keeper Experience** (see above), SeaWorld offers another interactive adventure: The **Beluga Interaction Program** offers participants the chance to touch, feed, and help train (through the use of hand signals) the park's beluga whales. While a wetsuit is provided (bring a swimsuit to wear underneath), the water is a chilly 55°F (13°C), which makes it a bit difficult to maneuver. The cost is $99 to $149, plus the required park admission. The program is not open to expectant mothers or kids younger than 10. Call © **800/432-1178** or 407/363-2380, or visit **www.seaworldorlando.com** for more information or to make mandatory reservations.

they can easily get lost in all the action—and unlike many other play areas in other parks, there are several escape routes here. Options that will assuredly entertain little ones include the **Shamu Express,** a kid-friendly coaster; the **Jazzie Jellies** samba tower that lifts and spins kids in jellyfishlike seats; and **Swishy Fishies,** a teacup-style ride, where kids spin round and round in buckets that surround a gigantic sandcastle. Recent additions include the **Flying Fiddler,** where a series of short drops are sure to surprise your little one; **Ocean Commotion,** a swinging tugboat that will surely invoke a squeal (or two); and a fan-sea-ful **Sea Carousel,** perfect for the wee ones.

Shark Encounter
Frommer's Rating: A
Recommended Ages: 3–adult
SeaWorld has added other species to this formerly shark-exclusive attraction—about 220 specimens in all. Pools out front have small sharks and rays (feeding isn't allowed here). The interior aquariums have big eels, beautiful but poisonous lionfish, hauntingly still barracudas, and bug-eyed puffer fish. This isn't a tour for the claustrophobic, as you have to walk through an acrylic tube, beneath hundreds of millions of gallons of water. Also, small fry may find the swimming sharks a little too much to handle.

Wild Arctic
Frommer's Rating: B+
Recommended Ages: All ages for exhibit; 6–adult for ride
Enveloping guests in the beauty, exhilaration, and danger of a polar expedition, Wild Arctic combines a high-definition adventure film with flight-simulator technology to display breathtaking Arctic panoramas. After a hazardous faux flight over the frozen north, you emerge into an exhibit where you can see a playful polar bear or two, beautiful beluga whales, and walruses performing aquatic ballets (on different levels—you can see them both above and below the surface). Kids and those prone to motion sickness may find the ride bumpy. There's a separate line if you want to skip the flight and just see the critters. **Note:** During the winter holidays, Wild Arctic transforms (practically overnight) into the Polar Express—offering guests a chance to ride on the train made popular by the charming children's book turned hit holiday movie of the same name.

Additional Attractions

The park's other attractions include **Pacific Point Preserve,** a 2½-acre natural setting that duplicates the rocky home of California sea lions and harbor seals. **Turtle Point** showcases sea turtles swimming in the lagoon or lounging on the beach and sand dunes. The **Extreme Zone** tests your climbing and jumping skills with a rock wall and trampoline jump (both for an additional fee). A ride on the **Sky Tower,** open only seasonally and at an additional fee, lets you look out over the entire park.

The **Makahiki Luau** is a full-scale dinner show featuring South Seas–style food (fish, chicken, and pork) while you're entertained by music and dance of the Pacific Islands. It's hardly haute cuisine or Broadway, but is very much on par with Disney's Spirit of Aloha Dinner Show (p. 319), minus the characters. It's held daily at 6:30pm. During the winter holidays, a Christmas Luau temporarily replaces the original experience. Park admission is not required. The cost is $46 for adults, $29 for children 3 to 9. Reservations are required and can be made by calling © **800/327-2424** or going online to **www.seaworldorlando.com**.

Shopping at SeaWorld

SeaWorld doesn't have nearly as many shops as Walt Disney World and Universal Orlando, but with the opening of the Waterfront has added some rather unique boutiques, including **Allura's Treasure Trove,** featuring fanciful dolls, mermaids, fairies, jewelry, and more. The **Waterfront Marketplace** is filled with handcrafted gifts made by artisans from exotic ports all over the world. At **Oyster's Secret,** visitors watch as pearl divers dive in search of just the right oyster, which will be pried open for the pearl inside. Guests can then have the pearls made into jewelry. There are, of course, also lots of cuddly toys for sale around the park. Where else but **Manatee Gifts** can you get a stuffed manatee? The **Friends of the Wild** gift shop, near Penguin Encounter, has one of the larger and more varied selections in the park. The shop attached to **Wild Arctic** is good for plush toys as well. The **Emporium,** near the entrance, is one of the largest stores in the park, featuring an array of souvenirs ranging from T-shirts to toys.

 Nighttime Fun

In addition to its regular productions, SeaWorld stages a few shows only seasonally, including *Reflections,* a nighttime spectacular combining fireworks and fountains on the lagoon. During summer months, guests are treated to the special-effects extravaganza nightly. While not on the same level as Disney's nighttime spectaculars, it adds an entertaining element to the experience—especially for those who prefer to visit well into the evening hours. If you're dining at the Spice Mill restaurant in the Waterfront, you can even enjoy dinner with the show; otherwise, seating at the Bayside Stadium is your best option. Other seasonal shows include **Elmo and Abby Cadabby's Treasure Hunt** (featuring Sesame Street characters singing and dancing their way into your toddler's heart), **Shamu Rocks** (an after-dark rock 'n' roll killer-whale show), and **Shamu's Christmas Miracles** (celebrating the holiday season).

SeaWorld's 5-acre **Waterfront** area, which debuted in 2003, added a seaport-themed village to the park's landscape. On High Street, look for shops, street shows, and the Seafire Inn restaurant, where lunch includes a musical revue. At Harbor Square, the Groove Chefs make musical mayhem with pots, pans, trays, and cans. New street performers include a crusty old captain who tells fish tales and makes music with bottles and brandy glasses. The array of Waterfront eateries includes the Spice Mill, Voyagers Smokehouse, Seaport Pizza, and the Seafire Inn.

Discovery Cove: A Dolphin Encounter

Former owner Anheuser-Busch spent $100 million building SeaWorld's sister park, **Discovery Cove** (☏ **877/434-7268;** www.discoverycove.com), which debuted in 2000. In 2011, millions more were poured into the park's very first expansion: the Grand Reef. Prices for the **All-Inclusive Day Experience** run $199 to $329 per person (plus 6.5% sales tax) for ages 6 and older if you want to swim with the dolphins. They run $129 to $169 if you just want to enjoy the fish and other sea life without having the dolphin experience, or are between the ages of 3 and 6. In order to make the experience a bit more tolerable in the price department, admission includes a 14-day consecutive pass to either SeaWorld, Aquatica, or Busch Gardens in Tampa Bay. The **Ultimate Experience** tickets—$359 if you swim with the dolphins, $259 if you don't—include a 14-day pass to both SeaWorld *and* Busch Gardens, then tack on admission to Aquatica, too. The prices have, in the past, varied seasonally, so double-check when you make your reservations (which are a requirement to enter this park).

If you've never gone for a dip with a dolphin, words hardly do it justice. It's exhilarating and exciting—exactly the kind of thing that can make for a most memorable vacation.

The actual dolphin encounter deserves an **A+ rating.** It's open only to those ages 6 and older. Younger guests or those who don't want to participate in the dolphin swim can take part in the other activities.

The park has a cast of more than two dozen dolphins, and each of them works from 2 to 4 hours a day. Many of them are mature critters that have spent their lives in captivity, around people. They love having their bellies, flukes, and backs rubbed. They also have an impressive bag of tricks. Given the proper hand signals, they can make sounds much like a human passing gas, chatter in dolphin talk, and do seemingly effortless 1½ gainers in 12 feet of water. They take willing guests for rides. They also wave "hello" and "goodbye" with their flippers and take great pleasure in roaring by guests at top speed, creating waves that drench them.

The dolphin experience lasts 90 minutes, about 35 to 40 minutes of which is spent in the lagoon with one of them. Trainers use the rest of the time to teach visitors about these remarkable mammals.

At press time, construction of the **Grand Reef** was ongoing, with an opening date set for the summer of 2011. The expansion brings with it an inviting palm-lined stretch of white-sand beach, plus underwater grottoes teeming with vibrantly colored tropical fish, moray eels, and reef sharks (among other denizens of the deep). Guests can venture below the surface in shallow waters surrounded by a variety of sea life; snorkel in deeper waters among velvety rays, angelfish, tangs, and an array of tropical fish; or dive even deeper into the park's newest interactive underwater adventure, **SeaVenture.** This underwater walking tour takes guests (who don diving helmets) along pathways that allow for an up-close and interactive experience unlike any other. Swimming right alongside you are thousands of schooling sardines and eagle rays, while some of the reef's more formidable inhabitants (including zebra, nurse, black-tip, and whitetip sharks as well as venomous lionfish) swim safely behind panoramic windows. Underwater pathways and bridges (for landlubbers) above the water allow visitors to view the waters below (and lead to various islands and hidden grottoes). This unique hour-long experience (limited to six people per group) runs an additional $59 per person.

The rest of the day won't be nearly as exciting, but it is wonderfully relaxing. Discovery Cove doesn't deliver thrill rides, water slides, or acrobatic animal shows; that's what SeaWorld, Disney, and Universal are for. This is where you come to get away from all that.

Here's what you get for your money, with or without the dolphin encounter:

○ A limit of *no more than 1,000 other guests a day.* (The average daily attendance at Disney's Magic Kingdom is over 41,000.) This ensures your experience will be more relaxing and private, which is really part of what you are paying for in the first place.

○ A continental breakfast, lunch, snacks, and beverages (throughout the day), a towel, locker, sunscreen, snorkeling gear including a flotation vest, a souvenir photo, and free self-parking.

○ Other 9am-to-5:30pm activities, including a chance to swim near (but on the other side of the Plexiglas from) **barracudas** and **black-tip sharks.** There are no barriers between you and the gentle rays (some of them 4 ft. in diameter) and brightly colored tropical fish in a new 12,000-square-foot lagoon. The 3,300-foot Tropical River is a great place to swim or float in a mild current—it goes through a cave, two waterfalls, and a large aviary where you can also take a stroll, becoming a human perch for some of the 30 exotic bird species. There are also beach areas for catching a tan.

○ As mentioned above, either 14 days of **unlimited consecutive admission** to SeaWorld, Aquatic, or Busch Gardens (park admission normally costs $48–$79.99 a day for adults, $42–$69.99 for kids 3–9), or to SeaWorld, Busch Gardens, and Aquatica if you purchase the **Ultimate Experience** (for $50 more).

Note: Private cabana rentals (tucked away amid the foliage for extra privacy) are available for an additional fee.

One other option is Discovery Cove's **Trainer for a Day** ticket, which, for $398 to $518 (depending on the day), allows guests 6 and older to also have a dolphin-training encounter, participate in guided snorkeling tours, feed fish, and interact with other critters, including rays. Kids ages 6 to 12 must be accompanied by a paying adult. The ticket also includes a waterproof camera, T-shirt, and 14-consecutive-day admission to either SeaWorld, Busch Gardens, or Aquatica.

You can drive to Discovery Cove by following the earlier directions to SeaWorld, and then following the signs to the park. Unlike other parks, Discovery Cove doesn't have a parking charge.

SeaWorld

If you're headed for this adventure, I recommend making a reservation far, far in advance. With the limited number of guests admitted and the number of people who want a chance to swim with the fishes (okay . . . mammals), this park gets booked very quickly. **Note:** There is an ever-so-small chance of getting in as a walk-up customer. The park reserves a small number of tickets daily for folks whose earlier dolphin sessions were canceled due to bad weather. The best chance for last-minute guests comes during any extended period of good weather.

Aquatica: SeaWorld's Water Park

Touted as a whimsical one-of-a-kind water park, **Aquatica,** 5800 Water Play Way (off International Dr., near the entrance to the Beachline Expwy.; ℂ **888/800-5447;** www.aquaticabyseaworld.com), is an innovative, family-oriented addition to the World of Discovery family of parks that combines the up-close encounters and eco-edutainment of SeaWorld and Discovery Cove (though on a much smaller scale) with water rides ranging from serene to extreme. Across Aquatica's 56 tropically land-scaped acres (a signature of SeaWorld's parks), amid a colorful South Seas–inspired setting, are 36 unique slides and rides, six winding rivers, hidden grottoes and lagoons, and stretches of white sandy beaches that seem like they go on for miles. Setting this park apart, aside from its innovative experiences, are its animal inhabit-ants: Calling Aquatica home are Commerson's dolphins (found in the exhibit near the Dolphin Plunge near the park's entrance), giant anteaters, brilliantly colored birds that travel throughout the park (expect to see them only sporadically throughout the day), and thousands of exotic fish (swimming about in the Fish Grotto).

GETTING TO AQUATICA BY CAR From I-4, take exit 75A/Highway 435 S., and follow the signs to the parking lot.

PARKING Parking is $12 for cars, light trucks, and vans; preferred parking (spots closest to the entrance) is $15.

TICKET PRICES Admission is $47.95 for adults, $41.95 for kids 3 to 9. You can rent single strollers ($10), double strollers ($15), wheelchairs ($10), ECVs (electric convenience vehicles; $38), lockers ($8–$10), and beach towels ($4, with a $2 refundable deposit); life vests are available at no charge throughout the park. Private cabanas run from $99 to $599 depending on size, location, and amenities included (think premium, ultimate, and private island). A less expensive option that includes two lounge chairs and an umbrella, set on a sandy strip along Roa's Rapids, costs a mere $20.

In addition to the admission prices above, Aquatica is part of the multiday **Flex-Ticket** that includes admission to SeaWorld, Universal Orlando, and Busch Gardens in Tampa (see p. 244 for more information). Combination tickets including admission to both Aquatica and SeaWorld are also available ($114.95 adults, $106.95 kids 3–9).

HOURS Hours vary seasonally, but the park is usually open from at least 10am to 6pm daily, often later, weather permitting. It's closed on select Mondays and Tuesdays in November and December, but is one of the few water parks open year-round, thanks to a constant water temp of 84°F (29°C).

EXPLORING THE PARK **Dolphin Plunge** (located near the entrance) is the park's signature ride; it takes riders down through 250 feet of clear tubes, under the water, and right through the dolphin habitat (those not willing to take the plunge can sneak a peak at Dolphin Lookout). Riders must be at least 48 inches tall. Other options include the **Taumata Racer,** an eight-lane 300-foot slide that has riders flying in and out of tunnels and around a 360-degree turn before crossing the finish line; **HooRoo Run,** one of the wildest flume rides anywhere around, with three— count 'em, three—drops straight down (riders must be at least 42 in. tall); and **Tassie's Twister,** a 129-foot flume that takes riders on single or double tubes spinning and splashing their way down through a gigantic bowl before dropping them into **Loggerhead Lane** below (a lazy river that, in addition to offering a relaxing ride through the park, has a great underwater view of the Commerson's dolphins as well as thousands of exotic fish). Riders must be able to hold on unassisted. **Omaka Rocka** was added to the park's lineup of wilder rides in 2010. Located near the wave pools and sharing an entrance with Whanau Way, this ride, inspired by skateboarding and snowboarding, has riders sliding and riding forward, backward, up the walls, and through high-speed tubes and half-pipe funnels before reaching the splashdown zone below.

You can also ride **Whanau Way,** a five-story, 340-foot multilane slide filled with drops, unexpected curves, water curtains, and other thrills before dropping riders into the pool below (riders must be able to hold on unassisted); and **Walhalla Wave,** a family raft ride that takes up to four riders down six stories of tunnels filled with twists and turns (42-in. minimum height). You can catch a wave (or two or three) at **Big Surf Shores** (best for older kids and adults thanks to its crashing waves) and **Cut-back Cove** (offering a gentler rolling surf that's more appropriate for kids), the world's only side-by-side wave pools. A tremendous stretch of beach with what seems like a sea of beach chairs and chaise lounges is right nearby—the downside, however, is that there's precious little shade to protect you from the searing hot sun. If you've got the cash to spare, I recommend renting one of the nearby cabanas, but only if you're here for the day.

If you're so inclined, you can zip through waterfalls and past geysers on more than 1,500 feet of rapids on **Roa's Rapids.** It's similar to a lazy river raft ride, but there's nothing lazy about it. The park also has a large family play area, **Walkabout Waters,** that sports one of the world's largest interactive water play areas—including a 60-foot rain fortress, family slides, water cannons, and plenty of fountains—as well as a children's area, **Kata's Kookaburra Cove,** for tinier tots with miniraft rides (Mom and Dad can ride along). Life vests are plentiful (with several racks scattered throughout the park) and free (a bonus, because they're required swimwear for those under 48 in. tall). If you enjoy the water, plan on spending a full day—and bring plenty of sunscreen.

Dining options include the **Banana Beach Cookout,** an all-you-can-eat buffet restaurant that serves burgers, hot dogs, barbecued chicken, and a selection of sides ($19.95 all-day pass for adults, $11.95 all-day pass for kids 3–9); the **Mango Market,** a grab-and-go market where you can pick up pizzas, salads, snacks, and other items (they'll even pack them up in a picnic basket); and the **WaterStone Grill,** selling a variety of freshly carved sandwiches (including a tasty Cuban pork sandwich), salads, and platters. Anheuser-Busch products (for those 21 and over) are available throughout the park.

There are a few gift shops scattered about the park; they sell sportswear, beachwear, trinkets, toys, sunscreen, and sundries.

OTHER AREA ATTRACTIONS

There are—surprise!—a number of cool things in Orlando that don't revolve around Mickey, the Hulk, or Shamu. Now that I've covered the monster parks, I'm going to explore some of Central Florida's best smaller attractions.

In Kissimmee

Kissimmee's main tourist strip is on Walt Disney World's southern border and extends about 2 miles west and 8 to 10 miles east. Irlo Bronson Memorial Highway/U.S. 192 is the highway that links the town to WDW and points west. Because it is so full of eateries and hotels, it can be hard to see some of the smaller destinations, though the roadway's guide markers can be quite helpful, as is the U.S. 192 map that you can pick up at any local hotel lobby. Check with your hotel's front desk or the attractions listings below for detailed directions and shortcuts that might make finding them a little easier.

Note: The following prices don't include the 6.5% to 7% sales tax, unless otherwise noted.

Gatorland ★★ 🏕 Founded in 1949 with only a handful of alligators living in huts and pens, Gatorland now houses thousands of alligators (including a rare blue one) and crocodiles on its 70-acre spread. Breeding pens, nurseries, and rearing ponds are situated throughout the park, which also displays snakes, toads, insects, turtles, and a Galápagos tortoise. Its 2,000-foot boardwalk winds through a cypress swamp and breeding marsh. Headliners include **Gator Wrestlin',** using the old "put-them-to-sleep" trick, but it's more of an environmental awareness program; **Gator Jumparoo,** a crowd-pleaser in which the park's largest reptiles lunge 4 or 5 feet out of the water to snatch a hunk of meat from a trainer's hand (with younger, more agile gators added to the act); **Up Close Encounters,** showcasing the park's toothy carnivores, slithery snakes, and other wildlife; and **Critters on the Go,** a mobile show that allows younger kids a chance to interact with the park's cuddlier critters. The **Mile of Monsters,** a self-guided walking tour, was added in 2010, showcasing 24 of the park's most notorious alligators and crocodiles (each with a sign that tells about its capture or unusual behavior). A **train ride,** a treat for younger children and tots, runs through the park ($2 per person); other kid-friendly attractions include the **Gully Gator Splash Park,** a new wet-and-dry play area; and **Allie's Barnyard,** a small petting zoo.

Making its debut in summer 2011 is the **Screamin' Gator Zip Line,** a 45-minute experience that takes adventurous guests zooming 65 feet above several exhibits—including the park's collection of Cuban jumping crocodiles!—at speeds of up to 30 mph. Combination tickets including park admission and the zipline run $70.

The **Trainer for a Day** program lets up to five guests get up close and personal with the gators for a day—or 2 hours, in this case. The $125 experience puts you side by side with trainers and includes a chance to wrangle some alligators (minimum age 12). Advance reservations are required, and admission to the park is included (and a 20% discount off a regular admission ticket is extended to up to six members of your party). A 1½-hour **Gator Night Shine** tour is also available ($19.99, regardless of age) and takes you along the wooden walkways with only a flashlight and a guide (insect repellent and gator food are included). Advance reservations are required.

Tip: Printable discount coupons and special Internet ticket prices are available at the park's website. Be sure to check it out before you leave home. Gatorland now offers a **Gator Grunt** package, which includes admission, all-day access to the train, the opportunity to get into the ring with the gators (along with a souvenir photo), and a package of gator food (all sold separately otherwise). Prices run $29.99 for adults and $23.55 for kids ages 3 to 12.

14501 S. Orange Blossom Trail (U.S. 441; btw. Osceola Pkwy. and Hunter's Creek Blvd.). ✆ **800/393-5297** or 407/855-5496. www.gatorland.com. Admission $23 adults, $15 children 3–12. Stroller rentals

International Drive

DINNER SHOWS ◆

Arabian Nights **12**
Medieval Times **14**
Pirates Dinner Adventure **7**
Sleuths Mystery Dinner Show **9**

ATTRACTIONS ●

Central Florida Zoo **1**
Fantasy Surf **13**
Forever Florida **16**
Gatorland **15**

Harry P. Leu Gardens **3**
Holy Land Experience **5**
Orlando Museum of Art **4**
Orlando Science Center **2**
Peabody Ducks **11**

Ripley's Believe It or Not! Odditorium **8**
Wet 'n Wild **6**
Wonder Works **10**

$7–$10. Wheelchair rentals $10–$20. Daily 9am–6pm, but closing times can vary by season. Free parking. From I-4, take exit 65/Osceola Pkwy. east to U.S. 17/92/441 and go left/north. Gatorland is 1½ miles up on the right.

In the International Drive Area

These attractions are a 10- to 15-minute drive from the Disney area and 5 to 10 minutes from Universal Orlando. Most appeal to special interests, but one is free (the Peabody Ducks' show) and another (Wet 'n Wild) is in a class with WDW's top two water parks, Typhoon Lagoon and Blizzard Beach.

Holy Land Experience 👆 This $20-million, 15-acre attraction near Universal Orlando is trying to court more believers by offering exhibits focusing on Jerusalem between the years 1450 B.C. and A.D. 66. Instead of thrill rides, visitors get lessons about Noah's Ark, the limestone caves where the Dead Sea Scrolls were discovered, and 1st-century Jerusalem. The trimmings include a display of old Bibles, a Bedouin tent where biblical personalities tell Old and New Testament stories, and a cafe serving Middle Eastern food. Recent additions include the Christus Gardens and the Church of All Nations as well as a multimedia production on worship through the ages; a small play area; and the Oasis Outpost, with a rock wall, archaeological dig, and misting station. The attraction has caused some controversy: Orlando-area rabbis, among others, believe it's a ploy to convert Jews to Christianity. I say, unless you're interested in a day dedicated to the history of the Bible, the high admission is pretty hard to swallow and this place is pretty skippable. Allow 3 to 4 hours.

4655 Vineland Rd. ✆ **800/447-7235** or 407872-2272. www.theholylandexperience.com. Admission $35 adults, $20 children 6–12. Mon–Sat 10am–6pm. Hours can vary by season, so call before coming. Free parking. From I-4, take exit 78/Conroy Rd. west to Vineland Rd. It's on Vineland at Conroy.

Peabody Ducks ★ 📷 One of the best shows in town is short but sweet, and, more importantly, *free*. The Peabody Orlando's five mallards march into the hotel's lobby each morning, accompanied by John Philip Sousa's "King Cotton March" and their own red-coated duck master. They get to spend the day splashing in a marble fountain. Then, in the afternoon, they march back to the elevator and up to their 4th-floor "penthouse." Donald Duck never had it this good. Allow 1 hour.

9801 International Dr. (btw. the Beachline Expwy. and Sand Lake Rd.). ✆ **800/732-2639** or 407/352-4000. Free admission. Daily at 11am and 5pm. Free self-parking; valet parking $14 (up to 3 hr.), $17 (day), $20 (overnight). From I-4, take exit 74A, Sand Lake Rd./Hwy. 528, east to International Dr., and then south. Hotel is on the left across from the Convention Center.

Ripley's Believe It or Not! Odditorium Do you crave weird science? If you're a fan of the bizarre, here's where you'll find lots of oddities. Among the hundreds of exhibits: a two-headed kitten, a five-legged cow, a three-quarter-scale model of a 1907 Rolls-Royce made of a million matchsticks, a mosaic of the *Mona Lisa* created from toast, torture devices from the Spanish Inquisition, a Tibetan flute made of human bones, and photos of Ubangi women with wooden plates in their lips. There are also exhibits on Houdini and films of people swallowing coat hangers. Visitors are greeted by a hologram of Robert Ripley. Allow 2 hours.

8201 International Dr. (1½ blocks south of Sand Lake Rd.). ✆ **407/363-4418.** www.ripleysorlando.com. Admission $20 adults, $12 children 4–12. Daily 9:30am–midnight. Free parking. From I-4, take exit 74A, Sand Lake Rd./Hwy. 528, and turn right on International Dr.

Wet 'n Wild ★★ Who knew people came in so many shapes and sizes? Stacked or stubby, terribly tan or not, all kinds come here, so there's no reason to be bashful

Amway Center **4**
Harry P. Leu Gardens **3**
Lake Eola Park **5**
Orlando Museum of Art **2**
Orlando Science Center **1**

about squeezing into a bathing suit and going out in public. The 25-acre Wet 'n Wild is America's third-most-popular water park (behind Blizzard Beach and Typhoon Lagoon, respectively). In 2007, the park's thrill lineup got a new addition: **Brain Wash** is a multiperson tube ride with a 53-foot drop into a 65-foot domed tunnel with areas of complete darkness; it has high-tech special effects that include video projection and special lighting. **Disco H20,** an enclosed flume ride where a four-passenger raft sends you flying through the sights and sounds of the '70s, complete with mirrored lights and disco tunes blasting in the background, debuted in 2005. Other options include the **Flyer,** a six-story, four-passenger toboggan run through 450 feet of banked curves; the **Surge,** which is one of the longest (580 ft. of curves) and fastest multipassenger tube

rides in the Southeast; and the recently renovated **Black Hole—The Next Genera-
tion,** a two-person spaceship-style raft that makes a 500-foot twisting, turning voyage
through the darkness—but watch out for an explosion of color and sounds that will
shock your senses along the way (each of the three rides carries a height requirement
of between 36 and 48 in., and adults are required to accompany children). You can also
ride the **Knee Ski,** a cable-operated half-mile knee-boarding course that's open in
warm-weather months only (56-in. height minimum); **Der Stuka,** a six-story free-fall
speed slide; and **Mach 5,** which has a trio of twisting, turning flumes, among other
thrillers. The park also has a large kids' area with miniature versions of the big rides. If
you enjoy the water, plan on spending a full day here.

Note: In addition to the admission prices below, Wet 'n Wild is part of the multiday
FlexTicket that includes admission to Universal Orlando (which owns this attraction), SeaWorld, and Busch Gardens in Tampa (see p. 244 for more information).

6200 International Dr. (at Universal Blvd.). © **800/992-9453** or 407/351-1800. www.wetnwild.com.
Admission $47.95 adults, $41.95 children 3–9. Hours vary seasonally, but the park usually is open at least
10am–5pm daily, often later, weather permitting (it's one of the few water parks open year-round). You
can rent towels ($4) and lockers ($5–$10); each requires a $3 deposit. Cabana rentals $90–$250. Parking is $10 for cars, light trucks, and vans. From I-4, take exit 75A/Hwy. 435 S., and follow the signs.

Elsewhere in Central Florida

The listings that follow are out of the mainstream tourist areas, meaning you won't
have to battle heavy crowds. The Central Florida Zoo, Orlando Museum of Art, and
Orlando Science Center are close enough to incorporate a visit to Winter Park, if you
choose to make a day of it.

Central Florida Zoo 🎏   This community zoo has come a long way since it was
born in 1923 when a circus came to town, leaving a monkey and a goat behind. The
monkey rode the goat in the earliest show. Today, the animal collection includes
beautiful clouded leopards, cheetahs, and black-footed cats, all of which are endangered. You'll also meet a ham of a hippo named Geraldine as well as black howler
monkeys, siamangs, American crocodiles, a banded Egyptian cobra, a Gila monster,
barred owls, bald eagles, and dozens of other species. Recent additions include the
alligator and crocodile viewing deck, an insect zoo, and a hyacinth macaw exhibit.
Allow 2 to 3 hours.

In 2010, **ZOOm Air Adventures** opened a zipline-style attraction at the zoo.
Adventurous park-goers will find two different courses comprising a series of rope
bridges, guide wires, ziplines, and various other tree-top challenges. Pricing is separate
from zoo admission and runs $22 to $46 for adults (each course is priced separately).
A kids' course costs $18. Night flights are also available at a slightly higher cost.

Tip: One-year memberships that include additional perks and free admission to this
and 100 other participating zoos and aquariums across the country are available. A family membership is $79, which, depending on your family's size, may be more economi-
cal than purchasing individual tickets, especially if there's a member zoo in your area.

3755 NW U.S. 17/92, Sanford. © **407/323-4450.** www.centralfloridazoo.org. Admission $11.95 adults,
$9.95 seniors, $7.95 children 3–12. Daily 9am–5pm. Free parking. Take I-4 exit 104 right onto Orange
Ave., turn left at the traffic light on Lake Monroe Rd., and then right on U.S. 17/92. The zoo is on the right.

Fantasy Surf ☺   Surf's up! Fantasy Surf, Orlando's newest (and only) indoor surf
park, brings the thrill of surfing to landlocked tourists (and locals, too). Cool off riding
the waves—produced by the patented FlowRider system—from morning till night.

Accommodating up to 30 riders at any one time, the $4-million, 14,000-square-foot aquatic facility features padded walls, a cushioned floor, and beach all covered by a sheet of water that's designed for wipeouts—making it perfect for beginners and pros alike to hang ten. Sessions are offered in 30-minute increments; the more sessions you purchase, the more money you save. With tickets valid for 18 months from the date of purchase, visitors heading back to Orlando can save a bundle by purchasing multiple sessions all at once. Be sure to check the calendar posted on the website, as Fantasy Surf plays host to pro tours and competitions throughout the year. If you forgot a suit, no worries—you can pick up the latest surf and swimwear at the Offshore surf shop, well stocked with swimsuits, board shorts, T-shirts, sunglasses, and other necessities. Onlookers and hungry riders can fill up at the Lull cafe (serving snacks, wraps, pizza, and beverages). Riders must meet the 42-inch height requirement for bodyboarding, or the 52-inch height requirement for flowboarding. Signed waivers are also required (and can be downloaded in advance from the website to save time).

5151 Kyngs Heath Rd., Kissimmee. ✆ **407/396-7433.** www.ultimateindoorwave.com. Each 30-min. session $25 adults, $20 kids 9 and under. Daily 9am–10pm (last session at 9:30pm). Free parking. Take U.S. 192, turn left on Poinciana Blvd., and look for Fantasy Surf on the right.

Forever Florida The 4,700-acre Crescent J Ranch is a nature preserve that offers a chance to see native wildlife, Florida flora, and a working cattle ranch by guided tour. Options include touring by horseback (reservations required at least 24 hr. in advance) or by Coach Safari, a funky buggy that puts riders on a perch 10 feet above sea level. Allow a half-day or longer to get here, take the tour, and see the grounds, which also include a pony-riding ring, hiking trails, and a petting zoo.

Note: Forever Florida has opened **Zipline Safari,** an eco-themed experience that allows guests an opportunity to experience Florida's more natural side from high above the treetops. The multistep course (with seven ziplines and two sky bridges above three unique ecosystems) takes 2½ hours to complete and is situated more than 50 feet above the ground. Participants must be at least 10 years old (and accompanied by an adult if age 17 or under) and weigh between 70 and 275 pounds.

4755 N. Kenansville Rd., St. Cloud (southeast of Kissimmee). ✆ **866/854-3837.** www.foreverflorida. com. Coach tours $28 adults, $22 kids 6–12; horseback $40–$99 per person, up to $199 for overnights; zipline tours $85. Daily tours at 10am and 1pm. Free parking. Take I-4 exit 64A/U.S. 192 east about 15 miles to U.S. 441, and then go south 7½ miles to Forever Florida on the left.

Harry P. Leu Gardens ★ ⚘ This 50-acre botanical garden on the shores of Lake Rowena offers a serene respite from the theme-park razzle-dazzle. Paths lead through giant camphors, moss-draped oaks, palms, and camellias—the latter represented by one of the world's largest collections: 50 species and some 2,000 plants that bloom from October through March. There are 75 varieties of roses in the site's formal gardens, as well as orchids, azaleas, desert plants, and colorful annuals and perennials. The attraction also has palm, bamboo, and butterfly gardens. Businessman Harry P. Leu, who donated his 49-acre estate to the city in the 1960s, created the gardens. There are $9 guided tours (a deposit of $25 is required) of his house and the gardens, built in 1888, on the hour and half-hour (at least 3 weeks' advance registration required). The interior has Victorian, Chippendale, and Empire furnishings and pieces of art. Admission is free Mondays from 9am to noon. It takes about 2 hours to see the house and gardens.

1920 N. Forest Ave. (btw. Nebraska St. and Corrine Dr.). ✆ **407/246-2620.** www.leugardens.org. Admission $7 adults, $2 children grades K–12; free the first Mon of every month. Gardens daily 9am–5pm; house daily 10am–4pm (closed July). Free parking. Take I-4 exit 85/Princeton St. and go east,

Repeated attempts were made to revive one of Florida's original attractions, but alas, their efforts were for naught as **Cypress Gardens** finally closed its doors in 2009. But don't think all of that prime real estate is going to waste: Merlin Entertainments Group (a British amusements operator with holdings that include Madame Tussauds and the London Eye) snapped up the property and announced plans to build **LEGOLAND Florida** (slated to open just as this guide hits bookstore shelves). Much like its popular counterpart in California, LEGOLAND Florida will feature between 40 and 50 main attractions that include giant LEGO brick models, kid-powered attractions, and more. If you visit, you may recognize a few remnants left behind by its predecessor—the water-ski show, botanical gardens, and possibly one of the wooden roller coasters are supposed to remain intact. Plans to keep the neighboring Splash Island water park operational (as a separately ticketed venue) are also in the works. Construction is ongoing, and specific details have yet to be released. An opening date is set for the fall of 2011. Check out www.legolandfloridaresort.com for the most up-to-date information before planning a visit.

right on Mills Ave., and then left on Virginia Dr. Look for the gardens on your left, just after you go around a curve.

Orlando Museum of Art ★   This local heavyweight handles some of the most prestigious traveling exhibits in the nation. The museum, founded in 1924, hosts special exhibits throughout the year, but even if you miss one, it's worth a stop to see its rotating permanent collection of 19th- and 20th-century American art, pre-Columbian art dating from 1200 B.C. to A.D. 1500, and African art. Allow 2 to 3 hours.

2416 N. Mills Ave. (in Loch Haven Park). © 407/896-4231. www.omart.org. Admission $8 adults, $7 seniors and college students, $5 children 4-17. Tues-Fri 10am-4pm; Sat-Sun noon-4pm. Closed Mon and major holidays. Free parking. Take I-4 exit 85/Princeton St. east and follow signs to Loch Haven Park.

Orlando Science Center ★★ 🏛   The four-story center, the largest of its kind in the Southeast, provides 10 exhibit halls that allow visitors to explore everything from Florida swamps to the arid plains of Mars to the human body. One of the big attractions is the **Dr. Phillips CineDome,** a 310-seat theater that presents large-format films, planetarium shows, and laser-light extravaganzas. At **KidsTown,** little folks wander in exhibits representing a miniature version of the big world around them. In one section, there's a pint-size community that includes a construction site, a park, an orange-juice processing center, and an automotive garage. **Dr. Dare's Laboratory** is a "classroom of tomorrow" that includes interactive computer displays, while **NatureWorks** uses replicated Florida ecosystems to teach kids about the environment. Dino Digs, H2Now, All Aboard, Science on a Sphere, SimMan, and the Science Park are some of the other exhibits that await you. Allow 3 to 4 hours, more if you have an inquiring mind.

777 E. Princeton St. (btw. Orange and Mills aves., in Loch Haven Park). © 888/672-4386 or 407/514-2000. www.osc.org. Admission (includes exhibits, CineDome film, and planetarium show) $17 adults, $16 seniors 55 and older, $12 children 3-11. Strollers and wheelchairs free (with photo ID or credit card) Sun-Tues 10am-5pm; Thurs-Sat 10am-5pm. Parking available in a garage across the street for $5. Take I-4, exit 85/Princeton St. east and cross Orange Ave.

STAYING ACTIVE

You will most likely burn more calories than you ever thought possible by simply strolling through the theme parks. Nevertheless, if you want some exercise other than walking the parks, Walt Disney World and the surrounding areas have plenty of recreational options. Most of the following are open to everyone, no matter where you're staying (exceptions are noted below). For further information about WDW recreational facilities, call ✆ 407/939-7529 or go to **www.disneyworld.com** (click the "recreation" link).

Outdoor Recreation

AIRBOATING   You can giddy-up-and-glide across the surface of local waters at **Boggy Creek Airboat Rides,** in Kissimmee (✆ 407/344-9550; www.bcairboats. com), where you'll pay $26 per adult and $20 per child ages 3 to 12 for half-hour tours; night tours and land-only wildlife safari tours are available as well. Another choice is **Old Fashioned Airboat Rides,** in Christmas, east of Orlando (✆ 407/568-4307; www.airboatrides.com), which charges $45 per adult and $35 per child age 12 and younger for 90-minute tours.

BALLOONING   There are several places in the area to experience an early-morning hot-air balloon flight, including **Orange Blossom Balloons,** in Lake Buena Vista (✆ 407/239-7677; www.orangeblossomballoons.com), and **Blue Water Balloons** (✆ 800/586-1884 or 407/894-5040; www.bluewaterballoons.com). Sunrise flights are available daily, and all flights, which last approximately 1 hour, are followed by a champagne toast (sorry, kids) at the conclusion of the flight and a breakfast buffet or picnic afterward. Children who make the age grade will probably be delighted with the view and the unique sensation, unless they (or you) don't see eye-to-eye with heights. Blue Water offers hotel pickup at no extra charge. Rates run approximately $175 per adult; children younger than 10 ride free (with a paying adult).

BICYCLING   Bike rentals (single- and multispeed adult bikes, tandems, baby seats, and children's bikes—including those with training wheels) are available from the **Bike Barn** (✆ 407/824-2742), at Disney's Fort Wilderness Resort & Campground. Rates for each bike are $9 per hour, $20 per day (surrey bikes run $21–$23 per half-hour), regardless of age. Fort Wilderness offers a lot of good bike trails. Many of the other Disney resorts also offer bicycle rentals at similar rates. Call your hotel in advance or inquire upon check-in.

BOATING   With so many man-made lakes and lagoons dotting the WDW landscape, it's no surprise Disney owns a navy of pleasure boats. **Capt. Jack's,** at Downtown Disney (✆ 407/828-2204), rents Sea Racers ($34 per half-hour, tax included), pontoons ($48 per half-hour, tax included), and sailboats ($21 per hour, tax included). The **Bike Barn,** at Disney's Fort Wilderness (✆ 407/824-2742), rents canoes and paddle boats ($7 per half-hour). At both sites, kids must be at least 12 to rent a boat; those younger than 18 cannot rent without a signed parental waiver.

The **Winter Park Scenic Boat Tour** (✆ 407/644-4056; www.scenicboattours. com) offers visitors another opportunity to see some of Central Florida's sights, this time while sailing along the city's historic lakes and canals. Tickets cost $12 for adults, $6 for kids ages 2 to 11.

FISHING   There are several fishing excursions offered on Disney waterways, including Bay Lake and Seven Seas Lagoon. The lakes are stocked, so you may catch

HITTING THE links

Walt Disney World operates five 18-hole, par-72 golf courses and one 9-hole, par-36 walking course, so if you want to work on your putting and need some time away from the kids (who will most likely prefer an outing on one of Disney's minigolf courses; see p. 240), you'll have plenty of options. All are open to the public and offer pro shops, equipment rentals, and instruction. The rates are $164 to $245 per 18-hole round ($25–$45 less if you're staying at a WDW property). Twilight specials are available in the spring for $55 to $70 per person; "After 10" and "After 3" specials are available during summer and fall for $49 to $59 per person. For tee times and information, call © **407/939-4653** up to 7 days in advance (up to 30 days for Disney resort and "official" property guests). Call © **407/934-7639** for information about golf packages.

Beyond Mickey's shadow, try **Celebration Golf Club** (© **888/275-2918** or 407/566-4653; www.celebrationgolf.com), which has an 18-hole regulation course (greens fees $39–$89; twilight specials $39; discounts apply for Florida residents and Celebration residents). Note that there is a dress code at the club—be sure to ask ahead so your kids are decked out in suitable attire. **ChampionsGate** (© **888/554-9301** or 407/787-4653; www.championsgategolf.com) offers 36 holes designed by Greg Norman, where greens fees will set you back $55 to $172, as well as the **David Leadbetter Golf Academy** (© **407/787-3330**; www.davidleadbetter.com). **Orange County National** (© **407/656-2626**; www.orangecountynationalgolf.com) has 36 Phil Ritson–designed holes; greens fees run $30 to $150.

Golf magazine recognized the 45 holes designed by Jack Nicklaus at the **Villas of Grand Cypress ★★★** (p. 70) as among the best in the nation. Tee times begin at 8am daily. Special rates

something, but true anglers probably won't find it much of a challenge. The excursions can be arranged 2 to 90 days in advance by calling © **407/824-2621.** A license isn't required. The fee is $235 to $270 for up to five people for 2 hours, $445 for up to five people for 4 hours ($110 for each additional hour), including refreshments, gear, guide, bait, and tax. Children above the toddler stage are permitted on these tours when accompanied by an adult; however, excursions just for kids ages 6 to 12 are available for $10 from Disney's Contemporary Resort, Polynesian Resort, and Old Key West Resort.

A less expensive alternative: Rent fishing poles at the **Bike Barn** (© **407/824-2742**) to fish in the Fort Wilderness canals. Pole rentals cost $6 per hour, or $10 per day (not including tax). Bait is $3.50 to $3.65. A license isn't necessary.

Outside the realm, **Pro Bass Guide Service** (© **407/877-9676**; www.probassguideservice.com) offers guided bass-fishing trips along some of Central Florida's most picturesque rivers and lakes. Hotel pickup is available; the cost is $250 for one or two people per half-day, $400 for a full day. A license is $17.

HANG GLIDING You'll get the chance to soar 2,000 feet in the air as you fly through the sky—with a little help from some instructors at the **Wallaby Ranch** (© **863/424-0070**; www.wallaby.com), located in Davenport, just south of Kissimmee. If you're a thrill-ride junkie, this is the real deal. Prices, starting at $120, depend on the number of lessons and type of flight you want (call or check the website for detailed information). Bring home a DVD of your flight for an additional $60.

are available for children younger than 17, and the resort even runs a 5-day summer golf program for kids interested in the game. For information, call ☎ 407/239-1909. The course is generally restricted to guests or guests of guests, but there's limited play available to those not staying at the resort. Fees run approximately $120 to $175.

With more than 150 courses located throughout the Orlando area, it's simply impossible to list them all. There are, however, several additional courses and academies worth noting: the **Shingle Creek Golf Club,** including the **Brad Brewer Golf Academy** (☎ 866/966-9933 or 407/966-9933; www.shingle creekgolf.com), located at the Rosen Shingle Creek Resort; **Hawk's Landing Golf Club and Academy** (☎ 407/238-8660) at the World Center Marriott; and the **Legacy, Independence,** and **Tradition** golf courses, as well as the **ANNIKA Academy,** all located at Reunion Resort

& Club of Orlando (☎ 888/418-9610 or 407/662-1000). The **Ritz-Carlton Golf Club** and **Grande Pines Golf Club,** both located at the **Grande Lakes Orlando** (☎ 407/393-4814), offer the only golf caddie concierge program around to make your game all it can be; the program offers advice, helpful hints, caddie services, food and beverage service, and much more.

Also consider **Golfpac** (☎ 800/848-8941 or 407/260-8989; www.golfpac travel.com), an organization that packages golf vacations with accommodations and other features and prearranges tee times at more than 40 Orlando-area courses. The earlier you call (months, if possible), the better your options. **Advanced Tee Times USA** (☎ 888/465-3356; www.teetimesusa.com) and **Golforlando** (☎ 866/342-4782; www. golforlando.com) are two other reservations services that offer packages and course information.

HAYRIDES A hay wagon departs **Pioneer Hall,** at Disney's Fort Wilderness, nightly at 7 and 9:30pm for 45-minute old-fashioned hayrides with singing, jokes, and games. Most kids will find it enjoyable, though some teens may think it corny. The cost is $8 for adults, $5 for children ages 3 to 9, and free for kids 2 and younger. An adult must accompany children younger than 12. No reservations are taken. Call ☎ 407/824-2832 for more information.

HELICOPTER TOURS For a bird's-eye view of Disney, Universal, SeaWorld, and beyond, fly sky-high with **International Heli-Tours** (☎ 407/239-8687 or 407/397-0226; www.internationalhelitours.com). Two locations—one on International Drive, the other in Kissimmee—offer tours 7 days a week (including a nighttime fireworks tour over Epcot). Prices, which vary depending on the number of locations included on the tour, range from $30 to $400 for adults, $20 to $200 for children 10 and under (with a two-adult-fare minimum and a four-passenger maximum).

HIKING The **Nature Conservancy's Disney Wilderness Preserve** (☎ 407/682-3664; www.nature.org/florida) is a 12,000-acre, little-discovered getaway from the theme-park madness. It has 7 miles of trails at the headwaters of the Everglades ecosystem, just south of Orlando. Self-guided trails range from a .5-mile interpretive trail good for younger kids to a 4.5-mile hiking trail for adults and teens. Picnic facilities are available along the trails. Admission costs $3 for adults, $2 for kids 6 to 17 and Nature Conservancy members. It's open year-round, Monday through Friday from 9am to 5pm. The preserve also features Sunday-afternoon **buggy rides** ($12 adults, $6 kids) from October through May.

HORSEBACK RIDING Disney's Fort Wilderness Resort & Campground offers 45-minute guided trail rides several times a day. The cost is $42 per person. Children must be at least 9 years old. Maximum rider weight is 250 pounds. If you or your children have never ridden before, the tame horses and gentle terrain make this ride a good introductory experience. For information and reservations up to 30 days in advance, call © **407/824-2832.**

Outside the world of Walt Disney are the **Horse World Riding Stables,** in Kissimmee (© **407/847-4343;** www.horseworldstables.com). Trail rides range in price from $44 for an easy hour on a nature trail to $75 for a 1¼-hour advanced-level ride.

HORSE-DRAWN CARRIAGE RIDES Disney offers evening carriage rides at two of its resort locations: **Fort Wilderness Resort & Campground** and the **Port Orleans Resort.** The 30-minute rides cost $45 for up to four people. Most kids will enjoy the ride and the sightseeing opportunity. For information, call © **407/824-2832.**

JOGGING Many of the Disney resorts have scenic jogging trails. For instance, the **Yacht** and **Beach Club** resorts share a 2-mile trail, the **Caribbean Beach Resort** has a 1.4-mile promenade encircling a lake, **Port Orleans** has a 1.7-mile riverfront trail, and **Fort Wilderness** has a tree-shaded 2.3-mile jogging path with exercise stations about every quarter-mile. Pick up a jogging trail map at any Disney property's Guest Services desk.

PARASAILING The **Sammy Duvall Watersports Centre,** at Disney's Contemporary Resort (© **407/939-0754;** www.sammyduvall.com), will take you up to 600 feet above Seven Seas Lagoon and Bay Lake on a flight that lasts 8 to 12 minutes. The cost runs approximately $95 for one rider and $170 for two riders. Kids older than 5 are eligible if they fly in tandem with someone else (minimum total weight of 125 lbs.), though you'll have to judge whether your child is up to such an experience. While older kids and teens would probably fare well, younger children likely wouldn't. Everyone who goes up has to sign a waiver, and parents have to sign off on their kids' participation. You can reserve a spot up to 90 days in advance.

SCUBA DIVING & SNORKELING Believe it or not, even in an inland location like Orlando, you can scuba and snorkel in the Florida waterways. **Fun 2 Dive Scuba and Snorkeling Tours** (© **407/322-9696;** www.fun2dive.com) and **Orlando Dive and Snorkel Tours** (© **407/466-1668;** www.floridamanateetours. com) both offer the chance to swim and snorkel with manatees (and other wildlife) as well as other ecotour opportunities. Prices run approximately $90 to $100 per person (with a maximum of six) to swim and snorkel. Fun 2 Dive also offers scuba lessons and deep-sea-fishing excursions.

SKATEBOARDING On the occasional rainy afternoon (or even in good weather), **Vans Skatepark** (© **407/351-3881;** www.vans.com) offers skateboarders (beginners or advanced) the chance to ride the day away on ramps, bowls, street courses, and more. Safety equipment is required (and available for rent if you don't have your own); those younger than 18 are required to have a parent or guardian sign a waiver (in front of a Vans employee or a notary). Rates run approximately $12 per session for nonmembers, $5 for members (requiring a 1-year commitment) on weekdays; $15 and $7, respectively, on weekends and holidays. Sessions are 2 hours long and run at scheduled times. Rental equipment, from boards to helmets and pads, is available for

$2 to $5. Private lessons, camps, and birthday parties are also offered. The park is located in the Festival Bay Mall at the far north end of International Drive.

SURFING It's true. The creative minds at Disney have added a way for you to learn how to catch a wave and "hang ten" at the Typhoon Lagoon water park (p. 236). On Tuesdays and Fridays, instructors from **Ron Jon Surf School** (*C* **407/939-7529**) show up for an early-bird session in the namesake lagoon, which has a wave machine capable of 8-footers. The 2½-hour sessions are held before the park opens to the general public and are limited to 14 people. Minimum age is 8. The $150-per-person cost (including tax) doesn't include park admission, which you'll have to pay if you want to hang around after the lesson. You'll also need alternative transportation to get here if you're staying in Walt's World, because the Disney Transportation System doesn't service Typhoon Lagoon until official park opening time.

Another good option (especially on a rainy day) is **Fantasy Surf** (*C* **407/396-7433;** www.ultimateindoorwave.com), the area's newest indoor surf park, located in Kissimmee in the midst of the tourist district along U.S. 192. Here you can catch a wave on the Flowrider, grab a bite to eat at the snack bar, and pick up the latest in surf wear at the small yet well-stocked shop. Rates per half-hour run $25 per adult and $20 per child younger than 9. Bodyboarding holds a height requirement of 42 inches, flowboarding a requirement of 52 inches.

SWIMMING Almost all of Orlando's resorts have their own pools, some of which are rather unique, others rather extensive (and discussed in more detail in chapter 3). If you're not satisfied with the one at your hotel, the **YMCA Aquatic Center,** 8422 International Dr. (*C* **407/363-1911;** www.aquaticcenterymca.com), has a full fitness center, racquetball courts, an indoor Olympic-size pool, and a heated 25m pool for kids. All pools have lifeguards. Admission is $10 per person, $25 for families.

TENNIS There are 20 lighted tennis courts scattered throughout the Disney properties and the **ESPN Wide World of Sports Complex.** Most are free and open to resort guests on a first-come, first-served basis. Call *C* **407/939-7529** for more information. The courts at **Disney's Grand Floridian Resort,** all lighted for evening play, will cost you $12.50 per hour to play; reservations are required. Private lessons are available for $90 per hour; group clinics run $15 per person. The courts at the Grand Floridian are for Grand Floridian guests only (Contemporary Resort guests will temporarily be allowed access until that resort's Bay Lake Tower has been completed).

The **Grand Cypress Racquet Club** (*C* **407/239-1944;** www.grandcypress.hyatt.com) features 12 courts, 5 of which are lighted. Racquetball courts, a clubhouse, and pro shop are available as well. Clinics are offered daily, with private lessons ($89 per hour, $49 per half-hour) and semiprivate lessons ($49 per hour) available as well.

WATER-SKIING & WAKEBOARDING Water-skiing trips (including boats, drivers, equipment, and instruction) can be arranged Tuesday through Saturday at Walt Disney World by calling the **Sammy Duvall Watersports Centre,** at Disney's Contemporary Resort (*C* **407/939-0754;** www.sammyduvall.com). Make reservations up to 14 days in advance. The cost for skiing is $185 per hour for up to five people. You can also arrange wakeboarding for up to four people; rates run $165 for an hour. There's no minimum age, though I wouldn't recommend this for children younger than 8; it's definitely not for those at all uncomfortable in the water.

Outside Disney, you can get some time behind a boat or at the end of an overhead cable at the **Orlando Watersports Complex,** 8615 Florida Rock Rd. (© **407/251-3100;** www.orlandowatersports.com), near Orlando International Airport, which has lights for nighttime thrill-seekers. Teens will likely think the nighttime option cool, but kids younger than 8 and those not completely comfortable in the water aren't the best candidates for this activity. Prices for skiing (including lessons) begin at about $22 an hour for a cable and $55 for a half-hour behind a boat. The complex offers a number of specials and discounts aimed at kids and families—call or check the website to see what's being offered during your visit. Rental fees run $2 to $45 depending on equipment and duration of rental.

Another good option is **Buena Vista Water Sports** (© 407/239-6939; www.bvwatersports.com); the setting is far more inviting, and it's located closer to all the action at Lake Bryan in Lake Buena Vista. It offers Sea-Doo rentals ($55 per half-hour, $98 per hour) as well as water-ski, wakeboard, and tube rides ($50 for 15 min., $85 for a half-hour, $145 for an hour).

SPECTATOR SPORTS

Disney doesn't want to give the competition a sporting chance. In 1997, it branched out with the multimillion-dollar **ESPN Wide World of Sports Complex** (known as Disney's Wide World of Sports in a previous life), a 200-acre facility. The Mouse hit a home run with a 7,500-seat baseball stadium—dubbed Cracker Jack Stadium in 2002—that's the spring-training home of the Atlanta Braves. In addition, there's a 5,000-seat field house featuring six basketball courts, a fitness center, and training rooms; major-league practice fields and pitching mounds; 4 softball fields; 12 tennis courts, including a 2,000-seat stadium center court; a track-and-field complex; a golf driving range; and more. The Hess Sports Fields include baseball, soccer, lacrosse, and football fields, while the Jostens Center (a state-of-the-art multisport field house) practically doubles the complex's capacity for indoor sporting events. Future additions include a 100-lane bowling center (one of the largest bowling facilities in the U.S.). A variety of events, from tennis tournaments to band competitions, has been held here since the center opened. For information about events taking place during your stay, call © **407/939-1500** or visit **www.disneyworldsports.com**.

So, if you and your kids are sports nuts, you won't have to forgo your fix while in Orlando. Even taking the above into account, Disney isn't the only show in town.

Arena Football

The **Orlando Predators** play from February to mid-May. For the uninitiated, arena football is a wide-open sport played by eight-man teams on a much-abbreviated field. You don't necessarily need to know the rules to enjoy the up-close crunching and beer-fest atmosphere. The Predators have a loyal and rowdy following, not to mention a few championships under their belts. Sold-out games are common, but single tickets ($7–$85) are often available the day of the game at **Amway Center.** Call © **407/447-7337,** or go to **www.orlandopredators.com** for more information. *Note:* At press time, the future of the Predators program was up in the air due to the instability of the entire AFL program.

Baseball

The **Atlanta Braves** began spring training at the ESPN Wide World of Sports Complex in 1998. There are 18 games played during a 1-month season that begins in

The Multisports Experience

The ESPN Wide World of Sports Complex at Walt Disney World has an expanded multisports venue that lets you test your skills at football, baseball, basketball, hockey, soccer, and volleyball. Admission is $11.31 for adults and $9.34 for kids 3 to 9. It's open on select days. For information, call ✆ 407/939-1500.

If you're a true sports fan, your best bet is to request in advance a package of information about the facilities and a calendar of events. Write to **ESPN Wide World of Sports**, P.O. Box 10000, Lake Buena Vista, FL 32830-1000, or call ✆ 407/939-1500. Online, check out **www.disneysports.com.**

March. The smaller setting makes for a far more intimate experience for kids than a regular stadium game would, and the atmosphere is usually a lot more relaxed. Tickets are $15 to $39. For information, call ✆ **407/828-3267.** You can get tickets through **Ticketmaster** (✆ **800/745-3000**).

Basketball

The Amway Center is the home court of the NBA's **Orlando Magic** (✆ **407/896-2442**; www.nba.com/magic), which plays 41 of its regular-season games here from October to April. To get there, take I-4 east to exit 83B, Highway 50/U.S. 17/92 (Amelia St.), turn left at the traffic light at the bottom of the off-ramp, and follow the signs. Single-game tickets ($13–$65 and on up to $1,500 for luxury seating) can be hard to get. The team schedules special theme nights and promotions throughout the season, many of them family related, and mascot Stuff the Magic Dragon (that really is his name) is a hit with kids. For up-to-the-minute parking information, turn your car radio to 1620 AM. On-site parking runs $10 (and can be prepaid), but spaces are limited.

SHOPPING

Whether you're looking for mouse ears and wizard wands or the latest and greatest in designer labels, you'll find it in Orlando (ranked fourth among the top shopping destinations in the country, falling in behind New York, Los Angeles, and Las Vegas). Walt Disney World itself is home to an almost endless array of shops spread throughout its parks, resorts, and Downtown Disney. The House of Mouse, however, is not the only game in town. If you venture beyond its boundaries, you'll discover first-rate shopping malls, outlet centers, and charming boutiques.

But before you break out your credit cards, do remember to keep your shopping wits about you. The malls and their upscale stores, at times, can charge extremely outrageous prices that you'll easily better at home. And the outlets, which once offered tremendous bargains, now at times discount only marginally. The key to getting the best possible deals is to know what is and *isn't* a bargain.

And now, a note on souvenir shopping. If, after exercising your credit cards elsewhere, you've still got energy (and money) to burn, the parks and entertainment districts at Walt Disney World, Universal Orlando, and SeaWorld feature some of the most distinctive souvenir shopping you'll find anywhere. Sure, many of the stores are filled with trinkets and T-shirts, but some offer more unique merchandise that you won't be able to find anywhere else—Orlando or otherwise. Besides the listings in this chapter, be sure to check out some unique shopping opportunities mentioned in chapter 5, "Exploring Walt Disney World," and chapter 6, "Exploring Beyond Disney: Universal Orlando, SeaWorld & Other Attractions."

THE SHOPPING SCENE

The hottest spots for tourists to shop are at Downtown Disney, CityWalk, and the larger themed shopping centers scattered along International Drive. Kissimmee, though a very busy area, has little to offer shoppers other than seashells and T-shirts that, at three for $10, are a good example of the old saying "you get what you pay for." I do, however, admit that I have on occasion found a hidden treasure or two among the trinkets, so if you're in the mood for a bargain and are willing to take the time to hunt for it, you may just get lucky. There are, of course, more than just a few of the same tourist traps located along I-Drive (mostly at the northern end) as well as along S.R. 535 in Lake Buena Vista. But don't despair; if you stick to the places listed in this chapter, you'll find plenty of quality merchandise.

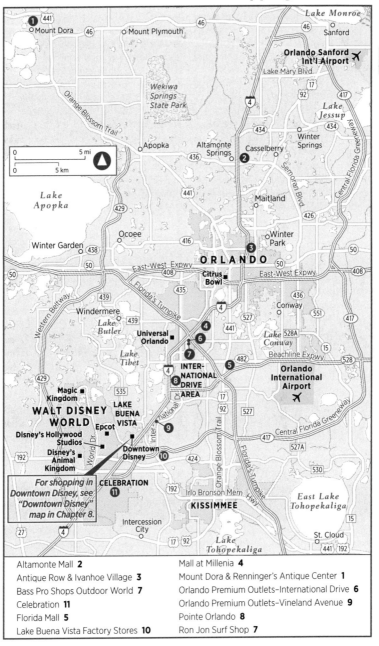

Altamonte Mall **2**	Mall at Millenia **4**
Antique Row & Ivanhoe Village **3**	Mount Dora & Renninger's Antique Center **1**
Bass Pro Shops Outdoor World **7**	Orlando Premium Outlets–International Drive **6**
Celebration **11**	Orlando Premium Outlets–Vineland Avenue **9**
Florida Mall **5**	Pointe Orlando **8**
Lake Buena Vista Factory Stores **10**	Ron Jon Surf Shop **7**

> **Ship It**
>
> Because Orlando is geared to travelers, many retailers offer to ship packages home for a few dollars more (Disney definitely does). So, if you're pondering an extralarge purchase, or even just one you would rather not have to carry (especially in the age of outrageous airline baggage fees), simply ask. If a retailer doesn't offer such a service, check with your hotel. Many a concierge or business center staffer can arrange a pickup by UPS, the U.S. Postal Service, or another carrier—or, at the very least, point you in the direction of the carrier located closest to the hotel. Anything's better than dragging that 6-foot stuffed Pluto through the not-so-friendly skies.

If you're looking for a quieter, out-of-the-way shopping experience, the quaint tree-lined streets of Winter Park—Park Avenue in particular—are filled with one-of-a-kind boutiques, well-known shops, and antiques stores. Closer to the action, yet still far enough off the beaten path to remain quaint and quiet, is Market Street in Celebration, which is home to a small collection of tiny shops. Downtown Orlando has its own unique shopping spots, with Antique Row (along Orange Ave.) and nearby Ivanhoe featuring antiques dealers, collectible shops, and better gift stores. If you're in search of a quiet retreat or an afternoon of simple indulgence, these shopping side trips should provide just the sort of peaceful experience you're seeking (you won't even mind coming away empty-handed).

Many Orlando area stores, particularly those in malls or other shopping centers, are open from 9 or 10am until 9 or 10pm Monday through Saturday, and from noon to 6pm on Sunday. It is always best to check before you go, as shopping hours, like those at the parks, can change during the holidays, as well as seasonally. Sales tax in Osceola County, which includes Kissimmee, the U.S. 192 corridor, and all of Disney's All-Star resorts, is 7%. In Orange County, which includes the International Drive area, SeaWorld, Universal Orlando, most (but not all) of Disney World, and most of the lesser attractions, it's 6.5%. In Seminole County, about 40 miles north of Walt Disney World, the rate is 7%. No matter where you are, plan on adding a few extra dollars in taxes to your bill when you get to the cash register.

One thing that's no different here than the rest of the country: If you arrive during the holiday season, from the end of November to January 1, it's best to avoid local shopping malls, especially on weekends. They're just as crazy and crowded as those back home—maybe even worse. And no matter what time of year it is, don't leave your good judgment at the door when you're shopping the outlet malls. Although there are some bargains to be found, the prices on many items aren't really much better than you can find at home in many cases. The selection, however, may be much larger than you're used to—especially if you're from outside the United States. Remember, though, that you still have to get it home with you somehow, so if you can buy the same item at home, do you really want to have to carry it all the way from Florida?

Great Shopping Areas

CELEBRATION Though not the best place to head if you're the shop-'til-you-drop type, this is a rather pleasant spot for a leisurely stroll along quaint streets filled with upscale shops, coffeehouses, and restaurants. Celebration, after all, is a

Disney-designed community, making it practically the perfect little town (or a facsimile thereof). It's a throwback to mid–20th-century mainstream America, when main-street shopping was in style. Market Street and the area just surrounding it are home to a dozen or so shops, a couple of art galleries, a handful of restaurants, and a three-screen movie theater. The storefronts, especially the galleries and gift shops, offer interesting and unique merchandise, though you'll find that there's a price to pay for perfection. Stores here include the **Market Street Gallery** (Swarovski crystal, collectibles, home decor, Yankee Candles, Christmas decorations, and more), **Day Dreams** (a shop filled top to bottom with dolls, teddy bears, books, and gift items), **Soft as a Grape** (comfy 100% cotton resort wear for the entire family), the **Lollipop Cottage** (clothing and gifts for children), **Confetti** (personalized gift baskets, sweets, treats, and party planning), **Unique Boutique** (designer labels mixing with one-of-a-kind fashions and accessories), **Downeast** (gifts, accessories, and clothing sporting labels such as Polo, Lacoste, Vera Bradley, and Cavalli, among others), the **Jewel Box** (an authorized Pandora dealer and purveyor of better baubles), **Sanrio Surprises** (a haven for Hello Kitty fans), the **Woof Gang Bakery** (homemade gourmet treats and an array of pet-care products for the pampered pet set), an art gallery and frame shop, a grocer, a post office, and others. The **Village Mercantile,** after 13 years in business, closed its doors in 2009, an unfortunate victim of the economy. The high prices here may make for more window-shopping than actual spending, but the real attraction in Celebration is the relaxing, picture-perfect atmosphere. If, by chance, Celebration reminds you of the film *The Truman Show,* you're not alone. The movie was filmed in Seaside, a Florida Panhandle community that inspired the builders of this burg.

DOWNTOWN DISNEY   With three distinct areas—West Side, Pleasure Island (soon becoming Hyperion Wharf), and the Marketplace—**Downtown Disney** (🕻 **407/939-2648;** www.downtowndisney.com) is chock-full of some of the most unique shops in Orlando, as well as many restaurants and entertainment venues.

The best shops in the Marketplace include the 50,000-square-foot **World of Disney,** the largest store in Downtown Disney (and the second-largest Disney store in the world). There are rooms and more rooms filled with everything Disney, from toys and trading pins to clothes and collectibles—and everything (and I mean *everything*) in between. **Bibbidi Bobbidi Boutique,** which arrived in 2006, is where little girls can have their hair styled, put on makeup, and have their nails done so they look like a princess (or their favorite Disney pop star) when they emerge. Girls can

 Getting Your Fill

The neatest way to buy toys at several Downtown Disney (and Disney theme park) stores (especially Once Upon a Toy) is in bulk . . . sort of. Toys such as Lincoln Logs and Mr. Potato Head, as well as a few others, can be purchased by the piece. Here's how it works: You pick out a box (often with two sizes to choose from) and fill it up with as many (or few) pieces as you can fit inside.

The only stipulation—you have to be able to close the lid properly. No matter how many pieces you've stuffed inside, the price of the box remains the same. If you've got good space-saving skills, buying your toys this way may net you a very good deal. (Here's a hint to get you started: Mr. Potato Head has a hole in his back, so fill it up and you'll fit more pieces in your box.)

play dress-up in the princess room, while the adventure room is geared more to boys—they can create their own pirate hat, play video games, and check out superhero, space explorer, and cowboy gear.

The **LEGO Imagination Center,** now larger and even easier to shop after a recent expansion, offers lots of play areas to entertain the kids (I'd hate to be the one cleaning up at night). The exterior sports several new, rather impressive LEGO models, while inside, shelves are filled with an array of LEGO blocks and play sets designed for everyone from toddlers to tweens, plus Bionicles, T-shirts, and trinkets. Check out the display behind the counter when you cash out—it's filled top to bottom with teeny tiny LEGO people (visible thanks to a nifty magnifying glass that runs back and forth across their little faces). **Once Upon a Toy** is one of the best stores in the Marketplace, and the best toy store I've ever been in. It's stocked from floor to ceiling with games and toys, many of them classics—you know, the ones you played with while growing up (most with a Disney twist, of course). The 16,000-square-foot space is divided into three sections: The first is filled with board games; the second is loaded with building sets and action figures; and the third is dedicated to techy toys (video games, movies, and other gizmos). The store's popular "build your own" and "fill your own" stations, including a "build your own lightsaber" station (where you can pick and choose from a variety of doodads, packing on as many pieces as possible), are sprinkled throughout the premises. *Note:* Inside the T-Rex restaurant is one of only five **Build-A-Dino** stores in the country (a younger sibling of the wildly popular Build-A-Bear stores). Here kids can pick out, stuff, dress, and accessorize their very own Paleolithic plush pal. Prices range from $15 to $22 (accessories and clothing cost extra).

Another custom-souvenir opportunity is at **Disney's Design-A-Tee** (presented by Hanes), which lets guests create their own souvenir T—from sleeve length to color to design (there are hundreds to choose from). Simply make your selection via touch screen and your personalized T-shirt will be ready within minutes. **TrenD,** as its name implies, is a hip and chic urban boutique that features an eclectic mix of Disney-inspired designer duds from the likes of Roxy, Tarina Tarantino, and Kidada Jones—a must for the fashion-conscious Disney diva. **Marketplace Fun Finds** replaces Mickey's Mart and Pooh Corner, its shelves lined with trinkets and treasures all priced under $20—the ever-popular Mickey grab bag among them. Across from Marketplace Fun Finds is **Little Miss Matched** (previously located at Disney's West Side), with colorful trinkets, apparel, and accessories (including signature socks sold in sets of three) lining the shelves. Other smaller but similarly interesting shops include the **Art of Disney,** featuring posters, limited-edition animation cels, and other collectibles; **Basin,** where slices of soap are sold in every scent imaginable; and **Team Mickey's Athletic Club,** which sells character clothing with a sporty spin.

At Downtown Disney West Side, **Hoypoloi** features contemporary glasswork, original sculptures, and an assortment of distinctive gifts. Other notable stores at West Side include **Magic Masters,** where you can load up on magic tricks for your budding Harry Houdini; **Magnetron,** which sells a huge variety of magnets (though, strangely enough, no Disney ones); and **D Street,** where the hip and trendy shop for edgy urban apparel and accessories with a vintage Disney-esque appeal, Vinylmation figures (the latest Disney collectible), and Disney art (created by local artists). At **Curl by Sammy Duvall** at Pleasure Island (soon to be Hyperion Wharf), you can pick up the hottest surf and skate wear, accessories, even the latest gear.

A DISNEY BARGAIN? THE WORLD'S BEST-KEPT secret

From a pink Cadillac to a 4-foot beer stein, tons of wacky treasures are regularly put on the auction block at Walt Disney World.

In addition to castoffs from the theme parks and WDW resorts, there are more routine items available, from over-the-hill lawn-maintenance gear to never-been-used stainless-steel pots and pans. If you're looking for a unique piece of Disney, the auctions are held six times a year. Some of the more unusual items sold in the past include a motorized surfboard and furniture from Miss Piggy's dressing room. The auction takes place on Disney's back lots. Call property control (☎ **407/824-6878**) for information, dates, and directions.

Bigger yet are trinkets sold at **www. disneystore.com** (what was once www. disneyauctions.com is now under the Disney shopping umbrella). Mainstream items, including artwork, figurines, cookie jars, pins, and snow globes (as well as other modest merchandise), are available on a regular basis (and sold at a set price). But sometimes things go big time, when limited-edition trinkets, movie props, costumes, Disney resort furniture, and theme-park artifacts go on the block on **www.mousesurplus. com** (a division of eBay). In the past, a dress Glenn Close wore as Cruella De Vil in *102 Dalmatians* sold for $5,000, a Dumbo car from the ride at WDW earned $9,000, and the Porsche from the Disney movie *The Kid* fetched $77,100. Recent items on the block include a FASTPASS sign from "it's a small world" ($3,499), a prop plane from the Animal Kingdom's Kilimanjaro Safaris ($5,999), and the Toy Story Van ($2,999) once used at Disney–MGM Studios (now Disney's Hollywood Studios).

INTERNATIONAL DRIVE AREA (*Note:* Locally, this road is almost always referred to as **I-Drive.**) Extending 8 or so miles northeast of Disney between Highway 535 and the Florida Turnpike, this busy thoroughfare is one of the most popular tourist districts in the area, in part because it is filled with so many restaurants, shops, hotels, and attractions. From indoor skydiving and glow-in-the-dark golf to dozens of themed restaurants and shopping spots, this is *the* tourist strip in Central Florida. Its two main shopping draws are the **Orlando Premium Outlets–Vineland Avenue,** just off south I-Drive (see below), and the **Orlando Premium Outlets–International Drive** (previously Prime Outlets Orlando), located at the northernmost end of I-Drive (see below). Another I-Drive shopping spot, **Pointe Orlando** (☎ **407/248-2838;** www.pointeorlandofl.com), features an ever-growing collection of upscale restaurants, clubs, and specialty shops in an outdoor setting. Thanks to extensive renovations, the completely re-created space includes winding walkways, shaded courtyards, fountains, and inviting lighting.

KISSIMMEE Skirting the south side of Walt Disney World, Kissimmee centers on U.S. 192/Irlo Bronson Memorial Highway, as archetypal of modern American cities as Disney's Main Street is of America's yesteryear. U.S. 192 is lined end to end with budget motels, smaller attractions, and almost every fast-food restaurant known to humankind (though a handful of good eateries can be found here as well). Kissimmee, however, does not offer the fabulous array of shopping options found elsewhere in Orlando. The shopping here is notable for the quantity, not necessarily the quality, but it's a good place to pick up some knickknacks, white elephant gifts, or those seashells I mentioned above.

WINTER PARK   Just north of downtown Orlando, Winter Park ((*C*) **407/644-8281**) is the place many of Central Florida's old-money families call home. It began as a haven for Yankees trying to escape the cold. Today, its centerpiece is **Park Avenue,** which has quite a collection of upscale retail shops along its cobblestone route: Eileen Fisher, Nicole Miller, Restoration Hardware, Crabtree & Evelyn, Williams-Sonoma, and Pottery Barn, among others (including several locally owned boutiques). No matter which end of the street you start at, there are more shops—over 140 in and around the Park Avenue area—than most can survive, but you're bound to find something here you'll not find anywhere else. Park Avenue is also home to a handful of unique upscale restaurants, cafes, and art galleries. *Note:* Leave the kids with a sitter if you plan to shop (or dine) here. You'll both be happier for it. To get here, take I-4 exit 87, Fairbanks Avenue/Highway 426, east past U.S. 17/92 to Park Avenue and turn left.

ORLANDO AREA OUTLETS & MALLS

Factory Outlets

Lake Buena Vista Factory Stores   The three dozen or so outlets here include Aéropostale, Carters, Character Outlet, Converse, Ecko Unlimited, Eddie Bauer, Fossil, Gap, Izod, Liz Claiborne, Nike, Nine West, OshKosh, Reebok, Tommy Hilfiger, Van Heusen, and the only Old Navy Outlet in the area. Savings can reach 75%, but most deals are much more modest. The plaza itself is very tasteful and inviting with a Mediterranean flair, and the location, just between the I-Drive and U.S. 192 areas on the lower end of Apopka–Vineland, means you can easily get here without having to face too much traffic (especially as 54 area hotels offer free shuttle service). This outlet center is a bit quieter and more relaxed than the Premium Outlets (see below), but its selection of shops is far smaller. It does, however, have a nicely done food-court area for a quick bite, a small playground, and even a salon if you are in need of a new 'do or a manicure. 15591 S. Apopka-Vineland Rd. (*C*) **407/238-9301.** www.lbvfs.com.

Orlando Premium Outlets–International Drive ★   Now a sibling of the Orlando Premium Outlets–Vineland Avenue (thanks to a recent change of ownership, and hence the name change from the former Prime Outlets Orlando), it should come as no great surprise that it, too, boasts a very inviting and meticulously landscaped atmosphere. This semicovered outdoor mall (similar to the way the Premium Outlets–Vineland Avenue is laid out, although this location is far larger and visually more impressive) offers a wide range of merchandise and over 200 of the hottest designer brands, which, in a few cases, can be gotten at a savings of up to 75% off retail prices. Still, as is the case with most outlets, most buys here are no better than what you'll find in discount houses in your hometown. There are well over a dozen shoe stores (Bass, Cole Haan, Nike, Nine West, Sperry, Vans, and so on); a handful of housewares shops (Calphalon, Le Creuset, and Le Gourmet Chef); a Disney Character Warehouse; and more than 100 clothing and accessories shops for men, women, and children (Neiman Marcus Last Call, Aéropostale, Burton Snowboards,

Oranges, grapefruit, and other citrus fruits rank high on the list of Florida's top local products. **Orange Blossom Indian River Citrus,** 5151 S. Orange Blossom Trail, Orlando (✆ **800/624-8835** or 407/855-2837; www.orange-blossom. com), is one of the top sellers during the late-fall-to-late-spring season.

Coach, DKNY, Dooney & Bourke, Ecko Unltd, Gap, Hugo Boss, Izod, J. Crew, Juicy Couture, Kate Spade, Kenneth Cole, Nautica, OshKosh, Pac Sun, Polo, Under Armour, Van Heusen, and a slew of others). You can also shop for electronics, cosmetics, luggage, jewelry, toys, gifts, accessories, and lingerie.

Thankfully, a recent top-to-bottom overhaul ensures that you no longer have to get in and out of your car to hop from building to building, an incredible inconvenience that once kept this shopping center off my list of favorites. The addition of numerous on-site dining options, ranging from snack spots to sit-down restaurants, is also a huge plus. It is, however, in an off-the-beaten-path location, so unless you're staying relatively close to Universal Orlando, the other outlet options make a much better choice. 5401 W. Oak Ridge Rd. ✆ **407/352-9600.** www.premiumoutlets.com/international.

Orlando Premium Outlets–Vineland Avenue ★★ 📦 This 440,000-square-foot outlet center offers shoppers the atmosphere of a beautiful outdoor shopping mall filled with landscaping and natural lighting. It's inviting rather than outlet-ish. Billed as one of only two upscale outlets in the city, it's by far the best choice for a great shopping experience in Orlando for visitors staying near Disney or SeaWorld. It currently has 150 tenants, including Disney outlets, Coach, Hollister, Kenneth Cole, Lacoste, Nike, Polo/Ralph Lauren, Talbots, Timberland, and Tommy Hilfiger. Others include DKNY, Fendi, Hugo Boss, Juicy Couture, Nautica, Salvatore Ferragamo, and Versace. Some of the best buys are at the more moderate options (including Banana Republic, Gap, and Sperry, among others), and the selection at all the stores is fabulous. Set just between S.R. 535 and I-Drive, it's easily accessible from either location. 8200 Vineland Ave. ✆ **407/238-7787.** www.premiumoutlets.com/vineland.

The Malls

Altamonte Mall   As surely as Disney brought new life to Orlando, this mall—the second largest in the area behind the Florida Mall (see below)—brought new life (and a ton of traffic) to the then-one-stoplight town of Altamonte Springs, north of Orlando. Relatively recent additions include a food court, an indoor play area for kids, and an 18-screen AMC movie theater with stadium seating. The lineup features anchor stores Macy's, Dillard's, JCPenney, and Sears; and 175 specialty stores, including the Body Shop, Foot Locker, Godiva, and Banana Republic. **Note:** Although the owners of the Altamonte Mall filed for bankruptcy protection back in 2009, there have been no apparent effects on mall operations thus far. 451 E. Altamonte Dr. ✆ **407/830-4422.** www.altamontemall.com.

The Florida Mall ★   This popular shopping spot's anchors include Nordstrom, Macy's, Dillard's, JCPenney, Sears, and Saks, to go along with the Florida Hotel & Conference Center and more than 260 specialty stores, restaurants (such as Buca di

Beppo, California Pizza Kitchen, and Crickets Bar & Grill), a food court, and entertainment venues. In order to keep up with the growing popularity of the area's open-air shopping centers, the Florida Mall unveiled a two-story, 300,000-square-foot open-air promenade in 2010. H&M, a trendy European retailer, is a standout among the mall's new "outdoor" tenants. 8001 S. Orange Blossom Trail. (C) **407/851-6255.** www.shop simon.com.

Mall at Millenia ★★ Anchors at this 1.3-million-square-foot upscale center are Bloomingdale's, Macy's, and Neiman Marcus. In addition to those heavyweight retailers, Millenia offers 200 specialty stores that include Cartier, Chanel, Crabtree & Evelyn, Giorgio's of Palm Beach, Gucci, Louis Vuitton, Swarovski, and Tiffany & Co. It also features some of the better dining options around, with restaurants ranging from fine dining to fast food; the Blue Martini, an upscale martini lounge, features regular live entertainment. The mall is 5 miles from downtown Orlando. 4200 Conroy Rd. (at I-4 near Universal Orlando). (C) **407/363-3555.** www.mallatmillenia.com.

OTHER SHOPPING IN ORLANDO

In Downtown Orlando

If you can think of nothing better than a relaxing afternoon of bargain hunting or scouring thrift and antiques shops, check out **Antique Row** and **Ivanhoe Village** on North Orange Avenue (stretching from Colonial Dr./Hwy. 50 to Lake Ivanhoe), in downtown Orlando. This collection is a long way from the manufactured fun of Disney. The shops are an interesting assortment of the old, the new, and the unusual. **Elephant Walk Antiques,** 1427-A Alden Rd. (near the intersection of Princeton and N. Orange Ave.; (C) **407/897-6022;** www.elephantwalkantiques.com); **A & T Antiques,** 1620 N. Orange Ave. ((C) **407/896-9831**); and **Oldies But Goodies,** 1907 N. Orange Ave. ((C) **407/893-5253**), sell traditional antiques.

Down the road, a handful of places offer less conventional items. The **Fly Fisherman,** 1213 N. Orange Ave. ((C) **407/898-1989;** www.flyfishermaninc.com), sells—no surprise—fly-fishing gear. Sometimes you can spot people taking casting lessons in the park across the street.

Most of these downtown shops are open from 9 or 10am to 5pm Monday through Saturday; the owners usually run them, so hours can vary. All are spread over 3 miles along Orange Avenue. The heaviest concentration of shops lies between Princeton Street and New Hampshire Avenue, although a few are scattered between New Hampshire and Virginia avenues. The more upscale shops extend a few blocks beyond Virginia. To get here, take I-4 exit 85/Princeton Street and turn right on Orange Avenue. Parking is limited, so stop wherever you find a space along the street.

Additionally, you can shop for fresh produce, plants, baked goods, and crafts every Sunday from 10am to 4pm at the downtown **Orlando Farmers' Market.** It's located at the intersection of Osceola and East Central. Get more information at **www. orlandofarmersmarket.com.**

A Homespun Alternative

Mount Dora 🛍 This haven for artists (and retirees) is also an enjoyable day trip, not to mention a wonderful alternative to all that is Disney. The town, established in 1874, has the genuine feel of Old Florida, with an authentic Main Street, far less crowded than the one Disney has re-created. The 19th-century buildings lining the streets are picture-perfect, leading to the calm, dark-green waters of Lake Dora. Unlike most of Florida, this town actually has rolling hills, adding to the charm. Highlights include **Renninger's Antique Center and Farmers' Market** (© 352/ **383-8393** for the antique center, 352/383-3141 for the farmers' market; www. renningers.com). The hundreds of shops and booths are open Saturday and Sunday. Up to 1,000 dealers attend Renninger's 3-day antiques extravaganzas held the third weekend of January, February, and November. After you've worked up an appetite, take a lunch break at the Beauclaire Dining Room at the historic **Lakeside Inn,** 221 E. 4th Ave. (© **800/556-5016** or 352/383-4101; www.lakeside-inn.com). Enjoy lemonade and cookies while rocking on the front porch overlooking the lake. Mount Dora. © **352/383-2165.** www.mountdora.com. Take I-4 exit 92, Hwy. 436, go west to U.S. 441, then north, and follow the signs to Mount Dora and its "business district."

Specialty Stores

Bass Pro Shops Outdoor World If you're looking for the retail version of fishing and hunting (including archery) heaven, schedule a visit to this store in the Festival Bay shopping center. The store also features areas for watersports equipment, camping gear, and outdoor apparel, as well as a golf pro shop and an aquarium. It's open daily, usually from 9am to 6pm (closed Christmas). 5156 International Dr. © **407/563- 5200.** www.basspro.com.

Ron Jon Surf Shop This local Florida retailer opened its second store in 2003 at Festival Bay, on the upper north end of International Drive. The 15,000-square-foot beach shop sports an island flair and offers a huge selection of its world-famous surf wear and beach gear, among its other unique (and occasionally offbeat) surfing-themed merchandise. 5156 International Dr. © **407/481-2555.** www.ronjons.com.

WALT DISNEY WORLD & ORLANDO AFTER DARK

8

or those of who you actually have the energy after a day at the parks and simply can't call it quits, Orlando has plenty of after-dark venues suitable for a night out on the town. That said, even if you're Orlando veterans and not first-timers (the ones most likely to overdo it), if you try to go-go-go from morning until night, you will be completely exhausted after only a few days and will end up needing a vacation after your vacation.

The success of Universal's **CityWalk,** a district filled with a variety of clubs, shops, and themed restaurants, shows that many visitors have the pizzazz to withstand life after a day of schlepping around the House of Mouse. But don't think **Downtown Disney West Side, Pleasure Island** (soon to be **Hyperion Wharf**), and the **Marketplace** (each filled with its own unique lineup of shops, themed restaurants, and attractions) are hurting for business. The clubs may have closed (a re-imagined Pleasure Island filled with upscale shops and trendy eateries is beginning to emerge, its appeal widened with every unique addition), but the shops and restaurants found throughout Downtown Disney are typically filled to capacity.

Check the "Calendar" section of Friday's *Orlando Sentinel* for up-to-the-minute details on local clubs, visiting performers, concerts, and events. Many of its listings are also online at **www.orlandosentinel.com**. The *Orlando Weekly,* published every Thursday, is a free magazine found in red boxes throughout Central Florida. It highlights more offbeat performances. You can see it online at **www.orlandoweekly.com**. Another good source on the Internet is **www.visitorlando.com**, operated by the Orlando/Orange County Convention & Visitors Bureau.

THE PERFORMING ARTS

While Disney occasionally hosts classical music acts, you'll usually have to go downtown to get a taste of the traditional arts.

Concert Halls & Auditoriums

The city continues to dream of getting the remaining financing necessary to complete its multimillion-dollar world-class performing-arts center (with groundbreaking for the Dr. Phillips Center for Performing Arts having begun in June 2011). While you're holding your breath, there are two existing facilities, both of which fall under the wand of Orlando Centroplex.

Amway Center   This new venue, which replaced the old Amway Arena, hosts the NBA's Orlando Magic (see "Spectator Sports," in chapter 6), the Orlando Predators arena football team, as well as big-name concert performers such as Garth Brooks and Bruce Springsteen. It also features family-oriented entertainment, including the Ringling Bros. Barnum & Bailey Circus in January, plus a slate of cultural offerings such as Broadway-style shows, ballets, plays, and symphony performances. 400 W. Church St. © **407/440-7000** (event information), 407/440-7900 (box office), 877/803-7073 or 800/745-3000 for tickets via Ticketmaster. www.orlandovenues.net. Parking $8–$10.

Florida Citrus Bowl   With 70,000 seats, the bowl is the largest venue in the area for rock concerts and, in the past, has starred such heavyweights as Elton John and the Rolling Stones. 1610 W. Church St. (at Tampa St.). © **407/849-2001** (event information), 407/849-2020 (box office), 800/745-3000 for tickets via Ticketmaster. www.orlandovenues.net. Parking $10–$15.

Theater

Bob Carr Performing Arts Centre   Touring Broadway productions frequently play this venue, so if you missed *Chicago, Wicked, West Side Story,* or *Hair* when it was playing in your local area (or if it didn't make it to you at all), you may be able to catch it here. 401 W. Livingston St. © **407/423-9999** or 800/950-4647. www.broadwayacross america.com. Tickets $12–$75, depending on show and seating. Parking $8–$10.

Orlando–UCF Shakespeare Festival 🎭   The company (celebrating its 22nd season) is known for staging traditional plays in contemporary settings and offers special programs geared toward students throughout the year. Shows currently scheduled range from *All's Well That Ends Well* to *Hamlet* to *Schoolhouse Rock.* Performances are held in three venues: the Ken and Trisha Margeson Theater, which has 324 seats that wrap around three sides of the stage; the Marilyn and Sig Goldman Theater, an intimate 118-seater; and the Walt Disney Amphitheater at Lake Eola, where the 936 seats give a view of Shakespeare under the stars. 812 E. Rollins St. © **407/447-1700.** www.orlandoshakes.org. Tickets $14–$38. Call ahead for reservations. Free parking for indoor theaters; metered parking for the amphitheater.

> ## The Fat Lady Sang
>
> The Orlando Opera Company sang its last note when it closed its doors in April 2009.

Theatre Downtown   These engaging local actors, some of whom have been working here since the group's formation in 1984, put on a range of Broadway-style plays, from *The Fantastics* to *Lend Me a Tenor* to *Sordid Lives.* Performances run Thursday through Saturday nights, plus Sunday matinees. 2113 N. Orange Ave. © **407/841-0083** for tickets. www.theatredowntown.net. Tickets $18, $15 for students and seniors. Parking is free along Orange Ave., south of the theater.

First-Run Films

Orlando has a number of movie multiplexes in the mainstream tourist areas. Most offer discounted tickets for children under 12 and discounted matinees; some also offer discounts to students and seniors (bring ID).

Some of the top draws include **AMC 24,** at Pleasure Island (🕿 407/298-4488), with the first EXT theater in the country (think floor-to-ceiling screen with 3-D technology); **Cinemark 20 Festival Bay,** on North International Drive (🕿 407/352-1042; www.cinemark.com); **Muvico Pointe 21 Theatres,** at Pointe Orlando on International Drive (🕿 407/926-6850; www.muvico.com), which also sports an IMAX screen; and **AMC Universal Cineplex 20,** at CityWalk (🕿 407/354-5998; www.amctheatres.com).

Dance

Orlando Ballet Formerly called the Southern Ballet Theatre, and celebrating its 38th season, this troupe stages traditional shows such as the *Nutcracker, Peter and the Wolf,* and *Carmen,* using guest artists to augment local talent. There has been a resurgence of interest in the ballet here in recent years, but performances rarely sell out. The season runs from October to May. Performances feature the Orlando Philharmonic Orchestra (see below) and are staged at the Bob Carr Performing Arts Centre. 401 W. Livingston St. 🕿 **407/426-1733** (information), 🕿 800/745-3000 for tickets via Ticketmaster. www.orlandoballet.org. Tickets $22–$80. Parking $8–$10.

Classical Music

Florida Symphony Youth Orchestra Kids get in on the classical action in a program with roots reaching back to 1957. Its musicians, from a radius reaching 40 or so miles from Orlando, play at the Bob Carr Performing Arts Centre. 401 W. Livingston St. 🕿 **407/999-7800.** www.fsyo.org. Tickets $8–$30. Parking $8–$10.

Orlando Philharmonic Orchestra The orchestra offers a varied schedule of classical and pop-influenced concerts throughout the year at the Bob Carr Performing Arts Centre. The musicians also accompany the Orlando Ballet (see above). A past family-oriented program set classical music to a host of kids' cartoons. 401 W. Livingston St. 🕿 **407/896-6700.** www.orlandophil.org. Tickets $13–$60 ($13–$46 for students). Parking $8–$10.

Film

Enzian Theater This not-for-profit alternative cinema features first-run independent films in a 250-seat theater. It also hosts a variety of special events, including March's 10-day run of the Florida Film Festival. 1300 S. Orlando Ave., Maitland. 🕿 **407/629-1088** or 407/629-0054 for tickets and showtimes. www.enzian.org. General admission $10, $8 students and seniors, $7.50 film society members. Prices vary for special events. Parking is free in the theater lot.

DINNER THEATER
In Walt Disney World

Disney does not turn into a pumpkin when the sun goes down, offering plenty of nighttime entertainment, including laser-light shows, fireworks, IllumiNations

8

WALT DISNEY WORLD & ORLANDO AFTER DARK | Dinner Theater

(p. 214), and Fantasmic! (p. 218). There are also two distinctly different dinner shows worthy of special note, the Hoop-Dee-Doo Musical Revue and Disney's Spirit of Aloha, and a third show that's an occasional player. *Note:* While they offer family-friendly entertainment, don't expect haute cuisine. The food, though good, takes a back seat to the show.

Disney's Spirit of Aloha Dinner Show
While not quite as much in demand as the Hoop-Dee-Doo, the Polynesian Resort's delightful 2-hour show is like a big neighborhood party. It features Tahitian, Samoan, Hawaiian, and Polynesian singers, drummers, and dancers who entertain while you feast on a menu that includes tropical appetizers, lanai roasted chicken, Polynesian wild rice, South Seas vegetables, dessert, wine, beer, and other beverages. It all takes place 5 nights a week in an open-air theater (dress for nighttime weather and bring sweaters) with candlelit tables, lanterns, and tapa paintings on the walls. Reservations should be made about 60 days in advance (but can be made up to 180 days in advance; full payment is expected when booking), especially during peak periods such as summer and holidays. Like the Hoop-De-Doo Musical Revue, the Spirit of Aloha is priced in tiers—the closer you sit to the stage, the higher the price you'll pay. Showtimes are 5:15 and 8pm Tuesday through Saturday. *Note:* Not all seats for this one are equal, so paying for a better seat is the way to go—but I must warn that the resulting price is really too high for the value received from the production as a whole. 1600 Seven Seas Dr. (at Disney's Polynesian Resort). ✆ **407/939-3463.** www.disneyworld.com. Reservations required. Adults $59.99, $54.99, and $50.99; kids 3–9 $30.99, $26.99, and $25.99, including tax and tip. Free parking.

Hoop-Dee-Doo Musical Revue ★★★
This is Disney's most popular show, so make reservations *early.* The reward: You'll feast on a down-home, all-you-can-eat barbecue (fried chicken, smoked ribs, salad, corn on the cob, baked beans, bread, salad, strawberry shortcake—all of it quite good, by the way—and your choice of coffee, tea, beer, wine, sangria, or soda). While you stuff yourself silly in Pioneer Hall, performers in 1890s garb lead you in a foot-stomping, hand-clapping, high-energy 2-hour show that includes a lot of jokes you haven't heard since second grade. *Note:* Be prepared to join in on the fun—or the singers and dancers, along with the rest of the crowd, will humiliate you until you do. This is entertaining for the entire family.

Reservations should be made the full 180 days in advance (at which time full payment is expected), especially during peak periods such as summer and holidays. Show times are 5, 7:15, and 9:30pm daily. The tiered pricing system means that the closer you are to the action, the higher the price you'll pay. Tier 1 seats are located on the first floor nearest the stage, tier 2 seats in the back half of the first floor and in the center of the balcony, tier 3 seats to the right and left sides on the balcony level. There's not a bad seat in the house, so don't feel the need to splurge. If you catch one

8

WALT DISNEY WORLD & ORLANDO AFTER DARK

Dinner Theater

It All Adds Up, Up, Up . . .

If you want to dine with your favorite Disney character during the holidays, expect to pay a bit extra. Holiday pricing, first instituted in 2007, is now the norm during peak seasons and the days (even weeks) surrounding most holidays—among them, Thanksgiving, Christmas, New Year's, Easter, Memorial Day, July 4th, and Labor Day. At press time, holiday pricing was running approximately $5 extra per person. For details and exact dates, go to www.disneyworld.com. To make Advance Dining reservations, call ✆ **407/939-3463.**

If You're Lucky . . .

Mickey's Backyard BBQ (☏ 407/939-3463; www.disneyworld.com) is offered at Pioneer Hall at Disney's Fort Wilderness Resort & Campground, where Tom Sawyer and Huck Finn allow you onto their home turf to have a thigh-slapping time and a feast in a covered outdoor pavilion. Expect Mickey and his pals to join you for a meal that includes barbecued pork ribs, chicken, cheeseburgers, hot dogs, corn on the cob, baked beans, mac and cheese, watermelon, beer, wine, lemonade, iced tea, and dessert. Meals are served at 6:30 and 9:30pm and cost $44.99 for adults, $26.99 for kids 3 to 9, including tax and tip. It happens only on Thursdays and Saturdays, generally from March through December, but the weather plays a big factor and shows are canceled at times, so *call ahead.* Advance Reservations are accepted up to 180 days ahead. Payment in full is expected at the time of booking.

of the early shows, consider sticking around for the Electrical Water Pageant at 9:45pm, which can be viewed from the Fort Wilderness Beach. 3520 N. Fort Wilderness Trail (at Fort Wilderness Resort & Campground). ☏ 407/939-3463. www.disneyworld.com. Reservations required. Adults $59.99, $54.99, and $50.99; kids 3–9 $30.99, $26.99, and $25.99, including tax and tip. Free parking.

Elsewhere in Orlando

Outside the Disney zone, Orlando has an active dinner-theater scene, but keep in mind that the city is a family destination—and the dinner shows are very reflective of that. You won't find the sophisticated offerings you would in major cultural centers such as New York, London, or Paris. Most of the local shows focus on pleasing the kids, so if you're looking for fun, you'll find it; but if you want critically acclaimed entertainment, look elsewhere. You also won't find four-star food, but dinners are certainly palatable enough. Attending a show is considered by many to be a quintessential Orlando experience, and if you arrive with the right attitude, you'll most likely have an enjoyable evening. Your children certainly will.

Note: Discount coupons to the shows can often be found in the tourist magazines that are distributed at gas stations and information centers; you'll also find them in many non-Disney hotel lobbies and sometimes on the listed websites.

Arabian Nights   If you're a horse fancier, this one's a must. One of the classier dinner-show experiences, it stars many of the most popular breeds, from chiseled Arabians to hard-driving Andalusians to beefcake Belgians. They giddy-up through performances that include Wild West trick riding, chariot races, slapstick comedy, and bareback bravado. Locals rate it number one among Orlando dinner shows, though my kids prefer the action of some of the other shows in town. On most nights, the 2-hour performance opens with a ground trainer working one-on-one with a black stallion. Dinner includes a choice of sirloin steak, chopped steak, grilled chicken, chicken tenders, or primavera penne pasta; salad; dessert; and soft drinks, wine, or beer. Special diets can be accommodated with advance notice. Showtimes vary, with at least one performance nightly. *Note:* Adult prices start at a whopping $64 for dinner and the show, but for those with extra cash to spare, $80 will get you a poster, priority seating, and a chance to meet the horses (I personally think that $16 could be better spent elsewhere). *Tip:* Book your tickets online to save $10 to $15 per person off the regular price. 6225 W. Irlo Bronson Memorial Hwy. (U.S. 192), Kissimmee. © **800/553-6116** or 407/239-9223. www.arabian-nights.com. Reservations recommended. $64–$80 adults, $31–$45 kids 3–11. Free parking.

Medieval Times Orlando has one of the nine Medieval Times shows in North America, and this is the show my kids rate tops in town. Inside, guests gorge on barbecued spareribs, roasted chicken, soup, garlic bread, potatoes, dessert, and beverages including beer. Vegetarian offerings include a stuffed mushroom cap with roasted veggies and a hummus dip. But because this is the 11th century, you eat with your fingers from metal plates while knights mounted on Andalusian horses run around the arena, jousting and clanging to please the fair ladies. Arrive 90 minutes early for good seats and to see the Medieval Village, a re-created Middle Ages settlement. Showtimes vary, but there is at least one performance nightly (7:30pm), two during peak seasons (6:30 and 8:30pm). Tickets are fairly pricy, but you're rewarded with substantial savings if you purchase online. Upgrades include preferred seating, photos, and various remembrances for an additional $16 to $20 per person. 4510 W. Irlo Bronson Memorial Hwy. (U.S. 192), Kissimmee. © **888/935-6878** or 407/396-1518. www.medievaltimes. com. Reservations recommended. $59.95 adults, $34.95 kids younger than 12. Free parking.

Pirates Dinner Adventure The special-effects show at this theater includes a full-size ship in a 300,000-gallon lagoon, circus-style aerial acts, a lot of music, and a little drama. Your kids may even get a chance to participate. Dinner includes an appetizer buffet with the preshow, followed by two rounds of drinks; your choice of roast chicken, pork, or garlic shrimp and scallops, with seasoned rice or roasted potatoes and mixed vegetables; dessert; and coffee. Kids' meals come with chicken fingers. After the show, you're invited to the Buccaneer Bash dance party, where you can

 PRIME RIB & A SIDE OF murder

Want to try your hand at playing Sherlock Holmes? **Sleuths Mystery Dinner Shows** ★★, 8267 International Dr. (© **800/393-1985** or 407/363-1985; www.sleuths.com), are interactive dinner shows staged in an intimate theater setting where guests play detective and try to solve a whodunit murder mystery.

A roster of suspects and impending victims (okay, they're really actors) interact with guests throughout the experience, which includes a preshow where you're introduced to the characters and served appetizers and a salad. When the actual performance begins, the actors both captivate and, at times, reduce you to hysterical laughter. Then it's time for dinner, which includes a choice of Cornish game hen, prime rib (for $3 more), or lasagna. While eating, you discuss clues with the other detectives at your

table (the round tables seat eight). Each table is given the opportunity to interrogate the suspects, who can get quite hilarious, depending on the amount of alcohol people have consumed before they get to ask their questions (you get unlimited wine and beer). The suspects duly questioned, a mystery dessert is served, and then the murderer is revealed. It makes for a very entertaining yet relaxing evening out.

Fourteen different productions (each about 2½ hr. long) are offered throughout the year. Admission costs $53 adults, $24 kids 3 to 11. Reservations are recommended. To get here, from I-4 W. take exit 75A; at the light, turn right onto Universal Boulevard, and follow it for 1 mile to Gooding's Plaza on the right. Parking is free.

mingle with cast members. This is a smaller production than the aforementioned shows, but it is nicely done, and the stadium and crowds are not as large and overwhelming. Showtimes vary, with at least one performance nightly. 6400 Carrier Dr. ℂ **800/866-2469** or 407/248-0590. www.orlandopirates.com. Reservations recommended. Dinner and show $59.95 adults, $39.95 kids 3–11; show only $29.95 for all ages. Free parking.

AT WALT DISNEY WORLD

The places described here can be located on the "Downtown Disney" map in this section.

Pleasure Island (Hyperion Wharf)

The 6-acre Pleasure Island complex, once home to an array of clubs and bars (all of which shut down in 2008), is currently in the end stages of a major redesign, with a completion date set for 2013 and a new name of Hyperion Wharf. Re-imagined in an effort to widen its appeal, in order to attract more than the 21-and-over clubbing set, the island now offers an array of themed restaurants, upscale shops, unique attractions (including **Characters in Flight,** a tremendous tethered balloon ride), a multiscreen movie theater (with an ETX theater, the first of its kind in the U.S.), a high-end surf shop, and a Harley-Davidson shop. The dining scene saw the addition in 2009 of **T-Rex Cafe** (p. 133)—think Rainforest Cafe with a prehistoric twist—and **Paradiso 37** (p. 134), an upscale eatery with a menu that reflects the 37 countries of the Americas (North, South, and Central). Other notable eateries include **Raglan Road** (see below); **Fulton's Crab House** (p. 132); **Portobello** (p. 132), once known as the Portobello Yacht Club; and **Planet Hollywood** (p. 132), which is just a few steps way, adjacent to Disney's West Side. Additional updates and enhancements are in the works, ensuring that those in search of an exciting, though more family-friendly, night on the town will not be disappointed. Guests can walk the grounds and enjoy the sights, sounds, and surroundings, making their way from one end of Downtown Disney to the other (all the way from the Marketplace to Hyperion Wharf to the West Side) with ease—and without having to worry about bringing along the kids.

For more information on Downtown Disney, call ℂ **407/939-2648** or go to **www. disneyworld.com**. Pleasure Island's existing shops and restaurants are currently

 The Luck of the Irish

The Great Irish Pubs of Florida, Inc. (the company that created the Nine Fine Irishmen pub in Las Vegas's New York–New York Hotel & Casino), brought the luck of the Irish to Downtown Disney in the form of **Raglan Road Irish Pub & Restaurant.** The pub is an impressive and inviting member of Disney's collection of unique eateries, immersing guests in a wholly Irish environment that includes custom-made furnishings direct from the Emerald Isles, incredibly high ceilings, rich woodwork, and leaded glass. The spirited atmosphere, where singing, dancing, and clapping are all encouraged, is enhanced by the live nightly entertainment. And the food's pretty good, too, thanks to the culinary creations of Kevin Dundon, one of Ireland's most celebrated chefs. Main courses at dinner are $15 to $30. Pub food is also plentiful and runs $8 to $18.

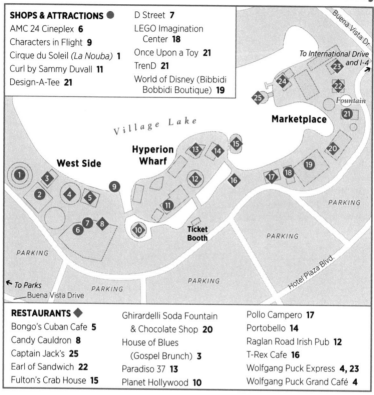

SHOPS & ATTRACTIONS ●

AMC 24 Cineplex **6**
Characters in Flight **9**
Cirque du Soleil (La Nouba) **1**
Curl by Sammy Duvall **11**
Design-A-Tee **21**

D Street **7**
LEGO Imagination
   Center **18**
Once Upon a Toy **21**
TrenD **21**
World of Disney (Bibbidi
   Bobbidi Boutique) **19**

Buena Vista Dr.
To International Drive
and I-4 **23**
24
22
25
Fountain
21
Village Lake
Marketplace
Hyperion
Wharf **13** **14** **15**
West Side **20**
1
3 **12** **16** **17** **18** **19**
2 **4** **5** **9**
PARKING
11
6 **7** **8**
10 Ticket
Booth PARKING
PARKING
← To Parks PARKING
Buena Vista Drive PARKING
Hotel Plaza Blvd.

RESTAURANTS ◆

Bongo's Cuban Cafe **5**
Candy Cauldron **8**
Captain Jack's **25**
Earl of Sandwich **22**
Fulton's Crab House **15**

Ghirardelli Soda Fountain
   & Chocolate Shop **20**
House of Blues
   (Gospel Brunch) **3**
Paradiso 37 **13**
Planet Hollywood **10**

Pollo Campero **17**
Portobello **14**
Raglan Road Irish Pub **12**
T-Rex Cafe **16**
Wolfgang Puck Express **4, 23**
Wolfgang Puck Grand Café **4**

open daily from 11am to midnight or later (and will remain operational throughout the reconstruction). There's free self-parking, but as the evening wears on (generally after the parks begin to close) spots can become very hard to find.

Disney's West Side

This area adjoins Pleasure Island (soon to be Hyperion Wharf) and offers additional shops, restaurants, and a 24-screen AMC Theater. Three of the most popular spots are the following:

Bongo's Cuban Cafe 🖐 Created by singer Gloria Estefan and her husband, Emilio, the cafe is Downtown Disney's version of old Havana. There are leopard-spotted chairs and mosaic bar stools shaped like bongo drums. There's no dance floor to speak of, though you can cha-cha on the patio upstairs, which overlooks the rest of the West Side. It's a great place to sit back and bask in the Latin rhythms and inviting surroundings. But while the mood is good, the food, and at times the service, is a little lacking. It's open daily from 11am to 2am, though it sometimes closes earlier. ✆ **407/828-0999.** www.bongoscubancafe.com. No cover. Free self-parking.

NOT YOUR ORDINARY circus

Lions and tigers and bears? Oh, no. But you won't feel cheated.

Disney's partnership with **Cirque du Soleil,** the famous Montreal-based, no-animals circus, is located in Downtown Disney West Side. The eye-popping **La Nouba ★★** (derived from the French for "to live it up"), set in a custom-built, state-of-the-art theater, is a Fellini-style amalgam of live music, dance, theater, and acrobatics that will have your jaw dropping. Highlights include a cyclist who does things with a bicycle that would make an X-Gamer jealous, a spectacular coordinated trampoline performance, and a pint-size troupe of Chinese acrobats who do tricks with diabolos (Chinese yo-yos) that bring the house down. I rank this one just beneath Las Vegas's Mystère, though the comedic interludes in this production are the best of all the permanent Cirque shows.

That said, though La Nouba is a ton of fun, it's also one of the priciest shows in town, so you need to decide if your budget can take the hit. Ticket prices vary according to location (don't feel you must spend extra for the expensive seats—nearly every spot in the theater offers a good view) and range from $71 to $124 for adults, $57 to $99 for children 3 to 9 (plus 6.5% tax). Yes, it's an expensive 90 minutes, but prices here are among the cheapest of all the Cirque productions in the U.S. Shows are at 6 and 9pm Tuesday through Saturday, though the show is dark 6 weeks each year. There are occasional matinees, so call ahead (© **407/939-7600**) or check **www.cirquedusoleil.com** for information and tickets.

House of Blues Several well-known artists have performed here, including One Republic, Natasha Bedingfield, the Charlie Daniels Band, and the Black Crowes. The barnlike building, with three tiers, may be a little difficult for those with limited mobility to maneuver in, but there isn't a bad seat in the house. The atmosphere is dark and boozy, perfect for the bluesy sounds that usually raise the rafters. The dance floor is big enough to boogie on without doing the bump with a stranger. You can dine in the adjoining restaurant (p. 135) on baby back ribs, Louisiana crawfish, jambalaya, and New Orleans–style shrimp. There's also a Sunday gospel brunch. © **407/934-2583.** www.hob.com. Cover varies by event and artist. Free self-parking.

Wolfgang Puck Grand Café ★★ While the wait can be distressing, the energized contemporary atmosphere, along with the eclectic menu, makes it worth the effort. An eye-catching exhibition kitchen in the more casual downstairs section allows you to watch as your food is prepared. A favorite stop is the sushi bar, an artistic copper-and-terrazzo masterpiece that delivers some of the best sushi in Orlando. The upstairs dining room has a more refined atmosphere with its own menu to match. Puck's is noisy, making conversation difficult no matter which level you choose. *Note:* In a hurry? Try the **Wolfgang Puck Express** at either the West Side or Marketplace. © **407/938-9653.** www.wolfgangpuck.com. Free self-parking.

AT CITYWALK

Located between the Islands of Adventure and Universal Studios Florida theme parks, this nightclub, restaurant, and shopping district had its coming-out party in

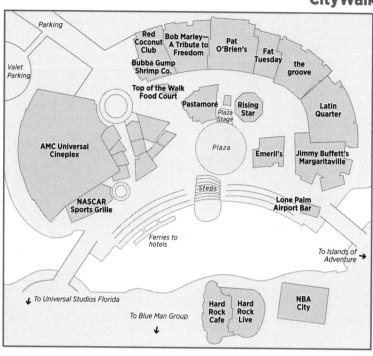

1999 and competes head-to-head with Disney's Pleasure Island (soon to be Hyperion Wharf). It opens daily at 11am, but the hours of many clubs and restaurants vary, so call in advance if you're interested in a specific venue. Most clubs stay open until 2am.

At 30 acres, CityWalk (© **407/363-8000;** www.citywalk.com) may be four times smaller than Downtown Disney, but it's the only remaining nightclub district now that Pleasure Island is in the midst of being "re-imagined," with its clubs closed for good. Alcohol is prominently featured here, as it's geared to an adult crowd; younger members of the family should always be accompanied by an adult if allowed to tag along. The nights can get pretty wild here. (**Note:** Some clubs won't allow anyone younger than 21 inside after a certain hour; see the listings below for details.)

You can walk this district for free at night or visit individual clubs and pay a cover. CityWalk also offers two **party passes.** A pass to all clubs costs $11.99 plus tax. For $15 plus tax, you get a club pass and a movie at Universal Cineplex (© **407/354-5998**). Universal also offers free club access to those who buy select multiday theme-park tickets (see chapter 6, "Exploring Beyond Disney"). There's also

Chilling Out

You can grab a margarita to go and "chill" in the brightly colored wooden chairs (think of the Adirondacks) outside Jimmy Buffett's Margaritaville. It's a perfect spot to watch the crowds scurrying to and from the theme parks.

Taking Center Stage

With a live band and backup singers, guests are invited to take to the stage and show off their talents (or, in some cases, the lack thereof) at **Rising Star** (℗ **407/224-3663**), CityWalk's latest addition to its lineup of clubs. Replacing CityJazz a few years back, this karaoke club features a live band, backup singers, and a host to get things going every Tuesday through Saturday. On Sunday and Monday the music's recorded, but the backup singers and host are live. There's a cover of $7 (no charge to sing) and a full bar if you need to loosen up before taking the stage.

a Meal & Movie Deal option; for $21.95, you get entrance to a movie at the Cineplex and dinner at one of the CityWalk restaurants (select menu items apply); see **www.universalorlando.com** for complete details.

Daytime parking in the Universal Orlando garages costs $14, but after 6pm self-parking is only $3. To get to CityWalk, take I-4 exit 74B (westbound) or 75A (eastbound) and follow the signs to the parks.

Bob Marley—A Tribute to Freedom   This hybrid bar/restaurant has a party atmosphere that will make the food more appealing as the night wears on. The clapboard building is said to be a replica of Marley's home in Kingston. Jamaican vittles—meat patties, jerk chicken, mango wings, and the brew of champions, Red Stripe beer—are served under patio umbrellas amid portraits of the original Rastaman. If you try an Extreme Measure, have a designated driver. Local and national reggae bands perform on a microdot stage. It's open daily 4pm to 2am. ℗407/224-3663. Cover $7 after 9pm, more for special acts. Must be 21 or older after 9pm.

the groove ★★   This often-crowded, multilevel club features a huge dance floor, a number of bars, and a handful of lounges for just hanging out. Three unique lounges are outfitted in blue, green, and red—each features its own decor, music, bar, and specialty drink. The high-tech sound system will blow your hair back; if you need a sound check, try the upper-level patio for a brief reprieve. A DJ plays tunes most nights, featuring the latest in hip-hop, retro hits, techno, and alternative music. Bands occasionally play the house, too. It's open daily from 9pm to 2am. ℗407/363-8000. Cover $7. Must be 21 or older to get in.

Hard Rock Live   The first concert hall to bear the Hard Rock name is next door to the largest Hard Rock Cafe in the world (p. 139). This building, fashioned to look like an ancient coliseum, has a 2,500-seat concert venue. The sightlines and the sound system are great. Recent performers have included the Backstreet Boys, Goo Goo Dolls, Duran Duran, and Joan Rivers. Tickets for big-name performers sell fast. Concerts generally begin about 8pm. ℗ 407/351-7655. www.hardrocklive.com. Tickets $6–$150, depending on concert.

Jimmy Buffett's Margaritaville   Flip-flops and flowered shirts are the proper apparel here. Music from the maestro is piped throughout the building, with live music performed on a small stage later in the evening. A Jimmy sound-alike strums on the spacious "back porch of indecision." True Parrot Heads know the lyrics at least as well as the singers. Bar-wise, there are three options: The Volcano erupts margarita mix; the Land Shark has fins hanging from the ceiling; and the 12 Volt, is, well, a little electrifying—I'll leave it at that. If you opt for dinner among the palm trees, go

8

WALT DISNEY WORLD & ORLANDO AFTER DARK | At CityWalk

for the true Key West experience. Early in the day that means a cheeseburger (in paradise); later, it's conch fritters, one of many kinds of fish (pompano, sea bass, dolphinfish), and Key lime pie. It's open daily from 11:30am to 2am. See p. 139 for more on the food here. ⓒ **407/224-2155.** www.margaritavilleorlando.com. Cover $7 after 10pm (waived if you come only to dine on the deck).

Latin Quarter This two-level restaurant/club offers you a chance to absorb the salsa-and-samba culture of 21 Latin nations in an Aztec-, Inca-, and Mayan-influenced setting. It's filled with the music of the merengue, the mambo, and the tango, along with a bit of Latin rock thrown in for good measure—a DJ spins the latest Latin dance tunes every Thursday through Saturday—so be prepared to move your hips. The surprisingly intimate atmosphere features mountainous architecture and waterfalls surrounding the dance floor; you'll feel like you're dancing in a Mayan temple. The sound system is loud enough to blow you into the next county. Out on the patio, a guitarist strums Spanish songs in the early evening hours; but before that happens, you can check out the club's Latin American art gallery. It's open daily 5 to 10pm. ⓒ **407/224-3663.**

NASCAR Sports Grille This recently redone (and renamed) NASCAR-licensed eatery is a must for race-car and sports enthusiasts alike. Table-side plasma screens (you pick the programming), high-tech simulators and games, and a huge plasma wall

LOUNGING around

Some of Orlando's most unique nightlife is located in its hotels. Even locals head to some of these places after dark. Consider any of the following and their parent hotels, all of which are listed in chapter 3.

Rix ★★, at Disney's Coronado Springs Resort (ⓒ **407/939-3806;** www.disneyworld.com), a surprisingly sophisticated un-Disney-like lounge, serves up gourmet appetizers and signature drinks in a trendy Mediterranean-inspired setting. **Todd English's bluezoo bar,** at the Walt Disney World Dolphin (ⓒ **407/934-1111;** www.thebluezoo. com), features classic cocktails in a hip and chic atmosphere. At **Disney's Grand Floridian** (ⓒ **407/824-3000**), a pianist and band alternate playing time from 3 to 9:45pm in the lobby. **Outer Rim,** at Disney's Contemporary Resort (ⓒ **407/824-1000**), is a trendy nightspot and close to the monorail. **Kimonos,** the sushi bar in the Walt Disney

World Swan (ⓒ **407/934-3000**), offers karaoke after 8:30pm. The entertainment is purely visual at **Mist Sushi & Spirits,** in the Renaissance Orlando Resort at SeaWorld (ⓒ **407/351-5555**), which overlooks the huge atrium, glass elevators, and trendy new interior.

Sit and sip one of the 25 signature martinis, accompanied by a menu of tapas-style treats and live entertainment, at the **Blue Martini,** in the Mall at Millennia (ⓒ **407/447-2583**). Or drink along to the sweet sounds of Ol' Blue Eyes in the **Starlight Lounge,** at Timpano Chophouse & Martini Bar (ⓒ **407/248-0429**). Over at the Gaylord Palms, **Auggie's Jammin' Piano Bar** (ⓒ **407/586-0000**) has live entertainment at 9pm nightly. And you can sit back and relax (in velvet chairs, I might add) at the **Velvet Lounge,** at the Hard Rock Hotel (ⓒ **407/503-3700**), where you can down cocktails while surrounded by rock-'n'-roll memorabilia and music.

create what Universal calls an "outdoor tailgating experience." The upgraded menu features such favorites as ribs, pasta, sandwiches, and more. It's open daily from 11am to midnight. ☏ **407/224-3663.**

NBA City If you're a fan of the NBA, this one's a must. Hoops and memorabilia hang from the walls, and TV monitors play seemingly every game on the airwaves. The mixed menu ($10–$22) ranges from steaks and chicken to fish, pasta, and sandwiches. Fans will love it, but if you're in search of better-than-average food and aren't a basketball junkie, look elsewhere. It's open daily from 11am to midnight (last seating at 10:30pm), later on Friday and Saturday (last seating 11:30pm). ☏ **407/363-5919.**

Pat O'Brien's Just like in the French Quarter—home to the original Patty O's—drinking, drinking, and more drinking are the highlights here. Creole treats and sandwiches ($8–$17) take up only a page or two of the menu—the rest is filled with wild alcoholic libations. Enjoy the piano bar or the flame-throwing fountain while you suck down the drink of the Big Easy, a Hurricane. If your plans for the evening fall anything short of full intoxication, this may not be the place for you. Pat O'Brien's is open daily 4pm to 2am. ☏ **407/224-2106.** www.patobriens.com. Cover $7 after 9pm. Must be 21 or older to enter after 9pm.

Free Ride

A free public transportation system called **Lymmo** (☏ **407/841-2279;** www.golynx.com) runs in a designated lane through the downtown area. But because Lymmo stops running at 10pm (midnight Fri–Sat), it may stop moving before you do. Stash enough cash for a taxi if you're going to party late into the night.

Red Coconut Club When it replaced the old Decades Café, locals wondered if the Red Coconut Club would be one more victim in City-Walk's revolving lineup of lounges, but this one looks like it's here to stay. A chic upscale interior with a retro flair, signature martinis, and live music draw a hip crowd—something previous tenants couldn't manage. Hours are Sunday through Thursday 8pm to 2am, Friday and Saturday 6pm to 2am. ☏ **407/224-3663.** Cover $7 after 9pm. Must be 21 or older to enter.

HOT SPOTS IN ORLANDO

Downtown Disney and CityWalk are the biggest nighttime draws for most tourists and some locals. However, the dozens of clubs and bars on International Drive, along Orange Avenue, and in the rest of downtown Orlando attract most homegrown night owls, business travelers who want to stay as far as possible from the Mickey madness, and a small number of enterprising tourists who venture north at night. These places can be located on the "Downtown Orlando Nightlife" map in this section.

The Beacham Inside a renovated theater, the downtown club formerly known as Tabu is now the Beacham. It holds a special appeal for members of the under-30 crowd who are on the prowl, or older cruisers who want to relive their glory days. DJs spinning dance and hip-hop hits are the featured attraction, while the VIP room offers a more intimate experience. The club has a "stylish dress" requirement; leave the shorts and tank tops at home. Doors open at 10pm every night. 46 N. Orange Ave.,

Downtown Orlando Nightlife

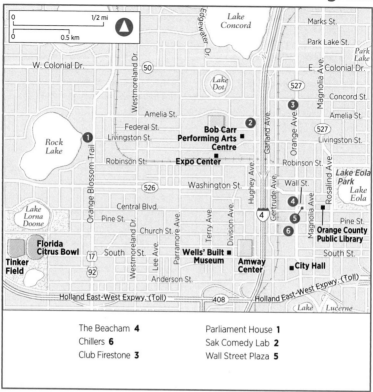

The Beacham **4**

Chillers **6**

Club Firestone **3**

Parliament House **1**

Sak Comedy Lab **2**

Wall Street Plaza **5**

Orlando. ☎ **407/246-1419.** www.thebeacham.com. Cover $5–$10 most nights. Parking $8–$10; metered parking available. Must be 18 or older to enter.

Club Firestone This concert venue/dance club draws a diverse crowd and keeps the dance floor busy. This is a serious club with dark lighting, three cavernous

On the Go

Fitting in nicely with the New Orleans theme of its next-door neighbor (Pat O'Brien's), **Fat Tuesday** (☎ **407/224-2236;** www.fat-tuesday.com) serves up a selection of frozen drinks street-side (at CityWalk you can walk about with your drink in hand, and clubs and restaurants won't turn you away). Order drinks off the menu or mix and match your own concoction from a variety of prefab flavors that line the back wall of this walk-up bar (think slushy machine). Drinks run $7, refills $6 if you purchase a refillable cup, and liquid toppers $1. Specialties include the 190 Octane (a mix of grain alcohol, orange juice, and orange punch). Unlike most frozen drinks, these really pack a punch. Cherry Jell-O shots, beer, and soda are also available.

Don't want to venture all the way downtown for comic relief? Head to **Fat Fish Blue**, at Pointe Orlando on International Drive (✆ **407/480-5233**; www.theimprovorlando.com or www.orlandofatfishblue.com), where the Orlando Improv Comedy Club (originally located on Church St. in downtown Orlando) has partnered with Fat Fish Blue (a casual eatery featuring Creole cuisine—and room for up to 400) to bring a lineup of live entertainment 5 nights a week. Think jazz and blues in addition to local and national comedy acts. Replacing Matrix and Metropolis, the restaurant/comedy club opened in August 2010.

rooms—each with its own style and sounds—and an outdoor patio. Orlando's biggest DJs mix it up nightly. It's open Thursday through Sunday from 8pm until 3am; showtimes vary. 578 N. Orange Ave. (at Concord St. in a converted garage that still bears a Firestone sign). ✆ **407/872-0066.** www.firestonelive.net. Cover $5 (live performances ticketed separately). Limited lot parking available for $3-$5.

ICEBAR Orlando　Kept at a chilly 27°F (–3°C), the ICEBAR (albeit only a small portion of the venue)—including the walls, the couch, the bar, and even the glasses themselves—has been created from over 50 tons of ice. Six entry periods, each lasting 45 minutes, are offered nightly (gloves and capes are provided), as space is limited (only a small number of people are allowed in at any one time). After you've been sufficiently chilled, head to the Fire Lounge, an ultrachic club that continues the arctic theme (sans ice), to warm up. The lounge is open throughout the evening, and there's no cover should you decide to skip the ICEBAR experience altogether (or simply miss the entry times). It's open nightly from 7pm to midnight (sometimes as late as 2am), and the first entry to the ICEBAR is at 7:15pm. 8967 International Dr. ✆ **407/426-7555.** www.icebarorlando.com. Admission $20. Free parking.

Sak Comedy Lab　Locals perform at this club, which launched the career of national improv artist Wayne Brady. Favorites include the Duel of Fools, where two teams face off in improvised scenes based on suggestions from the audience, and Lab Rats, where students play in improv formats. Shows usually take place Tuesday and Wednesday at 9pm, Thursday at 7:30pm, and Friday and Saturday at 7:30 and 9:30pm. Performances are now held at the CityArts Factory, at the corner of Pine and Orange. 29 S. Orange Ave. ✆ **407/648-0001.** www.sak.com. Admission $2-$15. Parking $8-$10.

GAY & LESBIAN NIGHTSPOTS

You can get all sorts of useful information on events from the **Gay, Lesbian, Bisexual, Transgender Community Center of Central Florida,** 946 N. Mills Ave., Orlando (✆ **407/228-8272;** www.thecenterorlando.org). **Gay Orlando Network** (www.gayorlando.com) and the **Gay Guide to Florida** (www.gay-guide.com) also feature a lot of nightlife entries.

Parliament House This is one of Orlando's wildest gay spots. Not a fancy place, the Parliament House has seen years of hard partying, and shows it. This is a place to drink, dance, and watch shows that include female impersonators and male revues. There are also DJs. A relatively large dance floor tends to get small pretty quickly as the crowd swells. The complex has six bars and includes a 130-room hotel with a courtyard, a small beach, and a restaurant. It's open daily 3pm to 2am; showtimes vary. 410 N. Orange Blossom Trail (just west of downtown). ✆ **407/425-7571.** www.parliamenthouse. com. Cover $2–$10. Free parking.

SPORTS BARS

ESPN Club If you're dying for a sports fix, this is it. Ninety monitors—there are even a few in the bathrooms—broadcast sporting events from around the world. There's a full bar, but there's also a restaurant (p. 131) and a small arcade, so you have an excuse to drag the family along. Daily hours are from 11:30am to 1am. In Walt Disney World at Disney's BoardWalk Resort. ✆ **407/939-3463.** www.disneyworld.com. Free self-parking.

ESPN Wide World of Sports Grill The Official All-Star Café in a previous life (revamped when the name of the complex changed), this casual sports-themed eatery is just a line drive away from the entrance to the stadium where the Atlanta Braves play their spring-training games (see "Spectator Sports," in chapter 6). There's also a ton of screens showing your favorite games, and kids will appreciate the PlayStation Pavilion (where plenty of PlayStation 3 games—sports-related, of course—and consoles are available at no additional charge). It's open daily from 11:30am to 9pm, though hours can vary according to scheduled events at the ESPN Wide World of

---

OTHER PLACES TO party

In addition to the clubs listed in this section, other downtown hot spots include **Chillers,** the **Big Belly Brewery,** and **Lattitudes,** 33 W. Church St. (✆ 407/939-4270)—three separate clubs located in a single tri-level building, all geared to the young-adult crowd with a very casual atmosphere.

Another complex lined with clubs and bars is **Wall Street Plaza** (www.wallst plaza.net), a "meet market" on Wall Street that's home to the **Globe** (✆ 407/849-9904), a European patio cafe; **Slingapours** (✆ 407/849-9904), a dance club with a patio for relaxing; **Waitiki** (✆ 407/849-0471), a retro Tiki lounge and restaurant; the **Monkey Bar** (✆ 407/849-0471), a hip martini bar; **One Eyed Jacks** (✆ 407/648-2050) and the **Loaded Hog** (✆ 407/649-1918), both party bars; the **Tuk Tuk Room** (✆ 407/849-9904), a cocktail and sushi lounge; and the **Wall Street Cantina** (✆ 407/420-1515), which serves mean margaritas.

Notable newcomers to the downtown scene include the **Other Bar** (✆ 407/843-8595), also on Wall Street (but not part of the conglomerate of clubs listed above), and **Bullitt Bar** (✆ 407/841-1068), where real rock 'n' roll—and a down-to-earth decor to match—replaces the usual top 40, dance, and techno found elsewhere.

Sports Complex; call ahead to make sure it's open. In Walt Disney World at ESPN Wide World of Sports Complex. ℂ **407/939-3463.** Free parking.

High Velocity   The interior is chockablock with signed photos, posters, and artifacts. Entertainment includes flatscreen TVs, pool tables, video games, Foosball, darts, and coin-op football and basketball. In addition, sporting events are aired on big-screen TVs and on smaller monitors around the room. High Velocity offers a fairly extensive bar-food menu. *Note to single women:* Men outnumber women about five to one. It's open daily 4pm to 1:30am. In Marriott Orlando World Center, 8701 World Center Dr. ℂ **407/238-8690.** Self-parking $12; valet parking $22.

UNSPORTSMANLIKE options

Disney's BoardWalk has a few options for folks searching for off-the-field nightlife. Street performers sing, dance, and do a little juggling and magic most evenings on the outdoor promenade. It can be a cheap night out if you enjoy strolling and people-watching. It has something of a midway atmosphere reminiscent of Atlantic City's heyday.

Atlantic Dance (ℂ **407/939-2444** for limited recorded information) features top-40 and '80s dance hits Tuesday through Saturday. It's open to everyone 21 and older; most of the clientele tend to be of the business-traveler variety. Hours are from 9pm to 2am; no cover.

The rustic saloon-style **Jellyrolls** (ℂ **407/939-5100**) offers dueling pianos and a boisterous crowd. Strictly for the 21-and-over set, it's open daily from 7pm to 2am, though it's busiest on weekends. There's a $10 cover.

The **Big River Grill & Brewing Works** (ℂ **407/939-5100**) serves microbrewed beer as well as steaks, ribs, chicken, fish, sandwiches, and salads. Prices range from $10 to $26. It's open Monday through Thursday from 11:30am to 1am; Friday through Sunday from 11:30am to 2am. It's near Atlantic Dance.

SIDE TRIPS FROM ORLANDO

Although many visitors to Orlando never venture outside the city while on vacation, an excursion away from the hubbub of the theme parks can allow you time to recharge your batteries, while still offering plenty of fun and enjoyment. One destination that many families will drive some distance to see is Tampa Bay's Busch Gardens, another major area kiddie attraction 1½ hours west of Orlando on I-4. But don't stop there: The city of Tampa is an exciting destination on its own.

Florida's very own city by the bay, Tampa is the commercial center of Florida's west coast—a major seaport and a center of banking, high-tech manufacturing, and cigar making (half a billion drugstore stogies a year). Downtown Tampa may roll up its sidewalks after dark, but a short ride will take you to Ybor City, the historic Cuban enclave, now an exciting entertainment and dining venue.

Visitors who opt to head southeast to the Space Coast may find themselves privy to the eye-popping spectacle of rockets blasting off from the Kennedy Space Center at Cape Canaveral. Nearby in Cocoa Beach, they can catch a wave with the surfing crowd.

TAMPA

85 miles SW of Orlando

Even if you stay on the beaches 20 miles to the west, you should consider driving into Tampa for a mild taste of metropolis. If you have children in tow, they may *demand* that you go into the city so they can enjoy the rides and see the animals at Busch Gardens (and if you have purchased the FlexTicket—see p. 244—you'll get free admission and shuttle service from Orlando to the park). Once there, you can also educate them (and yourself) at the Florida Aquarium and the city's other fine museums. And historic Ybor City has the bay area's liveliest and hottest nightlife.

Essentials

GETTING THERE Tampa International Airport (© 813/870-8770; www.tampaairport.com), 5 miles northwest of downtown Tampa, is the major air gateway to this area. Most major and many no-frills airlines

Tampa

HOTELS ■
Econo Lodge **13**
Embassy Suites Hotel and
  Conference Center **15**
Holiday Inn Suites Tampa
  Bay **16**
Hyatt Place **16**
LaQuinta Inn & Suites **12**
Saddlebrook Resort–
  Tampa Seminole Hard Rock
  Hotel & Casino **21**
Sheraton Tampa Riverwalk
  Hotel **30**
The Tampa All Suites Inn **14**
Tampa Marriott Waterside
  Hotel and Marina **33**
The Westin Tampa Harbour
  Island **34**

RESTAURANTS ◆
Bella's Italian Café **9**
Bern's Steak House **6**
Carmine's Seventh
  Avenue **24**
Channelside at the
  Garrison Seaport **32**
Columbia Restaurant **25**
Fly Bar & Restaurant **29**
Mel's Hot Dogs **20**
Mise en Place **28**
The Refinery **22**
Restaurant BT **8**
SideBern's **10**
Whiskey Joe's Bar & Grill **3**
Wine Exchange **7**

ATTRACTIONS ●
Adventure Island **18**
Big Cat Rescue **1**
Busch Gardens
  Tampa Bay **17**
Channelside at the
  Garrison Seaport **32**
Florida Aquarium **35**
Henry B. Plant Museum **26**
MOSI (Museum of Science
  and Industry) **19**
NY Yankees Spring
  Training Complex **4**
Tampa Bay History Center **31**
Tampa Bay Downs **2**
Tampa Museum of Art **27**
Tampa's Lowry Park Zoo **11**
Raymond James Stadium
  (Tampa Bay Buccaneers) **5**
Ybor City State Museum **23**

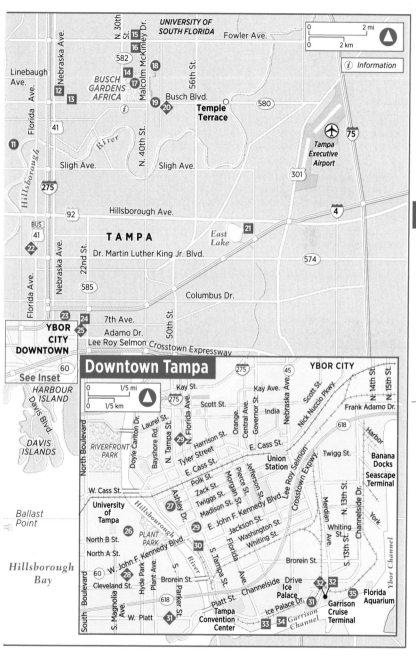

serve Tampa International (see "Airline Websites," p. 392), and all major rental-car agencies have operations here.

The **Limo/SuperShuttle** (✆ **800/282-6817** or 727/527-1111; www.supershuttle. com) operates van services between the airport and hotels throughout the Tampa Bay area. Fares for one person range from $40 to $60 round-trip. **Taxis** are plentiful at the airport; the ride to downtown Tampa takes about 15 minutes and costs $15 to $25.

Trains operated by **Amtrak** (✆ **800/872-7245**; www.amtrak.com) arrive downtown at Union Station, 601 Nebraska Ave. N.

VISITOR INFORMATION For advance information, contact the **Tampa Bay Convention & Visitors Bureau** (✆ **800/448-2672** or 813/223-2752; www.visit tampabay.com). If you're downtown, head to the bureau's **visitor information center** at 400 N. Tampa St. (Channelside), Ste. 2800 (✆ **813/223-1111**), open Monday through Saturday from 9:30am to 5:30pm.

Operated by the Ybor City Chamber of Commerce, the **Centro Ybor Museum & Visitor Information Center,** in Centro Ybor, 1514½ E. 8th Ave. (btw. 15th and 16th sts. E.), Tampa (✆ **813/248-3712**; www.ybor.org), distributes information and has exhibits on the area's history. A brief video will orient you to this area, an 8-block stretch of 7th Avenue. It's open Monday through Saturday from 10am to 6pm, Sunday from noon to 6pm.

GETTING AROUND Like most other Florida destinations, it's all but impossible to see Tampa's major sights and enjoy its best restaurants without a car. You can get around downtown via the **In-Town Trolley,** which runs north-south between Harbor Island and the city's North Terminal bus station on Marion Street at I-275. The trolleys run every 10 minutes from 6am to 6pm Monday through Friday. Southbound, they follow Tampa Street between Tyler and Whiting streets, and Franklin Street between Whiting Street and Harbor Island. Northbound trolleys follow Florida Avenue from the St. Pete Times Forum to Cass Street. The trolleys cost 25¢ and are operated by the **Hillsborough Area Regional Transit/HARTline** (✆ **813/254-4278**; www.hartline.org), which also provides scheduled **bus service** ($1.75–$2.75) between downtown Tampa and the suburbs. Pick up a route map at the visitor center (see above).

The transportation situation has gotten somewhat better, not to mention nostalgic, with the **TECO Line Street Car System** (✆ **813/254-HART** [4278]; www.teco linestreetcar.org), a new but old-fashioned 2⅓-mile streetcar system, complete with overhead power lines, that hauls passengers between downtown and Ybor City via the St. Pete Times Forum, Channelside, Garrison Seaport, and the Florida Aquarium. The cars run every 30 minutes; one-way fares are $2.50 for adults, $1.25 for seniors and children 17 and under. Check with the visitor center or call HARTline for schedules.

Taxis don't normally cruise the streets for fares, but they do line up at public places, such as hotels, the performing-arts center, and bus and train depots. If you need a taxi, call **Tampa Bay Cab** (✆ **813/251-5555**), **Yellow Cab** (✆ **813/253-0121**), or **United Cab** (✆ **813/253-2424**). Fares are $2 at flag fall, plus $2.25 for each mile.

Exploring Animal & Theme Parks

Adventure Island ☺ If the summer heat gets to you before one of Tampa's famous thunderstorms brings late-afternoon relief, you can take a break at this 30-acre outdoor water theme park near Busch Gardens (see below). You can also frolic here during the cooler days of spring and fall, when the water is heated. The Key West Rapids, Riptide, Gulf Scream, and other exciting water rides will drench the teens, while calmer rides are geared toward younger kids. Wahoo Run plunges up to five riders more than 15 feet per second as the half-enclosed tunnel corkscrews more than 600 feet to a waiting splash pool. There are also places to picnic and sunbathe, an arcade, a volleyball complex, and two outdoor cafes.

10001 Malcolm McKinley Dr. (btw. Busch Blvd. and Bougainvillea Ave.). ℰ **813/987-5600.** www. adventureisland.com. Admission at least $42 adults, $38 children 3–9, plus tax; free for children 2 and under. Pick Two tickets with Busch Gardens Tampa Bay (1-day admission per park) $80–$90, free for children 2 and under. Website sometimes offers discounts. Parking $12. Mid-Mar to Labor Day daily 10am–5pm; early Sept to mid-Oct Fri–Sun 10am–5pm (extended hours on holidays). Closed late Oct to early Mar; check website for exact opening dates. Take exit 50 off I-275 and go east on Busch Blvd. for 2 miles. Turn left onto McKinley Dr. (N. 40th St.); entry is on the right.

Big Cat Rescue ☺   Not your typical animal theme park, this one bills itself as an educational sanctuary in which visitors can get up close and "purrsonal" (groan) with more than 150 big wildcats. The world's largest accredited sanctuary for exotic cats, this one is a unique experience for animal lovers because not only can you view bobcats and tigers, but you can also feed them, take photo safaris, and even spend a night in one of the sanctuary's cabins.

12802 Easy St. ℰ**813/920-4130.** www.bigcatrescue.org. Day tours for ages 10 and over $25 per person Mon–Fri 9am–3pm; special kids' tour for all ages $15 per person Sat 9am; night tour for ages 18 and over $50 per person, last Fri of the month at dusk; feeding tours for ages 18 and over $50 per person, reservations required; Keeper for a Day tour for ages 18 and over $100 per person, reservations required. Take Busch Blvd. exit west off I-275 for 9 miles (it becomes Gunn Hwy.). Watch for the dirt road near the McDonald's.

Busch Gardens Tampa Bay ★★ ☺   Although its heart-pounding thrill rides get much of the ink, this venerable theme park (it predates Disney World) ranks among the largest zoos in the country. It's a don't-miss attraction for children and adults who can see, in person, all those wild beasts they've watched on *Animal Planet*—and they'll get better views of them here than at Disney's Animal Kingdom in Orlando (p. 226). Busch Gardens has more than 2,000 animals living in natural-style environments. Most authentic is the 65-acre plain, reminiscent of the Serengeti of Tanzania and Kenya, upon which zebras, rhinos, giraffes, and other animals graze. Unlike the animals on the real Serengeti, however, these grazing creatures have nothing to fear from lions, hyenas, crocodiles, and other predators, which are confined to enclosures—as are the hippos and elephants. The park's seventh roller coaster, **SheiKra** (see below), was the nation's first dive coaster, carrying riders up 200 feet at 45 degrees and then hurtling them 70 mph back at a 90-degree angle.

New in 2011 is **Cheetah Run,** a Linear Synchronous Motor (LSM) Launch Coaster, which uses the force of repelling magnets to launch riders from 0 to 60 in a matter of seconds. Located in the area that formerly housed the Budweiser Clydesdales, this new habitat will give visitors the opportunity to get closer to cheetahs than ever with elevated, glass-paneled viewing areas.

The park has eight areas (each with its own theme), animals, live entertainment, rides, kiddie attractions, dining, and shopping. A Skyride cable car soars over the park, offering a bird's-eye view of it all. Turn right after the main gate and head to **Morocco,** a walled city with exotic architecture, crafts demonstrations, and an exhibit featuring alligators and turtles. Over in **Egypt,** you can visit King Tut's tomb, with its replicas, and youngsters can dig for their own ancient treasures in a sand area.

Adults and kids 54 inches or taller can ride **Montu,** the tallest and longest inverted roller coaster in the world, with seven upside-down loops.

From Egypt, walk to the **Edge of Africa,** home to most of the large animals. Go to the Adventure Tours tent and see if you can get on a Serengeti Safari, one of the park's most popular zoologist-led wildlife tours.

Next stop is **Nairobi,** where you can see gorillas and chimpanzees in their lush rainforest habitat in the Myombe Reserve. In the middle of all the excitement, you will find **Timbuktu,** where two of the smaller roller coasters are located; **Scorpion,** a high-speed number with a 60-foot drop and 360-degree loop (42-in. height minimum); and **Cheetah Chase,** a five-story "wild mouse"–style coaster (46-in height minimum). For visual amusement, there's Sesame Street Presents "Lights, Camera, Imagination!"

Now head to the **Congo,** where the highlights are the rare white Bengal tigers that live in **Jungala,** the park's 4-acre attraction within the Congo, featuring a colorful village hidden deep in the jungle, up-close animal interactions, multistory play areas, rides, and live entertainment. The Congo is also home to **Kumba,** which plunges riders from 110 feet into a diving loop, where you get a full 3 seconds of feeling weightless while spiraling 360 degrees, before tearing through one of the world's largest vertical loops (54-in. height minimum). You will also get drenched—and refreshed on a hot day—by riding the **Congo River Rapids,** where you're turned loose in round boats that float down the swiftly flowing "river" (42-in. height minimum).

From the Congo, walk south into **Stanleyville,** a prototype African village, with a shopping bazaar and the Stanleyville Theater, featuring shows for all ages. Two more water rides here are the **Tanganyika Tidal Wave** (48-in. height minimum), where you'll come to a very damp end, and the **Stanley Falls Flume** (an aquatic version of a roller coaster). If you're really crazy, check out the floorless **SheiKra,** where for 200 feet up and 90 degrees straight down, you can view the world—from a floorless perspective and a water-feature finale, all packed into a half-mile of steel track. The Zambia Smokehouse serves ribs and chicken—some of the best chow in the park.

Up next is **Sesame Street Safari of Fun** for the young ones and those, ahem, too frightened to partake in some of the other rides. You'll see Sesame Street characters in a family-friendly African adventure where you can dip and dive through the desert on the Air Grover junior coaster, climb and play in Elmo's Tree House, and splash in Bert and Ernie's water play area. The Sesame Street characters take part in shows, and you can have a meal with them, too.

The next stop is **Bird Gardens,** the park's original core, offering rich foliage, lagoons, and Florida flamingos. New this year is **Walkabout Way,** an immersive animal attraction that gives an up-close look at animals indigenous to the Land Down Under. Hand-feed kangaroos and wallabies in Kangaloom during scheduled feedings throughout the day. Laugh with a kookaburra and other Australian birds in the free-flight aviary, Kookaburra's Nest.

If your stomach can take another hair-raising ride, try **Gwazi** (48-in. minimum height), an adrenaline-pumping attraction in which a pair of old-fashioned wooden roller coasters (named the Lion and the Tiger) start simultaneously and whiz within a few feet of each other six times as they roar along at 50 mph and rise to 90 feet.

Added up-close tours are available, including a 6-hour zookeeper-for-a-day program and a nighttime safari by lantern light. Tour components and prices are subject to change without notice and park admission is required, but not included. For reservations, call ✆ **813/984-4043.**

You can exchange foreign currency in the park, and interpreters are available. **Note:** Daily round-trip transportation is available from Orlando to Busch Gardens Tampa Bay (a 1½-hr. ride or so). Shuttle buses pick up at Orlando-area hotels between 8:30am and 9:40am, with a return trip at park close or 7pm during peak seasons. Round-trip fares are $10 per person, free with Busch Gardens combination tickets. Call ✆ **800/221-1339** for schedules, pickup locations, and reservations.

3000 E. Busch Blvd. (at McKinley Dr./N. 40th St.). ✆ **888/800-5447.** www.buschgardens.com. **Note:** Admission prices and hours vary, so call ahead, check website, or get brochure at visitor centers. Admission $75 plus tax adults, $65 plus tax children 3–9, free for children 2 and under. Prices subject to change without notice. Combination tickets and Passport Memberships available. Discounts available for guests with disabilities, seniors, military personnel, and AAA members. Normal park hours daily 10am–6pm; hours extended during select weekends, summer, and holidays. Parking $12 for cars, $14 for trucks and campers. Take I-275 north of downtown to Busch Blvd. (exit 50) and go east 2 miles. From I-75, take Fowler Ave. (exit 54) and follow the signs west.

Florida Aquarium ★★ ☺ There are more than 20,000 aquatic animals and plants at this entertaining attraction. The exhibits follow a drop of water from the springs of the Florida Wetlands Gallery, through a mangrove forest in the Bays and Beaches Gallery, and out onto the Coral Reefs, where an impressive 43-foot-wide, 14-foot-tall panoramic window lets you look out at schools of fish and lots of sharks and stingrays. Also worth visiting are the educational Explore a Shore playground, a deepwater exhibit, and a tank housing moray eels. You can look for birds and sea life on 90-minute Eco Tour cruises in the *Bay Spirit II*, a 72-foot catamaran. The aquarium also offers a program called **Dive with the Sharks** (✆ **813/273-4015**), which gives certified divers the chance to swim with blacktip, sand tiger, and nurse sharks for 30 minutes. The $175 price tag includes a souvenir photo and T-shirt. The Penguin Promenade allows you to get up close and personal with the cute creatures. Also popular is Ocean Commotion, a high-tech gallery utilizing state-of-the-art technology like "smart Wi-Fi," floor-to-ceiling interactive displays, virtual dolphins and whales, animation, and multimedia presentations. Guests can even upload their own videos to become part of the exhibit. Also fun for the adventurous: **Swim with the Fishes,** in which you can scuba through the half-million-gallon Coral Reef Exhibit. Kids must be 6 or older, and those age 8 and under must have an adult with them. The cost is $85 per person, which includes aquarium admission. Accompanying parents must pay, too. Expect to spend 3 to 4 hours here.

701 Channelside Dr. ✆ **813/273-4000.** www.flaquarium.org. Admission $20 adults, $17 seniors, $15 children 3–11, free for children 2 and under. Eco Tour $22 adults, $20 seniors, $18 children 3–11, free for children 2 and under. Combination aquarium admission and Eco Tour $36 adults, $32 seniors, $28 children 3–11, free for children 2 and under. Website sometimes offers discounts. Daily 9:30am–5pm. Eco Tour Sun–Fri 2 and 4pm; Sat noon, 2, and 4pm. Parking $6. Closed Thanksgiving and Christmas.

Tampa's Lowry Park Zoo ★ ☺ Recognized as the number-one zoo in the U.S. by *Parents* magazine (2009) and *Child* magazine (2004), Tampa's Lowry Park features 2,000 animals from Africa, Asia, Australia, South America, and Florida, on nearly 60 acres of natural outdoor habitats. Guests will find many interactive exhibits and opportunities to get closer to wildlife—feed a giraffe, ride a dromedary camel, hold a lorikeet, touch a stingray, and more. The **Manatee and Aquatic Center** and **David A. Straz, Jr., Manatee Hospital** focus efforts on critical care for injured, sick, and orphaned wild manatees. The zoo also offers water play areas, rides, educational shows, and a variety of eateries. Guests can enhance their experience by going on the

River Odyssey EcoTour, a relaxing 1-hour journey up the Hillsborough River aboard the zoo's own vessel, the *Sirenia,* to view animals and plant life that abound along the river's path. EcoTour tickets are $14 for adults, $13 for seniors, and $10 for children 3 to 11. Combo tickets (Zoo/EcoTour) and group tickets are available.

1101 W. Sligh Ave. ⓒ **813/935-8552.** www.lowryparkzoo.com. Zoo admission $21 adults, $19 seniors, $16 children 3–11, free for children 2 and under. Zoo daily 9:30am–5pm. Free parking. Closed Thanksgiving and Christmas. Take I-275 to Sligh Ave. (exit 48) and follow the signs.

Visiting the Museums

Henry B. Plant Museum   Built in 1891 by railroad tycoon Henry B. Plant as the chichi 511-room Tampa Bay Hotel, this ornate building is worth a trip across the river from downtown to the University of Tampa campus. Its 13 silver minarets and Moorish architecture, modeled after the Alhambra in Spain, make this National Historic Landmark a focal point of the Tampa skyline. Although the building is the highlight of a visit, don't skip its contents: art and furnishings from Europe and Asia, plus exhibits that explain the history of the railroad resort, Florida's early tourist industry, and the hotel's role as a staging point for Theodore Roosevelt's Rough Riders during the Spanish-American War. During December's **Victorian Christmas Stroll,** the museum is transformed into a holiday wonderland, with 19th-century Yuletide decor, carolers, and Dickens-style stories.

401 W. Kennedy Blvd. (btw. Hyde Park and Magnolia aves.). ⓒ **813/254-1891.** www.plantmuseum.com. Admission Jan–Nov $10 adults, $7 seniors and students, $5 children 4–12. Special pricing in Dec for Victorian Christmas Stroll. Tues–Sat 10am–4pm; Sun noon–4pm. Closed Thanksgiving, Christmas Eve, and Christmas Day. Take Kennedy Blvd. (Fla. 60) across the Hillsborough River.

MOSI (Museum of Science and Industry) ★★ ☺   MOSI is the largest science center in the Southeast, with more than 450 interactive exhibits. Step into the Gulf Hurricane to experience 74-mph winds, explore the human body in the Amazing You, and, if your heart is up to it, ride a bicycle across a 98-foot-long cable suspended 30 feet above the lobby. (Don't worry: You'll be harnessed to the bike.) You can also watch stunning movies in Florida's first IMAX dome theater. Outside, trails wind through a nature preserve with a butterfly garden. The museum is one of very few in the world to feature the articulated remains of a Sauropod dinosaur.

4801 E. Fowler Ave. (at N. 50th St.). ⓒ **813/987-6100.** www.mosi.org. Admission $21 adults, $19 seniors, $17 children 2–12, free for children 1 and under. Admission includes IMAX movies. Daily 9am–5pm or later. From downtown, take I-275 N. to Fowler Ave. E., exit 51. Take this 2 miles east to museum on right.

Tampa Bay History Center ★ ☺   Opened in early 2009, this 60,000-square-foot museum covers everyone from Native Americans to tycoons and sports legends who have inhabited Tampa. It features interactive exhibits, theaters, a map gallery, research center, museum store, and Columbia Cafe, a branch of the internationally acclaimed Columbia Restaurant. The permanent exhibits explore approximately 500 years of recorded history and 12,000 years of human habitation in the region.

801 Old Water St. ⓒ **813/228-0097.** www.tampabayhistorycenter.org. Admission $12 adults, $10 seniors and children 13–17, $7 children 4–12. Mon–Fri 9am–5pm.

Tampa Museum of Art ★   The museum recently moved into a 66,000-square-foot space in downtown's $43.6-million Curtis Hixon Waterfront Park, with state-of-the-art gallery spaces featuring translucent ceilings and polished stone floors. The new space is an impressive site, art notwithstanding. You'll find five interior galleries, one exterior sculpture gallery, and a high-tech classroom. The museum features world-class traveling exhibitions and a growing collection of contemporary and classical art.

120 W. Gasparilla Plaza, downtown. (C) **813/274-8130.** www.tampamuseum.com. Admission $10 adults, $7.50 seniors, $5 children 6–18 and students with ID, free for children 5 and under; "pay what you will" 2nd Sat of the month 9–11am and Thurs 5–9pm. Mon–Wed and Fri 11am–7pm; Thurs 11am–9pm; Sat–Sun 11am–5pm. Take I-275 to exit 44 (Ashley Dr.).

Ybor City

Northeast of downtown, the city's historic Latin district takes its name from Don Vicente Martinez Ybor (*Eeee*-bore), a Spanish cigar maker who arrived here in 1886 via Cuba and Key West. Soon, his factory and others in Tampa were producing more than 300,000 hand-rolled stogies a day.

It may not be the cigar capital of the world anymore, but Ybor is still a smokin' part of Tampa, and it's one of the best places in Florida to buy hand-rolled cigars. It's not on par with New Orleans's Bourbon Street, Washington's Georgetown, or Miami's South Beach, but good food and great music dominate the scene, especially on weekends when the streets bustle until 4am. Live-music offerings run the gamut from jazz and blues to rock.

At the heart of it all is **Centro Ybor,** a dining-shopping-entertainment complex between 7th and 8th avenues and 16th and 17th streets ((C) **813/242-4660;** www.centroybor.com). Here you'll find a multiscreen cinema, a comedy club, several restaurants, and a large open-air bar. The Ybor City Chamber of Commerce has its visitor center here (see "Essentials," earlier in this chapter), and the Ybor City State Museum's gift shop is here as well (see below).

Check with the visitor center about walking tours of the historic district. **Secret Ybor: Scandals, Crimes, and Shady Ladies** ((C) 813/831-5214; http://historicguides.com/secretybor.htm) explores the more scandalous side of the city. Tours depart at various times from locations throughout Ybor City. The tours are prearranged and only for groups of 20 or more; minimum fee is $200 for 20 people.

Even if you're not a cigar smoker, you'll enjoy a stroll through the **Ybor City State Museum ★,** 1818 9th Ave., between 18th and 19th streets ((C) 813/247-6323; www.ybormuseum.org), housed in the former Ferlita Bakery (1896–1973). You can take a self-guided tour to see the collection of cigar labels, cigar memorabilia, and works by local artisans. Admission is $4, free for children 6 and under. Walking tours of Ybor City are held Saturday at 10:30am, cost $8 (which includes museum admission), and start at the Ybor City Museum State Park. Depending on the availability of volunteer docents, admission includes a 15-minute guided tour of **La Casita,** a renovated cigar worker's cottage adjacent to the museum; it's furnished as it was at the turn of the 20th century. The museum is open daily from 9am to 5pm, but you have the best chance for the guided tour if you visit between 11am and 3pm. Better yet, plan to catch a cigar-rolling demonstration (ongoing; no specific schedule), held Friday through Sunday between 10am and 3pm.

Like any area with trendy bars and restaurants, things are always changing, opening, and going out of business, so you may want to check **www.ybortimes.com** for the latest in Ybor City.

Organized Tours

Check out the **Tampa Bay Visitor Information Center,** 3601 E. Busch Blvd. (© 813/985-3601), opposite Busch Gardens, which operates guided bus tours of Tampa, Ybor City, and environs. Tampa native Jim Boggs will guide you through the city on 4-hour tours, which are given from 10am to 3pm daily, with a stop for lunch at the Columbia Restaurant in Ybor City. The tour costs $45 for adults and $40 for children 12 and under. The full-day tours (10am–5pm) of Tampa, Clearwater, and St. Petersburg give a good overview of the cities and the beaches; this tour costs $75 for adults and $65 for children. Reservations are required at least 24 hours in advance; passengers are picked up at major Tampa hotels.

Ghost Tours of Tampa Bay (© 727/398-5200; www.ghosttour.com) offers candlelight walking tours of Tampa Bay's most haunted locations, with nightly tours in Tampa, St. Petersburg, and John's Pass Village. Reservations are required; cost is $15 for adults and $8 for kids 4 to 12.

Outdoor Activities & Spectator Sports

BIKING, IN-LINE SKATING & JOGGING   Bayshore Boulevard, a 7-mile-long promenade, is famous for its sidewalk right on the shores of Hillsborough Bay and is a favorite with runners, walkers, and in-line skaters. The route goes from the western edge of downtown in a southward direction, passing stately old homes in Hyde Park, a few high-rise condos, retirement communities, and houses of worship, ending at Ballast Point Park. The view from the promenade across the bay to the downtown skyline is matchless. Bayshore Boulevard is also great for a drive.

BOATING   Check out the Hillsborough River by canoe with **Canoe Escape of Tampa** (© 813/986-2067; www.canoeescape.com), which offers all sorts of paddling programs, from a 3-hour religious journey and moonlight trips to a 3-hour nighttime tour down the river. Or rent your own canoe or kayak and take a self-guided tour through Wilderness Park, a 16,000-acre wildlife preserve. Guided tours range from $130 per person to $60 per person for groups of six or more; self-guided rentals range from $25 to $56 per person.

FISHING   For charters, try **Captain Jim's Inshore Sportfishing Charters,** 512 Palm Ave., Palm Harbor (© 727/439-9017; www.captainhud.com), which offers private sport-fishing trips for tarpon, redfish, trout, and snook. Rates are $350 to $625 for two anglers. Call for schedule and reservations. Rave reviews have come in for **Capt. Gus's Crabby Adventures** (© 813/645-6578; www.crabbyadventures. com), whose 4-hour boating, eating, and eco-experience includes interaction with blue crabs, stone crabs, and all the creatures of the bay, including manatees, dolphins, laughing gulls, pelicans, herons, egrets, and osprey. Gus instructs guests on how crab traps are pulled and baited. You'll also learn to grade, clean, steam, and eat blue crabs and stone crabs at the Bay Chop Villa, an open-air waterfront shack and gazebo. Parties of two pay $300; additional passengers are $50 each. The boat leaves at 8am and 2pm.

GOLF   Tampa has three municipal golf courses where you can play for about $30 to $35, a relative pittance compared to fees at private courses. The **Babe Zaharias Municipal Golf Course,** 11412 Forest Hills Dr., north of Lowry Park (© 813/631-4374; www.babezahariasgc.com), is an 18-hole, par-70 course with a pro shop, putting greens, and a driving range. It is the shortest of the municipal courses, but its small greens and narrow fairways present ample challenges. Water provides obstacles on 12 of the 18 holes at **Rocky Point Golf Course,** 4151 Dana Shores Dr. (✆ **813/673-4316;** www.rockypointgc.com), between the airport and the bay. It's a par-71 course with a pro shop, practice range, and putting greens. On the Hillsborough River in north Tampa, the **Rogers Park Golf Course,** 7910 N. 30th St. (✆ **813/673-4396;** www.rogersparkgc.com), is an 18-hole, par-72 championship course with a lighted driving and practice range. All of the courses are open daily from 7am to dusk, and lessons and club rentals are available.

You can book starting times and get information about area courses by calling **Tee Times USA** (✆ **800/374-8633;** www.teetimesusa.com).

If you want to do some serious work on your game, the **Arnold Palmer Golf Academy World Headquarters** is at Saddlebrook Resort, 5700 Saddlebrook Way, Wesley Chapel, 12 miles north of Tampa (✆ **800/729-8383** or 813/973-1111; www.saddlebrookresort.com). Half-day and hourly instruction are available, as well as 2-, 3-, and 5-day programs for adults and juniors. You have to stay at the resort or enroll in the golf program to play at Saddlebrook. See p. 346 for more information.

For course information online, go to **www.golf.com** or **www.floridagolfing.com,** or call the **Florida Sports Foundation** (✆ **850/488-8347**) or **Florida Golfing** (✆ **866/833-2663**).

SPECTATOR SPORTS Major-league baseball fans were thrilled when the **Tampa Bay Rays** made it to the World Series against Philly in 2008. Although they lost, the games remain a huge draw for fans flocking to **Tropicana Field,** 1 Tropicana Dr., St. Petersburg (✆ **727/825-3250**). Tickets range from as low as $10 to as high as in the hundreds, depending on how well the season is going. In 2009, the Rays moved to a new spring-training facility in Port Charlotte.

New York Yankees fans can watch the Bronx Bombers during baseball's spring training, from mid-February to the end of March, at **George Steinbrenner Field** (✆ **813/879-2244** or 813/875-7753; www.steinbrennerfield.com), opposite Raymond James Stadium. This scaled-down replica of Yankee Stadium is the largest spring-training facility in Florida, with a 10,000-seat capacity. Tickets are $10 to $20. The club's minor-league team, the **Tampa Yankees** (same contact info), plays at Legends Field from April through August.

National Football League fans can catch the **Tampa Bay Buccaneers** at the modern 66,000-seat Raymond James Stadium, 4201 N. Dale Mabry Hwy., at Dr. Martin Luther King, Jr., Boulevard (✆ **813/879-2827;** www.buccaneers.com), from August through December. Single-game tickets are very hard to come by, as they are usually sold out to the plethora of season-ticket holders. This is a huge football city!

The National Hockey League's **Tampa Bay Lightning,** winners of the 2004 Stanley Cup, play in the St. Pete Times Forum starting in October (✆ **813/301-6500;** www.tampabaylightning.com). You can usually get single-game tickets ($30–$349) on game day.

The only thoroughbred racetrack on Florida's west coast is **Tampa Bay Downs,** 11225 Racetrack Rd., Oldsmar (✆ **800/200-4434** in Florida, or 813/855-4401; www.tampadowns.com), home of the Tampa Bay Derby. Races are held from December to May ($2 general admission, $3 clubhouse), and the track presents simulcasts year-round. Call for post times.

TENNIS Sharpen your game at the **Saddlebrook Tennis Academy,** at the Saddlebrook Resort (p. 346). You must be a member or a guest to play here.

Shopping

Hyde Park and Ybor City are two areas of Tampa worth some window-shopping, perhaps sandwiched around lunch at one of the fine restaurants (see "Where to Eat," below).

On the mall front, there's the upscale **International Plaza** (© 813/342-3790; www.shopinternationalplaza.com), near Tampa International Airport, where the headliners include Neiman Marcus and Nordstrom.

CIGARS Ybor City is no longer a major producer of hand-rolled cigars, but you can still watch artisans making stogies at the **Columbia Cigar Store.** Rollers are on duty Monday through Saturday from 10am to 6pm. You can stock up on domestic and imported cigars at **El Sol,** 1728 E. 7th Ave. (© 813/247-5554), the city's oldest cigar store; **King Corona Cigar Factory,** 1523 E. 7th Ave. (© 813/241-9109); and **Metropolitan Cigars & Wine,** 2014 E. 7th Ave. (© 813/248-3304).

SHOPPING CENTERS **Old Hyde Park Village,** 1507 W. Swann Ave., at South Dakota Avenue (© 813/251-3500; www.oldhydeparkvillage.com), is a terrific alternative to cookie-cutter malls despite the fact that it's almost always inexplicably devoid of people. Check out Hyde Park, one of the city's most historic neighborhoods, and stroll the cluster of 50 upscale shops set in a village layout. The selection includes Williams-Sonoma, Pottery Barn, Restoration Hardware, Brooks Brothers, Crabtree & Evelyn, and Godiva, to name a few. There are also several restaurants, including the Wine Exchange, Timpano Italian Chophouse, the Cobb CineBistro movie theater and restaurant, and the highly recommended Restaurant BT (see below). There's a free parking garage on South Oregon Avenue. Most shops are open Monday through Saturday from 10am to 7pm, Sunday from noon to 5pm. Throughout the year, the village hosts various events, from concerts to art festivals.

The centerpiece of the downtown seaport renovation is the massive tourist trap known as **Channelside at Garrison Seaport,** on Channelside Drive between the Garrison Seaport and the Florida Aquarium (© 813/223-4250). It has stores, restaurants, bars, a **Splitsville Lanes** bowling alley (© 813/514-2695; www.splitsvillelanes.com), and a multiscreen cinema with an IMAX screen.

In Ybor City, **Centro Ybor,** on 7th Avenue East at 16th Street (© 813/242-4660; www.centroybor.com), is primarily a dining-and-entertainment complex, but you'll find a few chains, such as American Eagle and Urban Outfitters.

Where to Stay

The listings below are organized into two geographic areas: near Busch Gardens and downtown. If you're going to Busch Gardens, Adventure Island, Lowry Park Zoo, or the Museum of Science and Industry (MOSI), the motels near Busch Gardens are much more convenient than those downtown, about 7 miles to the south. The downtown hotels are geared to business travelers, but staying there will put you near the Florida Aquarium, the Tampa Museum of Art, the Henry B. Plant Museum, the Tampa Bay Performing Arts Center, scenic Bayshore Boulevard, and the dining and shopping opportunities in the Channelside and Hyde Park districts.

The Westshore area, near the bay, west of downtown, and south of Tampa International Airport, is another commercial center, with a wide range of chain hotels catering to business travelers and conventioneers. It's not far from Raymond James Stadium and the New York Yankees' spring-training complex. Check with your favorite chain for a Westshore-Airport location.

Room rates at most hotels in Tampa vary little from season to season. This is especially true downtown, where the hotels do a brisk convention business year-round. Hillsborough County adds 12% tax to your hotel bill.

Discount Packages

Many Tampa hotels combine tickets to major attractions such as Busch Gardens Tampa Bay in their packages, so always ask about special deals.

NEAR BUSCH GARDENS

The chain motels nearest to the park (1½ blocks east of the main entrance) are the **Econo Lodge,** 1701 E. Busch Blvd. (℅ **813/933-7681;** www. econolodge.com), and the **Comfort Inn,** 820 E. Busch Blvd. (℅ **813/933-4011;** www.comfortinn.com). Stay at either if it's your last resort (no pun intended) or if you're on a supertight budget. The 500-unit **Embassy Suites Hotel & Conference Center,** 3705 Spectrum Blvd., facing Fowler Avenue (℅ **800/362-2779** or 813/977-7066), is the plushest, most expensive establishment near the park. The **Tampa All Suites Inn,** 3001 University Center Dr. (℅ **813/971-8930**), features a heated pool and fun Tiki bar. Nearby stands **LaQuinta Inn & Suites,** 3701 E. Fowler Ave. (℅ **800/687-6667** or 813/910-7500). Just south of Fowler Avenue are side-by-side branches of **Hyatt Place,** 11408 N. 30th St. (℅ **813/979-1922**), and **Holiday Inn Suites Tampa Bay,** 11310 N. 30th St. (℅ **813/971-7690**).

DOWNTOWN TAMPA

Seminole Hard Rock Hotel & Casino ★   Despite its location in a somewhat run-down part of town, Tampa's Seminole Hard Rock is full of nonstop action. Rooms in the 12-story building have modern amenities and large bathrooms. The casino has 178,000 square feet of Vegas-style slots, as well as blackjack, baccarat, Pai Gow poker, Asia poker, Let It Ride poker, and minibaccarat. You'll also find Florida's largest (and smoke-free) poker room, with 92 live-action tables—52 dedicated to no-limit, high-stakes Texas Hold 'em, Omaha Hi-Lo, and Seven-Card Stud. The pool area is fine, but not as nice as those at the Hard Rock in Vegas or in Hollywood, Florida. The fitness center is top-notch and even does outdoor treatments in its Zen garden. A recent expansion added new restaurants, including the swanky **Council Oak Steaks & Seafood** and **Fresh Harvest,** with a live-action show kitchen.

5223 Orient Rd., Tampa, FL 33605. ℅ **866/502-PLAY** (7529) or 813/627-7625. Fax 813/623-6862. www.seminolehardrocktampa.com. 250 units. Winter $169–$329 double; off season $219–$309 double. AE, DC, DISC, MC, V. **Amenities:** 5 restaurants; 5 bars; Jacuzzi; heated outdoor pool; full-service spa. *In room:* A/C, TV, CD player, fridge, hair dryer, high-speed Internet access.

Sheraton Tampa Riverwalk Hotel ★   Set on the east bank of the Hillsborough River, this six-story Green Lodging hotel remains one of Tampa's better bets. Half the rooms face west and have views from their balconies of the Arabesque minarets atop the Henry B. Plant Museum and the University of Tampa across the river—lovely at sunset. These rooms cost more but are preferable to units on the east side of the building, which face downtown's skyscrapers and lack balconies. All rooms feature Sweet Sleeper beds. Set beside the river, the **Ashley Street Grille** serves indoor-outdoor breakfasts and lunches, then offers fine dining in the evenings. Unless you're here on business or need to stay downtown, there's not much here to entice a mainstream traveler. *Note:* The hotel is completely smoke free.

200 N. Ashley Dr. (at Jackson St.), Tampa, FL 33602. ℅ **800/333-3333** or 813/223-2222. Fax 813/221-5929. www.sheratontampariverwalk.com. 277 units. Winter $249–$299 double, $425–$450 suite; off

9

SIDE TRIPS FROM ORLANDO

Tampa

season $229–$279 double, from $240 suite. AE, DC, DISC, MC, V. Valet parking $16. Pets up to 80 lb. accepted. **Amenities:** 2 restaurants; bar; concierge; concierge-level rooms; exercise room; access to nearby health club; heated outdoor pool; limited room service; sauna; Wi-Fi. *In room:* A/C, TV, hair dryer, Internet access.

Tampa Marriott Waterside Hotel & Marina ★★   This luxurious 22-story hotel occupies downtown's most strategic location in the emerging Channel District— beside the river and between the Tampa Convention Center and the St. Pete Times Forum. Opening onto a riverfront promenade, the three-story lobby is large enough to accommodate the many conventioneers drawn to the two neighboring venues and to the hotel's 50,000 square feet of meeting space. The third floor has a fully equipped spa, modern exercise facility, and outdoor heated pool. About half of the guest quarters have balconies overlooking the bay or city (choice views are high up on the south side). Although spacious, the regular rooms are dwarfed by the 720-square-foot suites. In 2009, the hotel wrapped up a $12-million renovation to all guest rooms, which now feature flatscreen TVs and new bathrooms. There's also a 32-slip marina.

700 S. Florida Ave. (at St. Pete Times Forum Dr.), Tampa, FL 33602. © **800/228-9290** or 813/221-4900. Fax 813/221-0923. www.tampamarriottwaterside.com. 719 units. Winter $259–$285 double, $399–$575 suite; off season $179–$259 double, $350–$500 suite. Weekend rates available. AE, DC, DISC, MC, V. Valet parking $21; self-parking in garage across the street $10–$25. **Amenities:** 3 restaurants; 3 bars; babysitting; concierge; concierge-level rooms; health club; Jacuzzi; heated outdoor pool; limited room service; spa. *In room:* A/C, TV, fax, fridge, hair dryer, high-speed Internet access.

Westin Tampa Harbour Island ★★★   Close enough to downtown but still worlds away on its own 177-acre island, the Westin insists that you're here on vacation and not stuck in some downtown convention hotel. Rooms overlook the harbor and are hypercomfortable, with pillow-top mattresses and large bathrooms featuring dual shower heads. The elegant waterfront restaurant, **725 South,** is popular for business dinners and power lunches. A new Westin Workout gym is a highlight for those into working out. Stroll the boardwalk to fully appreciate your surroundings.

725 S. Harbour Island Blvd., Tampa, FL 33602. © **877/999-3223** or 813/229-5000. Fax 813/229-5322. www.starwoodhotels.com. 299 units. $249–$399 double; $495–$895 suite. Weekend rates available. AE, DC, DISC, MC, V. Valet parking $16; self-parking $14. **Amenities:** Restaurant; 3 bars; babysitting; concierge; access to nearby health club; Jacuzzi; heated outdoor pool; limited room service; access to spa. *In room:* A/C, TV, fax, hair dryer, high-speed Internet access.

A NEARBY SPA & SPORTS RESORT

Saddlebrook Resort–Tampa ★★ ☺   Set on 480 rolling acres of countryside, Saddlebrook is a landlocked condo development off the beaten path (30 min. north of Tampa International Airport). But if you're interested in spas, tennis, or golf, this resort offers complete spa treatments, the **Saddlebrook Tennis Academy** (Jennifer Capriati pitches a tent here), and the **Arnold Palmer Golf Academy** (see "Outdoor Activities & Spectator Sports," earlier in this chapter). Guests are housed in hotel rooms with Tommy Bahama–esque decor or one-, two-, or three-bedroom suites. Much more appealing than the rooms, the suites come with a kitchen and either a patio or a balcony overlooking lagoons, cypress and palm trees, and the resort's two 18-hole championship golf courses. There are shops, restaurants, a half-million-gallon "super pool," and a kids' club with supervised activities.

5700 Saddlebrook Way, Wesley Chapel, FL 33543. © **800/729-8383** or 813/973-1111. Fax 813/973-4504. www.saddlebrookresort.com. 800 units. Winter $259–$399 suite; off season $159–$249 suite. Packages available. AE, DC, DISC, MC, V. Valet parking $10. **Amenities:** 4 restaurants; 3 bars; bike rental;

children's program; concierge; 2 golf courses; health club; Jacuzzi; heated outdoor pool; limited room service; sauna; spa; 45 grass, clay, and hard tennis courts. *In room:* A/C, TV, hair dryer, Internet access, kitchen, minibar.

Where to Eat

The restaurants below are organized by geographic area: near Busch Gardens, in or near Hyde Park (across the Hillsborough River from downtown), and in Ybor City. Although Ybor City is better known, Tampa's trendiest dining scene is along South Howard Avenue—"SoHo" to the locals—between West Kennedy Boulevard and the bay in Hyde Park.

NEAR BUSCH GARDENS

You'll find national fast-food chains and family restaurants east of I-275 on Busch Boulevard and Fowler Avenue.

Inexpensive

Mel's Hot Dogs ☺ AMERICAN   Catering to everyone from businesspeople to hungry families, Mel Lohn's red-and-white cottage offers everything from traditional Chicago-style and "bagel-dogs" to bacon/cheddar Reuben-style hot dogs. All choices are served on poppy-seed buns and can be ordered with fries and a choice of coleslaw or baked beans. Even the decor is dedicated to wieners: The walls and windows are lined with hot-dog memorabilia, and a wiener-mobile is usually parked out front. Mel's chili is outstanding, too. And just in case hot-dog mania hasn't won you over, there are a few alternatives (chicken, beef, and veggie burgers, plus terrific onion rings).

4136 E. Busch Blvd., at 42nd St. ⓒ **813/985-8000.** www.melshotdogs.com. Most items $2.75–$11. No credit cards (but there's an ATM on the premises). Sun–Thurs 11am–8pm; Fri–Sat 11am–9pm.

HYDE PARK
Expensive

Bern's Steak House ★★ STEAK   The exterior of this famous steakhouse is so unassuming, you'd never know you were about to enter meat—and wine—heaven. The interior is an opulent foodie fantasyland, containing eight ornate dining rooms with themes such as Rhône, Burgundy, and Irish Rebellion. This is a carnivore's paradise. At Bern's, you order and pay for grilled steaks of perfectly aged beef according to the thickness and weight (the 60-oz. strip sirloin can feed six adults). A surprisingly good deal for a fancy steakhouse, all entrees come with French onion soup, salad, baked potato, onion rings, and organic vegetables. Bern's also offers a seasonal "Kitchen within a Kitchen" specials menu, which changes every 3 weeks. The wine list—one of the restaurant's most famous attributes—has more than 6,500 labels, many available by the glass. Upstairs, the **Harry Waugh Dessert Room** has 50 romantic, semiprivate casks paneled in aged California redwood; each can privately seat from 2 to 12 guests. All of these little chambers are equipped with phones for placing your requests with the piano player. The dessert menu has 35 to 40 tough choices—and with ice-cream flavors, choices become 100 times harder—plus some 1,400 after-dinner drinks, wines, and spirits. You can go here just for dessert, but the dessert room is first come, first served unless you have dinner, which will get you a coveted cask upstairs. For those who love cheese, Bern's has two indoor caves storing artisanal cheeses from around the world.

Tip: The big secret here is that steak sandwiches are available at the bar but are not mentioned on the menu.

SideBern's, 2208 W. Morrison Ave., at South Howard Avenue (© **813/258-2233**), is the restaurant's New American offshoot. It's quite good, but if you have only a single night, choose the original: Missing Bern's would be like watching the remake of *Psycho* without seeing the original. If you have 2 nights or more, then do *not* miss the stellar seasonal menus created by Executive Chef Chad Johnson, who uses only locally grown ingredients. There's also an exceptional cheese-and-wine-pairing menu.

1208 S. Howard Ave. (at Marjory Ave.). © **813/251-2421.** www.bernssteakhouse.com. Reservations recommended. Main courses $21–$70. AE, DC, DISC, MC, V. Sun–Thurs 5–10pm; Fri–Sat 5–11pm. Closed Christmas and Labor Day. SideBern's: Mon–Thurs 6–10pm; Fri–Sat 6–11pm. Valet parking $5.

Restaurant BT ★★★ VIETNAMESE   One reviewer called this one of the hippest, most innovative Vietnamese restaurants in the U.S. Chef Trina Nguyen-Batley creates a chic, sophisticated oasis of French Vietnamese fare that's as gorgeous as it is delicious. An appetizer of filet mignon tartare with ginger, garlic, chili, opal basil, cilantro, peanuts, shallots, and lime juice prepares the palate for an outstanding onslaught of flavors and textures to come. A Vietnamese bouillabaisse of Gulf prawns, Manila clams, calamari, salmon, pineapple, okra, bean sprout, lily stem, and tomato in a tangy aromatic seafood broth is equally spectacular. Come to think of it, you can't go wrong with anything here.

1633 W. Snow Ave. © **813/258-1916.** www.restaurantbt.com. Reservations recommended. Main courses $20–$38. AE, DC, DISC, MC, V. Mon–Thurs 11:30am–2:30pm and 5:30–9:30pm; Fri–Sat 11:30am–2:30pm and 5:30–10:30pm.

Moderate

Fly Bar & Restaurant ★★ TAPAS   A trendy hot spot in downtown Tampa, Fly Bar & Restaurant is in a restored building and features a buzzing rooftop bar and lounge that's hot with the après-work crowds. The San Francisco import is all about small plates, to be shared in the dining room, on the sidewalk tables, at the bar, or on the rooftop. Among the options: fish tacos with roasted tomatillo salsa; Kobe beef sliders with Gruyère, sautéed mushrooms, and onions; shrimp and grits with chorizo and spring onions; and truffled mac and cheese. There's usually live music, too.

1202 N. Franklin St. (at E. Royal St.). © **813/275-5000.** www.flybarandrestaurant.com. Reservations recommended. Tapas $6–$13. AE, DC, DISC, MC, V. Mon–Sat 5:30–11pm.

Mise en Place ★★ NEW AMERICAN   Look around at all those happy, stylish people soaking up the trendy ambience, and you'll know why Chef Marty Blitz and his wife, Maryann, have been among the culinary darlings of Tampa since 1986. They present the freshest of ingredients in a creative, award-winning menu, which changes weekly. Main courses often include such choices as mole-crusted duck breast with Kabocha squash pork-belly posole, blackberry ancho gastrique, and haricot vert chayote chili salad; or *sous vide* halibut, fennel salsify asparagus, bay scallops, trumpet mushroom ragout, golden lentil marcona almond quinoa, verjus vinaigrette, Maldon sea salt, and roast grapes. Ingredients may read like an unabridged culinary dictionary, but the mouthfuls are worth every word. The tasting menus, with wine, are listed on the menu under "Get Blitzed" (four courses) and "Get a Little Blitzed" (three courses).

In Grand Central Place, 442 W. Kennedy Blvd. (at S. Magnolia Ave., opposite the University of Tampa). © **813/254-5373.** www.miseonline.com. Reservations recommended. Main courses $19–$35; 4-course tasting menu $69 with wine, $49 without; 3-course tasting menu $44 with wine, $29 without. AE, DC, DISC, MC, V. Tues–Thurs 11:30am–2:30pm and 5:30–10pm; Fri 11:30am–2:30pm and 5:30–11pm; Sat 5–11pm.

The Refinery ★ GASTROPUB The Refinery's culinary M.O. is "sustainably and ethically right." Ingredients come from farmers, not cans. And those ingredients are assembled into menus that change every week, though on any given night you may be offered a starter of pork belly with tamarind, roasted radish, pumpkin mole, pepitas, and polenta cake; a main course of roasted chicken with black-eyed peas, collards, pedron cornbread, and honey-Crystal lacquer; and a dessert of cardamom pound cake. Housed in a restored Craftsman-style home, the Refinery's cuisine may be refined, but its vibe is pure laid-back casual.

5137 N. Florida Ave. ℭ **813/281-0770.** www.thetamparefinery.com. Reservations recommended. Main courses $10–$20. AE, DC, DISC, MC, V. Tues–Thurs 5–10pm; Fri–Sat 5–11pm; Sun brunch 11am–3pm.

Whiskey Joe's Bar & Grill ★ BARBECUE Gorgeous ocean views trump the bar menu at Whiskey Joe's (formerly known as Castaway), where pan-seared grouper, whole snapper, po' boy sandwiches, fried chicken, and barbecue ribs reel in a steady crowd of locals and visitors alike. Insist on sitting on the deck and time your meal around sundown; the vantage point for sunsets here makes developers drool. Live reggae on Sunday and daily happy hours make Whiskey Joe's a popular gathering spot for locals.

7720 Courtney Campbell Causeway. ℭ **813/281-0770.** www.whiskeyjoestampa.com. Reservations recommended. Main courses $10–$20. AE, DC, DISC, MC, V. Daily 11am–11pm.

Wine Exchange ★★ MEDITERRANEAN This Tampa hot spot is an oenophile's dream come true, as each dish is paired with a particular wine available by the bottle or the glass. The menu is rather simple, featuring pizzas, pastas, salads, and sandwiches, but daily specials are more elaborate, including macadamia nut–crusted mahimahi, stuffed pork chop, or chili-rubbed flank steak. The outdoor patio is a great place to sit. There's almost always a wait—and free Wi-Fi—at this buzz-worthy eatery.

1611 W. Swan Ave. ℭ **813/254-9463.** www.wineexchangetampa.com. Main courses $17–$24; pizza and pasta $9–$18. AE, DC, DISC, MC, V. Mon–Fri 11:30am–10pm; Sat 11am–11pm; Sun 11am–9pm; brunch Sat–Sun 11am–3pm.

Inexpensive

Bella's Italian Cafe ★ ITALIAN While trendy restaurants come and go, Bella's has been open for more than 20 years—and for good reason. A casual, rustic ambience with a wood-fired oven and indoor-outdoor seating attract a sophisticated crowd of foodies of all ages. The authentic Italian fare is delicious, from the paper-thin carpaccio (with garlic, olives, capers, and basil) to the old-fashioned spaghetti and meatballs to the pizzas cooked in the oak-burning oven. For those who like a strong drink with dinner, the Bellarita is a popular potion of Conmemorativo tequila and Grand Marnier. On second thought, save that for after dinner so you can at least appreciate your meal as it's going down!

1413 S. Howard Ave. ℭ **813/254-3355.** www.bellasitaliancafe.com. Reservations recommended. Main courses $13–$26; pizza $9–$12. AE, DC, DISC, MC, V. Mon–Wed 11:30am–11:30pm; Thurs 11:30am–12:30am; Fri 11:30am–1:30am; Sat 4pm–1:30am; Sun 4–11:30pm.

YBOR CITY
Moderate

Columbia Restaurant ★★★ SPANISH Columbia celebrated 100 years in 2005. Its tile building occupies an entire city block in the heart of Ybor City. Tourists flock here to soak up the ambience, as do the locals because it's so much fun to clap along during the fire-belching flamenco floor shows Monday through Saturday evenings ($6 per person extra on top of the cost of dinner). You can't help coming back time after time for the Spanish bean soup and original "1905" salad. The *paella a la Valencia* is outstanding, with more than a dozen ingredients ranging from shrimp and calamari to chicken and pork. Another favorite is *boliche* (eye of round stuffed with chorizo), accompanied by plantains and black beans and rice. Entrees come with a crispy hunk of Cuban bread with butter. Lighter appetites can choose from a 16-item tapas menu. The decor throughout is graced with hand-painted tiles, wrought-iron chandeliers, dark woods, rich red fabrics, and stained-glass windows.

2117 E. 7th Ave. (btw. 21st and 22nd sts.). ✆ **813/248-4961.** www.columbiarestaurant.com. Reservations recommended, especially for flamenco shows. Main courses $15–$30. AE, DC, DISC, MC, V. Mon–Thurs 11am–10pm; Fri–Sat 11am–11pm; Sun noon–9pm.

Inexpensive
Carmine's Seventh Avenue ★ CUBAN/ITALIAN/AMERICAN Bright blue poles hold up an ancient pressed-tin ceiling above this noisy corner cafe. It's not the cleanest joint in town, but a variety of loyal local patrons gathers here for genuine Cuban sandwiches—smoked ham, roast pork, Genoa salami, Swiss cheese, pickles, salad dressing, mustard, lettuce, and tomato on crispy Cuban bread. There's a vegetarian version, too. The combination of a half-sandwich and choice of black beans and rice or a bowl of Spanish soup made with sausages, potatoes, and garbanzo beans is a filling meal just by itself. Main courses are led by Cuban-style roast pork, thin-cut pork chops with mushroom sauce, spaghetti with a blue-crab tomato sauce, and a few seafood and chicken platters.

1802 E. 7th Ave. (at 18th St.). ✆ **813/248-3834.** Main courses $10–$20; sandwiches $5–$10. AE, MC, V. Mon–Tues 11am–11pm; Wed–Thurs 11am–1am; Fri–Sat 11am–3am; Sun 11am–6pm.

Tampa After Dark

Artsline (✆ **813/229-2787**) is a 24-hour information service providing the latest on current cultural events. Racks in many restaurants and bars have copies of *Creative Loafing Tampa* (**www.tampa.creativeloafing.com**) and *Accent on Tampa Bay* (**www.ampubs.com**), two free publications detailing what's going on in the area. You can also check the "BayLife" and "Friday Extra" sections of the *Tampa Tribune* (**www.tampatrib.com**), as well as the Thursday "Weekend" section of the *St. Petersburg Times* (**www.sptimes.com**).

THE CLUB, BAR & MUSIC SCENE Ybor City is Tampa's favorite nighttime venue. Stroll along 7th Avenue East between 15th and 20th streets, and you'll hear music blaring from the clubs. On Friday and Saturday, from 9pm to 3am, the avenue is packed with high-school kids and 20-somethings; you'll also find something going on Tuesday through Thursday, and even on Sunday. The clubs change names frequently, so you don't need names or addresses; your ears will guide you. With all of the sidewalk seating, it's easy to judge what the clientele is like and make your choice from there.

The center of all things nightlife still remains **Centro Ybor,** on 7th Avenue East at 16th Street (✆ **813/242-4660;** www.centroybor.com), the district's large dining-and-entertainment complex. The restaurants and pubs in this family-oriented center tend to be tamer than many of those along 7th Avenue, at least on nonweekend nights. You don't have to pay to listen to live music in the center's patio on weekend afternoons

In the Hyde Park area of town, restaurant bars buzz with late-night activity. Most recently, the downtown scene has been on the verge of a hipster takeover thanks to

Parking can be scarce at night in Ybor City, and the area has seen an occasional robbery in the late hours. Play it safe and use the municipal parking lots behind the shops on 8th Avenue East, or try the new parking garages near Centro Ybor, on 7th Avenue East at 16th Street.

such places as **Fly Bar & Restaurant** (see above) and a slew of new watering holes frequented by the young and fabulous. Among them: **Tapas Wine & Beer Merchants,** 777 N. Ashley Dr. (© 813/463-1968); **Club Underground,** a popular hip-hop club at 802 E. Whiting St. (© 813/857-5872; www.clubunderground tampa.com); and **Kelly's Pub,** 206 N. Morgan St. (© 813/228-0870).

THE PERFORMING ARTS   With a prime downtown location on 9 acres along the east bank of the Hillsborough River, the huge **David Straz, Jr., Center for the Performing Arts ★**, 1010 N. MacInnes Place (© 800/955-1045 or 813/229-7827; www.strazcenter.org), next to the Tampa Museum of Art, is the largest performing-arts venue south of the Kennedy Center in D.C. This four-theater complex presents a wide range of theater, classical and pop concerts, operas, and special events.

The restored **Tampa Theatre,** 711 Franklin St., between Zack and Polk streets (© 813/274-8286; www.tampatheatre.org), dates from 1926 and is on the National Register of Historic Places. It presents a varied program of classic, foreign, and alternative films, as well as concerts and special events (and it's said to be haunted!).

The 66,321-seat **Raymond James Stadium,** 4201 N. Dale Mabry Hwy. (© 813/673-4300; www.raymondjames.com/stadium), is sometimes the site of headliner concerts. The **USF Sun Dome,** 4202 E. Fowler Ave. (© 813/974-3111; www.sundome.org), on the University of South Florida campus, hosts major concerts by pop stars, rock bands, jazz groups, and other artists.

One of the busiest spots in town for live music, rustic style, is **Skipper's Smokehouse,** 910 Skipper Rd. (© 813/971-0666; www.skipperssmokehouse.com), a Key West–style former smokehouse turned blues, jazz, zydeco, ska, and reggae hot spot.

Ticketmaster (© 800/745-3000; www.ticketmaster.com) sells tickets to most events and shows.

A DAY TRIP TO THE SPACE COAST ★

46 miles SE of Orlando

The "Space Coast," the area around Cape Canaveral, was once a sleepy place where city dwellers escaped the urban centers of Miami and Jacksonville. But then came NASA. Today, the region draws hordes who come to visit the Kennedy Space Center and enjoy the area's 72 miles of beaches (this is, after all, the closest beach to Orlando's mega-attractions). And although the shuttle program is winding down, the area isn't completely kaput.

Thanks to NASA, this is also a prime destination for nature lovers. The space agency originally took over much more land than it needed to launch rockets. Rather than sell off the unused portions, it turned them over to the **Canaveral National**

9

SIDE TRIPS FROM ORLANDO

A Day Trip to the Space Coast

Seashore and the **Merritt Island National Wildlife Refuge** (www.nbbd.com/godo/minwr), which have preserved these areas in their pristine natural states.

A handful of Caribbean-bound cruise ships departs from Port Canaveral. The south side of the port is lined with seafood restaurants and marinas, which serve as home base for gambling ships and the area's deep-sea charter and group fishing boats.

Essentials

From Orlando, it's an easy 45-minute drive to the beaches via the Beachline Expressway (Fla. 528). A car is essential in this area. **Space Coast Area Transit** (*©* **321/633-1878;** www.ridescat.com) operates buses ($1.25 adults, 60¢ seniors and students), but routes tend to be circuitous and extremely time-consuming.

For information on the area, contact the **Florida Space Coast Office of Tourism/Brevard County Tourist Development Council,** 8810 Astronaut Blvd., Ste. 102, Cape Canaveral (*©* **800/872-1969** or 321/868-1126; www.space-coast.com). The office is in the Sheldon Cove building, on Fla. A1A a block north of Central Boulevard, and is open Monday through Friday from 8am to 5pm. It also operates an information booth at the Kennedy Space Center Visitor Complex (p. 352).

Attractions

In addition to the two attractions below, Brevard College's **Astronaut Memorial Planetarium & Observatory,** 1519 Clearlake Rd., Cocoa Beach (*©* **321/634-3732;** www.brevardcc.edu/planet), south of Florida 528, has its own International Hall of Space Explorers, but its big draws are sound-and-light shows in the planetarium. Call or check the website for schedules and prices.

Brevard Zoo ★★ ☺ This delightful small-town zoo houses more than 550 animals, including white rhinos, red kangaroos, cheetahs, alligators, siamang gibbons, giant anteaters, jaguars, wallabies, crocodiles, howler monkeys, bald eagles, red wolves, and river otters. Enjoy a 10-minute train tour of the grounds ($3); hand-feed gentle giraffe and lorikeets in a free-flight aviary; get friendly with the wildlife at the Paws On play area, featuring a 22,000-gallon aquarium, water play, and petting zone; and kayak around an animal exhibit or through a 22-acre restored wetlands ($6). For an up-close view of the animals, try the rhino encounter, offered daily from noon to 1pm ($15). The zoo also offers ecotours on the Indian River Lagoon (www.lagoonadventures.org). For $50, you get kayak rental, instruction, snacks and drinks, a trained environmental educator guide, lunch on an island, and close viewing of manatees, dolphins, and wading birds. Plan to spend 1 to 4 hours here.

8225 N. Wickham Rd., Melbourne (just east of I-95 exit 73/Wickham Rd.). *©* **321/254-9453.** www.brevardzoo.org. Admission $14 adults, $13 seniors, $10 children 3–12, free for children 2 and under. Daily 9:30am–5pm (last admission 4:15pm).

John F. Kennedy Space Center ★★★ Whether or not you're a space buff, you'll appreciate the sheer grandeur of the facilities and technological achievements displayed at NASA's primary space launch facility. Astronauts departed Earth from here in 1969 en route to the most famous "small step" in history—the first moon walk—and space shuttles recently lifted off from here on missions to the International Space Station. Today, military and commercial rockets regularly launch from Cape Canaveral Air Force Station.

Because all roads other than S.R. 405 and S.R. 3 are closed to the public in the Space Center, you must begin your visit at **Kennedy Space Center Visitor Complex.** A bit like an amusement theme park, this privately operated complex is

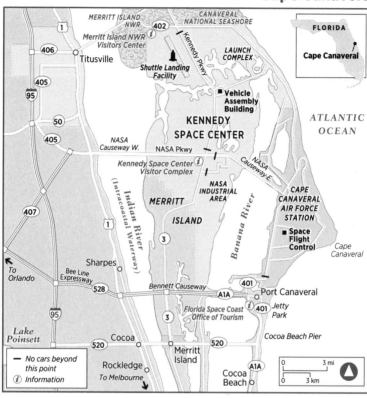

MERRITT ISLAND
NWR
Merritt Island NWR
Visitors Center
Titusville
Shuttle Landing
Facility

CANAVERAL
NATIONAL SEASHORE

Kennedy Pkwy

LAUNCH
COMPLEX

FLORIDA

Cape Canaveral

Vehicle
Assembly
Building

KENNEDY
SPACE CENTER

ATLANTIC
OCEAN

NASA
Causeway W.
NASA Pkwy

Kennedy Space Center
Visitor Complex

NASA
Causeway E.

MERRITT

ISLAND

Indian River
(Intracoastal Waterway)

NASA
INDUSTRIAL
AREA

CAPE
CANAVERAL
AIR FORCE
STATION

Space
Flight
Control

Cape
Canaveral

Banana River

To
Orlando

Sharpes

Bee Line
Expressway

528

95

Lake
Poinsett

Bennett Causeway

401

A1A

Port Canaveral

401

Jetty
Park

Florida Space Coast
Office of Tourism

3

Cocoa Beach Pier

Cocoa

520

520

Merritt
Island

Cocoa
Beach

A1A

Rockledge
To Melbourne

— No cars beyond
this point
ⓘ Information

0   3 mi
0   3 km

constantly under renovation, so check beforehand to see if tours and exhibits have changed since press time. Call ahead to see what's happening the day you intend to be here and arrive early. You'll need at least 2 hours to see the Space Center's highlights on the bus tour, up to 5 hours if you linger at stops along the way, and a full day to see and do everything. If you buy a copy of the *Official Tour Book,* you can take it home as a colorful souvenir (though the bus tours are narrated and the exhibits have good descriptions).

The Visitor Complex has real NASA rockets and the actual Mercury Mission Control Room from the 1960s. Exhibits portray space exploration in its early days and where it's going in the new millennium. There are hands-on activities for kids, a daily "encounter" with a real astronaut, dining venues, and a shop selling space memorabilia. IMAX movies shown on five-and-a-half-story-high screens are both informative and entertaining.

While you could spend an entire day at the Visitor Complex, you must take a **KSC Tour** to get a behind-the-scenes glimpse of Kennedy Space Center. Buses depart every 15 minutes or so, and you can reboard as you wish. They stop at the LC-39 Observation Gantry, with a dramatic 360-degree view over launchpads where shuttles once blasted off into space, and the Apollo/Saturn V Center, a tribute to the Apollo moon program, which includes artifacts, shows, photos, interactive exhibits, and the 363-foot-tall Saturn V, the most powerful rocket ever launched by the United States.

Don't miss the **Astronaut Memorial.** Dedicated in 1991, it honors the U.S. astronauts who gave their lives for space exploration. The 43×50-foot "Space Mirror" brilliantly illuminates the names cut through the monument's black granite surface.

Today, the U.S. Air Force operates Cape Canaveral Air Force Station on Cape Canaveral, the barrier island east of the Banana River, where military and commercial rockets are launched. Launch days are great days to visit the Visitor Complex. Rocket launches taking place during operating hours can be viewed from the main Visitor Complex with the regular admission price of $41 plus tax per adult and $31 plus tax per child (ages 3–11).

For an out-of-this-world experience, do **Lunch With an Astronaut,** a once-in-a-lifetime opportunity available every day ($23 plus tax for adults, $16 plus tax for kids 3–11, in addition to Visitor Complex admission). Astronauts who have participated in the past include some of the greatest, such as Jim Lovell, Al Worden, Story Musgrave, and Jon McBride. Seating is limited; call ✆ **877/313-2610** to make a reservation.

Kennedy Space Center Visitor Complex also offers the **Astronaut Training Experience,** a combination of hands-on training and preparation for the rigors of spaceflight. You'll hear first-hand from veteran astronauts as you progress through an authentic half-day of mission simulation and exploration and even get to check out true-to-training simulator exercises. Due to the program's highly interactive nature, ATX crews are small and advance reservations are required. Cost is $145 per person; call ✆ **877/313-2610** to reserve.

Note: Make sure to stop by the **U.S. Astronaut Hall of Fame,** on S.R. 405, on your way to Kennedy Space Center Visitor Complex or on your way home. The Hall of Fame, approximately 6 miles west of the main Visitor Complex, is included with regular admission to the Visitor Complex. The Hall of Fame features exhibits and tributes to the heroes of the Mercury, Gemini, Apollo, and Space Shuttle programs. There's also the world's largest collection of personal astronaut memorabilia and a Mercury Sigma 7 capsule on display. Separate admission to the Hall of Fame only is $20 plus tax for adults, $16 plus tax for children 3 to 11.

NASA Pkwy. (S.R. 405), 6 miles east of Titusville, ½ mile west of S.R. 3. ✆ **877/313-2610** for general information and reservations. www.kennedyspacecenter.com. Admission $41 plus tax adults, $31 plus tax children 3–11, free for children 2 and under. Annual passes $53 plus tax adults, $43 plus tax children 3–11. Audio guides $6 plus tax per person. Daily 9am to closing times that vary according to season. Bus tours depart daily beginning at 10am. Closed Dec 25.

Beaches & Wildlife Refuges

To the north of the Kennedy Space Center, **Canaveral National Seashore ★★★** is a protected 13-mile stretch of barrier-island beach backed by cabbage palms, sea grapes, palmettos, marshes, and Mosquito Lagoon. This is a great area for watching herons, egrets, ibises, willets, sanderlings, turnstones, terns, and other birds. You might also glimpse dolphins and manatees in Mosquito Lagoon. Canoeists can paddle along a marked trail through the marshes of Shipyard Island; and backcountry camping is possible November through April (permits required; see below).

The main **visitor center** is at 7611 S. Atlantic Ave., New Smyrna Beach (✆ **321/867-4077,** or 321/867-0677 for recorded information), on Apollo Beach, at the north end of the island. The southern access gate to the island is 8 miles east of Titusville on S.R. 402, just east of S.R. 3. A paved road leads from the gate to undeveloped **Playalinda Beach ★★★**, one of Florida's most beautiful. Though illegal, nude sunbathing has long been a tradition here (at least, for those willing to walk a few miles to the more deserted areas). The beach has toilets, but no running water or other amenities. There's a **pontoon boat tour** of the Indian River Lagoon for $20 per person and a turtle-watch program for $14 per person. For those looking for a little more history, the **Eldora Statehouse** is a well-preserved example of earlier life along Mosquito Lagoon. It is in Canaveral National Seashore's Apollo district and is open year-round. The seashore is open daily from 6am to 8pm during daylight saving time, daily from 6am to 6pm during standard time. Entry fees are $3 per person. National Park Service passports are accepted. Backcountry camping permits cost $10 for up to six people per day and $20 for more than six people per day, and must be obtained from the New Smyrna Beach visitor center (© **386/428-3384,** ext. 10). For single-day access to backcountry beaches between Playalinda and Apollo beaches, it's $2 per day. For advance information, contact the seashore headquarters at 308 Julia St., Titusville, FL 32796 (© **321/867-4077** or 321/267-1110; www.nps.gov/cana).

Canaveral National Seashore's neighbor to the south and west is the 140,000-acre **Merritt Island National Wildlife Refuge ★★**, home to hundreds of species of shorebirds, waterfowl, reptiles, alligators, and mammals, many of them endangered. Pick up information and a map at the visitor center, on S.R. 402 about 4 miles east of Titusville (it's on the way to Playalinda Beach). The center has a quarter-mile boardwalk along the edge of the marsh. Displays show the animals you may spot from 6-mile Black Point Wildlife Drive or from one of the nature trails through the hammocks and marshes. The visitor center is open Monday through Friday from 8am to 4:30pm, Saturday and Sunday from 9am to 5pm (closed Sun Apr–Oct). Entry is free. For more information and a schedule of programs, contact the refuge at P.O. Box 6504, Titusville, FL 32782 (© **321/861-0667;** www.nbbd.com/godo/minwr).

Note: Parts of the national seashore near the Kennedy Space Center and all of the refuge close 4 days before a launch and usually reopen the day after.

Another good beach area is **Lori Wilson Park,** on Atlantic Avenue at Antigua Drive in Cocoa Beach (© **321/868-1123**), which preserves a stretch of sand backed by a forest of live oaks. It's home to a small but interesting nature center, and restrooms are available. The park is open daily from sunrise to sunset; the nature center is open Monday through Friday from 1 to 4pm.

The beach at **Cocoa Beach Pier,** on Meade Avenue east of A1A (© **321/783-7549**), is a popular spot with surfers, who consider it the East Coast's surfing capital. The rustic pier was built in 1962 and has 842 feet of fishing, shopping, and dining overlooking a wide, sandy beach (see "Where to Eat," below). Because this is not a public park, there are no restrooms other than the ones in restaurants on the pier.

Jetty Park, 400 E. Jetty Rd., at the south entry to Port Canaveral (© **321/783-7111;** www.jettypark.org), has a fishing pier with bait shop, lifeguards, playground, volleyball court, horseshoe pit, picnic tables, snack bar, grocery store, restrooms, changing facilities, and the area's only campground. From here, you can watch the big cruise ships as they enter and leave the port's narrow passage. The park is open daily from 7:30am to dusk; the pier is open 24 hours for fishing. Admission is $10 per car for nonresidents of Brevard County ($5 for residents), $15 per RV. The 150 tent and RV campsites (some of them shady, most with hookups) cost $25 to $47 a night, depending on location and time of year. Properly vaccinated pets are allowed in some areas of the park.

Where to Eat

On the **Cocoa Beach Pier** (www.cocoabeachpier.com), at the beach end of Meade Avenue, you'll get a fine view down the coast to accompany the seafood offerings at **Atlantic Ocean Grill** (✆ 321/783-7549) and the mediocre pub fare at adjacent **Marlins Good Times Bar & Grill** (same phone). The restaurants may not justify spending an entire evening on the pier, but the outdoor, tin-roofed **Mai Tiki Bar ★**, where live music plays most nights, is a prime spot to have a cold one while watching the surfers or a sunset.

Rusty's Seafood & Oyster Bar, 628 Glen Cheek Dr., Port Canaveral (✆ 321/783-2033; www.rustysseafood.com), a lively sports bar on the south side of the harbor, serves inexpensive chow ranging from spicy seafood gumbo to a pot of seafood that will feed two. The raw bar, weekday lunch buffet, and daily happy hour (3–6pm) are good values. Seating is indoors or out.

The **Surf Bar & Grill ★**, 2 S. Atlantic Ave. (at Minuteman Causeway Rd.), Cocoa Beach (✆ 321/783-2401; www.thesurfbarandgrill.com), offers seafood specials in its fine-dining room, the Surf; fried combo platters and pub fare in its less expensive Surf Bar & Grill; and oysters and outdoor seating in Shuckleberry Fin's Oyster Bar.

PLANNING YOUR TRIP TO WALT DISNEY WORLD & ORLANDO

Winging it once you arrive simply won't do when your destination is Walt Disney World. Without some type of advance preparation, you'll likely find yourself so overwhelmed upon arriving in Orlando that you'll miss out on exactly what it was you came for in the first place—fun. In this chapter, you'll find just about everything you need to know before you go, including tons of helpful information to get you started. In addition to the information contained in the following pages, you'll find more useful tips and information in chapters 3 through 6—those covering the area's best hotels, restaurants, theme parks, and smaller attractions.

10

For additional help in planning your trip and for more on-the-ground resources in Orlando, please turn to "Fast Facts," later in this chapter.

GETTING THERE
By Plane

THE MAJOR AIRLINES There are more than 50 scheduled airlines and several more charter companies serving roughly 35 million passengers who land in Orlando each year. **Southwest** (© **800/435-9792;** www. southwest.com) continues to maintain the top spot, claiming just under 24% of the flights in and out of the **Orlando International Airport (MCO).** Second place goes to **AirTran Airways** (© **800/247-8726;** www.airtran.com), at just over 12.4% (the merger of AirTran and Southwest in 2011 assuring that they will continue to retain the lion's share of flights in and out of MCO), while **Delta** (© **800/221-1212;** www.delta. com) and **JetBlue** (© **800/538-2583;** www.jetblue.com) tie for third, each with slightly more than 11% of the flights (after the Delta/Northwest merger back in 2010, flights now operate solely under the Delta name).

Some major airlines offer transatlantic or transpacific passengers special discount tickets under the name **Visit USA**, which allows mostly one-way travel from one U.S. destination to another at very low prices. Unavailable in the U.S., these discount tickets must be purchased abroad in conjunction with your international fare. This system is the easiest, fastest, and cheapest way to see the country. Inquire with your air carrier.

Several so-called no-frills airlines (those offering lower fares but providing few or no amenities) fly to Orlando, including **Spirit Airlines** (✆ 800/772-7117; www.spiritair.com).

To find out which airlines travel to Orlando, see "Airline Websites," on p. 392.

ORLANDO'S AIRPORTS   **Orlando International Airport** (MCO; ✆ 407/825-2001; www.orlandoairports.net) offers direct or nonstop service from 81 U.S. cities and more than two dozen international destinations. Rated one of the top airports in the country, it's a thoroughly modern and user-friendly facility with tons of restaurants, shops, a 445-room on-premises Hyatt Regency hotel, and centrally located information kiosks. All major car-rental companies are located at or near the airport.

   Orlando Sanford International Airport (SFB; ✆ 407/585-4000; www.orlandosanfordairport.com) is much smaller than the main airport, but has grown a bit in recent years, thanks mainly to a small fleet of carriers that serve it, including Allegiant Air, Direct Air, Monarch, and Thomson Airways. Sanford has on-site Alamo, Avis, Budget, Dollar, Enterprise, Hertz, National, and Thrifty rental-car desks. It is also served by Mears Transportation shuttles (see below).

GETTING INTO TOWN FROM THE AIRPORT

Orlando International Airport is 25 miles east of Walt Disney World and 20 miles south of downtown. At rush hour (7–9am and 4–6pm), the drive can be torture and take up to an hour or more; at other times, it's about 30 to 40 minutes, depending on your exact destination. **Orlando Sanford International Airport** is roughly 35 miles northeast of Walt Disney World and about 18 miles northeast of downtown.

   Mears Transportation Group (✆ 407/423-5566; www.mearstransportation.com) has vans that shuttle passengers from Orlando International (catch them at ground level) to the Disney resorts and official hotels, as well as most other Orlando properties. These air-conditioned vehicles operate around the clock, departing every 15 to 25 minutes in either direction. Rates vary by destination. From Orlando International, round-trip fares run $30 for adults ($24 for kids 4–11) to International Drive, $46 ($37 kids) to Walt Disney World/Lake Buena Vista or West U.S. 192. Children 3 and under ride free. From Sanford International, Mears offers transportation via luxury van (seating up to 8) or town car (seating up to 4). Fares run $120 each way (or $240 round-trip) whether your destination is International Drive, Walt Disney World, or West U.S. 192.

   Quicksilver Tours and Transportation (✆ 888/468-6939 or 407/299-1434; www.quicksilver-tours.com) is a bit more personal. Its folks greet you at baggage claim with a sign bearing your name—they'll even help with your luggage. The bonus is a 30-minute grocery stop and free phone call included in the price. While a bit more expensive than Mears, they're coming for you. And they're only going to *your* resort. This is a good option for four or more people. Rates run from $125 (up to 10 people, round-trip) to I-Drive, $130 to Universal Studios, and $130 to $135 for the Disney empire.

Tiffany Towncar (© **888/838-2161** or 407/370-2196; www.tiffanytowncar. com) offers a $125 round-trip rate for up to seven people ($135 for 8–10 people) from Orlando International to I-Drive, Universal, Disney, and U.S. 192. Drivers will meet you right at baggage claim, and a free 30-minute grocery stop is included. Booster and car seats are available upon request (at no charge).

If you're renting a car, to get from Orlando International to the attractions, take the **north** exit out of the airport to **Hwy. 528 W.** Follow signs to **I-4;** it takes about 30 to 40 minutes to get to Walt Disney World if the traffic isn't too heavy (however, double that if it's rush hour or if there's been an accident). When you get to I-4, follow the signs **west** toward the attractions. From Sanford International, exit onto Lake Mary Road and follow the roadway to the I-4 interchange and follow signs **west** toward the attractions. Another option would be to take S.R. 417 **south** (though a toll road, it's a bit more direct if your destination is Walt Disney World); then follow signs to the attractions. Most Orlando car-rental agencies (regardless of location) will provide you with maps that will show how to get to your hotel; be sure and ask for one at the rental counter.

Note: It's always a good idea when you make reservations to ask about transportation options between the airport and your hotel. Also be sure to ask how far you have to travel to pick up and drop off a rental car. Some lots are miles from the airport, and you could potentially spend lots of time waiting in line and catching shuttles before you actually get to the airport on your day of departure.

By Bus

While not the most efficient or cost-effective form of transportation (especially when traveling from more than just a few hours away), **Greyhound** (© **800/231-2222** in the U.S.; 001/214/849-8100 outside the U.S. with toll-free access; www.greyhound. com) is the sole nationwide bus line. International visitors can obtain information about the **Greyhound North American Discovery Pass,** which offers unlimited travel and stopovers in the U.S. and Canada. This pass can be obtained outside the U.S. from travel agents or through **www.discoverypass.com**.

By Car

If you're visiting from abroad and plan to rent a car in the United States, keep in mind that foreign driver's licenses are usually recognized in the U.S., but you may want to consider obtaining an international driver's license.

Also be advised that many rental agencies in Florida will rent only to drivers 21 and older, and that drivers younger than age 25 may have to pay a young renter's fee of up to $25 a day.

All of the major car-rental companies are represented in Orlando and maintain desks at or near each of the airports. *Note:* Disney has an Alamo car-rental desk (© **800/327-2996**) right on property, so if you're interested in renting for only a few days instead of your entire vacation, this may be a good option for you.

Many agencies provide discount coupons in publications targeted at tourists, though you should keep in mind that AAA discounts and online offers are often better. You may also want to ask your travel agent if he or she has a recommendation, or

PLANNING YOUR TRIP

Getting There

whether a discount is included in any vacation package. Also, it never hurts to ask about specials.

International visitors should note that insurance and taxes are almost never included in quoted car rates in the U.S. Be sure to ask your rental agency about additional fees for these—they can add a significant cost to your car rental.

For full details on the ins and outs of renting and driving a car in Orlando, see "Getting Around," later in this chapter.

THE LAY OF THE LAND

Orlando's major artery is Interstate 4. Locals call it **I-4,** or that #@$*%^#!! highway! It runs diagonally across the state (though directional signs are always marked east or west) from Tampa to Daytona Beach. The exits along this route will take you to Disney, Universal, SeaWorld, International Drive, U.S. 192, Kissimmee, Lake Buena Vista, and north to downtown Orlando and Winter Park. Most exits are well marked, but construction is common and exit numbers have been changed through the years. If you get directions by exit number, always ask the name of the road to help avoid getting lost. (Cellphone users can dial 📞 **511** to get a report of I-4 delays.)

The **Florida Turnpike,** a toll road, crosses I-4 and links with I-75 to the north and Miami to the south. **U.S. 192/Irlo Bronson Memorial Highway** is a major east-west artery that reaches from Kissimmee to U.S. 27, crossing I-4 near World Drive, the main Walt Disney World entrance road. Construction has widened this stretch of highway and made driving a bit easier, while the addition of large numerical markers has made locating hotels, restaurants, and attractions much easier as well. The **Beachline Expressway** (Hwy. 528; previously the Bee Line Expwy.), also a toll road, goes east from I-4 past Orlando International Airport to Cape Canaveral and Kennedy Space Center. The **East–West Expressway** (also known as Hwy. 408) is a toll road that can be helpful in bypassing surface traffic in the downtown area. The **417,** also a toll road, runs from north of the Orlando International Airport to I-4 just below U.S. 192. This route is a good alternative to I-4 if you are staying on the lower end of International Drive, World Center Drive, or areas east of the I-4, as it is far less traveled than the main highway.

If you're jockeying between Disney and Universal, one of the lesser traffic evils is **Apopka–Vineland Road.** It tends to be less cluttered than I-4 or International Drive. Follow it north from Lake Buena Vista and the northeast side of Disney to Sand Lake Road, then go right/east to Turkey Lake Road, and then left/north to Universal Orlando. Another way to avoid the highway when driving between Universal Orlando and Disney is to take the Palm Parkway (just off Apopka–Vineland Rd.) to Turkey Lake Road, which will take you right to Universal.

I-4 and Highway 535 roughly bound **Walt Disney World** to the east (the latter is also a northern boundary), and U.S. 192/Irlo Bronson Memorial Highway bounds it to the south. World Drive is WDW's main north-south artery. Epcot Center Drive (Hwy. 536/the south end of International Dr.) and Buena Vista Drive cut across the complex in a more or less east-west direction; the two roads cross at Bonnet Creek Parkway. Despite a reasonably good highway system and explicit signs, it's easy to get lost or miss a turn here—even if you think you know the roads. I've gotten lost or passed an exit on Disney property at least once or twice on every trip. Again, pay attention and drive carefully. Don't panic or pull across several lanes of traffic to make an exit, especially once you're on Disney property—there's always another exit just ahead where you can turn around. All roads lead to the parks, and you'll soon find another sign directing you to the same place. It may take a bit longer, but Goofy will still be there.

Clever landscaping hides the fact that many parts of WDW are very close together. It took me several trips to discover that Disney's Hollywood Studios is just behind the BoardWalk, which is right next to the WDW Swan and the WDW Dolphin, which is across the lake from Disney's Yacht and Beach Club resorts, which are next to Epcot—you get the picture. Walking can occasionally be the most efficient way to get from one place to another; it's always worth looking at a map to check before you set out anywhere. *Note:* One of the best maps of WDW's parks and roadways, although not nearly as detailed as it once was, can be found on the back of the "Orlando, Florida, and Vicinity" map provided by Alamo (Disney's official rental-car company). The map is available (upon request) to those staying on Disney property—it lays out the entire WDW roadway system as well as the theme parks and resorts.

AAA (© **800/222-1134;** www.aaa.com) and other auto club members should call their local offices for maps and optimum driving directions.

For information on car rentals and gasoline (petrol) in Orlando, see "Getting Around by Car" and "Fast Facts: Gasoline," later in this chapter.

By Train

Trains operated by **Amtrak** (© **800/872-7245;** www.amtrak.com) pull into stations at 1400 Sligh Blvd., in downtown Orlando (23 miles from Walt Disney World), and 111 Dakin Ave., in Kissimmee (15 miles from WDW). There are also stops in Winter Park, 10 miles north of downtown Orlando at 150 W. Morse Blvd.; and in Sanford, 23 miles northeast of downtown Orlando, at 800 Persimmon Ave., which is also the end terminal for the Auto Train (see below).

International visitors can buy a **USA Rail Pass,** good for 15, 30, or 45 days ($389–$749) of unlimited travel on Amtrak. The pass is available online or through many overseas travel agents. See Amtrak's website for the cost of travel within the western, eastern, or northwestern United States. Reservations are generally required and should be made as early as possible. Regional rail passes are also available.

AMTRAK'S AUTO TRAIN This option offers the convenience of bringing your car to Florida without having to drive it all the way. It begins in Lorton, Virginia—about a 4-hour drive from New York, 2 hours from Philadelphia—and ends at Sanford, 23 miles northeast of Orlando. (There are no stops in between.) Reserve early for the lowest prices. Round-trip fares *average* $1,200 ($2,000 with a berth) for two passengers and an auto. Call © **800/872-7245** for details.

GETTING AROUND

In a city that thrives on its attractions, you won't find it difficult to get around—especially if you have a car. Don't count on the city bus system to get you where you want to go—not quickly or efficiently, anyway. If you're traveling outside the tourist areas, avoid the 7-to-9am and 4-to-7pm rush if at all possible. Commuter traffic (recently ranked as fourth-worst in the nation) can be bad anywhere, but here the complication of tourist traffic makes it even more of a headache. And don't expect weekends to be any better—the locals who run the hotels, restaurants, and attractions still have to get to work, making commuter traffic a 7-day-a-week problem. Most of the parks don't open until 9am or so, and they usually stay open at least until dusk; you won't miss much by leaving a little later. (The exception is Animal Kingdom, where the animals move around early and then seek shelter and shade for the remainder of the day; see "Animal Kingdom" in chapter 5, "Exploring Walt Disney World.")

Besides driving, there are two alternate means of getting around the International Drive area—walking and taking the I-Ride Trolley. I don't recommend the former in the area around Sand Lake Road because, though there are plenty of sidewalks, you quite literally may be taking your life in your hands if you try to cross this extremely busy road. The farther south you move along I-Drive, however, the easier walking becomes. The **I-Ride Trolley** (© **407/248-9590;** www.iridetrolley.com) is a safer bet. It makes 77 stops between Orlando Premium Outlets–International Drive (formerly known as Prime Outlets), on the north end of the drive, and SeaWorld to the south. The trolley runs every 20 minutes, from 8am to 10:30pm, and costs $1.25 for adults, 25¢ for seniors, and is free to kids younger than 12; exact change is required. There's an unlimited 1-day pass available for $4 per person. Thanks to I-Drive's high traffic volume, the trolley offers a decent (and fun) alternative to the bumper-to-bumper traffic.

The good news, if you are driving, is that road signs throughout the area are more accurate than they were a few years back. But to make sure you're heading the right way, follow the directions supplied for the various attractions and hotels later in this book. Call ahead to your destination to check if there is any construction you should be aware of before heading out. Most attractions give recorded directions as an automated option when you call the main number, but you can also ask for an operator to get clarification.

Several hotels offer transportation to and from the theme parks (some to WDW, others to Universal Orlando, with a select few offering transportation to both) and other tourist destinations; the service may or may not be free, however, so be sure to check with your individual hotel for details. Depending on your itinerary, and the shuttle service offered at your hotel, you may find renting a car to be the least expensive option. It's not difficult getting around town, but it can be expensive, so know your options when you're deciding on your hotel.

By Disney Transportation System

If you plan to stay at and spend most of your time at Disney, there's an extensive, free transportation system that runs throughout the entire WDW property.

Disney resorts and official hotels offer unlimited free transportation via bus, monorail, ferry, or water taxi to all WDW properties throughout the day, and at times well into the evening. If, however, you want to venture elsewhere (say, to Universal or SeaWorld), you'll have to pay extra to do so.

If you're staying at the Disney resorts, using the system can save you money on a rental car, insurance, and gas, as well as all those parking fees ($14 a day at the WDW theme parks, though Disney resort guests are exempt from parking charges). The drawback, however, is that you're at the mercy of Disney's schedules, which are often slow and, at times, *very* indirect; bus trips from the outlying resorts (especially Fort Wilderness) to the various parks (and vice versa) can take over an hour during peak times.

Along with the maps in this guide, pick up a guide map when you land at the Guest Services desks at any of the Disney resorts and theme parks, or download a more generic map at **www.disneyworld.com**.

The best rule when using Disney transportation: Ask the driver or someone at your hotel's front desk to help you take the most direct route. Keep asking questions along

Look Both Ways

Traveling on foot anywhere in Orlando, especially on International Drive, can be tricky. If you have to walk across a parking lot or street, *be careful.* The Surface Transportation Policy Project's pedestrian safety report has named Orlando the most dangerous city in the country for pedestrians. Drivers here pay far more attention to their maps and street signs, not the people in front of them. Though walking up and down the sidewalks on I-Drive or U.S. 192 can be an enjoyable way to get to a restaurant or minigolf course without having to pack up the car, you need to pay strict attention when it comes to crossing the street, and you should avoid crossing multiple-lane roads altogether.

the way. Unlike missing a highway exit, missing a bus stop means you may reach your pension before you reach your destination.

By Car

Whether or not to rent a car while in Orlando is one of the most important decisions you will make when planning your trip (just behind selecting your hotel). First, think about your vacation plans. If you're planning on going beyond the boundaries of Disney to Universal, SeaWorld, or anywhere along I-Drive, a rental car is a necessity. If you want to head out in the evenings to smaller attractions, dinner shows, or other activities not located within the realm of Disney, a car will allow you the most flexibility. If you plan to limit your vacation only to WDW, then a car might prove an extra and unnecessary expense ("might" being the operative word here).

If you've decided to stay right on Disney property, the question to ask yourself is how, exactly, will you get to the parks? If the Magic Kingdom is accessible only by taking a bus, switching to the monorail, and then catching a ferry, you may want to opt for a car. The least expensive properties, the All-Star resorts, are among the farthest from the Disney parks. Wait times between buses can be considerable, if not unendurable, even with recent enhancements to the dispatch system.

During peak hours in the busiest seasons, you may have trouble getting a seat on the bus, so keep that in mind if you're traveling with seniors or companions with disabilities. Also, if you're bringing along children and strollers, consider the frustration factor of loading and unloading strollers and all of the paraphernalia that comes with them on and off buses, ferries, and trams.

A car may drastically cut the commute time between the parks and hotels not directly on the monorail routes, so decide how much your time is worth and how much the car will cost plus the $14-per-day theme-park parking charge (Disney resort guests, however, are exempt from parking fees) before making a decision about renting.

In general, if you're going to spend all of your time at Disney and you're ready, willing, and able to handle the transportation network's schedules, there's no sense renting a car that will sit in the parking lot. But if you're on an extended stay—a week or more—you'll probably want a car for at least a day or two to venture beyond the tourist areas. You can discover downtown Orlando, visit museums, or tour the Space Coast (see chapter 9); leaving the parks behind may be necessary for your sanity, not to mention your survival. After heading from park to park, day after day, a reality check may very well be in order, and there's no better way to come back down to earth than to enjoy some of Florida's more natural offerings.

10

PLANNING YOUR TRIP

Getting Around

If you are going to be spending the majority of your vacation outside the House of Mouse, a car is an absolute necessity (unless you plan on staying solely within the bounds of Universal Orlando for your entire trip). While there are plenty of transportation options such as shuttles, trolleys, and taxis, utilizing them every time you venture outside of your hotel can't be done without losing your sanity (and lots of cash).

All the major car-rental companies are represented in Orlando and maintain desks at or near the airport (and even inside select hotels and resorts throughout the tourist district). Many agencies provide discount coupons in publications targeted at tourists, though AAA discounts and online offers are often better. You may want to ask your travel agent if he or she has a recommendation, or whether a discount is included in any vacation package. Also, it never hurts to ask about specials. Be advised that many rental agencies in Florida will rent only to drivers 21 and older, and that drivers younger than age 25 may have to pay a young renter's fee of up to $25 a day.

Note: Disney has an Alamo car-rental desk (📞 **800/327-2996**) right on property, so if you're interested in renting for only a few days instead of your entire vacation, this may be a good option for you.

Good rental deals can also be obtained through such online sources as Expedia, Travelocity, Priceline, and CarRentals.com. Keep in mind, however, that pricing often varies from day to day. The further out you can book a car, the less expensive your rental is likely to be. I've paid as high as $690 per week for the very same class of car that, weeks earlier, was listed at just under $200 per week. And that same car, the one I rented for $690 (during the now lengthier spring-break season)—a no-frills, sub-economy-class Matchbox car—I later rented for only $79 (through the very same rental agency). And if that isn't enough to make your head (or bank account) spin, if you're intent on renting a specific car such as a Dodge Caravan, you'll need to book as far out as possible thanks to limited inventories.

CAR-RENTAL INSURANCE

Car-rental insurance usually costs $25 or more a day. If you hold a private auto insurance policy, you are *probably* covered in the U.S. for loss or damage to the car, as well as liability in case a passenger is injured. The credit card you use to rent the car also may provide some coverage. Double-check with your insurance company and your credit card company regarding what may or may not be covered on both ends. **Note:** Many car-rental companies now charge steep out-of-service fees, if the car is out of commission for any reason after its return. Also note that some car-rental companies have been known to lie about the amount of coverage you need in order to get you to sign up for policies that make them quite a bit of profit. Always do your homework on what is and isn't covered by your policy before you get to the rental counter.

Car-rental insurance probably does not cover liability if you cause an accident (some companies, however, may offer supplemental liability insurance for an additional daily fee). Check your own auto insurance policy, the rental-company policy, and your credit card coverage for the extent of coverage: Is your destination covered? Are other drivers covered? How much liability is covered if a passenger is injured? (If you rely on your credit card for coverage, you may want to bring a second credit card with you. Damages may be charged to your card, and you may find yourself stranded with no money.) You don't need any surprises spoiling your vacation, so look at your coverage before reaching the rental counter.

DRIVING IN TOWN

SPEED LIMITS Obey posted speed limits. On highways and interstates, they're usually 55 or 65 mph, but as high as 70 mph in some rural areas. In residential areas,

30 or 35 mph is usually the case. **Note:** The corridor between the attractions and downtown Orlando is a speed trap, with fines for speeding starting at $81 (and reaching as high as $306). Fines double in construction areas and school zones. It is best to stick to the speed limit for safety reasons as well, not just because of the threat of a monetary penalty. With so many tourists, most of them with no idea where they're going (and who are probably paying more attention to their maps than their driving), you'll be able to react more quickly to any surprises if you're not speeding along.

SEAT BELTS Seat belts are required for all passengers. Children ages 3 and younger must be buckled into a car seat, and those ages 4 and 5 must be in a safety restraint (whether a car seat, booster seat, or seat belt). Police will issue tickets to parents who don't put their children in the proper restraints while driving. Many car-rental agencies offer car-seat rentals; however, if you'll be here for more than just a few days, you may want to consider bringing your own, as the rental cost will almost add up to the price of a new car seat.

AIR BAG SAFETY Children, in or out of car seats, should ride only in the back seats of cars that are equipped with air bags. Air bags have been linked to the deaths of several young passengers in the U.S. If you don't know if your car is equipped with passenger-side air bags, you'll need to ask the car-rental attendant; air bags are, however, a standard feature on most new-model cars.

DRINKING & DRIVING Don't. It's that simple. Florida's rules are strict and strictly enforced. If you're planning to drink (alcohol, that is), especially after an exhausting day in the theme parks, designate a sober driver or find an alternative means of transportation (there are plenty of options). Some clubs even provide free soft drinks to designated drivers. If you don't obey the law, your accommodations may change from a four-star hotel room to a Florida jail cell in short order.

DEFENSIVE DRIVING Drive with extra care in tourist-heavy areas. It's not uncommon for drivers to make sudden turns or to slow down unexpectedly when reading road signs. People often come to near stops on the highway while attempting to read their maps and decipher the Disney signs, which can be confusing. The tourist areas in Orlando are doubly difficult: The locals are in a hurry to get to their jobs, and tourists are scurrying to be the first to the fun. Assume all other drivers have no idea where they're going—which is often close to the truth—and you'll do fine. One of the best things to remember: Keep a safe distance between you and the car ahead of you. And, while it may sound like common sense, don't read a map while driving (you'd be surprised how many drivers do). Get your co-pilot to do it, use this book to determine your exit in advance, or call ahead to your destination to find out which exit you should take. Stay in the far right lane, the slow lane, when you begin to get near your exit. If you miss your exit, don't panic—there are plenty of others (especially around Disney) that can get you where you want to go.

DRIVING IN THE RAIN Watch out for a hazardous condition where oil on the road creates slick patches when the road gets wet. Rainstorms in Florida are intense and frequent; they're almost a daily occurrence in summer. Exercise extreme caution and drive in the far right lane when driving much slower than the speed limit. Don't pull off onto the shoulder of the road. If visibility is especially poor, pull off at the first exit and wait out the storm; they seldom last more than an hour. Florida law requires drivers to turn on their headlights whenever they turn on their windshield wipers.

IF YOU GET LOST Exit numbers continue to change and signs continue to be confusing. On interstates or Orlando's toll roads, don't try a U-turn across the grassy

PLANNING YOUR TRIP

Getting Around

Cars, Cars Everywhere

If the traffic outside isn't enough for you, you can find cars inside as well. The **NASCAR Sports Grille** at Universal's CityWalk (p. 327) is loaded with racing memorabilia and high-tech driving-related video games.

median. Go to the next exit and reenter the highway by accessing the on-ramp near where you got off. Avoid pulling over to ask directions from people on the street. Instead, stop at a convenience store or gas station and ask the clerk. Don't forget, you can get maps ahead of time from the Orlando CVB. If you are renting a car, most agencies will provide a map (some even provide computer-generated directions). Some rental-car agencies offer GPS navigational systems with their rentals as an add-on; inquire when you rent your car. Most of the hotels have maps located in the racks with all of the brochures. They are usually inserts in the local tourist magazines.

SAFETY WHILE DRIVING   Question your rental agency about personal safety or ask for a brochure on traveler safety tips when you pick up your car. Obtain written directions from the agency or a map with the route marked in red, showing how to get to your destination. And, if possible, arrive and depart during daylight hours.

If you drive off a highway and end up in a dodgy-looking neighborhood, turn around and leave the area as quickly as possible. If you have an accident, even on the highway, stay in your car with the doors locked until you assess the situation or until the police arrive. If you're bumped from behind on the street or are involved in a minor accident with no injuries, and the situation appears to be suspicious, motion to the other driver to follow you. Never open the window or get out of your car in such situations. Go directly to the nearest police station, well-lit service station, or 24-hour store.

You may want to look into renting a cellphone on a short-term basis if you don't already have one. One recommended wireless rental company is **InTouch USA** (© **800/872-7626;** www.intouchusa.com). Another option, if you plan on renting a car, is to rent a cellphone right from the car-rental company. Be sure to inquire about availability and rates when making your reservations.

If you see someone else on the road indicating a need for help, don't stop. Take note of the location, and call the police by dialing © **911** to make them aware of the situation.

Park in well-lit, well-traveled areas whenever possible. Keep your doors locked, whether you're inside the car or not. Look around before you get out and never leave packages, pocketbooks, or any kind of valuables in sight. Although theme-park lots are patrolled, it's best to secure your valuables at all times. For an added measure of security, you can store items in the lockers available near all of the park entrances. If it is an item you really don't need with you that day, use the hotel safe for storage and don't even bring it along.

If someone tries to rob you or steal your car, don't resist. Report the incident to the police immediately.

By Bus

Stops for the **Lynx** bus system (© **407/841-5969;** www.golynx.com) are marked with a paw print. It will get you to Disney, Universal, and I-Drive, but it's generally not very tourist-friendly. One-way fare is $2 for adults, $1 for kids 7 to 18, and free for kids 6 and younger (up to three per paying adult); express passes and day passes are available as well.

Mears Transportation (☎ **407/423-5566;** www.mearstransportation.com) operates buses to all the major attractions, including Kennedy Space Center, Universal Studios, SeaWorld, and Busch Gardens (yes, in Tampa), among others. Its service is the largest in the area, and with good reason. Rates will vary based on where you are going and where you are coming from, so call ahead for the particulars. Many of the area hotels use Mears for their shuttle service to the parks and attractions. If your hotel does not provide free shuttle service, make sure you compare the costs of taking shuttles to the cost of renting a car before deciding on your transportation; the car will often be the cheaper way to go.

By Motorcycle

The increasing popularity of Bike Week in nearby Daytona Beach and a growing number of weekend road warriors have sparked an increase in places specializing in motorcycle rentals. The Harley-Davidson, in all shapes and sizes, is the most popular. You must be at least 21 and sometimes 25 years of age, have a motorcycle license, and have a major credit card. Rental fees can run between $489 and $1,179 for a week or between $99 and $199 per day (event pricing runs slightly higher), including helmets and raingear (insurance is extra). You can rent bikes at **American V Twin,** 5101 International Dr. (☎ **888/268-8946** or 407/903-0058; www.amvtwin.com); **Orlando Harley-Davidson,** 3770 37th St. (☎ **407/423-0346**); **South Orlando Harley-Davidson,** 7786 W. Irlo Bronson Hwy. (☎ **407/994-3700**); and **Eaglerider Motorcycle Rentals,** 1233 Sand Lake Rd. (☎ **407/316-8687**). Reserve your bike months in advance if you're going to be here during Bike Week, late February to early March, or Biketoberfest (also in Daytona) in mid-October.

By Taxi

Taxis will line up in front of major hotels in addition to a few smaller properties. The front desk will be more than happy to hail one for you. If you wish, you can also call **Yellow Cab** (☎ **407/699-9999**) and **Ace Metro** (☎ **407/855-1111**) on your own. Both are good choices; however, rates can run as high as $3.25 for the first mile and $1.75 per mile thereafter, though occasionally you can get a flat rate if you ask. Yellow Cab (a division of Mears Transportation) features a fare estimator on its website, **www.mearstransportation.com**—just click on "Taxi Service" and the "Taxi Fare Estimator" icon will come up. In general, cabs are economical only if you have four or five people aboard and aren't going very far. You could actually rent your own car (depending on the model) for the price of just a few taxi rides.

FAST FACTS: ORLANDO

Area Codes The area code for Orlando is 407. **Note:** Because of its growth spurt, Orlando uses 10-digit dialing. If you're making a local call in Orlando's 407 area code region, even across the street, *you must dial the 407 area code followed by the number you wish to call,* for a total of 10 digits.

Automobile Organizations Motor clubs will supply maps, suggested routes, guidebooks, accident and bail-bond insurance, and emergency road service. **AAA** is the major auto club in the U.S. If you belong to a motor club in your home country, inquire about AAA reciprocity before you leave. You may be able to join AAA even if you're not a member of a reciprocal club; to inquire, call AAA (☎ **800/222-4357;** www.aaa.com). AAA has a nationwide emergency road service phone number (☎ **800/AAA-HELP** [222-4357]).

Babysitters Many Orlando hotels, including all of Disney's resorts, offer in-room babysitting, usually from an outside service such as **Kid's Nite Out** (☎ **800/696-8105** or 407/828-0920; www.kidsniteout.com) or **All About Kids** (☎ **800/728-6506** or 407/812-9300; www.all-about-kids.com). Rates for in-room sitters usually run $14 to $16 per hour for the first child and another $2 to $3 per hour for each additional child. A premium fee of $2 per hour (not per child) is often added for services provided during unusually early or late hours. A transportation fee of approximately $10 to $12 is usually charged as well. Several resorts offer child-care facilities with counselor-supervised activities right on the premises, including select Disney resorts (for kids ages 3–12; ☎ **407/939-3463**) and Universal Orlando's on-site resorts (for kids ages 4–14; ☎ **407/503-2230,** 407/503-2236, or 407/503-1200). This type of child care usually costs between $10 and $15 per hour, per child.

Reservations are highly recommended and are often required for either type of service.

Business Hours Theme-park operating hours vary depending on the time of year, even on the day of the week. Although most open at 8 or 9am and close at 6 or 7pm, you should call or check the park's website for its most current schedule before arriving. Other businesses are generally open from 9am to 5pm, Monday through Friday. Bars are usually open until 2am, with some after-hours clubs staying open into the wee hours of the morning (though the alcohol stops flowing at 2am).

Car Rental See "Getting There: By Car," earlier in this chapter.

Cellphones See "Mobile Phones," later in this section.

Crime See "Safety," later in this section.

Customs What You Can Bring into the U.S. Every visitor 21 years of age or older may bring in, free of duty, the following: (1) 1 U.S. quart of alcohol; (2) 200 cigarettes, 50 cigars (but not from Cuba), or 3 pounds of smoking tobacco; and (3) $100 worth of gifts. These exemptions are offered to travelers who spend at least 72 hours in the U.S. and who have not claimed them within the preceding 6 months. It is forbidden to bring into the country almost any meat products

(including canned, fresh, and dried meat products such as bouillon, soup mixes, and so on). Generally, condiments including vinegars, oils, pickled goods, spices, coffee, tea, and some cheeses and baked goods are permitted. Avoid rice products, as rice can often harbor insects. Bringing fruits and vegetables is prohibited, as they may harbor pests or disease. International visitors may carry in or out up to $10,000 in U.S. or foreign currency with no formalities; larger sums must be declared to U.S. Customs on entering or leaving, which includes filing form CM 4790. For details regarding U.S. Customs and Border Protection, consult your nearest U.S. embassy or consulate, or go online to **U.S. Customs** (www.customs.gov).

What You Can Take Home from Orlando For information on what you're allowed to bring home, contact one of the following agencies:

o **U.S. Citizens: U.S. Customs & Border Protection (CBP),** 1300 Pennsylvania Ave. NW, Washington, DC 20229 (☎ **877/287-8667;** www.cbp.gov).

o **Canadian Citizens: Canada Border Services Agency,** Ottawa, Ontario, K1A 0L8 (☎ **800/461-9999** in Canada, or 204/983-3500;

www.cbsa-asfc.gc. ca).

- **U.K. Citizens: HM Customs & Excise,** Crownhill Court, Tailyour Road, Plymouth, PL6 5BZ (📞 **0845/010-9000;** from outside the U.K., 020/8929-0152; www.hmce. gov.uk).

- **Australian Citizens: Australian Customs Service,** Customs House, 5 Constitution Avenue, Canberra City, ACT 2601 (📞 **1300/363-263;** from outside Australia, 612/6275-6666; www.customs. gov.au).

- **New Zealand Citizens: New Zealand Customs,** The Customhouse, 17–21 Whitmore St., Box 2218, Wellington, 6140 (📞 **04/473-6099** or 0800/428-786; www.customs. govt.nz).

Disabled Travelers

Most disabilities shouldn't stop anyone from traveling in the U.S. Thanks to provisions in the Americans with Disabilities Act, most public places are required to comply with disability-friendly regulations. Almost all public establishments in Orlando (including hotels, restaurants, museums, and so on, but not including certain National Historic Landmarks) and at least some modes of public transportation provide accessible entrances and

other facilities for those with disabilities.

Accommodations Every hotel and motel in Florida is required by law to have a special room or rooms equipped for wheelchairs. A few have wheel-in showers. Disney World's Coronado Springs Resort has 99 rooms designed to accommodate guests with disabilities. Disney's Polynesian and Grand Floridian resorts are both particularly well suited to guests who use wheelchairs, as the location of the resorts on the monorail system makes travel to the Magic Kingdom and Epcot a bit easier. Make your special needs known when making reservations. For other information about special Disney rooms, call 📞 **407/939-7807.**

If you don't mind staying 10 to 15 minutes or so from Disney, check out one of the area's various vacation homes. **All Star Vacation Homes** (📞 **800/592-5568** or 407/997-0733; www.all starvacationhomes.com) is one of the best around, offering, among other things, several handi-capped-accessible homes that have multiple bedrooms, multiple bathrooms (including accessible showers), full kitchens, and pools. Most cost less than $300 a night and are located in Kissimmee (though you'll find a handful of villas and town houses near I-Drive). **Medical Travel Inc.**

(📞 **800/778-7953;** www. medicaltravel.org) is another source of rental homes, plus scooters, vans, and medical equipment. It can satisfy the needs of travelers with disabilities, including those with terminal illnesses, and their families.

Transportation Public buses in Orlando have hydraulic lifts and restraining belts for wheelchairs. They serve Universal Orlando, SeaWorld, the shopping areas, and downtown Orlando. Disney shuttle buses accommodate wheelchairs, as do the monorail system and some of the watercraft that travel to the parks and resorts.

If you need to rent a wheelchair or electric scooter for your visit, **Walker Medical & Mobility Products** (📞 **888/726-6837** or 407/331-9500; www.walkermobility.com) offers delivery to your room of models that fit into Disney's transports and monorails as well as rental cars. **CARE Medical Equipment** (📞 **800/741-2282** or 407/856-2273; www.caremedical equipment.com) offers similar services. **Disney** (📞 **407/934-7639;** www. disneyworld.com) offers wheelchair rentals at the parks, at Downtown Disney, and, in more limited numbers, at the resorts. A very limited number of Electric Convenience Vehicle scooters are also available for rent at the parks.

Note: Although the Segway is becoming increasingly popular as a mode of transportation for those with disabilities, neither Disney nor SeaWorld permits them inside any of their parks. Universal Orlando does allow them inside its parks. Segways can be rented near the Orange County Convention Center at **Orlando Gliders,** 8990 International Dr. (*✆* **866/611-9398**); rates run from $60 (2 hr.) to $125 (a full day).

Amtrak (*✆* **800/872-7245;** www.amtrak.com) provides redcap service, wheelchair assistance, and special seats if you give 72 hours' notice. Travelers with disabilities are also entitled to a 15% discount off the lowest available adult coach fare (though they cannot book online). Documentation from a doctor or an ID card proving your disability is required. Amtrak also provides wheelchair-accessible sleeping accommodations on long-distance trains. Service dogs are permitted aboard and travel free. TDD/TTY service is also available at *✆* **800/523-6590,** or you can write to P.O. Box 7717, Itasca, IL 60143.

Theme Parks Many attractions at the parks, especially the newer ones, are designed to be accessible to a wide variety of guests. People with wheelchairs and their parties are often given preferential treatment so they can avoid lines. The assistance available is outlined in the guide maps you get as you enter the parks. All of the theme parks offer some parking close to the entrances for those with disabilities. Let the parking-booth attendant know your needs, and you'll be directed to the appropriate spot. Wheelchair and electric-cart rentals are available at most major attractions, but you'll be most comfortable in your chair or cart from home if you can bring it. Keep in mind, however, that wheelchairs wider than 2 feet may be difficult to navigate through some attractions. And crowds may make it tough for any guest.

At Walt Disney World
Disney's many services are detailed in each theme park's *Guidebook for Guests with Disabilities.* You can pick one up at Guest Relations near the front entrance of each of the parks, or go online to **www.disneyworld.com** (click through to the site map, and then select "Travelers with Disabilities"). You can also call *✆* **407/934-7639** or 407/824-2222 with questions regarding special needs. Examples of services are as follows:

- Almost all Disney resorts have rooms for those with disabilities.
- Braille guidebooks, cassette tapes, and portable tape players are available at City Hall in the Magic Kingdom and Guest Relations in the other parks (a $25 refundable deposit is required).
- Service animals are allowed in all parks and on some rides.
- All parks have special parking spots near the entrances.
- Assisted listening devices are available to amplify the audio at select attractions at WDW parks. Also, at some attractions, hearing-impaired guests can use hand-held wireless receivers that allow them to read captions about the attractions. Both services are free but require a $25 refundable deposit.
- Wheelchairs and electric carts can be rented at all of the parks.
- Downtown Disney West Side, with crowded shops and bars, may be a bit difficult to navigate in a wheelchair. The movie theater, however, is wheelchair accessible.
- For information about Telecommunications Devices for the Deaf (TDD) or sign-language interpreters at Disney World live shows, call *✆* **407/827-5141** (TDD/TTY). You can usually get an ASL interpreter at several

events and attractions if you call no later than 2 weeks in advance.

At Universal Orlando Parks Guests with disabilities should go to Guest Services, located just inside the main entrances, for the *Rider's Guide for Rider Safety and Guests with Disabilities* booklet, a TDD, or other special assistance. Wheelchair and electric-cart rentals are available in the concourse area of the parking garage. Universal also provides audio descriptions on cassette for visually impaired guests and has sign-language guides and scripts for its shows (advance notice of 1–2 weeks is required); call *℡* **888/519-4899** (TTY) or 407/224-5929 (voice) for details. You can also get information online at **www.universalorlando.com**—from the main page, click on either "Universal's Islands of Adventure" or "Universal Studios Florida" (both under "Theme Parks"), then scroll down the left side to "ADA Info."

At SeaWorld The park has a guide for guests with disabilities, although most of its attractions are easily accessible to those in wheelchairs. SeaWorld also provides a Braille guide for the visually impaired and a very brief synopsis of its shows for the hearing impaired. Sign-language interpreting services are available at no charge, but must be reserved by calling *℡* **407/363-2414** at

least a week in advance. Assisted listening devices are available at select attractions for a $20 refundable deposit. For information, call *℡* **407/351-3600** or check out **www.seaworld.com**.

Other Resources You can get information online at **www.visitorlando.com**, the website of the Orlando/Orange County Convention & Visitors Bureau (Orlando CVB). *Wheelchairs On the Go,* by Michelle Stigleman and Deborah Van Brunt, is a comprehensive guidebook that lists information on accessibility in Florida, from ground transportation to medical-equipment rentals, accommodations, and attractions. *PassPorter's Open Mouse* (www.passporter.com/wdw/specialneeds) offers extensive information on accessible travel throughout Walt Disney World and on the Disney Cruise Line.

If you plan on visiting the **Canaveral National Seashore** (p. 354) as a side trip while in Orlando, know that the **America the Beautiful—National Park and Federal Recreational Lands Pass—Access Pass** (formerly the **Golden Access Passport**) gives visually impaired people or those with permanent disabilities (regardless of age) free lifetime entrance to federal recreation sites administered by the National Park Service, including the Fish and Wildlife Service, the Forest Service, the Bureau of

Land Management, and the Bureau of Reclamation. This may include national parks, monuments, historic sites, recreation areas, and wildlife refuges. The America the Beautiful Access Pass can be obtained only in person at any NPS facility that charges an entrance fee. You need to show proof of a medically determined disability. Besides free entry, the pass also offers a 50% discount on some federal-use fees charged for facilities such as camping, swimming, parking, boat launching, and tours. For more information, go to **www.nps.gov/fees_passes.htm** or call the United States Geological Survey (USGS), which issues the passes, at *℡* **888/275-8747.**

Doctors & Dentists

There are basic first-aid centers in all of the theme parks. There's also a 24-hour, toll-free number for the **Poison Control Center** (*℡* **800/282-3171**). To find a dentist, contact the **Dental Referral Service** (*℡* **800/235-4111;** www.dentalreferral.com).

Doctors on Call Service (*℡* **407/399-3627**) makes house and room calls in most of the Orlando area, including the Disney resorts. **Centra Care** has several walk-in clinics listed in the Yellow Pages, including ones on Sand Lake Road, near Universal (*℡* **407/851-6478**); at Lake Buena Vista, near Disney (*℡* **407/934-2273**); and on U.S. 192 (W. Irlo

10

Doctors & Dentists

Bronson Hwy.), in the Formosa Gardens shopping center (℗ **407/397-7032**). The **Medical Concierge** (℗ **407/648-5252;** www.themedicalconcierge.com) makes "hotel house calls," has a walk-in clinic (listed in the Yellow Pages), arranges emergency dental appointments, and rents medical equipment.

Also see "Hospitals," later in this section.

Drinking Laws The legal age for purchase and consumption of alcoholic beverages is 21; proof of age is required and often requested at bars, nightclubs, and restaurants, so it's always a good idea to bring ID when you go out. No liquor is served in the Magic Kingdom at Walt Disney World. Alcoholic drinks are available, however, at the other Disney parks, at SeaWorld, and are quite evident at Universal Orlando's parks (even more so at its seasonal celebrations). Bars are required to stop serving alcohol at 2am, but don't necessarily close at that time. Do not carry open containers of alcohol in your car or any public area that isn't zoned for alcohol consumption—the police can fine you on the spot. Florida blue laws prohibit the sale of alcohol on Sundays before noon in Orange County and before 1pm in Osceola County. And nothing will ruin your trip faster than getting a citation for DUI ("driving under the influence"), so don't even think about driving while intoxicated.

Driving Rules See "Getting Around," earlier in this chapter.

Electricity Like Canada, the United States uses 110 to 120 volts AC (60 cycles), compared to 220 to 240 volts AC (50 cycles) in most of Europe, Australia, and New Zealand. Downward converters that change 220 to 240 volts to 110 to 120 volts are difficult to find in the United States, so bring one with you.

Embassies & Consulates All embassies are in the nation's capital, Washington, D.C. Some consulates are in major U.S. cities, and most nations have a mission to the United Nations in New York City. If your country isn't listed below, call for directory information in Washington, D.C. (℗ **202/555-1212**) or check **www.embassy.org/embassies**.

The embassy of **Australia** is at 1601 Massachusetts Ave. NW, Washington, DC 20036 (℗ **202/797-3000;** www.usa.embassy.gov.au). Consulates are in New York, Honolulu, Houston, Los Angeles, and San Francisco.

The embassy of **Canada** is at 501 Pennsylvania Ave. NW, Washington, DC 20001 (℗ **202/682-1740;** www.canadainternational. gc.ca/washington). Consulates are in Buffalo (N.Y.), Detroit, Los Angeles, New York, and Seattle.

The embassy of **Ireland** is at 2234 Massachusetts Ave. NW, Washington, DC 20008 (℗ **202/462-3939;** www.embassyofireland. org). Consulates are in Boston, Chicago, New York, San Francisco, and other cities. See the website for a complete listing.

The embassy of **New Zealand** is at 37 Observatory Circle NW, Washington, DC 20008 (℗ **202/328-4800;** www.nzembassy.com). Consulates are in Los Angeles, Salt Lake City, San Francisco, and Seattle.

The embassy of the **United Kingdom** is at 3100 Massachusetts Ave. NW, Washington, DC 20008 (℗ **202/588-6500;** http://ukinusa.fco.gov.uk). Consulates are in Atlanta, Boston, Chicago, Cleveland, Houston, Los Angeles, New York, San Francisco, and Seattle.

Emergencies Call ℗ **911** to report a fire, contact the police, or get an ambulance. This call is free from all public telephones and should be the first call made in case of any serious medical emergency or accident.

The Florida Tourism Industry Marketing Corporation, the state tourism promotions board, sponsors a **help line** (℗ **800/647-9284**). With operators speaking more than 100 languages, it can provide general directions and help with lost travel papers and credit cards, minor medical emergencies, accidents, money transfer, airline confirmation, and more.

Family Travel   No city in the world is geared more to family travel than Orlando. In addition to its theme parks, Orlando's recreational facilities provide an abundance of opportunities for family fun. Most restaurants have lower-priced ($4–$9) children's menus (if not, the appetizer menu works just as well) and fun distractions such as place mats to color while younger diners wait for their food. Many of the hotels and resorts offer children's activity centers (see chapter 3, "Where to Stay," for details).

Keep an eye out for coupons discounting meals and attractions; they can be found practically everywhere. The "Calendar" section in Friday's *Orlando Sentinel* newspaper often contains coupons and good deals. Many restaurants, especially those in tourist areas, offer great discounts that are yours for the clipping. Check the information you receive from the Orlando/Orange County Convention & Visitors Bureau (see "Visitor Information," in chapter 2), including free or cheap things to do. Additionally, many hotel lobbies and attractions have free coupon books for the taking.

Most of the major theme parks offer parent-swap programs in which one parent can ride without the children, then switch off and let the other parent

ride without having to return to the end of the line. Inquire at Guest Services or Guest Relations, near the park entrances, for details on which rides are included.

To locate accommodations, restaurants, and attractions that are particularly kid-friendly, refer to the "Kids" icon throughout this guide.

Here are more suggestions for making traveling with children easier:

○ **Are Your Kids Old Enough?**   Do you really want to bring an infant or toddler to the parks? If you plan on visiting Disney several times as your children grow, then the best age for a first visit to Disney is just about 3 years old. Why? Because the kids are old enough to walk around and enjoy the sights and sounds, as well as a good deal of the rides and shows. The thrill rides would most likely frighten them, but most inappropriate rides for the tiny-tot set have height restrictions that prevent any unfortunate mistakes. If, however, this is going to be a one-time trip, then I recommend waiting until your children are between 7 and 10. They'll still be

able to appreciate the wonder of the experience but won't have reached the stage where all they'll want are chills and thrills.

Some of the characters walking about may make young kids a bit nervous, though most will run right up to Donald or Mickey and give them a big hug. Younger kids may need a nap just when you want to see a show or hop on an attraction, but if you have kids this is nothing new to you. When you plan your day's activities, be sure to account for necessary breaks and naps. Will your whole family be able to enjoy the experiences that Disney and other parks have to offer? This is something you will have to decide. My five kids range in age from 9 to 17, and we have traveled with just about every age combination you can think of. On our first family trip, my oldest (now 17) was 4, and his two younger siblings were ages 3 and 1. While the 1-year-old has absolutely no recollection of the trip, he was thoroughly amused by the sights and sounds everywhere we went. The 3-year-old (now 15) still remembers plenty. You'll need to take into account your kids' stamina, interests, and tolerance levels before you decide whether to make the trip and when planning your daily itineraries. My kids could go well into the evening inside the parks, but many other children can't, so it may take you longer to cover a park (it took me 2–3 days to do Magic Kingdom when my youngest was 2). At the time, my nephew was 7, and he was petrified by some of the rides in the parks; even my own kids, who'll try anything once and have never been wary of rides, freak out at attractions involving sensory effects. It may be repetitious, but I'll say it again: Know your own child before deciding whether he or she is ready for this sort of trip. Not every child will fall in love with Disney World at first sight, and it's a rather large expense to incur if Junior's going to be

frightened, sleepy, or cranky for the entire trip.

○ **Planning Ahead** Make reservations for character breakfasts at Disney (see chapter 4, "Where to Eat") as soon as possible. Disney usually accepts them up to 180 days in advance (recently changed from 90 days), and many are booked minutes (I'm not kidding!) after the 180-day window opens, so mark your calendar to call (and be sure you keep in mind that the line opens for calls at 7am EST). Also, in any park, check the daily schedule for character appearances (all of the major ones post them on maps or boards near the entrances), and make sure the kids know when they're going to get to meet their heroes. It's often the highlight of their day. (Be wary, however, of promising specific characters, as schedules and character lineups can change.) Advance planning will help you avoid running after every character you see. The "in" thing of late is getting character autographs. The

lines can be quite long, so you may want to pick and choose just a couple of favorite characters to do this with.

○ **Packing** Although your home may be toddler-proof, hotel accommodations aren't. Bring blank plugs to cover outlets and whatever else is necessary to prevent an accident from occurring in your room. Most hotels have some type of crib available; however, they are usually limited in number. Some hotels can also supply bedrails, though they are not as readily available as cribs are. Outside of hotel supplies, your biggest packing priority should be sunscreen. Locals can spot tourists by their bright-red sunburns. Both parents and children should heed this reminder: *Don't forget to bring and use sunscreen with an SPF rating of at least 30.* If you do forget it, it's available at convenience stores, drugstores, and some theme-park shops. Young children should be slathered, even if they're in a stroller. Be sure to pack a wide-brim hat for infants and toddlers. Adults and children alike should drink plenty of water to avoid dehydration.

- **Accommodations** Kids younger than 12, and, in many cases, those as old as 17, stay free in their parent's room in most hotels, but to be certain, ask when you book. Most hotels have pools and other recreational facilities that will give you a little no-extra-cost downtime. If you want to skip a rental car and aren't staying at Disney, International Drive and Lake Buena Vista are the places to stay. Hotels often offer family discounts; some offer Kids Eat Free programs, and some provide free or moderate-cost shuttle service to the major attractions. International Drive also has the I-Ride Trolley, which travels the length of the road and makes numerous stops along the way.

- **Ground Rules** Set firm rules before leaving home regarding things such as bedtime and souvenirs. It's easy to get off track as you get caught up in the excitement of Orlando, but don't allow your vacation to seize control of your better judgment. Having the kids earn their own money or at least allotting a specific prearranged amount for them to spend works wonders. Making them part of your decisions also works well. They'll be far more cooperative when they understand that everyone in the family gets a say in the plan for the day and that they will eventually get to do something or go somewhere that they want to.

- **At the Parks** Getting lost is all too easy in a place as strange and overwhelming as the theme parks. Toss in the crowds and it's amazing it doesn't happen more often. For adults (yes, they get lost, too) and older kids, arrange a lost-and-found meeting place before you arrive in the parks, and if you become separated, head there immediately. Make sure your kids know to find a staff member (point out the special name-tags worn by the staff) to help them. Attach a name-tag with the child's first name and your cellphone (or hotel) number to the inside of younger kids' T-shirts and tell them to find a park employee (and only a park employee) immediately and show them the tag if they become lost.

- **Read the Signs** Most rides post signs that explain **height restrictions,** if any, or identify those that may unsettle youngsters. Save yourself and your kids some grief before you get in line and are disappointed. (The ride listings in chapter 5, "Exploring Walt Disney World," and chapter 6, "Exploring Beyond Disney: Universal Orlando, SeaWorld & Other Attractions," note any minimum height requirements, as do the guide maps you can get at the parks.) A bad experience, whether it be a dark, scary section of a ride, the loop-de-loop of a roller coaster, or too big of a drop, can cause your child long-lasting anxiety. It can also put a damper on things for the rest of your day (and possibly even your vacation).

I've often explained to my children—irrespective of their ages—that if they hear screaming, that's a pretty good indication that a ride may not be the best choice for them. With younger kids, you have to be steadfast in your decisions, though most height restrictions will keep those who really shouldn't be riding at bay. With the older ones, well, you may have to indulge them a bit and let them ride just one—they likely won't make the same mistake twice. Note that once you get past the height restriction, age is not always as much of a deciding factor when it comes to rides as one might think. It really depends on your child's previous experiences and personality. I've seen 5-year-olds squeal with glee on rides that I can't even stomach; on the other hand, I've observed kids as old as 8 or 10 walk out of some of the attractions with "touchy feely" effects practically in tears.

- **Take a Break** The Disney parks, Universal Orlando, and SeaWorld have fabulous interactive play areas offering both parents and young kids a break. By all means, take advantage of them. They allow kids to expend some of their pent-up energy after having to wait in lines and not wander far from Mom and Dad all day long. They offer a nice break for you, too (if you can sit down to watch them, that is). Note that many of these kid zones are filled with water squirters and shallow pools, and most of the parks feature a fair number of water-related attractions, so getting wet is practically inevitable—at least for the kids. It's advisable to bring along a change of clothes or even a bathing suit. You can rent a locker ($10 or less) for storing the spares until you need them. During the summer, the Florida humidity is enough to keep you feeling soggy, so you may appreciate the change of clothing even if you don't go near any water.

- **Show Times** Schedule an indoor, air-conditioned show two or three times a day, especially during midafternoon in the summer. You may even get your littlest tykes to nap in the darkened theater. For all shows, arrive at least 20 minutes early to get the better seats, but not so early that the kids are tired of waiting (most waits are outside in the heat at Disney; Universal has covered queue areas at most attractions).

- **Snack Times** When dreaming of your vacation, you probably don't envision hours spent standing in lines, waiting and waiting (unless you have done this before, that is). It helps to store some lightweight snacks in a backpack, or in the stroller if you have one, especially when traveling with small children. This may save you some headaches, as kids get the hungriest just when you are the farthest from food. It will also be much healthier and will certainly save you money, as the parks' prices are quite high.

- **Bring Your Own?** While you will have to haul it to and from the car and on and off trams, trains, or monorails at Disney, having your own stroller can be a tremendous help. It will be with you when you need it—say, back in the hotel room as a highchair, or for an infant in a restaurant when a highchair is inappropriate. Remember to bring the right stroller, too. It should be lightweight and easy to fold and unfold with one hand, have a canopy, be able to recline for naps, and have plenty of storage space. The parks offer stroller rentals for around $10 to $31 per day (depending on size); however, these are often hard and uncomfortable (and rental fees could easily exceed the cost of a purchasing a stroller after just a few days). They do not recline and have little or no storage space for the gear that goes along with bringing the kids. They are good, however, if you have older kids who may just need an occasional break from walking. For infants and small toddlers, you may want to bring a snugly sling or backpack-type carrier for use in traveling to and from parking lots and while you're standing in line for attractions (where strollers are not allowed). And while many parks now have a small number of infant-friendly strollers on hand, I still highly recommend bringing your own if your kids are younger than 3 or 4.

- **Recommended Reading** *The Unofficial Guide to Walt Disney World* is a good source of additional information, as is *Frommer's Walt Disney World with Kids.* I've also listed some additional tips for tackling the theme parks in the "Making Your Visit More Enjoyable" sections in chapters 5 and 6.

Gasoline At press time, in the U.S., the cost of gasoline (also known as gas, but never petrol), was once again on the rise, with prices hovering at around $3.79 a gallon. Taxes are already included in the printed price. One U.S. gallon equals 3.8 liters or .85 imperial gallons. Fill-up locations are known as gas or service stations.

Health Orlando doesn't have any particular health risks to watch out for (except sun exposure—see "Common Ailments," below). Vaccines are not required to enter the U.S.; however, when traveling to Orlando (or anywhere for that matter), it is always a good idea to pack an assortment of over-the-counter remedies for common travel-related ailments. Sunscreen and sunburn cream will help to ward off and/or soothe an Orlando sunburn; Pepto-Bismol and antacids will lessen an array of stomach ailments that often pop up when traveling; eye drops will relieve tired and dry eyes (whether from the plane ride or all the plant life lurking at the parks); and a supply of bandages will help to protect the inevitable blisters, minor scrapes, and scratches.

You should, of course, pack any prescription medications that you require while vacationing—and keep the phone numbers of your family's various physicians handy in case you need a prescription refilled or called into a local pharmacy. Pharmacies are plentiful throughout the Orlando area (many of them are open 24 hr. and offer drive-through service). Most are stand-alone stores, but pharmacies can often be found inside the area's larger grocers as well. **Turner Drug Store** has two locations that serve the tourist districts (the first near Downtown Disney at 12500 Apopka–Vineland Rd., © **407/828-8125;** and the other in Celebration, © **407/566-9060**) and will deliver prescriptions (for a small fee) right to your hotel. Additional pharmacies can be found in the local phone book. If you have your prescription filled at a national chain (such as Eckerd, CVS, or Walgreens, among others), it's likely that you can easily obtain refills or replacement prescriptions if yours becomes lost. If, however, you use a pharmacy not in a national network, you may still be able to call your physician, who can then call in a refill good for the duration of your trip. Note that while pharmacies and several grocers are well stocked with over-the-counter medications, many hotels often stock a very small supply of trial-size over-the-counter medicines in their gift shops, though prices are generally astronomical.

Common Ailments: Sun/ Elements/Extreme Weather Exposure
Limit your exposure to Florida's strong sun, especially during the first few days of your trip and, thereafter, during the hours from 11am to 2pm, when the sun is at its strongest. Use a sunscreen with the highest sun protection factor (SPF) available (especially for children), and apply it liberally. If you have children under a year old, check with your pediatrician before applying sunscreen—some ingredients may not be appropriate for infants.

The hot Orlando sun (coupled with high humidity in the summer months) can easily cause you to overheat—even to the point of dehydration. Drink plenty of liquids (water is preferable to sugary or alcoholic drinks) throughout the day, even if you don't feel thirsty, to prevent any ill effects. Dehydration can sneak up on you very quickly.

Seek protection indoors or in a safe location during the city's not-infrequent summer electrical storms. Central Florida is the lightning capital of the U.S., and while the storms are often stunning to watch, you do not want firsthand experience with a lightning strike.

Disney, Universal, and SeaWorld all have at least one first-aid station (usually staffed with medical personnel who can provide basic medical care) at each of the parks. If you feel ill or get injured while at your hotel, call ☎ **911** if the situation is life-threatening; otherwise the hotel concierge will be happy to put you in touch with the appropriate medical personnel and/or services. Select hotels, including the Grande Lakes Orlando resort (p. 87), have their own on-site doctors.

What to Do if You Get Sick Away from Home
Always carry a list of phone numbers that includes your hometown physician, your hometown pharmacy, and your insurance provider, as all will likely be necessary if you find yourself in need of medical attention while away from home. If you suffer from a chronic illness (or even if you're just under the weather prior to your departure), consult your doctor before leaving home. Always pack prescription medications in your carry-on luggage (so they are readily available even if your checked luggage isn't), and carry them in their original containers, with pharmacy labels—otherwise they won't make it through airport security.

If you do need medical assistance while traveling in or around Orlando, there are several options. Emergency rooms are available at the institutions listed under "Hospitals," below. **Centra Care** (www.centra care.org) operates walk-in-care facilities in Lake Buena Vista (12500 S. Apopka–Vineland or S.R. 535, near Downtown Disney; ☎ **407/934-2273**), and in Kissimmee (7848 W. Irlo Bronson Hwy. or U.S. 192, in the Formosa Gardens Plaza; ☎ **407/397-7032**). Additional centers (slightly farther from the tourist district) are listed in the local yellow pages. A free **pickup service** (☎ **407/938-0650**) for those in need of transportation to one of these facilities is available, as is in-room care for minor injuries and ailments (☎ **407/238-2000**).

Another good source in the Orlando area is the **Medical Concierge,** a division of the EastCoast Medical Network (☎ **407/648-5252;** www. themedicalconcierge.com), with board-certified physicians available 24 hours a day, 7 days a week, for good old-fashioned house calls in the comfort of your hotel room. They also provide same-day emergency dental appointments as well as medical equipment rentals. Insurance receipts, insurance billing, and foreign-language interpretation are provided.

Keep in mind that if you require medical assistance while traveling, it is always best to contact your hometown physician (or pediatrician) as well as your insurance provider as quickly as possible, preferably before you seek outside medical attention, to ensure that you are fully aware of what is covered, what is not, and what your financial responsibility will likely be. Many insurance companies require some type of preapproval for out-of-town services, or they may not cover any or all of the expenses incurred.

Hospitals **Dr. P. Phillips Hospital** (formerly the Sand Lake Hospital), 9400 Turkey Lake Rd. (② **407/351-8500**), is about 2 miles south of Sand Lake Road. From the WDW area, take I-4 east to the Sand Lake Road exit and make a left on Turkey Lake Road. The hospital is 2 miles up on your right. To avoid the highway, take Palm Parkway (off Apopka–Vineland near Hotel Plaza Blvd.); it turns into Turkey Lake Road. The hospital is 2 miles up on your left. **Florida Hospital Celebration Health,** 400 Celebration Place (② **407/303-4000**), is

located in the near-Disney town of Celebration. From I-4, take the U.S. 192 exit. At the first traffic light, turn right onto Celebration Avenue. At the first stop sign, take another right.

Insurance The outlay for an Orlando vacation can be considerable, especially if you're buying a vacation package or renting a home while in the city. If you're traveling during hurricane season, have a medical condition, have to shell out a lot of money in advance of your trip, or if your vacation package is nonrefundable, do consider obtaining travel insurance. For information on traveler's insurance, trip-cancelation insurance, and medical insurance while traveling, please visit **www. frommers.com/planning**.

Internet & Wi-Fi The Orlando International Airport (now with its own 4G wireless network serviced by Verizon and AT&T), most Orlando area hotels, and a select number of local restaurants offer some form of Internet access (whether Wi-Fi or high-speed). Be prepared to pay a fee for the service (generally between $10–$13 for a 24-hour period—though select hotels may offer short-term connections at a slightly lesser cost, with access often restricted to the lobby), unless you have a wireless card (with a valid subscription) allowing you access at any time, from anywhere. Several hotels,

especially those catering to the business set, have public computers available to guests (fees vary) or in-room computers (some with Web TV, others with an actual computer station). T-Mobile, Wayport, and Boingo are among the most popular hot-spot providers (see www.wi-fi hotspotlist.com for a comprehensive list of both providers and properties in the area).

Kennels The major theme parks offer animal boarding, usually for about $12 to $15 per day. At Disney, a single facility, **Best Friends Pet Care,** on the Bonnet Creek Parkway (② **877/493-9738**), opened in 2010, replacing the numerous facilities once scattered about the resort. Overnight boarding, day care, and a slew of specialized services are offered for the pampered pet set. Resort guests can board their pets overnight for $10 to $34 ($12–$37 for those not staying at Disney), depending on the size and type of pet (larger, more luxurious accommodations go for a higher price). Pets are also welcome to stay overnight at Disney's Fort Wilderness Campground (at select campsites) for a nightly fee of $5. SeaWorld ($15) and Universal Orlando ($15) also offer kennels, but overnight boarding is not available (though all Universal Orlando resorts welcome pets to stay with you right in your room for a small fee). A current vaccination record is a must at all kennels. **Note:** For more information on traveling with your pet in Orlando, see "Pets," below.

Laundromats   Stand-alone laundromats are not widespread throughout the tourist districts; however, there are two within a relatively close drive: **Coin-A-Magic,** 1415 John Young Pkwy. (at the intersection of Irlo Bronson Memorial Hwy.), Kissimmee (✆ **407/933-1828**); and **Laundry Express & Cleaner** (closest to International Dr.), 5360 S. John Young Pkwy. (✆ **407/345-4777**). Several area hotels and resorts do have on-site self-service laundry facilities. Generally, these are coin-operated and charge about $1.50 to do a load of wash and another $1.50 to dry.

Legal Aid   While driving, if you are pulled over for a minor infraction (such as speeding), never attempt to pay the fine directly to a police officer; this could be construed as attempted bribery, a much more serious crime. Pay fines by mail, or directly into the hands of the clerk of the court. If accused of a more serious offense, say and do nothing before consulting a lawyer. In the U.S., the burden is on the state to prove a person's guilt beyond a reasonable doubt, and everyone has the right to remain silent, whether he or she is suspected of a crime or

actually arrested. Once arrested, a person can make one telephone call to a party of his or her choice. The international visitor should call his or her embassy or consulate.

Lost Children   Every theme park has a designated spot for adults to be reunited with lost children (or lost spouses—it happens). Ask where it is when you enter the park (or consult the free park guide map), and instruct your children to ask park personnel (not a stranger) to take them there if they get separated from you. Point out what park personnel look like so they will know whom to go to. Children age 7 and younger should wear name-tags inside their clothing (if you're carrying a cellphone, put the number on the tag).

LGBT Travelers
Orlando is a Southern town, but the entertainment industry and the theme parks have helped in the building of a strong gay and lesbian community. Same-sex dancing won't draw any unwelcome attention at clubs in the area such as those located at Universal's CityWalk or in downtown Orlando. The tenor of crowds can change, however, depending on what's going on in town, so respect your own intuition.

The popularity of Orlando with gay and lesbian travelers has been confirmed by the expansion of the June "Gay Day"

celebration at Disney World into a weekend event that includes Universal Orlando and SeaWorld. Park-goers can wear red on Gay Day to signify their support of the gay and lesbian community. Additional information on the event can be found at **www.gay days.com**.

For information about events for that weekend and throughout the year, contact the **Gay, Lesbian, Bisexual, Transgender Community Center of Central Florida,** 946 N. Mills Ave., Orlando (✆ **407/228-8272;** www.thecenterorlando.org). Welcome packets usually include the latest issue of the *Triangle,* a quarterly newsletter dedicated to gay and lesbian issues, and a calendar of events. Though not a tourist-specific packet, it includes information and ads for local gay and lesbian clubs. **Gay Orlando Network** (www.gayorlando.com) is another planning resource for travelers. *Watermark* (✆ **407/481-2243;** www.watermarkonline.com) is a gay-friendly publication that can be found in many bookstores.

Mail   At press time, domestic postage rates were 29¢ for a postcard and 44¢ for a letter. For international mail, a first-class letter of up to 1 ounce costs 98¢ (80¢ to Canada and Mexico); a first-class postcard costs the same as a letter. For more information go to **www.usps.com**.

If you aren't sure what your address will be in the U.S., mail can be sent to you, in your name, c/o General Delivery at the main post office of the city or region where you expect to be. (Call ☎ **800/275-8777** for information on the nearest post office.) The addressee must pick up mail in person and must produce proof of identity (driver's license, passport, and so on). Most post offices will hold mail for up to 1 month, and are open Monday to Friday from 8am to 6pm, Saturday from 9am to 3pm.

The post office most convenient to Disney and Universal is at 10450 Turkey Lake Rd. (☎ **407/351-2492**), open Monday through Friday from 9am to 7pm, Saturday from 9am to 5pm. A smaller location, closer to Disney, is at 8536 Palm Pkwy., in Lake Buena Vista, just up the road from Hotel Plaza Boulevard (☎ **407/238-0223**). If all you need is to buy stamps and mail letters, you can do that at most hotels.

Always include zip codes when mailing items in the U.S. If you don't know your zip code, visit **www.usps.com/zip4**.

Maps Maps of the Orlando area can be found online at **www.visitflorida.com** and **www.visit orlando.com**, as well as at the official visitor center and at most area hotels. Maps of the Disney, Universal, and SeaWorld parks

can be found on their respective websites, as well as at the theme parks themselves.

Medical Requirements Unless you're arriving from an area known to be suffering from an epidemic (particularly cholera or yellow fever), inoculations or vaccinations are not required for entry into the United States. Also see "Health," above for general health information while in Orlando.

Mobile Phones Just because your cellphone works at home doesn't mean it'll work everywhere in the U.S. (thanks to our nation's fragmented cellphone system). It's a good bet that your phone will work in Orlando, but take a look at your wireless company's coverage map on its website before heading out.

If you're not from the U.S., you'll be appalled at the poor reach of the **GSM (Global System for Mobile Communications) wireless network,** which is used by much of the rest of the world. Your phone will probably work in Orlando; it definitely won't work in many rural areas. To see where GSM phones work in the U.S., check out www.t-mobile.com/coverage. And you may or may not be able to send SMS (text messaging) home.

If you need to stay in touch and you know your phone won't work in Orlando, you can rent a phone that does from **InTouch USA** (☎ **800/872-**

7626; www.intouchglobal.com). Make arrangements in advance, as rentals aren't readily available within the Orlando area. Note that you'll pay $1 a minute or more for airtime in addition to the initial rental fee, and there are often significant restrictions (and high fees for overages) regarding the number of minutes available to you. If you only plan on making calls within the U.S., a good solution is to purchase a pay-as-you-go phone. They don't require a lengthy contract or monthly plan to use, and you pay only for the calls you make. **Cricket** (www.mycricket.com) and **T-Mobile** (www.t-mobile.com) are among the most widely known for offering this type of service; however, others (such as **AT&T** and **Verizon**) are beginning to jump on the bandwagon.

If you have Web access while traveling, consider a broadband-based telephone service (in technical terms, **Voice over Internet Protocol,** or **VoIP**), such as **Skype** (www.skype.com) or **Vonage** (www.vonage.com), which allows you to make free international calls from your laptop or in a cybercafe. Neither service requires the people you're calling to also have that service (though there are fees if they do not). Check the websites for details.

Money & Costs Frommer's lists exact prices in the local currency. The currency conversions provided were correct at press time.

MONEY-SAVING tips

For the budget conscious (and those who prefer not to completely deplete their financial portfolio), here are a few helpful suggestions and reminders:

- **Become a member.** Joining travel-related programs (including, but not limited to, AAA), participating in select reward programs (such as hotel and airline reward programs), and obtaining the Orlando Magicard (through the Orlando CVB) can save you a fair amount of money on hotel stays, restaurant meals, attraction tickets, and merchandise at select retailers (even in the theme parks)—but you have to remember to present your credentials when making reservations, checking in, and/or paying your bill to see the savings.

- **Bring your own stroller.** Or consider purchasing an inexpensive model while you're in town—the rental fees at the theme parks can easily exceed the cost of a new stroller in just a couple days.

- **Pack snacks and drinks.** While it is part of the Disney experience to purchase the occasional Mickey bar, pail of popcorn, turkey leg, or souvenir cup filled with the soda of your choice, bringing your own supplementary stash of snacks and bottled water (purchased at area grocers, not at your hotel) into the parks will save you a bundle in the end. Theme-park prices for such items are beyond believable.

- **Budget for souvenirs.** Also an integral part of the Disney experience is souvenir shopping. If you want to save a few dollars, it's helpful to create a budget for souvenir shopping before you go. Make sure to allow for the occasional must-have one-of-a-kind item that you and your kids will likely discover along the way, in addition to the traditional T-shirts and trinkets that you'll see everywhere. Even the little items add up quickly, so keep track of your spending as you go.

- **Remember those baggage fees.** If you do decide to splurge on souvenirs, remember that the

However, rates fluctuate, so before departing, consult a currency exchange website such as **www.oanda.com/currency/converter** to check up-to-the-minute rates. For help with tip calculations as well as currency conversions, download Frommer's convenient Travel Tools app for your mobile device. Go to **www.frommers.com/go/mobile** and click on the Travel Tools icon.

As a whole, Orlando is no more expensive than any other major city in the U.S. That said, in the theme-park zones, expect to be charged high prices for just about everything (that $1 bottle of water in the outside world will cost $2.50 and up in the tourist areas). If you plan on spending most of your time at the parks, budget accordingly.

THE VALUE OF THE U.S. DOLLAR VS. OTHER POPULAR CURRENCIES

US$	C$	£	€	A$	NZ$
1.00	0.97	0.61	0.70	0.93	1.27

items you purchase will have to be packed (leave room in your luggage or pack a spare bag just for such purchases)—and keep in mind the high cost of baggage fees if you're traveling by plane.

○ **Time your meals.** When dining at the parks, try to eat your big meal of the day at lunch, when prices are generally lower (though there are a few exceptions). Character meals and dinner shows, like souvenirs and specialty snacks, are part of the whole Disney experience, but choose wisely—the characters, experience, and prices vary considerably. If you have toddlers, head to the Crystal Palace (Magic Kingdom), Tusker House (Animal Kingdom), Cape May Café (Disney's Beach Club Resort), Chef Mickey's (Disney's Contemporary Resort), or 1900 Park Fare (Disney's Grand Floridian Resort & Spa). If you have school-age kids, add Cinderella's Royal Table (Magic Kingdom), Princess Storybook (Epcot's Akershus Royal Banquet Hall), and 'Ohana (Disney's Polynesian Resort) to the list of choices. *Note:* Breakfast is the least expensive meal (relatively speaking), followed by lunch, followed by dinner (which can reach as high as $60 per adult and $36 per child depending on the experience). Dinner shows, while definitely entertaining, are best saved for kids ages 8 and up; the younger children (especially toddlers) tend to lose interest—which, given the price tag, would be less than ideal.

○ **Consider the Disney Dining Plan.** This option is only available to those staying at an official WDW hotel—but it can add up to substantial savings when compared to purchasing your meals a la carte. See p. 102 for details. At times, the Disney Dining Plan has been offered as a free perk when purchasing a Disney vacation package, so be sure to check **www. disney.com** for details.

When it comes to carrying currency, although many Orlando establishments do accept traveler's checks, I still recommend using a credit card, debit card, and/or cash because it's far less of a hassle (but if you do opt for traveler's checks, make sure they are denominated in U.S. currency—foreign-currency checks will likely be refused). Be sure you have enough petty cash to cover airport incidentals, tipping, and transportation to your hotel (you can do this before leaving home, or you can get cash at an airport ATM).

ATMs In Orlando, the easiest and best way to get cash away from home is from an ATM (automated teller machine), sometimes referred to as a "cash machine" or "cashpoint." The **Cirrus** (© **800/424-7787**; www.mastercard. com) and **PLUS** (© **800/ 843-7587**; www.visa.com) networks span the globe.

Go to your bank card's website to find ATM locations at your destination. Be sure you know your daily withdrawal limit before you depart. In addition, international travelers should check with their bank before departing to ensure that their PIN (personal identification number) will be valid in the U.S. (though most major U.S. banks generally accept the same four-digit PINs commonly accepted worldwide). It is also a good

WHAT THINGS COST IN ORLANDO	US$
Taxi from airport to Walt Disney World (up to four people)	60.00
Shuttle from airport to Walt Disney World (two adults, two kids)	122.00–135.00
Double room at Disney's Grand Floridian Resort & Spa (very expensive)	440.00–1,145.00
Double room at Disney's Animal Kingdom Lodge (expensive)	250.00–615.00
Double room at Disney's Caribbean Beach Resort (moderate)	154.00–309.00
Double room at Staybridge Suites Lake Buena Vista (moderate)	129.00–289.00
Double room at Disney's All-Star Music Resort (inexpensive)	82.00–179.00
Six-course fixed-price dinner for one at Victoria & Albert's, *not* including tip or wine pairing (very expensive)	125.00–200.00
Adult all-you-can-eat buffet dinner at the Disney theme-park restaurants, not including tip or wine (moderate)	23.00–40.00
Roll of ASA 100 Kodak film, 36 exposures, purchased at Walt Disney World	16.00
Tube of sun block in the theme parks	12.00
Evening movie tickets at AMC, Pleasure Island	8.00–15.00
Adult 4-day + Park Hopper admission to Walt Disney World	298.00
Child 4-day + Park Hopper admission to Walt Disney World	279.00
Adult 1-day, one-park admission to Walt Disney World	85.00
Child 1-day, one-park admission to Walt Disney World	79.00
Adult 1-day, one-park admission to Universal Orlando	85.00
Child 1-day, one-park admission to Universal Orlando	79.00
Adult 1-day, one-park admission to SeaWorld	79.99
Child 1-day, one-park admission to SeaWorld	71.99
Adult five-park, 14-day Orlando FlexTicket	274.95
Child five-park, 14-day Orlando FlexTicket	254.95
Admission 1-day to Discovery Cove with Dolphin Swim	199.00–319.00
Adult admission to Orlando Science Center	17.00
Child admission to Orlando Science Center	12.00
Adult admission to Gatorland	23.00
Child admission to Gatorland	15.00

idea to alert your bank of your travel plans in an effort to avoid any possible difficulties using your card while in the U.S.

ATMs can be found on Main Street in the Magic Kingdom and at the entrances to Epcot, Disney's Hollywood Studios, and Animal Kingdom (where you'll find another one located across from the TriceraTop Spin in DinoLand). They're also at Pleasure Island (soon to be Hyperion Wharf), in Downtown Disney Marketplace, at Disney resorts, and in the Crossroads Shopping Center. There are also ATMs near Guest Services at Universal Studios Florida, Islands of Adventure, SeaWorld, and Aquatica. Outside the parks, most malls have at least one ATM, and they're in some convenience stores, such as 7-Elevens and Circle Ks, as well as in grocery stores and drugstores.

There are frequently extra charges for using nonbank ATMs or bank ATMs not affiliated with your home branch. Depending on your institution, those charges can range from $1 to $3.50 per transaction—the average is $2.75 across Florida. To compare banks' ATM fees within Orlando, use **www. bankrate.com**. Visitors from outside the U.S. should also find out whether their bank assesses a 1% to 3% fee on charges incurred abroad (most will, unless they are

associated with the Global Alliance).

Be *very* careful when using ATMs, especially at night and in areas that are not well lit and heavily traveled. Don't let the land of Mickey lull you into a false sense of security. Goofy and Pluto won't mug you, but some of their estranged neighbors might. Cuddly characters aside, this is a big city and the crime rate here is the same as in comparable locations. When entering your PIN at an ATM, make sure you shield the keyboard from others in line. And if you're using a drive-through, keep your doors locked.

In addition to getting cash out of an ATM, you can also buy **Disney dollars** while visiting Walt Disney World. This currency, with images of Mickey, Minnie, Pirates of the Caribbean, and so on, comes in $1, $5, and $10 denominations. The dollars are good at WDW shops, restaurants, and resorts, as well as Disney stores everywhere. This is a great way to give a preset allowance to kids for their souvenirs. If you have any leftover dollars, you can exchange them for real currency upon leaving WDW or keep them as a souvenir. *Note:* Pay close attention if you have a refund coming. Some items, such as strollers, wheelchairs, and lockers, require a deposit, and Disney staffers will frequently use Mickey money for

refunds. If you don't want it, just let them know and they'll be happy to give you real cash.

Credit Cards & Debit Cards **Credit cards** are the most widely used form of payment in the U.S., and most Orlando establishments accept the following: **Visa** (Barclaycard in Britain), **MasterCard** (Euro-Card in Europe, Access in Britain, Chargex in Canada), **American Express, Diners Club,** and **Discover.** Credit cards also provide a convenient record of all your expenses and offer relatively good exchange rates. You can withdraw cash advances from your credit cards at banks or ATMs, but high fees make credit-card cash advances a pricey way to get cash.

It's highly recommended that you travel with at least one major credit card in Orlando. You must have a credit card to rent a car, and hotels and airlines usually require a credit card imprint as a deposit against expenses. International visitors using chip-and-PIN cards (or smart cards, as they are often called) will have to have their cards swiped (they still have a magnetic strip), and in most cases sign for their purchases (no PIN required), as the U.S. has no plans to implement a chip-and-PIN system anytime soon.

Disney, Universal, and SeaWorld parks, shops, restaurants (but not most fast-food outlets) and resorts (Disney and Universal) accept all five major credit cards mentioned above. Additionally, the WDW and Universal resorts will let you charge purchases made in their respective park shops and restaurants to your hotel room, but you must settle up when you check out. Be sure, however, to keep track of your spending as you go along so you won't be surprised when you get the total bill.

Debit cards are also a commonly accepted form of payment in most Orlando stores and restaurants as well as select resorts. Debit cards draw money directly from your checking account. Be aware that fees (generally $1–$3, though sometimes a percentage of the transaction) are usually imposed on most debit transactions, both foreign and domestic. Also note that most resorts deduct up to $200 (or more) from your debit account each and every day of your stay, greatly reducing the amount of money you have available in your bank account (until it is credited back some 10 or so days after you've settled your bill and checked out), so be sure to ask exactly what the policy is before handing over your card at check-in. Some stores enable you to receive cash back on your debit card purchases as well. The same is true at most U.S. post offices.

The main lesson here is to beware of hidden fees

when traveling. Check with your credit or debit card issuer to see what fees, if any, will be charged for overseas transactions. Recent reform legislation in the U.S., for example, has curbed some exploitative lending practices. But many banks have responded by increasing fees in other areas, including fees for customers who use credit and debit cards while out of the country—even if those charges were made in U.S. dollars. Fees can amount to 3% or more of the purchase price. Check with your bank before departing to avoid any surprise charges on your statement.

Newspapers & Magazines The *Orlando Sentinel* is the major local newspaper, but you can also purchase the Sunday editions of other papers (most notably, the *New York Times*) in some hotel gift shops or bookstores such as Barnes & Noble or Borders. Don't count on finding daily editions of West Coast papers, such as the *Los Angeles Times,* without making special arrangements. The Friday edition of the *Sentinel* includes extensive entertainment and dining listings, as does the newspaper's website, **www. orlandosentinel.com**. *Orlando Weekly* is a free alternative paper that has a lot of entertainment and art listings focused on events outside tourist areas.

Packing Airline baggage fees being what they are, packing light has become a financial requirement. There are, however, a few items that you should definitely pack: a sweater or sweatshirt (no matter what time of year, Orlando evenings can range from cool to downright cold, and when restaurants blast the air-conditioning, it can get quite uncomfortable to dine while shivering in short sleeves); a swimsuit; comfortable broken-in shoes and several pairs of socks (pounding the theme-park pavement in a pair of new shoes—or shoes without socks—will almost always result in painful blisters); a hat; and a big bottle of sunscreen (a must to protect from the strong sun). In an effort to make life a bit easier, most area hotels offer some sort of laundry service (whether self-serve or valet), so if you don't mind doing the wash, you can easily cut down on the amount of clothing you bring along. Leave room in your suitcase (if at all possible) to bring home souvenirs, or pack a small collapsible bag to accommodate your purchases on the trip home. Only a select few restaurants (such as Victoria & Albert's) and nightclubs carry a dress code—otherwise casual clothing is in order, no matter where you go. For more helpful information on packing for your trip, download Frommer's convenient Travel Tools app for your mobile device. Go to **www.frommers.com/go/mobile** and click on the Travel Tools icon.

Passports Virtually every air traveler entering the U.S. is required to show a passport. All persons, including U.S. citizens, traveling by air between the United States and Canada, Mexico, Central and South America, the Caribbean, and Bermuda are required to present a valid passport. *Note:* U.S. and Canadian citizens entering the U.S. at land and sea ports of entry from within the Western Hemisphere must now also present a passport or other documents compliant with the Western Hemisphere Travel Initiative (WHTI; see www.getyouhome.gov for details). Children 15 and under may continue entering with only a U.S. birth certificate or other proof of U.S. citizenship.

It is always advised to have at least one or two consecutive blank pages in your passport to allow space for visas and stamps that need to appear together. It is also important to note when your passport expires: Many countries require your passport to have at least 6 months left before its expiration in order to allow you into the destination. For more information, contact the following agencies:

○ **Australia** Australian Passport Information Service (🕻 **131-232;** www.

passports.gov.au).

○ **Canada Passport Office,** Department of Foreign Affairs and International Trade, Ottawa, ON K1A 0G3 (🕻 **800/567-6868;** www.ppt.gc.ca).

○ **Ireland Passport Office,** Setanta Centre, Molesworth Street, Dublin 2 (🕻 **01/671-1633;** www.foreignaffairs.gov.ie).

○ **New Zealand Passports Office,** Department of Internal Affairs, 47 Boulcott Street, Wellington, 6011 (🕻 **0800/225-050** in New Zealand or 04/474-8100; www.passports.govt.nz).

○ **United Kingdom** Visit your nearest passport office, major post office, or travel agency or contact the **Identity and Passport Service (IPS),** 89 Eccleston Square, London, SW1V 1PN (🕻 **0300/222-0000;** www.ips.gov.uk).

○ **United States** To find your regional passport office, check the U.S. State Department website (travel.state.gov/passport) or call the **National Passport Information Center** (🕻 **877/487-2778**) for automated information.

Petrol Please see "Gasoline," above.

Pets For those of us who wouldn't dream of going on vacation without our pets, more and more lodgings are going the pet-friendly route. Be aware, however, that policies vary from property to property in Orlando, so call ahead to find out the particulars of your hotel.

None of the Disney resorts allows animals (except service dogs) to stay on the premises or has its own on-site kennel (the only exception being Disney's Fort Wilderness Campground, where you can have your pet at the full-hook-up campsites), but resort guests are welcome to board their animals overnight in the new **Best Friends Pet Care** facility on Bonnet Creek Parkway (see "Kennels," above). Universal Orlando and SeaWorld will board small pets during the day only, not overnight.

Universal's three Loews-run resorts do allow pets on the property. In fact, "Loews Loves Pets" is a program that caters to pets and their families by offering such amenities as food, leashes, bedding, toys, and more. Pet walking, pet pagers, and door hangers (to let the resort staff know that there is a pet in the room) are also available.

An excellent resource is **www.petswelcome.com**, which dispenses medical tips, pet-friendly lodgings

It is illegal in Florida to leave your pet inside a parked car, windows rolled down or not. The sweltering heat can easily kill an animal in only a few minutes. All of the major theme parks have kennel facilities available, so if you have brought your pet along, take advantage of these kennels.

Make sure your pet is wearing a name-tag that includes your name and phone number, as well as the phone number of a contact person who can take the call if your pet gets lost while you're away from home.

and campgrounds, and veterinarians. Also check out **www.dogfriendly.com**, which features links to Orlando accommodations, eateries, attractions, and parks that welcome canine companions.

Photography   Orlando is a magnet for shutterbugs. If you're still shooting film, 2-hour film processing is available at all major parks. Look for the PHOTO EXPRESS signs. You can buy film, batteries, and disposable cameras in all of the theme parks, but you'll save money on almost everything if you shop at drugstores, such as Walgreens, or local grocery stores. These places often run specials for discounted processing or free double prints, saving you a significant amount of money. They're listed in the yellow pages under "Photo Finishing." The parks carry only a small selection of memory cards for digital cameras; if you need rechargeable batteries, you will have to go to one of the many camera shops found just outside park property.

Police   Call ☎ **911** in an emergency.

Safety   Just because Minnie, Mickey, Donald, and Goofy all live here doesn't mean that a few seedy characters aren't lurking about as well. Even in the most magical place on earth, you shouldn't let your guard down; Orlando has a crime rate that's comparable to that of other large U.S. cities. Stay alert and remain aware of your surroundings. It's best to keep your valuables in a safe. Most hotels today are equipped with in-room safes or offer the use of a safety-deposit box at the front desk. Keep a close eye on your valuables when you're in public places, including restaurants, theaters, and even airport terminals. Renting a locker at the theme parks is always preferable to leaving your valuables in the trunk of your car. Be cautious, even when in the parks, and avoid carrying large amounts of cash in a backpack or fanny pack, which could easily be accessed while you're standing in line for a ride

or show. And don't leave valuables unattended under a stroller—that's pretty much asking for them to be stolen.

If you're renting a car while in Orlando, read the safety instructions provided by the rental company. Never stop for any reason in a suspicious, poorly lit, or unpopulated area, and remember that children should never ride in the front seat of a car equipped with air bags. See "Getting Around: By Car," earlier in this chapter, for more safety tips.

Senior Travel   In Orlando, people older than the age of 60 (sometimes 65) often qualify for reduced admission to theaters, museums, and other attractions (generally the smaller attractions and cultural venues, including the Orlando Science Center, Central Florida Zoo, Orlando Museum of Art, and others—but not on tickets to the biggies such as Disney and Universal), as well as discounted fares on public transportation, including the Lynx bus system and the I-Ride Trolley.

Keep in mind that area restaurants often offer discounts to seniors (though sometimes only at special hours or on special days).

You can order a copy of the *Mature Traveler Guide,* which contains local discounts mainly on hotel rooms but also on attractions and activities, from the **Orlando/Orange County Convention & Visitors Bureau,** 8723 International Dr., Ste. 101, Orlando, FL 32819 (℃ **800/643-9492** or 800/551-0181; www.visitorlando.com). You can also find it online at the CVB's website (click the "Senior Citizens Discounts" link on the site map).

The U.S. National Park Service offers an **America the Beautiful—National Park and Federal Recreational Lands Pass—Senior Pass** (formerly the **Golden Age Passport**), which gives seniors 62 years and older lifetime entrance to all properties administered by the National Park Service—national parks, monuments, historic sites, recreation areas, and wildlife refuges—for a one-time processing fee of $10. If you're going to the Cape Canaveral National Seashore on an excursion out of Orlando, it's a good bet. The pass must be purchased in person at any NPS facility that charges an entrance fee. Besides free entry, the America the Beautiful Senior Pass also offers a 50% discount on some federal-use fees charged for such facilities as camping, swimming,

parking, boat launching, and tours. For more information, go to **www.nps. gov/fees_passes.htm** or call the United States Geological Survey (USGS), which issues the passes, at ℃ **888/275-8747.**

Smoking If you're a smoker, light up where and when you can. Smoking is prohibited in many of Florida's public places. While some bars have smoking areas and most hotels have smoking rooms, many are eliminating them. You're still permitted to inhale in most outdoor areas, but these areas are limited to restricted spots at Disney, Universal, and SeaWorld parks. *Note:* Don't expect to light up during dinner. In 2002, Florida voters approved a constitutional amendment that bans smoking in public work places, including restaurants and bars that serve food. Stand-alone bars that serve virtually no food as well as designated smoking rooms in hotels are exempt.

Taxes The United States has no value-added tax (VAT) or other indirect tax at the national level. Every state, county, and city may levy its own local tax on all purchases, including hotel and restaurant checks and airline tickets. These taxes will not appear on price tags. In Orlando, a 6% to 7.5% sales tax (depending on the local county you happen to be in) is charged on all goods, with the exception of most

edible grocery-store items and medicines. Hotels add another 5% to 6% in resort taxes to your bill, so the total tax on accommodations can run up to 13.5%.

Telephones   **Local calls** in Orlando require that you dial the area code **(407)** followed by the seven-digit local number, even when calling just across the street.

Many convenience groceries and packaging services sell **prepaid calling cards** in denominations up to $50. Many public pay phones at airports now accept American Express, MasterCard, and Visa. **Local calls** made from most pay phones cost either 25¢ or 35¢. Most long-distance and international calls can be dialed directly from any phone. **To make calls within the United States and to Canada,** dial 1 followed by the area code and the seven-digit number. **For other international calls,** dial 011 followed by the country code, city code, and the number you are calling.

Calls to area codes **800, 888, 877,** and **866** are toll-free. However, calls to area codes **700** and **900** (chat lines, bulletin boards, "dating" services, and so on) can be expensive—charges of 95¢ to $3 or more per minute. Some numbers have minimum charges that can run $15 or more.

For **reversed-charge or collect calls,** and for person-to-person calls, dial the number 0, then the area code and number; an operator will come on the line, and you should specify whether you are calling collect, person-to-person, or both. If your operator-assisted call is international, ask for the overseas operator.

For **directory assistance** ("Information"), dial 411 for local numbers and national numbers in the U.S. and Canada. For dedicated long-distance information, dial 1, then the appropriate area code plus 555-1212.

Time   Orlando is in the **Eastern Standard Time (EST)** zone, which is 1 hour later than Chicago, 3 hours later than Los Angeles, 5 hours earlier than London, and 12 hours earlier than Sydney. The continental United States is divided into **four time zones:** Eastern Standard Time (EST), Central Standard Time (CST), Mountain Standard Time (MST), and Pacific Standard Time (PST). Alaska and Hawaii have their own zones. For example, when it's 9am in Los Angeles (PST), it's 7am in Honolulu (HST),10am in Denver (MST), 11am in Chicago (CST), noon in New York City (EST), 5pm in London (GMT), and 2am the next day in Sydney.

Daylight saving time is in effect from 1am on the second Sunday in March to 1am on the first Sunday in November, except in Arizona, Hawaii, the U.S.

Virgin Islands, and Puerto Rico. Daylight saving time moves the clock 1 hour ahead of standard time.

For help with time translations, and more, download Frommer's convenient Travel Tools app for your mobile device. Go to **www.frommers.com/go/mobile** and click on the Travel Tools icon.

Tipping   In hotels, tip **bellhops** at least $1 per bag ($2–$3 if you have a lot of luggage) and tip the **chamber staff** $1 to $2 per day (more if you've left a big mess for him or her to clean up). Tip the **doorman** or **concierge** only if he or she has provided you with some specific service (for example, calling a cab for you or obtaining difficult-to-get theater tickets). Tip the **valet-parking attendant** $1 to $2 every time you get your car.

In restaurants, bars, and nightclubs, tip **service staff** and **bartenders** 15% to 20% of the check, tip **checkroom attendants** $1 per garment, and tip **valet-parking attendants** $1 to $2 per vehicle.

As for other service personnel, tip **cab drivers** 15% of the fare; tip **skycaps** at airports at least $1 per bag ($2–$3 if you have a lot of luggage); and tip **hairdressers** and **barbers** 15% to 20%.

For help with tip calculations, currency conversions, and more, download

Frommer's convenient Travel Tools app for your mobile device. Go to **www.frommers.com/go/mobile** and click on the Travel Tools icon.

Toilets   You won't find public toilets or "restrooms" on the streets in most U.S. cities, but they can be found in hotel lobbies, bars, restaurants, museums, department stores, railway and bus stations, and service stations. Large hotels and fast-food restaurants are often the best bet for clean facilities. Restaurants and bars in resorts or heavily visited areas may reserve their restrooms for patrons.

VAT   See "Taxes," above.

Visas   The U.S. State Department has a **Visa Waiver Program (VWP)** allowing citizens of the following countries to enter the United States without a visa for stays of up to 90 days: Andorra, Australia, Austria, Belgium, Brunei, Czech Republic, Denmark, Estonia, Finland, France, Germany, Greece, Hungary, Iceland, Ireland, Italy, Japan, Latvia, Liechtenstein, Lithuania, Luxembourg, Malta, Monaco, the Netherlands, New Zealand, Norway, Portugal, San Marino, Singapore, Slovakia, Slovenia, South Korea, Spain, Sweden, Switzerland, and the United Kingdom. (This list was accurate at press time; for the most up-to-date list of countries in the VWP, consult http://travel.state.gov/visa.) Even though a visa isn't necessary, in an effort to help U.S. officials check travelers against terror watch lists before they arrive at U.S. borders, visitors from VWP countries must register online through the Electronic System for Travel Authorization (ESTA) before boarding a plane or a boat to the U.S. Travelers must complete an electronic application providing basic personal and travel eligibility information. The Department of Homeland Security recommends filling out the form at least 3 days before traveling. Authorizations will be valid for up to 2 years or until the traveler's passport expires, whichever comes first. Currently, there is a US$14 fee for the online application. Existing ESTA registrations remain valid through their expiration dates. **Note:** Any passport issued on or after October 26, 2006, by a VWP country must be an **e-Passport** for VWP travelers to be eligible to enter the U.S. without a visa. Citizens of these nations also need to present a round-trip air or cruise ticket upon arrival. E-Passports contain computer chips capable of storing

biometric information, such as the required digital photograph of the holder. If your passport doesn't have this feature, you can still travel without a visa if the valid passport was issued before October 26, 2005, and includes a machine-readable zone; or if the valid passport was issued between October 26, 2005, and October 25, 2006, and includes a digital photograph. For more information, go to **http://travel.state.gov/visa**. Canadian citizens may enter the U.S. without visas, but will need to show passports and proof of residence.

Citizens of all other countries must have (1) a valid passport that expires at least 6 months later than the scheduled end of their visit to the U.S.; and (2) a tourist visa. For information about U.S. visas, go to **http://travel.state.gov** and click on "Visas." Or go to one of the following websites:

Australian citizens can obtain up-to-date visa information from the **U.S. Embassy Canberra,** Moonah Place, Yarralumla, ACT 2600 (✆ **02/6214-5600**), or by checking the U.S. Diplomatic Mission's website at http://canberra.usembassy.gov/visas.html.

British subjects can obtain up-to-date visa information by calling the **U.S. Embassy Visa Information Line** (✆ **09042-450-100** from within the U.K. at £1.20 per minute; or ✆ 866/382-3589 from within the U.S. at a flat rate of $16, payable by credit card only) or by visiting the American Embassy London's website at http://london.usembassy.gov/visas.html.

Irish citizens can obtain up-to-date visa information through the **U.S. Embassy Dublin,** 42 Elgin Rd., Ballsbridge, Dublin 4 (✆ **1580-47-VISA** [8472] from within the Republic of Ireland at €2.40 per minute), or by going to http://dublin.usembassy.gov.

Citizens of **New Zealand** can obtain up-to-date visa information by contacting the **U.S. Embassy New Zealand,** 29 Fitzherbert Terrace, Thorndon, Wellington (✆ **644/462-6000**), or going to http://newzealand.usembassy.gov.

Visitor Information

Please see "Visitor Information," on p. 34, and the box "Orlando's Best Websites," on p. 9.

Wi-Fi   See "Internet & Wi-Fi," earlier in this section.

AIRLINE WEBSITES

MAJOR AIRLINES

Alaska Airlines/Horizon Air
www.alaskaair.com

American Airlines
www.aa.com

British Airways
www.british-airways.com

Continental Airlines
www.continental.com

Delta Air Lines
www.delta.com

Frontier Airlines
www.frontierairlines.com

JetBlue Airways
www.jetblue.com

Midwest Airlines
www.midwestairlines.com

United Airlines
www.united.com

US Airways
www.usairways.com

Virgin Atlantic Airways
www.virgin-atlantic.com

BUDGET AIRLINES

AirTran Airways
www.airtran.com

Frontier Airlines
www.frontierairlines.com

JetBlue Airways
www.jetblue.com

Southwest Airlines
www.southwest.com

Spirit Airlines
www.spiritair.com

WestJet
www.westjet.com

Index

See also Accommodations and Restaurant indexes, below.

General Index

A

AAA (American Automobile Association), 361, 367–368
  package deals, 99
  tickets through
    Universal Orlando, 253
    Walt Disney World, 162
A & T Antiques (Downtown Disney), 314
Accommodations, 42–99, 375. *See also* Accommodations Index
  bed & breakfasts in Orlando, 95–96
  best, 10–12, 42–45
  condo-hotels and vacation homes, 74–75, 83
  daily resort fees, 67
  for disabled travelers, 369
  downtown Orlando, 94–95
  "green," 33
  International Drive area, 84–94
  Kissimmee, 77–83
  Lake Buena Vista, 69–77
    "official" WDW hotels, 64–69
  lounges at, 327
  practical information, 96–99
  price categories, 44
  reservation services, 98–99
  Tampa, 344–347
  timeshare resorts and apartments, 86
  tipping, 390
  Walt Disney World, 45–64
    checking in ahead of time, 64
    perks of staying at, 45, 48–49
    reservations services, 98–99
    restaurants, 124–131
    transportation to the theme parks, 97
    value seasons or lowest rates, 97
Ace Metro, 367
Adults. *See* Grown-ups
Advanced Tee Times USA, 301
Advance Reservations, 101, 108
Adventure Island (Tampa), 336–337
Adventureland (Magic Kingdom), 178–181
Africa (Animal Kingdom), 233–234
Air bag safety, 365
Airboating, 299

AirTran Airways, 357
Air travel, 357–359
Akershus Castle (Epcot), 213
Aladdin's Magic Carpet Ride (DisneyQuest), 241
All About Kids, 368
Allie's Barnyard (Aquatica), 292
All Star Vacation Homes, 369
Altamonte Mall, 313
A'lure—The Call of the Ocean (SeaWorld), 282–283
The Amazing Adventures of Spider-Man (Islands of Adventure), 8, 267–268
AMC 24, 318
AMC Universal Cineplex 20, 318
American Adventure (Epcot), 213–214
American Express Lounge (Universal Studios), 258
American Express Vacations, 99
American Film Institute Showcase (Disney's Hollywood Studios), 217
American Idol Experience (Disney's Hollywood Studios), 223
America the Beautiful Access Pass, 371
America the Beautiful Senior Pass, 389
Amtrak, 361, 370
  Tampa, 336
Amway Arena, 304, 317
Animal Actors on Location! (Universal Studios), 254
Animal Kingdom, 226–236
  Africa, 233–234
  arriving in, 228
  Asia, 234–236
  Dinoland U.S.A., 231–232
  Discovery Island, 230–231
  Hidden Mickeys, 221
  hours, 228
  The Oasis, 229–230
  Picnic in the Park, 125
  restaurants, 123–124
  services and facilities in, 228–229
  suggested itinerary, 171
  ticket prices, 228
  tip sheet, 230
Animal-rights issues, 33–34
Animation Academy (DisneyQuest), 241
Animation Courtyard Shops (Disney's Hollywood Studios), 226
ANNIKA Academy, 301
Annual passes to Walt Disney World, 164–165
Apartment rentals, 86
Apopka–Vineland Road, 360
Aquatica, 244, 290–291
Arabian Nights, 320–321
Area codes, 367
Arena football, 304

Arnold Palmer Golf Academy World Headquarters (near Tampa), 343
Arnold Palmer Invitational, 28
Art of Disney
  Downtown Disney, 310
  Epcot, 207
Artsline (Tampa), 350
Asia (Animal Kingdom), 234–236
Astronaut Memorial (near Titusville), 354
Astronaut Memorial Planetarium & Observatory (Cocoa Beach), 352
Astronaut Training Experience (Kennedy Space Center), 354
Astro Orbiter (Magic Kingdom), 193
Atlanta Braves, 28, 242, 304–305
Atlantic Dance, 332
ATMs (automated-teller machines), 383, 385
  Animal Kingdom, 228
  Disney's Hollywood Studios, 216
  Epcot, 198
  Islands of Adventure, 265
  Magic Kingdom, 175
  SeaWorld, 281
  Universal Studios, 253
  Walt Disney World, 172
Attendance levels, 2
Attractions and rides
  for disabled travelers, 370
  Frommer's ratings, 178
  height restrictions, 166, 375–376
  International Drive Area, 294–296
  Kissimmee, 292–294
  SeaWorld, 282–286
  Universal Studios, 245, 254–259
  Walt Disney World, 160–245. *See also specific parks, attractions and rides*
    best days to visit, 166
    best time of year to visit, 165
    Extra Magic Hour, 192
    FASTPASS, 167
    information in advance, 161
    itineraries, 166–171
    maintenance and repairs, 190
    operating hours, 165
    parking, 162
    planning your visit, 166
    security, 161
    services and facilities, 172–173
    tickets, 162–165
    tours, 204
    for travelers with special needs, 173–174

GENERAL INDEX

Accommodations

Restaurants